CADOGAN GUID

Other titles in the Cadogan Guides series:

AMSTERDAM
AUSTRALIA
BALI
BERLIN
CARIBBEAN
ECUADOR,
  THE GALÁPAGOS
  & COLOMBIA
GREEK ISLANDS
INDIA
IRELAND
ITALIAN ISLANDS
MEXICO
MOROCCO
NEW YORK
NORTHEAST ITALY
NORTHWEST ITALY
PORTUGAL
PRAGUE
ROME
SCOTLAND

SOUTH OF FRANCE: PROVENCE,
  CÔTE D'AZUR &
  LANGUEDOC-ROUSSILLON
SOUTH ITALY
SOUTHERN SPAIN: GIBRALTAR &
  ANDALUCÍA
SPAIN
THAILAND
TUNISIA
TURKEY
TUSCANY, UMBRIA & THE MARCHES
VENICE

Forthcoming:

CENTRAL ASIA
CYPRUS
GERMANY
MALTA
MOSCOW & ST PETERSBURG
PARIS
SICILY

ABOUT THE AUTHORS

Getting soaked by freezing rain half-way up a volcano, hitching lifts in bullet-riddled buses, or drinking Cuba Libres in gringo bars was all in the line of research for Natascha Norton, who spent over a year based in Central America. A seasoned Latin American traveller, she thought she knew what to expect—everything, that is, except meeting her future husband in Guatemala.

Mark Whatmore agreed to join this project with almost indecent haste, always ready for another bumpy ride on a Central American 'chicken bus' or the mean streets of El Salvador and Panamá. A man with boundless energy and enthusiasm, no flea-ridden mattress ever stopped him from enjoying a good beach or mountain village.

ACKNOWLEDGEMENTS

From Natascha Norton
In England: I would like to thank Rachel Fielding, Vicki Ingle and Chris Schüler of Cadogan Books; the Expedition Advisory Centre of the Royal Geographical Society; my mother for a roof over my head as well as encouragement and advice; Benoît LeBlanc for constructive criticism of first drafts and hours of patient map-making; Tony Davies and Gill Bloyce for their sitting-room floor; and thanks especially to my friend and co-author, Mark Whatmore.

In Guatemala: thanks to Susan Horn; Tony Evans; the INGUAT staff in Guatemala City; Lisa and Steve Parker; Kevin Savage; Antonio Ramos of Viajes Tivoli; and Claudio and Lies for a beautiful place to live and plenty of excellent meals.

In Belize: thanks to Alfredo Villoria and Chet Schmidt in Punta Gorda; Rose O'Doherty; Bob Jones in San Ignacio; Josie Pollard in San Pedro; Meb Cutlack; Tom Brown on Caye Caulker; and Joy Vernon of the Belize Tourist Office, Belize City.

In Honduras: thanks to the staff of the Honduran Tourist Office in Tegucigalpa, especially Adriana María Salgodo.

Mark Whatmore would like to thank the staff of the Tourist Offices in El Salvador, Nicaragua, Costa Rica and Panamá. Also, the many people who shared kindness and enthusiasm, and offered hospitality whilst he was researching and writing the guide.

CADOGAN GUIDES

CENTRAL AMERICA

NATASCHA NORTON
and
MARK WHATMORE

CADOGAN BOOKS
London

THE GLOBE PEQUOT PRESS
Old Saybrook, Connecticut

Cadogan Books Ltd
Mercury House, 195 Knightsbridge, London SW7 1RE

The Globe Pequot Press
6 Business Park Drive, PO Box 833, Old Saybrook, Connecticut 06475–0833

Cover design by Keith Pointing, adapted by Ralph King
Cover illustration by Povl Webb
Maps © Cadogan Books Ltd,
drawn by Thames Cartographic Services Ltd

Managing Editor: Victoria Ingle
Editorial Director: Rachel Fielding

First published in 1993

A Catalogue record for this book is available from the British Library

ISBN 0–947754–37–7

Library of Congress Cataloging-in-Publication Data

Norton, Natascha
   Central America—Guatemala, Belize, Honduras, Costa Rica, Panamá, El Salvador,
Nicaragua / by Natascha Norton and Mark Whatmore.
      p.   cm.—(Cadogan Guides)
   Includes bibliographical references and index.
   1. Central America—Guidebook.   2. Central America—Description and travel—1981–
I. Norton, Natascha and Whatmore, Mark.   II. Title.   III. Series.
F1429.N6   1992   92–28245
917.2804′53—dc20   CIP
   ISBN 1–56440–070–0

Photoset in Ehrhardt on a Linotron 202
Printed in Great Britain by BPC Wheatons Ltd, Exeter

CONTENTS

Part VI: Honduras *Pages 234–98*

Part VII: El Salvador *Pages 300–38*

Part VIII: Nicaragua *Pages 339–76*

Part IX: Costa Rica *Pages 377–444*

Part X: Panamá *Pages 445–501*

Language *Pages 502–10*

Further Reading *Pages 511–12*

Country Index *Pages 513–26*

General Index *Pages 527–30*

LIST OF MAPS

INTRODUCTION

Huevosiy frijoles *(eggs and beans) and* tortillas *are staples of Central American cuisine*

A glance at the world map reveals Central America as one of the most shattered regions on the face of the globe. Here, on the bridge of the Americas, seven tiny nations are strung out on a slither of land, binding together two vast continents. It's a region in which a fantastic range of political, geographical, ethnic and environmental forces have collided, producing a magical hybrid. In the big cities a version of Coca-Cola culture moves to the rhythm of Colombian *salsa*, while, deep in the forests, species of birds, beasts and plants from north and south live beside local species that are found nowhere else in the world. A complex network of historical and cultural connections cross country borders, but the deepest political and racial divisions slice up nations.

Despite its awesome reputation for death squads and squalor, daily life in Central America is astonishingly normal. Most people live close to the land, carving a simple existence from steep hillsides, cutting fields from the forest or working on large coffee, banana or cotton plantations. The great driving forces are not politics and violence, but land, family and religion. Nevertheless a fiery Latin heart beats just below the surface and once a year every village and town explodes into an annual fiesta, with an orgy of drink, dance and wild celebration.

Scattered throughout the isthmus are pockets of indigenous culture, united by a rigid adherence to pre-Columbian traditions. These groups of indigenous Indians have managed to preserve their cultural integrity with astonishing tenacity. Virtually untouched by almost five hundred years of white, Catholic rule Guatemala's Quiché Indians still sacrifice animals in honour of ancient gods, while Panamá's Kuna Indians have formed a self-governing province and have little contact with the outside world. These groups, along with many others, are united by ancient traditions which transcend modern borders, while the monumental Maya ruins rising out of the jungles in Guatemala, Belize and Honduras, are a haunting reminder that the area supported sophisticated cultures long before the arrival of the Spanish, perhaps as early as 1500 BC.

Colonial rule also stamped its mark firmly on Central America, establishing patterns of oligarchic rule, religious hierarchy and exploitative economics which still persist, as well as scattering the isthmus with superb churches and instilling a deep current of racism. Meanwhile, in today's cities a furious swirl of 20th-century chaos mixes all these influences, sweeping up everything in its path and creating a culture that is breathless with energy. Buses growl through the traffic, pot-bellied policemen flirt with young girls, shoeshiners hustle for business, and tower blocks rise above the smog.

Contrary to popular belief Central America is also a land of great subtlety and tremendous beauty. Soft mists rise off the purple peaks of Guatemalan volcanoes, while herds of Panamanian cattle send dust clouds drifting across the rice fields. Large tracts of land remain empty, including great swathes of undisturbed rainforest in Guatemala, Belize, Costa Rica and Panamá; a string of volcanic peaks runs from Guatemala to Costa Rica; massive crater lakes nestle in rugged mountain ranges, all hemmed in by a pair of extremely beautiful coasts. Offshore islands are ringed by spectacular coral reefs, while the entire Belizean coastline is sheltered by a huge barrier reef. Beneath the surface a kaleidoscope of tropical fish are accompanied by sharks, swordfish, marlin and ray.

Visitors to Central America should expect the unexpected. While you're sure to stumble across stereotypes, including bizarre religious ceremonies and stone-faced soldiers bristling with firepower, you'll also find that surprises lurk around every corner. Many with a special interest—whether it's ornithology or archaeology, beaches or butterflies, politics or pirates—will find that Central America has a great deal to offer. Those who are open to the experience may find themselves seduced by any of these, or led down new and unexpected paths.

A Guide To The Guide

Part I provides general information about Central America as a whole with regard to getting there, getting around and some of the things you might want to consider before you set out.

Next comes a general history of Central America until its independence from Spain in 1821 (after which the individual countries took on more specific identities); and then the Topics, short pieces on some of the main issues and characters of Central American history including the Maya, Central American music and literature, ecotourism and banana republics.

Each subsequent chapter, or 'Part', covers a single country, opening with an introduction, followed by the post-Independence history of the country; then comes detailed practical information, including how to get there, the various entry requirements, what you might expect to eat and where you might expect to sleep. In the second part of each chapter the countries are laid out geographically, and practical information which is specific to each region given as it is described.

At the back of the guide you'll find a glossary, suggestions for further reading and the index.

The Best of Central America

Artesanía; Guatemalan weavings, Costa Rican leather goods.

Beaches: Manuel Antonio National Park, Costa Rica or West End Beach, Roatán, Honduras.

Birdwatching: Costa Rican and Belizean National Parks.

Books: *Sweet Waist of America* by Anthony Daniels or, for an old-world account, *Incidents of Travel in Central America, Chiapas and Yucatán* by John Lloyd Stephens (see p. 511).

Bookshop: The Bookshop, San José, Costa Rica, or Argos in Panamá City.

Buses: at their most furious and decorative on the streets of Panamá City.

Colonial Architecture: Antigua in Guatemala or León in Nicaragua.

Cup of Coffee: Café La Perla, San José, Costa Rica or the Café Tirol, Cobán, Guatemala.

Diving: Belizean Cayes, Bay Islands in Honduras and various sites in Costa Rica, including Cocos island.

Fiestas: Holy Week in Antigua, Guatemala is the most sombre, carnivals everywhere are wild, particularly in Puerto Limón, Costa Rica, Belize City and Las Tablas, Panamá. November 1st in Todos Santos, Guatemala is among the best Indian fiestas, including drunken horse races, while early December in Chichicastenango is also very good.

Heroes: Sandino, the man with the oversized hat; no one else carries this much weight.

Villains: it all depends who you're talking to and could be anyone from President Bush to Manuel Noriega; however, if asked which you prefer, it's always a good idea to go second.

Hot Springs: Fuentes Georginas, Guatemala.

Jungles: the Petén in Guatemala, Costa Rican National Parks or, for the adventurous, Panamá's Darién Gap.

Lakes: Lake Atitlán in Guatemala is unrivalled for beauty and tourism.

Man-made Wonder: Panamá Canal.

Markets: Chichicastenango in Guatemala.

Month of the Year: the end of rains bringing sunshine and flowers to the entire isthmus, this is November in Guatemala, December in Costa Rica and Panamá.

Mountain Road: the Cerro de la Muerte—hill of death—Costa Rica, or the climb from San Marcos to Tacana, Guatemala.

Murals: the church of Santa María de los Angeles in Managua.

Museums: the gold museum in San José, Costa Rica or the Popol Vuh archaeological museum in Guatemala City.

National Parks: Costa Rica has a superb network of parks, offering a rare opportunity to see Central American wildlife in the wild. Elsewhere the best is the Cockscomb Jaguar Reserve in Belize.

Political Graffiti: the walls of El Salvador and Nicaragua are coated with it.

Pre-Columbian Ruins: Tikal in Guatemala, Caracol in Belize and Copán in Honduras.

Railways: if it's still in action, Costa Rica's jungle train offers the best ride on the isthmus, while Puerto Cortés to Tela in Honduras is also a spectacular ride.

Rum: Belize and Nicaragua.

Volcanoes: erupting peaks include Pacaya in Guatemala—although this is now dangerous due to armed robberies—and the Arenal volcano, Costa Rica.

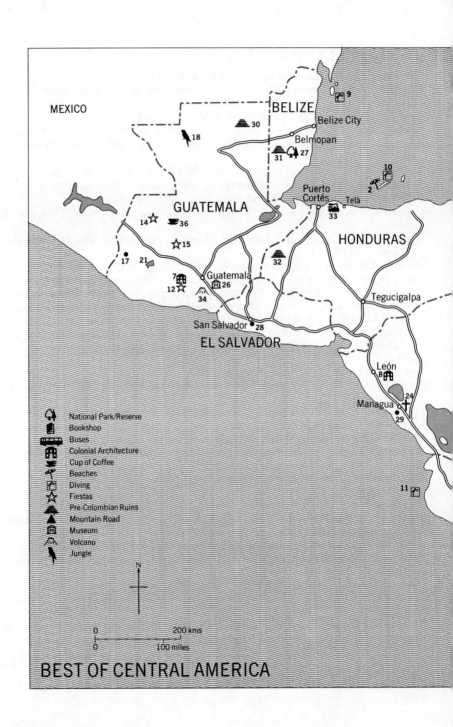

MEXICO

BELIZE

Belize City

30

Belmopan

18

31 27

GUATEMALA

Puerto
Cortés   Telá

10

2

33

HONDURAS

14 36

15

32

17   21

7

Guatemala

12   26

34

Tegucigalpa

San Salvador 28

EL SALVADOR

León

8

24

Managua

29

National Park/Reserve
Bookshop
Buses
Colonial Architecture
Cup of Coffee
Beaches
Diving
Fiestas
Pre-Colombian Ruins
Mountain Road
Museum
Volcano
Jungle

N

11

0   200 kms
0   100 miles

BEST OF CENTRAL AMERICA

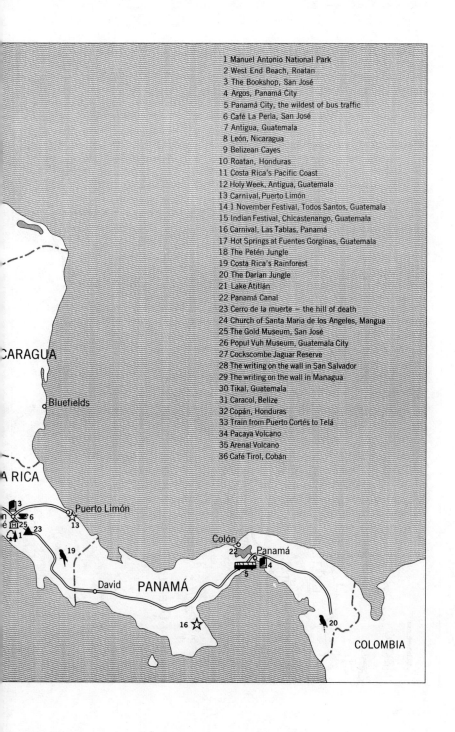

1 Manuel Antonio National Park
2 West End Beach, Roatan
3 The Bookshop, San José
4 Argos, Panamá City
5 Panamá City, the wildest of bus traffic
6 Café La Perla, San José
7 Antigua, Guatemala
8 León, Nicaragua
9 Belizean Cayes
10 Roatan, Honduras
11 Costa Rica's Pacific Coast
12 Holy Week, Antigua, Guatemala
13 Carnival, Puerto Limón
14 1 November Festival, Todos Santos, Guatemala
15 Indian Festival, Chicastenango, Guatemala
16 Carnival, Las Tablas, Panamá
17 Hot Springs at Fuentes Gorginas, Guatemala
18 The Petén Jungle
19 Costa Rica's Rainforest
20 The Darían Jungle
21 Lake Atitlán
22 Panamá Canal
23 Cerro de la muerte – the hill of death
24 Church of Santa Maria de los Angeles, Mangua
25 The Gold Museum, San José
26 Popul Vuh Museum, Guatemala City
27 Cockscombe Jaguar Reserve
28 The writing on the wall in San Salvador
29 The writing on the wall in Managua
30 Tikal, Guatemala
31 Caracol, Belize
32 Copán, Honduras
33 Train from Puerto Cortés to Telá
34 Pacaya Volcano
35 Arenal Volcano
36 Café Tirol, Cobán

CARAGUA

Bluefields

A RICA

Puerto Limón

San José

13

1   23

19

Colón

22   Panamá

4

5

David   PANAMÁ

16

20

COLOMBIA

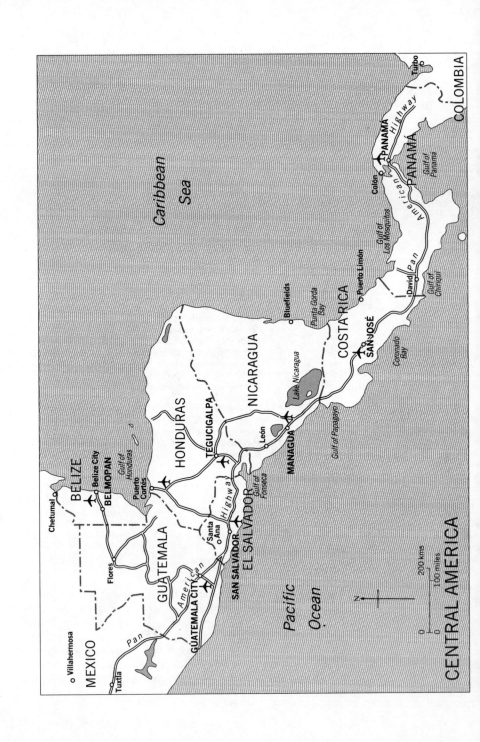

CENTRAL AMERICA

GENERAL INFORMATION

The Pan-American Highway

Before You Go

Tracking down information about Central America around the world is a tricky business as only the most popular countries can afford any representation abroad, so in most places you'll have to rely on the embassy for meagre scraps of information. The addresses of Tourist Offices and embassies in the UK and US are given in the introduction to the country chapters, although even if you can get hold of one you may find it easier to wait until you get to Central America where they are sure to be better informed.

Essential Geography

Broadly speaking the geography of Central America conforms to a simple pattern and a cross-section of the isthmus, taken anywhere from Guatemala to Panamá, has many similar characteristics. The Pacific coast is a sweltering flat land, which is mostly intensely fertile and heavily farmed, producing the crucial cash crops of sugar cane and rice, and also cattle. In the north, most notably in Guatemala, the coast itself is depressingly straight, with great Pacific rollers dumping onto black volcanic sand, although further south the beaches improve rapidly as the coast becomes more complex, reaching a peak in Costa Rica's soft sands and beautiful bays. Heading inland from the Pacific the highlands rise up into a central chain of mountains (reaching some 3000 metres) and volcanic peaks which form the backbone of the isthmus and provide a welcome break from the heat of the lowlands. The mountains are at their highest and broadest in Costa Rica and Guatemala, where the highlands are home to the bulk of the population and the capital cities nestle in massive open valleys. In Nicaragua the hills are a great deal lower and individual volcanoes stand alone, rising straight off the coastal plain. Over the other side of the mountains a vast area of empty swamp and jungle reaches towards the Caribbean. In some areas this land has been colonized and farmed, often planted with great tracts of banana palms, while elsewhere it remains wild and empty, particularly in northern Nicaragua, Guatemala, Panamá and southern Honduras.

Climate

Climate in Central America is governed by season and altitude. At any time of year the lowland areas are stiflingly hot; during the rainy season high humidity makes it particularly sticky. Meanwhile up in the highlands it is always pleasantly cool in the shade, although the sun is even sharper. The seasons in Central America are very simple indeed: it's either raining or it isn't. The rains start around May and end anywhere between November (in Guatemala) and December (in Panamá). The rains can be very heavy, particularly towards the end of the rainy season, but they need not stop you travelling; you'll just get less of a tan.

Average Temperature and Rainfall

	Jan	Feb	Mar	Apr	May	June	July	Aug	Sep	Oct	Nov	Dec
Guatemala City	23	25	27	28	29	27	26	26	24	23	23	22
	11	12	14	14	16	16	16	16	16	15	14	13
	2	*2*	*2*	*5*	*8*	*20*	*17*	*16*	*17*	*13*	*6*	*2*
Managua	30	30	30	30	32	31	31	31	31	31	30	30
	23	24	26	28	27	26	26	25	26	24	24	24
	0	*0*	*0*	*0*	*6*	*12*	*11*	*12*	*15*	*16*	*4*	*1*
Panamá City	31	31	32	32	31	30	30	31	30	30	29	30
	21	21	22	23	23	23	23	23	23	22	22	23
	4	*2*	*1*	*6*	*15*	*16*	*15*	*15*	*15*	*16*	*18*	*12*
Costa Rica	24	24	26	27	27	27	26	26	27	26	25	24
	14	14	15	16	16	16	16	16	16	15	15	15
	1	*0*	*1*	*4*	*17*	*20*	*18*	*19*	*20*	*22*	*14*	*4*
San Salvador	30	31	32	32	31	31	30	30	30	29	29	29
	16	16	17	19	19	19	18	18	19	18	17	16
	0	*3*	*2*	*5*	*12*	*20*	*21*	*20*	*18*	*14*	*4*	*1*
Honduras	25	27	29	30	030	28	28	28	29	27	26	25
	14	14	15	16	18	19	17	17	17	17	16	15
	4	*2*	*1*	*3*	*14*	*18*	*10*	*10*	*17*	*16*	*8*	*4*
Belize City	27	28	29	30	31	31	31	31	31	30	28	27
	19	21	22	23	24	24	24	24	23	22	20	20
	12	*6*	*4*	*5*	*7*	*13*	*15*	*14*	*15*	*16*	*12*	*14*

The first line is the average maximum temperature per month in degrees Celcius, the second the average minimum; and the last line, the average number of rainy days.

When to Go

The year in Central America is dominated by the rains, which start around May and end between November (in Guatemala) and December (in Panamá). The end of the rains ushers in the finest weather of the year—fresh, clear and warm, and prompts a few weeks, if not months, of indulgence among local people, who like to take it easy towards the end of the year.

Major Events

Local holidays and fiestas are listed in the introductions to each chapter, however, the big events of the Central American year as a whole are as follows:

Easter Week or *Semana Santa*—at its best in Antigua, Guatemala, where the streets are carpeted with coloured sawdust and the Crucifixion is re-enacted.
May 1 (Labour Day)—marching by unions, labour organizations and left-wingers throughout the isthmus, at its most elaborate and unstable in San Salvador.
September 15 (Independence Day)—marked by military parades throughout the isthmus.
October 12 (*Día de la Raza* or Columbus Day)—big on the Caribbean coast where drunken fiestas last for days.
November 1 (All Saints' Day)—superb in Todos Santos Cuchumatán, Guatemala, where a drunken horse race is the centrepiece in a furious three-day fiesta.
Christmas Day—a fairly subdued, private affair.
New Year—drunken, loud and vaguely international.

Earthquakes and Volcanoes

Earthquakes and volcanoes are a real problem for the residents of Central America, particularly the former which regularly claim lives and from time to time destroy cities and villages. There's absolutely nothing you can do to avoid the danger; your chances of getting caught up in a really dangerous earthquake are extremely scarce and certainly no worse than in Los Angeles. Smaller tremors are very common indeed and you are fairly likely to feel one or two while in Central America, but there is really nothing to worry about and with all that heavy traffic it's easy to get confused. Active volcanoes are dotted throughout Central America, running from Guatemala to Costa Rica, but again the risk of coming to any harm is very remote. However, if you happen to be close to an erupting cone, particularly at night, with sensible precautions it's an exhilarating and relatively harmless experience.

Health

Medical preparation for a trip to Central America should begin with a visit to your doctor at least six weeks before you plan to go as he or she will be able to offer the most up-to-date information. The standard vaccinations for Central America are yellow fever, rabies, typhoid, tetanus, polio, hepatitis, and hepatitis B. In spite of the cholera epidemic that began in 1990, even medical experts advise against a vaccination as it is generally agreed that it has little effect and it's simply better to take precautions as you travel—drinking bottled water and avoiding unwashed fruit and vegetables. Malaria pills are only essential for the Guatemalan Petén, Honduran Mosquitia and Panamanian Darién. Otherwise the risks are minimal and it is not necessary to take malaria pills in cool mountainous regions, but only on the tropical plain and in the jungle.

The most common complaint is 'bad guts', and it's a good idea to bring medicine for this, though it is widely available throughout Central America. Good medical labs operate in all cities and towns, so help is always easy to find. Your embassy can recommend English-speaking doctors in the various capitals. When it comes to theories on avoiding intestinal problems travellers are divided: some insist that you can eat any street vendor's snack and survive, others prefer to avoid street food and fresh salads in all but the best restaurants; however, there are no fixed or guaranteed guidelines.

Sunburn is another problem, and sun screen is not always on sale so do bring your own. Hats are available cheaply anywhere in Central America. Contraceptives, tampons and sanitary pads are all available, though again, it is best to bring your own contraceptives or tampons. (Remember that severe diarrhoea can diminish the effectiveness of the contraceptive pill.) Contact lens soaking and cleaning solutions are also best brought with you, as well as insect repellent. If you intend to do a lot of hiking, remember to bring your own padded foot plasters which make open blisters easier to bear. Finally, if you would like a detailed, personalized vaccination assessment and up-to-the-minute advice, contact the excellent Medical Advisory Service for Travellers Abroad (MASTA), at the London School of Tropical Medicine. In the UK British Airways run clinics at 32 locations from Aberdeen to Plymouth; their phone numbers are obtainable from a recorded message on 071–831 5333.

Insurance

Travel insurance, available through any travel agent, is always a good idea. Make sure the policy covers both theft and medical expenses and if you're particularly worried about ending up in a Central American hospital then make sure that the policy includes a flight home should you get seriously ill. Good insurance policies are available through all the main operators, including Thomas Cook and American Express (for their customers only).

Passports and Visas

The visa requirements for all Central American countries are slightly different and each is listed in the introduction to the individual chapters.

UK citizens do not need visas for any of the countries but Americans, New Zealanders and Australians will not be allowed into parts of the region without one. If you do need visas then try and get hold of them before you go, rather than spending half your holiday queueing at the Salvadorean embassy in Guatemala City.

Baggage Checklist

Suitable Apparel: The contents of one steamer trunk and one suitcase, and with a handbag for soiled linen, meet the ordinary requirements of one person.

The South American Handbook, 1925

Certain items are vital for Latin American travel; however, before you leave home take another look at your luggage. The chances are you have packed too much; many things such as hats and light clothing can be bought cheaply and easily when and if you need them. If you intend to go walking you should bring sturdy footwear as suitable boots are difficult to find in Central America. You will also need something to ward off the rain, cold and wind, all of which can strike with a vengeance.

Ideally, use a small rucksack or shoulder bag which can be padlocked. This is no guarantee of security but at least it hinders pickpockets. The advantage of small luggage is that you can keep it with you inside buses instead of having it thrown on the roof. In general your things are safe on the roof, but it is better to be safe than sorry.

Always keep with you your passport, vaccination booklet, flight ticket, traveller's cheques, insurance papers, and photocopies of relevant pages in your passport and the counterfoils of your traveller's cheques. Some people find a pocket calculator invaluable for making sense of fluctuating currency values and assessing prices of goods.

Use a money pouch or belt: either a leather belt with a concealed zip, or a wider cotton version that is concealed under your clothing and can fit your money and passport. Pouches can be sewn on to an elasticated armband and worn under clothing.

A basic medical kit should include insect repellent, flea powder, antiseptic, Lomotil for diarrhoea and a rehydration powder like Dioroalyte, antihistamine cream, essential personal medicines, and preferred contraceptive. Foot plasters, sun screen and toilet paper are also very useful. Remember that toilet paper is generally not provided in Central American toilets and should always be carried with you.

Flip-flops are excellent for dubious showers and for general use. Also very useful are a small alarm clock for those 4 am buses, a torch, a camping knife, and sunglasses.

Other things you might want include:
A universal plug.
An electrical adaptor.
Water purification tablets.
Earplugs.
Writing materials.
A simple sewing kit.
Water bottle.

Getting to Central America

By Air

From Europe

Several major airlines operate a service between Europe and Central America and the price of a return ticket will probably be between £500 and £600. More precise details of flights are given in the introduction to each chapter. It is generally cheaper to fly into the more popular destinations such as Guatemala City and San José. Flights to Mexico can be as much as £100 cheaper than those to Central America so it's worth considering starting your trip there, although you've still got a good distance to cover to reach the Guatemalan border. Good travel agents will also be able to offer 'open jaws' tickets, taking you into one city and out of another, which shouldn't cost any more than a straightforward return flight, while flights between Central American countries are reasonably priced. Two excellent London travel agents specializing in flights to Latin America are: Journey Latin America, 14–16 Devonshire Road, London W4 (tel 081 747 3108) and Latin American Travel, 28 Conduit Street, London W1 (tel 071 629 1130).

From the US

There are good connections between all Central American capitals and Miami, New York, Los Angeles, Houston, Washington DC as well as several other cities, with daily flights to most of these. Return fares from Miami and Los Angeles are priced at around US$400, but expect to pay twice that if coming from New York. Do shop around as special deals are often available. Among those offering the cheapest fares are Council Travel: in New York at 35 West 8th Street, New York 10011 (tel 212 254 2525); in California at 2846 Channing Way, Berkeley, CA 92093 (tel 510 415 848); and in Washington at 1314 Northeast 43rd Street, Suite 210, Seattle, WA 98105 (tel 206 632 2448).

By Sea

Finding a space on a ship bound for Central America is a time-consuming and uncertain business. Plenty of cruise ships head there and a great many freighters make their way to the Panamá Canal; however, few of these will be enthusiastic about taking on casual passengers. If you do get lucky the journey by sea takes at least two weeks from Europe or a week from the US. If your heart is set on arriving by boat then your best bet is to work as a crew member on a yacht. Boats heading for Central America leave Gibraltar and the Canary Islands in October and November and are often searching for an extra pair of hands, while in the US you'll just have to search around the large marinas and keep an eye of yacht club notice boards.

By Rail

Travellers coming from the US can at least get some of the way to Central America by train, covering the huge expanse between the US border and Mexico City. Reasonably comfortable sleepers operate on this line. However, if you plan to sleep your way out through the boredom then make sure you're absolutely exhausted as the trip takes at least 30 hours, often more!

By Road

Again the overland routes between the US and Central America are relatively direct, with good highways covering the main routes, although they do demand a degree of stamina. From Texas the most direct route cuts down the side of the Gulf of Mexico, bypassing the horrors of Mexico City. From California the drive is almost twice as long. By car you should expect to take at least a week to get through Mexico, even if you do use the most direct route. By bus you'll almost certainly have to travel via Mexico City and change buses. If you're sleeping on the bus it's just possible to make it through Mexico in four or five days, but don't expect to arrive in a fit state to enjoy yourself.

Agents and Specialist Operators

In the UK

Explore Worldwide (small-group exploratory holidays often using local transport, with the emphasis on discovering local cultures and wildlife); 1 Frederick Street, Aldershot, Hants GU11 1LQ, tel (0252) 319448.

Journey Latin America (large range of bespoke and package tours including environmental expeditions and economy journeys); 14–16 Devonshire Road, Chiswick, London W4 2HD, tel 081–747 8315.

Exodus Expeditions (escorted tours to Guatemala, Mexico and Belize); 9 Weir Road, London SW12 0LT, tel 081–675 5550.

Twickers World (tailor-made individual and group itineraries); 22 Church Street, Twickenham, Middlesex TW1 3NW, tel 081–892 8164.

Steamond Latin American Travel (tailor-made special-interest tours and itineraries including bird-watching, scuba-diving, etc); 278 Battersea Park, London SW11 3BS, tel 071–978 5500.

South American Experience (tailor-made packages); 47 Causton Road, London SW1P 4AT, tel 071–976 5511.

Worldwide Journeys (tailor-made holidays to Belize and Guatemala with emphasis on activity: jungle exploration, river-rafting, diving, etc); 146 Gloucester Road, London SW7 4SZ, tel 071–370 5032.

In the US

Himalayan Travel (fishing, bird-watching, river-rafting, natural history tours to Costa Rica); P.O. Box 481, Greenwich, CT 06836, tel (800) 225 2380.

Sobek Expeditions (river-rafting, sea-kayaking, and wildlife tours); P.O. Box 1089–60, Angel's Camp, CA 95222, tel (800) 777 7939.

Voyagers (natural history and photography tours to Belize and Costa Rica); Department EC, Box 915, Itaca, NY 14851, tel (607) 257 3091.

Wildland Adventures Inc. (ecotravel specialists); 3516 NE 155th, STE WT, Seattle, WA 98155, tel (800) 345 4453.

On Arrival

Entry Formalities

Formalities must be arranged before you set off but once your plane touches down in Central America you'll face immigration and customs. If you have not got a visa and do not need one then you will be presented with a tourist card. Once you've filled this in it is stamped, along with your passport and you must keep the two together until you leave the country. All this is usually very straightforward and you're through in a matter of minutes, queues permitting.

The main airports have banks and you should get hold of some local currency if the bank is open, and track down a taxi to take you into town. If the bank is closed then you should be able to find a taxi driver who will accept US dollars.

Tourist Information

The national tourist boards have offices at the main airports in Panamá City, Guatemala City and San José, although they have a strong tendency to remain closed all day. The best tourist information is provided by the main offices, which are all in the centre of the capital cities, and their addresses are listed in the country chapters, so it's best to wait until you have settled into a hotel before you rush off in search of information.

Maps

Local maps are generally available from Tourist Offices in each country while the best overall map of Central America is published by International Travel Map Productions, P.O. Box 2290, Vancouver, BC, V6B 3W5, Canada. Its European distributor is Bradt Publications, 41 Nortoft Road, Chalfont St Peter, Bucks, SL9 0LA, England and it is available from bookshops in San José in Costa Rica and in Antigua, Guatemala.

Getting Around

This section provides a general guide to the principles of travel within the isthmus. Information that is particular to each individual country—from car hire to bus time-tables—is given at the beginning of the relevant country chapter.

Unless you're staying for a year or two you'll have to be selective; many people like to choose a couple of countries and fly between them, avoiding long-haul overland trips. For exploring individual countries the best options are either car hire or bus travel, while other options, including boats, donkeys and pick-up trucks, provide a touch of spice.

By Air

Flying is easy and always the most convenient option, though certainly not the cheapest or most interesting; however, if time is short you can quickly reach any of the countries' capitals, saving days of bus travel. Prices for return flights tend to be double the single fare, so there is rarely money to be saved on return tickets. You will also find that foreigners often pay a different, more expensive, fare than local nationals. Don't worry, this is standard. Short journeys, such as from Guatemala City to Belize City, cost around US$80 one way, to San José it's nearer US$150 one way. It is always worth comparing prices between airlines offering the same routes.

Aviateca flies between Guatemala City, Managua and San José; **Taca** flies between Guatemala City, San Salvador, San José and Panamá; **Sahsa** flies between Guatemala City, San Salvador, San José and Panamá; **Aeronica** flies between Guatemala City, Managua, San José and Panamá; **Lacsa** flies between Guatemala City, San Pedro Sula, San José and Panamá; **Copa** flies between Guatemala City, San Salvador, Managua and Panamá. There are also connections for Belize City and Tegucigalpa.

By Boat

Except for the ferry route between Puerto Barrios, Guatemala and Punta Gorda, Belize, this is rarely a practical or safe way of getting from one country to another. There is an occasional boat service between Mango Creek, Belize and Puerto Cortés, Honduras, but schedules are haphazard and the danger from bad seas makes it an uncertain option.

By Train

There are no longer any train routes in Central America crossing international borders, although there are domestic services still operating in Guatemala, Nicaragua and Costa Rica, the details of which are given in the text on the relevant countries.

By Bus

This is the standard mode of transport for most travellers, and certainly the cheapest, if not the most comfortable. Adequate compensation for the inconveniences and delays, however, is provided by the pleasure of meeting local people and staying close to the region's endlessly varied landscapes.

The international **Tica Bus** route from San José to Guatemala City, via Managua and Tegucigalpa has now reopened, so you should be able to find out about it in any of the capitals it passes through. On the other hand, you can take local buses to the relevant border crossing and change for another bus once through customs. There are usually good connections to and from border posts and the details are outlined in each chapter.

There is an excellent international first class bus service between Guatemala City and San Salvador, operated by several companies. Buses depart every hour from a block south of the Zona 4 bus terminal in Guatemala City and in San Salvador from the Terminal Occidental.

By Car or Motorbike

Driving around Central America by hired car or your own vehicle gives you the advantage of complete freedom of movement. However, when weighing the obvious advantages against possible disadvantages, it is worth remembering that the police earn very little and often supplement their income by corruption. Foreigners are easy prey and it is essential that your papers are in perfect order and available for inspection at all times.

It is also much easier to deal with official hazards if you develop an easy-going attitude about checkpoints and border crossings. Usually everything runs smoothly and your way. Repair facilities outside the capital cities are rare, and it is a good idea to have plenty of spare parts with you.

By Bicycle

Central America is getting ever more popular with cyclists. The roads are often rough and unsurfaced, the terrain can be anything from sand to mud to rocks and pebbles, but few other modes of travel allow such a close contact with the land and its people. Bicycles are common throughout the region, so basic repairs are no problem, but it is worth carrying essential spares. Insurance against theft is vital. Unfortunately, few places outside Managua and the tourist centres of Guatemala and Costa Rica hire out bikes. If you are a serious cyclist, take your own (sturdy) machine, and contact the Cyclist's Touring Club, 69 Meadow, Godalming, Surrey, tel (0483) 417217.

Disabled Travellers

Travel in Central America can be quite rough, and no specific concessions or provisions are made to smooth the way for those with a physical handicap. Unfortunately, due to poverty and malnutrition, many more people suffer from disabilities here than in the West. If you or your travelling companion have special needs, you can make life much easier if you can afford to book organized tours and travel, where all aspects of transport are arranged for you, and provided in comfortable vehicles. You will find that the more developed countries, particularly Costa Rica, are better equipped to help.

There are quite a few organizations which advise and encourage international travel for disabled people. To mention a few: DIVE (Disabled International Visits and Exchanges), c/o The Central Bureau for Educational Visits and Exchanges, Seymour Mews House, Seymour Mews, London W1H 9PE; SATH (Society for the Advancement of Travel for the Handicapped), International Head Office, Suite 1110, 26 Court Street, Brooklyn, NY 11242, USA.

Specialist guide books or publications include: *Access to the World*, Louise Rice, Facts of File, London (1985); *Disabled Traveller's International Phrasebook*, Ian McNeil, Disability Press, 60 Greenhayes Avenue, Banstead, Surrey; *A List of Guidebooks for Handicapped Travelers*, The President's Committee on Employment of the Handicapped, 1111 20th Street, NW, Washington, DC 20036, USA.

Money and Official Currencies

The best currency to bring with you is the US dollar, since the entire region is economically dominated by it and always accepts it as payment. For safety's sake, you should bring at least half your money in traveller's cheques, which can be cashed at banks, as well as up-market hotels and even selected shops (except in Nicaragua, where only one bank in Managua will change cheques and dollar cash makes things a great deal easier). It's also a good idea to bring some dollar cash for border crossings and emergencies, or to clinch a bargain, or in case you need to change money outside banking hours. Dollar cash, and sometimes cheques, can also be changed on the black market, which is widely tolerated but illegal. Black-market dealers operate in the streets and usually offer a slightly better rate than the banks, although they often indulge in sharp practices and well rehearsed rip-offs. Up-market hotels usually accept and exchange traveller's cheques, but at a poor rate.

Once in Central America it can be very difficult to buy US dollars, and few banks are willing to break down large bills for you, so avoid US$100 notes, unless you intend to change that much at each transaction. Credit cards are only useful at top hotels and shops, travel agents, and car hire agencies. American Express, Diners, Visa and Access are the most commonly accepted plastic.

A word of advice: do invest in a money pouch that can be discreetly kept under your clothing, and never leave valuables unattended. Most hotels have safes for customers' money and papers, which you should use. The money belt remains the safest place to keep your valuables but is by no means infallible. Everyone knows gringos keep their money around their waist these days, but there is still no need to draw attention to yourself. Purses, wallets and handbags really are a bad idea, since pickpockets are many and expert.

Local Currencies
The relevant local currencies are best bought and sold on arrival in Central America as you'll find that they are hard to get hold of elsewhere, with the notable exception of Miami, where Central American currencies are easily obtained and off-loaded. Avoid bringing local currencies out of their relevant countries, as you will find it very difficult to get rid of them. The Central American currencies are as follows:

Guatemala:	Quetzal
Belize:	Belize dollar
Honduras:	Lempira
El Salvador:	Colón
Nicaragua:	Córdoba Oro
Costa Rica:	Colón
Panamá:	US dollar/Balboa

Manners and Mores

Crime and Police Business
Perhaps the best way to ensure your safety in Central America is to avoid carrying unnecessary valuables and accept the fact that they may be stolen. Most visitors to Central America have no real trouble at all, although petty theft and pickpocketing are widespread and irritating. There's little you can do to prevent this except keep your wits about you and avoid putting your money in easily accessible pockets.

Far more serious and a lot less likely is violent crime. If you are careful to avoid the worst spots—most notably Colón in Panamá and the Pacaya volcano in Guatemala—then you're very unlikely to fall victim to violent crime. Nevertheless women should avoid going out alone at night wherever possible, particularly in the big cities and seedy

Caribbean ports. Here the danger of theft and assault, while small during the day, is very real at night.

One last danger is that of getting caught up in political conflict. Although peace is breaking out all over the isthmus there are still some dangerous areas, particularly some remote sections of the Guatemalan, Nicaraguan and Salvadorean highlands. If you plan to venture into these areas then check with the local tourist office before you do so. More precise information on which areas to avoid and where to take particular care is given in the relevant country chapters.

Sexual Attitudes

> Some travellers don't wear underpants under their shorts with the result
> that when they sit cross-legged on the floor, anyone sitting opposite is
> subjected to a view of their genitals; this is usually unpopular.
>
> John Hatt, *The Tropical Traveller* (Pan, 1985)

This being Latin America, *machismo* is alive and well, and the concept of sexual equality is generally not even paid lip service. The traditional roles of women are defined by their place in the family, even though circumstances force the majority of them to work outside the home as well. Men are considered the natural head of the family, though this is often not the case in practice.

However, while sexism has obvious faults, there are also some, more positive aspects. Patronage of females means there is always a man around who is willing to help a woman, and even protect her from the advances of other men. Single women travellers often find themselves inundated with advice and help they didn't even ask for, which is often friendly and useful without any expectation of favours in return.

As far as foreign women are concerned, there is a general assumption among Latin Americans that Westerners are sexually easy, a quality which is both admired and despised. Certainly foreigners are popular conquests in certain circles. Male travellers will find themselves untrammelled by local mores, and cheap prostitution appears a real attraction for some. Women, on the other hand, are advised to think carefully about wearing sexy shorts or no bras, since they will undoubtedly attract attention and possibly disgust. Latin American society is astonishingly conservative and the display of naked flesh is regarded as bad manners, with the notable exception of the beach, where anything goes. Men in shorts are often considered to look ridiculous, while walking about bare chested is also inappropriate away from the beach. Topless sunbathing is not a good idea in the local context, though it may be accepted in certain luxury resort hotels, far from the gaze of local people. Among indigenous people you should try particularly hard to keep yourself under wraps although things tend to be a little more lax in Panamá and Costa Rica where creeping westernization has cut deepest. To give you an idea of local custom: women often submerge in the waves fully dressed, trousers and all.

Homosexuality is as much a part of Latin American society as it is of any other, though the demands of *machismo* are strongly repressive and it remains confined to a subculture of known bars in the capital cities and tourist towns like Antigua, Guatemala. Officials, such as the police and military, are well known for their brutality against gays, and foreign travellers should be careful not to draw attention to themselves. Homosexual and lesbian

12

couples will have no trouble with accommodation arrangements since it is very common for travellers of the same sex to share rooms. Double beds are rare anyway. Public opinion on the subject is characterized by a mixture of contempt and amusement.

Tipping

Throughout Central America tips are given in hotels and restaurants and to taxi drivers, porters and chambermaids. However, as in all Central American matters, there are no hard and fast rules and you're free to do as you please, responding to the situation as it arises. Generally speaking the staff in more up-market establishment will expect to be tipped, while those in cafés and cheap restaurants may be pleasantly surprised but will appreciate the gesture. In some countries, including Costa Rica and Guatemala, a 10% service charge is sometimes added to restaurant bills, and a 10–15% tourist tax added to hotel bills, although again this by no means rules out an additional tip.

Beggars

Beggars are a depressing reminder of Central America's desperate circumstances and are to be found on the streets of all main cities from Panamá to Guatemala. They are widely accepted by local people, who are usually willing to give them a coin or two. Beggars are also occasionally allowed to wander into restaurants and bars, becoming very much a part of the everyday chaos, although there is no doubt that their presence takes some getting used to.

Drugs

Drugs of all varieties, quantities and qualities are widely available throughout Central America, washed up on these shores as they travel north to the US. Dance floors in Belize are suffused with the sweet smell of marijuana, while Costa Rican teenagers and Panamanian street children use the ever present white powder to loosen up on a Saturday night. The use of soft drugs is widely tolerated in some parts of Central America, particularly Belize and the Caribbean coast of Costa Rica, although foreigners must still be discreet to avoid enraging local law enforcement officers. Elsewhere you should be very wary of having anything to do with drugs or those who deal in them, as dealers generally regard tourists as easy money and official penalties are steep, particularly when applied to outsiders.

Photography

From the vivid colours of Guatemalan costumes to the soft moods of Costa Rican rainforests, Central America is a photographers' paradise. Bear in mind that the range of light is enormous; in the clear sunshine of the highlands it can be searing, while little light penetrates beneath the canopy of the forest. So bring a wide range of film, as anything beyond the 100–400 ASA range is not available here. Standard slide and black and white film is available, although only in Guatemala City, Panamá City and San José.

Photographing sensitive subjects, including police and soldiers, can easily land you in deep trouble and you should make a point of asking local people if they mind being photographed. Photographing Indian religious ceremonies is deeply offensive, unless you are invited to do so.

Communications and Services

Throughout Central America all normal services are available to a reasonable standard in the capital cities, although it is worth noting that they deteriorate rapidly as you move out into the smaller towns and villages.

Post Offices and Telephones

In all of Central America these services are provided by state-owned companies which have a main office in the capital and small offices in most towns and villages. The service is usually good and it is well worth making the trip to a large office, where staff are used to establishing long-distance links. It is also possible to make international calls from a private phone or hotel room, although there is a greater degree of uncertainty attached to the process. The international phone service is at its best in Costa Rica and Panamá and at its least predictable in Nicaragua and El Salvador.

Postal services are similarly variable and again it's always a good idea to make a point of using main Post Offices. Letters should take around 10 days to reach the US and 2 weeks to Europe, but it can be a lot longer. Parcels tread a very unpredictable path and are more likely to go missing than letters, particularly if you send them from small, remote post offices.

Details of services available are given at the relevant point in the text.

Newspapers and the Media

English-language newspapers—usually *The Miami Herald* or *International Herald Tribune* or *New York Times*—are sold in Guatemala and Costa Rica; elsewhere you'll have to make do with local papers. There is also an English language weekly newspaper, *The Tico Times* published in Costa Rica. Otherwise you can keep in touch via CNN which is available in hotel rooms throughout the region.

Electricity

The current runs at 110 volts throughout Central America. This means North Americans can use all their electrical equipment without any problems. Europeans, however, will need adaptors for everything electrical bought in their own countries. Adaptors are not always easy or cheap to find in Central America, so do bring your own if you really need one.

Where to Stay

Central America offers the full range of accommodation, from luxury resort hotel to open-air hammock shelter. There are many local variations with a broader range of up-market accommodation in the more visited countries, particularly Costa Rica and Guatemala, although whatever kind of holiday and expense you have in mind, you will find something suitable in most places. Your choice will be far greater, however, in or near capital cities and if you are not looking exclusively for first-class hotels.

The widest range of accommodation lies in the band from inexpensive to moderate, which broadly speaking encompasses prices as low as US$4 per night to US$30 per night, for a double room. Camp sites are very rare, and guest houses are so cheap that you save no money camping anyway, the only advantage being to get off the beaten track or stay at official sights in distant reserves or up volcanoes.

Prices in the book are grouped under four price bands, which refer to the average price of a double room. (Like everywhere else, single travellers are generally penalized by having to pay almost the same as couples.) To find out what sort of accommodation you might encounter in each bracket look in the general introduction to the country chapters. Some countries, such as Guatemala, are very cheap for the traveller. Others, like Costa Rica or Belize, are expensive by the region's standards. Top-class hotels in Panamá City are the most espensive of all, because of the high number of business travellers to the Canal region.

To reflect this variety of accommodation within the isthmus, and to avoid a confusion of detail, the price bands used in this guide are quite wide, giving a general indication of what is cheap or expensive in Central America.

Remember that local inflation is rampant and prices change constantly in this region. All prices are therefore quoted in US dollars.

Category	*Double room*
LUXURY:	US$90–US$130
EXPENSIVE:	US$30–US$90
MODERATE:	US$12.50–US$30
INEXPENSIVE:	US$4–US$12.50

If you are travelling on a budget, keep your ear to the travellers' grapevine: the state of places to stay in this bracket changes all the time—and the addition of a (workable) shower, or laundry facilities, can make all the difference. Generally speaking, good value accommodation will be found around bus and train stations, markets, and truckers' stopping places (near gas stations).

Note that room prices will vary according to the season; and wherever you stay, it's worth booking in advance by fax, telex or registered mail.

Eating Out

Central American cuisine is commonly characterized by *huevos y frijoles*, eggs and beans, with cheese and meat as optional extras. This is not the most exciting meal in the world, but at least it's filling, and there is always a bottle of hot sauce (*salsa picante*) to liven things up. *Tortillas*, toasted patties of corn, are added to almost any dish, and are usually placed on the table automatically. Regional specialities, such as Belizean seafood or jungle cuisine, are covered in the relevant chapters.

In general, meat-eaters are much better catered for than vegetarians, who get stuck with eggs and beans, pasta, pizza and rice, with few vegetables or salads to choose from safely. Tropical fruit is some compensation for this, and wandering about any Central American market will show you the amazing variety on offer.

Salads should be avoided except if you are certain they have been cleaned properly, which usually means sticking to expensive hotels for that kind of food. The choice of international cooking is good in the capital cities, with Chinese the most frequent option. Italian, French and Mexican restaurants are also quite common. In provincial areas you will find your choice of foreign meals limited to Chinese, and in villages food is exclusively local fare.

Do try the local *comedores*, where you will find standard Latin meals and a good opportunity to mix with the local people and practise your Spanish. Dishes are simple and cheap and help to make your money go a long way. Another option for enjoying local fare is to head for the market, where boisterous ladies run open-air kitchens; huge pots of soup bubble away next to mountains of fried chicken. The local Chinese restaurants are often very good, but do tend to look rather grubby.

Drinks

Soft drinks (*jugos*)—or *aguas* if they're fizzy, canned or bottled—tea, and coffee are commonly available wherever you go. While travelling by bus, you will also encounter a myriad of homemade drinks, such as *agua de coco* (coconut water), with a lump of cooling ice in it. These are delicious and tempting, but the ice is invariably made from unsafe water. The same goes for any homemade, water-based drink, whether sold on the streets or in local *comedor* eating venues. For your own protection, it is also worth drinking straight from the bottle, rather than using possibly dirty glasses.

Local beers, *cervezas*, are cheap and rather watery, but refreshing in the tropical heat without causing too much drowsiness. Rum, *ron*, is also cheap and often quite good, while regional 'firewaters', *aguardientes*, burn a mean trail down your throat—an effect similar to drinking distilled alcohol. Regional brews are mentioned in the relevant country sections.

Restaurants and Comedores

There is a clear divide in Central America between local establishments, where the food is cheap and the atmosphere can be distinctly rough and ready and a rather slicker range of up-market establishment. In the former, it's the setting that provides most of the flavour, while the latter, generally a great deal more expensive, provides your only hope of gastronomic indulgence. These tourist and foreign-run restaurants are bound to be quite expensive by local standards, but the variety of meals is greater and sanitary conditions are usually better. Up-market hotels and restaurants offer an international menu and prices to match.

Shopping and Bargaining

Shopping conditions vary greatly within Central America, ranging from the small village markets of the Guatemalan highlands, where hand-woven cloth is sold alongside a family of pigs, to the swish boutiques of Panamá City, which offer designer clothes in industrial quantities.

Brightly coloured friendship bands from Guatemala are popular souvenirs

Generally speaking the best *artesanía* (craft work) and most spontaneous markets are found in Guatemala, while things are more contained in the calm of Costa Rica, but go wild again amidst the rampant commercialism of Panamá. Among the best locally produced goods are Guatemalan weavings, Costa Rican coffee and leather goods, Nicaraguan rocking chairs (which pack down into small wooden boxes) and Panamanian *molas*, blouses embroidered by the Kuna Indians, although the selection is endless. Western consumer goods, of all sorts and from all parts of the world, are at their cheapest in Panamá, where many a crate falls off the back of a passing ship.

Central Americans have a tremendous capacity for business and take great pleasure in shopping, whether it's toothpaste or tangerines and whether they're buying or selling. Bargaining is always part of the process, particularly in rural markets, and involves an exchange of formalities in which both buyer and seller must preserve their dignity. Bear in mind that the middle ground always exists; it's just a question of reaching it.

Sports and Activities

Sport in Central America is in the early stages of development, although Costa Rica is well ahead in the game. Here is a simple list of the best that's on and an indication of which way to head if you're looking for a particular activity. For more information see the individual country chapters.

Amateur Archaeology

Maya ruins are scattered throughout Belize, Guatemala and Honduras and offer a fascinating insight into the area's pre-Columbian history. For those in search of ancient history the best countries to head for are Guatemala and Belize, where the concentration of ancient sites is at its highest.

17

Diving

Both Central American coasts provide ideal waters for diving and there are many companies offering diving courses and days out. The sport is at its most developed in Costa Rica and Belize, which boasts one of the longest barrier reefs in the world, although it is also possible to dive in Honduras and Panamá. There's no need to bring your own equipment as there are companies catering to tourists in all of these countries.

Fishing

Superb river and sea fishing is available throughout Central America. The sport has been well developed in Costa Rica and Belize, where specialist companies offer ever more imaginative types of fishing from big-game blue marlin to rainbow trout in the mountains.

Hiking

There are excellent opportunites for hiking throughout Central America. The range of scenery gives you the option of a short stroll along a sandy beach, the gruelling ascent of a volcanic peak, or wading through jungle mud. In Costa Rica and Guatemala it is possible to hire camping equipment and there are well developed trail systems and National Parks, particularly in the latter. Elsewhere in the isthmus you'll have to bring your own equipment and by and large find your own way. In the UK walking trips to Costa Rica are organised by High Places (tel 0742 822333), Globe Works, Penistone Road, Sheffield S6 3AE.

Natural History

Central America offers superb bird and animal watching, and in Costa Rica alone there are said to be as many species of bird as in the entire United States. There are excellent National Parks in Costa Rica, Guatemala and Belize, which all provide the best opportunities for ornithology.

Potholing

Central America's limestone interior is said to provide some of the finest potholing in the world, although as yet the sport has not been developed in any systematic way. Caves in Guatemala and Costa Rica have been explored, although if you're planning an expedition you'll still need to bring all your own equipment.

River Rafting

Again, this is an up and coming sport in Central America which has been widely developed in Costa Rica. You'll need to no expert training and can simply book a day out once you arrive. Several companies in San José offer trips ranging from an afternoon to a week on the water. For more experienced rafters the rivers of Costa Rica offer some superb challenges, while the sport is slowly being taken up in Belize and Guatemala.

Surfing

Pacific rollers pound the eastern side of Central America and attract a steady stream of surfing enthusiasts. The most popular destination is Costa Rica, although the surf in Panama and El Salvador is also said to be superb. Many surfers bring boards with them although it is possible to hire a board at some of the more popular beaches in Costa Rica.

Environmental Issues

The Central American isthmus is riddled with instability. Here the meeting of north and south funnels a range of opposing forces into close contact, generating a tension which manifests itself in volcanic eruptions, earthquakes and political upheaval. However, this uncomfortable relationship has also created a rich and varied environment in which species of animals and plants from both north and south coexist with local species that are found nowhere else in the world.

The region contains an amazing range of environments. The far south, where Panamá merges into Colombia, is one the the most impenetrable jungles in the world, a rugged landscape of low hills, swamps, tortuous rivers and towering rainforest, in which tropical downpours and scorching sunshine conspire to keep the air heavy with humidity. At the other end of the isthmus the Cuchumatanes mountains roll across the border between Guatemala and Mexico, reaching a height of some 3600 metres. Here the jagged granite peaks are regularly bitten by frost and occasionally dusted with snow, while the altitude keeps the air fresh and clear.

Between these extremes a chain of volcanic peaks forms the backbone of the isthmus, including at least seven active volanoes. The best of these are Pacaya in Guatemala and Arenal in Costa Rica, both oozing a steady plume of sulphurous smoke and sporadically spraying fountains of fire into the night sky. A series of broad highland valleys are strung up between the volcanoes, some containing beautiful lakes, others occupied by sprawling moden cities such as San José, San Salvador and Guatemala City. In amongst the volcanoes are several mountain ranges, the largest in Costa Rica and Guatemala, their upper slopes supporting an almost Andean environment of sparse scrub and coarse bushes. The lower slopes, however, are richly fertile, their acid volcanic soils coated in enormous coffee plantations. A few small areas, saved by the difficult terrain and poor infrastructure, are still covered by magical cloud forests, in which the trees are wrapped in moss, their branches dripping with ferns and bromeliads.

Stretching out beneath the highlands a wide coastal plain runs down the Pacific side from Guatemala to Panamá. It's an area of scorching heat and intense fertility now monopolized by commercial agriculture. Huge plantations of cotton and sugar have replaced most of the original vegetation, although in Costa Rica the Santa Rosa National Park preserves the only remaining area of dry tropical forest which once covered the entire coastline. Meanwhile on the other side of the highlands, reaching to the shores of the Caribbean, much of the land remains inaccessible and uninhabited. In Belize and Honduras some regions are now well developed, although in Nicaragua and Panamá the

Caribbean coast is a great forested frontier, hundreds of tiny rivers cutting through a tangle of tropical vegetation as they make their way to the sea.

Lying a few miles off the Caribbean coast are several small clusters of islands and coral reefs, the largest running parallel to the coast of Belize and ranking as the world's second longest barrier reef. The seas on both sides of Central America are teeming with a kaleidoscope of tropical fish including rays, sharks, barracuda, swordfish and marlin. If you're snorkelling or diving, the display is incredibly impressive, while the marine life also makes superb eating, served up with spicy creole sauces and sweetened with coconut.

Flora and Fauna

This range of environments in Central America is matched by an equally varied selection of wildlife. In Costa Rica alone there are some 760 species of birds, which is around the same number as are found in the entire United States. In the dense tropical forests **scarlet macaws** waft between the treetops, squawking at uninvited intruders while thumb-size **hummingbirds** buzz among the flowers and flocks of brilliant green **parakeets** chatter as they spin through the trees. Central America is an ornithologist's paradise and even for the uninitiated the variety and beauty of the birds is a real source of fascination. Perhaps the most infamous of all Central America's birds is the **resplendant quetzal**, which was sacred to the Maya and still has a certain magical aura. With its bright green plumage and long, snaking tail the quetzal is an astonishing sight in the wild, its vivid colours providing a sudden flash amidst the soft greys and misty greens of the cloud forest.

Animal life is also profuse, with the remaining swamps, grasslands and forests providing a home to **jaguars**, **crocodiles**, **deer**, a weird selection of lizards and **iguanas**, four types of **monkey**, **coatimundi**, **armadillos**, **tapirs**, **otters**, **peccary** and more than 15 species of **poisonous snake**, including the deadly fer-de-lance, coral snake and bushmaster. Most of the large animals are extremely elusive, although from time to time they pop up just when you're not expecting them. Nevertheless when wandering through the jungle you get a strong sense of being in somebody else's territory. The rustle of leaves or crack of branches may be all that you hear of a disappearing **deer**, although other species do like to make their presence felt, particularly the monkeys. The acrobatic **spider monkeys** are the most assertive, screeching at you from the treetops and shaking branches to send dead limbs tumbling to the forest floor. Their aim can be extremely accurate and spider monkeys have been known to defecate on intruders, scoring a direct hit from some 30 metres up.

Among the most regular visitors to Central America are the huge sea **turtles**, of which four species come ashore on the Pacific and Caribbean coasts. The females nest during the rainy season, hauling themselves up onto the beach and digging a small hole with their flippers. They then deposit about a hundred eggs as large as a ping-pong balls and cover them in sand before dragging themselves back into the sea. The young turtles emerge a few months later and must make a desperate dash for the surf, many of them being picked off by seabirds before they make it. Turtles' eggs are also sold in the markets and served in bars, where they are eaten raw with a touch of lemon juice and tabasco and are said to have aphrodisiac qualities.

National Parks

The distribution and development of National Parks in Central America mirror the region's political and social problems. The poorer, troubled nations, such as Nicaragua and El Salvador have done little to protect the environment, attending first to more pressing problems. Meanwhile Belize and Costa Rica have led the way, identifying their most important environmental assets and taking concrete steps to preserve them.

If you're keen to see some of Central America's birds and beasts or visit a wide range of untouched environments then Costa Rica is certainly the most rewarding destination. Around 20% of the country is protected in a network of private reserves and government-funded National Parks, most of which are well established with facilities for visitors and a choice of excellent trails. The parks include several active volcanoes, a couple of cloud forests, a slice of the high mountains, swamps, open grassland, dry tropical forest, beaches and some incredibly well preserved sections of tropical rainforest. The accessibility of the parks varies enormously. Some can be visited easily by car and make comfortable day trips from San José, while others, such as the Corcovado National Park, require quite a commitment, including some tough jungle-hiking and several nights of camping. The more remote parks offer a unique opportunity to see exotic birds and animals in the wild, while the forest itself is tremendously impressive.

A little smaller are the National Parks of Belize. Here several specific species are protected, including howler monkeys at the Community Baboon Sanctuary and jaguars at the large Cockscomb reserve to the south of Dangriga. Again every effort has been made to include the full range of environments, from the high mountains to the offshore coral reef, and to provide facilities for visitors, making Belize a close rival to Costa Rica for amateur naturalists and ornithologists.

Across the border in Guatemala the national parks are still in their early days. The country's most important reserve embraces the forest surrounding Tikal in the Petén. The forest here is well preserved and makes a fitting backdrop for the ruins, although sadly much of the surrounding area is now being plundered for oil, while new roads and cattle farms are eating into virgin territory. Guatemala has three other impressive reserves. The first at Monterrico, on the Pacific coast, where a superb black sand beach provides an ideal nesting sight for turtles and a maze of mangroves is alive with fish and birds. Over on the Caribbean coast is the Río Dulce reserve, where the river of the same name cuts through a dramatic steep-sided gorge before spilling into the ocean. Last, but by no means least, is Lake Atitlán, Guatemala's scenic jewel, its turquoise waters ringed by volcanic peaks, although the scale of development is starting to have a damaging impact here.

Elsewhere in Central America National Parks are often little more than large tracts of empty land, and in El Salvador some are not even known to the tourist board. Honduras has several National Parks, including vast empty areas in the west and the beautiful Bay Islands arching out into Caribbean. In Nicaragua the only park of any note is Masaya National Park, which is well developed for tourism, while in Panamá several large areas are protected although they are all inaccessible, protected from tourists and developers by mile upon mile of impenetrable forest.

21

Ecotourism

Ecotourism has become a catch phrase for a new kind of travel which is committed to minimizing the impact of tourism on sensitive natural environments and their traditional human and animal inhabitants. Belize is at the forefront of this movement in Central America. Government and local agencies have combined to coordinate a programme of development for the country's areas of outstanding natural beauty, both on land and under water. That is the ideal. In practice, 90% of the country's coastal developments are foreign owned, and the risk of unscrupulous exploitation is still high.

Not every package advertised under the 'ecotourism' banner is truly committed to its ideals, and travellers are advised to check carefully what exactly they are being offered. Ecotourism is big business and there is a tendency to overcharge travellers just because a tour is advertised under its label. In particular it should be noted how many people any one group contains, since only small groups can claim to have a low impact on local environments and people. Another good question is to what extent the local people benefit, either financially or in developmental needs for the community.

In Belize itself there are two organizations which offer excellent information, as well as help with organizing visits to areas of interest. The **Belize Audubon Society**, 29 Regent Street, P.O. Box 1001, Belize City, tel (02) 77369 has been given responsibility for the administration of nine of the country's reserves, and can advise on natural resources and conservation in Belize. **Programme for Belize**, 1 King Street, Belize City, tel (02) 75616 is a consortium of British and American organizations concerned with ecological preservation in Belize. In particular they are running a programme of buying Belizean rainforest as a measure to protect it. The Río Bravo Conservation Area is also one of their projects. Specifically concerned with southern Belize is the **Toledo Eco Tourism Association**, which you can contact via Chet Schmidt, Nature's Way Guest House, 65 Front Street, tel (07) 2119.

Whether you choose to join an ecotour or not, you should note that Belize has certain laws to protect its natural resources, though sadly they are not effectively enforced, so it is up to the visitor to support the country's efforts at preservation. The following are the most important prohibitive laws:

1. Removing and exporting black coral
2. Hunting without a licence
3. Picking orchids in forest reserves
4. Spear-fishing while wearing scuba diving gear
5. Camping overnight in any public place, including reserves

Specialist Operators
Concentrating on adventurous journeys and promoting ecotourism from England are **Wild West Expeditions**, Ashes Farm Cottage, Hayfield, Derbyshire SK12 5LL, tel (0663) 741578; **EcoSafaris**, 146 Gloucester Road, London SW7 4SZ, tel 071–370 1085; and **Twickers World**, 22 Church Street, Twickenham, London TW1 3NW, tel 081–892 8164/7606, fax 081–892 8061.

Part II

CENTRAL AMERICAN HISTORY BEFORE INDEPENDENCE

> Land as slim as a whip,
> Hot as torture,
> Your step in Honduras, your blood
> In Santo Domingo, at night,
> Your eyes in Nicaragua...
>
> Pablo Neruda, *Centro América*

Flying across Central America, the view is astonishing, especially over Panamá. Far below, you see the Atlantic and Pacific oceans at the same time, only a narrow strip of land keeping them apart—a narrow strip which also separates (or connects) the great land masses of North and South America. Central America has somehow always been viewed like that: a ragged bridge connecting two huge continents, or worse still, simply a peninsular extension of North America, giving credence to the modern idea of 'America's Back Yard'—after all, the Darién Gap is a dead end in terms of overland travel. The jungle there is so inaccessible and the land so swampy that no road or rail has yet succeeded in penetrating to the South American mainland. The only way to proceed is on foot or to fly.

Yet there is nothing homogeneous about this region that stretches from the Mexican/ Guatemalan border all the way to the swampy jungles of the Panamanian border with Colombia. What looks like a geographical unity is in fact a collection of seven very different countries. There are features which they all have in common, such as the Spanish language, certain tropical export crops, and a subtropical climate. But the human history of the region could hardly be more dissimilar. From prehistoric times quite distinct cultures have emerged, largely defined by the regional differences in geography and vegetation. Even the effect of the Spanish Conquest was regionally disparate.

Prehistory

During the last Ice Age, such vast expanses of ocean were frozen that the earth's general sea level was lowered. One effect of this was that Asia and North America were at times connected by a land bridge, known as the Bering Passage, and it is believed that humans first came into the Americas via this route about 60,000 years ago. Radiocarbon dates from polished bone tools suggest that the entire North and South American continents were populated by 11,000 BC.

The people who lived here in those times were hunter-gatherers, who lived a nomadic existence, following a seasonal cycle after a large variety of animals and easily gathered fruits, nuts and roots. Small family groups would have roamed the landscape, only occasionally coming together into larger camps in order to hunt the giant mammals of the age, such as mammoth, mastodon or bison. But there were many smaller animals they hunted too, such as rabbits, foxes, squirrels, turtles, lizards and quail.

Between 11,000 and 6000 BC the climate gradually became warmer and drier. Huge lakes dried up, grasslands became deserts, and the woodlands shrank, so that slowly the giants of prehistory became extinct. New kinds of food eventually had to be found by humans, and very, very slowly, people evolved new ways of life, where food came from a greater variety of sources.

In the time from 7000 to 1500 BC domesticated plants played an increasingly important role, and larger camps of people developed in response to the greater numbers needed for effective food gathering and hunting. In particular near rivers, lakes and oceans, sedentary groups emerged, who supplemented their fishing culture with gathering a great variety of other food, such as wild cereal plants, fruit, nuts, avocados, squashes, chilli peppers and prickly pears.

The Origin of Agriculture

The evidence for how and when humans first developed agriculture in the Americas is hotly debated. By its nature, plant evidence is hard to come by, and archaeologists have had to make do for their clues with a few cave sites in dry areas, such as in Oaxaca in central Mexico or the Ayacucho basin in the Peruvian Andes. It is at those sites that they have analyzed the ground layers relating to different ages, as well as studying coprolites (fossilized faeces) and human bones. From these combined studies scientists have been able to establish that a major change took place in human diet after 4500 BC and it is only from this time onwards that agriculture can be said to have been important.

To look for an exact point at which hunting and gathering stopped and agriculture began is fruitless. Development is the key word, and the transition from a nomadic hunting way of life to a sedentary agricultural life was gradual. The cultivation of certain plants may not have resulted from the extinction of the larger animals, nor because of the changing climate or population pressure, but for simple practical reasons. For example, one of the earliest domesticates was the bottle gourd for carrying water, and other plants were cultivated for dyes. Some plants, such as the tomato, are believed to have been domesticated incidentally, when genetic changes in the plant, such as increased size, made it a more important and easily gathered food source.

This must particularly apply to the all-important food plant, maize. Whatever the plant ancestor of maize, its cob would not have been larger than a thumbnail, and its use as a food source cannot have been obvious to early man. Instead, the combined effect of incidental domestication and genetic changes in the plant gradually made it more and more useful, and eventually people would have begun to cultivate it in an agricultural way, planting and gathering it specifically for the purpose of food. That these changes must have been slow is underlined by the fact that by 1500 BC maize was still only one-fifth of its present size. What is certain, however, is that man's changed relationship to the environment eventually allowed the first settled cultures to develop.

Early Societies

The earliest evidence for settled communities comes from household tools and crafts, such as simple pottery, and cotton fibre cloth was probably also used, though it has not often survived. From 3000 BC onwards, and certainly from 1500 BC settled communities of between twelve and several hundred people gradually developed a new culture that included ritual and religious belief. Small figurines, believed to relate to ancestor worship or fertility rites have been found from this time. Homes were probably window-less houses made of pole and wattle, with roofs thatched by palm leaf. In the highlands, houses would have been made of mud bricks (adobe), and thatched with straw or coarse grasses. Both these types of housing can still be seen in traditional Indian villages today.

Elite centres appear by around 1000 BC when flat temple platforms indicate ceremonial sites, and unequal burials testify to a stratified society. Some were simply wrapped in a sleeping mat and buried under the family house, while others were buried with great fineries and even human retainers.

One of the earliest Mesoamerican civilizations were the Olmec, who existed between 1200 and 100 BC with their heyday from 900 to 600 BC. However, their territory was almost entirely restricted to the Gulf Coast and the Tuxla Mountains of modern Mexico. The only significant satellite further south was at Izapa, on the Mexican Pacific coast near modern Tapachula. Another Mesoamerican people were the Toltecs, whose capital was the Yucatán ceremonial centre of Tula, and yet another were the Mixtecs, who ruled the area around modern Mexico City after the demise of the nearby city of Teotihuacan. The only Mesoamerican civilization to develop further south was that of the Maya, whose earliest beginnings go back as far as 2000 BC. Their territory is generally divided into three different zones: the Highland Maya of the Guatemalan highlands, the Lowland Maya of the Guatemalan Petén and adjacent Maya Mountains, and the Northern Lowland Maya of the Mexican Yucatán.

The Maya

The history of Maya civilization is divided into three periods: the Pre-Classic (2000 BC to AD 250), the Classic (AD 250 to 900), and the Post-Classic (AD 900 to 1530). They are generally held to represent the development, maturity and decadence of the civilization.

Pre-Classic Maya: 2000 BC to AD 250

From 2000 BC to around AD 150, Maya ancestors lived in the small communities already described. In particular along the Pacific plain of Guatemala, were villages established to harvest both the land and the sea. Their inhabitants lived off shellfish, crab, fish, turtles and iguanas, as well as maize from cultivated fields. The earliest village culture in this region is known as Ocos, and flourished from 1500 BC onwards. Later came the Cuadros village culture, which lasted until around 850 BC. Both evolved fine pottery skills, making a variety of bowls, pots and figurines. A common artefact of the period was the tripod bowl or jar, often decorated with crisscross and zigzag designs, and—uniquely in Central America—patterns made by pressing rope or twine into the wet clay.

Another important centre of early civilization, Kaminal Juyu, lies in the central valley of Guatemala, close to the modern capital. A significant ceremonial centre from earliest Pre-Classic times, it eventually developed into a huge site of at least one hundred buildings, with political and trading links reaching all the way to Mexican Teotihuacán. Even the inhospitable Petén lowlands show evidence of early cultures, and sites such as Altar de Sacrificios, Ceibal, Tikal and Uaxactún were certainly inhabited by 400 BC.

Eventually, some time between 250 BC and AD 300, these simple village cultures scattered across the Maya territory developed the traits of a great civilization. Monumental architecture, sophisticated art forms, timekeeping and elaborate calendars, writing, and the science of astrology were all components of that development. Society became structured by an official religion and a rigid, hereditary class system where even slaves were a hereditary group.

Kaminal Juyu developed into a vast and prestigious city. Temple platforms were raised from the ground, reaching up to 18 metres, and on these stood the simple temples of pole and thatch that so disappointed the Spanish in their search for riches. For those were not to be found in the temples, but in the burial chambers underneath them and around the pyramid platforms.

Classic Maya: AD 250 to 900

The Classic Age was a Golden Age for the Maya civilization, and their sophistication in architecture, art and science can easily match that of the ancient Egyptians or Greeks. Their astronomers could accurately predict lunar and solar eclipses and had recognized many planets, while the Maya calendar reached far beyond the Christian calendar and the complexity of their writing system has yet to be fully understood (see p. 34).

It is during this age that Maya lords built the imposing pyramids of Tikal and Caracol, and sculptural art reached its peak at sites like Copán and Quiriguá. Often these sites are referred to as cities, since as many as 50,000 people once lived in and around them. But that is a misleading term, imposing modern conceptions on the past. It is now generally accepted that it is better to speak of ceremonial centres, since Maya civilization was fundamentally ruled by religious faith and ritual, and all aspects of life, whether the planting season, dates for war, or people's names, were decided by the Maya

baktun *katun* *tun* *kin*

astronomers and diviners. They were at the heart of all decisions, and the position of every person in society was dominated by their interpretation of the celestial and divine cycle.

Only a very small elite of nobles and priests lived at the core of what we see today: the great plazas and pyramids. Nearby there were quarters of artisans, craftsmen and slaves, and spreading out over a much larger area were the dwellings and clustered communities of the peasant majority, who were involved exclusively in food procurement and processing for the central elite, who then redistributed it among the population.

Post-Classic Maya: AD 900 to 1530

Between 790 and 889 AD the Classic Maya civilization abruptly disintegrated. Within a hundred years, the Lowland Maya populations seem to have left, state architecture and monumental building stopped, and even the Maya hieroglyphics appear to have degenerated into simpler forms of pictographic symbolism. Many explanations have been put forward for this collapse: earthquakes or hurricanes, epidemics, ecological disasters, social revolt, foreign invasion or economic decline. Certainly, the warlike Toltecs seem to have moved in from the north around 900, but the evidence from some sources suggests that the decline began before then. Until the Maya script is fully understood, we shall never know more than a fraction of the story.

All we can say for sure is that the Classic Maya civilization did collapse, and from the 10th century onwards, the glorious temples and plazas of most lowland ceremonial centres were left to itinerant squatters, who camped among the abandoned buildings, periodically looting the royal burial chambers or using masonry for their own building needs. Soon the great buildings were reclaimed by surrounding jungle, and by the time the Spanish arrived, the temples and pyramids of the Maya had been derelict for over 500 years, remnants of a 'lost civilization'. The surviving Maya Indians could not shed much light on the magnificent art and architecture of their ancestors, nor adequately explain their culture's historic knowledge of astronomy, science and writing.

But while southern lowland centres of power, such as Tikal, declined, northern lowland centres, such as Chichen Itzá in modern Mexico, expanded. They developed a new style of art and culture, and traded goods along the coast in canoes. Much of this phase of Central American history remains obscure, though Post-Classic culture may have been a fusion of Maya and Toltec. By the time the Spanish arrived, however, Chichen Itzá was also in ruins. In the Western Highlands of Guatemala, though, the Quiché Maya had their powerful kingdom with its capital at Utatlán, the Mam Maya ruled their domains from Zaculeu, and the Cakchiquel Maya governed theirs from Iximché. All these peoples preserved many aspects of Classic Maya culture, and continued to do so after the Conquest.

27

European Discovery and the Colonial Era

Europeans first came to Central America on Columbus' fourth and final voyage in 1502. His ship dropped anchor at Guanaja, one of the Honduran Bay Islands, and much to the excitement of his teenage son, his forces captured a Maya trading canoe, filled with exotic goods such as quetzal plumes, cacao beans, shells and fine pottery. Soon Columbus set sail once more, heading east around the Mosquito Coast, and discovered the Veragua region, which yielded enough gold finds to encourage a steady stream of expeditions to beach on today's Nicaraguan and Panamanian Atlantic coasts.

In 1513, the conquistador Balboa discovered the Pacific Ocean while travelling inland near the Darién forest, and soon Panamá City (1519), León and Granada (1524) were founded. They were some of the earliest colonial settlements in Central America, and flourished as bases from which to explore, as well as exploit local minerals and the Indians. Slavery was good business, and many thousands of Indians were shipped off to South American silver and gold mines. Most died of European diseases and malnutrition before they reached their destination, and once arrived, they were found to be unsuitable for heavy mine work. It was then that the Spanish began importing the stronger African slaves, thus introducing a significant black society to Central America.

Spanish forces were also penetrating south from Mexico City, soon to discover and conquer the Highland Maya of Guatemala and establish the brutal reign of Pedro de Alvarado. It was he who founded the most glamorous colonial city of Central America: Antigua Guatemala, situated in a beautiful highland valley embraced by three volcanos. Meanwhile Spanish forces also traced the Atlantic coast southwards from the Yucatán, establishing strategic forts near the Honduran ports of Puerto Cortés and Trujillo, as well as inland at San Pedro Sula. These were important in repelling Portuguese and English expeditions, and also as bases from which to exploit the fertile interior for cacao.

After the Conquest, population centres followed the ancient patterns so that the main centre of Spanish rule grew up in the Guatemalan highlands. From there it spread thinly south, neglecting the traditionally 'empty' regions, such as the swampy jungles of the Atlantic littoral, as well as many inland areas, such as the inaccessible Honduran highlands. Much of the interior was left to its own devices by the colonial authorities, with the exception of vital ports along the Pacific, such as Colón in Panamá, and fortifications along the Atlantic, such as Omoa and Trujillo in Honduras.

The Spanish were too preoccupied with extracting the riches of Mexican silver and Peruvian gold to bother much with Central America; its mineral resources were limited, and its largest asset was an enslaved Indian population which did little to increase the wealth of Spain itself. Since the conquistadors had little interest in farming, the great agricultural potential of the region was not exploited intensively until after Independence, although indigo and cacao were relatively lucrative exports from El Salvador and Guatemala. Soon the region became a colonial backwater. Panamá was lumped in under the jurisdiction of New Granada, ruled by the Viceroy of Peru, while the rest became the Captaincy-General of Guatemala in 1543, beholden to the Viceroy of New Spain, the forerunner of modern Mexico. This political division still influences Central American politics today and Panamá retains a unique position, not least because of the US-controlled Panamá Canal.

Unlike the Europeans in North America, the Spanish came as soldiers, not settlers. They did not bring their families, but married and had children by Indian women. The mestizos who resulted from this union soon formed the majority of colonial society. The Spanish crown, however, reserved the positions of highest authority for *peninsulares*—those born in Spain, who brought their families with them—a division that was eventually to spark off the independence movement. Along the Atlantic coast, the presence of African slaves led to a significant society of blacks and mulattos. Added to these peoples were small but coherent groups of Chinese, East Indians and white settlers, usually of religious groups, such as the Mennonites, as well as non-Maya indigenous groups, like the Miskitos or Darién Indians, who survived by nature of their inaccessibility. The Maya themselves succeeded better than any other indigenous people of the Americas in retaining their racial and cultural heritage, and to this day they make up over half the population of modern Guatemala.

Neglect by the Spanish authorities allowed others to make inroads into the territory. English, Dutch and French pirates made their homes along the Bay of Honduras, and by the 17th century, English pirates had even helped their country establish claims to what became known as the Crown Colony of British Honduras. Their legacy still exists in Belize, which has only been independent from Britain since 1981, and the English-speaking inhabitants of the Honduran Bay Islands.

Independence from Spanish Rule

Central America gained independence on the coat-tails of Mexico in 1821. There was no battle for independence in the region, and there were plenty among the economic elite who remained loyal to Spanish authority. They were virtually let go against their will; once the rest of Latin America had gone, the Spanish colonial authorities had no further interest in a region that had always been one of the least profitable possessions.

It was a confusing time, when such disparate groups as the mine owners from Honduras, cacao planters of El Salvador and cattle ranchers of Panamá found themselves in a territory with no political authority and little common ground. As a result the various regions turned inwards, trying to consolidate their own interests, while sporadic battles raged between forces loyal to Spain and those with ambitions for wider political control of the region. A limited consensus was reached in 1823, when all but Chiapas decided not to become part of Mexico, and instead founded the United Provinces of Central America, whose capital was to be Guatemala City. This union was made up of five newly founded provinces: Guatemala, El Salvador, Honduras, Nicaragua and Costa Rica, whose borders were more or less the same as those of the countries of today. British Honduras remained outside the union, while Panamá became a part of Colombia. It was a recipe for political fragmentation, and the union was soon rent by conflicting economic and political interests, falling apart completely in 1839.

Ever since, Central American unity has been a lost cause. Honduras and Guatemala soon emerged as the original 'banana republics', their economic and political destiny closely supervised by US interests such as the United Fruit Company. Panamá declared its independence from Colombia in 1904, supported by the US to facilitate the building of the canal. Central America's role as the 'back yard' of the US has been a constant theme of its history since Independence, and on several occasions economic and political influence has spilled over into direct military intervention: the US occupation of Nicaragua from 1909 to 1933, the CIA-backed coup in Guatemala in 1954, or the invasion of Panamá in 1989. Admittedly this has produced a level of economic investment which the local governments could never have generated. But the price has been high, and remains the foremost cause of political instability in the region.

Part III

TOPICS

WHITE — NORTH

BLACK — WEST

GREEN   RED — EAST

YELLOW ~ SOUTH

Glyphs for the world directions and associated colours

The Maya Universe

These are the names of the First People who were made and modelled...
Thoughts came into existence and they gazed; their vision came all at once.
Perfectly they saw, perfectly they knew everything under the sky, whenever
they looked.

The *Popol Vuh* of the Quiché Maya, translated by Dennis Tedlock

Miraculously surviving the ravages of time and the depredations of the conquistadors,
the manuscripts, the stone inscriptions, the pottery, the pyramids and temples, and above
all, the living tradition itself allow us a glimpse into the extraordinary universe of the
Maya.

Maya Gods

The pantheon of the Classic Maya period (AD 250–900) has roots
stretching back more than a thousand years earlier to the Olmecs, and
continued to be worshipped long after the Spanish Conquest. Because
of this long history, and because the Maya were not a centralized empire
but a collection of independent peoples, some of the gods have several aliases.

According to some traditions, the original omnipotent spirit was Hunab Ku. He
created Itzamná, god of fire, and the inventor of writing; and Ixchel, goddess of medicine
and the Old Moon. They created all the other gods, including Chac, the goggle-eyed

31

rain god; the four Bacabs, who stood at the points of the compass and supported the heavens; the maize god, an ever-present symbol of renewal; and a rather cuddly character known as the Fat God. The monkey-men gods were the special patrons of the scribes.

Of special importance was 'God K'; he was the wind god and the special protector of the Maya rulers, who carried his image on their sceptres. After the arrival of the Toltecs around AD 900, he seems to become identified with Kukulkan. God of the primordial wind, he was known to the Quiché as Gucumatz and worshipped by the Aztecs as Quetzalcoátl—the plumed serpent.

Among the gods of the underworld (Xibalbá), who sent forth owls to summon mortals to their final ball game, were the skeletal Huna-hau, the Death God; his assistants Tatan Holon ('Father Skull') and Tatan Bak ('Father Bones'); the Jaguar God; the long-nosed Ek Chuuah, god of merchants; and Ixtab, the goddess of suicides, who is shown hanging from a noose in Maya manuscripts.

Itzamná

Creation Myths

There are many different accounts of the creation from the Maya lands. One version, inscribed on two stones at Quiriguá in Guatemala and Palenque in Mexico, lay unnoticed for millennia until it was deciphered by two US scholars, Linda Schele and David Freidel, in 1992. On 13 August, 3114 BC, the gods lit the flame from which the universe was created, in a hearth of three stones. The fire can still be seen in the sky today—the red Orion nebula, which hangs between the three brightest stars of that constellation. At the moment of creation, though, the sky lay flat upon the surface of the earth in a two-dimensional universe. The gods then used the Milky Way as a great tree to lift the sky up above the earth.

Ixchel, the old Moon Goddess

The creation of human beings is recorded in the Quiché Maya's Book of Creation, the *Popol Vuh*. It took the gods Tepeu and Gucumatz four attempts to accomplish this difficult task. Their first creatures were fashioned out of the earth's mud, but soon disintegrated. The second versions were made of wood, but were stupid and had to be destroyed as unworthy. The third attempt promised well; the creatures were made of living flesh, and had minds too. Disappointingly, they failed to honour their creators (which was supposed to be their main purpose in life) and were punished by being turned into monkeys. The fourth creations, made from maize, at last proved satisfactory, knowing their place and worshipping the gods.

Sun God

Maya Society

At the apex of a Maya city was a ruler who claimed to be descended from the gods. At Copán and Quiriguá, carvings show the new king as the sun rising from the jaws of the earth, while his predecessor is

Chac, the Rain God

swallowed up. To prove that the blood of the gods flowed in their veins, members of the ruling family would shed their blood before their subjects; the men by piercing the penis with a bone spike, the women by dragging a thorn-studded cord through a hole in their tongue. After his death, a ruler would be interred in one of the great pyramids, along with many human sacrifices of men, women and children. Some were undoubtedly captured victims of war, but others would have been kept for sacrifice, especially the children.

An elite caste of scribes descended from the Monkey Man gods recorded every aspect of their society. They kept and consulted the sacred calendars and astronomical tables, which dictated every detail of public and private life. The palace household also included nobles and military officers, who could be sent out to govern conquered cities. Further down the hierarchy were the artisans, artists and traders. Of the ordinary people— builders and farmers, peasants and slaves—we know even less than we do of their ancient Egyptian counterparts.

The Maya cities were extremely militaristic, and in a constant state of conflict with neighbouring centres of power. Their aim was not to expand their territory but to capture high-ranking individuals from rival cities, who would then be sacrificed to the gods. This conflict was also ritualized in the Ball Game. The two rival teams were kitted out in helmets and heavy padding, not unlike modern American footballers. The game was played on stone courts with vertical hoops, such as the one which can still be seen at Copán (see p. 272). The stakes were high: the losers often ended up on the sacrificial altar. In the *Popol Vuh*, two young men are challenged to a ball game with the lords of the underworld. After the defeat and death of the two young men, the severed head of one of them impregnates Lady Blood by spitting in her hand. She gives birth to the Hero Twins, who defeat the underworld gods in a return match.

Art and Architecture

For the modern traveller in Central America, the most visible remnants of the Classic Maya civilization are the great temples that rise so dramatically from the forests of Guatemala, Honduras and Belize. The most characteristic structures are nearly always known as 'pyramids'. This is a somewhat misleading term, however, as it conjures up visions of Egypt, where the pyramids are buildings in their own right. In Central America, they are simply the platform on which a temple was constructed. Sometimes the 'pyramids' are wide and relatively low, as at Copán (see p. 272); sometimes they soar almost vertically, as at Tikal (see p. 168). They are usually surrounded by a complex of smaller temples, plazas, ceremonial avenues, and sometimes a ball court.

Maya architecture never achieved the carefully worked, accurately interlocking masonry so characteristic of the Incas of Peru. Maya buildings usually consist of a core of rubble and cement, faced with a thin cladding of dressed stone, and they stay up by sheer mass rather than geometry. The cladding, however, was covered with intricate relief carving and mosaics, and where the stone was too hard to be easily worked, stucco was moulded into spectacular relief. The principle of the arch was unknown to Maya architects; instead, they constructed their massive vaults by overlapping stone slabs until they met in the centre of the roof. The peak of the vault was often crowned by a highly ornamented 'roof comb'. We are accustomed to the mellow hues of weathered stone, and

33

it takes some effort of imagination to picture the temples in their heyday: painted blood red, with the relief moulding picked out in bright colours.

A prominent feature of Maya monumental art was the stela. These large oblong stones, rising up to 10 metres above the ground, usually stood planted before a circular altar slab in the temple plazas. The stelae were intricately carved with stylized portraits of noble rulers; the sides or back recorded crucial dates in Maya hieroglyphs. Only a fraction of the stelae have been deciphered, but it is generally agreed that they record royal lineages, and the dates of important battles, accessions to the throne, royal birthdays and other significant events.

The Maya 'cities' were home only to the gods, the priests, the ruler, and his dead ancestors. The great mass of the population would have lived nearby, in thatched wooden buildings not unlike the ones their descendants inhabit today. It was for the dead, too, that the Maya reserved their finest pottery and artefacts of jade, obsidian, crystal and other minerals and precious stones. Many surviving vases illustrate scenes of the underworld, and pottery figurines of gods, humans and animals are frequently recovered from graves. The National Museum of Archaeology and Ethnology and the Popol Vuh Museum in Guatemala City (see p. 82) have excellent collections of Maya ceramics, jade and other artefacts.

The Maya Alphabet

Shield Jaguar   *Accession Glyph*   *Birthday Glyph*   *Bird Jaguar*   *Prefix—Female Names and Titles*

Ever since their first discovery by Europeans, the complex inscriptions on Maya architecture and monuments have baffled even the most expert epigraphers. We know far less about the Maya script than we do about Egyptian hieroglyphics, but from what we do know, it is even more complicated than Chinese. Maya scribes made virtuosic use of a complex system. They had a phonetic symbol for every syllable, but also used pictographic images—a flame to signify the word hot, for example. They would also use pictographs to represent the sound or meaning of individual syllables in a word. Furthermore, there are many homonyms in the Maya script, so that the same symbol can have very different meanings depending on the context. For example, the words 'sky', 'four', 'snake' and 'captive' are all pronounced identically and can only be distinguished in the proper context.

Many studies have failed because they have tried to bend this system to the concept behind the Western alphabet. Bishop Landa was one of the first to try this, but never realized that his Maya informant was often giving him the name for a letter, but not the variety of meanings it could carry. Eventually the Maya nobleman's patience wore thin, and he wrote 'I don't want to' in the bishop's book.

Among the small groups of symbols whose meaning the experts agree on are the emblem glyphs for a number of important Classic centres such as Tikal, Yaxchilán, or Quiriguá, and the glyphs relating to noble lineages and important events in their dynastic history. The symbols for birth, death, and accession to power have been recognized, and often their dates have also been found in surrounding glyphs or pictures. Symbols found at Yaxchilán, on the river Usumacinta in the Petén jungle, tell us that the city was ruled by the Jaguar dynasty, fathered by the great lord Shield Jaguar, during the 8th century. The extent of a city's military and political power is often demonstrated by the appearance of its unique emblem glyph at other sites, representing conquest or an advantageous royal marriage.

Maya Arithmetic

The concept of zero, so essential to any advanced mathematics, has been thought of only twice in human history: once in India around 600 BC, and once in Central America. Exactly when it first appeared in Central America is not certain, but it was already in use by the time the Maya came on the scene.

The system of Maya arithmetic was vigesimal, based on factors of 20, but had been adjusted to fit in with the calendar. The numerals were arranged in vertical columns, which increased in value from bottom to top. There were just three symbols: a dot signified 1, a horizontal bar signified 5, and a stylized shell signified zero.

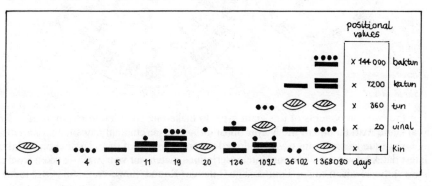

The Maya Calendar

The Maya were obsessed with time, and the keeping of time. The fate of each person was ordained by the date and timing of their birth, and the interpreters of the celestial and divine cycles held immense power over the population, including the nobility. One of the four surviving pre-Conquest books, the Dresden Codex, contains an extraordinarily accurate table of the movements and eclipses of the planet Venus.

From Pre-Classic times, the Maya used two different calendars. Who invented them is uncertain, but most believe that it was probably the Olmecs, and that the Maya simply refined the existing systems handed down to them. The Long Count is a system that hinges on a fixed date in the past, like the Christian calendar, and begins at

4 Ahau 8 Cumku, the equivalent of a day in 3113 BC. According to their belief, this was the beginning of a historic cycle of 13 baktuns (periods of 144,000 days). This cycle is due to be destroyed in the year equivalent to the Christian year of AD 2012, when a new age will begin.

The Maya also used the Calendar Round, which estimated time in cycles of 260 days, each of which held important information for fortunes and ceremonials. This system involved the use of two calendars which ran concurrently. The first consisted of 20 named days with 13 numbers; the second of 365 days, divided into 18 months of 20 days each, with five extra days, called Uayeb, which were considered highly unlucky.

The best way to understand this system in operation is to imagine two interlocking cogwheels of different sizes:

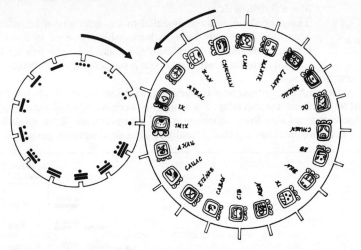

For the two components of this giant cycle to make one completion required 52 solar years, and marked one of the Mayas' most important ceremonial dates.

Use of the Long Count was abandoned towards the end of the Classic Age, and the latest dates known from monumental inscriptions match our year AD 909, taken from a stela at the Mexican site of Tonina. The Calendar Round, however, is still in use today.

The Living Heritage

Although much Maya learning has been lost, centuries of persecution have failed to eradicate it entirely. The Maya Indians survive, and their languages, culture and religion are still a part of their everyday lives. The daykeepers or shamans living in the Western Highlands of Guatemala still keep the sacred knowledge of the Calendar Round. Predominantly Indian towns and villages, such as Chichicastenango, Santiago Atitlán, and Momostenango, are well known for their periodic festivals. But since secrecy has been the key to survival, foreigners are unlikely to witness any ritual ceremonies relating to the Calendar Round. In **San Andrés Itzapa**, however, you can experience the cult of Maximón, a strange hybrid of Maya and Catholic ritual. In a side-street chapel, the cigar-toting effigy of the saint is liberally anointed with rum under the benevolent gaze of the priest. Outside the celebrations continue as fireworks are let off under the auspices of the Maya daykeeper. It is this resilience and power of adaptation that has kept the Maya tradition alive, and makes it one of the most exciting features of Central America today.

Central American Literature: an Introduction

Mis ojos miraban en hora de ensueños
La página blanca.
Y vino el desfile de ensueños y sombras.

It was the hour of dreams. In front of me
A snow-white page outspread I seemed to see.
And a procession came of dreams and shades.

Rubén Darío, *The White Page*

Central American literature has an ancestry at least as old as the Maya civilization itself. The lowland Maya were writing books on deerskin, or paper made from pulverized bark as early as AD 500, and the knowledge they contained stretched back far further. Some, like the *Book of Chilam Balam* and the *Popol Vuh*, recorded creation myths, prophesies and acts of the gods. Others dealt with crop cycles and astronomical calculations. There were histories, biographies, atlases, almanacs and calendars. Written on sheets of paper anything up to 6 m long and folded into pages like a concertina, the manuscripts were elaborately and exuberantly illustrated.

When Franciscan monks arrived bearing the Bible, the Indian priests replied that they preferred to trust their own sacred texts. What followed was a literary holocaust comparable to the destruction of the library at Alexandria. The Spanish burned the 'books of the idolatrous priests' wherever they could find them, often consigning their owners to the flames as well. Only four Quiché Maya manuscripts survive today. The Spanish-Tlaxcalan mestizo Diego Muñoz Camargo recorded the scene in a drawing that accompanies his *History of Tlaxcala*. As two Spanish friars torch a pile of books, gods and animals leap from the flames, as if liberated from the page to inhabit the air.

The Colonial Era
The first colonial writers of Spanish America were the conquistadors themselves and the hard-headed priests who accompanied them. At his house in Antigua, Guatemala, Bernal Díaz del Castillo (1495?–1584), veteran of 119 battles, wrote his argumentative *True History of the Conquest of New Spain* to refute all other accounts. The conquistadors' arch-critic, Father Bartolomé de las Casas (1474–1565), also lived in Antigua for a while. His *Brief Account of the Destruction of the Indies* (1552) described Spanish atrocities in horrific detail, and caused much liberal hand-wringing back in Madrid. To show that the Highland Maya of Guatemala could be converted to Christianity by peaceable means, he composed hymns in their Quiché language.

Early colonial bards penned ponderous epics extolling the feats of Cortés and Alvarado in the heroic style of ancient Rome and Renaissance Italy, while the church churned out devotional tracts, often in Nahuatl and other indigenous languages. The enterprising priests also wrote and staged sacred dramas (*autos sacramentales*). Like the medieval mystery plays, these were based on Bible stories and performed in the native language with singing, dancing, comic interludes and audience participation.

But New Spain was not a propitious environment for the development of literature. All publications had to be vetted by the censors in Madrid, and Spanish printers held a monopoly which allowed them to flood the provinces with their work. Under these conditions it is hardly surprising that the bulk of Central American literature was provincial and derivative. Little poetry of note was written, and no novels at all.

Meanwhile, the gods and animals that flew from the burning pages of the sacred books still hovered in the air. Storytellers handed down ancestral knowledge from one generation to the next. From sympathy or curiosity, some of the Spanish priests began to write down, from the memories of the Indians, the texts they had themselves destroyed. Even Bishop Diego Landa, the most zealous of the book burners, turned his hand to ethno-history. It is thanks to their activities that the *Popol Vuh* survives today; the earliest copy dates from around 1700.

The *autos sacramentales*, meanwhile, began to assume a life of their own in the hands of their Indian performers. Fables, allegories, parables and satire became important weapons against censorship, and a means of protest against oppression. Brutal landlords could be hidden in animal or mythical characters, ignominiously defeated and held up to ridicule. The comic interludes, often based on Indian folklore, gradually became longer, and in some cases supplanted the Christian element altogether. One such play, the *Baile del Güegüence* from Nicaragua, was written down in the 19th century, although it is probably older. The knockabout plot concerns a Spanish governor who can't afford to stage the customary songs and dances for the Royal Council. He arrests the *güegüence* (village elder) and tries to extort money from him. After much singing, dancing and bawdy farce, the wisecracking elder outwits his blustering overlord.

From Independence to Modernismo

Just as Central America was slow to be drawn into the independence movement of the early 19th century, it was slow to be drawn into the literary tumult that followed. Writers to the north and south, from Mexicali to Tierra del Fuego, produced a torrent of poems, plays and novels celebrating revolution and erotic love, the Aztec warriors of the past and the gauchos of the present. They lurched giddily from the romantic idealism of Byron and Shelley to the gritty realism of Zola. They devoured the latest European authors while proclaiming *americanismo* in literature.

By the time Central America got in on the act, young writers had found a new creed: *modernismo*. The movement began in Cuba and Mexico, but the Nicaraguan Rubén Darío (1867–1916) became its brightest star and acknowledged leader with the publication of his volume of poems *Azul* in 1888.

Modernismo was a far cry from what the name might suggest to a 20th-century reader. A reaction against realism, it was intended to be 'art for art's sake'. Refined, sensual and otherworldly, it owed much to the French symbolists. But Darío, whose ancestry combined Amerindian, Spanish and African, successfully fused the contradictory heritage of the continent into a truly Latin American literature. The beauty of the Nicaraguan landscape suffuses his work, and although Walt Whitman and Edgar Allan Poe were among his literary heroes, this did not prevent him from taking a stab at Yankee imperialism in his poem 'A Roosevelt'.

Darío's fame took him all over Latin America, where his prestige was enormous; to France, where he met Paul Verlaine; and to the United States, where he caught the pneumonia that killed him shortly after his return to Nicaragua. He was Central America's first poet of international stature. 'To enter the city of Nicaraguan poetry,' Steven F. White has written in *Poets of Nicaragua*, 'one must first pass the landmark that guards the gates—Rubén Darío'.

The 20th Century: Magical Realism and Political Commitment

Modern Latin American literature conjures up famous names like the Chilean Isabel Allende, the Argentinean Jorge Luis Borges, the Peruvian Mario Vargas Llosa, the Colombian Gabriel García Márquez, or the Mexican Carlos Fuentes. Yet that peculiarly Latin American form of literature we call magical realism was invented almost single-handed by the Guatemalan novelist Miguel Angel Asturias (1899–1974). As a young man in Paris, he assisted in the translation of the *Popol Vuh*, which was to influence all his future writing; wrote his first important book, *Leyendas de Guatemala* (Legends of Guatemala, 1930); and completed his novel *El señor Presidente* (The President). He returned to Guatemala in 1933, to spend a miserable decade struggling with political repression, alcoholism and an unhappy marriage. *El señor Presidente* remained unpublished until 1946.

These experiences found an outlet in his best-known book, *Hombres de maíz* (Men of Maize, 1949). This ambitious novel draws on Maya legend, the theories of Marx and Freud, and the literary techniques of Joyce and Eliot, to give a form and a voice to the traumatized subconscious of Guatemala. Like Darío, Asturias conjures up a 'procession of dreams and shades', testifying to the colonization of the spirit as well as of the land; to the loss of identity and masculine pride; and to the powerlessness to keep a woman or refuse a drink. Ariel Dorfman, the Chilean author of *Death and the Maiden*, has described *Hombres de maíz* as 'both the fountainhead and the backbone of all that is being written in our continent today.' Although driven into exile by the 1954 coup, Asturias had recovered his confidence as a writer. Many other novels followed, including his 'Banana Trilogy', which satirizes the activities of the United Fruit Company in Guatemala, and in 1967 he won the Nobel Prize for Literature.

Throughout the 20th century, Central American literature has been closely allied to politics. The Nicaraguan poetic renaissance kindled by Rubén Darío soon turned to political protest in the work of Salomón de la Selva (1893–1958) and the group of poets known as the Vanguard. Inspired by the guerrilla leader Augusto César Sandino, the Vanguard combined poetic avant-gardism with the rhythms of popular songs in a celebration of daily lives and work of the *campesinos* (peasant farmers). One major figure stands outside this mainstream: Alfonso Cortés (1893–1969), affectionately known as *el poeta loco*. After a mental breakdown in 1927, Cortés inscribed his startling, otherworldly poetry on minute pieces of paper while chained to the wall in the house, which had once belonged to Rubén Darío, where he lived with his sisters.

When the Sandinistas came to power in 1979, it seemed as though the poets had actually become the *acknowledged* legislators, if not of the world, at least of Nicaragua.

The vice-president was novelist Sergio Ramírez (1942–), whose compelling tales of the influence of North American culture on his country, *Stories* and *To Bury our Fathers*, were published by Readers International in 1976 and 1984 respectively. The internationally respected poet Ernesto Cardenal (1925–), a veteran of the Vanguard movement, was minister of culture; their ambassador to Brazil was the poet Ernesto Gutiérrez (1929–); even the president, Daniel Ortega, was a published poet. Among the fine poets who emerged during these years were Giaconda Belli and Vidaluz Meneses. The daughter of a general in Anastasio Somoza's loathed National Guard, Meneses attempted to come to terms with this painful relationship in her poem 'Last Postcard for my Father'.

Throughout Central America, writers have continued to publish clandestinely in the face of state repression. Quite a few have been the target of assassination or forced into exile. Some, like Salvadoreans Manlio Argueta (1935–)—the author of *One Day of Life* and *Cuzcatlán*—and Jacinta Escudos (1961–) or the Panamanian Bertalicia Peralta (1939–), have been translated into English. Many others have not. *And We Sold the Rain*, edited by Rosario Santos (Ryan Publishing, 1989), provides a good general introduction for English-speaking readers. This collection of short stories offers a glimpse into the lives of the men, women and children of Central America: Maya Indians, Marxist guerrillas and *campesinos*, living, through war and poverty, at the edge of life and death.

Music

Central America's natural history is an interesting blend of the immediate north and south, but its musical roots are far more widespread, combining the rhythms of Africa, native America, the Caribbean, Europe and the US to create a series of unique and energetic hybrids. The entire isthmus is rocked by rhythm, and whether you are in a café, on a bus or walking down the street you'll never be far from the sound of a radio. Central Americans have a passion for music and and a great talent for dance. Their various tastes reflect the region's main historical and cultural divisions. From the steamy, erotic dance-floors of Managua to the misty villages of Guatemala, music is a means of communication and self-expresssion, an essential ingredient in daily life.

Music also played an important role in the region's pre-Columbian cultures, although few details are known. The only surviving instruments are small clay ocarinas which make a high-pitched whistling sound. Nevertheless, archaeologists believe that animal-skin drums, rattles and flutes were all in use and that music enhanced the impact of religious ceremonies, increasing the sense of awe upon which the power of the religious elite depended. It is a theory supported by the murals at the Maya site of Bonampak (on the border between Guatemala and Mexico), which clearly show an assembled orchestra alongside the portrait of a ruler and his assistant.

These ancient traditions doubtless feed the music of today's Indian groups, who still use music in their fiestas and religious ceremonies, although these days they have absorbed a wide range of influences. Most Indian bands still include drums, flutes and whistles, but the principal instrument is now the marimba, a long xylophone-type instrument sometimes played by three or four musicians. The marimba features in most Central American styles, favoured by Indian groups and farmers from Guatemala to Costa Rica and sometimes accompanied by guitars and singers. It's a soft, lilting style of music, appropriate enough to the highlands and to local fiestas, but rarely heard in the cities. Meanwhile, in the wilds of Panamá they have developed a unique and haunting style called *típica*, in which a wailing woman is accompanied by a furious African drum beat. To an outsider the music is disturbing but local people seem to enjoy it, picking out enough rhythm to dance enthusiastically.

The marimba is, in fact, of African origin, having arrived in Central America via Jamaica and the slave trade, although Central America's black communities, based on the Caribbean coast, have now moved on to the more modern sounds of calypso and reggae. The English influence is strong here and many of the local bands sing in English, taking their lead from heroes such as Bob Marley. A local Belizean variation is *Brukdown* which is firmly rooted in creole culture and includes the guitar, banjo, accordion and drums. In Bluefields, Nicaragua, local people still dance the *Palo de Mayo*, replacing its English refrain with a more blatant sexual style. Here the big bands are Dimensión Costeña and Caribe, both churning out a specifically Latin reggae which is big in dance-halls across the isthmus.

Classical music has never really taken off in this part of the world, although the Costa Ricans have struggled to introduce high culture to Central American listeners. Back in the 1940s President Figueres declared 'why have tractors without violins?' and Costa Rica now has the only National Youth Symphony in Latin America. It's not a musical style that has spread to the streets but nevertheless they do stage a series of concerts every year and musicians from around the world perform in San José's Teatro Nacional, undoubtedly the most beautiful theatre on the isthmus.

Back in the world of mestizo popular culture it's *salsa* and *meringue* which are the great Latin sounds, booming out across the dance-floors from Guatemala to Panamá. A lot of the big hits come up from Brazil, Venezuela and Colombia, while other styles, including traditional *mariachi*, which is sometimes played in the streets, come south from Mexico. Meanwhile modern rock and pop music from Europe and the US is also extremely popular with the likes of Madonna and Michael Jackson competing for air-time. Songs come and go here as quickly as anywhere else and the importance of radio ensures that they are widely known. On a typical dance-floor contemporary Latin sounds are mixed evenly with pop and rock, and in this, as in most things, Central America is walking the tightrope, unsure where it belongs.

Some Central American Stereotypes

Banana Republics

Bananas have been one of the great shaping forces in modern Central America. Introduced as a sideline by the company which built Costa Rica's Atlantic railway, banana plantations still dominate much of the Pacific coast from Belize to Panamá, although the political power of the banana companies is not what it once was. The

companies grew and developed during the thirties and forties, reaching their zenith in 1955 when the almighty United Fruit Company was able to engineer a coup in Guatemala after the government threatened the compulsory puchase of its unused land. (The coup was backed by the CIA, who have always played a key role in keeping the world safe for banana producers.) Today bananas are still grown in the steamy lowlands of all Central American republics and in many areas the banana company still dominates the economy. Towns such as Bananera in Guatemala and Almirante in Panamá are almost entirely owned by banana companies and come complete with company housing, shops and transport; in Bananera there is even a small golf course for ex-pat executives.

The Oligarchy
The Generals. Central America's generals have a long history of manipulating the political agenda and it is only in Costa Rica that they remain excluded from power, thanks to the abolition of the armed forces. Elsewhere the men in uniform have always played a major role and at one time or another the army has ruled every one of the republics.

The generals were at their most powerful and eccentric in the early years of this century. Jorge Ubico, who ruled Guatemala from 1930 to 1944 believed that he was a reincarnation of Napoleon, surrounded himself with replica cannons and had the Guatemalan symphony orchestra dressed in military uniform. Meanwhile in El Salvador General Maximiliano Hernández Martínez, a classic Latin American despot who combined extremes of eccentricity and brutality, hung coloured lights in San Salvador in a bid to prevent the spread of smallpox.

In more recent times the generals have shown themselves capable of horrific brutality, killing hundreds of thousands in civil wars in Nicaragua, El Salvador and Guatemala. Thankfully the troops are currently in the process of returning to their barrack. Yet, ousted in Panamá and pushed to one side in Nicaragua, Guatemala and El Salvador, the army still manages to cast a strong shadow over the political agenda and retains a great deal of power. This may not be apparent at first, for techniques have become increasingly

42

sophisticated and the sight of tanks on the streets appears to be a thing of the past. These days the generals flex their muscles through the press, and rumours of a coup serve to keep the government on the straight and narrow.

The last general to be in direct control of his country was the infamous General Manuel Noriega, who used Panamá as a warehouse for the storage and shipment of drugs, guns and money, but was finally deposed by US troops in December 1989.

Coffee Barons. Throughout Central America coffee remains the golden bean and a flicker in the coffee price sends shock waves through the governments of Costa Rica, El Salvador and Guatemala—where the economy is still rooted in coffee production and the coffee producer is a significant man. While light industry is the territory of tomorrow's entrepreneurs, the coffee barons remain a very influential section of the traditional right-wing oligarchy. They are traditional in all they do with a strongly conservative streak and a deep disregard for the workforce (who are mostly press-ganged peasants in El Salvador and Guatemala, while in Costa Rica the relatively high standard of living threatens to undermine the coffee harvest and impoverished labourers now have to be imported from Nicaragua to prevent the beans rotting on the bushes). Ironically it is extremely difficult to get a good cup of coffee in Central America, although the Café La Perla in San José, Costa Rica, or Café Tirol in Cobán, Guatemala are recommended.

The Fourteen Families. El Salvador's tight-knit oligarchy is perhaps the most in-famous and ruthless in Central America. Although light industry and the army have provided opportunities for those outside the original clique, the big names do still dominate the larger industries and main sources of capital. And though the original grouping has now expanded to a hundred families or more, there is still a small group that pulls the strings and rakes in the cash. If you're interested to find out what they're up to then take a look in any daily newspaper. In amongst the tales of death and mutilation you'll find the irrepressible society columns, telling you who has just made an excellent match, and who's off to Miami this week.

Death Squads. Despite the much vaunted sweeping tide of democracy the death squads are still very much in operation, particularly in Guatemala and El Salvador. Responding to international pressure, the armed forces have adopted a new respectable image but old habits die hard and the traditional means of control are still employed on a regular basis. Off-duty policemen and soldiers still act as judge, jury and executioner, when dealing with those they consider their enemies. Their targets have changed little since the early 1960s: the victims are still union leaders, left-wing politicians and human rights workers.

Costa Rican Women

Among a certain select group of North American men there is a strange belief that Costa Rican women make ideal and exotic wives. Classified advertisements in Costa Rican newspapers testify to this traffic, as do up-market brothels and frustrated, drunk men who prop up bars in San José. There are, apparently, no claims made about Costa Rican men making ideal husbands—no doubt their time will come.

Drugs

Latin America's main producers of marijuana and cocaine remain the giants of Colombia, Peru and Bolivia, with limited production in Central America itself. Nevertheless the isthmus plays a key role as a link with the lucrative northern markets and the shipment of drugs is a growth industry. Cocaine by the ton is regularly intercepted in Central America, with light aircraft, lorries and small boats shuttling merchandise from south to north. Cheap, high-quality drugs are available throughout the isthmus and drug abuse is widespread, taking a heavy toll in certain areas, particularly Colón, Panamá City, Belize City and Puerto Limón, where crack use is now widespread and has spawned an epidemic of violent crime.

Sex, Sleaze and the Graham Greene Factor

To many, Central America is a fly-blown bar frequented by washed-up soaks, sleazy ex-patriots and US writers down on their luck. These elements are certainly there, although these days writers can afford the sanctity of Antigua's secure drinking holes and the slick nightclubs of San José. Meanwhile it's largely Central America's poor who live amidst the horrors of drugs and violence, condemned to a life of hard graft and an early grave. If you'd like to join them or are in search of a location for a new novel then try the hell-holes of Panamá where sleaze is in plentiful supply. However if it's just good music you're after then you'll find it in every corner of the isthmus.

Colón

Yes, it's true, Colón is undeniably the most dangerous city in Central America. However it does not match the rumours that you may encounter in Costa Rica, where Colón is now famous as a city in which the entire population wanders around in a crack-induced trance, stealing and killing as a matter of course. There is, nevertheless, a great deal of crime, drug abuse and desperation and it's a city in which tourists are a prime target. Stick to Panamá City unless you're a member of the dangerous sports club, in which case it's right up your street.

Some Key Players

Don Pedro de Alvarado

Handsome, blond, muscular, brave, restless and deeply ruthless, Don Pedro de Alvarado was the archetypal conquistador, tearing through Central America in search of gold and laying waste to all that stood in his way. Alvarado arrived in Guatemala in 1523, sent south by Cortés to claim Central America for the Spanish and instructed to 'preach matters concerning the Holy faith'. Once in Guatemala Alvarado adopted his own approach. Almost immediately his meagre army was confronted by some 30,000 Quichéan warriors. However, he was able to play one faction off against another and used the warring tribes to fight his battles for him. According to Maya accounts the first epic battle ended in a personal duel between Alvarado and the Quichéan king, Tecún Umán, who wore a headdress of Quetzal feathers. Alvarado eventually triumphed. Following their defeat the Quichés invited Alvarado to their capital, Utatlán, but before he entered the city he grew suspicious and had the entire place burnt to the ground.

From 1524 until his death in 1541 Alvarado ruled Guatemala as a personal fiefdom, rewarding his followers with vast tracts of land and the right to use the Indians as they saw fit. He established his headquarters in what is now Antigua, which became the colonial capital for all of Central America. Meanwhile, disappointed by the lack of gold, Alvarado grew increasingly restless and took part in a series of other expeditions, travelling as far as Peru and Mexico. In 1541, on the way to the Spice Islands, he was killed under a rolling horse.

When news of Alvarado's death reached his wife, Beatriz de la Cueva, she plunged Antigua into mourning, had the royal palace painted black, inside and out, and ordered the city authorities to appoint her as the new governor. Then, for several days the entire area was swept by furious storms and, on 10 September 1541, a powerful earthquake shook the valley, releasing a massive volume of water that had built up in the cone of the Agua volcano. A tide of mud and water swept down the mountain and the city was buried beneath it.

William Walker

The Nicaraguan presidency is a job that is generally speaking taken by an unexpected outsider, although few could have predicted that William Walker, the self-proclaimed 'grey-eyed man of destiny' would ever end up in the hot seat.

Born in Nashville, Tennessee, in 1824, Walker got off to a flying start entering the University of Nashville at the age of 12. Graduating seven years later he soon grew tired of the medical profession and moved on to study law in New Orleans. Bored with law he turned his hand to journalism, becoming foreign editor on a liberal newspaper. Here he fought vigorously for the abolition of slavery and devoted his spare moments to the love of his life, who was deaf and mute. However, the death of his girlfriend and the closure of the newspaper soon sent Walker off in yet another direction, this time following the gold rush to San Francisco in 1850. Unlike other miners Walker wasn't content to strike a claim and dig, but decided instead to form a small private army and march into Mexico, where he set about forming a democracy in the province of Sonora. His efforts were not well received by the Mexicans and he was lucky to escape with his life, limping home to an American border post where he turned himself in. He was later charged with breaking the Neutrality Act and put on trial in the US, but was mysteriously acquitted.

Nevertheless Walker had now found his vocation: released from the petty confines of a single profession, his heart was set on military intervention. Encouraged by the US millionaire Cornelius Vanderbilt, who operated a steamship company on Lake Nicaragua, Walker put together a second army and set sail for Nicaragua, where he intervened in the civil war, giving his support to the Liberals of León in their battle against the Granada-based Conservatives. Walker's men, known as 'the immortals' marched up from the south, fighting their first battle in Rivas and then storming Granada. Within a year Walker declared himself president and, much to the surprise of his Liberal supporters, made English the official language and reintroduced slavery. Armies from Guatemala, Honduras and Costa Rica all rose against this imposter on the isthmus and 'the immortals' were finally defeated at the battle of Rivas in 1856, thanks to the efforts of a Costa Rican drummer boy—now a national hero—who set fire to their ammunition. Walker himself managed to flee but was eventually captured by the British in Honduras, handed over to the Honduran army and shot by a firing squad on the beach.

Pirates

'Gold constitutes treasure and he who possesses it has all he needs.' So said Christopher Columbus, and although he himself found little in the way of riches on his travels, he did open the door to untold wealth for the Spanish. In the 16th century, as the flow of gold from Latin America became a flood, the French and English became enraged and jealous. Afraid to engage the Spanish in open conflict they fostered teams of privateers and freewheeling thugs, who operated under their guidance but soon developed their own distinctive style and were joined by an unruly assortment of independent operators.

The narrow isthmus of Panamá was the weak link in Spain's communications and as the gold built up on land, awaiting the arrival of a fleet of Spanish ships, it presented a target for the pirates. **Sir Francis Drake** was among the first to make a successful raid here, storming the town of Nombre de Dios in 1572, after which the Spanish rebuilt their forts at Portobelo. (Drake sailed on around South America and across the Pacific; the second man to sail around the world, he returned to Central America and, in 1596, died at sea off Portobelo, falling victim to that all too common travellers' complaint, dysentry. His lead coffin, dumped into the water somewhere along the coast, has yet to be located.)

Following in Drake's footsteps was perhaps the most famous and audacious pirate, **Sir Henry Morgan**, who launched a series of bold and unprovoked attacks against Spanish colonial cities. Morgan operated with the full approval of the Council of Jamaica, charged 'to draw together the English privateers and take prisoners of the Spanish nation.' He was legally permitted to attack Spanish ships but, true to pirate tradition he stepped beyond the bounds and began looting towns and cities. With his men, who became known as the 'Brethren of the Coast', Morgan launched a daring attack on Portobelo in 1668, landing three miles from the town and coming at it from behind so as to avoid the formidable coastal defences. Two years later he returned to the Panamanian coast, and having captured the castle at San Lorenzo he sailed up the Chagras river and led his men on a gruelling march across the isthmus to attack Panamá City itself. Morgan's boldness so impressed Charles II that he was knighted and returned to Jamaica as Deputy Governor, where he died of dropsy.

Ronald Reagan

Although he rarely visited Central America, Ronald Reagan had the most profound and destabilizing effect on the isthmus and contributed to much of the political turmoil that still persists today. A deep commitment to right-wing politics and fear of communism lead Reagan to take an uncompromising stance on Central America, redirecting US policy from Panamá to Guatemala.

He was dogmatically against the Sandinista regime in Nicaragua, to which he devoted a great deal of energy, eventually bogging himself down in the Irangate scandal. And, although the previous US president, Jimmy Carter, had offered the olive branch to the Sandinistas, Reagan, beginning in 1982, laid siege to the country, providing enormous funds for the rebel Contra army and imposing a trade blockade which crippled

Nicaragua's economy. The conflict forced the country into ruin and eventually destroyed the Sandinista government.

In Guatemala he also reversed US policy. In the seventies President Carter cut off US aid in protest against the mounting tide of human rights abuse, but in 1981, with the generals still in power, Reagan lifted the ban on arms sales, ensuring that the army remained a formidable force in Guatemalan politics. Almost a decade later President Bush again suspended arms sales after the army was implicated in the 'death squad' killing of Mike Devine, a US citizen living in Guatemala.

In El Salvador the Reagan administration dropped US support for a seventies programme of limited agrarian reform and put itself behind the army in a commitment to the war of attrition being waged against the FMLN (Farabundo Martí National Liberation Front). The policy increased the intensity of the conflict and deepened the divisions which continued to tear the country apart until long after the end of the Reagan administration.

With regard to Panamá, Reagan was equally determined. Of the canal, he said: 'We bought it, we paid for it, it's ours and we should tell Torrijos and company that we are going to keep it.' It was an attitude which hardened anti-US sentiment in Panamá; thus, when General Torrijos was replaced by his bright young officer, Manuel Noriega, the two countries were locked on collision course. This was the origin of yet another Central American time bomb, which President Reagan eventually handed on to Bush and which has left another corner of Central America in tatters.

Manuel Noriega

Born the son of an accountant and a domestic servant, Manuel Noriega's double-dealing got off to an early start—he was informing for the CIA while still in high school. He failed to get into medical school and used family connections to get himself a job in the Panamanian embassy in Lima, where he continued to work for the Americans and managed to use his connections to evade conviction after he was arrested for battering a prostitute.

Returning to Panamá at the age of 28, Noriega went straight into the army, rising swiftly through the ranks in the Colón garrison, under the leadership of Major Omar Torrijos. The two men worked closely together and Torrijos found Noriega a trusty subordinate, if a little overenthusiastic, and he was forced to relieve him of his duties for ten days following complaints of brutality. Nevertheless when Torrijos seized power in 1968 it was with the support and assistance of Noriega, whom he appointed as the head of G2, military intelligence. Noriega used and abused the position to its absolute maximum, consolidating his own power base and working on behalf of Torrijos, FMLN guerrillas in El Salvador, the Sandinistas in Nicaragua, the Colombian cartels, Fidel Castro, M19 guerrillas in Colombia and, of course, the CIA, who paid him $110,000 in 1977.

When, in July 1981, Torrijos died in a plane crash Noriega was in a powerful position. At first he was forced to strike a power-sharing deal with two other high-ranking officers, but by 1987, having further consolidated his position, he had persuaded his rivals to retire and assumed overall control. Meanwhile, however, Noriega was able to exploit every opportunity. For example, when a small-time US dealer bought cocaine in Colombia the cartels would send word to Panamá, where he would be detained. The cocaine was then sold on the open market and the dealer ransomed to his family in the US. All the while, Noriega continued to operate as an overpaid double or triple agent, buying and selling information and goodwill to the highest bidder. When the Colombian cartels paid him $5 million so that they could build a laboratory in southern Panamá, Noriega informed the CIA, cashing in his credit in Colombia to earn a little in Washington. But he became increasingly heavy handed and gradually lost his balance in this delicate double game. In 1987 the Reagan administration, unable to ignore Noriega's other associations, instituted sanctions against Panamá.

The anti-Noriega campaign was a catalogue of failures: in 1988 Noriega fought off a coup attempt; in 1989 he overrode the outcome of elections and his supporters beat up his opponents; and so, in 1990, the Americans were forced to send in the troops, who drove the general to ground in the papal nunciate.

He is currently languishing in jail, having been convicted on charges of drug trafficking and other corruption offences.

Melodrama on the Buses

Of all the Central American melodramas the bus journey is perhaps the most gripping. The show opens with the bus quietly ticking over as the bus-boy hustles business. Rushing around the bus terminal he generates a real sense of urgency, hurrying passengers onto the bus. His priorities are clear: it doesn't matter who you are or where you're going provided you take a seat. Passengers are packed in, waiting in the heat for hours, and the tension steadily mounts. Finally the bus-boy steps into the driver's seat and revs the engine; but this first roar is almost always a false alarm, a little taster to remind the passengers that the bus still works and will eventually leave. More passengers are then packed in, accompanied by chickens, goats and pigs. Here the skills of the bus-boy are stretched to the limit as he attempts to fill the bus to more than double its capacity. Once he is satisfied with his handiwork he again takes the driver's seat, but this time he sounds the horn, summoning the leading man.

Rolling out of a nearby bar, like an overweight prima donna, the bus driver steps onto the stage. He lingers, perhaps airing his belly or picking food from his teeth, and helps a pretty young girl into the seat beside him. As the passengers start to murmur and fidget he pauses to share a joke with another driver, reminding everyone that they're totally dependent on him.

Then, finally in position, the driver is transformed, overcome by a furious sense of urgency. Heading out of town and onto the open road he races through the streets, scattering private cars and pedestrians. On the highway he considers himself the undisputed king of the road, and uses every blind corner to flex his machismo, overtaking with hair-raising confidence. The driver's biggest problem is that both the police and truck drivers also consider themselves the undisputed kings of the road. In most countries truck and bus drivers have formed an alliance and use a complex series of hand signals to warn each other of impending danger, while police are held at bay by healthy backhanders. Meanwhile others, including cyclists and car drivers, soon learn that they are unwelcome intruders. In El Salvador road signs plead with drivers to watch out for cyclists, reminding them that 'he could be your brother'.

Having driven as though every second counted, barely pausing to scoop up waiting passengers, the bus screeches to a halt at a roadside café. Here a special room is often set aside for the driver and he eats an enormous amount of food, whatever the time of day, lingering over a last bowl of soup as the passengers sweat it out in the bus, eager to move on.

Contact between the driver and his passengers is usually quite limited. However, in the event of a breakdown, things often change swiftly as everyone on the bus unites in hardship. With any luck it won't happen to you, although do bear in mind that these are dangerous roads. High in the Guatemalan highlands many a bus has tumbled over the side, and their rusting carcases are still there to be seen. It's a sight to make you wonder why on earth you embarked on this journey; while to a driver it is a tribute to his immense bravery, and a reminder that they need men like him more than ever.

Part IV

GUATEMALA

Guatemala is a small country, known for volcanoes and cruelty. When I crossed the frontier from Mexico I alternately lifted up my eyes to the hills, and scanned the roadside for corpses. There weren't any, and I felt slightly cheated by the books about Guatemala I had read.

Anthony Daniels, *Sweet Waist of America*

Guatemala is like that. On the one hand you know that terrible things have happened here, still happen here, but on the other hand, you almost never see any evidence of it. Human rights violations usually occur behind closed doors, in remote areas of the country or at night, and are rarely reported in the local press. Instead you see a country whose beauty is unmatched in Central America: a country where smouldering volcanoes rise above green and golden highland valleys, mysterious cloud forests are shrouded in swirling mists, and seemingly endless tropical jungles hide ancient pyramids of the lost Maya civilization. It only takes a few hours to travel from temperate highlands to steamy jungle, another aspect of this tiny country that confuses and delights.

Roughly the size of Ireland or the American state of Connecticut, Guatemala's northern frontier is with Mexico. To the northwest, the Pacific plain soon rises up into the highest mountain range in Central America, the Cuchumatanes, and the border roughly follows this chain northeast until it sinks into the Petén jungle, at which point the official border turns a sharp east before bulging out again to encompass a large area of the Petén lowlands, which make up a third of the entire country. If it wasn't for Belize, most of Guatemala's eastern border would be the Caribbean Sea. Instead an almost

50

vertical borderline divides the two countries, and Guatemala's share of the Caribbean is limited to a tiny bite at the beginning of the Gulf of Honduras. Running diagonally from northeast to southwest, Guatemala's southern border is first with Honduras and then with El Salvador, while the western border is made up by the Pacific coast.

The country divides into distinct geographic regions. The west is characterized by a slim Pacific plain which soon rises into the Western Highlands punctuated by a string of volcanoes towering above a fertile landscape of maize and bean fields, and dotted with countless Indian hamlets and villages. This is the heartland of the modern Maya. Just over half the population are pure descendants of the Maya tribes who have inhabited the region for millennia, speaking their own languages, wearing their finely embroidered weaving, and stubbornly holding on to their traditions. Many of their ancient customs have become mixed with Catholic rituals, and the result is an annual calendar peppered with riotous festivals, where pagan dances accompany huge processions for Christian saints, and acts of worship can include anything from smoking cigars to sacrificing chickens. The weekly markets, which form the cornerstone of Maya social life, are also notable. Every town and village has its own market day, when the Indians come to sell their produce—predominantly maize, beans, cereals and other vegetables, while exchanging the latest gossip or discussing possible marriages.

Eastern Guatemala is clearly divided into two parts: the southeast is cut in two by the desert valley of the Motagua river, which is the main corridor from the Western Highlands to the Atlantic coast, with dry hills leading up towards the borders with Honduras and El Salvador on one side, and the moist Verapaz highlands rising towards the north. In these regions you will find mainly *ladino* culture, which is characterized by a strong Spanish influence. Fiercely Catholic, the people are mestizos, representing all shades of colour from European to Indian, with the occasional black descendant from the West Indies, though most of those live in one single place: the Atlantic settlement of Livingston which can only be reached by boat. *Ladino* is not a racial term, however. Even a pure Indian is a *ladino* if he has abandoned his traditional dress and language in favour of the Spanish inherited culture, and it is a sad fact that many feel pressured to do so to avoid discrimination and abuse.

Beyond the Motagua valley and the Verapaz, the landscape descends onto the Petén plain and the dense jungle that eventually melts into the Mexican Yucatán peninsula. This is the least populated area of Guatemala, though once it was home to the famous civilization that built the giant pyramids of Tikal, now only inhabited by tropical birds, such as toucans and scarlet macaws, and troops of howler monkeys whose loud grunts fill the air at every dusk.

Travelling by bus is the best way to explore this little country. Services are frequent and extremely cheap, making it possible to get from one end of the country to the other in no more than a day, for less than US$5. The distance from the Pacific to the Atlantic coast by road is just 403 km, while from the Mexican to Salvadorean border is no more than 299 km. To reach the Maya pyramids is also easy, since at least three flights daily connect the capital with the jungle town of Flores, near the ruins of Tikal. Because of the country's accessible nature, a short visit of two weeks would still be plenty of time to see a great deal of the country, and if you stayed for six weeks, you would have no trouble seeing the entire country and much of what it has to offer.

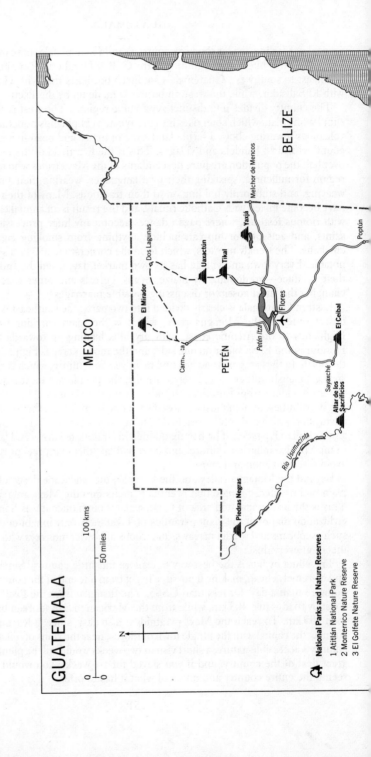

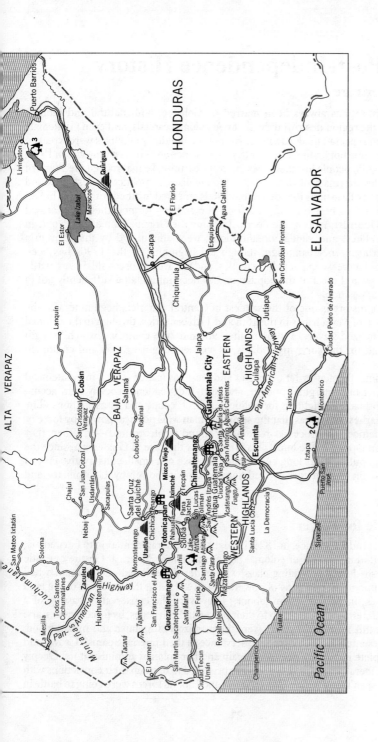

Post-Independence History

A Tragic Heritage

Guatemala's history has always been marred by violence, both natural and human. Earthquakes in the region destroyed the first two colonial capitals, and even Guatemala City has suffered repeated quake damage. Every time buildings and lives were wrecked political change came hot on the heels of physical destruction. The last time was in 1976, when around 25,000 people lost their lives in a huge earthquake that rocked the Western Highlands. In the aftermath of social and economic distress, political unrest grew and the struggling guerrilla groups founded in the 1960s emerged fortified with a new Indian support base. For the first time in centuries, the Indians formed their own armed resistance: the Guerrilla Army of the Poor (EGP) and the Organization of the People in Arms (ORPA). They, and similar organizations, were annihilated by the army in a 10-year counterinsurgency campaign, though the beginning of the 1990s has been marked by a small increase in guerrilla activities, and the armed forces still have a battle on their hands, even if most of the population has been intimidated sufficiently not to support armed opposition.

The country's history is one of the saddest in Central America, beginning with the brutal destruction of Maya tribes in the 16th and 17th centuries, through to the colonial era of institutionalized slavery, and on to the 19th and 20th centuries, which brought more loss of land for the surviving Indians, as well as marginalization and continued abuse.

In the meantime, the new order of creoles and mestizos (called *ladinos* in Guatemala) treated each other only marginally better, and post-Independence society grew accustomed to warring factions fighting for political control, coups and assassinations. The tradition from earliest times was that the strongest man wins political power, by force or fraud, so that democratic processes have never found fertile ground—or rather, they have always been nipped in the bud. This is especially the case in Guatemala, since the majority of the population has long been under the yoke of a small, conservative elite of landowners and the armed forces, traditionally kept in power by US military and economic aid.

The Struggle for Power

The aftermath of Independence, in 1821, brought political fragmentation to Guatemala, which was the traditional seat of colonial power in Central America. On the one side were the Spanish-descended ruling class, who under the colonial administration had always held all important positions of power, as well as having the best pick of the land and its resources, including Indian labour. They were the conservative bastion of a fading empire, determined to hold on to their power and privileges, by force if necessary. Ranged against this formidable group were the mestizos, of Spanish and Indian blood, who had long resented their enforced subservience to the Imperial Spanish Crown and dreamt of complete independence from Spain and her colonial administrators. Deeply influenced by Liberal ideology, they too were prepared to back up their convictions with force, and so it wasn't long before Conservative and Liberal forces were going to battle in various parts of the region. Meanwhile the Maya Indians were at best helpless spectators to the civil war, and at worst forcibly conscripted into armies fighting a cause that had no truck with their concerns.

In 1829, the Liberal forces of Honduran general Francisco Morazán invaded Guatemala, and a year later he became President of the United Provinces of Central America, which had been founded in 1823, though the fighting had never allowed it to develop properly. This marked the temporary end for Guatemalan Conservative forces. The Central American federation, however, did not survive, breaking up into separate republics in 1839, while Francisco Morazán was executed in 1842.

In the new Guatemalan republic the Conservatives once more gained the upper hand, and the country's first *caudillo* (leader), José Rafael Carrera, ruled intermittently from 1844 until his death in 1865. He succeeded in this by playing both factions of Central American politics against each other, and it was not until Justo Rufino Barrios brought down his successor, in 1871, that Liberals regained the political centre stage.

The Age of Liberal Reforms

The Conservative mid-19th-century rulers of Guatemala only succeeded in strengthening their power base to a limited extent. The traditional Spanish-born elite found itself sharing with the *caudillos* and, increasingly, the limited progress of the country's economic expansion meant that the *ladino* population was forever dissatisfied and always ready to mount opposition. Once chemical substitutes had been found for the country's major export crops of indigo and cochineal, a new economic base had to be found and it was the Liberals who seemed to offer the best solutions.

Justo Rufino Barrios (1871–85) instituted a major reform programme that was intended to modernize Guatemala and make it a competitive force on the world market. This development included building a national road and railway network, founding a professional army, and crucially, promoting new export crops, of which coffee was the most important. To do this much Indian land was confiscated, which sowed the seeds for widespread rural poverty and popular discontent for the coming century. Church land was also confiscated, which was a convenient punishment for the Church's traditional support for the Conservatives.

Foreign investment was encouraged by offering huge tracts of land and no export duties, and by 1900, coffee took up 85% of the country's exports, while the new coffee oligarchy came to dominate not just Guatemala's economy, but also her politics. The Indians were brutally forced off their land and pressed into a system of debt-peonage, whereby they had to work as agricultural labourers with no land of their own to sustain them.

The Liberal dictator presidents succeeded in staying in power for many decades, forging a deadly alliance with the military which ensured their survival. Thus two of Guatemala's most dominant traditions were cemented: the landed coffee oligarchy and the military as political power-broker. State terror ensured that any kind of opposition was crushed, and dictators distinguished themselves by their brutality. A prime example was Manuel Estrada Cabrera (1898–1920), who was such a picture-book baddie that Miguel Angel Asturias used him for the basis of his novel on repression called *El Señor Presidente*.

After the world economic collapse in 1929, the Guatemalan leadership sought to broaden its economic base once more, and foreign investment was further encouraged, especially from the United States. One of the American companies that benefited most was the United Fruit Company, who gained outrageously huge land concessions from both Cabrera and the later dictator president Jorge Ubico (1931–1944). The company came to own more land in Guatemala than anyone else, and controlled not only the Pacific railways, but also the ports, the shipping, and all communications and electric power in its territory. Needless to say it also had decisive political influence, which established another Guatemalan tradition: an economy and government closely tied to North American interests. Under Ubico the government stole a great deal more land from the Indians, and further enslaved them to the new system by creating 'vagrancy laws' which made it illegal for Indians not to work on the coffee and banana plantations for a certain period each year. He also repressed any political opposition, as well as labour unions and rural co-operatives. Death or exile were standard punishments for dissenters, another tradition that has survived to this day.

The Spiritual Socialist

Ubico, however, was overthrown by a military coup in 1944, largely because he lost the support of the US, and also because he made the mistake of alienating sectors of the Guatemalan oligarchy and military, frustrated once more by slow economic progress. Worse still, the carve-up of riches and power between United Fruit and the landed oligarchy left little hope for advancement to ambitious young officers, as well as the country's emergent middle class. Thus Ubico was removed and for the first time elections took place, and Juan José Arévalo was elected.

Arévalo was a teacher and writer, who had spent the Ubico years in exile, and returned to his country determined to right the balance of power and welfare. He espoused a doctrine of what he called 'Spiritual Socialism', and under his five-year presidency many reforms were carried out. Social security was established for the first time, as well as a labour code and rural cooperatives, a national educational and health programme was set up, and open elections were encouraged.

His successor, Jacobo Arbenz, continued Arévalo's reforms and even legalized the Communist Party and allowed other political opposition to thrive. This was revolutionary in the Guatemalan context. But like a moth to the flame, Guatemalan democracy was quickly burnt up by traditional power. What finally made the Arbenz administration unacceptable was the 1952 Agrarian Reform Law, which sought to redistribute land to the rural poor. Only uncultivated land was to be taken, but the small group of landowners resented every inch taken from them, most of all the foreign land owner, United Fruit, who found 400,000 acres of its uncultivated land nationalized in 1953.

The company quickly sought to use its contacts in Washington to lobby the US government and put pressure on the Guatemalan administration. There followed a short period of financial sanctions, diplomatic pressure and covert CIA destabilization tactics. But, finally, it was easier to mount a coup and, in 1954, the CIA's 'Operation Success' helped Colonel Castillo Armas take the Presidential Palace. The Guatemalan army refused to defend Arbenz, and thus the humiliated president left for exile and democracy was at an end. Castillo Armas was confirmed as president a year later, and three decades of murderous repression ensued.

The Military Reign of Terror

Armas only lasted a couple of years before he was assassinated, but he had already returned all nationalized land to its former owners, dismantled the labour unions and peasant associations, and mounted anti-communist propaganda backed up by an armed counter-revolution which left thousands dead. US foreign aid flowed freely once more, and the traditional alliance between the agro-export elite and the military was soon re-established.

Armas was followed by the hated General Miguel Ydígoras Fuentes, who had been head of the Secret Police under Ubico. The military put him in power after the 1957 elections had resulted in uncontrollable riots, and from then onwards, the military was firmly in charge of who ran the country. Ydígoras, however, turned out to be too despotic, even for his military supporters, and reformist officers mounted a coup against him in 1960. They were not successful, but those that escaped the firing squad founded the first armed rebel group in Guatemala: the Revolutionary Armed Forces (FAR). Also founded at this time was the 13th November Revolutionary Movement (MR–13), and both groups turned to Marxism-Leninism and Castro's example for their ideology. Ydígoras was finally overthrown in 1963, and while US military aid increased sharply, so did a brutal counterinsurgency programme, which made any kind of open dissent a life-threatening activity.

The 1960s saw the military tighten its grip on the country, and while presidents occasionally denounced the army's violence, the counterinsurgency campaign remained as virulent as ever. The most notorious campaign of the decade was led by Colonel Carlos Arana Osorio, whose 1968 Zacapa campaign was responsible for the deaths of at least 10,000 civilians. Right-wing death squads also emerged in these years, as certain sectors of the Conservative elite became impatient with the army's inability to wipe out armed rebellion completely. Between the years 1966 and 1970, these squads alone are believed to have killed over 30,000 people. Such was the atmosphere of violence and terror that political opposition was all but silenced, and the 1970 'elections' brought the 'Butcher of Zacapa', Carlos Arana Osorio into power.

The 1970s saw a continuation of the previous decade, the Guatemalan military ruling with US support and vital military aid. Only the 1976 earthquake brought disturbance to the army's tight control over the country, and in the wake of high casualties and even higher numbers of homeless and destitute, guerrilla groups re-emerged and found support from the population's Indian majority. Until this time, the revolutionaries had never considered the needs of the rural Indians nor seen them as natural allies, peasants being traditionally conservative rather than leftist revolutionaries. However, they now began to establish themselves in the Western Highlands and remote north, organizing armed resistance and educational propaganda.

The result of the rebels' move into the countryside was tragic for the Indians. The military subjected them to a genocide of such magnitude that it is only now being fully assessed. They devised a scorched earth policy, and entire villages were razed to the ground, their inhabitants tortured and murdered in the most hideous ways imaginable. A common tactic was to herd the women and children into their local church or community hall, and then set the building on fire, leaving their husbands to listen to their death cries before being murdered themselves. The manner of the army's killings were unspeakable, and the files of Amnesty International are full of horrific eyewitness reports from the few survivors that made it to Mexican and Belizean refugee camps.

In the first months of 1981, 1500 Indians were killed in the Chimaltenango Department alone, and the devastation of land and human life continued. In June 1982, one of the country's most notorious generals took power: General Efraín Ríos Montt. He was installed by the military to reduce corruption and lead the country back towards civilian rule. But instead he launched his 'Beans and Guns' counterinsurgency campaign, and the World Council of Churches reported that the government was responsible for the death of 9000 people between the months of March and July that year. He was an extraordinary character who, while the armed forces were murdering in the countryside, harangued Guatemalans with Sunday sermons on television, when he told them not to fornicate or drink, and lead a Christian life. He was deposed by coup in 1983, and has since returned to preaching for the Church of the World in Guatemala City.

Civilian Rule

The army finally handed government back to civilian rule in 1985, and the Christian Democrat Vinicio Cerezo Arévalo became the first civilian president of Guatemala in 31 years. Naturally the democratic process was initiated on the army's terms and the years of Cerezo's government continued to see military offensives mounted in the countryside, and massacres of civilians still occurred, such as the massacre of 22 peasants in the village of Aguacate, near San Andrés Itzapa, in November 1987, and of 14 Indians in Santiago Atitlán in December 1990.

Cerezo's government was followed by the election of Jorge Serrano Elías in January 1991, who is leader of the right-wing Movement of Solidarity Action (MAS) and won a resounding victory with 68% of the vote. This result, however, must be set against a 55% abstention by registered voters, which reflects widespread disillusion with the democratic process in Guatemala and does not bode well for the future. Guatemala is still ranked high by America's Watch for human rights violations, and the UN Human Rights Commission has also condemned the country for the high number of disappearances. Thus the Guatemalan government lives under the pall of human rights violations by the armed forces and also the constant threat of international sanctions because of it, which will severely hamper the country's economic progress.

The Maya Indians, meanwhile, continue to survive in spite of the genocide of the late 1970s and 80s, and their economic, social and political marginalization. Despite continued exploitation and extreme poverty, the Maya culture and traditions are alive in the countryside, especially in the highlands, and a revitalized tourist industry is taking full advantage of the considerable riches they have to offer. To what extent tourism can replace the continuing urgent need for agrarian reform is debatable. But in some regions, at least, controlled tourism can help Indian communities survive where their traditional economic base has been denied them. However, tourism being volatile and dependent on many things, it can never be considered a long-term solution to the needs of Guatemala's rural population, who make up the vast majority of her people.

General Information

Getting to Guatemala

By Air

The main airlines with regular connections to Guatemala City (La Aurora airport) from Europe or North America are British Airways, KLM, Iberia and Eastern. Coming from Europe, there are only two direct flights, KLM from Amsterdam and Iberia from Madrid, otherwise you usually change planes in Miami or Houston. Coming from North America, there are direct flights from Miami, Houston, New Orleans and Los Angeles, with a greater choice of airlines.

Prices are cheaper if you travel on weekdays, between Monday and Thursday, and tickets with fixed dates are always cheaper than open ones. Scheduled return flights from Europe to Guatemala hover around the £654 mark for the cheapest fare, while bucket shops may be able to knock off up to £100. From North America, expect to pay around $350 return from Miami, and double that figure if coming from New York or Canada.

By Boat

The only maritime connection is from the Belizean port of Punta Gorda to the Guatemalan port of Puerto Barrios, on the Atlantic coast. There are two ferries a week, leaving on Tuesdays and Fridays.

By Train

For hardy and patient travellers coming from North America, there is always the train (see Paul Theroux's *The Old Patagonian Express*). The journey from Mexico City onwards becomes extremely slow and hot, with delays a regular occurrence. Once in Guatemala, the trains are even slower than in Mexico, and officially twelve-hour journeys often end up taking twenty-four hours instead, with no food served on the train. There is no longer a public train connection between Guatemala and San Salvador.

By Bus

Bus connections from North America to Guatemala are cheap and regular, but not direct and it will take you a few days to cross Mexico alone, with another day to reach Guatemala City from the Mexican border. Coming from El Salvador, there is a reliable bus route direct from San Salvador to Guatemala City. Coming from Honduras, there are buses to the border posts of either Agua Caliente (best) or El Florido from the Honduran city of San Pedro Sula, and Guatemalan buses will take you to the capital from there. Coming from Belize, there is a very rough dirt road over the Maya Mountains and through the jungle, connecting Belize City and Belmopan to Flores (occasionally impassable during the rainy season). Normally there are no direct buses, so you can expect a change at the border, where you are at the mercy of unscrupulous bus drivers.

By Car

Driving south from North America in your own car is an option you will only want to consider if you like long-haul driving and your nerves can stand the vagaries of Latin American border officials. You will need faultless documents and separate insurance for each country, and if you find yourself leaving Guatemala without your vehicle, you will have a lot of explaining to do and a heavy import duty to pay—even if it was stolen or destroyed in a crash.

Embassies and Consulates

In the UK: 13 Fawcett Street, London SW10 9HN, tel (071) 351 3042.
In the US: Embassy of the Republic of Guatemala, 2220 R Street, NW Washington DC 20008, tel (202) 745 4952.
9700 Richmond Avenue, Suite 218, Houston, TX 77042, tel (713) 953 9531.
584 South Spring Street, Office 1030, Los Angeles, CA 90013, tel (213) 489 1891.
300 Sevilla Avenue, Oficina 210, Coral Gables, Miami, FL 33134, tel (305) 443 4828.
10405 San Diego Mission Road, Suite 205, San Diego, CA 92108, tel (415) 282 8127.
In Canada: The consulate in Montreal is now closed, but there is an embassy in Ottawa at: 294 Albert Street, Suite 500, Ottawa, Ontario K1P 6E6, tel (613) 237 3941.
In Australia: 39 Ocean Street, Woollahra, Sydney NSW 2025, tel (02) 322 965.
In Mexico: Avenida Esplanada 1025, Lomas de Chapultepec 11000, Mexico D.F. 4, tel (05) 520 2794.

Tourist Offices

Guatemala Tourist Commission in the USA: P.O. Box 144351, Coral Gables, FL 33114–4351, tel (305) 854 1544, fax (305) 854 4589, telex 153877 LMART/MIA.
Consulates and embassies in other countries should be able to supply you with at least some brochures, if no maps. In general, however, the best information available is from the national tourist office in Guatemala City itself (see p. 61).

Passports and Visas

Nationals of member countries of the EC (except Greece), Canada, or the United States, have to obtain either a visa, which is valid for one month and can be extended monthly for a total of six months in all, or a tourist card, which airlines or border officals issue for a US$5 fee. The tourist card is preferable because it is possible to request 90 days in one go, thus only requiring one visit to the immigration office for long-term visitors who wish to stay up to six months. Both types of documentation can also be issued by the Guatemalan consulates abroad. It is always advisable to check with them for the latest entry requirements.

Nationals from Australia or the Republic of Ireland must have a visa to enter Guatemala, available from the nearest consulate or embassy. Applications should be handed in at least a week before travelling, along with your passport and one passport photo, plus the relevant fee.

In the USA you also have the option of applying for a one-year visa, where you get three months on entry, renewable every three months, though it is preferable to leave the country for 72 hours since the extension procedure involves filling in many forms, being finger-printed at the police station, and having to leave your passport with the officials for an indeterminate number of days.

The Immigration Office (*Departamento de Migración*) in Guatemala City is at 41 Calle 17–36, Zona 8, tel (71) 7640. Ask at the INGUAT tourist office for the best bus to take from the city centre. The building is not marked, but you can recognize it for its white square shape, about four storeys high.

Customs

Visas or tourist cards can be issued on entry, but it is better to get them before to avoid delay. Leaving by air, there is an exit fee of about US$4, payable in local or US currency. Leaving by land the exit fee is usually about US$1. Officially you must be in possession of a return flight ticket to enter Guatemala by air, and most airlines in the US will not allow you on the plane without a return ticket. On arrival, you may be asked to show you have enough funds for the duration of your intended visit. Normally a credit card or travellers' cheques worth a few hundred US dollars is enough evidence. In practice, arriving passengers are almost never asked about funds.

On Arrival

Tourist Offices

National Tourist Office (INGUAT), Centro Cívico, Avenida 7 y Vía 1, Ciudad de Guatemala, C.A., tel (502) 2 31 1333/47, fax (502) 2 31 8893, telex 5532 INGUAT GU. (Open Mon–Fri, 8.30–4.30 and Sat, 8.30–noon.)

The only other places where you will find INGUAT offices in Guatemala are Antigua, Panajachel, Quezaltenango and Flores.

Orientation

All Guatemalan towns, including the capital, are laid out in a grid system, whereby calles run north to south, and avenidas run east to west. Additionally, the bigger towns are divided into different zones, and the street numbers are repeated in each zone, so it is vital to know which zone you need. Addresses are written so that the street the place is actually on comes first, then comes the number of the nearest crossroad, and then the house number. For example, the El Dorado hotel is at 7 Avenida 15–45. This means the building is located on 7 Avenida, between junctions 15 Calle and 16 Calle, at number 45. It's easy once you get used to it.

Maps

The best and cheapest map available is the one sold by the Guatemalan Tourist Board, though you will undoubtedly be able to find others in map shops before you leave home. This map not only features the country, but also small street maps of the capital and a few major towns and tourist attractions.

Large-scale topographical maps are produced by the Guatemalan Military, which you can inspect, but need special permission from the Ministry of Defence to buy. The address is Instituto Geográfico Militar, Avenida Las Américas 5–76, Zona 13; open weekdays 7–4. Alternatively, the Casa Andinista bookshop in Antigua will sell you photocopies without any problems.

Getting Around Guatemala

By Air
The only internal flight route in operation is the one connecting Guatemala City with the jungle-bound town of Flores. There are three or four flights daily in either direction, and tickets are available at most travel agencies or at the two airports. There are four airlines operating the route: Aviateca, Aerovías, Aeroquetzal, and Tapsa. Prices should be the same whoever you fly with, but always check, because sometimes the agents slap on extras, selling the same ticket at substantially different prices, depending on which airline they use. A return flight costs about $100, and the journey time is about 80 minutes. If possible, you should try to make reservations at least a few days ahead, as flights can be heavily booked, especially during Easter Week or Christmas and New Year.

By Train
As one passenger put it: you'd be faster walking! Nobody uses the Guatemalan trains unless they have no choice or believe it is their kind of adventure. However, they can be a useful option when the country is suffering one of its recurrent national bus strikes.

There is one route running from the Mexican border at Tecún Umán to Guatemala City, via the Pacific towns of Coatepeque, Retalhuleu, Mazatenango and Escuintla. It should take 12 hours, but often takes double that time. The only other remaining passenger service connects the capital with the Atlantic port of Puerto Barrios, a journey that is supposed to take 8 hours, but usually takes nearer 20. (The bus takes 6 hours.)

The train route to the Pacific port of San José no longer takes passengers, nor can you travel to El Salvador by train any more. There is also a strong chance that the two passenger services described above will be discontinued.

By Bus
This is undoubtedly the fastest, cheapest and easiest way to explore most of Guatemala. The country's towns and many villages are linked by good paved or passable dirt roads everywhere except in the Petén, where appalling mud roads regularly disintegrate completely during the rainy season. Bus connections are regular and extremely cheap, though you should always try to travel in the morning, since public transport generally stops by late afternoon. It is also much safer to travel during daylight hours, and less daunting to arrive in a new place before nightfall. Tickets are bought on the bus, and to avoid 'gringo prices', it is always a good idea to ask a local passenger what the fare is, before the ticket man gets to you.

On some routes it is possible to travel by Pullman buses, which are more comfortable than the local 'chicken buses' (old Blue Bird buses or retired US school buses, crammed to bursting point with people and often small livestock too). Pullmans are a bit more expensive, but you get a reserved seat to yourself, and the bus makes fewer stops.

By Car

The roads in Guatemala, excepting the Petén, are generally good, and normal passenger cars have no trouble here. If you intend to go off the beaten track, you will find mostly dirt and gravel roads, where high-clearance vehicles are recommended. Should you want a real adventure and wish to drive to Tikal in the Petén, nothing less than a tough four-wheel-drive vehicle will do, and even then it is not advisable to attempt the journey during the rainy season from May to December.

Be sure to take a spare wheel and any other essential spare parts that may be unavailable here, and a large canister of petrol would be a good idea as well, as petrol stations are few and far between. The Guatemalan Tourist Office (INGUAT) sells a useful road map, which has all petrol stations marked on it, as well as a mileage chart. It is advisable to use secure parking facilities wherever possible, since theft and vandalism is a problem—especially in towns and cities or near tourist attractions.

Traffic outside the cities is very sparse, so driving is relatively relaxed, bar the occasionally hazardous local driving or military checkpoint. These checkpoints are nothing to worry about, however, and normally you will be waved on. Hassle is more likely to come from the police and Guardia de Hacienda (rural police), who like to stop cars with foreign licence plates. There will always be the occasional corrupt officer looking for a bribe, but that is a risk you take driving anywhere in Latin America.

Car Hire

Hire cars are available in the capital and most major towns, though they are expensive at US$55 per day for the smaller cars, and often you have to pay the first $800 of any damage, or there is no insurance at all. Read the small print! This is especially important as foreigners have to pay all damages, whether the accident was their fault or not. To hire any vehicle, you will need a current driving licence and a credit card, regardless of how you intend to pay the final bill. Motorbikes can be hired in Guatemala City, Antigua and Panajachel, for around $20 per day.

Major car hire offices in Guatemala City are the following, and all except Tally have airport representatives: **Avis**, 12 Calle 2–73, Zona 9, tel 316990; **Budget**, Avenida La Reforma 15–00, Zona 9, tel 316546; **Dollar**, 6 Avenida A 10–13, Zona 1, tel 67796; **Hertz**, 7 Avenida 14–76, Zona 9, tel 680107; **National**, 14 Calle 1–42, Zona 10, tel 680175; **Tabarini**, 2 Calle A 7–30, Zona 10, tel 316108; **Tally**, 7 Avenida 14–60, Zona 1, tel 514113.

By Bicycle

Travellers on bicycles are becoming an increasingly common sight in Guatemala, and many locals use them too. There are bike rental shops in most large towns, and there is always someone to be found who can help you fix your bike. The best kind of bike is clearly a mountain bike, with tough wheels and plenty of gears. Should you get tired of cycling, you can always travel on the local buses, which will transport your bike on the roof, normally at no extra charge.

Embassies and Consulates

All embassies and consulates are in Guatemala City, and are normally only open on weekdays, in the mornings. Onward travellers to other Central American countries may need visas, so the relevant offices are listed, where they exist.

UK: Edificio Centro Financiero, 7 Avenida 5–10 (7th floor), Zona 4, tel 321601; (Mon–Thurs, 10–noon and 2–4, Fri, 1–5).

US: Avenida Reforma 7–01, Zona 10, tel 311541/4.

Canada: 7 Avenida 11–59 (6th floor), Zona 9, tel 321411.

Costa Rica: Avenida Reforma 8–60 (third floor), Zona 9, tel 319604.

El Salvador: 12 Calle 5–43 (7th floor), Zona 9, tel 325848.

Honduras: 16 Calle 8–27, Zona 10, tel 373919.

Mexico: 13 Calle 7–30, Zona 9, tel 363573.

Nicaragua: 10 Avenida 14–72, Zona 10, tel 680785.

Panamá: Edificio Maya (7th floor), Via 5 4–50, Zona 4, tel 325001.

Money Matters

Guatemalan currency is the quetzal, and one quetzal is made up of 100 centavos. Notes come in denominations of 100, 50, 20, 10, 5, 1, and 0.50. It is worth trying to avoid notes of 100 and 50 quetzals, since people do not like changing them; and torn or damaged notes should never be accepted because you will get stuck with them.

Exchange rates are volatile in this region of rampant inflation and regular devaluations, but you can be sure that your money will go a long way here. The best currency to have is US dollars, either in cash or travellers' cheques, which you can exchange at most banks and on the black market. You will get a slightly better rate on the black market, though you must be careful: avoid showing your passport, which could be stolen in the process; don't hand over your cash first; and don't go into an unknown house with a supposed money changer. Exclusive hotels and some shops and restaurants also change money.

Guatemalan banks do not charge commission for cashing travellers' cheques, but it can take at least half an hour to get your money because of interminable queues and forms. Make sure you are in the right queue. Every town has at least one bank, and often there are a few to choose from, such as the Banco de Guatemala, Banco del Ejército, Banco del Agro, Banco Industrial, and Lloyds Bank. The daily exchange rate is displayed, and is fixed by the government so it is the same in all banks. Banking hours are normally Mon–Fri, 9–3, though some open as early as 8 am.

Wiring money from abroad should be avoided if possible, since delays and other trouble is virtually guaranteed. If you have no choice, then you will be paid in local currency and can rarely buy back US dollars at the bank. Best use Lloyds Bank International, 8 Avenida 10–67, Zona 1; or Bank of America, 5 Avenida 10–55, Zona 1. Another bank that has been known to pay out in US dollars or travellers' cheques is Banco Internacional, 7a Avenida 11–20, Zona 1; telex 5488 BANCOIGU; tel 518066. Amex card holders can also get dollars at their office, simply by writing a personal cheque.

Credit cards, such as American Express and Visa, are generally accepted. Diners Club and Access/Mastercard can also be used. Of course plastic money will only help in the most expensive hotels, shops and restaurants, for hiring cars or buying flight tickets.

Post Offices

There are post offices (*correos*), open Mon–Fri, 8–6 in the capital, 8–4 everywhere else, in every major town, and often even in the smaller places. When sending letters, it is always best to send them airmail and express—they will still take up to six weeks to reach Europe and a couple less to North America. Generally the postal service is slow but safe, and even parcels arrive back home eventually. To send any parcel which weighs over 2 kg, you will have to take it to the main post office in Guatemala City open for inspection, so take string and sticking materials to finish wrapping at the counter. There are strict regulations about the way parcels should be wrapped. If you can afford it, you may prefer to use DHL or UPS offices for extra safety and speed. Or you could use the services of the **Get Guated Out** agency in Panajachel (see p. 113).

Receiving mail is straightforward via the *lista de correos* at any Guatemalan post office. The central post office in Guatemala City is the safest. Letters from Europe or North America normally arrive in ten days. To avoid mix-ups, make sure letters are addressed to you by your surname only, with no initial or title prefixed. That way there is only one choice of letter under which to sort your mail. To get your post you will need your passport, and will be charged a tiny fee for each piece of mail. The address for the central post office in the capital is: Lista de Correos, Correo Central, 7 Avenida and 12 Calle, Zona 1, Guatemala City, Guatemala, C.A.

Alternatively, members of American Express, or even holders of their travellers' cheques, could have their mail sent to the offices of American Express, Avenida Reforma 9–00, Zona 9, Guatemala City, Guatemala, C.A. They keep mail longer than the post office and are probably a bit safer, though there's not much in it.

Telecommunications

Payphones do exist, for which you will need plenty of 25 and 10 centavo coins, but more numerous are the offices of the national telephone company, GUATEL, open daily 7–10. Often chaotic places, they are nevertheless the best choice for making local and international calls. Be warned that international calls are very expensive, and just three minutes to Europe will cost you over US$20. Reverse charge calls can only be made to the US, Canada, Italy and Spain.

The main GUATEL office in Guatemala City is near the main post office, at 7 Avenida 12–39, Zona 1; there are a number of others, including one on Avenida Reforma 6–29, Zona 9. Your other option is to use the luxury hotels, who will allow you to phone at exorbitant rates.

Police and Military

In spite of Guatemala's appalling human rights record, its waning guerrilla war and other horrors, it is extremely unlikely that you will be affected. As a foreigner you are not a target for terror. It is the Indians and street children who are in danger.

In fact, Guatemala is one of the safest Latin American countries to travel in, as long as you take the normal care and attention necessary anywhere in this part of the world. Watch out for pickpockets at markets and bus terminals. Although you should guard your baggage while travelling, do not worry too much if your pack is on the roof during bus journeys. Unless it falls off, it will most likely still be there when you arrive at your destination (you have to be much more careful in South America).

You will see guards armed with machine guns in all government offices, banks, and many commercial stores, and although intimidating at first, they are quite harmless as far as you are concerned. Most uniformed officials will be very courteous and only too pleased to help you if they can. Should you get stopped, for example at one of the standard military road blocks, or need to report a theft, always remain calm and polite, no matter what. Bribes should never be more than a last resort, and best avoided by unpractised players.

The police wear uniforms of dark blue trousers and light blue shirts. The military are in familiar khaki, with high-ranking members in olive or dark green uniforms. The chaps in grass-green, with the strange hats, like Canadian mounties gone wrong, are members of the Guardia de Hacienda, and responsible for policing the countryside.

Also in the countryside, mainly in the Western Highlands, you will see groups of civilian men armed with rifles, guarding villages, markets or strategic roads. These are not bandits, but civil defence units organized by the military, their job being to defend their village against lurking guerrillas.

Medical Matters

Farmácias, as chemists are known, stock all types of drugs, many without a prescription, and many that are banned in Europe and North America. Clearly, it is best to bring your own medicines with you, but you should be able to buy most things you need here. If you plan on visiting the jungle, don't forget to bring the relevant malaria pills. Contraceptives, such as the pill or condoms, are readily available. Sanitary towels can be bought anywhere in the country, and tampons in the cities. Two items you will have difficulty finding are earplugs and contact lens soaking solutions, and mosquito repellent is also rare. (In the capital you can buy contact lens solution at Optica Moderna, 12 Calle 4–48, zone 1.)

Should you suffer an attack of persistent bad guts, you would be well advised to visit one of the many biological labs, which will analyze your problem and prescribe the appropriate remedy. In most cases these labs will be better qualified to recognize what is wrong than your doctor back home, so do trust them to help you, rather than suffer until returning to your own country. There are good labs in Guatemala City, Antigua and Quezaltenango. Alternatively, go to the nearest private hospital you can find, which will always be better than the state's institution, and not that expensive.

Public Holidays and Opening Hours

Banks and government offices close on official holidays, though public transport can always be found even when officially not running.

New Year's Day
6 January—Epiphany
Easter Week (*Semana Santa*)—most important festival
1 May—Labour Day
30 June—Anniversary of 1871 revolution
15 August—Assumption, celebrated only in the capital
15 September—Independence Day
12 October—Discovery of America
20 October—Revolution Day
1 Nov—All Saints' Day
24 Dec—Christmas Eve
25 Dec—Christmas Day
31 Dec—New Year's Eve

Most places are open Mondays to Fridays, 9–4, and slightly shorter hours at the weekend. Many places close over lunchtime, and some are shut on Mondays and weekends. Check opening times before setting out as there is considerable local variation. Archaeological sites are open daily, usually 8–4, though this also varies. Shops tend to open at 8 and close at 5.30; markets normally run from dawn until 4, with most of the action over by lunchtime.

Festivals

Guatemala is rightly famous for its traditional Indian festivals, times when the air is thick with incense and resounds to the constant blast of earpiercing firecrackers. You will see the Maya heritage at its most vibrant, with people decked out in their best native costumes, outrageously drunk, yet with untiring energy for another dance or song or candle-lit procession. These festivals are normally in honour of a Christian saint, but contain elements of earlier Indian celebrations that the colonial church was incapable of supressing. What we see today is a remarkable mixture of two very different heritages.

The festivals of the *ladino* population are no less riotous, with plenty of colour and noise, and a bullfight or two. Both kinds of festival usually have attendant fairs and markets, and normally go on for a week, the last two days being the most important and interesting for visitors.

The most famous Indian festival in the country is the December one in Chichicastenango, while Easter Week in Antigua is celebrated with an extravagance you are unlikely to find anywhere else in Central America. There are many others worth making an effort to see as well, such as the horse races in Todos Santos, or the kite-flying in Santiago Sacatepéquez, both on 1 November. Every town and village has at least one special day for a festival, which will be listed in the text. For the two most famous events, you will need to book accommodation well in advance or get there at least a day early.

BEST OF THE FESTIVALS

January
1–5 Jan **Santa María de Jesús**, a small Indian village near Antigua.

15 Jan Annual pilgrimage to **Esquipulas**, a *ladino* town near the Honduran border and home to the famous Black Christ.

19–25 Jan Traditional dances at **Rabinal**, a small Indian village in the department of Baja Verapaz.

22–26 Jan **San Pablo la Laguna**, a normally quiet Indian village on Lake Atitlán.

February
1st Friday of Lent **Antigua**, former colonial capital near Guatemala City.

March
Easter Week (*Semana Santa*) This is one of the most interesting times to be anywhere in Guatemala, when the whole country is celebrating, and nowhere more so than in **Antigua**.
Easter Saturday Indians from all around Lake Atitlán come to be baptized in its waters at **Panajachel**.

April
Whitsun **Aguacatán**, a small place near the town of Huehuetenango, celebrates Whitsun with a festival and interesting market.

May
2–3 May **Amatitlán**, near the lake of the same name, has its annual pilgrimage across the waters.
8–10 May **Santa Cruz la Laguna**, a small Indian village on Lake Atitlán.

June
12–14 June **San Antonio Palopó**, Indian village on Lake Atitlán.
24–29 June **San Pedro Carchá**, outside Cobán, a mainly *ladino* festival with plenty of traditional dancing.
27–30 June **San Pedro la Laguna**, Indian village on Lake Atitlán.
28–30 June **Almolonga**, a bustling Indian village near Quezaltenango, with nearby hot springs in which to recover if needed.

July
1–4 July **Santa María Visitación**, a village near Sololá, above Lake Atitlán.
16–22 July **Puerto Barrios**, port city on the Atlantic coast, has a *ladino* festival, very loud and with plenty of sleaze.
20–25 July **Cubulco**, a remote *ladino* farming community in the Baja Verapaz, whose festival still includes many traditional Indian dances.
21 July–4 Aug **Momostenango**, a remote Indian town in the mountains near Quezaltenango, holds a traditional festival and has beautiful woven blankets at its market.
23–27 July **Santiago Atitlán**, the country's most visited Indian village, on the shores of Lake Atitlán, with a very popular festival.
31 July–6 Aug **Cobán**, coffee capital of Guatemala, has its annual festival at this time, and also hosts the **National Festival of Folklore**, where representatives come from all over the country to show their native costumes and participate in many traditional dances. **An agricultural fair is also held.**

August

6–15 Aug **Joyabaj**, an out of the way town east of Santa Cruz del Quiché, where you will see traditional dances rarely performed elsewhere.

11–17 Aug **Sololá**, perched above Lake Atitlán, springs to life for its annual festival, with a good market attached.

12–15 Aug **Nebaj**, northeast of Huehuetenango, where the Indians wear one of the most beautiful costumes in the country.

12–18 Aug **Cantel**, an Indian village outside Quezaltenango, located in a gorgeous valley.

22–28 Aug **Lanquín**, a remote town east of Cobán.

September

12–18 Sep **Quezaltenango**, the country's second city.

24–30 Sep **Totonicapán**, near Quezaltenango, a traditional town with one of the largest markets.

October

1–6 Oct **San Francisco el Alto**, a hillside settlement near Quezaltenango, with an interesting animal fair.

2–6 Oct **Panajachel**, favourite gringo spot on Lake Atitlán.

20–26 Oct **Iztapa**, a small town on the Pacific coast, and one of the few places worth visiting there.

21 Oct–1 Nov **Todos Santos**, a remote Indian village northwest of Huehuetenango, with chaotic horse races 29 Oct–1 Nov, worth making an effort to see.

November

1 Nov **Santiago de Sacatepéquez**, near the highway between the capital and Chimalte-nango, where giant kites are flown in the cemetery as part of the Day of the Dead celebration.

22–26 Nov **Zunil** is a small village outside Quezaltenango, where the local costume is all shocking pinks and purple.

23–25 Nov **Nahualá**, a rarely visited Indian settlement, halfway between Los Enquentros and Quezaltenango, has a very drunken and colourful festival, where men sport their traditional skirts.

25 Nov **Santa Catarina Palopó**, a small village on Lake Atitlán.

27 Nov–1 Dec **San Andrés Itzapa**, a small town near Antigua, interesting for its shrine to Maximón, the notorious Indian saint.

December

5–8 Dec **Huehuetenango**, the largest town to the northwest of Guatemala City.

7 Dec The Burning of the Devil takes place symbolically, as bonfires of rubbish are lit throughout the country, but mainly around **Quezaltenango** and in **Guatemala City**. (Very smelly.) **Antigua** also has a ceremonial burning, usually attended by a street party and fireworks.

13–21 Dec **Chichicastenango**, a staunch Indian town, where Catholic and Maya traditions have merged into a unique festival of worshipping, dancing, processions, and live music, accompanied by the richest handicraft market you will find in Guatemala. Of the dances, the most famous is the *Palo Volador*, which is not so much dancing as dicing with death: pairs of men swing from the top of a 60-foot pole on the end of an unravelling rope.

24–31 Dec **Livingston**, the only black community in Guatemala, on the Atlantic coast, celebrates Christmas with occasional live singing of African songs on the streets, and a couple of good reggae discos at night.

31 Dec New Year's Eve resounds to the deafening noise of dynamite firecrackers, with the best parties happening in **Antigua, Panajachel** and **Livingston**.

Markets

If you cannot make it to one of the festivals, then there are always the markets as consolation. Every town and village in Guatemala has a weekly market, and that is always the best time to be there. The most interesting are in the Western Highlands, where the majority of Indians lived, who flock to their nearest market, bent double by the wares carried on their backs. Walking around the stalls and baskets of farm produce and small livestock, you will notice that the atmosphere is refreshingly tranquil. This is because Guatemalan Indians come to market foremost to socialize: to keep up with the latest news from distant hamlets, establish family ties, and set up potential marriages. Buying and selling is just by the by for these people, who live off the land and are almost outside the money economy of the rest of the country.

Of course the *artesanía* or *típica* markets are quite different: here the Indian traders, usually women, drive a tough bargain, and are uncharacteristically pushy in getting you to look at their goods. The best craftware and textile markets are in Guatemala City (daily), Antigua (daily, but weekends best), Panajachel (daily), Chichicastenango (Thursday and Sunday), Momostenango (Wednesday and Sunday), Nebaj (Sunday) and Todos Santos (Wednesday and Sunday). There are many others well worth seeing, and all other market days are listed in the text.

Shopping

The markets are the best places for shopping—if you know how to bargain. The big attraction is the Indian hand-woven textiles, which are made into anything from rugs, blankets, bags, *huipiles* (blouses), skirts and hats, to wall-hangings. These textiles are often also elaborately embroidered, showing the traditional patterns of each region or village, and thus half the pleasure of buying these things is identifying them with a particular place or region, where you have seen them worn or used in their original context.

Hand-made linen tablewear is another good buy, with an almost infinite variety of colours and styles available. There is also delicate hand-made pottery, which is rather brittle, so difficult to transport; also a large array of carved wooden masks used during the Indian festivals; wooden furniture; wickerwork and rush mats and baskets; leather belts, bags and suitcases; plenty of silver-leaf filigree jewellery, as well as coral and glass bead necklaces; and finally, in Antigua, there is a great deal of Guatemalan jade for sale, made into anything from reproduction Maya statues to pendants. Watch out for soapstone fakes in the markets, and only buy jade from reputable shops.

A 7% government tax is added to most commercial transactions in shops, though almost never in the markets, where you do not get a bill anyway.

The Media

The two most widely available national newspapers are *El Gráfico* and *La Prensa Libre*, of which the latter is slightly less populist and celebrity orientated, but both are fundamentally right-wing in their political stance. As papers critical of the usually right-wing governments get closed down, this is no surprise. *La Hora*, published in the afternoons and only available in and near Guatemala City, has the most balanced news analysis; *Siglo XXI* is on a par with La Hora and published in the mornings. The weekly magazine *La Crónica* also aims to present a critical and broad analysis of Guatemalan and Latin American events in general. There are a number of other newspapers as well.

Going to the cinema is a favourite cheap pastime in Guatemala, and most large towns have at least one. The programme is often dominated by porn, violent or horror films, but most places usually run the latest North American film releases as well. Foreign films are run with subtitles, not dubbed, but the sound and film quality can be dreadful; unscheduled breaks in the programme or sound are frequent.

TV and radio stations abound in Guatemala, where over 60% of the population is illiterate, and many restaurants and hotels have radios and TVs permanently switched on, so you will soon get to know them well. Satellite and cable TV are also quite common here, and 'gringo' bars and restaurants in Antigua even show American CNN news.

Where to Stay

There are luxury hotels of international standard in Guatemala City, Antigua, Panajachel, Chichicastenango outside Tikal, and in El Relleno on Lake Izabal; first-class hotels in Quezaltenango and Livingston; and otherwise perfectly good standard hotels and guest houses in most of the places you will want to visit, with a price that suits your pocket easy to find. Should you go off the beaten track to remote Indian towns or villages, you will find very basic guest houses, or sometimes none at all. Where there is no official guest house, your best option is to find the local *alcalde* (mayor), who will either find you a reputable private house to lodge in, or let you sleep on the floor in the local council building or school. If you plan on visiting remoter places in the Highlands, remember your sleeping bag, since it can get very cold at night.

Prices for even the cheapest hovel are fixed by the national tourist board (INGUAT), so you can always see what the correct price is supposed to be. However, many places neglect to get their annual review, so don't be surprised if the price notice is a few years out of date, and expect to be flexible. Officially, there is a 17% tax added to all hotel bills, so always check if a price is inclusive or not. Cheap accommodation normally has taxes already included. Guatemala has the cheapest accommodation in Central America: the most basic double rooms cost around US$2, reasonable guest houses offering rooms for as little as US$7, while slightly up-market hotels charge from US$14 for two.

There are many different names for accommodation, but they basically all mean the same thing and do not necessarily indicate differences in standard. *Hotel, pensión, posada, hospedaje* and *huésped* are standard descriptions of the whole gamut of Guatemalan accommodation. Although phone and fax numbers have been listed in the text where available, most places will not accept verbal reservations, and even written ones are difficult to get with any but the most expensive. All you can do is phone to see if rooms are free and then turn up and try your luck.

There are no youth hostels in Guatemala, and only two places where you can camp with reasonable facilities and safety: Panajachel and Tikal. But accommodation is so cheap that there really is no advantage in camping, and the only time you might need a tent is climbing one of the volcanoes or hiking in remote mountain or jungle areas. If you do not want to bring your own, you can hire most camping equipment in Antigua, either from the *Casa Andinista* or the many tour agencies.

Commercial renting of holiday homes or flats is not an established business here, but you can find long-term lets in the two gringo centres of Antigua and Panajachel, and possibly in Quezaltenango. Again, unless you plan on staying for months on end, you will not save much money by renting, when you can find pleasant, cheap guest houses and meals too.

Eating Out

Food is not Guatemala's strong point. The basic dish is eggs and black beans (*huevos y frijoles*), usually greasy and fried. These mostly come with fried chicken (*pollo frito*) or beef (*lomito*); and then there are the other two standard foods, which are actually Italian: pasta and pizzas. All these dishes are usually served with warm tortillas, which are roasted cornflour patties, or with tasteless white bread. You do, however, have a good choice of international cuisine in most towns, with at least one Italian or Chinese restaurant, and plenty of fast-food burger places.

Having said this, there are a few tasty local snacks to try, such as the *tamale*, which is an envelope of banana-leaf (not edible) with steamed maize paste inside, often mixed with other vegetables or bits of meat. *Tamales negros* are sweet, made with prunes. *Chiles rellenos* are peppers stuffed with bits of meat and vegetables, often served with hot sauce—as is everything here, unless you say otherwise. *Antojito* is a small tortilla 'sandwich', usually filled with a thin piece of fried beef, onion and tomato. *Enchiladas* are another standard, composed of crispy tortillas piled high with chopped vegetables, salad or meat, or a bit of each. And finally, the *fiambre* is not a snack but a giant salad of meats, fish, and cheese with assorted greenery, all piled up together, normally only eaten on 1 November.

All these dishes (except the last) are commonly served by vendors on the streets or at bus stations, but you would be safer eating them in restaurants, where hygiene is marginally better, or in the markets, where food is freshly made on the day. The best places to try them is in the *comedores*, which are typical Guatemalan restaurants that serve a limited range of local food at the cheapest prices you will find in the country.

More up-market restaurants rarely serve traditional food, unless they specialize in 'typical' dishes. One of the best restaurant chains of this type, only in the capital, is **Los Antojitos**, listed in the text. There are also restaurants which serve traditional Maya food, which adds some exotic meats to the standard eggs and beans. For example, you could eat stewed armadillo, turkey (*pavo*) or *tepezcuintle*, which is a jungle animal that looks like a strange mini-deer, but is in fact the largest member of the rodent family: delicious when not overcooked. A good alternative to the eggs and beans are *plátanos fritos*, which are fried savoury bananas.

On either coast, you will also find delicious fresh seafood, usually fish, shrimp or squid, and a special dish you should try here is *ceviche*, which is chopped pieces of fish and onions marinaded in lemon juice, served cold. (Avoid as long as there is a cholera problem.) Tropical fruit of all kinds is sold all over the country, but is best here, and the local coconut bread (*pan de coco*) is very good, though do not eat too much unless constipation is the desired effect. A 10% service tax is added to all restaurant bills.

Drink

The most common drinks available are canned or bottled fruit juices, fizzy drinks or watery local beers. For the climate, the local beer is ideal; served very cold it is refreshing without making you dozy. *Gallo* or *Moza* are the most common, the latter a dark beer. *Cabro* beer is brewed in Quezaltenango and usually only available in and around that town. Avoid the delicious freshly-made shakes made with water (*licuados*), until you feel your stomach can cope with the local microbes. In the better restaurants, fruit juices and shakes are made with sterilized water, but always ask to make sure, since local tap water is generally not safe. Guatemalan wine tastes like a cross between vinegar and petrol, and is best avoided. But the rum is cheap and all right if mixed. Best buy is *Ron Colonial*, while *Ron Botran* and *Venado Especial* will give you a severe hangover (*goma*). Hardened drinkers will appreciate the local firewater called *Quetzalteca*, which blasts a burning trail down your throat.

In spite of the fact that Guatemala is a coffee-growing country, the drink is almost universally weak, normally made of instant powder and tasting like dishwater. This is a pity, because when you get the real thing, it is very good. The most likely places to find real coffee are the gringo joints of Antigua and Panajachel, or exclusive restaurants. Tea is also disappointingly weak, but a good alternative is the locally produced hot chocolate.

Itineraries

The Western Highlands

Most visitors to Guatemala head for the Western Highlands, and rightly so. This is where the scenery of volcanoes, lakes and pine-clad highland scenery is at its most captivating. It is also where you will meet the majority of the country's Indian inhabitants. The standard circuit would first take you west from the capital to the small town of **Antigua**, with a beautiful setting and fine colonial architecture. From here the Pan-American Highway leads you northwards to beautiful **Lake Atitlán**. Next the road continues to **Quezaltenango**, the country's second city and an excellent base for exploring remoter villages and markets and a bit of easy hiking. Beyond here, the northwestern town of **Huehuetenango** has very little to offer, except that the remote and rough terrain around it is spectacular at times, and if you want to visit the Indian village of **Todos Santos**, you will have to pass this way. Heading south again, there are two routes you could take: either you can return via the paved Pan-American Highway, or you can continue on dirt roads via Sacapulas (east of Huehuetenango), and Santa Cruz del Quiché, meeting the paved highway again beyond **Chichicastenango**. The latter choice is slow but scenicly terrific, and either way, you will want to make sure you visit Chichi, as it is known.

Pacific and Atlantic Beaches

Do not bother coming to Guatemala for the beaches. What you will find on the Pacific side is a 60 km belt of flat plantation country, with little access to the sea itself. Where there are roads to the beach you will find a grey strip of sand, often separated from the mainland by mangrove swamps and a water canal. On the Atlantic side, there is only one place worth going to, and that is **Livingston**, a Caribbean community descended from African slaves, Carib Indians, and the odd shipwrecked sailor. The place is located at the mouth of the River Dulce, and while the beach may not be memorable, the river is, with jungle vegetation and plenty of wildlife to see during boat trips, which can take you all the way to **Lake Izabal**, and waterside **El Relleno**, dotted with some of the country's most exclusive hotels and private holiday villas.

The Jungle

The ruined Maya city of **Tikal** is the most awe-inspiring place in the country. From the present-day town of **Flores**, there are also a number of opportunities to go on jungle tours or organize guides for individual itineraries to distant archaeological sites in the jungle, only accessible on foot, horseback or via the rivers.

The Verapaz Mountains

This large region is the least visited area of Guatemala. Roads are good for the most part, yet you are off the beaten track here. The mountains hide two particular spots worth making an effort to see: the **Quetzal Reserve**, where you might see the country's extremely rare national bird; and the gorgeous forest pools of **Semuc Champey**, an arduous place to reach, beyond Cobán, but well worth it.

The back road connecting **Cobán** in the northeast with **Huehuetenango** in the northwest is unrivalled for its spectacular setting, snaking its way along the edges of a terrifyingly steep river valley and into the **Cuchumatán Mountains**. The last time a bus actually fell off the road was in the mid-seventies.

Guatemala City

Try as it might, Guatemala City just cannot muster the atmosphere of a capital city. Its two million inhabitants are spread thinly throughout the seemingly endless grid of avenidas and calles, and except for Zona 1's Avenidas 5 and 6, the city is strangely quiet—more reminiscent of a provincial town.

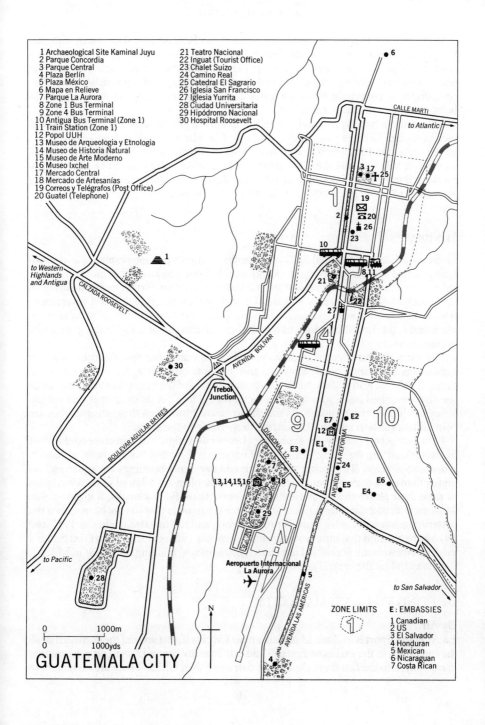

1 Archaeological Site Kaminal Juyu
2 Parque Concordia
3 Parque Central
4 Plaza Berlín
5 Plaza México
6 Mapa en Relieve
7 Parque La Aurora
8 Zone 1 Bus Terminal
9 Zone 4 Bus Terminal
10 Antigua Bus Terminal (Zone 1)
11 Train Station (Zone 1)
12 Popol UUH
13 Museo de Arqueologia y Etnologia
14 Museo de Historia Natural
15 Museo de Arte Moderno
16 Museo Ixchel
17 Mercado Central
18 Mercado de Artesanías
19 Correos y Telégrafos (Post Office)
20 Guatel (Telephone)

21 Teatro Nacional
22 Inguat (Tourist Office)
23 Chalet Suizo
24 Camino Real
25 Catedral El Sagrario
26 Iglesia San Francisco
27 Iglesia Yurrita
28 Ciudad Universitaria
29 Hipódromo Nacional
30 Hospital Roosevelt

6

CALLE MARTI
to Atlantic

3 17
25

1

19
20
2
26
23

10

21
22
8 11

27

9

to Western
Highlands
and Antigua

CALZADA ROOSEVELT

AVENIDA BOLIVAR

30

Trebol
Junction

9

E7 E2
12
E1

E3

10

BOULEVAR AGUILAR BATRES

DIAGONAL 12

AVENIDA LA REFORMA

24

E5

E6
E4

13,14,15,16   18
7

to Pacific

29

Aeropuerto Internacional
La Aurora
5

to San Salvador

28

N

0   1000m
0   1000yds

GUATEMALA CITY

AVENIDA LAS AMÉRICAS

4

ZONE LIMITS   E : EMBASSIES
1   1 Canadian
                2 US
                3 El Salvador
                4 Honduran
                5 Mexican
                6 Nicaraguan
                7 Costa Rican

In the expensive southern quarters of Zonas 9 and 10, it is particularly quiet, with only the guards hanging around at the entrances of walled compounds that hide the city's finer residences. As in Latin America generally, exclusive usually means boring and empty, since any existing life is rigorously kept behind high walls and barbed wire. The so-called *zona viva* could hardly be less so, the restaurants, bars and occasional clubs being dull, though always expensive.

In fact, there is really no good reason to stay long in Guatemala City, known as *Guate* locally, though foreigners soon dub it 'Grotty'. Three or four days is plenty of time to see all the museums and churches, and stroll along the hybrid streets of Zona 1, the centre, where you will also find the city's most colourful places: the squares and the central markets. Bar the appalling pollution, this is painlessly done, since the city is 'an extremely horizontal place ... like a city on its back.' (Paul Theroux).

History

Guatemala City was founded in 1774, after the country's previous capital, like the two before it, had been destroyed by an earthquake. It was not an auspicious moment, and in spite of the desolation and disease which racked Antigua, their former capital, many of its survivors had no desire to up and leave. The rich and the ecclesiastical and government bodies were loath to start from scratch, developing a new city from nothing on an open plain near Lake Amatitlán, while the townfolk and Indian peasants had nothing to gain by moving away.

However, the government made it compulsory to move, and thus the country's new capital was reluctantly filled. Slowly, a new city was built, designed on the standard Spanish colonial grid system, which has gradually spread out to cover the entire plateau the city is perched on. Today its edges teeter on the brink of dusty ravines that cut the sandy earth like giant wrinkles. As the shanty towns grow, even these steep gashes are being filled, rubbish and shacks clinging desperately to the sides.

Perhaps not surprisingly, the exuberant glamour of Antigua's architecture could never be re-created on the same scale, and Guatemala City has always been a visually monotonous place. This being earthquake country, most buildings are squat and no higher than a few storeys, though 20th-century technology has allowed some skyscrapers to raise their glassy shoots, and these have become useful landmarks, if nothing else. Most architecture dates from this century, since Guatemala City has not been spared the battering quakes any more than its predecessors, and the massive quakes in 1917 and 1976 have ensured that little remains of the 18th and 19th centuries. What you find is a modern city with the occasional old church or municipal building, the finest of which is the cathedral on the central square.

GETTING TO GUATEMALA CITY

By Air
La Aurora airport is in Zona 13 of Guatemala City itself, just around the corner from all the top hotels in the exclusive Zonas 9 and 10. The city centre (Zona 1) is a 10-minute drive away, and the taxi there should not cost more than US$5. There are no meters so

always fix a price before the journey begins. Buses nos. 5 and 6 run from near the airport exit to the city centre every 30 minutes during daylight hours. Note that the airport shuts down at night, so you cannot sleep there.

There are regular flights from the following Central American and Caribbean cities: San Salvador, Tegucigalpa, Mexico City, Belize City, Managua, San José, Panamá and San Andrés. Most flights from South America are via Panamá/San José. There are no direct flights from Peru or Ecuador.

Aeronica, 10 Calle 6–20, Zona 9, tel 325541.
Aeroquetzal, Avenida Hincapie and 18 Calle, Zona 13, tel 365214.
Aerovías, Avenida Hincapié and 18 Calle, Zona 13, tel 347935.
Aviateca, Avenida Hincapié, Zona 13, tel 318227.
British Airways, Avenida Reforma 8–60, Zona 9, tel 312555.
Continental, at airport, tel 312051/5.
Iberia, Avenida Reforma 8–60, Zona 9, tel 373914/5.
Eastern, at airport, tel 321325.
KLM, 6 Avenida 20–25, Zona 10, Edificio Plaza Marítima, tel 370222.
PanAm, 6 Avenida 11–43, Zona 1, tel 532523.
Taca, 7 Avenida 14–35, Zona 9, tel 322360.
Tapsa, Avenida Hincapié, Zona 13, tel 314860.
Virgin Atlantic, Avenida Reforma 9–00, Zona 9, Edificio Plaza Panamericana, tel 312070.

By Train
The train station is on the same square as the Zona 1 bus terminal, though you would never know it. It is the wooden building behind all the buses, away from the main street. You have two choices of destination only: to Puerto Barrios on the Atlantic coast (Tues, Thurs and Sat, at 7.30 am) or Tecún Umán on the border with Mexico (Tues and Sat, at 7 am). The journey to the coast can take up to 20 hours, through hot and arid country-side, with no restaurant carriage. The journey to Tecún Umán can be equally slow, but the countryside is much more interesting, as you pass over the Western Highlands and then along the foothills bordering the tropical Pacific plain. Again, there is no food provision on board, and delays are frequent. Best buy your ticket in advance, and always check days and times of departure, since these can change at any time.

By Bus
The **main bus terminal** is in Zona 4, where you will find 2nd-class buses going to almost all parts of the country, as well as nearby places, such as Lake Amatitlán. These buses are normally in good repair, though they do get very crowded and the seats are tight. It is best to turn up in the mornings for long-distance journeys. **Zona 1 bus terminal** is on a square, on the corner of 18 Calle and 9 Avenida, and here you will find 2nd-class buses and Pullman-style buses leaving for destinations in the Eastern High-lands and the Atlantic coast. All tickets, except those for long-distance Pullman buses, can be bought on the bus. (You *can* travel on the Pullmans without buying a ticket first, but because seats are booked, you will most likely have to stand for the whole journey.)

If you are heading for the former colonial capital of Antigua, one hour from the present capital, you will find buses leaving every half an hour (5 am–8 pm coming from Guatemala City, but 5–5 coming from Antigua), from the junction of 18 Calle and 4 Avenida in Zona 1, and more from the small terminal on 20 Calle, between 2 and 3 Avenue, Zona 1.

The following Pullman companies are recommended for a more comfortable journey, but please note that the journey times are approximate. Buses leave from outside the offices:

To Cobán or the Quetzal Reserve: Escobar/Monja Blanca, 8a Avenida 15–16, Zona 1, tel 511878. Daily 5–4.30; the journey to Cobán takes 4 hrs, to the Reserve 3 hrs.

To Esquipulas: Rutas Orientales, 19 Calle 8–18, Zona 1, tel 537282. Daily every half hour, 4 am–6 pm; the journey takes 3 hrs.

To Flores (for Tikal): Fuente del Norte, 17 Calle 8–46, Zona 1, tel 86094/513817. Daily at 1, 2, 3, 7 am and 11 pm, officially a 14-hr journey, but normally nearer 24. Reservations are essential.

To Huehuetenango: Los Halcones, 15 Calle 7–66, Zona 1. Buses run daily, 7–2; the journey takes 6 hrs.

To Puerto Barrios: Litegua, 15 Calle 10–42, Zona 1, tel 27578. Daily every hour, 6–5; the journey takes 6 hrs. Their best Pullman service leaves for the coast at 10 and 5 daily, which should be non-stop and a bit faster.

To Panajachel: Rebuli, 3a Avenida 7–36, Zona 9. Daily every hour, 6–3; the journey takes 3 hrs.

To Quezaltenango: Transportes Galgos, 7a Avenida 19–44, Zona 1, tel 23661, and **Líneas Américas**, 2a Avenida 18–74, Zona 1. Both companies run daily buses, 5.30–9; the journey takes 4 hrs.

To San Salvador (El Salvador): Quality, 6 Avenida 9–85, Zona 9. 1st-class Pullmans run daily from Guatemala City, departing from Hotel Villa Española 6 am, Hotel Fiesta 6.30 am, arriving in San Salvador at the Hotel Fiesta 10.45 am, Hotel Camino Real 11 am, and at Hotel Presidente 11.15 am. Tickets can be bought at the main office and the hotels where the buses stop. Buses leave San Salvador for Guatemala daily at the same time, 6 am.

Melva Internacional, 4a Avenida 1–20, Zona 9, tel 367248. Daily, 6–11 am, 12 and 1 pm; the journey takes 5 hrs. The Salvadorean borders are open daily, 6–8.

To El Florido (for Honduras): Rutas Orientales, 19 Calle 8–18, Zona 1, tel 537282. Buses run daily, every half hour, 4–6; the journey takes 4 hrs as far as Chiquimula. There you must change buses for El Florido, taking a **Vilma** bus, which leaves from the back of the market. Last bus from either Chiquimula or the border leaves at 4.30 pm and takes around 2 hrs. From the border, a Honduran minibus will take you to the town of Copán Ruinas in 40 min. The Honduran borders are open daily, 6–6.

To La Mesilla (for Mexico): El Condor, 19 Calle 2–01, Zona 1, tel 28504. Daily buses 4, 8, 10 am, 1 and 5 pm; the journey takes at least 7 hrs. You travel faster by taking a **Los Halcones** bus to Huehuetenango, and changing there for a bus to the Mexican border. **Cristóbal Colón** buses connect with Mexico City and all cities along the way on the Mexican side, the first one leaving around 8 am.

There are also bus routes to the Mexican border towns of Talismán run by **Transportes Galgos** (see Quezaltenango route) and to Tecún Umán, run by **Fortaleza**, 19 Calle 8–70, Zona 1, tel 517994. The Mexican borders open daily from 6–6.

GETTING AROUND GUATEMALA CITY

By Bus

There are **municipal buses** (*buses urbanos*) running to all parts of the city from around 6 am until 8 pm. Fares are ridiculously cheap, so it is always worth having small change in your pocket rather than having to bring out high denomination notes in public. Unfortunately, there is no such thing as a bus timetable or even a brochure outlining which bus goes where. The whole system changes constantly, and nobody can claim to know its logic or routes. The good news is that there are probably only three buses you will want to use, remembering always to confirm with the driver that he is going where you want to go.

Bus no. 5 not only connects the airport to Zona 1, but also connects the centre with the city's most important complex of state-run museums. If you are coming from the airport, you want to make sure the bus says *Parque Central* in the window. Another bus connecting Zona 1 with the airport is **no. 100**, which is usually an orange colour.

If coming from Zona 1, the best place to catch this and the other buses, is beneath the hilltop Teatro Nacional, which is on the continuation of 6 Avenida, beyond 18 Calle. The no. 5 is normally a dark-green colour, and if it is going to the airport, it should say *aeropuerto* in the window. It will also take you to the cluster of the **Museo Nacional de Arqueología y Etnología**, the **Museo Nacional de Arte Moderno** and the **Museo de Historia Natural**, all next door to each other. Best ask to be dropped off here, otherwise you are likely to miss it first time.

Bus no. 2 is also normally a green colour, and stops at the same place underneath the Teatro Nacional. This one will take you from Zona 1 to Zonas 9 and 10, travelling along the Avenida Reforma, which is the main dual carriageway through the southern quarters of the city. Returning from Zonas 9 and 10, the bus drops you off just past the city's tourist office INGUAT, one street east of the Teatro Nacional. If you are heading further into the centre of Zona 1, stay on the bus and it will most likely take you all the way to the Parque Central. Any bus stopping at the Teatro Nacional which says *terminal* in the front window, will take you to the city's main bus terminal in Zona 4. Ask to be dropped off at the appropriate place, and you will find yourself right in front of the terminal.

By Taxi

Taxis can be flagged down anywhere, but there are two regular stands worth knowing about, both in Zona 1: on the **Parque Concordia** and the **Parque Central**. There are also always taxis at the airport and around the bus terminals. Always agree a price before getting into the car, as there are no meters. If you cannot face the buses, and do not wish to hire a car, you can use taxis for journeys as far as Antigua. You should not pay more than $25 one-way for the journey to Antigua, while inner-city journeys should never come to more than $4 for a long run.

TOURIST INFORMATION

Instituto Guatemalteco de Turismo (INGUAT), Centro Cívico, 7 Avenida 1–17, Zona 4, tel (502–2) 31 1333/47, (Mon–Fri, 8–4.30 and Sat 8–1).

The office has very helpful staff, who speak English as well, and can offer a limited range of brochures and listings, make hotel bookings, and assist in route planning around Guatemala.

ORIENTATION

Guatemala City is not that large, but because it is on a grid of numbered streets, it can be a confusing place at first. The city is divided into zones, and the system for numbering avenidas and calles is repeated in each zone so that the same number of avenida can be in very different parts of the city, and very different kinds of neighbourhood. Consequently you must first find the right zone before you look for the right street. Occasionally street signs are missing, which does not help, but if you always keep counting as you walk, you will have a rough idea where you are. See p. 61 for an explanation of Guatemalan addresses.

WHAT TO SEE

Zona 1: the City Centre

Zona 1 is the city centre, which is basically an oblong box of streets defined by the Parque Central to the north, and 18 Calle to the south, Avenida Elena to the west, and the railway track to the east. It takes about half an hour to walk its length, so even if you do get lost, it will not take long to find a familiar spot. The main arteries of commerce are Avenidas 5, 6 and 7, as well as 18 Calle.

Around here you will see the hub of the city's life, from seedy bars and strip joints near 18 Calle and 9 Avenida, to shops and stalls, cinemas and hotels, to street performers and shoeshine boys around the Parque Concordia on 6 Avenida and 15 Calle; and finally there is some interesting architecture, not only the Palacio Nacional and cathedral, but also the churches of San Francisco and Santa Clara on 6 Avenida.

Heading up 6 Avenida, you come to the courtyard of **San Francisco** church on the junction with 13 Calle. It is not a large building, yet the chunky colonial Baroque columns of the entrance are attractive, and as you pass the wrought-iron gates, you find yourself in a peaceful gloom. The most famous sculpture here is the 'Sacred Heart', which was brought from Antigua. Across 13 Calle, the church of **Santa Clara** is even smaller and more unassuming, a quiet haven for tired beggars, not often visited by anyone else. Other churches in Zona 1 worth visiting include **La Merced** (11 Avenida and 5 Calle), which has a very fine interior brought from ruined Antigua churches—note especially the organ, pulpit and altars—and the **Santuario Expiatorio** (26 Calle and 2 Avenida), which is extraordinary for its exterior, shaped like a fish, as well as the modern mural on the inside.

Reaching the **Parque Central**, you get a refreshing sense of space after the claustrophobic streets behind you. It is not particularly attractive: a large expanse of concrete surrounded by the washed-out colours of modern buildings to the west and older architecture to the east. The most important modern building is the **Biblioteca Nacional**, which is situated behind the bandstand and shrub terraces, known as the

Parque del Centenario, though there is little to separate it from the rest of the main square except a road. Directly opposite is the **cathedral**, its brown façade valiantly standing despite the cracks. Inside, the interior is all whitewashed pillars and dour Passion paintings, though there is a certain Baroque elegance about the place, and hundreds of flickering candles before the altars create a festive atmosphere.

At a right angle to the cathedral stands the **Palacio Nacional**, which suffers from being the pale green of mouldy bread, but is otherwise inoffensive neo-colonial. It was begun by President Ubico in 1939, and completed just in time for his enforced removal from office, in 1944. If you bring your passport, you can enter the palace up the left-hand flight of steps, to find two elegant fountained courtyards, lined by three storeys of balconies. Surprisingly, you can wander about freely, and may just bump into a cavalcade of important generals or ministers, in starched uniforms and dark glasses. On the first floor, facing the street, you may be allowed to take a peep into the reception rooms, with their chandeliers and parquet floors. The stained-glass windows remain shattered from the last bomb attack a few years ago.

Worth visiting while you are up this end of town is the **Mercado Central**, in a concrete bunker immediately behind the cathedral. The lowest levels, which are underground, hold the food market and many *comedores*, where you can eat local food freshly cooked. The higher level holds the craft market, where you will find excellent examples of Guatemala's Indian costumes from every corner of the country. There are textiles, basketry, leatherware, jewellery, clothes, shoes, trinkets and tat—almost anything you can get in Guatemala's markets can be bought here. Naturally prices are slightly higher than elsewhere, but they are still very reasonable. It would be a shame to buy here when you first arrive, since you would get no sense of the places and people that make these lovely things. But it will whet your appetite for things to come, and if there is anything you wish you had bought before you leave, you can pop back here and buy it then. On Sundays there is also an open market on the Parque Central itself.

Heading south along 6 or 5 Avenida, you will eventually come to Zona 1's best square: the **Parque Concordia**. Slightly elevated above the black air of the streets, a tree-lined promenade surrounds a small patch of greenery and a central fountain, where instant-photo men, shoeshine boys, preachers, hustlers and street performers vie for your attention. The best time to be here is at the weekends, when you can do some good people-watching or check out the market stalls that cluster alongside. Just a block away, on the corner of 7 Avenida and 12 Calle, the grand, pink, Moorish building is the **Central Post Office**; the GUATEL office is next door.

Finally, there are two undistinguished museums you can visit in Zona 1: the **Museo de Arte e Industria**, 10 Avenida 10–72 (Tues–Fri, 9–4; Sat–Sun, 9–noon and 2–4; nominal fee) and the **Museo Nacional de Historia**, 9 Calle and 10 Avenida (Tues–Fri, 8.30–4; Sat–Sun, 9–noon and 2–4; free).

Zona 4

18 Calle marks the border of Zonas 1 and 4, where the scene is immediately a mess of dual carriageways, flyovers, and lung-choking traffic easing its way around the elevated fortress of the **Teatro Nacional** on one side, the large indoor food market in the middle, and the highrise buildings of the **Centro Cívico**, which holds the tourist office and various government offices.

There are three places you will want to locate here: firstly, the extension of 4 Avenida past 18 Calle, where the Antigua buses leave; secondly the urban bus stop at the foot of the National Theatre; and thirdly, the **Tourist Office**, whose entrance is just past the elevated walkway crossing the continuation of 7 Avenida, on the left-hand side. Otherwise you may enjoy exploring the **food market** and hardening your sensibilities with the sights and smells of rotting vegetables and unprettified animal anatomy. Be warned that pickpockets are a danger here, so take nothing with you. Further into the depths of Zona 4, the main bus terminal is best reached by bus or taxi, there being no particular pleasure to exploring this part of town.

Lastly, and probably least, if you continue past the tourist office on 7 Avenida and turn left on Ruta 6, you will find the **Iglesia Yurrita**. Unfortunately it is closed most days, but the exterior is memorable enough, and surely deserves a prize for bad taste. It was built in 1928, with private funds, to look like a Russian Orthodox church, and is a higgledy-piggledy of mosaics and onion-domed towers, with a bit of Gothic pointiness added for good measure.

Zonas 9 and 10

This is one indistinguishable large area cut down the middle by the spacious **Avenida La Reforma**, with Zona 9 to the west and Zona 10 to the east. It is a relatively new part of the city and is the favoured home of the capital's wealthier residents, as well as their concomitant trappings, such as exclusive shops, restaurants, clubs and hotels. Most of the city's embassies are located around here too, as are some fine private museums.

Coming from Zona 4, the first point of interest on the Avenida Reforma is the **Jardín Botánico y Museo de Historia Natural** (8–noon and 2–6, closed Sat & Sun and National Holidays, free). The best part of this place is the botanical garden, which is small but attractive, while the museum is small and bedraggled; neglected stuffed animals contrast sadly with the living garden outside. Across the road is a slate-grey turreted wall, which encloses a whole block and hides a military training school.

The Avenida Reforma is a couple of kilometres long, so hopping on and off the frequent buses may be a good idea to explore its environs along the whole length. A few blocks on from the military academy, a museum you will want to see if you are interested in Maya sculpture and pottery is the **Museo Popol Vuh** (Mon–Sat, 9–5.30, $1 fee). It is located on the sixth floor of a black office block, at Avenida Reforma 8–60. Consisting of one large room, the museum does not take long to explore.

The main exhibit centres on a collection of Maya funerary vases, ranging from enormous urns the size of beer barrels, to miniature household ones. The museum has few explanatory notices, making it hard for the layman to appreciate the significance of what is on view. Still, the delicate craftsmanship is obvious, and as beautiful now as it was two thousand or so years ago. Additionally, there is a small collection of colonial religious art and icons, as well as many stone carvings from Maya sites in the Petén jungle and the Pacific lowlands. A tiny, well-stocked bookshop is attached, where you will find excellent publications on many Guatemalan subjects. Access to the bookstore only is free.

Travelling southwards on Avenida Reforma, the most exclusive quarter of Guatemala City—called the **zona viva**—begins east of the Reforma, between Calles 10 and 14, and up to 4 Avenida. There is really nothing much to set it apart from the other streets, except that there are a high number of luxury boutiques, hotels and restaurants bunched together. An excellent place for cheap snacks is the **Miga** delicatessen shop (7 Avenida 14–44), which is set back from the road, on the parking lot of a shopping mall and does great bagels.

One of the city's best museums is the **Museo Ixchel** at 4 Avenida 16–27 (Mon–Fri, 8.30–5.30, Sat, 9–5.30, $1 fee). Just like the Popol Vuh, this is a small private museum. Here you will find superb changing exhibitions on Guatemalan Indian costumes, with pieces collected from often remote regions, and presented in an imaginative and informative way. Maya textiles, their method of production and the significance of design and colour are presented here, and make the museum a valuable introduction to the country's rich living heritage. A large shop is attached, where many of the finest textiles can be bought, as well as plenty of trinkets too.

The end of Avenida Reforma, and Zonas 9 and 10, is marked by the large busy roundabout called **Parque Independencia**, beyond which the road becomes the Avenida Las Américas, heading into Zonas 13 and 14, ever more exclusive and residential, until it ends up at the **Plaza Berlín**. This is more or less where the city comes to an end, and if it wasn't for recent building and the smog, you could see Lake Amatitlán directly south, and the rumbling Pacaya volcano beyond.

State Museums in Aurora Park

On the western edge of **Aurora Park**, which is a vast expanse accommodating the airport, a military base, the national hippodrome, a zoological park (depressing and filthy), and an artisan market (tourist trap), there is also a cluster of three state-run museums. The whole complex of Aurora Park is located just southwest of Zona 9, and is best reached on bus no. 5 from the city centre.

The **Museo Nacional de Arqueología y Etnología** (Tues–Fri, 9–4; Sat–Sun, 9–noon and 2–4; nominal fee) is without doubt the best state museum in the country. For a newcomer to Maya history and art, this is the place to be introduced to the subject. Rooms are laid out in chronological order, starting with an assortment of theories on the original population of the Americas, moving swiftly on to the emergence of Maya culture, displayed by a mixture of model scenes from daily life, to pottery, tools, and decorative art from each era.

Archaeologists have established three phases for Maya cultural history, and as we encounter each one, we see the increased sophistication in art, pottery and sculpture. Major sites, such as the jungle city of Tikal, coastal Quiriguá and highland Utatlán, are rebuilt in miniature, giving the visitor a helpful idea of what these places once looked like. One whole room (closed at weekends) is wholly dedicated to Maya jade artefacts and jewellery, including the famous mosaic mask from Tikal. Also on view is a collection of Indian costumes, craftwork and utensils from various parts of the country. As you head for the exit, you pass a pleasant circular patio with a fountain in the middle, where ancient stelae stand tall and enigmatic. They are large stones and sculptured slabs, covered in Maya hieroglyphs, still only partly deciphered.

The **Museo de Arte Moderno** (same times, free) is opposite, and well worth a quick visit. The earliest paintings are from the 19th century, and begin with a rather distasteful anonymous picture of Mary, her heart stuck full of daggers. The exhibition quickly moves on into the 20th century, and although the museum is small, it has a good variety of Guatemalan painters and styles. A couple of artists are particularly memorable. Roberto Ossaye died very young and painted most of his pictures in his twenties, which makes his breadth of technique and use of materials all the more impressive. Rolando Ixquiac Xicara has only three of his works on show, but they are enough to show off his haunting talent. Finally there are about twenty sculptures in metal, stone and wood. One of the best is by Roberto Cabrera, which is an odd assemblage of female torsos and other anatomy, boxed in compartments.

The **Museo Nacional de Historia Natural** (same times, free) is just around the corner from the other two, and not worth visiting. Almost none of its glass boxes of flora, fauna and palaeolithic collections originate in Guatemala, or even Central America.

Parque Minerva and Kaminal Juyu

If you would like a graphic idea of Guatemala's geography, then why not head out to the Parque Minerva, where you will find a giant relief map of the country. It must be said, however, that this is no beauty spot, and the horizontal and vertical scales differ considerably. To get there, take bus no. 1, which runs along 5 Avenida in Zona 1.

Kaminal Juyu, today engulfed by one of the capital's western suburbs, was formerly an important Maya city. In fact, it was once the largest city in the country's highlands, with a sophisticated level of art and writing as early as 400 BC. In later centuries, the city is believed to have had close links with the great city state of Teotihuacan, and declined around the same period that city did, soon after AD 600. The archaeological remains of Kaminal Juyu have only been partly excavated, and the present-day visitor unfortunately gets little sense of the site's scale or importance because what you see is mainly mounds of overgrown earth. The site is open daily (8–6), and can be reached by taking bus no. 17, which runs along 4 Avenida in Zona 1.

WHERE TO STAY

The full range, from sleazy to first class, can be found in Zona 1, the best of which are listed here. There are many more, so you will always find something. If you prefer to stay away from the city centre, or require a luxury hotel, then your choice will most likely be in Zonas 9 and 10. The telephone and fax code for Guatemala is 502; for the capital it is 2.

In Zona 1

EXPENSIVE

Please note that the top range hotels usually add tax to your bill. **Pan American**, 9 Calle 5–63, tel 26807–9, fax 26402, is the best hotel in the city centre. Run by friendly staff, the decor is traditional Guatemalan, the standard of the rooms and restaurant very good. **Ritz**, 6 Avenida A 10–13, tel 81871–5, fax 24659, is a modern hotel of international standard, conveniently located, but nothing special. **Posada Belén**, 13 Calle A 10–30, tel 29226, 513478, is overpriced, but nevertheless the most beautiful and secure guest house in this price range. (Look for the street number as there is no sign.) **Colonial**, 7 Avenida 14–19, tel 26722, 22955, has a guard at the entrance, and clean rooms ranged around a pleasant courtyard. **Hogar del Turista**, 11 Calle 10–43, tel 25522, is quiet, clean and secure, though it offers less than the Colonial for the same price. No breakfast or other meals.

MODERATE

Hotel Excel, 9 Avenida 15–12, tel 532709, is a clean, modern place with secure parking, and all rooms have private bathrooms and TV.

INEXPENSIVE

Hotel San Francisco, 6 Avenida 12–62, tel 25125–28, is central and good, but noisy because of its location. Best of the cheapies is **Chalet Suizo**, 14 Calle 6–82, tel 513786. Spotless and safe, this place is always oversubscribed. **Hernani**, 15 Calle 6–56, tel 22839, is well-kept and close to Parque Concordia. **Fénix**, 7 Avenida 15–81, tel 516625, is clean and very reasonably priced. **Pensión Mesa**, 10 Calle 10–17, tel 23177, lives on the old rumour that Che Guevara stayed here once. Basic but relaxed and friendly, with a sunny courtyard. **Centroamericana**, 9 Avenida 16–38, tel 26917, is close to the Zona 1 bus station. Dingy rooms and sagging beds around a light, covered patio. It is safe and convenient, though the surrounding area is the red-light quarter.

In Zona 4

EXPENSIVE

Hotel Plaza, Vía 7, 6–16, tel 363173, 316337, fax 22705, is a medium-range hotel, with secure parking and restaurant; clean but close to noisy roads. **Sheraton**, Vía 5, 4–68, tel 341212, fax 347245, is conveniently located, but surrounded by noisy roads.

In Zonas 9 and 10

LUXURY

This region of the city is much quieter, less polluted and also safer. **Camino Real**, 14 Calle and Avenida Reforma, tel 334633, fax 374313, is the capital's most exclusive hotel, matching top international standards. Singles from $110, doubles from $140, plus tax. **Hotel El Dorado**, 7 Avenida 15–45, tel 317777, fax 321877, rivals the Camino Real in every way, and charges the same prices. **Cortijo Reforma**, Avenida Reforma, 2–18, tel 366712, fax 366876, is near the border with Zona 4, better quality and location than the nearby Sheraton, and cheaper. **Fiesta**, 1 Avenida 13–22, tel 322572, fax 682366, is near the *zona viva* and is a top hotel. Singles from $80, doubles from $90, plus tax.

EXPENSIVE

La Casa Grande, Avenida Reforma 7–67, tel and fax 310907, is not as grand as it appears. A beautiful villa set back from the road, this is a small hotel with personal service and a good restaurant.

EATING OUT

As mentioned in the introduction, Guatemala is no place for great food. Having said that, it is possible to find perfectly good international cooking. Vegetarians are not generally catered for, and will most likely find themselves restricted to eggs and beans, or pasta. The cheapest restaurants and *comedores* are in Zona 1, with literally hundreds to choose from. Fast food joints are everywhere; hamburgers and hotdogs are always to be found. **McDonald's** (10 Calle 5–56, Zona 1; 7 Avenida and Vía 3, zone 4; and elsewhere) and **Pizza Hut** (6 Avenida and 12 Calle, Zona 1) are represented here, as well as many local chains, such as **Pollo Campero**.

In Zona 1
The best restaurant for trying Guatemalan cuisine is **Los Antojitos**, 15 Calle 6–28 (closed Sunday), which does delicious steaks and plenty of traditional dishes, at reasonable prices. Try also **Arrin Cuan**, 5a Avenida 3–66, and **Ranchón Antigueño**, 13 Calle 3–50, for typical meals.

A good Italian restaurant in the centre is the **Picadilly**, 6 Avenida and 11 Calle. Three more worth trying are **Bologna**, 10 Calle 6–20; **Giovanni Canessa**, 12 Calle 6–23; and **A Guy from Italy**, 12 Calle 6–33, and also 5 Avenida 5–70. A popular Mexican restaurant is the **El Gran Pavo**, 13 Calle 4–41. Two Spanish restaurants to try are **Altuna**, 5 Avenida 12–31, and **Isaisas**, 9 Calle 3–59. Chinese food is widely available in Zona 1, usually good and cheap. **Fu Lu Sho**, 6 Avenida 12–09, is recommended. For North-American-style food, try **Danny's Pancakes**, 6 Avenida 9–45, or the **Europa** bar and restaurant, 11 Calle 5–16, which is a reasonably popular gringo bar.

The best place for breakfast is **Delicadezas Hamburgo**, 15 Calle 5–28, which faces onto the Parque Concordia, popular with gringos and locals alike. Others recommended for breakfast or afternoon breaks are: **American Doughnuts**, 5 Avenida 11–47; **Pastelería Austria**, 12 Calle 6–58; **Pastelería Jensen**, 14 Calle 0–53; **Pastelería Bohemia**, 11 Calle 8–48; **Pastelería Lins**, 11 Calle 6–12; and **Pastelería Los Tilos**, 11 Calle 6–54.

In Zonas 9 and 10
Some of the best restaurants in Guatemala City are steakhouses, and a well-priced one is **El Rodeo**, 7 Avenida 14–84, Zona 9. If you want something special, try **Hacienda de los Sanchez**, 12 Calle 2–25, Zona 10. There are plenty of others, such as: **Gauchos**, 13 Calle 1–20, Zona 10; **Nim-Guaa**, Avenida Reforma 8–01, Zona 10, and **Tambasco 2**, 7a Avenida 9–15, Zona 9.

For typical Guatemalan dishes, there is **El Parador**, Avenida Reforma 6–70, Zona 9. Two very good Italians are **Ciao Italia**, 15 Calle 3–48, and **La Trattoria**, 13 Calle 1–55. Fancy French food at fancy prices can be had at **Estro Armónico**, 15 Calle 1–11, Zona 10, and **La Boheme**, 3a Avenida 10–41, Zona 10. Vaguely French and easily affordable is **La Crepe**, 14 Calle 7–49, Zona 9, which does a huge variety of crêpes, both sweet and savoury. Fish and seafood specialities are served at two recommended restaurants: **La Mariscada**, 6a Avenida 9–64, Zona 9; and **Marina del Rey**, 16 Calle 0–61, Zona 10. If you do not want to travel to Nicaragua, but would still like to taste its national dishes, why not visit **Caprichos**, 1a Avenida 13–74, Zona 10. You have a wide choice of Chinese restaurants in this part of town. Some of the favourites are: **China Queen**, 6a Avenida 14–04, Zona 9; **Palacio de Oro**, 8a Calle 6–01, Zona 9; **Palacio Royal**, 7a Avenida 11–00, Zona 9; and **Real Capitol**, 6a Avenida 9–11, Zona 9. Last, but not least, there is **Arbol de la Vida**, Avenida Reforma 12–01, Zona 10, which is your only choice for a vegetarian restaurant.

Cafés and cake shops are in good supply, and if you cannot find one, you can always try the luxury hotels. A personal favourite for chocolate cookies is **Q Kiss**, Avenida Reforma 3–80, Zona 9. Just as delicious are the sweets at **Pastelería Zurich**, inside the shopping centre at 4 Avenida 12–09, Zona 10. Other good places to try are: **Café Milot**, Avenida Reforma 13–70, Zona 9; **Pastelería Los Alpes**, 10 Calle 1–09, Zona 10; and **Pastelería Jensen**, 7 Avenida 12–13, Zona 9.

ENTERTAINMENT AND NIGHTLIFE
Guatemala City at night can be a dangerous place, especially in Zona 1, and it is not a good idea to walk the streets alone whether you are male or female. Zonas 9 and 10 are quieter, but even there it would be best to take a taxi to your destination, unless it is just around the corner from your hotel. Having said this, the capital is strangely quiet very early on. Public transport becomes rare after 8pm, and there is a distinct lack of obvious nightlife other than the girlie bars around the Zona 1 bus station.

Your choices for nightclubs are almost entirely restricted to the ones attached to the exclusive hotels of Zonas 9 and 10, which are predictably middle-aged in atmosphere, and have nothing Guatemalan about them. The best music bar is **El Establo**, Avenida Reforma 11–83, Zona 10. Favourite discos in town are **Kahlua**, 1 Avenida 13–29, Zona 10; **Le Pont**, 13 Calle 0–48, Zona 10; **Dash Disco**, 12 Calle 1–25, Zona 10; **Basco's Disco**, 16 Calle 0-55, Zona 10; and the city's newest hotspot is **Sherlock's Home**, Avenida Las Américas 2–14, Zona 13.

There are numerous cinemas throughout the city, including four on 6 Avenida in the centre. Films are usually in English with Spanish subtitles.

SHOPPING
The **Central Market** behind the cathedral has an entire floor of native textiles and crafts. **La Placita** by Guadalupe Church at 5 Avenida and 18 Calle is recommended. **4 Ahau**, 11 Calle 4–53, Zona 1, is good for textiles and crafts, and **Pasaje Rubio**, 9 Calle, near 6 Avenida, Zona 1 has antique silver trinkets and coins.

USEFUL INFORMATION
Emergencies
Police: large building on 6 Avenida and 14 Calle, Zona 1; emergency tel 120.
Medical: see your embassy for a list of English-speaking doctors and best hospitals.

Archaeological Tour Agencies
Turismo Kim'Arrin, Edificio Maya, Office 103, Vía 5 4–50, Zona 4.
Panamundo, Guatemala Travel Service, 3 Avenida 16–52, Zona 10.
Clark Tours, 7 Avenida 6–53, Zona 4; also has representatives in the Camino Real and Sheraton Hotels.

Further addresses (including tour agencies) can be found in the *Tourist Directory*, supplied free by INGUAT.

Money Matters
Apart from the banks and exchange offices, there is a daily exchange service at the airport (weekdays 7.30–6.30; weekends 8–11 and 3–6). The black market exchange is on the

streets around the central post office, in Zona 1. Best to use cash only, and get them to hand over the money before you give them yours. Remember that the exchange rate here is always negotiable and should at least match the bank's. Another place to change dollars is at the reception of large hotels.

The **American Express** office is at Banco del Café, Avenida Reforma 9–00, Zona 9, tel 311311 or 347463.

Books
English literature can be bought at Arnel, in the Edificio El Centro, 9 Calle and 8 Avenida, Zona 1. International newspapers and magazines (American usually) are best found at the exclusive hotels.

Post Office
The main post office is on 7 Avenida and 12 Calle, Zona 1.

Telecommunications
International telegrams are sent from the GUATEL office at 8 Avenida and 12 Calle, Zona 1, or any other GUATEL office.

Day Trips from Guatemala City

Guatemala City is not a place you will want to spend much time in, and it is highly unlikely that you will use it as a base. However, **Lake Amatitlán** is just half an hour away, by bus or car, and certainly deserves a visit—not least for the surrounding views of the Pacaya and Agua volcanoes, or a relaxed boat trip across the waters. If you turn up during a weekend, you also have the opportunity to take the **bubble-lift** up to the **Parque de las Naciones Unidas** (if it's working), where you definitely get the best views of all.

The lake is just west of the main highway connecting the capital with the Pacific lowlands, and there are frequent daily buses that leave either from the Zona 4 bus terminal, or you can flag down the appropriate bus on the corner of 20 Calle and 3 Avenida, in Zona 1. You could also go on an organized tour to the lake, and the *Tourist Directory*, supplied by INGUAT, lists recommended agencies.

On the southern shores of Lake Amatitlán rises the small but active cone of Pacaya, which still erupts regularly, occasionally hitting careless tourists over the head with bits of flying debris. At night, the orange haze from its bubbling mouth is particularly mesmerizing, most dramatically visible if you camp out near the summit. Organized trips are the easiest and safest way to explore Pacaya, and there are plenty of agencies which do both day trips and overnight tours (camping equipment can be hired). The Agua volcano is best climbed while based in Antigua, an hour's journey into the highlands from Guatemala City.

Mixco Viejo

A Maya fortress town, **Mixco Viejo** lies 58 km north of Guatemala City, and was once the capital of the Pokomam nation. Of the highland sites, it is one of the best preserved, and is located on a high ledge, surrounded by steep ravines on all sides, making it one of the most impregnable Maya capitals. In fact, Alvarado was only able to conquer this city with the help of an Indian traitor. Squat temple pyramids of stone make for excellent vantage points, and it is the views across the highland countryside that really impress today.

To reach the site is still difficult, and the only way on public transport is to take the Pachalum bus from the Zona 4 bus terminal, leaving around 10 am daily. Ask the driver to drop you at the entrance of the site, where you will have to camp for the night, since the return bus passes the entrance at around 3 am in the morning. A much better option is to hire a car or arrange for a travel agent to take you on a day trip.

THE WESTERN HIGHLANDS

The Western Highlands are the most populated region of Guatemala, home to the Maya Indians, as well as a wonderful landscape of mountains punctuated by volcanic peaks and expansive lakes. Towns and villages cluster among rolling fields of corn and vegetables, bursting into life on market days and during their annual festivals. The tiny cities of Antigua and Quezaltenango make ideal bases from which to explore the area and get to know the indigenous culture. Geographically, the Highlands form a ridge along Western Guatemala from Mexico to El Salvador, with the Pacific Lowlands to the southwest, and the Eastern Highlands and dry valleys heading towards the Caribbean coastal plain. The road network reaches almost everywhere you will want to visit, and whatever transport you choose to use, journey times will never be very long.

The majority of people in the Western Highlands are descendants of the Maya tribes that have always lived here: the Quiché, Mam, and Pocomam. These three indigenous groups are made up of many small related tribes, such as the Cakchiqueles and Tzutujiles of the Quiché group; the Ixil and Aguacateca of the Mam group; and the Kekchi and Pocomam, of the Pocomam group. There are many other tribes too, such as the Jacalteca, Chuj and Kanjobal. But they are much less in evidence, and you will probably not meet any of their members.

Each tribe has its own language and dialects, which can vary even from one village to the next. However, the most common Indian languages to be heard in the markets are those of the Cakchiquel, Tzutujil, Kekchi, Ixil and Quiché. Undoubtedly, the untrained ear will be unable to distiguish one Indian language from another, let alone one tribe from another. What you will learn to distinguish, as you travel the Highlands, is which costume comes from where, fitting together the pieces of a rich puzzle that maps out Indian culture in this part of the country.

Virtually all Indians can speak some Spanish in Guatemala, so they can communicate not only with you, but also with their 'foreign' neighbours. Bear in mind, however, that in a few cases it may be just as difficult for the Indian from a remote village to speak Spanish, as it may be for you. (Although the English word is not loaded, the Spanish equivalent, *indio*, is considered a term of abuse by most Indians in Latin America, who prefer the word *indígena*.)

Antigua

Antigua (altitude 1530 m) nestles in a fecund valley close to the volcanoes Agua, Fuego and Acatenango, with stunning views beyond the tiled roofs. At street level too, the views are picturesque, with cobbled streets lined by chunky colonial houses, ornate wooden window grilles and inviting entrances to green-clad courtyards. Although the town is laid out on the standard colonial grid, finding your way around can be a bit of a torment at times, since there are very few street signs. But Antigua is small enough to comfortably walk from one end to the other in twenty minutes, so wandering about is no hardship. The majority of 'sights' are ruined churches, of which there is an abundance. But even if you are not interested in ruins, the very special atmosphere of Antigua will undoubtedly make it one of your favourite places. After the frenzy of Guatemala City's traffic, Antigua will seem a real haven: the air is clean, the town peaceful, and full of pleasant places to stay, eat and drink.

Inevitably, Antigua is a powerful magnet for gringos, not least because of the twenty or so language schools here. If you do want to learn Spanish, or refresh your existing knowledge, you are spoilt for choice; and in some ways, the preponderance of gringos is very comforting. Antigua is an excellent place to recover from rigorous travel or ease yourself gently into the Guatemalan environment. But after a while, the place can seem a little artificial, so overtaken by gringo needs and tastes that one is undeniably remote from Guatemalan culture and life.

History

The conquistador Pedro de Alvarado founded Guatemala's first capital, Santiago de los Caballeros, in 1524, near the former Cakchiquel capital of Iximché east of Lake Atitlán. In 1527, his brother Jorge de Alvarado decided to move the capital in his absence, mainly due to the difficulties he was having keeping the Cakchiqueles servile. Thus the first permanent colonial capital was founded in the valley of Almolonga, close to the Agua and Fuego volcanoes. The city, now called Ciudad Vieja, took the name of its predecessor, and flourished for almost twenty years before disaster struck.

The pathologically avaricious Alvarado, bent on conquering new lands in Indonesia, began having a new fleet of ships built in 1538. By the time the ships and crew were ready, Alvarado changed his plans. In June 1541 he joined in a battle in Mexico, where he was squashed by a falling horse. His grieving wife, Doña Beatriz, quickly cheered herself up by proclaiming herself 'Governess of the Americas'. She was only 22, and her reign was to last just one day. On 10 September 1541, two earthquakes, accompanied by torrential rains, triggered off a massive landslide which smothered the capital and killed Doña Beatriz along with many of her subjects. *La sin ventura* (the unlucky one)—as she had called herself—was the first and last female ruler of the colonial Americas.

This was the end of the administrative body's second capital. Two years later, in 1543, Antigua was finally inaugurated when the city council held its first meeting in the uncompleted Palace of the Captains General. Antigua was to become one of the most glamorous and sophisticated cities of Spanish America—a place where both clergy and nobility vied for positions, and the most ostentatious convents, churches and palaces

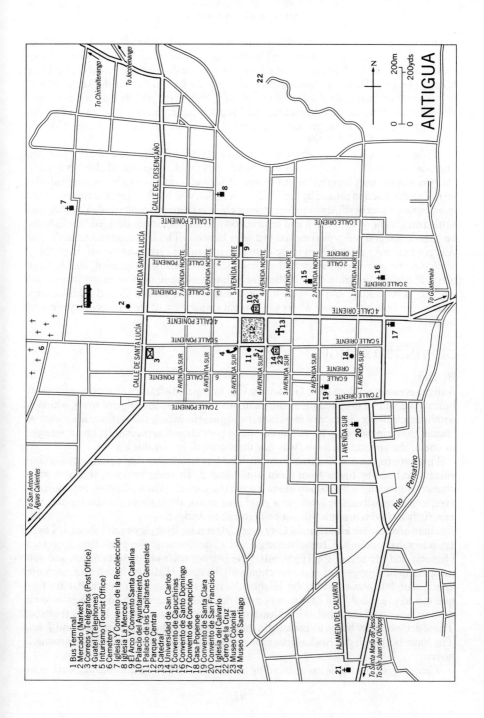

ANTIGUA

1 Bus Terminal
2 Mercado (Market)
3 Correos y Telégrafos (Post Office)
4 Guatel (Telephones)
5 Inturismo (Tourist Office)
6 Cemetery
7 Iglesia Y Convento de la Recolección
8 Iglesia La Merced
9 El Arco Y Convento Santa Catalina
10 Palacio del Ayuntamiento
11 Palacio de los Capitanes Generales
12 Parque Central
13 Catedral
14 Universidad de San Carlos
15 Convento de Capuchinas
16 Convento de Santo Domingo
17 Convento de Concepción
18 Casa Popenoe
19 Convento de Santa Clara
20 Convento de San Francisco
21 Iglesia del Calvario
22 Cerro de la Cruz
23 Museo Colonial
24 Museo de Santiago

were built; where schools, hospitals, and government buildings provided excellent services for the colonial residents, and life was eased with cheap Indian labour. Violent earthquakes continued throughout the 17th century, but this only increased the building boom. The great Baroque churches and palaces were built with ever thicker walls and better reinforcements. By the end of the century, there were no less than ten convents, three parish churches, five hermitages and four churches, a university, as well as the cathedral, which was the grandest in Central America. All this for a city that was designed for 5000 inhabitants.

By the mid-18th century, there were nearer 50,000 inhabitants, and after just two centuries of existence, Antigua was experiencing its Golden Age: its inhabitants lived in the greatest comfort imaginable at the time. But it all came to an abrupt end with the terrifying destruction caused by the 1773 earthquake, which left Antigua in rubble, many dead buried underneath, and epidemics soon claiming those who survived. The dust had settled on a scene of such death and destruction that the authorities decided the city must be abandoned and the capital moved to a safer location. The subsequent dismantling of Antigua may have caused even more destruction than the earthquake itself. Everything that could be transported away for building the new capital was removed, and Antigua was left defiled and gutted. It is therefore almost miraculous how much of colonial Antigua is left today, and in spite of continued seismic batterings and 20th-century architectural sins, it is a place where the opulent atmosphere of the 18th century remains intact.

GETTING TO ANTIGUA

By Bus

Antigua is easily reached from Guatemala City by bus, which takes about one and a half hours. You will be dropped off at the main bus terminal on the edge of town, which is within easy walking distance of most hotels and guest houses. Usually, there are plenty of 'guides' hovering about, who will direct you to your chosen accommodation, or straight to one of the language schools, who pay them a small fee for this service.

There are frequent daily buses from the local bus terminal to the capital, surrounding villages and nearby towns from dawn until about 3. By late afternoon, you have little chance of catching a bus to anywhere except the capital. When planning any journey, even to nearby villages, it is always a good idea to ask about times the day before, and especially to find out when the last bus returns to Antigua.

There are buses to **Guatemala City** every 20 minutes from dawn until about 5. There are buses every hour to **Chimaltenango** and all destinations along the Pan-American Highway and the rest of the Highlands. The journey takes about 40 minutes, and you must ask to be dropped off at the junction with the main Highway, in order to catch the appropriate bus onwards into the Highlands. Buses coming from the capital are frequent, and you should not have to wait more than half an hour for a connection to such destinations as Panajachel, Chichicastenango, Quezaltenango or Huehuetenango. There are two daily buses to **Esquintla** on the Pacific Highway, leaving at 6 and 7 am. The route is a rough dirt road, skirting the Agua volcano, and the journey takes around 2 hours.

There are regular buses to surrounding villages such as San Andrés Itzapa, San Lucas

Sacatepéquez, Alotenango (for Ciudad Vieja), Duenas (nearest village to starting point for climbing Acatenango and Fuego), Jocotenango, Santa Lucía Milpas Altas, San Antonio Aguas Calientes, Sumpango, San Juan del Obispo, Pastores, Santa María de Jesús (for climbing Agua), San Pedro las Huertas, and San Luis de las Carretas.

Buses Inter-Hotel and Tourism (B.I.T.) run a private shuttle service operating daily between Antigua and the airport in Guatemala City. On Tuesdays, Thursdays and Sundays there is also a shuttle between Antigua and Panajachel. For prices and timetables, see notice boards at the tourist office, Casa Andinista, and at many hotel reception desks and restaurant notice boards.

GETTING AROUND ANTIGUA

Antigua is too small to have its own municipal transport, and most people get around on foot. Bicycles, motorbikes and cars can be hired for excursions, as can horses. (See Useful Information below.) There is a taxi stand by the bus terminal and on the main square, in front of the cathedral.

TOURIST INFORMATION

The local **INGUAT** office is located in the former Palace of the Captains General, across the street from the cathedral. Its opening hours are daily, 8–noon and 2–6. The office not only provides brochures and general help but can also advise on which language schools are currently the best value.

An excellent source of information on anything from accommodation to tours and travellers' messages is the notice board in the courtyard of **Doña Luisa's**, 4 Calle Oriente 12.

WHAT TO SEE

The Plaza Mayor

As with all Spanish colonial towns, the heart of Antigua is its main square, from which calles and avenidas spread out in straight lines. In former times it was an open expanse where festivals and market days were held. These days you find a landscaped park, centred around a fountain. Visitors relaxing on the park benches and cathedral steps are frequently accosted by the charming but relentless Indian hawkers. *Compra algo* (buy something) will soon become a familiar refrain, or even *toma una foto* (take a picture). But be warned, they expect to be paid—an unfortunate practice that should not be encouraged.

Around the square are ranged the grandiose buildings of the cathedral on the east side, the City Hall (Ayuntamiento) on the north side, the Palace of the Captains General on the south side, with Agua's cone towering behind, and an arcade hiding a bank, shops and cafés along the west side. The square is quite small, and the whole effect is almost cosy.

The whitewashed façade of the **cathedral** sadly shows the scars of many tremors and quakes, and the interior is mostly ruined. Completed in 1680, what we see today is just a small reflection of what was once not only the grandest cathedral in Central America but also a magnificent Archbishop's Palace. Originally there were twelve naves, and the present church is made up of just two chapels of the original cathedral, while the palace is no more than fallen masonry and broken columns, some of which still retain their intricate stucco. Wandering among the debris, you might even find the odd human bone, excavated from the many crypts underfoot, where Alvarado and his wife lie buried, as well as the famous chronicler of the conquest, Díaz del Castillo. Entrance (small fee) to the ruined palace is via the gate on 5 Calle Oriente.

The **Palace of the Captains General** stands at right angles to the cathedral. It is now home to the local police headquarters, municipal offices, and the tourist office. The covered arches provide welcome shade as you walk around to the commercial west side of the square, where street vendors and shoeshine boys sit in wait of custom.

Completing the square is the elevated walkway that fronts the **Ayuntamiento**, again shaded by covered arches, which date from the 18th century. The two-storeyed Tuscan columns neatly mirror those of the Palace opposite. In fact, they are the only part of the square's buildings that survived the earthquake of 1773 relatively intact. Originally, this building not only housed the City Hall, but also offices of the police, and the 'Jail for the Poor', which had a chapel attached where death row prisoners were given their last rites before being publicly hanged on the square.

Today the building houses two museums: in the former prison is the **Museo de Santiago** (daily, 9–4, small fee); and part of the former City Hall now houses the **Museo del Libro Antiguo** (same times, no fee), with a replica of Central America's first printing press and a selection of early religious and scientific books. The Museo de Santiago is ranged around the old prison courtyard which has impressive four-foot-thick walls and heavy iron-grilled doors. There is a small collection of colonial uniforms, and the walls are hung with various portraits, rusty spikes and war regalia, including Alvarado's sword.

East of the Plaza

Heading past the right-hand side of the cathedral, along 5 Calle Oriente, the first building across the street is one of Antigua's finest examples of colonial Baroque, best viewed from the elevated entrance to the Archbishop's Palace opposite. The most ornate stucco is around the entrance of what was once the University of San Carlos de Borromeo. Today it houses the **Museo de Arte Colonial** (Mon–Fri, 9–4; Sat and Sun, 9–noon and 2–4, free), which you should see just for the beautiful inner courtyard. The nine rooms inside contain a range of 17th- and 18th-century colonial art and statuary, as well as an example of the dyed sawdust carpets Antigua is decked out with during Easter Week.

Turning right, down 3 Avenida Sur, you soon come to Antigua's most picturesque square, where two columns of palm trees lead the way to a chunky fountain and arcaded wash basins, where Indian women come to do their laundry. As you reach the square, the San Pedro church immediately in front of you gleams in freshly restored splendour. Next door is the **San Pedro Hospital**. Founded for members of the clergy in 1663, it has long since been open to the general public, not least because of the recurrent need to tend earthquake casualties, most recently in 1976. At the other end of the square, behind the washing arcade, is the church of **Santa Clara** and the ruins of the attached convent. Founded in 1699 by nuns from Puebla, Mexico, the convent was built up to its present proportions after the 1717 earthquake, only to be destroyed in 1773. What remains are the cloisters ranged around a spacious plaza and elegant fountain, which is still beautiful.

Past Santa Clara, heading east on 7 Calle Oriente, you come to the high walls hiding the **San Francisco Church**, by far the most impressive of the town's churches—no plain wooden altars here, but richly gold-leafed and intricately carved ones. Founded by the Franciscans in the late 16th century, the attached monastery was once an important centre of religious teaching, and also included a printing press, hospital, and music and art rooms.

Along the left aisle, plaque upon plaque testifies, in good Catholic manner, to the intervention of Antigua's favourite saint, **Pedro de Betancourt**: 'Thank you for releasing me from a vicious woman'. His tomb is newly restored, placed on shiny terracotta-coloured marble. St Pedro, originally from the Canaries, lived in Antigua during the mid 17th century, devoting himself to the poor and sick with such zeal that he is said to have miraculously cured septic wounds by licking them clean with his tongue. Not one to make life easy, he flagellated himself daily, and during Easter Week, he would crawl past the twelve altars of the Stations of the Cross (see below) on his knees. He died in 1667. A small museum (small fee) adjoins the church, dedicated to St Pedro, where you can see a few old books and some of the man's garments, including his ancient underpants.

Continuing on 7 Calle Oriente and turning left on Calle del Hermano Pedro, you come to the ruins of the **Concepción Convent**, which was the first and grandest nunnery in Antigua. Sadly, the ruins offer little idea of its former splendour, but there are some attractive colonial tiles near its main entrance. Founded in 1578 by a Mexican abbess, it attracted large numbers of nuns from the wealthiest families, and the convent expanded rapidly, thus becoming the richest and largest of its kind. Over a thousand women lived here at one time, including the numerous slaves that tended the religious ladies' every need. The most notorious inmate was Doña Juana de Maldonado, who brought the convent into disrepute by regularly entertaining a bishop in her quarters. Thomas Gage, writing in the early 17th century, commented that 'here is not only idolatry, but fornication and uncleanness as public as in any place of the Indies.' However, this statement has to be set against the fact that Gage was an English lapsed Catholic turned fanatic Protestant. Moreover, he wasn't a very savoury character himself: in 1640s England it was illegal to preach a Catholic mass, and Gage testified so effectively against former Catholic friends that three were hung, drawn and quartered.

Finally, a short walk away, at the corner of 1 Avenida Sur and 5 Calle Oriente, the Casa Popenoe (Mon–Fri, 2–4) offers an immaculate colonial house, complete with original furnishings, domestic tools and a lovely garden.

North of the Plaza

5 Avenida Norte, easily recognizable by the clock-tower arch that spans the street, takes you north of the Plaza, past a number of Antigua's favourite cafés and restaurants. The arch, a few blocks away from the main square, is part of the **Santa Catalina Convent**, now a hotel and restaurant. It was founded in 1609 by four nuns from the crowded Concepción convent, and the arch was built in 1693, so that nuns could pass unseen to the connected property across the street, acquired to house the ever-increasing numbers of nuns and novices. Now a private residence, it is perhaps one of the most famous landmarks of Antigua, framing the cobbled street and views beyond.

At the end of 5 Avenida Norte is the **Church of La Merced**. It has the most ornate stucco of all the churches in Antigua, with twirls of vines, leaves and flower patterns delicately sculpted onto its columns and walls, their creamy colour perfectly highlighted against an ochre backround. On the small square in front of the church, a few Indian women normally sell their textiles under the shade of pine and palm trees. The beautiful fountain nearby dates from the late 17th century, and originally stood in the cloister of San Francisco.

Heading one block east, along 1 Calle Poniente, you reach the remains of **Santa Teresa Convent**, originally home to Carmelite nuns from Peru, but now a gloomy prison for local criminals. Passing swiftly by, the street opens up into a tree-lined avenue, a peaceful corner of Antigua, where some of the town's most desirable residences hide behind thick wooden doors. To the right, down one block of 2 Avenida Norte, a deceptively nondescript entrance leads into **Las Capuchinas**. The spacious ruins, in rather better repair than most, now house the National Council for the Protection of Antigua, which also organizes regular exhibitions of local artists' paintings and sculptures.

The convent was founded in the early 18th century, with only a short life, brought to ruin by the 1773 earthquake. Today the convent is the subject of a tantalizing mystery. What was the circular structure just north of the cloister for? Centered around a supporting tower, a second-floor patio is ringed by eighteen nuns' cells, while underneat, there is a large open room which is bare on the inside, but whose wall contains unexplained niches all around the outside, some containing stone rings on their sides. Was this building for torture, a bath house or a store room? The experts continue to argue.

After a while, ruin-fatigue may set in, and a refreshing antidote is a stroll up to the **Cerro de la Cruz**. This is a hill-top cross, perched directly north of town, a short half-hour walk away, and with a great view of all Antigua and the surrounding countryside. To get there, follow 4 or 3 Avenida Norte to its northern conclusion, turn right, and then left, up the hill and beyond the last houses. It is probably a good idea to ask directions along the way, but you should come to some paved steps and a path winding through some pine trees to your left, which eventually comes out onto an open clearing overlooking Antigua. Although so close to town, this path is regularly dogged by thieves and muggers. It is therefore advisable not to go alone, and not in the late afternoon or after dark.

West of the Plaza

Leaving the Plaza along 4 Calle Poniente, three blocks ahead leads you to Antigua's lively bus terminal and permanent market, located beyond the tree-lined road of Alameda Santa Lucía. '*Guate! Guate!*' shout the bus conductors, as you approach, and black clouds blast from revving engines. Market stalls spill out from the purpose-built wooden shacks: cigarettes, fruit and vegetables, hardware, Indian *artesanía*—almost anything can be bought here. It is one of the country's best markets for buying Indian craftwork at reasonable prices, so it is worth taking the time to shop around here.

One block south of the bus terminal, the extension of 5 Calle Poniente crosses the Alameda Santa Lucía, and ends at the entrance to Antigua's **cemetery**, which is a good place for a quiet walk among gaudy shrines to the dead, complete with plastic flowers and glittering streamers. You will notice a lot of blue and green paint here, as in every other cemetery. These are the traditional colours of mourning for the Indians. For a slightly less morbid pastime, the **Casa Kojom** (Mon–Fri, 9–5, US$1) is not far away, and an excellent museum dedicated to Guatemala's indigenous musical heritage. It is reached by turning right, into Calle de los Recoletos, just before the cemetery. The museum is a small bungalow, set back from the dirt road, in a well-kept garden. It displays many of the Maya Indians' musical instruments, and shows how these were either given up or adapted to colonial tastes after the Spanish arrived. Some instruments, such as the marimba, are still in common use today. The museum has an audiovisual show, demonstrating music from many of the instruments displayed. There are also useful books on traditional Maya festivals and religious ritual.

Continuing past the museum on the dirt road, you soon reach yet another of Antigua's abundant ruins. This one is known as **La Recolección**, after the Recolect friars who came to found a mission here in the late 16th century. Until the 1976 earthquake, its ruins and one remaining arch were considered some of the most evocative by romantics. Now the crumbling walls and weathered boulders tend to get used as a convenient toilet facility or shelter for the destitute.

South of the Plaza

The southern quarter of Antigua has the least to offer in the way of monuments and ruins, and so gets fewer visitors, which is a relief after the crowds around the main square. As you walk its peaceful streets you will see the wonderfully photogenic ruined church of **San José el Viejo**, framed in greenery by nearby trees. It is located at the junction of 5 Avenida Sur and 8 Calle Oriente.

Following 8 Calle Oriente east, past four blocks, will bring you out on the Alameda del Calvario, that runs directly south from the gates of San Francisco. Probably one of Antigua's most unattractive streets, with regular traffic throwing up swirls of dust, it becomes a focal point during the famous Easter Week processions, when ceremonial floats are carried past the twelve altars built along the road representing the Stations of the Cross, and ending up at the church of **El Calvario**, which is still in use today. By the entrance you will see a gnarled old tree, planted by Pedro de Betancourt on 19 March 1657—another place where the Indians come to pay their respects to him. The altars are neglected, and there is really little reason to come out this far, apart from the beautiful stone fountain, which is set into the road in front of El Calvario. It too is neglected, but some of the delicate carving remains.

One of the best detailed introductions to Antigua's historical buildings and monuments is *Antigua Guatemala*, by Elizabeth Bell and Trevor Long, originally written in 1978, and revised in 1990.

SEMANA SANTA IN ANTIGUA
Easter Week in Antigua is one of the most dramatic and colourful festivals in Latin America, and the largest in Central America. Thousands of Guatemalans and foreigners gather to fill the cobbled streets and cram the hotels. Almost all of Antigua's inhabitants

are involved in some aspect of the huge processions, biblical re-enactments and religious services that take place throughout the week, and many more come from far and wide to participate as musicians and singers at the numerous concerts and parties. It's a time of wild celebration and joy—deeply religious fervour mixes easily with drunkenness and dancing. Firecrackers blast in the streets day and night, and the squares are decorated with beautiful flowers, and crammed with people.

The tourist office annually publishes a detailed programme of events. However, a few things are worth knowing in advance: events often happen hours later than stated; banks operate a half-day on Wednesday, and close from Thursday to the following Monday; the food market closes down after Wednesday; from Thursday to Sunday, restaurants and bars often reduce their menus to a few items, usually the most expensive ones, and prices can double; and all accommodation prices double and even triple, and booking in advance or arriving a few days early is essential.

Palm Sunday: Begins early, with 7, 8 and 9 am processions setting off from the major churches after Mass. The main procession of the day starts at 2 (approx.), from outside La Merced church. Jesus' entry into Jerusalem is re-created for the **Jesús Nazareño de la Merced** procession, and his effigy is carried on a huge float (*anda*), which weighs many thousands of pounds. The men shuffle in slow unison, gently swaying as they take turns in shouldering the impossible weight. Eventually, at around 10, the procession of many hundreds of participants wends its way around the main square and returns to La Merced. This final stage is the most dramatic, as the many faces are lit by flaming torches, purple-robed Israelites swing great copal burners, spreading thick clouds of incense and firecrackers explode all around.

Monday: See the freshly decked out altars at La Merced church.

Tuesday: Festivities, mass and worship centre around San Francisco church from 6 am to 11 pm, honouring the city's patron saint.

Wednesday: Main action centres around Escuela de Cristo church, from 6 am to 11 pm.

Thursday: This is one of Easter Week's highlights, and you certainly will not want to miss the night, during which the famous dyed sawdust, pine needle, seed, and flower carpets are delicately sprinkled onto the streets, only to be destroyed by the most dramatic procession of them all: the 3 am **Procession of the Roman Soldiers**. They run around the city's streets, announcing the *sentencia*, the death sentence for Jesus. Others gallop on horseback, and behind them come the modern-day Guatemalan military, giving the spectator an almost too realistic sense of the fearful drama. Meanwhile marimba bands play all over town. It really is worth staying up—or rising early—to see this memorable performance of religious theatre. Some restaurants and bars stay open 24 hours to help you get through the night.

Good Friday: The Procession of the Roman Soldiers comes to a bleary-eyed end around 6 am, only for yet another procession to set off from La Merced church an hour later, passing through town, and eventually returning to its starting point sometime around 3. As a mark of devotion, many of Antigua's inhabitants lay yet more perishable carpets before their front doors.

At midday, the re-enactment of the Crucifixion takes place at the Escuela de Cristo church, while at 2 pm, the Song of Pardon is sung in front of the City Hall, as part of the La Merced procession that began in the morning. After the singing, a lucky prisoner from the local jail is released. Meanwhile, there are many other ceremonies taking place all over town.

Easter Eve: The streets are quiet, but more carpets are laid out, and the procession of mourning, **la procesión de la Virgin de la Soledad** , in the evening, is one of the most moving you will see. Women dressed in black carry enormous floats of the virgin, draped in black and bedecked in long-stemmed red roses.

Easter Sunday: A 'morning after the night before' atmosphere pervades the town, as the festival comes to an end and the majority of visitors quickly depart.

WHERE TO STAY

There are almost as many hotels and guest houses as there are private homes in Antigua, so your range of choices is excellent. No place listed is more than a short walk away from the main square; they are given in order of price in each category, and all prices are inclusive of tax. Remember that Antigua is always popular, so you may have to hunt around, and that during Christmas and Easter Week it can be very hard to find anywhere at all. It is best to get there a few days early, or book in advance where possible. The telephone code for Antigua is 0320.

LUXURY

The **Ramada Hotel**, 9 Calle Poniente and Carretera Ciudad Vieja, tel 011–015, fax 287, has standard North-American hotel facilities in a predictably neutral atmosphere; pleasant garden with pool (open to non-residents for US$3); also sauna, jacuzzi and vapour room. **Panza Verde**, 5 Avenida Sur, is a colonial house with a good and expensive restaurant; there are only four rooms. **Hotel Antigua**, 5 Avenida Sur and 8 Calle Oriente, tel 331/288, fax 807, is the best large hotel in town. Housed in a colonial-type building, the hotel has a beautiful garden and swimming pool. By the time you read this the **Hotel Casa Santo Domingo**, 3 Calle Oriente, tel 102, should also have opened. Located in one of the oldest convents, this will be a very glamorous place to stay, with stunning gardens containing ruined arches and beautiful fountains. Unfortunately, at the time of writing, the restaurant cannot be recommended for anything other than salads and cocktails.

EXPENSIVE

Posada de Don Rodrigo, 5 Avenida Norte 17, tel 291/387, is without doubt one of the most beautiful colonial residences in Antigua, and all rooms and furnishings are period, often even originals. The cobbled main courtyard has two resident macaws who give a tropical flavour, and the restaurant in another courtyard is excellent, though expensive. **Hotel Santa Catalina**, 5 Avenida Norte 28, is housed in an immaculately restored convent, bright rooms and restaurant ranged around a spacious courtyard. Excellent value. Very peaceful, **Aurora**, 4 Calle Oriente 16, tel 217, is housed in a large colonial residence, spacious rooms opening onto a private courtyard.

MODERATE

Posada San Sebastián, 7 Avenida Norte 67, tel 465, is in a newly restored colonial house, a very peaceful place with a wonderful orchard attached. The same owners also run the **Posada San Sebastian**, centrally located at 3 Avenida Norte 4. Rooms are immaculate, but there is no garden. **Posada Asjemenou**, 5 Avenida Norte 31, tel 865, is the best value guest house in this range. A lovingly restored colonial house, with clean and attractive rooms around a spacious courtyard. Delicious breakfast available. **Hotel El Descanso**, 5 Avenida Norte, tel 142, is a delightful small hotel, with rooftop terrace and clean rooms. **Hotel Santa Clara**, 2 Avenida Sur, tel 342, is an immaculate little place, not far from the San Francisco church.

INEXPENSIVE

La Casa de Santa Lucía, Alameda de Santa Lucía 5, is one of the most popular in this category. Clean rooms around a cool courtyard. **Posada Landivar**, 5 Calle Poniente, has modern rooms, immaculately kept, and a rooftop terrace. **Posada de Doña Angelina**, 4 Calle Poniente 33, has rooms around a verdant courtyard. Standards vary, depending on what you wish to pay. **El Placido**, Calle del Desengaño 25, is unfortunately located on the thundering road all buses use coming from Guatemala City. However, rooms are around a lovely courtyard, and you have use of the kitchen. **El Pasaje**, Alameda Santa Lucía 3, is basic but friendly, with great views from the rooftop terrace. **Posada El Refugio**, 4 Calle Poniente 28, has no frills, but serves cheap breakfasts.

EATING OUT

Antigua has some of the best cafés and restaurants in the country, with a wide choice of local and international cuisine, many run by resident foreigners. New places are opening all the time, and the following is just a selection from many more. For example, all the top hotels and guest houses have restaurants, and are not mentioned here.

For cheap snacks and simple *comedor*-style food, try the market and nearby spots on the Alameda Santa Lucía, past the new shopping arcade, but on the same side. **Peroleto** does good snacks and lots of fruit juices. Along 4 Calle Poniente, places like **Panificadora Colombia** and **Antigua Capri** can be recommended for simple fare, as well as **San Carlos**, which is on the main square. For quick take-away snacks of filled bagels and the like, try the American-run **Deliciosa**, 4 Avenida Norte 100.

Some of the best foreign food in Antigua is Italian. **Queso y Vino**, 5 Avenida Norte (closed Tuesdays), has pasta made fresh on the premises, as well as excellent pizzas. **Asjemenou**, 5 Calle Poniente (closed Mondays), has good pizzas, as well as delicious breakfasts and the best cappuccinos and coffee in town. **Martedino**, 4 Calle Poniente, is consistently excellent value for all types of Italian food—in spite of the neon light and bathroom tiles on the wall. **El Capuchino**, 6 Avenida Norte, is expensive but good.

Delicious German food, such as *schnitzel*, can be enjoyed to the sounds of classical music at the **Oasis del Peregrino**, 7 Avenida Norte. Good, but more expensive and thin on atmosphere is **Welten**, 4 Calle Oriente. The hotels **Santa Catalina**, 5 Avenida Norte, and **Panza Verde**, 5 Avenida Sur, both have expensive but highly recommended restaurants serving German and international dishes. For something really special, international cuisine is served at **El Sereno**, 6 Calle Poniente, in the refined ambience of a colonial house. Newly opened, and competing against the latter, is the **Fonda del Pinzón**, just past the cinema on 5 Avenida Sur.

Mistral, 4 Calle Oriente, serves bland French and international meals in a pleasant covered courtyard, and also has a comfortable bar with cable TV. **Doña Luisa**, 4 Calle

Oriente, is in a restored colonial house with a beautiful courtyard, and is a long-standing favourite in Antigua. It is one of the best places for breakfast, but also serves a few meals, such as chilli con carne or soup. Added features include American cable television, a small library, *Time* and *Newsweek* on sale from the cashier, and the travellers' notice-board. A strong contender for Doña Luisa's business is **Sueños del Quetzal**, 5 Avenida Norte, which has a sunny balcony instead of a courtyard. Good but over-priced, meals are vegetarian, and snacks include fresh bagels, with a choice of fillings. An extra attraction (or deterrent!) is the American cable TV. Next door is **La Fonda de la Calle Real**, which does good meals, including Guatemalan fare, but has excruciat-ingly slow service. For excellent service and meals try **Coma y Punto**, on the corner of 6 Avenida Norte and 2 Calle Poniente, which also has a small bar and good music. On 6 Avenida Norte, near La Merced, you will find the **Tecún** restaurant, which regularly presents Maya art and culture with exhibitions and live performances of dance and music.

El Churrasco on 4a Calle Poniente has good cheap steaks. **Los Gauchitos**, on the same street, is good for the money, in spite of the fast-food atmosphere. **Las Antorchas**, on 3a Avenida Sur, is expensive and excellent. Finally, there is the Japanese restaurant **Zen**, on 3 Avenida Norte, which gets very mixed reports for its food, but is located in a pleasant colonial courtyard; it is worth trying at least once, but especially on New Year's Eve, when the best party is traditionally held here.

There are a few excellent cafés (excellent for cakes and pastries—not coffee). The best is **La Cenicienta**, 5 Avenida Norte, closely followed by **Las Américas**, on the corner of 6 Avenida and 5 Calle. Also worth trying is **Café Jardín**, on the west side of the main square. Just for cookies, see **Cookies etc**, on 3 Avenida Norte, which is the only place that serves good coffee as well.

ENTERTAINMENT AND NIGHTLIFE
With so many resident and visiting foreigners, Antigua's nightlife is rapidly expanding. Apart from restaurants that double up as drinking spots, there are eight music bars, most conveniently in the same street, and open until one in the morning, while the law remains forbidding the sale of alcohol after 1 am.

La Chimenea, on the corner of 4 Calle Poniente and 7 Avenida Norte, has comfort-able sofas and chairs and an atmosphere reminiscent of an English pub. The music is standard American pop. Heading north, up 7 Avenida Norte, **Café Latino** hosts regular live bands, including reggae from Belize. On the same side of the street, **La Boheme** is now a restaurant/bar, and only has music in the early evening. A few stumbles further, **Picasso's** is the best bar in town, and certainly has the best range of taped Western music. Virtually across the street is **Bota Tejana**, which is a no-frills bar and the only one where you can mix more with local people than foreigners. Out of favour these days, and too expensive, is **Moscas y Miel**, on 5 Calle Poniente, which also has a tiny dance-floor. Equally ignored is the **El Cabildo**, on 7 Avenida Sur, though it certainly deserves more foreign custom than it gets. The newest bar is **Macondo**, in the Santa Catalina convent on 5 Avenida Norte, catering to a middle-aged crowd who can afford the expensive drinks. Finally, the Ramada Hotel has a small disco.

The cinema is on 5 Avenida Sur, near the main square and usually shows English-language films with subtitles. **Cinemala**, at 3 Avenida Norte 9, shows three videos a day on a large TV screen, though often the tape quality is appalling and Q5 seems too much for what you get. The programme is widely advertised around Antigua. **Cinecafé Oscar**, on the same street, but behind the cathedral, offers a similar service for the same price. Its programmes are also widely advertised. A third option is **Cine Elektra**, 7 Avenida Sur, next to Govinda's. New places open all the time.

SHOPPING
Antigua's market, near the bus terminal, is one of the best for Indian handicrafts. People come from all over the country to sell here, especially at weekends, when most of the action transfers to the corner of 4 Calle and 6 Avenida. Prices at weekends will be slightly higher, but a practised haggler can still get a good bargain.

USEFUL INFORMATION

Travel Agents:
Viajes Tivoli, above Un Poco de Todo, is the best agent in town, and can book any type of international flight for you, as well as book tours (including to Tikal); and you will find very friendly service at **Centro de Viajes**, on 5 Avenida Norte.

Emergencies
The tourist office can help with recommending English-speaking medics, or anyone local will be able to direct you to the private hospital.

Money Matters
Banco de Guatemala and Banco del Agro on the main square are the best places to change money during the week. The Banco del Agro branch on Alameda Santa Lucía is open Mon–Sat, until 6 pm. For exchange outside banking hours, try the door to the right of Roly Hairdressers, 4 Avenida Sur. The address is well known and the rates for cash or cheques are good. Lloyds Bank International have an office on the main square at 4 Calle Oriente.

Books
A wide selection of books on many Guatemalan subjects, both in English and Spanish, is available at **Casa Andinista**, 4 Calle Oriente; another good place is the **Librería Pensativo**, on 5 Avenida Norte, though most of their books are in Spanish; last choice because of bad prices and abrasive staff is **Un Poco de Todo** in the shopping arcade on the main square.

    CIRMA: The Centro de Investigaciones Regionales de Mesoamerica, 5 Calle 5, (Mon–Fri, 8–6, Sat 9–1) is an excellent research library open to the public, where you can find all types of publications in both English and Spanish.

Post Office
This is located on the Alameda Santa Lucía, virtually opposite the bus terminal.

Telecommunications
The GUATEL telephone office is on 5 Avenida Sur, just off the main square. There are many places offering a **fax service** but the cheapest is the J.C. Librería, 6 Calle Poniente 21.

Car and Bike Rental
Avis have an office at 5 Avenida Norte 22, tel (0320) 291387. Mountain **bikes** as well as ordinary bikes can be hired from apt no. 9, Rosario Lodge, 5 Avenida Sur. Prices are steep, with mountain bikes going for $8 per day. Accompanied tours around Antigua and environs have been highly recommended and cost $3.50 per hour. Long-distance cycling tours are also available. **Motorbikes** can be hired from 6 Avenida Sur, 8.

Laundry
There are two places on 5 Calle Poniente, near the main square.

Language schools
The most prestigious and expensive of the lot has long been the **Proyecto Lingüístico Francisco Marroquín**, 4 Avenida Sur 4, whose clientele is overwhelmingly North American. **Maya**, 5 Calle Poniente 20, is equally good, and for some reason favoured mostly by a European clientele. Other establishments that are repeatedly recommended are the **Professional Spanish Language School**, 7 Avenida Norte 82, and **Tecún Umán**, 6 Calle Poniente 34. There are many more schools to choose from, offering every kind of teaching option you might want, as well as accommodation with a local family, if required. Prices range around $60–120 per week for one-to-one teaching, and full-board accommodation with a family usually costs $30 per week extra. If you hire a private teacher, you should expect to pay around $2 per hour.

Volcanoes
Information, maps, hiking equipment and guides are best found by either going to the **Casa Andinista**, 4 Calle Oriente, which also sells photocopies of topographic military maps to the northern Ixil region otherwise unavailable and can give you the latest news on safety (this is also a good place to enquire about travel) or **Club Chigag**, 6 Avenida Norte 34, though the latter gets very mixed reports.

Excursions from Antigua: Villages and Volcanoes

Once you get to know Antigua you will find it hard to tear yourself away; however, there are plenty of excursions worth taking, ranging from energetic volcano climbing to gentler pastimes like soaking in hot springs. The highland valley surrounding Antigua is strewn with Indian hamlets and sleepy villages, while in between, rich farming country is covered with crops such as coffee, maize, cereals, vegetables and fruit trees. Towering above are the three volcanoes of Agua, Acatenango and Fuego, the last of which is still active. Nearer Guatemala City, but usually visited on a tour from Antigua, the active Pacaya volcano is the most dramatic, since for years it has not just been fuming, but actually erupting at regular intervals.

It is a beautiful area, and the inhabitants are friendly too. Armed robbery and rape do occur sporadically, however, particularly on the volcanoes, where it is always best to take a local guide with you or go in a group. Most times everything goes well, so do not let yourself be put off, but it is very worthwhile finding out the latest news on security, either from the tourist office or the local hiking organizations. All villages mentioned can be reached by public transport from Antigua bus terminal, or by taxi; you should always remember to agree on a price first.

Villages

One of the nearest villages is **San Juan del Obispo**, just a couple of kilometres southeast of Antigua. It is chiefly interesting for the restored palace of Francisco Marroquín, who was the first bishop of Guatemala, in the days of Alvarado. The nuns who now occupy the palace do not mind showing visitors around. The church contains some very fine colonial religious artwork from the 16th century. You could walk to the village in an hour, or any bus going to or from Santa María de Jesús can drop you off. Heading onwards to **Santa María de Jesús**, a journey that will take just under an hour from Antigua, you reach one of the best vantage points from which to survey the whole valley that has Antigua at its heart. The views of the twin peaks of Fuego and Acatenango are terrific. The village itself is mainly inhabited by Indians, who sell high-quality *huipiles*, with the best choice on market days: Mondays, Thursdays and Saturdays.

Southwest of Antigua, less than six kilometres away, is the village of **Ciudad Vieja**, which is not really interesting for what it is today, but rather for being near the spot where Guatemala's second capital perished. It was here that the ill-fated town of **Santiago de los Caballeros** was swept away in 1541, when a huge mudslide, caused by an earthquake, came off the slopes of Agua. There are no remains. Also out this way, but clinging to the lower slopes of Acatenango, is **San Antonio Aguas Calientes**, where the Indians have turned their superb weaving into a commercial cottage industry, selling their wares all along the village street. If you are interested, there are plenty of women here who will give you weaving lessons on their backstrap looms—just ask around if no one approaches you first. Trying it yourself, you quickly appreciate the immense amount of time and effort that goes into Guatemalan weaving.

For a change from the swimming pools of Antigua's posh hotels, you could luxuriate in the hot springs of **San Lorenzo el Tejar**, about five kilometres from Antigua. The springs are open daily, 6–5, except Tuesday and Friday afternoons; small fee. To reach them, take any bus heading for Chimaltenango, and ask to be dropped off nearest the village of **San Luis Carretas**, from where it is a short walk. You will find a communal pool, but also private tubs, which you can have all to yourself for as long as you wish. A few kilometres further on by bus, you pass a tiny lake, popularly known as **Los Aposentos**, set amongst a grove of pine trees, and a good place for a leisurely turn in a rowing boat.

Finally, if you only have time to make one day trip, **San Andrés Itzapa** on a Sunday is well worth staying on for. The reason for this lies not in the village itself, which is a dust-blown sort of place that suffered terrible damage during the 1976 earthquake; rather, it is interesting for the local cult of **Maximón**, one of the Maya Indians' most notorious saints, also known as St Simón. A controversial saint, not least because he is supposed to be evil, New World colonists have always tried to suppress the Indians' attachment to him.

In most cases, Maximón is dressed up in Western clothing, often with a fat cigar in his mouth, and Mafia-type sunglasses. The origin of his evil reputation is uncertain, but it may have been propaganda spread by the earliest conquistadors. One theory is that Maximón (pronounced 'Mashimon') was an Indian holy man at the time of the conquest, who was murdered by the Spanish because they feared his influence over the Indians. As a result of his martyrdom, however, he became one of the Indians' most revered saints—a symbol of their oppression as well as of the power they implored against it. Today, there are only a handful of villages left where he is worshipped, and the chapel in San Andrés Itzapa is one of the least visited by outsiders.

Every Sunday, Indian worshippers flock from as far away as Guatemala City, to pay tribute to Maximón. This elaborate ritual necessitates liberal splashings of rum, as well as the smoking of fat cigars (women only), candle-lighting, praying, and even fireworks. People queue to take their turn in front of Maximón's altar, where they will pray to him, all the while splashing him with rum and throwing money into his lap. Occasionally a daykeeper (a traditional shaman) will accompany someone, rubbing their head and neck with rum, and stroking their bodies with special laurels from head to toe.

Afterwards the worshipper will normally choose one of the many stone tables in the chapel on which to light candles. The candles are all different colours, and signify different prayers: red is for matters of love, faith or desire; green is for business or wealth; pink is for health and hope; black is for warding off enemies and jealousy; purple is against vicious or bad thoughts; blue is both for luck in matters of money, journeys or learning, and for anything to do with work; yellow is for the protection of adults; and white is for the protection of children. Once outside again, the burning of fireworks and rum is used to divine fortune, and this part is normally performed with the help of a daykeeper, who is paid for his service.

You will find the chapel easily by turning up an unpaved street, that leads off to the right, just past the main square. Anyone can tell you where if you get lost. Do not take your camera in case it causes offence.

Volcanoes

Two of the volcanoes, Agua and Pacaya, can be climbed on organized day trips, which cost anything from $15 upwards. To find out about the range currently available take a look at the notice board at Doña Luisa's. For official information on the latest security situation, reputable guides, and equipment, compare what is offered at Casa Andinista and Club Chigag, before coming to any decisions. Most people prefer the services of Casa Andinista. If not planning to stay overnight, strong walking shoes, food and water, toilet paper, sun cream and sun glasses are all you need. Remember also, that the temperature at high altitudes is very cold, more so because of the wind chill.

The easiest volcano to climb nearby is **Agua** (3760 m), immediately south of Antigua, which has a clear path leading up it, beginning outside the village of Santa María de Jesús. The slopes of this perfectly symmetrical cone are steep, and the ascent takes a good four to five hours. The high altitude makes it even harder, but once at the crater, you will be rewarded with the extraordinary sight of a football pitch inside the mountain, and views to take away what little breath you have left. The descent is obviously much quicker, and if you set off at 6 am, you can do Agua as a tough but rewarding day trip. If you plan to stay the night near the summit, there is a shelter, but you will certainly need a warm sleeping-bag, and preferably a tent. The dawn viewed from up here is magical, and on a clear day you can see all the way to the Pacific, as well as the surrounding valleys and neighbouring volcanoes of Pacaya, Fuego and Acatenango.

Acatenango (3960 m) and **Fuego** (3835 m), to the southwest of Antigua, are twin volcanoes that only the toughest attempt to climb. The ascent of Acatenango can take anything up to nine hours. You have a choice of two craters to view, as well as a superb panorama stretching from Agua across the valley, to the distant cones surrounding Lake Atitlán. If you have the energy left to climb Fuego as well, you will have to stay the night beneath Acatenango's craters, and continue for another foot-crunching day the next morning. Unfortunately, you have to descend quite a way before you can start climbing Fuego, so you are in for a long day. Near the summit, the crater is continuously spouting sulphurous fumes, so do not be tempted to get too close. You must go back via Acatenango, so the return journey is no easier.

Pacaya (2544 m), rising above Lake Amatitlán near Guatemala City, is a popular day trip—not least because you can drive a good long way before walking, and then the volcano is pretty small. Up top, you will enter a blackened world of burning earth and witches' fumes, petrified lava and strange shapes, the mountain reminding you of its vitality by spouting clouds of smoke and occasional rocks. At night, the volcano's display is the most dramatic, as its cone is wrapped in a haze of orange light. Clearly you need to be careful on Pacaya, never getting too close if the eruptions are fierce. It is also an unfortunate fact that the volcano's popularity makes it most prone to bandit activity, and in 1991 all tours were suspended after a particularly brutal attack. With any luck, things will have improved by the time you arrive, but even an armed guard is unlikely to help, should you meet with robbers prepared to use their guns.

Iximché

Capital of the Cakchiqueles, Iximché was once a city of 10,000 people, founded by proud noble families who had seceded from the greater Quiché empire only 50 years before the Spanish arrived. As happened elsewhere in Latin America, the internal divisions between the Indian nations helped the Spanish in their conquest. In Guatemala, it was the Cakchiqueles who sided with Alvarado and his troops. He arrived in Iximché in 1524, and declared it the first Spanish capital of Guatemala.

It did not take long before the Spanish alienated their Indian allies by demanding ever more labour, riches and women, and by 1526 Alvarado had burnt this Indian city, and its inhabitants were forced to flee. It's a depressingly familiar story, and today the site gives little away of what it once looked like. It may have little to offer as a ruin, but it is a tranquil place and surrounded by beautiful countryside. Its location, about halfway between Chimaltenango and Los Encuentros, make it an easy day-trip away from Antigua, or a short detour from the Pan-American Highway.

It is quite easy to get to the site, though it does involve a good hour's walk if you don't have private transport. Catch any bus to Chimaltenango (40 mins), and wait there for a Tecpán bus (1hr). From Tecpán, it is then a few kilometres' pleasant walk to the site of Iximché (small fee).

Lake Atitlán

> The Indians consider the Atitlán basin the navel of the earth and sky, for as one enters it the sky becomes defined by its rim of smoking cones.
>
> Ronald Wright, *Time Among the Maya*

Lake Atitlán is most extraordinary at sunset. As the cool mountain air turns all the shades from blue to dusty pink to grey, so the waters of the lake change their hues of greenish blue. Every time you watch it happen, the scene will be different. Add to this spectacle the setting of the lake: 18 km long and about 10 km wide, at the feet of three volcanoes piercing white clouds, and you can understand why some people get carried away and insist this is the most beautiful lake in the world. It lies at an altitude of 1562 m, and is ringed by mountains on all sides, often with steep rock faces falling straight into the water, and only a few stretches where the ground is level for any distance. Although dramatic storms occasionally whip up on the lake, the weather here is generally temperate.

The former Indian village of **Panajachel** has long been a popular resort for retired and visiting foreigners. Dotted around the lake are a number of traditional Indian villages, of which Santiago Atitlán is the most famous. But there are plenty of others, less enslaved to tourism, and there are also long distances of the shoreline that are not inhabited at all, perfect for tranquil hiking or boating.

During the sixties, Panajachel was 'discovered' by hippies, who have left an indelible mark on the place. The Indians still sell custom-made waist jackets and skull caps none of them would be seen dead in, and have even mastered the art of tie-dying. All this has

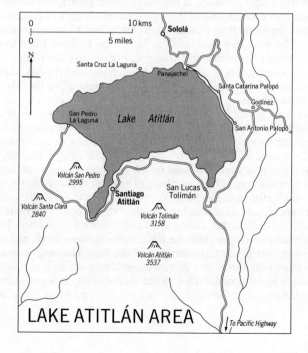

meant that Panajachel has long since stopped being a quiet village and is now a buzzing resort with every kind of accommodation, and a lively nightlife second only to Antigua. Restaurants and lakeside stalls cater to a wide range of tastes, ranging from local fish to Swiss delicacies or health food.

You may find all this commercialism a touch depressing. However, Panajachel is still a very small place, and in spite of Lake Atitlán being one of Guatemala's foremost tourist attractions, you will find yourself in another world almost as soon as you leave the settlement. With luck, the fact that the entire basin is a national park will help to keep it that way.

GETTING TO LAKE ATITLÁN

By Bus
Coming from the capital, the **Rebuli** company runs daily buses, 6–3, from its offices at 3 Avenida 2–36, Zona 9, and the journey takes about 3 hrs. Coming from Antigua, catch a local bus to Chimaltenango, and get off at the junction with the main Highway. From there, flag down any bus with either Panajachel or Sololá painted on the front window. This journey should not take more than 3 hrs either. Bus tickets are very cheap, but always compare with your fellow passengers to make sure you are not paying an inflated 'gringo price'.

GETTING AROUND LAKE ATITLÁN

The road is paved as far as Panajachel, but after that it becomes a very rough dirt road, extremely steep in places, as it follows ridges above the shoreline. Panajachel is located on the northeast shore of Lake Atitlán, and the dirt road curves around the eastern side of the lake, to San Lucas Tolimán, in the southeastern corner, all the way to Santiago Atitlán and San Pedro La Laguna on the southwestern shore. The road is so bad that if you tried to drive the 55 km from Panajachel to San Pedro La Laguna, it could easily take you half a day. There is a new paved road to San Lucas Tolimán, but it leaves the lake, going via San Andrés Semetabaj and Godinez. For an easy day's hike, take an early morning bus from Panajachel to Godinez, and then walk down the mountainside to San Antonio (takes about one hour), and follow the dirt road along the lake for another 11 km, back to Panajachel.

The best way of reaching the lake's southern villages is by taking one of the morning ferries or launches, which leave from the beach in front of Panajachel every day. There are ferries between 8 and 5. To Santiago Atitlán, the crossing takes 45 minutes, and the price is usually around $3 for a return ticket. Do not be conned into buying a return ticket, however, since they are only valid on the boat you bought it on, which may not travel back when it suits you. There are plenty of boats and you can always buy a single if you ask for it. For morning ferries (same times, but check at the tourist office) direct to San Pedro or Santa Cruz La Laguna, head for the jetty just before the **Hotel Tzanjuyu**. A road leads off the main street, taking you straight down to the water. The returning ferry drops in at all the villages along the inaccessible western shore, and the two-hour journey is a lovely way to see this quiet part of the lake. You can, of course, hire the services of a boatman. Agree on a price before setting off and, if possible, go with someone who has been recommended by the tourist office. It is not unknown for the occasional tourist to end up swimming home because of mid-lake renegotiations.

Lake Atitlán

It is possible to travel all the way around the lake by a combination of bus rides, boat trips and walking (not a good idea to go alone). This would take you about four days, and you would need to take your own provisions and tent, though there are simple guest houses in some villages, namely San Lucas Tolimán, Santiago Atitlán, San Pedro La Laguna, and Santa Cruz. To cut this journey by half, you could take a bumpy bus ride from Panajachel to Santiago Atitlán one day (check time with the tourist office, but it is very early), catch a boat to San Pedro La Laguna the next morning, and from there spend two days walking back to Panajachel via Santa Cruz.

Panajachel

The road that turns off the Pan-American Highway for Panajachel and Lake Atitlán is a dramatic short drive. One of the first things you see is the bizarre sight of a giant soldier's helmet set on a pair of boots, which marks the entrance to a large military base. Before you have time to wonder whether you imagined it, you find yourself transported to Sololá, a small town perched high above the lake's basin. Up to here the road is relatively level. But from now on, you are in for a rollercoaster ride, plunging 500 metres in 8 km, on hairpin bends and along steep ridges, with short flashes of the lake below and superb views of the surrounding mountains and volcanoes. A number of *miradores* (viewpoints) have been set up along the road, which are good places to take panoramic photographs.

Panajachel itself is flat and strung out along a dusty main road, lined with hotels, gas stations and restaurants. There are almost no traces of the original Indian village. The 'village' spreads from the main road down to the lake shore, its two main thoroughfares lined with more restaurants and guest houses, and a bustling street market on Avenida Santander, where you will find an excellent range of Guatemalan **artesanía** and textiles.

109

Prices are not bad either. The waterside is newly landscaped, with a tiny stretch of sand, and a number of wooden shack restaurants, where you can eat delicious food right by the lake. The best beach for relaxed sunbathing is beyond the River Panajachel, just east of the main waterfront, and easily reached by crossing the pebbly estuary of the shallow river.

Avenida Santander branches off the main road by the **bank**, which is also where all buses stop. If you continue straight on, you soon come to the edge of Panajachel and the local market, where the region's indigenous inhabitants retain a vital part of their way of life, with no concessions to tourism. This is the place to buy fresh fruit and vegetables. Apart from this area, Panajachel is dominated by the floating population of foreigners, and the place is often referred to as 'Gringotenango'. However, as a base for exploring the lake it is ideal, and if you prefer to be away from the crowds, you have a number of choices in villages such as Santa Catarina, San Pedro La Laguna, Santiago Atitlán and Santa Cruz.

TOURIST INFORMATION
The **INGUAT** office (Mon, 8–noon; Wed–Sun, 8–noon and 2–6) is located near the bank. They can do little more than tell you departure times for boats and buses, and any other information you require is best picked up from other travellers.

GETTING TO AND FROM PANAJACHEL
There are daily direct buses to Chichicastenango (2 hrs) and Quezaltenango ($2\frac{1}{2}$ hrs) in the early mornings (see the timetable in the tourist office). Otherwise, there is a constant flow of minibuses between Sololá and Panajachel, or to the Los Encuentros junction, where you can easily get an onward connection, either back towards Guatemala City, or heading west. If you are waiting for one of the early morning buses, and the waiting crowd worries you, you have a better chance of getting onto the bus if you wait for it by the old market, where all the early buses stop first. For local buses around the eastern shore of the lake, check with the tourist office for the latest schedule. Normally there is just one bus heading towards San Lucas Tolimán, and the return leaves about the same time from the other end, making it virtually impossible to return the same day.

WHERE TO STAY
You have plenty of choices here, and the only times you might have a problem are over Christmas and Easter, when the place is not only full, but prices can double. Equally, prices can sink very low at quiet times—they are always negotiable, even in the top hotels. The telephone code for Panajachel is 0621.

Directly on the Lakeshore

EXPENSIVE
Hotel del Lago (tel 555/60), at the end of Avenida Rancho Grande, is a largish hotel, with all modern conveniences, including a pool. **Hotel Playa Linda** (tel 159), on the public beach, has a lovely garden and verandah, with most rooms facing the lake. The best private beach belongs to **Hotel Monterrey** (tel 126), off a side road of Avenida Santander. Quite a way from the hub of things, one of the oldest hotels here is the **Hotel**

Tzanjuyu (tel 318), with two storeys facing the water, and an atmosphere and decor that recall 1940s Hollywood movies.

On a small bay at the beginning of Panajachel, there are a couple of good hotels, one dusty kilometre from the centre of Panajachel. **Hotel Atitlán** (tel 441) is the most luxurious hotel on the lake itself, with all the services you would expect, such as private beach, swimming pool and restaurant, as well as plenty of water-sport options laid on. **Hotel Visión Azul** (tel 419/374) is nearest the main road on the bay, a pretty little hotel with private beach and pool and much cheaper than Hotel Atitlán.

The lakeside hotel in Santa Catarina, **Villa Santa Catarina** (tel 291) has an excellent location, though the hotel does clash somewhat with the village, arrogantly spreading itself out on the shore, its back to the Indian inhabitants who used to wash their clothes there.

INEXPENSIVE

The **Arca de Noé**, below Santa Cruz, is a lovely place with excellent meals for guests only, at $3 for five courses. Bungalows with private bathroom (two to three people) go for $10, and simple rooms, sharing shower and toilets, are $5 for two. Get there early in the morning if you want any chance of getting a room or bungalow. Up in the village there's the basic but clean **Hospedaje Hernández**, which charges less than $2 for a room.

In Panajachel

EXPENSIVE

Hotel Regis, Avenida Santander, tel 149/152, is a friendly, well-kept hotel with private garden, right in the middle of Panajachel. **Hotel Primavera**, on Avenida Santander, is clean and has an excellent Swiss restaurant. **Cacique Inn**, Calle Real, tel 205, is expensive for what it offers, but does have a small pool.

MODERATE

Hotel Paradise Inn (tel 021) on Calle del Río offers motel-style accommodation, as near to the lake as possible, without being on it. **Hotel Galindo,** on the main road towards the local market, has a lovely garden and a good restaurant. New bungalows in their own grounds are offered at **Rancho Grande**, Avenida Rancho Grande, tel 554.

INEXPENSIVE

Hotel Fonda del Sol (tel 162), right next to the tourist office, is basic but clean, and excellent value for the price. Of the other cheapies, the favourite is **Las Casitas**, opposite the market on the main road, which has clean rooms around a private garden, breakfast restaurant and very friendly management. **Hotel Naya Kanek**, also on the main road near the market, is less friendly but all right. Finally, anywhere saying 'Rooms' will offer basic accommodation, sharing cold showers at rock bottom prices.

In San Lucas Tolimán

There are a few basic but clean guest houses here—ask for directions: **Pension Central**; **Hospedaje El Exito**; **Pensión Las Conchitas**; and **Cafetería Santa Ana**.

In Santiago Atitlán

First choice has got to be the moderately priced **Posada de Santiago**, just one kilometre outside the village, near the Texaco station. Described by one traveller as 'a little piece of heaven', rooms include private bathrooms and beautiful fireplaces. Meals are excellent if not cheap.

In the village itself there is the **Hospedaje Chi-Nim-Ya**, and also the **Pensión Rosita**, which is a bit cheaper and much grubbier.

In San Pedro La Laguna

Chuasinahi is a basic guest house near the waterfront, offering rooms for $2. Next door are the wooden shacks that make up **Ti-Kaaj**, favoured by the young hippie set. Also popular with them is the **Pensión Johanna**, located on an inlet beneath the village, where there is another landing stage (ask for directions).

EATING OUT

Most of the top hotels have restaurants, where you can enjoy expensive meals. Apart from them, the choice is good, and one of the best is **Al Chisme** on Calle de los Arboles, which also does good pastries. For excellent vegetarian meals, try **La Unica Deli**, on the main road, up towards the market. A bit further on this way, **Ranch Market** is best for breakfast and pastries, serving good coffee. It also has the added attraction of an English lending library, and American magazines to read.

For delicious steaks and the like, try **El Patio**, on Avenida Santander, where, as the name suggests, you can sit outdoors on balmy nights. Also on Avenida Santander is the Swiss restaurant of **Hotel Primavera**, which offers immaculate over-priced meals. **The Last Resort** (left after the GUATEL office, if you are coming from the main road, down 14 Calle de Febrero), on the other hand, serves a wide range of filling meals, including breakfast, at rock bottom prices. The atmosphere is relaxed here, as customers listen to the steady beat of reggae or play ping-pong in the back. There are plenty more places to try, and new establishments are opening up all the time.

ENTERTAINMENT AND NIGHTLIFE

For an evening of drinking, the most popular bar these days is **La Casa del Pintor**, Calle los Arboles. Good pizzas are also served here. **Circus Bar**, under the same management, across the street, functions more like a disco, and has live music at weekends. There are also two video bars: **Café Xocomil**, on the main road, near the market; and **Video Bar**, on Avenida Santander, near the GUATEL office; more places open up all the time. Finally there is the disco **Past Ten**, opposite the Hotel del Lago on Avenida Rancho Grande, which is having trouble competing with the Circus Bar.

SPORTS AND ACTIVITIES

There are opportunities for water sports on the lake. Boats, canoes and windsurfers can be hired via the top hotels or direct on the Panajachel waterfront. At weekends the water is invaded by speedboats and water-skiers as many wealthy Guatemalans have lakeside retreats.

USEFUL INFORMATION

Money Matters
The only bank is the Banco Agrícola Mercantil, but there are always moneychangers hanging around outside. Remember that Panajachel is the only place around the lake where you can change money.

Post Office
This is on a small turning off the main road, just after the village church. No parcels can be sent from here, and your best bet is to use **Get Guated Out**, which is next to Al Chisme restaurant on Calle de los Arboles (the office is upstairs). They will charge you around $25 for a 2kg parcel, postage extra. They use the national postal service, so there is nothing safer about their service; it is just a matter of expensive convenience.

Telecommunications
The **GUATEL** office is located halfway down Avenida Santander.

Bike and Motorbike Hire
Bikes can be hired opposite the tourist office, on the main road. They cost about $3 per day, but are available by the hour as well. For **motorbikes**, ask at the tourist office; prices will be around $25 per day.

Art Gallery
La Galería is an interesting art gallery, where Guatemalan painter Nan Cruz has a permanent exhibition, and other artists from all over the world show their locally inspired work.

Volcanoes
There are three volcanoes around Lake Atitlán, and all of them can be climbed. The easiest is San Pedro (3000 m), which can be ascended by a steep trail in about three or four hours; begin from the village of the same name. Tolimán (3120 m), above Santiago Atitlán, takes a few hours longer to climb, while the Atitlán volcano (3535 m) is a tough one that will take all day. It is advisable to take a guide, since trails are not clear, and there are said to be occasional groups of guerrillas camping out up there. Either go via the tourist office in Panajachel, or ask for the *alcalde* (mayor) in the relevant village, and he will recommend someone. Always fix the price first, and remember that you are expected to feed your guide.

Some Indian Villages Around Lake Atitlán

Two Indians tribes lived here before the Spanish Conquest. The western shore, from Santiago Atitlán to San Pedro La Laguna, was inhabited by the Tzutujil, whose capital was on the slopes of San Pedro volcano, but has long since disappeared, destroyed by Alvarado as early as 1524. The rest of the shoreline was the domain of Cakchiquel Indians, who helped Alvarado, only to be subjected themselves. The descendants of these two tribes still speak their different languages, and also wear extremely beautiful clothes, each village distinct from the next. There are about twelve villages around the lake, and only the most interesting and accessible are mentioned here.

Santiago Atitlán

Diagonally across the lake from Panajachel, Santiago Atitlán hides in a protected inlet of the lake, the village and surrounding fields sandwiched in between the volcanoes of Tolimán, Atitlán and San Pedro. Arriving by boat, you pass small reedy islands and fishermen in their dugout canoes, called *cayucos*. By the water's edge, women stoop, washing clothes, while men and boys work in the neatly kept gardens beyond. It is a tranquil and idyllic scene. If you venture up into the village, however, you will be surrounded by women and children trying to sell you their wares, their fierce selling technique only outdone by their aggressive competitiveness towards each other.

The reason for the hard sell is obvious. The villagers of Santiago Atitlán wear the most famous 'costume' of Guatemala's Indians. It is very glamorous as well as superbly made, and tourists often pay a lot of money for the weavings and embroidery. (The average wage for agricultural labourers can be less than US$2 a day, yet selling a small piece of embroidered weaving can net US$10.) All males, young and old, traditionally wear white, knee-length trousers, with dark blue stripes, intricately embroidered with colourful flowers and birds around the knee. A dark red waistband, and white shirt complete the outfit. Today, many men wear jeans and modern shirts, which is a shame. The women are better at keeping to their customary dress, the most famous detail being the headdress—a red ribbon wound round and round the head, eventually sticking out so far that it looks just like a halo. It is called a *tocayal* and is depicted on the 25-centavo coin.

As well as the daily market, another attraction here is the chapel to Maximón, for this is one of the few places in the country where he is worshipped. Unlike in San Andrés Itzapa, Maximón does not have a fixed home here. Instead, a different member of the *cofradía* (religious brotherhood) has the honour of keeping him in his house each year. If you would like to visit him, just ask for the *Casa de Maximón*, and make sure you bring an offering of some rum and a few cigarettes, which will be shared by Maximón and his keeper. Maximón looks quite different here, made of wood and clad in delicate scarves, but still with the dark glasses and cigar. Some have suggested that Maximón is, in fact, a reincarnation of the Maya God, Mam, who also used to be represented as a human, wooden figure.

The local church on the main square has a simple interior of whitewashed walls and wooden benches. It has always been the focus of local rallying against army oppression on this side of the lake, and just by the entrance you can see a stark reminder of it: a small paper cross is fixed on the wall for every member of the community murdered in recent years.

If you can time your visit to be here on Good Friday, you will witness an extraordinary ritual of a both pagan and Catholic nature, when Maximón and Christ are paraded together, though never facing each other. Both are also ritually taken down from their respective crucifixes, testifying to the equal importance the Indians attach to both Christian and pagan saints, and the Catholic Church's inability to eradicate traditional religion in spite of centuries of indoctrination.

Just northeast of the village, there is also a small nature reserve (**Parque Nacional Atitlán**), designated to protect the *poc*, a kind of grebe. Lake Atitlán was the only place in the world where it existed, and strictly speaking it is now extinct, because the bird you see today is a hybrid of the original grebe with the pied-billed grebe. Visiting the reserve by hired canoe from Santiago Atitlán is a very pleasant way to spend a quiet hour or so, though there really isn't anything much to see.

San Pedro La Laguna
Of the many other villages dotted around the lake, San Pedro La Laguna, at the foot of the San Pedro volcano, is a refreshingly quiet place, with none of the frenzied tourism of its neighbour. The main reason for this is no doubt the lack of traditional costume, as most villagers seem to have *ladinized*. However, the reedy shoreline, dotted with gigantic boulders lapped by gentle waves from the lake, make for relaxed days and peaceful nights. No wonder some people head straight for San Pedro, preferring the simple life here to the bustle and noise of Panajachel. There is nothing to do except sunbathe, swing in a hammock or paddle in the water. In between these pastimes, you can eat and drink simple fare at one of the three waterfront restaurants.

Santa Catarina and San Antonio
Following the old dirt road east of Panajachel takes you through a beautiful grove of trees and then out into the sun and along the contours of the lake. If you do not wish to walk, the best way to cope with the steep mud road, slippery pebbles and large potholes is to hire a motorbike, though it is possible to take cars along this route. The first village is 4 km away, the second 11 km.

The first village you reach is **Santa Catarina** (officially Santa Catarina Palopó), nestling in a tight dip between dusty mountain folds. Nothing much goes on here, but the views of the lake in its mountainous frame are terrific. The women wear intricately embroidered *huipiles*, coloured green and blue, with blue skirts. You may have seen them selling their clothes at the Panajachel market on Avenida Santander.

Further on, the road twists and turns, up and around the craggy shoreline, until it reaches **San Antonio** (officially San Antonio Palopó), its mud houses stacked on the hillside above the lake. A lovely crumbling church perches in the middle of the village, and in front of its steps, women and children sell mainly fruit and vegetables. Passing the open doors of some of the homes, you might see one of the giant foot-looms, used exclusively by the men to weave large blankets. The women wear a simple but elegant costume here: red *huipiles* and dark blue skirts, with plenty of silver-leaf necklaces and coloured beads.

Chichicastenango and the Ixil Triangle

The junction of Los Encuentros, on the Pan-American Highway, marks an important turning point for the traveller: the main Highway turns west, passing Lake Atitlán on its way to the city of Quezaltenango, and northwards from there. The equally large branch road heads directly north, taking you to the unique Indian town of Chichicastenango, and the nearby departmental capital of the Quiché region, Santa Cruz del Quiché. Here the paved road comes to an end, continued by a rugged dirt road, which takes the hardy traveller on a five-hour bus journey to a remote region known as the Ixil Triangle.

This distant area in the northern reaches of the Western Highlands is a wild place, where the landscape has something almost alpine about it, beautiful farming valleys nestling in wide bowls between forested mountains. The Indians here favour geometric designs on their clothes, and the *huipiles* of Nebaj rank among the country's most stunning.

Chichicastenango

Famous for its fabulous market on Thursdays and Sundays, and the spectacular festival of St Thomas, *Chichi*, as it is known, has an atmosphere all of its own. This is because most of the inhabitants are pure Maya, and their traditional culture and way of life permeate every aspect of the place.

Set on top of a hill, cobbled streets meander steeply up and around the main square. Adobe houses huddle together and their red-tiled roofs contrast beautifully with the whitewashed walls and rich green pastures all around.

The Church of Santo Tomás

On the main plaza, the church of **Santo Tomás** was brutally plonked on top of an existing Maya temple by the Spanish in 1540. It is one of the best places to observe how the Indians adapted to enforced Christianity by worshipping the Christian god alongside their traditional gods and saints in an unorthodox mixture of Catholic and pagan rites.

The steep flight of steps that leads up to the main church entrance is almost always enshrouded by wisps of incense and smoke, as people burn offerings to the gods or to Saint Thomas, the local patron saint, before entering the church. Foreign visitors should never enter by the main entrance, but by the side, since they have made no offering. The perfumed air is even heavier inside the church, where *brujos* (shamans, also known as daykeepers) swing incense burners up and down the aisles. Low altars, raised slightly off the ground, line the centre aisle all the way to the front. Each one is used for invoking a different blessing: there is the one for the well-being of pregnant women, the one for not feeling sad after the death of a relative, another to remember the victims of the 1976 earthquake, one for weddings, one for Maya priests, one for Catholic priests, and there are quite a few more. Flower petals are offered and candles lit—a set number for each altar. The coloured candles are often lit in pairs. This is a way of communicating with the spirits of the dead: one candle for the living, one for the deceased.

The church is divided along the central aisle. When you are facing the main altar, the left-hand side is dedicated to Maya gods and spirits, while the right-hand side of the nave is for Christian saints. Both groups are given equal reverence, with offerings of candles, flowers, incense and alcohol. On first impression, the altars on either side may look the same, but closer inspection will show otherwise. For example, note the first altar on the left, near the main entrance: the figures are an extraordinary mixture of Christian images and Maya gods. The nubile ladies on the far side are, in fact, the saints of pregnant women, while the angel-type figures in front, each with an arm missing, represent the god Hunahpu, who had his arm ripped off by Seven Macaw, when he was fighting Hunahpu for his sin of self-glorification:

116

Suddenly Hunahpu appeared, running. He set out to grab him, but actually it was the arm of Hunahpu that was seized by Seven Macaw. He yanked it straight back, he bent it back at the shoulder. Then Seven Macaw tore it right out of Hunahpu. Even so, the boys did well: the first round was not their defeat by Seven Macaw.

The Quiché bible, *Popol Vuh*, translated by Dennis Tedlock

When visiting the church, always keep your distance from any rites in progress inside. Bus loads of tourists come here every week, and the Indians have become very sensitive to disrespectful behaviour by visitors. Photography is obviously out of the question. If you would like to know more about the interior of the church or the rituals performed, you will always be able to find someone near the side entrance, who will oblige for a small fee. Each person will give you a very personal explanation that is true for them.

El Calvario and the Museum

While both Indians and *ladinos* worship in the main church, the smaller church, directly opposite, is just for Indian worshippers. Called **El Calvario**, it is a whitewashed church with a very plain interior. The most important feature is the glass coffin holding the black Christ, who is paraded about the streets during Easter Week. To one side, you will also find a small shrine to the God of Chickens, where the faithful often leave an egg or other offerings, when their chickens are not laying well.

The small museum, on the south side of the main square (8–noon and 2–5; may be closed on Mon and Tues), has an interesting collection of Maya jade artefacts, as well as pottery. The collection belonged to Father Rossbach, who was so popular and trusted by the local people that they made him presents of their precious pieces, kept by their home altars and passed on from one generation to the next. They were collected over a period of 50 years, and left to the town on the priest's death.

The Shrine of Pascual Abaj

Traditionally, the Quiché Indians worship their gods and spirits in many places. Often these are open-air shrines, set on sacred hilltops, in forests, or by streams. Nature is an integral part of Maya religion, with its own spirit and power that must be respected. The hills around Chichi are full of such shrines, most of them secret to outsiders. However, the shrine of Pascual Abaj is well known and regularly visited by foreigners. Just a short walk out of town, you will find it by walking down the hill from the main square, taking the street leading away from Santo Tomás church. Then follow the first right turn, where you will come to an open field, and the path leads off to the left, through someone's yard, and up onto a pine-clad hill.

Most times there is nothing much to see, other than patches of burnt earth around a collection of stones, where fires are lit and chickens ritually sacrificed. Tufts of feathers blow around in the breeze, and most likely children will come scurrying up to sell you some trinkets. But the view of town and the surrounding hills is worth the walk in itself.

THE FESTIVAL OF SANTO TOMAS

Probably the most famous festival in Central America, next to the Easter Week celebrations, the *fiesta de Santo Tomás* takes up a whole week, 13–21 December. It is accompanied by a large market on the main square and endless processions and firework displays. The last three days are the best time to be here, with the town really packed out on 20 and 21 December.

The first processions get under way as early as 6—some are just continuations of ones from the night before—with the participants, both men and women, distinctly the worse for alcohol.

All through the day the sudden crack of fireworks will blast your eardrums, and the town is a constant hum of music and voices. Traditional dances are performed on the main square, the participants dressed in their finest regional costume. At these times you can see virtually all the costumes of the Quiché region in one place, the Chichi dress being one of the most elaborate: the men wear knee-length trousers and jackets made of bark-brown wool and embroidered with red, pink and green silk around the edges. Their shirts are white, but on their heads they wear a triangle of cloth, of the same material as that of their suits, and tied behind the head. The women wear a brown-based costume too, their *huipiles* distinguished by the heavy embroidery of large-petalled flowers of mainly orange, yellow and green.

On the second to last day of the festival all the official dancers assemble on the square to be introduced to the spectators: each couple from each region will perform a short twirl, and then take off their masks to reveal that both of them are, in fact, men. It is an extraordinary transvestite show for deeply Catholic and conservative Guatemala. On the last day the Indians form a large procession of their holy shrines and altars, candle-holding women and children behind each one.

A rare spectacle you will see throughout the festivities is the pole dancers, jumping off a 20-metre pole, tied to a long rope. This dance with death is known as *Palo Volador*, and sounds rather more dramatic than it actually is, since the men's rope is wrapped tightly around the top of the pole, and their body weight slowly unwinds it, allowing them to circle gracefully to the ground. Only occasionally is there some real drama, when one of the participants is so drunk that he falls off his perch before tying the rope on.

GETTING TO AND FROM CHICHI

By Bus
From **Guatemala City** (3 hrs), there are regular daily buses leaving from the Zona 4 bus terminal, from dawn until around 5 pm. Most of them will be heading for the town of **Santa Cruz del Quiché**, *Quiché* for short, and all go via Chichicastenango, as do the buses to **Joyabaj**. Destinations, written in their shortened version, are marked above the front window of all buses.

From **Antigua** (3 hrs), there are no direct buses, but the connection is easily made by flagging down passing buses at the Chimaltenango junction. From **Panajachel** (2 hrs), there are daily direct buses to Chichi at 7, 8, 9 am and 4 pm. At other times, you can easily travel by getting any bus to the Los Encuentros junction, from where you can catch passing buses coming from the capital.

If you are heading for the **Ixil** region, you will need an early start to catch the Nebaj buses leaving Quiché between 8 and 10 am. Buses leave roughly every half an hour for Quiché, and the journey takes around thirty minutes. Wait for them passing just past the Pensión Chuguila, at the top of the steep downhill road leading out of town.

There is a direct bus leaving for the town of Quezaltenango (it will say Xela on the bus), in the northwestern highlands, between 9 and 10 am every morning, journey time 3 hrs; wait for it opposite the Pensión Chuguila. Do make enquiries to check that this bus is still running when you are here. If it is not, you can quickly connect with regular buses for Quezaltenango, Panajachel, or Guatemala City, by taking any bus heading for the Los Encuentros junction.

WHERE TO STAY
The choices for accommodation and eating out are rather limited, considering this is one of the country's most famous tourist attractions. On the other hand, there is something to be said for the fact that Chichi is not enslaved to tourism. Except during the festival, accommodation is easily found. The telephone code for Chichi is 0561.

EXPENSIVE
The **Hotel Santo Tomás**, tel 061/316, fax 306, is the newest hotel in town. Housed in a restored colonial mansion with a courtyard, rooms have modern facilities and open fireplaces, and there is also a good restaurant. Prices are wildly flexible so do negotiate. The **Maya Inn**, tel 176, is near the main square, on the street leading out past the museum. It is the longest established quality hotel, with a lovely atmosphere of colonial splendour frayed at the edges. Spacious rooms are ranged around a variety of courtyards, complete with macaws and tropical foliage.

MODERATE
Maya Lodge, tel 167, is right on the main square, housed in a colonial building, clean but basic. It is not really worth the price it asks. Much better value is **Pensión Chuguila**, tel 134, which has pleasant rooms around its own courtyard and patio restaurant. Secure parking available. Bar those of the top two hotels, the restaurant here is the best in town, which is still only acceptable rather than good. Officially singles are $35, doubles $40. Out of season they are as little as $8 and $9 respectively. **Pensión Girón** is friendly but the rooms, set around a large car park, are bare concrete with ancient beds.

INEXPENSIVE
Most popular of the cheapies is **El Salvador**, conspicuously painted blue and white and overlooking the main square from a nearby rise (down the hill, on the street leading away from the church, and then second right turn). Rooms are grubby, bathrooms dirty, but the place is convenient and friendly. Ask around for other cheap hostels.

EATING OUT
Restaurants are overpriced and low in quality, and you are almost better off eating the freshly cooked meals made in the market. Otherwise try **Txiquan Tinamil**, on the corner of 5 Avenida and 6 Calle; **El Torito**, in the same building as Pensión Girón; or **Tapena**, 5 Avenida, near Pensión Chuguila.

Around Chichicastenango
Just half an hour's bus journey away is the town of Santa Cruz del Quiché, which is the departmental capital of the Quiché region. If you want to head on towards the Ixil region,

you will have to come here for the morning buses. The town itself has little to offer the visitor, except a stroll around the large covered market. However, it is near the pre-Columbian capital of the Quiché tribe, **Utatlán**, which certainly merits a visit.

The site can be reached by following 10 Calle west out of town, where a dirt road makes for an enjoyable short walk past corn fields, and on to a small hilltop covered in pine trees. The atmosphere is wonderfully tranquil, and it can be hard to imagine the scene when this was a great city. Before the Spanish arrived, **K'umarcaah**, as the Quiché called it, was a relatively new capital, built for the elite, and incorporating many fine palaces and elaborate fortifications built of stone and covered in white plaster. Twenty-four noble families lived here, with a great many servants, craftsmen and other employees, as well as a large number of warriors who patrolled the city.

Yet Alvarado's forces still managed to burn the city to the ground. He came here in 1524, invited by the Quiché king, who planned to ambush the Spaniards. But Alvarado suspected foul play when he saw only men and soldiers in the city, so attacked immediately. The king's sons, Oxib Queh and Beleheb Tz'i were then publicly burned in the main plaza. There is not much left to see today, though the main plaza is obvious enough. For a clearer idea of what the city looked like, it's worth visiting the small museum on site, where there is a large model, as well as a helpful guardian to answer questions.

The most intriguing aspect of Utatlán is the couple of tunnels below the site. Perhaps they were a secret hideout for the Quiché? Or perhaps they were symbolic entrances to the Underworld, and places of worship? Bring a torch and ask for directions at the museum, since the path is steep and rather obscure. The first tunnel you reach is very narrow, its walls blackened by the Indian shamans, who regularly come here to worship, burning candles and incense. The lower tunnel is more spacious, but the hint of chants and ritual sacrifice teases the imagination, as the smell of burnt copal fills your nostrils.

The Ixil Triangle

Beauty cloaks Guatemala the way music hides screams.

R. Wright, *Time among the Maya*

This area, in the northern region of the department of Quiché, is wild in more than landscape. The entire northwest of Guatemala was and is the main battlefield on which the guerrilla and state forces have been locked in a deadly struggle since the seventies. Although the violence has waned since 1985, sporadic armed conflict does still occur. Some of the most horrific massacres the country has seen have taken place in the Ixil Triangle, defined by the area between the Indian villages of Nebaj, Chajul and San Juan Cotzal, in the northern region of the department of Quiché.

The perpetrators of these crimes come from both sides of the conflict; their victims are almost always the innocent Indian farmers, caught between two forces who alternately try to use them for their own ends, or justify their violence in the name of the indians. Many villages were razed to the ground, only to be rebuilt by the government as 'model villages'. Those inhabitants who survived the nightmare of the eighties are deeply scarred by it.

At the time of writing, the area around the Ixil Triangle is peaceful enough, and for those wishing to learn something of Guatemala's recent history, as well as hike in some of its most gorgeous countryside, there are few better places to visit. Remember, however, that peace in this particular region is deceptive, and violence could erupt again at any time. Understandably, amenities for visitors are very simple indeed. Before visiting the area, it would be a good idea to get advice from the **Casa Andinista** in Antigua. Mike Shawcross, the owner, runs an aid programme in the Ixil region, and he or his staff are well-placed to advise you.

Nebaj

The approaching dirt road takes you over a cold and windy pass, before twisting and turning down towards Nebaj, spread out on the floor of a wide highland valley ringed by steep mountains. It is the largest of the three villages of the Ixil Triangle, and the only one that can offer commercial accommodation for the steady trickle of anthropologists, aid workers and tourists. If you arrive on any day other than Thursday's or Sunday's market, you will find a very quiet sort of place, where the only noise is likely to come from a chicken scratching in the dirt road, or children chasing home-made hoops.

It is a beautiful, crumbling village, where most of the inhabitants still cook on log fires, the smoke rising picturesquely through red-tiled roofs. Nearby, the market is housed in an area of purpose-built wooden shacks, which fill to bursting on Sundays, with more vendors lining up their goods in the surrounding streets. The inhabitants of the surrounding mountainsides and valleys come to sell their vegetables, and small livestock, such as chickens, turkeys and the odd goat. It is then that you get the best chance to see the full glory of local dress, particularly the women's headdress, which is a wide band, folded into knots and bows as it is wrapped around the head, and ending in bushy pompoms, piled on top of their turbans, or hung loosely by the side of the head.

Apart from market day, the other attraction is the beautiful countryside, which offers many walking and hiking opportunities (always given that you have checked the area is safe at your time of travelling). A two-hour walk to the 'model village' of **Acul**, in a neighbouring valley, is highly recommended. The original village was razed to the ground by the army, and then rebuilt, gathering survivors in one easily-supervised location. The neat and orderly rows of houses belie the fact that they are difficult to live in, and the allocated kitchen gardens too small and too close together. People and animals live in unhealthy proximity, making diseases and infection a recurrent problem.

The track is wide and clear, the views reminiscent of the Swiss Alps, and when you get there, you can even purchase home-made cheese at the farm of an ancient Italian, nearing the 100 mark. His homestead is just outside the village; ask anyone for directions.

Another pleasant, less strenuous walk is to a nearby waterfall (*las cascadas*). Follow the road heading to Chajul, and turn left before crossing the bridge where a well-worn dirt track will take you to the falls. You know when you are close when the track takes a sharp bend left and goes steeply downhill before levelling out in front of the waterfall, which dramatically shoots off a ledge to pound the rocks about 15m below. If you are tempted to picnic in the field near the base of the falls, be warned that the mosquitoes will drive you crazy. If staying longer, you could also visit the markets of **San Juan Cotzal** (Saturdays) and **Chajul** (Fridays).

121

GETTING TO AND FROM NEBAJ

Two or three direct buses for Nebaj (5 hrs) leave daily from **Santa Cruz del Quiché**, between 8 and 10 am. The journey will be long, the ride bumpy, the seating space minimal, but the scenery will be superb.

Buses returning to Quiché leave daily at 1, 3, and 4 am, all of which pass through the town of **Sacapulas**, where you will have to change if you want to take back roads northeast (for **Cobán**) or northwest (for **Huehuetenango**). If you are heading for Cobán, you can catch a noon bus to Uspantán, where you will probably have to stay the night. (For more on this route see p. 00.) If you are heading for Huehuetenango, you will most likely have to wait until the next morning, for the 5 am bus, though you might make it in one go if you catch the 1 am bus from Nebaj.

WHERE TO STAY AND EAT

Undoubtedly the best and friendliest place to stay is **Las Tres Hermanas**, near the main square. (The three ancient sisters who run this place have recently become only two.) A handful of damp, windowless rooms line a pleasantly chaotic courtyard, where a central wash basin stands amongst rose bushes, fluttering washing lines and chicken droppings. Prices are just over US$1 each, and excellent cheap meals are provided on request. Another option is **Hotel Ixil**, on the main road coming into Nebaj, where the standard of rooms is just slightly better, but which does not have the same charm; singles from $4, doubles from $6.

Other than eating at Las Tres Hermanas, you have a choice of two *comedor*-style shacks on the main square, and during market day there are always snacks to be had there.

From Chichi to Quezaltenango

The drive west, from Chichi to Quezaltenango—or *Xela* (pronounced 'shella'), as it's commonly known—must rank as one of the most lovely in Guatemala. Returning to the Pan-American Highway at Los Encuentros, the road sweeps up and around forests and fields, giving you a brief glimpse of Lake Atitlán, lying deep in its rocky cushion of volcanoes and hillsides. An hour passes, while the landscape unfolds into cornfields and thatched hamlets, the occasional cluster of pines or eucalyptus trees swaying in the ever-present breeze.

A small Indian town along here is **Nahualá**, easily missed from the main road, and rarely visited by tourists, other than on 25 Nov, when the place turns into a terrific chaos of drunkenness and revelry for its annual fiesta. The men here wear distinctive thick, knee-length woollen skirts of brown and white checks, together with pink or red shirts. During the festival you will see them in their very best outfits, but another good time to visit is for the Sunday market. This is a staunchly traditional place, and one where the Indian cult of Maximón is alive and well. Sculpted out of one piece of wood, two feet high, the figure here is the least well known in Guatemala. Dressed in a white tunic he has the unusual feature of an open mouth with his tongue sticking out, and is kept in his own permanent chapel.

Beyond Nahualá, the road loops up and onto a sparse and windswept highland plateau, where the cold thin air allows only hardy grasses to grow, but the earth is a rich and fertile black. It's a refreshing contrast to the vibrant colours and sunbaked scene so far, providing a short spell of misty clouds and boggy fields before you descend back into the open sunshine of the Quezaltenango valley. It seems almost to be completely flat—a great open plain, ideal for agriculture, and therefore a region busy with towns and villages. At its heart lies Quezaltenango, Guatemala's second city and an excellent base for excursions to Indian markets and beautiful countryside.

It was here that Alvarado fought one of his most decisive battles against the Indians, and personally slew the great warrior king, Tecún Umán, in 1524. His headdress was made up of splendid quetzal feathers, and the conquistador was so impressed by its beauty, that he declared the present city must be named Quezaltenango—Quetzal Citadel.

Quezaltenango (Xela)

Xela is a rather extraordinary place, giving itself the airs of a city, when it is, in fact, undeniably provincial. Regardless of this inconvenient detail, the burghers have always considered themselves guardians of a notable cultural and economic centre and duly built themselves a Grecian temple (sadly derelict now), and a grand main square, surrounded by columns and steps, and a large cathedral. There is a large theatre as well, fronted by columns and its own small square. All the ingredients of a proper city are there, but somehow they look out of place, and most of the buildings are neglected, lending an air of pleasant melancholy. The weather can often add to this feeling, since Xela's altitude of 2335 m ensures a noticeable chill, and it frequently rains. In fact, the town really is an imitation of its former glory, since it was destroyed by an earthquake in 1902. Wandering along the streets around the main square, you have a chance to see great colonial mansions, unrestored or partially rebuilt, and imagine how they might once have looked.

The actual sights of Xela can easily be seen in one day, and consist of the cathedral and municipal museum on the main square, the outrageously tasteless San Nicolás Church, and the local zoo. Of these, the church is the most diverting: it is a Gothic-style building reminiscent of an overdressed Christmas cake, all pinks, blues, silver and white. The zoo is decidedly unpleasant, as you look at desperately bored felines pacing around in their own droppings. To get to either, take a bus heading for the terminal via San Nicolás, the zoo being just beyond the dilapidated temple that stands by the edge of the market.

One advantage of the pretension to grandeur here is that there are a number of good restaurants, most notably Chinese, and the hotels are some of the best value for money in the country. Local entertainment is thin on the ground, though there are three cinemas and the theatre. The most popular films are either violent or pornographic, but you do stand a good chance of seeing an American movie with Spanish subtitles at the cinema next to the theatre. These last two venues are worth a look in themselves; the buildings are slightly bedraggled but still splendid. In all, Xela is a good place to use as a base for exploring the surrounding region, which has a great deal to offer, and you can easily spend a whole week here, taking a different trip each day. It is also an excellent place to learn Spanish, since there are few tourists and thus plenty of opportunities to use your new language.

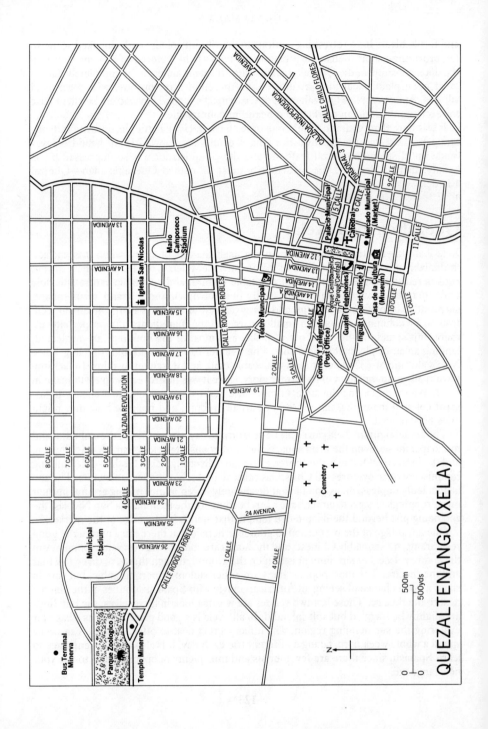

QUEZALTENANGO (XELA)

Bus Terminal Minerva
Parque Zoológico
Templo Minerva

Municipal Stadium

8 CALLE
7 CALLE
6 CALLE
5 CALLE
4 CALLE
3 CALLE
2 CALLE
1 CALLE

CALZADA REVOLUCION

CALLE RODOLFO ROBLES

13 AVENIDA
14 AVENIDA
15 AVENIDA
16 AVENIDA
17 AVENIDA
18 AVENIDA
19 AVENIDA
20 AVENIDA
21 AVENIDA
23 AVENIDA
24 AVENIDA
25 AVENIDA
26 AVENIDA

Iglesia San Nicolas

Mario Camposeco Stadium

Teatro Municipal

CALLE RODOLFO ROBLES

19 AVENIDA

2 CALLE
3 CALLE
4 CALLE

Cemetery

1 CALLE
4 CALLE

24 AVENIDA

Correos Y Telegrafos (Post Office)

12 AVENIDA
14 AVENIDA
14 AVENIDA A
14 AVENIDA A

Parque Centroamérica (Parque Central)
Guatel (Telephones)
Inguat (Tourist Office)
Casa de la Cultura (Museum)

Palacio Municipal
Catedral
Mercado Municipal (Market)

15 CALLE
6 CALLE
9 CALLE
10 CALLE
11 CALLE

DIAGONAL 3

AVENIDA
CALZADA INDEPENDENCIA
CALLE CIRILO FLORES

N

0   500m
0   500yds

GETTING TO AND FROM XELA

By Bus

From Guatemala City, there are fast and regular Pullmans, the best of which are from the **Galgos** company (see p. 78), and the journey takes around 4 hours. The sign in the bus window will always use the abbreviation Xela. Coming from Antigua, Panajachel or Chichi, all you need to do is get to the nearest junction with the Pan-American Highway, and wait for the relevant bus to pass by. As always, your best chance of catching a bus like this is in the morning and early afternoon.

Arriving at the bus terminal on the edge of town, you can find regular municipal buses heading for the centre if you walk through the market next to the terminal, and cross the main road for the bus stop. The buses are an easily recognizable yellow, and you should ask for one going to the Parque Central.

As the capital of the Western Highlands, Xela is a major transport centre, with buses arriving and leaving for almost all corners of the Highlands, as well as for the Mexican border and down to the Pacific Coast.

The local **Galgos** office (for Guatemala City, and any of the main junctions along the way) is at Calle Rodolfo Robles 17–43, which is also where their buses arrive and leave town. This is within easy walking distance of the main square. **Líneas Américas** have their office on Calzada Independencia, between 5 and 6 Calle, which is the main road coming into town from the Cuatro Caminos junction. **Rutas Lima** are on the same road, near 4 Calle.

If all buses are full or you don't mind the chicken buses, then just head for the main bus terminal, on the edge of town, where regular buses leave from dawn until late afternoon. On the rare occasion when no bus is heading direct to Guatemala City (or Huehuetenango, if you're heading north), take any bus to the Cuatro Caminos junction, outside town, and wait there.

The main **Minerva bus terminal** is the place to wait for regular buses to Huehuetenango (Huehue $2\frac{1}{2}$ hrs) and San Marcos (2 hrs), where you can also change buses for the Mexican border posts of La Mesilla and Talismán respectively. There are frequent buses to regional destinations such as San Francisco el Alto (El Alto, 1 hr), Momostenango (Momo, 2 hrs), and Totonicapán (Toto, 30 min); and also to the Pacific towns of Mazatenango (Masate, $1\frac{1}{2}$ hrs), Retalhuleu (Reu, $1\frac{1}{2}$ hrs), and Coatepeque (Coa, $1\frac{1}{2}$ hrs). If you are heading for the Mexican border town of Talismán, it is quickest to take a bus to Retalhuleu, or any of the large towns on the Pacific Highway, and change there.

Apart from the main bus terminal, there is also a small one, round the back of the cathedral, where you can catch buses to Totonicapán and San Francisco el Alto. Just beyond, by the Shell station, buses leave for Zunil and Almolonga.

GETTING AROUND XELA

In spite of being the country's second largest city, Xela has the proportions of a small and compact town, and walking from the bus terminal to the central park only takes half an hour, though the dusty main road is hardly inviting. Everything you will need or want to see is closely ranged around the main square, so the only time you will need the bus is to travel between the centre and the bus terminal.

TOURIST INFORMATION

The **INGUAT** tourist office is on the south side of the main square in Xela (Mon–Fri, 9–noon and 2.30–5). The helpful and friendly staff can offer information on buses and excursions to the surrounding area, in particular hiking on the nearby Santa María volcano.

WHERE TO STAY

EXPENSIVE

Pensión Bonifaz, 4 Calle 10–50, tel (061) 4241 and 2959. Opened in the 1930s, its refined atmosphere dates from that time also, the furnishings unchanged. It is very quiet, with a good restaurant and café.

MODERATE

Los Alpes, on the road past the Minerva bus terminal, towards San Martín Sacatepéquez (tel 6327) is only worth staying at if you have your own transport. **Modelo**, 14 Avenida A 2–31, tel 2529, is the best medium-priced hotel, with a very good restaurant, centrally located. **Hotel Centro Americana**, on the corner of 14 Avenida and Minerva Boulevard, tel 4901, looks a bit grubby on the outside, but rooms are of a good standard. Secure parking is available.

INEXPENSIVE

Hotel Río Azul, 2 Calle 12–15, located near the main square, is a new hotel with clean, bright rooms and parking facilities. The same prices are to be found at **Pensión Andina**, 8 Avenida 6–7, tel 4012.

Best of the budget places is **Casa Kaehler**, 13 Avenida 3–33, tel 2091, which is very close to the main square and most of the best restaurants. It also really does have hot water—important in this cold town. The only drawback is the paper-thin walls. **Radar 99**, next door, is dirty and very basic. **Posada Belén**, 15 Avenida, is a new guest house on the top floor of a shopping centre, right by the city centre market. There are many more cheap places to stay, so just ask around if the above are full.

EATING AND DRINKING OUT

There are some good places to eat and reasonable spots to drink, though they generally close down by 10.

A favourite Chinese restaurant is the **Shanghai**, just off the main square, on 4 Calle, where you can also eat international and the odd Guatemalan dishes—excellent value. Pizzas are another specialty in Xela, and the best two places to eat them are: **Pizza Ricca**, 14 Avenida, and **Don Benito's**, on the corner of Calzada de la Revolución and 15 Avenida. For steaks try **La Rueda**, next to the market near the Minerva temple. The restaurant of the **Modelo** hotel serves good meals in a quietly refined atmosphere, though not cheap. The same can be said for the **Hotel Bonifaz** restaurant. Finally, if you prefer vegetarian food, try the **El Señor Sol**, 9 Avenida 6–12.

For breakfast, your best bet is one of the café-restaurants along 14 Avenida, one of the most popular being in the **Gran Hotel Americano** (accommodation not recommended, however). Another good place is the **Deli Crepe**, further up the road. If you feel like being civilized and taking afternoon tea, there's hardly a better place than the **Hotel Bonifaz**, which serves great cakes and reasonable coffee too. Rather a long way out, but very good, is the Swiss **Café Berna**, on Calle Rodolfo Robles 23, next to the private hospital.

ENTERTAINMENT AND NIGHTLIFE

Don Rodrigo's Taberna, on 14 Avenida, is the best bar in town, which isn't saying much, but it is a friendly little place. Other than that, you have a choice of small drinking holes near the main square and around the central market at the far end of 15 Avenida.

The best central **cinema** is on 14 Avenida A, next to the municipal theatre. There is also a modern cinema, in the shopping mall on the corner of Calzada Revolución and 24 Avenida, leading out to the Minerva bus terminal.

USEFUL INFORMATION

Money Matters
There are four banks to choose from on the main square.

Post Office and Telecommunications
The post office is on the corner of 15 Avenida and 4 Calle, Zona 1. The GUATEL office is on 15 Avenida A and 4 Calle (opposite the post office).

Language Schools
One of the best schools anywhere in Guatemala is the **Proyecto Lingüístico Quezalteco de Español**, 5 Calle 2–40, Zona 1, tel (061) 8792. One-to-one teaching as well as films and discussions on anything from local politics to Guatemalan culture costs about $100 per week, living with a family (full board).

Laundry
Minimax laundry is on 14 Avenida, Zona 1.

Mexican Consulate
This is in the Hotel Bonifaz, just off the main square, 4 Calle 10–50 (weekdays, 8–noon).

Volcanoes
The beautiful **Volcán Santa María** is visible from most parts of town. It can be climbed in about five very tough hours. If you are already fit, then this is a rewarding expedition, with terrific views of the Guatemalan string of volcanoes (the active Santiaguito just next to you), as well as the surrounding valleys and lush Pacific foothills. Topographic maps for the climb are best bought in the **Casa Andinista**, Antigua. Check with the local tourist office for the latest security report and how to hire a guide, if you would prefer one; the ascent is marked, but the path isn't always easy to follow. To reach the beginning of the trail, catch a bus from 17 Avenida and 1 Calle, to **Llanos del Pinal**, and ask the

driver to drop you at the relevant crossroads. Follow the dirt road until you see painted signs leading to a trail off to the left.

Excursions from Xela

Zunil and Fuentes Georginas
One of the friendliest markets you will encounter is in the village of **Zunil**, just 20 minutes from the city. This is a small Indian settlement spread around a disproportionately large white church, situated in a lovely valley. The market sells mainly vegetables, though there is a cooperative behind the church which sells the unique Zunil textiles. These do not seem to be sold in any of the country's other markets. In fact, the main pleasure of visiting the Monday market is in seeing the local women in their brilliantly pink, purple and puce clothing sitting behind their freshly harvested goods, quietly chatting to one another.

While you are here, you should also have a look in the great Spanish church, its dark interior hiding an unusually precious **silver altar**. The annual fiesta is on 25 November, which is certainly worth visiting if you are in the area; and another special occasion is Palm Sunday. To reach Zunil, catch a bus from the Shell station, beyond the cathedral bus terminal. The last bus back to Xela leaves between 5 and 6 pm.

On the hillside, 8 km above Zunil, are the **Fuentes Georginas** (closed Mondays)— undoubtedly the best hot spring and pool in the country. To get there, you can either walk uphill for two or three hours, or hire a pick-up in the village, which will take you for $4. The mountain is covered in thick tropical foliage, an indication that you are not far from the steamy Pacific. In a fern-clad niche in the mountain a few small bungalows are perched on a ridge with two steaming pools, and a bar-restaurant.

There is a small entrance fee if you do not plan to stay the night, but you'll certainly be tempted by one of the bungalow rooms, each with their own fireplace, bathtub, and barbecue outside. Plenty of firewood is provided to keep you warm all night, as there is a problem with the damp up here. It is a good idea to bring firelighters, sold in any of the markets and, just in case, extra blankets. The price is $10 per night, singles pay $7.

If you don't wish to go all the way to the Fuentes Georginas, you could visit the hot baths in the village of **Almolonga**, on the way to Zunil. These are, however, very much public bathhouses and only worth visiting if you are yearning for a hot soak, rather than a romantic swim.

Lake Chicabal
This small lake, tucked inside the cone of an extinct volcano, is an ideal place for a picnic. The nearest village to the lake is San Martín Sacatepéquez, also known as San Martín Chile Verde, on one of the roads leading to the Pacific. You can reach it by taking any bus from the Minerva bus terminal heading for Coatepeque via this route (check this, as there are others), and the journey takes about 45 minutes. The last returning bus passes by at around 5.15 pm, though if you're lucky there may be one at around 7 pm.

The village of San Martín is an unusual place, since the inhabitants speak a rare Mam dialect that isolates them from the rest of the Indians in this region. Traditional life is strong in this closed community, and the men wear a distinctive white, knee-length tunic, held by a red sash. The nearby lake is considered a holy place, and on 2 and 3 May, shamans gather to perform sacred ceremonies by the water's edge. It is advisable to keep a low profile, particularly at this time, and best not to offend by swimming in the lake if any local people are present.

The walk begins via a small path (ask directions), a little way to the right of the church, and leads gently up and past the last homesteads of the village. Do not turn off until you reach a small concrete bridge, where you take a right, following the track uphill for some time. Your path will take you through the forest and across a small savannah, and then up through forest again, until it ends on a wide dirt track. Take a left and follow the large trail, ignoring smaller ones leaving it, and after a couple of kilometres, you will head over the last hill and into the cone itself, a steep and sandy path leading through dense vegetation to the lakeshore. Often a milky cloud sits low on the crater and you do not see the water until you are virtually in it.

It should only take you about one and a half hours to reach the lake, but it can feel a lot longer as it's mostly uphill. There are not many people up this way, but if you do meet someone, it is worth checking that you are on the right path. Sitting in this cool and beautiful place, the soothing silence all around, it is easy to understand why the Indians chose it as a place of worship.

Some Local Markets

The short drive to the highland town of **Totonicapán** takes you swiftly up to Cuatro Caminos, and the edge of the great plateau. Leaving the dust and commercial straggle behind, the bus enters a beautiful avenue of pines and conifers, the road rising gradually to the town itself, tucked at the far end of a dead-end valley, at a cool 2500m, surrounded by tree-covered hills and craggy, mountainous outcrops on all sides.

The town is an important centre of weaving and pottery, and the large market held on Tuesday and Saturday is filled to bursting with all shapes and sizes of the distinctive orange-glazed pottery. Unfortunately, it is very brittle, so it is unlikely that you will want to carry it home. However, you may be tempted by some of the weaving (though much of it is machine-made) to be found on the second floor of the main market building. There is also fine woodwork, basketry and ropes. The annual fiesta is held 26–30 September.

About an hour's drive from Xela, **San Francisco el Alto** (2640 m) is a small market town, perched on a ledge overlooking the Quezaltenango valley. On the way, the bus crosses a river at the village of San Cristóbal de Totonicapán, remarkable for the huge colonial church, which is famed for its precious altars and fine silver. Market day here is Sunday, and since this is not an obvious place to visit, you may find a good bargain. Continuing on, the road climbs steeply to the windswept San Francisco el Alto, and on Fridays the place is jammed with traders from all over the Highlands, come to sell anything from textiles, crafts, food produce, or animals. One of the largest live-animal markets in Guatemala, the chaotic scenes of pigs being wrestled by men checking their teeth are quite something, though the way the animals are treated is enough to turn you into a vegetarian, if you are not one already.

There is a new guest house here, the **Los Altos** (at the top end of the town), which is clean and friendly, and a good place to stop over if you will be visiting Momostenango market, two days later. The price is just over US$1 per person, and secure parking is available.

The **Momostenango** market is held on Wednesdays and Sundays (main day), so it is not possible to combine it with the one just described. However, it is certainly worth your time to make the two-hour journey to this special Indian village.

After San Francisco el Alto, the road becomes a wide dirt track, bumping the bus slowly up through a pine forest, and down into a remote highland valley that must have taken many days to reach before the road was made. The scenery along the way is beautiful, and it is not surprising to discover that this region is full of sacred hilltops and altars. Momostenango means just that: the place of many altars, and it was here that the American translator of the Maya bible, Dennis Tedlock, spent time as an apprentice daykeeper. Traditions of Maya faith are practised here, more than in many other parts, as it is an important centre for daykeepers, who still keep time by the Maya calendar. They ensure adherence to its annual festivals, in particular the Maya New Year, celebrated every 260 days. To discover when these festivals might be is very difficult, and even if you turned up by chance, you would probably not be welcome—these are secret celebrations, jealously guarded against outsiders, who have so often sought to destroy them. (To learn more about the Maya Calender, see Tedlock's *Popol Vuh*, and Michael Coe's *The Maya*.) The church here is similar in atmosphere to the one in Chichi, mixing pagan and Catholic images and worship, and is the best place to take in the religious significance of this town.

In the market you will see some of the best and cheapest examples of the distinctive woollen blankets that are sold all over the country. Made only here, the blankets come in all shapes and sizes, some natural creams and browns, some interwoven with rich dyes of red, blue and green, with traditional Maya images on them. There are two varieties: thick, woven rugs, most suitable as wall hangings; and the long-haired, soft blankets, which make beautiful bedspreads.

There are plenty of beautiful walks you can take in the surrounding area, and there is very simple accommodation available if you wish to stay. Try either **Hospedaje Paclom** or **Hospedaje Roxane**, but neither has much to recommend it.

Towards the Pacific

Even if you have no intention of going to the Pacific Lowlands, you should consider taking any Mazatenango bus as far as **San Felipe**. The reason is not so much this dilapidated roadside town, but the journey getting there. The drive is spectacular, and you get a real sense of climate being tied to altitude as you travel from Xela's early morning chill down to the hot and humid Pacific coast. As the road plunges ever downwards, the vegetation becomes thicker and greener, and the heat and humidity increase. Every now and then, the view stretches out towards the Pacific, but all you will see is a hazy horizon, the quivering air obscuring the ocean. Behind you tower the Guatemalan Highlands, and looking north and south, you may still see the volcanic cones, rising above all.

San Felipe is the first tropically hot settlement you come to, and although still high up, the atmosphere already belongs to the Pacific. Peeling wooden shutters protect its inhabitants from the worst of the heat, and the place has a dusty, neglected character. There's not really any reason to continue to the Pacific Highway, unless you want to sweat it out in the commercial hubbub of **Mazatenango**, or any of the other dusty towns along there. Plenty of buses pass for Quezaltenango, so you should have no trouble returning.

Huehuetenango and the Cuchumatanes Mountains

Huehuetenango is the last major town before you reach the Mexican border post of La Mesilla, and the focal point for the northern Highlands. There is little to detain you for more than a day, but it is a stepping stone for connections into the remote Cuchumatanes Mountains, the highest range in Central America, offering superb scenery and remote Indian and *ladino* villages. The most famous Indian village is Todos Santos, whose inhabitants have been beautifully portrayed in a black and white photographic book called *Los Todos Santeros* by Hans Namuth. For hiking and walking, there are few places to rival this region, and if you have the time and energy to come here, you will encounter a world quite different from the Western Highlands—wilder and more dramatic.

Huehuetenango

Huehuetenango, or Huehue, as most refer to it, is a small but bustling provincial town with an economy centred on agriculture and some mining. The main square, just five minutes from the busy local market around 1 Avenida, is the most attractive part of town. A colonnaded walkway offers a short stroll in front of the municipal building, while almost opposite, a grand church promises more than its interior rewards. In the middle of the square a neglected relief map of the Cuchumatanes gives you a vague idea of the rugged mountains though most of the flags marking settlements have disappeared.

The town is close to one of the Highlands' more important archaeological sites: **Zaculeu**, ancient capital of the Mam people, located 5 km away—take a minibus from outside the **Hotel Maya** (3 Avenida). For some reason all the surfaces were smoothed over with white plaster in the late 1940s, leaving you with a sense of climbing over giant building blocks rather than the remains of Maya temples. The view of the Cuchumatanes and surrounding countryside is some consolation for this crass restoration.

Pedro de Alvarado's brother, Gonzalo, came here to wreak horrible revenge for the plot to ambush the Spanish in Utatlán, said to have been suggested by the Mam leader, Kaibil Balam. Warned of the approach of over two thousand Spanish troops, the Indians barricaded themselves inside Zaculeu. Two inconclusive battles were fought and, in the end, the Mam were beaten by a bitter six-week siege that almost brought both sides to starvation. (It is an outrageous irony that the infamous counterinsurgency troops—well documented as the perpetrators of the country's worst horrors—are named Kaibiles, after the Indian leader.)

USEFUL INFORMATION

There is no tourist office here, but hotel staff are sometimes a good source of information. The **post office** and **GUATEL** office are next to each other on 2 Calle, opposite the Hotel Mary. **Banks** can be found by the main square. **Mexican visas** or **tourist cards** can be bought from the Honorary Consul at the **Farmacia del Cid**, on 5 Avenida and 4 Calle. If you are continuing north, this is the last **laundry** (8 Avenida 2–39). The telephone code for Huehue is 0641.

GETTING TO AND FROM HUEHUE

From Guatemala City, you face a long, 6-hr bus drive that takes you the length of the Western Highlands, so it is worth booking a seat on a Pullman bus (see p. 78 for the address in the capital). Returning in this direction, you will find the **Los Halcones** office at 7 Avenida 3–62 (buses at 7 am and 2 pm); alternatively try **Rápidos Zaculeu,** on 3 Avenida 5–25 (buses at 6 am and 3 pm).

From Xela, there are frequent direct buses from the Minerva terminal; or head to the Cuatro Caminos junction and connect there. Coming from anywhere else in the Highlands, you will easily connect from any main junction along the Pan-American Highway.

Leaving Huehuetenango, you will find most buses on 1 Avenida by the market: for example to Sacapulas (2 hrs) heading east; Soloma (4 hrs), high in the Cuchumatanes; and La Mesilla (2 hrs) on the Mexican border, for which there are hourly buses departing until 4 pm. For Sacapulas and Soloma there are only one or two buses, late in the morning, so best check the day before, and preferably buy your ticket then as well. Unlike elsewhere, seat tickets are sold in advance for the local buses, and you may have trouble getting on unless you buy your ticket a few hours before departure.

For the spectacular back road that connects the Western Highlands with the eastern Verapaz range, either catch a direct bus to Sacapulas, or a minibus to Aguacatán, and change there. You will need an early start to make the noon bus from Sacapulas to Uspantán, which is the furthest you are likely to get in one day, and the only place which offers basic accommodation. The bus for Cobán leaves at the antisocial hour of 2.30 am, so take your alarm clock. Alternatively, try hitchhiking on one of the trucks that regularly use the route. The whole point of this adventurous journey is enjoying the scenery and the gut-wrenching road, so avoid travelling at night.

Sacapulas is also where you can pick up buses for Nebaj, coming from Quiché. If you reach Sacapulas by noon, you should have a good chance of catching one of the Nebaj buses. Equally, you can head down south from here, the buses for Quiché passing at dawn.

WHERE TO STAY

INEXPENSIVE

The best hotel in town is the **Hotel Zaculeu,** on 5 Avenida 1–14, tel 068, which is a colonial house with a pleasantly overgrown courtyard. **Hotel Mary,** 2 Calle 3–52, tel 569, is a concrete three-storey building, noisy, but rooms are clean and the water hot. **Gran Hotel Shinula,** on the busy 4 Calle, has the same prices as Hotel Mary, but is worse value for money.

Pensión Astoria, 4 Avenida 1–45, tel 197, is the best guest house, with clean rooms and restaurant attached. **Hotel Central,** 5 Avenida 1–33, is the favourite cheapie, with double rooms only. There is also a restaurant attached. Other, horrible, accommodation is available, but since tourist numbers are low, you should have no trouble finding a place to stay among the above.

EATING OUT

Other than in the hotel restaurants, your choices are limited here. A number of restaurants are along 2 Calle, off the main square: **Ebony,** right by the square, and **Mini Ebony** further on, sell cheap snacks and good fruit juices. A popular pizzeria is **Pizza Hogareña** on 6 Avenida, between 4 and 5 Calle; under the same management is **Rincón Hogareño,** a block further down the street, a *comedor*-style restaurant, good but no pizzas (closed on Mondays). Another place worth trying is the **Café Jardín**, on the corner of 6 Avenida and 4 Calle.

The Cuchumatanes Mountains

Like the remote Ixil Triangle, this distant region of high mountains and desolate plateaus was the stage for unspeakable atrocities during the eighties. Many people, both guerrilla and Indian peasant, fled to its furthest reaches and on into Mexico to live in miserable refugee camps. The remaining Indian men were press-ganged into civil defence patrols by the army. Often armed only with machetes or ancient rifles with hardly any bullets, they were supposed to guard their villages and the roads against insurgents. You will still see members of these patrols now, though local people will tell you that all is *tranquilo*, and the bad times over.

In the early mornings, the earth is white with frost. The altitude hovers around 3000 m, and in many ways the landscape recalls the Andes: trees are short and wind-bent, the sparse grassland strewn with crusty boulders and rocks, and many dwellings are no more than wooden huts thatched with rough grasses. Yet it is still beautiful, and it is hard to reconcile knowledge of the recent nightmarish past with the magnificent landscape all around.

There is only one major dirt road that threads its way past Indian and *ladino* towns and villages to Barillas, a frontier town to Mexico and the mainly uninhabited jungle. There is no road to the border or onwards, so there is little reason to travel this far. The furthest Indian village, of interest only during its market days on Thursdays and Sundays, is **San Mateo Ixtatán**. It takes at least six, very rough, hours by bus, and once there you will find accommodation with straw matresses and very simple food. In your own four-wheel drive, with provisions and camping equipment, you could have a very adventurous time getting here, and plenty of chances to explore far from the beaten track. Without your own transport, the journey as far as **Soloma** will be plenty adventurous, and the scenery is spectacular.

The Journey to Soloma

Leaving Huehuetenango, the bus takes you past the small town of Chiantla, in colonial times a rich silver-mining town, whose church holds one of the country's most precious altars to the Virgin. Protected in glass casing, she is dressed in priceless silver and adornments, which pilgrims come to visit from all over the country.

Once past the last checkpoint, you could ask to continue the journey perched on the roof with the luggage, the most exciting place from which to enjoy the scenery to come. (The driver will think you are mad, but it is definitely worth it.) The dusty road turns back and forth, winding up into the mountains, eventually coming out onto a highland plateau, where the distinctive landscape of the Cuchumatanes first comes into its own. The houses are raggedy wooden or adobe, with a variety of roofs made either of tiles, grass, or wood shingles. Sheep graze in the rocky fields, and if it wasn't for the bus thundering by, all you would hear is the occasional bird, hovering over the stunted trees.

A knobbly pass leads to a steep track descending around mountainous creases and down into a valley containing several small villages, until you eventually reach Soloma, after four hours of having your bones crunched by the bumpy ride. The town is populated mostly by *ladinos*, but you will see a few Indian women, who wear long, white *huipiles* that look rather like nighties. There really isn't anything to do here, except spend half the night in the basic **Hospedaje Central**, by the market square (US$1 each), and get the 4 or 5 am bus back towards Huehuetenango. The adventure is undoubtedly exhausting, but the scenery is worth the aching bones and little sleep. On the return, you can get off at the Paquix junction (referred to as *cruce*), and wait for transport heading to the famous Indian village of **Todos Santos**. On any day other than Sunday, you should have a good chance of flagging down a vehicle. If not, you can always catch something heading back to Huehuetenango until around 3 pm.

Todos Santos

The steep helter-skelter ride down into the valley of Todos Santos is only suitable for tough four-wheel-drive vehicles and very difficult for motorbikes. The sheer mountain-sides are terraced with agricultural fields, in between what is left of the pine forest, and deep gashes of eroded ground bear witness to a serious problem. But the people here need the land for food and the wood for cooking and house-building, and it is the government who should be helping with reafforestation programmes.

Todos Santos is a large Indian village, the heartland of the Mam people. The villagers wear one of the most distinctive traditional costumes to be seen. The men are as glamorous as the women, wearing jolly red and white striped trousers held up by a handwoven belt, ending in bobbles. Their shirts of thin white and blue stripes are embroidered around the neck and cuffs with intricate designs in pink, red, purple and blue. They also wear a kind of mini straw bowler, perched above the ears.

The women wear gorgeous *huipiles* made of red or purple cloth, embroidered with complicated designs in the same fashion as the men's shirts. Visitors come from all over to buy them in the local co-op shop, which helps the community in the face of increased land shortage. Prices are rightly high, but still cheaper than in any of the more accessible markets. The crochet bags, used mainly by the men, are also made by them. You see them standing in doorways, chatting, while their hands move with expert speed without so much as a glance at what they're doing. Actual market days are on Wednesday and Saturday.

The location of the village is on a small promontory, overlooking the continuing valley below, so the shingled houses are tightly packed and the narrow streets curl steeply up and around the main square, hemmed in by steep hillsides. The atmosphere is peaceful and friendly, and while there is nothing much to do here, the surrounding countryside offers some beautiful walks.

The only times the village bursts into action are during Easter Week, and the more famous All Saints' festival on 1 November, when the men stage death-defying horse races. Bravado dictates that a rider must not just race his horse but drink great swigs of alcohol as well, with often painful results. During Easter, the most interesting day to be here is Easter Friday, when Romans, dressed in what look like pink and yellow bin liners, and cardboard helmets, run about the streets searching for Jesus. There is much shouting and laughing as the soldiers are pursued by hordes of excited children, until eventually Christ is led away to the Calvario church—fake beard, rosy cheeks and long white gown. One of the strangest sights of all is a resident family of American missionaries, who seem to think they blend in by wearing Indian costume.

GETTING TO TODOS SANTOS
Buses from Huehuetenango leave from 1 Avenida, by the former Pensión San Jorge, at around 11 am. Get there early if you want to be sure of getting on. Alternatively, take any bus heading into the Cuchumatanes, and get off at the Paquix junction, where you might be lucky enough to hitch a lift. Be warned, however, that this is the 'middle of nowhere', and many hours can pass without a vehicle in sight. You could always walk—but from the junction it would be a tough full-day's hike, though mostly downhill.

Buses leave Todos Santos at the painful hours of 3 and 5 am, and failing that, you just have to try your luck with the occasional private vehicle that may be leaving for Huehuetenango. During Easter Week, there are officially no buses at all from Thursday to Sunday.

WHERE TO STAY AND EAT
The better of two very simple places is **La Paz** on the main street. About US$1 per person, the *pensión* (guest house) is basic but friendly, and the best rooms have a balcony looking out over the street. Second choice is **Las Olguitas** (same price), which is also a *comedor*, but the rooms are in a wooden contraption above the kitchen, and the place is not only loud, but very dirty too.

First choice for meals of beans, eggs and tortillas is the *comedor* **Katy** (7 am–8 pm), on the hill above the main square, beyond the small park. You might get bored with the same food three times a day, but it is certainly preferable to the filthy tables at Las Olguitas, and the meals there are made up of the same ingredients anyway. Your best chance of alternative meals is on market days, when a few kitchens operate inside the market building.

Walks Around Todos Santos

Towards San Juan Atitán (2 hrs)
The path leading up the hill past the *comedor* **Katy** will take you up a steep trail, by an open-air shrine hiding among a small outcrop of conifers. There are a couple of crosses here, one of which is of ancient wood and not a Christian cross at all, but a Mam cross signifying Holy Earth. Like Momostenango and Chichicastenango, this is a place where the Maya daykeepers still practise their rites, and in spite of everything in the recent past, tradition is as strong as ever. Some grassy mounds nearby testify to the remains of the small Maya site, **Tojcunanchén**.

From here the dirt track widens and takes you to a pass, where the view across two valleys invites you to take a rest and enjoy the beauty all around. Larks and other birds buzz by, and the fecund fields are riddled with little paths where women patter swiftly past on tough bare feet, usually followed by a gaggle of children and the odd duck. You can either turn back here or continue for another two hours of exhausting walking to the village of San Juan Atitán (Thursday market). Here the men wear a quite different dress from their neighbours: white linen trousers, covered by a brown, woollen tunic, and a red belt around the waist. There is nowhere to stay in San Juan so you need your own camping equipment and provisions. This makes a very rewarding short hike, returning the next day.

Down the Todos Santos Valley (3 hrs)

Following the dirt road out of the village, past the dentist's, you come to a large path leading off to the right, once you have passed the last straggle of houses. Follow this downhill for a while, and you will find yourself walking parallel to the deep ravine that hides a busy river at its base. Past cactuses and the occasional shepherd with his flock, this is a great way to see the nearby countryside and meet the local farmers too. Eventually, you descend to cross the river, and over three more bridges before a dirt track takes you up to the other side of the valley, and a road leading back to Todos Santos. On this side you will pass small homesteads, some of which have roadside stands selling warm sodas, which are very welcome.

THE PACIFIC COAST

Our driver slowed down at last. We were in a street of decrepit shanties; there were children in the dust and wandering pigs. Then, suddenly, vast and blank under a glaring white sky, the Pacific.

Aldous Huxley, *Beyond the Mexique Bay*

From Mexico to El Salvador some 250 km of the Pacific coastal plain lies leadenly flat; with endless dreary plantations cut by potholed excuses for roads, which finally end on grey banks of sand that sink into the sea. You will not find the white beaches of tropical brochures—the sand here is black and volcanic. Nor are there picturesque towns and exotic palm-fringed villages. The towns along the Pacific Highway are intolerably sweaty and choking with pollution and commerce. The villages are some of the most depressing anywhere, populated by underpaid plantation workers. This is a region entirely given over to the country's rich tropical farming, which accounts for the most part of Guatemala's wealth, but especially for that of the landowners, who buzz down from the capital in their private planes, rarely staying overnight to brave the heat and bugs.

Having said this, the Pacific coast does hide some surprises, and although the area is in no way developed for tourism, lacking all facilities in most places, the adventurous traveller will think this an advantage. What the beaches lack in tropical glamour they make up for with their sheer size: one giant sand dune stretching endless and empty into the horizon. The bedraggled fishing villages, with their forlorn streets and neglected huts have a melancholy attraction, and the people are more open, curious to discover what on earth you're doing here. Most are *ladino*, with some migrant Indian labourers, and the markets and festivals are characterized by Spanish heritage rather than Indian.

After the touristic bustle of the Western Highlands, you might find silent days swinging in a hammock just what you want: by day you can watch lizards and iguanas basking in the sun; by night, you will see an explosion of insects around any light and crowds of toads flashing their tongues to catch them. If you would like to see what the coast looked like before it was drained and deforested for agriculture, the **Monterrico Nature Reserve** is the only place where you will find the original mangrove swamps and some of the attendant wildlife. You can see the unique archaeological remains of the coastal civilizations near Santa Lucía Cotzumalguapa. Or you might prefer the energetic sleaze of Guatemala's second port, Puerto San José, where weekend crowds from the capital regularly cause a riot of music and streetlife.

The Pacific Highway actually runs parallel to the coast, 50 km inland, along the foothills of the Highlands; and although you cannot see the sea, it is the country's best and fastest road, and travel is easy as long as you stay on it. Off the Highway, the roads are abysmal, the buses excruciatingly slow and hot. The only exceptions to this rule are the main roads leading to Quezaltenango (from Retalhuleu, Coatepeque or Mazatenango), and to the ports of Champerico and Puerto San José.

The best time to visit the Pacific is during the dry season, normally from October to April. April to July are the hottest months, and at this time the heat and humidity can reduce even the most energetic to brain-dead panting. At any time of year, mosquito repellent is essential, and during the rainy season you should consider taking malaria pills. Protection from the sun is always vital.

Along the Pacific Highway

Connecting with Guatemala City, the Pacific Highway is a major commercial artery. Vast plantations truck out their produce, such as coffee (from the foothills rising off the plain), sugar cane, cotton, rubber, and much more. The towns along here exist almost exclusively on the commerce connected with these primary products, and their markets are sweet with pineapples, papayas, bananas in all shapes and sizes, coconuts, oranges, and plenty besides. The bus terminals are hectic with traders from all over the country, and the black exhaust fumes sit chokingly low in the heat. None of the towns have anything to detain the visitor, and most likely you will see them from a bus window, on your way to somewhere else. You may even pass by in the rattling train, with stations in Escuintla, Santa Lucía Cotzumalguapa, Cocales, Mazatenango, Cuyotenango, Retalhuleu, and Coatepeque before reaching the Mexican border.

Towards Mexico

Coming from Guatemala City, the first major town on the Pacific plain is **Escuintla** (1 hr journey from Zona 4 bus terminal), which is a busy place with a huge market and crowded streets lined with crumbling old buildings. Next to Retalhuleu, it is the best of a ragged bunch—not for its beauty but for sheer chaotic energy. It is also an important junction for many other destinations, such as a back-road connection to Antigua (7 am and 1 pm from the main bus terminal; 2 hrs). Regular buses leave or pass through for Taxisco (2 hrs) and the Salvadorean border (4 hrs), and also for Puerto San José (2 hrs). If you should find yourself having to stay the night, try **Hotel Izcuintla**, 4 Avenida 6–7; or **Campo Real**, on 10 Calle. There is a **Lloyds Bank** on 7 Calle 3–9, and a **Banco de Guatemala** on the corner of 7 Calle and 4 Avenida.

137

Continuing northwest, you pass dusty Siquinalá (change for Sipacate beach), and then **Santa Lucía Cotzumalguapa,** referred to as *Cotz* and only worth stopping in if you plan to visit the archaeological collection nearby (see p. 142). From here the buses thunder along the Highway, past dusty palms and rows of banana trees, and endless roadside shacks.

The next large town is **Mazatenango** (*Masate* in conversation and on the bus windows), which is unbearably hot and sticky, and the only possible reason to get off the bus is to change for one heading to the remote fishing village of Tulate, two to three hours away through the plantations; or for one of the regular buses to cool Quezalte- nango (regular buses, 8–5, 2 hrs). Cuyotenango quickly follows, but the Highway cuts brutally through its middle and leaves it behind, taking you to **Retalhuleu** (*Reu,* pronounced 'ray-oo', for short), a small distance off the main road, and the richest and grandest of the Pacific towns.

Here old colonial splendour mixes with the exclusive new villas of wealthy plantation owners, and the road into town is lined with fortified entrances leading to immaculate lawns and tropical gardens. By no means a beautiful town, the crumbling buildings around the main square are pleasant enough, and the streets around the market are alive with commerce. Unlike the Indian markets, *ladino* ones are definitely there to buy and sell, to spend and make hard cash. Pushing and shoving, shouting and haggling are the norm around here, and it is fun to walk among the overflowing stalls.

Should you wish to stay the night, there are three central hotels to recommend, all around US$5 per person and near the main square: **Posada de Don José, Hotel Astor,** and the **Modelo.** If you have your own transport, there are a few motels along the entrance road to town. Change buses here either for regular connections to Quezalte- nango (2 hrs) or the small port of Champerico (1 hr). Banks, a post office and GUATEL office are all on or near the main square. A **Mexican consulate** (Mon–Fri, 4–6) selling visas and tourist cards can be found at 5 Calle and 3 Avenida. This is your last chance to purchase these before you reach the border.

Finally, almost an hour later, the last town before the Mexican border is **Coatepeque** (*Coa* for short), a seething place that you will want to leave as soon as possible. However, coming from the Mexican border posts of Tecún Umán (34 km) or Talismán (60 km), this is the first town with hotels, a bank, post office and GUATEL office. You can also change here for frequent buses to Quezaltenango, if you are heading straight for the Highlands.

The Mexican border post by **Tecún Umán,** being the nearest, is the busiest crossing, and most of the heavy trucks and private vehicles take this route. The train also crosses here. Unless you need a visa, you can buy tourist cards for Mexico from immigration officials, and the post is operational 24 hrs a day. Buses leave regularly for the six-hour journey to Guatemala City, and on the Mexican side the town of Tapachula is half an hour away by bus. If not in your own transport, you need to arrive during daylight hours to connect onwards. The border by the **Talismán** bridge (long walk across the bridge) is also open 24 hrs a day, and buses on the Mexican side quickly connect with Tapachula. If arriving from Mexico and heading straight for the Highlands, it is quickest to get any bus to Retalhuleu, and connect there for Quezaltenango.

Towards El Salvador

From Guatemala City, the Highway branches southeast by Escuintla, taking you past the familiar lowland scenery of plantations and dust-covered roadsides, with the occasional view of a towering volcano peering through the clouds to your left. About two hours later, **Taxisco** is the first town of any note, and the place to change buses if heading for the **Monterrico Nature Reserve** (see p. 142). Shortly afterwards, the bus arrives in **Chiquimulilla**, yet another commercial centre, and your last chance to head somewhere other than the border.

One choice is to catch a bus to the fishing village of **Las Lisas**, though there are easier beaches to reach than this one. Another possibility would be to take a bus heading north, for the town of Cuilapa. This is a back road that twists up through coffee plantations and onwards, to the dusty hills of the **Oriente**, the range of heat-cracked, sandy hills and valleys that runs almost the entire length of Guatemala's eastern border from the Pacific to the Atlantic. From there you could either make for the capital once more, or travel further into the country's eastern region.

After Chiquimulilla the Highway heads towards El Salvador. The **Salvadorean border** (open daily 6–8) is by a small settlement grandly entitled Ciudad Pedro de Alvarado, and very quiet, since almost nobody uses this route. In El Salvador, regular buses (until 6) take you onwards to Sonsonate, where you can change for San Salvador. The more usual and faster route for travelling to El Salvador is on a direct bus connecting the two capitals, via the Pan-American Highway.

Ports and Beaches

While no one has yet come to Guatemala for its beaches, there are nevertheless a few worth visiting, always bearing in mind that accommodation and facilities will normally be very basic—unless you happen to be near one of the rare hotels and want to pay a lot of money. There are two ports on the Pacific: Champerico is a forgotten place, not far from the Mexican border, while Puerto San José is the country's second largest port, and what Brighton is to Londoners, or Coney Island to New Yorkers.

The Western Pacific

In the 1930s when Aldous Huxley visited **Champerico**, it was Guatemala's third port. Yet even then he wrote about 'the unspeakable boredom of life at Champerico'. These days very little commercial shipping comes here at all—it is even duller. It would be a good place to drink oneself to death, strolling occasionally along the crumbling remains of the port, sniffing the fishy smells from the occasional small boat, wandering the beach—suitably grey—and then returning to the bar of the **Hotel Martita**.

The town is easily visited from Xela, with daily direct buses from the main terminal, or else head for Reu and change there. The journey takes about 2½ hours, and the last returning bus is at 2.30 pm, so you may want to stay overnight before heading back. If you do not like the Martita (about US$3), try the **Miramar**. Do try some of the seafood while you visit the beach, the fried fish or shrimps are often delicious.

Not far south of Champerico (in fact, you could ask one of the boatmen there to take you, a wet trip of 40 min), **Tulate** is a tiny fishing village of pole-and-thatch huts. It is perched on a sandbank, separated from the mainland by a narrow canal, and the inhabitants live either side of one sandy path leading to the ocean. The Pacific's white waves pound the sand that drops steeply to the water, and as far as the eye can see in either direction there is nothing but empty beach and distant palm trees waving in the quivering heat. Even the pigs go swimming to cool off, though they prefer the black water of the canal. Except at the weekends, there are no visitors at all, and there is absolutely nothing to do here except doze, swim, eat fried fish, and chat with the locals.

Unless you're prepared for the extremely basic accommodation on offer, you will probably not wish to stay the night. The branch road that leads off the Pacific Highway at Cuyotenango is one of the worst tarmac roads in the country, so ideally you would come this way in your own transport, and then the 60 km or so should take only 1½ hours. There are regular buses from Mazatenango, the last one returning at around 5 pm. From Cuyotenango onwards, a drearily straight road cuts through the plantations, though the potholes and discarded sugar canes guarantee a zigzag ride that is very hot and can take up to three hours.

By far one of the easiest beaches to reach is near the village of **Sipacate**, about two hours' bus journey from Escuintla. You can be on the beach in as little as four hours from either Guatemala City or Antigua (taking the direct bus to Escuintla). Coming from Escuintla, take any bus along the Highway, and get off at Siquinalá, where buses to Sipacate leave from behind the market. The branch road is not bad at all, and the sweltering bus, packed with plantation workers and women returning from the market, takes you quite painlessly past the settlement of La Democracia (see p. 143 for archaeological remains here), the small town of La Gomera, and finally on to Sipacate. There are plenty of pick-ups travelling this road, so there is also a good chance of a fast lift for hitchhikers.

Sipacate is a forlorn place. The nearest beach is the other side of the Chiquimulilla Canal that stretches from here all the way to the Salvadorean border. Along this entire stretch, the mainland is cut off from the beaches, necessitating a short trip in a *cayuco*.

If you want to eat here, rather than on the beach, your best bet for fried fish is **El Guayacán**. Otherwise follow the main street left, for a water taxi (small fee) to **Rancho Carillo**, a wooden collection of beach huts and restaurant, perched high above the waves. To stay here will set you back an outrageous US$8, for a double *cabaña* with private bathroom.

An alternative is to hitch a lift with the locals to **La Empalizada**, 5 km up the coast. There are two dirty and overpriced places to stay immediately you reach the beach, but if you ask to be dropped off at **El Coco**, a short distance further along, you find yourself with an entirely deserted beach and possibly a place to stay, depending on whether it is operational or not (secure parking available). There's even a swimming pool there, though you'll be lucky if it has water in it. The rooms are tiny concrete saunas and food, if any, is limited.

The Southern Pacific

Much more populated than the rest of the Guatemalan Pacific, the stretch between Puerto San José and the border offers its very own attractions. **Puerto San José**, the country's second port, is surprisingly small, but busy with commerce, military, and sleazy bars. A concrete maze of streets by the sea, it's certainly not beautiful in any way. It is, however, a very loud and boisterous place, and the beachside shacks and restaurants invite you to sample all the seafood delights you can stomach. At weekends and holidays the town is filled with sweaty families from the capital, and soon the beach is a mass of bodies and garbage . . . If the new road ever opens it should take no more than two hours to get here from the capital. The old road, however, is dreadful, and from Escuintla alone it can take 2½ hours, bumping around potholes. Direct buses leave Guate from the main Zona 4 terminal.

Outside San José there are some exclusive holiday enclaves favoured by the Guatemalan rich, each with their fortified and guarded entrances and expensive waterside villas or hotel rooms. Here you will find such things as swimming pools, restaurants and manicured lawns—safe and clean, but also far removed from anything remotely Guatemalan. To get there you will need your own transport, or pay through the nose for a taxi. West of the town is the posh hotel **Club Palmeras de Chulamar**, and you can book rooms by calling tel 313782 in the capital. East of San José is the **Turicentro Likín** (call tel 512190 or 518490 in the capital to book), which has bungalows lined along short canals. Not much of a beach here, more a place to sunbathe by the pool or go on boat trips; restaurant and supermarket on site.

For another peaceful and clean place to laze at the beach, catch a bus to **Iztapa**, one hour from San José (direct buses from Guate also). This too was once a port, though you would never guess it. Its shipbuilding days came to an end well before Independence, and since then its sandy streets have been enlivened only by snoring drunks and panting dogs. Some of the buildings and most of the beach shacks across the canal are made of wood, giving the place a slightly romantic, wind-crooked look. As usual, the beach is impressively wide, and you can enjoy it here from the comfort of a good hotel—the **María del Mar**, with clean rooms around a swimming pool, charges $7 singles, $10 doubles during the week; and $8 singles, $12 doubles at weekends. (You can book rooms in the capital, via **ECA Tours**, 5 Avenida 13–21, Zona 9; tel 343908/343970.) Nearby, the **Hotel Brasília** charges half the price, but has no pool. A good place to eat is the **Pollo Andra**, which is also a clean and inexpensive guest house.

The coastal road is interrupted here by the mouth of the River Naranjo. You can, however, cross to the village of Pueblo Viejo by *cayuco*, and take a bus from there to Monterrico Beach and Nature Reserve. The journey along a sandy road is maddeningly slow. Coming from the capital, take a bus to Taxisco (Zona 4 terminal), and change there for the ten-minute ride to the village of La Avellana, from where water taxis take you through the mangroves and set you down by the beachside village.

Monterrico is perhaps the best-known beach on the Guatemalan Pacific, and this has a lot to do with the fact that it is the only place commercially advertised by the tourist board, because of the **nature reserve** all around. The large village is set along black sandy paths, with assorted humans and animals lazing under the shade of palm trees or porches. The beach is generously wide and stretches in either direction as far as the eye can see, with great waves crashing in on a never-ending roll.

You can stay directly on the beach here, and the best place is **Hotel Baule Beach**, although the basic rooms are overpriced at around $8 for doubles. A pleasant terrace with hammocks looks out to sea—a great place to watch the sunsets. To get there walk through the village to the beach, and then turn left. On the way you pass **Jonny's Place**, which is slightly cheaper, and worth checking out. The alternative to these two is **Las Margaritas** in the village, which offers straw mats on wooden beds, and is simply horrible. The best place to sample the local seafood is at **Divina Maestra** in the village, where the cooking lives up to the name. As usual, the main occupations here are dozing, eating and sunbathing, with the single alternative of a canoe trip around the surrounding mangrove swamps. You can hire canoes by the jetty—haggle out a price in advance.

The **Monterrico Nature Reserve** is an area of the coast that has been left more or less how it was originally, and supports an isolated ecosystem of plants and wildlife. Originally, mangroves protected the entire coast, and a swampy hinterland was covered in forest and impenetrable thickets. Only in this century has deforestation and draining changed the landscape forever. But here can you get an idea of what it was like, although you are unlikely to see anything other than birds and butterflies. The INGUAT office in the capital provides a special brochure on the reserve's flora and fauna.

Archaeological Sites

In pre-Conquest times, the Pacific Lowlands of Guatemala were colonized in part by people migrating south from Mexico. One of these groups was the **Pipile**, who probably arrived sometime during the Early Post-Classic period (AD 900–1200). Their language was close to the Aztec tongue of Nahuatl, and although they became extinct around the time of the Spanish Conquest, many names of Guatemala's towns and villages bear the mark of their linguistic influence. For example, the familiar ending -*nango* is Nahuatl for 'place of'. Most of the archaeological sites in this region have been destroyed by the relentless development of plantations. However, there are a few scattered remains hiding among the sugar-cane fields, and two locations in particular are worth seeking out.

The most interesting site for remains of Pipile sculpture is at **El Baúl**, located in a working plantation (*finca*), about 6 km outside the town of Santa Lucía Cotzumalguapa. Without your own transport the only convenient way of visiting this site is by taxi from the nearby town. The site is really only for enthusiasts, though you do have the added attraction of entering one of the country's huge *fincas*, normally closed to outsiders. Walking through you will see the machinery and migrant labourers who literally work for slave wages to create the immense wealth of the agro-export elite. El Baúl operates one of the ten largest sugar mills in the country, belonging to the powerful Herrera family, which is reputedly the second wealthiest in Guatemala.

The most significant stela found here was the 'Herrera Stela', which was discovered in 1923, and shows a plumed Maya warrior. Much disagreement rages about its age, but the Maya expert Michael Coe believes it to be the oldest dated sculpture in the Maya territory, dated AD 36. Apart from the stone carving to be seen on the *finca*'s land (ask for directions), there is also a small collection of bits and pieces held in the administrative buildings, which you can view on request.

A separate sculptural tradition in this region has strong links with the Mexican Olmec style. Unlike the ornate carvings of the Pipile, who adapted to the Maya style, the sculptural remains of these people are quite different and uniquely grotesque. They are believed to have been a subsidiary cult of the **Izapan civilization**, who were based near the Mexican town of Tapachula, by the present-day border with Guatemala. Small bulbous heads and figures stare blankly at you, and after visiting Maya sites around the country, these sculptures will seem very alien indeed. The best collection is in the small town of La Democracia, a short bus ride away from the Pacific Highway at Siquinalá. Most of the sculptures are ranged around the main square, but there is also a small **museum** (Tues–Sun, 9–noon and 2–5).

Although it is somewhat off the beaten track, you can easily stop off here on the way to the beach at Sipacate, whether in your own vehicle or on a bus, as you pass right by.

THE VERAPAZ MOUNTAINS

The Verapaz region is the heartland of Guatemala's coffee-growing industry, based around the town of Cobán, and is also one of the last areas where the quetzal's habitat of cloud forest remains to sustain it. A reserve has been set up, where you can wander about the forest and perhaps sight the bird, though the chances are slim at the best of times, which is during the April to June nesting season. A visit is still highly worthwhile, however. Once past Cobán, the roads degenerate into mud and gravel, but the scenery is superb, easily making up for the discomforts and the almost daily drizzle of rain. (You can avoid the worst of the weather by visiting from November to April.) If you have three or four days to spare, a visit to the remote pools of **Semuc Champey** will undoubtedly be one of the highlights of your journey—a truly magical place hiding in the forests east of Cobán. Alternatively, you could test your nerves on one of the country's most spectacular back roads, connecting Cobán to Huehuetenango.

History

Just one region eluded the Spaniards in the early years of conquest: the highland area covering the northeast of the country. Bordered by the Western Highlands and jungle to the north and east, and the arid Motagua valley to the south, this was the land that many Indians fled to, joining the bellicose Rabinal nation in successful defence against the invaders. Thick forests covered undulating highlands, deep river beds cut through the countryside, and crops flourished on the fertile land, enabling the Mayas to sustain themselves for many years of guerrilla warfare. They were so successful that the Spanish dubbed the region *Tierra de Guerra* (land of war), and more or less avoided it.

In the meantime, news of Alvarado's massacres had reached the Spanish Court, denunciations coming from his former leader, Hernán Cortés, as well as the first campaigner for Indian rights, Friar Bartolomé de Las Casas. Later to be known as the Apostle of the Indies, Las Casas came to Guatemala in 1533, ten years after the Conquest, and took up the Indian cause with great vigour.

His writings had such influence at the Spanish Court that he managed to gain a royal charter to attempt a peaceful Christianization of the Indians. He argued that the Indians were fellow human beings, and as such, could be reasoned with, and were capable of being converted without violence. To achieve his goal of peaceful conversion, he needed to establish two vital points: total separation of the secular Spanish from the Indians in

143

the region he would work in; and a ban on converted Indians being forced into slavery, as was the custom.

He was granted his wishes, and the area in which he was to attempt his pacification was the notorious *Tierra de Guerra*, where the conquerors had failed. Thus, in 1536, he finally set to work. Based in present-day Antigua, his first step was to compose hymns in the Maya dialects which told the story of Christian Creation and the life of Jesus Christ. Christianized Indian merchants were then sent to the region, the following year, where they performed the novel songs before the Indian leaders they were trading with. It is said that the merchants sang eight nights in a row, their hymns becoming more popular each day, until the Indians were learning to sing them too. An emissary was sent back with the merchants, inviting one of Las Casas' friars to visit the highlands, and this was duly done.

By 1539, the friars had achieved what the conquerors had failed to do, and the region was renamed Verapaz (true peace) to honour Las Casas and his men. Or one could say that the Catholic Church successfully pacified the territory for the Spanish colonists to move in later. In the long run, the results for the Indians were not dissimilar from those elsewhere: appropriation of their land and loss of human rights. It was a tactic the Spanish and Portuguese Crowns were to use successfully for all intractable regions. Las Casas meanwhile had to flee for his life a few years later, pursued by irate conquistadors who resented their supply of Indian slaves being cut, and most of all, the idea of giving back the land they had stolen.

Baja Verapaz

Although the lower Verapaz range is situated just north of Guatemala City, it is reached by taking the Atlantic Highway east, and then heading up into the hills by the El Rancho junction. The road is excellent and bus connections between the capital and Cobán, passing through Baja Verapaz, are fast and regular.

The stretch along the Atlantic Highway takes you along the brown desert landscape of the Motagua valley. Past the El Rancho junction, a dust-covered collection of shacks and petrol stations, the bus begins the winding ascent. There is almost no colour here except for the shades of rusty brown to faded yellow, and the few thorny plants that grow are covered by layers of dust, blown up by the winds.

A crossroads marks the turning west, into the valley of Salamá, and the town of the same name. Beyond the town lies the smaller settlement of Rabinal, the first place founded by Las Casas; and beyond that, lies remote Cubulco. There is no real reason to travel this way unless you happen to be passing for the local fiestas (Salamá: 17–21 Sep; Rabinal: 25–29 Jan; Cubulco: 23 Jan). Unlike the Western Highlands, this region has a very low Indian population, and traditional clothing and colourful markets are a rare sight. On the other hand, you do have a chance to explore an area of the country where outsiders seldom stray. Ideally you would come here in your own transport, and there's a nice place to stay in Salamá, the **Hotel Tezulutlán**, which makes a good base. The Sunday market in Rabinal, the most traditional of these three settlements, is a good place to look for bargains, though the variety of textiles and embroidery is limited.

Past the Salamá crossroads, the landscape changes quite suddenly to pine forests and green pastures. Small homesteads hide in the countryside, surrounded by neat fields and grazing animals, and the scent of pines drifts into the bus. But this impression only lasts an hour or so, before you pass into the strange world of epiphytes clinging to giant trees, damp mists draped over the treetops, as the road winds into the chilly heights of a cloud forest.

The Quetzal Reserve

Three hours from the polluted capital you find yourself in the moist atmosphere of the **Biotopo del Quetzal** (daily, 8–4, free). The Cobán road leads right by the entrance; just ask to be dropped off there. A visitors' centre, with a small exhibition and a helpful guardian to answer questions, is the starting point for two paths leading through the forest. Both are very clearly marked, so there is no chance of getting lost. One route takes you on a brief 2 km tour, the other on an 8 km hike, up and down the steep mountainside.

Even the short path is a good introduction to the wonders of this special environment, and soon you find yourself padding along a soft trail, inhaling the musty smell of rotting leaves. Light is subdued by the roof of tangled leaves and branches, high above, and only the occasional clearing allows shafts of sunrays to glitter on wet foliage. Cool streams bubble down over moss-covered boulders, and if you pause in the stillness of the forest, you'll begin to discern some of the many sounds and animals that are really all around. Looking up into the vast canopy, you might be lucky enough to focus on a monkey, comfortably perched to eat some fruit. Most likely, you'll see some of the huge variety of birds that flit among the branches, the butterflies and insects of all shapes and sizes. There are other animals here too, though few of them will let you know it: there is the small green toucan, his feathers an excellent camouflage; there are mini ocelots, tapirs, and of course, snakes.

If you are up at dawn or waiting quietly at dusk, you might see the gorgeous quetzal, the tiny body of the male trailing his famous tail plumes. The small avocado fruit of the aguacatillo trees is a favourite food of the quetzal, so it is a good idea to wait near one of these trees. Your chances of seeing one are greatly reduced outside the nesting season of April to June, and even in season, the number of people around and traffic on the road may scare these lovely birds away. As Jonathan Maslow puts it, sighting a quetzal is 'one part knowledge, one part patience, and three parts willingness to get wet.'

The head and body of the quetzal is a magical array of greens, blues and turquoise, depending on how the sun lights up the feathers, while the breast is crimson red. Legend has it that when Alvarado slew Tecún Umán, a quetzal bird fell from the sky to cover the warrior's dead body. Next morning, it rose up once more, but its breast was forever stained by the Indian's blood, and so it is to this day. Guatemala's national emblem, namesake for its currency, and symbol of freedom, has always held a special place. Long before the Spanish arrived, or the independent nation made it a symbol, the bird was sacred to the Mayas. To kill it was a capital offence, and only Maya lords had the right to decorate their battle headdress with the male's arching tail feathers. Nor was the bird only for decoration: it was considered spiritual protector of Indian chiefs, accompanying them to battle, and dying with them, if they were beaten.

If confined in a cage, the quetzal dies—most apt for a symbol of freedom. Yet in spite of the fact that hunting the bird has been banned since 1895, ornithologists believe that the quetzal will probably be extinct by the year 2000. The reason is quite simply the destruction of its only habitat, the cloud forest. By 1981, the Guatemalan cloud forest had been reduced from 30,000 sq km to 2500 sq km, and land shortages and lack of alternative cooking fuel mean that squatters are still cutting down the remaining forests, even in the reserve. There are also reports of people killing the bird for food, quite apart from selling its feathers for profit. It is a sad prospect for one of the world's most exquisite birds.

GETTING THERE
From Guatemala City, there are regular Pullmans leaving every day (see p. 78), and the journey takes 3 hrs to the reserve. Ask to be dropped off, because the bus does not stop automatically. Cobán is only an hour away, so you can easily visit coming from that direction as well. Leaving the reserve by bus, you just stand by the road, and flag down the first bus heading your way.

WHERE TO STAY AND EAT
There are three choices for staying near the reserve. The most comfortable is the **Posada Montaña del Quetzal** (reservations in the capital, tel 313079/322923), which has a restaurant and swimming pool, and charges around $12 for doubles. Located 4 km from the reserve itself, this is not a good choice if without private transport. A few steps from the reserve entrance is a simple **hospedaje**, made up of two log cabins with ten beds each, communal showers and toilet. This is very basic and you will need your own sleeping bag and torch, but the location is convenient. Finally, there is a beautiful **campsite** (tents only) set in the reserve itself, behind the visitor's centre, right next to a pool fed by freezing spring water. Barbecue facilities, shower and toilets are provided.

When it comes to eating, you can either have eggs and beans at the *hospedaje*, or walk 4 km up to the Posada. So if you plan on staying more than one night, you might want to bring some food.

Alta Verapaz

Beyond the Quetzal Reserve, you are soon in coffee-growing country, with wonderfully lush valleys steaming in the sun, and farms (*fincas*) of all shapes and sizes dotting the landscape. Coffee is the mainstay of the country's economy today, and not only its number one export, but also the largest generator of employment. In spite of this, the industry is still virtually a private enterprise under the control of a small group of families, and the coffee oligarchy are a powerful force, with strong ties to the military, who protect their interests against governmental attempts at land reform. One common estimate is that 4% of coffee-growing farms produce and control 83% of Guatemala's national production. Formerly, the landowning families lived in their regional capital of Cobán, but these days the town is a rather damp and forgotten place, its high society decamped to the exclusive suburbs of Guatemala City.

History

It was only in the late 19th century, when the craze of coffee-drinking took hold in Europe, that coffee began to be cultivated in these parts; before then, the Verapaz was a relatively remote region of Indian and Church lands. But under the rule of Justo Rufino Barrios (1871–1885), who instigated the so-called Liberal Revolution, the Church was separated from the State, and most of its lands—as well as that of the Indians—was confiscated by the government and sold to foreign investors. Many of these were German immigrants, who were brought in to develop the burgeoning coffee industry, and by 1900, 95% of Guatemala's coffee farms were owned by Germans.

To provide the necessary labour force for this new industry, the president decreed that Indians should work in the plantations, as and when required by the coffee barons, and duly used the army to round them up. Made landless by the government, the Indians were now forced to work in the labour-intensive coffee plantations. From sunrise to sunset they were supervised in work teams, and at night locked up. It was an outrage that even touched the newspaper-reading Guatemalans of the time, and protests were voiced against the virtual slavery existing around the Cobán area. But the president legalized debt-peonage, and the Indians became trapped in a never-ending cycle of borrowing and debt, inherited from one generation to the next, and tying them permanently to the farm they worked on. In practice, little has changed to this day, though many of the huge plantations no longer allow permanent settlement on their lands, sending the seasonal labourers away when they are not needed. (Naturally, many of these people become squatters, having no land to work and live off, and thus deforestation continues unabated, clearly marking the quetzal and other species for extinction.)

For the Mayas, the worst of this development was not the slavery—forced labour was an integral part of the Maya empire—but the denial of their land and traditional way of life, which fundamentally attacked the whole reason and meaning for their existence. Farming the *milpa* (field) was not merely for feeding the family, but an act of worship in itself. Traditionally it was a sacred duty to grow maize, closely tied to the good will of the gods and the proper balance of the elements. It is based on the idea that the person belongs to the land, not the other way round, and it is his duty to look after it as best he can:

> To be ... exiled from the *milpa*, was to be separated from the self, to become a shiftless ghost, no longer part of the Maya weave, no longer quite human.
>
> J. E. Maslow, *Bird of Life, Bird of Death*

In the long run, most of the German immigrants fared badly also. The onset of the Second World War, and the immigrants' open support for the German side, incurred the wrath of the United States, who duly pressured the Guatemalan government into deporting the Germans and confiscating their lands. Much of this land is still in government hands today, and few Germans returned or managed to stay. But there were some who assimilated, intermarried and learnt Spanish, and were able to start again in the 1950s. This German heritage still shows in the names of some of the largest landowners such as Daetz Villela and Diesseldorf.

Cobán

A small provincial town these days, Cobán was once at the hub of the coffee-growing industry, and many of its inhabitants were wealthy landowners who gave the town an air of countrified sophistication. Now most of the grand buildings are damp and crumbling, and this is a quiet place, with little for the visitor to see or do. All around there is a rich patchwork of plantations, fields, and the odd scrap of cloud forest clinging to the hillsides, yet the white mists that sit heavily on the hilltops can create a chilly atmosphere. Here, more than anywhere else in the country, you get a sense of the permanent change that people are inflicting on the countryside. The Western Highlands suffer the same problems, yet the atmosphere is quite different. The farming terraces, pine forests, blue skies and sunshine inspire joy. By contrast, the Verapaz around Cobán can be a melancholy world of fine drizzle and milky clouds. Dead tree stumps stubbornly remind you of the displaced forest, and wooden huts topped with corrugated iron stand mud-stained by the roadside, home to the landless squatters.

The one time Cobán springs into life is during Easter Week and the National Festival of Folklore (22–28 Aug). The latter is, however, more an attempt by the tourist board to draw some action to the town than an indigenous fiesta.

WHERE TO STAY
Cobán will probably only be a stopover to somewhere else, but since most of the interesting journeys from here require an early start, you will find yourself staying at least one night. Note that during Easter Week and the National Festival of Folklore, accommodation can be scarce.

INEXPENSIVE
The top hotel in Cobán is **La Posada**, 1 Calle 4–12, tel 0511495, which is on the entrance road to town, just before the main plaza. A lovely colonial house with a restful garden, it also has an excellent restaurant. All rooms have a private bathroom.

Of the guest houses, the **Central**, 1 Calle 1–79, has modern rooms around a large courtyard, and a good restaurant. Next choice, and for the same price, would be **La Paz**, 6 Avenida 2–19, a short walk from the town's triangular plaza, next to the **Pizzeria**, which serves horrible and expensive pizzas. **Hospedaje Maya**, opposite the local cinema, is also recommended, and there are a few other places, but they are generally grubby.

EATING OUT
Apart from the restaurants attached to accommodation, there are *comedores* along the market, behind the cathedral, and also on the main road into town. Just above the bus terminal, **El Refugio** is a good place for a meal and has a bar until 11. The best coffee in Guatemala can be had at **Café Tirol**, which is diagonally across the street, from La Posada, just by the tip of the triangular plaza. You can also change dollars here if the banks are closed.

Adventurous Journeys beyond Cobán

Semuc Champey

About three hours east of Cobán, by bus, you come to the remote village of **Lanquín**, and the closest you can get to the fabulous pools of Semuc Champey. (The bus leaves at 5.30 am from outside the bank behind the cathedral, on the same street as the Pensión Central.) The road to Lanquín is rough but beautiful, passing the pretty village of San Pedro Carchá shortly after setting off. From there the stony road twists and turns along the sides of steep valleys, their slopes covered with glistening coffee bushes and the floppy leaves of banana trees. The road finally descends into the valley of Lanquín, passing a few grand *fincas* on the way.

In Lanquín you have three choices of accommodation: just by the entrance of the village is the newly opened **El Recreo**, which is attractively set on a small hillock, and is undoubtedly the best choice if you want creature comforts. In the village, the **Hospedaje Divina Providencia** is run by a very friendly man, who has been blind for many years, though he does not let that stop him tending to his coffee bushes himself. Squeaky beds go for $1 per person, and though facilities are basic, the food is good, and is your only option around here. **Tienda Mary**, on the main square, charges the same money but is not as nice.

To reach the pools, you can either get up early, and hope for a lift with a truck any time from 7 am onwards, or you can walk. (If in your own transport you should only attempt the road in a high clearance, four-wheel-drive vehicle.) If you walk it will take up to four hours along a road littered with sharp stones, winding steeply out of the valley, down into another and up again before descending to the swift waters of the River Cahabón, and your final reward. Along the way you will pass lone homesteads of Indian families, who are very reserved and often do not speak Spanish. An unusual feature is the women's habit of smoking fat cigars, and you will see them shyly turning away to light up.

It's an exhausting walk, though not difficult, and you know you are close when the suspension bridge over the River Cahabón comes into view. Just beyond it, a squashy mud path leads off to the right, taking you slipping and sliding through the undergrowth. You can hear the seven steps of pools gushing, one into another, minutes before you see them. There can be few sights lovelier in Guatemala: glass-clear, turquoise water fills a natural cascade of large pools, surrounded by massive trees covered with drooping lianas. If you had to walk twice as long, you would still think it was worth it, and a cooling swim soon refreshes tired legs. To get the best view, walk to the top pool, where there's also a clearing to camp on. Bring your own food and water, since there is nothing along the way; and if you plan to camp, be careful, since robbery does happen and it is probably better not to be alone. If you were lucky enough to get a lift in the morning, you will be fresh for the walk back, since there is almost no traffic passing towards Lanquín in the afternoon.

Only half an hour's walk from Lanquín, you can also visit a huge cave (*cueva*) here (small fee). Dark, wet, and home to thousands of bats, you cannot see very much without good lighting, and the paths are very slippery. The municipal building in the village has a switch to light up the cave (ask before setting off to have it turned on), but usually it's not working. The cave is said to go on for many miles, and locals will tell you that they've spent weeks walking into the interior and some have never returned. The walk along a river is pleasant, though, and near the entrance to the cave is a good spot for a swim. Leaving Lanquín, buses set off from the main square for Cobán at 5.30, 7 am and 1 pm.

A Back Route Towards the Petén Jungle

For the hardy traveller only, there is a tough two-day route into the northern jungles, which passes quite close to Lanquín. (If coming from Lanquín, catch the 5.30 am bus and ask to be dropped off at the Pajal junction, where you can wait for the morning bus heading for the Sebol road junction and Fray Bartolomé de Las Casas.) Coming from Cobán, you need to be in the village of San Pedro Carchá early, to catch the 6am bus to Fray Bartolomé de Las Casas, a long eight hours away. Once arrived, you will have to spend the night in one of the basic *pensiones* here. Next day, look for a lift with the trucks and pick-ups that leave for the five-hour journey to jungle-bound Sayaxché, in the southern Petén.

The only possible reason for inflicting this journey on yourself is if you plan to visit the ruined Maya temples of the Petén, the most accessible of which are near Sayaxché and Flores, and you do not want to return to the capital to either fly or catch a direct bus to Flores. It is worth bearing in mind that this route is not only exhausting but potentially hazardous, since the remote northern foothills of the Verapaz are one of the last regions where guerrillas are still holding out. Occasionally they block the road and demand 'contributions' to their cause from the passengers. It is unlikely that you would be hurt, since the guerrillas do not make a habit of harming foreigners, but it would be extremely nerve-racking, at the very least.

Towards the Western Highlands: Cobán to Huehuetenango

If you enjoy spectacular scenery as well as being scared witless, then this is the trip for you: the dirt road that connects the east and west of northern Guatemala is one long rollercoaster ride, best done sitting on the roof of the bus where you get the best views. During the week it is possible to hitch a lift with large trucks that use this road. But normally you will need two days by public transport. If in your own transport, remember that petrol stations are few and far between in this region, and you will need a tough vehicle.

The journey begins in the small town of **San Cristóbal Verapaz**, reached by regular local bus from the Cobán bus terminal. An excellent place to stay here is the **Hospedaje Oly**, on the main street, which is a beautiful home turned guest house, with a very friendly owner who charges $3 for a double (coming from the other direction, this is the best place to end the journey and stay the night before heading onwards).

In the morning, you can either try your luck hitching, with the most likely destinations being Uspantán, Sacapulas, Nebaj or Huehuetenango, or you can wait for the bus to Uspantán, leaving between noon and 1. The drive will take about six hours, and the gut-churning begins when you find yourself packed into the bus and know there is no way you could get out in an emergency. Sitting on the roof rack of the bus, lodged among sacks of grain and baskets of fruit, is infinitely preferable to staying inside, not just for the space and fresh air, but your bird's-eye view. Of course, you do get the worst of the vehicle's terrifying swaying, the bus leaning just far enough for you to see the sheer drop to the river below.

The bus alternately hurtles and crawls along mountain ledges and around hairpin bends, and when you're not wondering whether to jump off immediately and walk, you can enjoy the heart-stopping vista of jagged mountain chains framing a deep river valley. The lower stretches of land are covered in the greens and golden browns of farming fields, while the river is a stunning aquamarine in places, its giant loops winding around grey rocks and boulders. Ignore the rusting wreck of a bus at the bottom of the valley.

In Uspantán, a small town, you can stay at the **Viajero**, a basic place three blocks east of the main square, or the **Golinda** *pensión*. Ask on arrival what time the buses leave for Sacapulas, where you have a choice of either staying on the bus, and ending up south in Santa Cruz del Quiché, or you can change here for buses to either Nebaj to the north-west (see p. 121), or Huehuetenango to the west (see p. 131). Again, the journey on the dirt road will be spectacular, and by the end of the day you will have a real sense of achievement: not only did you survive, but you travelled on one of Guatemala's most beautiful roads.

Heading East to Lake Izabal

Finally, there is a back road to **El Estor**, on Lake Izabal, where you can catch a ferry to Mariscos, and buses heading for the Petén jungle or the Caribbean. This is a rough option that bumps you along the Polochic valley, past coffee villages and the town of Panzós, and down to the lowlands of the lake. It is, however, off the beaten track, and the bus journey along the River Polochic is beautiful, as is the ferry trip across the great lake. The only hitch is that sometimes the ferry does not turn up for a few days, especially if the weather is bad and the water too rough.

Valenciana buses for El Estor leave the Cobán bus terminal at 5, 8, and 10 am (returning at the same times), and the journey takes around eight hours. The **Brenda Mercedez** company also runs buses on this route.

You will have to stay at least one night in El Estor, either in the lakeside **Vista del Lago**, doubles US$9 with or without private bath, or the **Hotel Villela**, behind the other one, which is simple and friendly, and charges US$5 for a double with private bath. In the unlikely event that these are full, try **Hotel Los Almendros**, and there are a few others besides that. The best places to eat in El Estor are the **Ranchón Centenario**, just past the market, and the **Bambú**, near the waterfront.

If you find yourself enchanted by the backwater atmosphere of El Estor, there is a trip you can make to a nearby canyon, a popular swimming spot with the locals. There are also some fine beaches, reached by hiring a motorized canoe, though this can be comparatively expensive (US$10). Inland, there are some traditional Kekchí villages you could visit, but you would need your own transport for that.

The ferry to **Mariscos** is supposed to leave daily at 5 am (departs at 1 pm from the other direction; journey takes 2 hrs), and there are usually buses waiting there, heading for Guatemala City. If your destination is either the Caribbean or the Petén, just get off at the junction with the Atlantic Highway, and wait for a connection. Mariscos itself is a sleepy little place, set at the foot of hills covered in tropical forest and rubber plantations, where there's nothing much to do except visit some nearby beaches. The area is still undeveloped touristically, but that is bound to change, and some wealthy Guatemalans have already built their holiday homes along the lake, west of Mariscos.

THE ORIENTE AND CARIBBEAN COAST

This was Death Valley. The earth here was finer and duller than sand... There
was a dusting of it on all the cactuses, which gave them the look of stumps.

Paul Theroux, *The Old Patagonian Express*

Theroux was talking about the Motagua Valley, which leads from the capital all the way
to the Atlantic. But the description fits just as well for most of Guatemala's eastern range
of hills, which trace the borders with El Salvador and Honduras. Known as the *oriente*,
the scorched hills and valleys rising east of the capital are cowboy country. Few Indians
live in this region, and even fewer retain their traditional custom of dress. Instead there
are busy market towns, full of *ladinos* going about their business, which holds little
interest for the tourist. Towns like Cuilapa, Jutiapa, Jalapa, and Chiquimula are all much
of a muchness. The only town that enjoys a regular stream of visitors is the pilgrimage
city of Esquipulas, famous for its Black Christ, which draws the largest number of
pilgrims in Central America.

If, however, you enjoy spectacular bus journeys, there is one trip in this region you
could consider. It is the route from Jalapa to Chiquimula, which takes you for five long
hours through the most dramatic part of the region. Broad valleys are flanked by
imposing mountains, and unlike the rest of the Oriente, the landscape is green and rich
in wild flowers that line the roadside. The road is not paved, which accounts for the long
journey time, but if you have two days to spare, this is certainly a trip worth taking.
Frequent buses leave from the capital's Zona 4 bus terminal for Jutiapa (2½ hrs), where
there are connections for Jalapa (1½ hrs). The best place to stay in Jalapa is the **Hotel
Casa del Viajero**, which charges US$5 for doubles with a private bath. Buses from
Jalapa to Chiquimula leave the market terminal at 6, 8, 10, 11 am and 1 pm, and from
Chiquimula there are constant buses back to the capital, or onwards to Honduras or the
Caribbean coast.

Other than to visit Esquipulas, most visitors who pass this way are en route to
Honduras, crossing the frontier either beyond that city or near Chiquimula, usually
using the latter route, because it leads directly to the famous Maya city of Copán, just
inside Honduran territory. Even if you do not plan to travel in Honduras, you can easily
visit this special site from Guatemala City, either by organized tour or on your own.
Border formalities are minimal, and even those normally requiring visas can obtain
72-hour permits to visit the ruins.

Another important Maya site is just off the Atlantic Highway, not too far from the
Caribbean coast: Quiriguá, which is treasured for its stelae, rose to prominence in a very
short time in the 7th century, yet only flourished for 138 years. Now it is hidden among
banana plantations, and as you travel closer to the coast, so the landscape comes alive
again with the green of floppy-leaved banana trees. Past the junction turning northwest,
for the Petén, the landscape becomes humid and tropical, remnants of forest and spongy
swamps giving way to cattle ranches. The distance to the coast is not far, but the journey
is slowed down considerably by stretches where the tarmac disintegrates into dirt and
gravel. Eventually you find yourself in the fetid heat of Guatemala's largest port, named
Puerto Barrios after one of the country's most famous presidents. Here you can catch
ferries to either Livingston in Guatemala, or Punta Gorda in Belize.

152

Guatemala's share of the Caribbean coast is less than 100 km long, and has few settlements apart from the large port. Livingston, however, is unique in Guatemala, since it is inhabited almost entirely by blacks, descended from African slaves and Carib Indians, who mainly arrived from the Eastern Caribbean in the 18th century. As with the Pacific, this is no place to come for spectacular beaches, but it is a very interesting place culturally, and an excellent setting-off point for journeys up the beautiful Río Dulce, and into the jungles of the Petén.

The Holy City of Esquipulas

Described as a 'religious Brighton' in Anthony Daniel's *Sweet Waist of America*, Esquipulas draws huge numbers of pilgrims from all over Latin America, but in particular from Central America, and it is true that the city lives off little else. There is a kind of religious fairground outside the great basilica, which caters for the visitors' every possible taste in trinkets, from candles and plastic flowers to straw hats; and each 15 January the place is solid with pilgrims.

The first building you set eyes on when approaching Esquipulas is the huge gleaming, white basilica. The rest of the town huddles around its elevated position, and visitors rarely bother to explore its streets. All eyes are on the church, and in particular the Black Christ behind the altar. A small side entrance by the back leads visitors single-file behind the encased wooden statue, where there is an opening so that the faithful can kiss the figure's feet, and deposit money down a conveniently placed tube. The Christ, beautifully carved out of balsam wood by the renowned colonial sculptor, Quirio Cataño, is nailed to a heavy silver cross.

Each person stays for a short time, and then gets shuffled on by the waiting line, usually retreating backwards, savouring every last minute of the pilgrimage. Around the base of the figure, you will also see endless plaques, notes and photos, testifying to the miraculous help the Black Christ has given. The figure has been here since 1595, perhaps made in dark wood to appeal better to the Indians. But its fame for miraculous healing, and the reason for its immense popularity, dates from the mid-18th century when the bishop of Guatemala, Pardo de Figueroa, recovered from a severe illness while visiting here.

Inside the church itself the cavernous dark is lit by hundreds of candles, while hanging above the main aisle are some glamorous chandeliers, which would look more at home in an exclusive restaurant than in here. Outside the church are numerous shops selling chains, votives, cards, candles, books and anything else that has even the remotest association with this place.

History

Esquipulas briefly hit the headlines in 1954, when it was invaded by a mercenary army hired by the American CIA to bring down the Guatemalan government. The cause of this intervention was ostensibly the 'communist tendencies' of the Jacobo Arbenz government. He had tried to institute land reform and come into direct conflict with the powerful United Fruit Company, who had close links with the US government.

The American company first came to Guatemala at the turn of the century, and by 1929 it had already established a monopoly control over the banana industry there. A powerful economic force, United Fruit not only owned huge parts of Guatemala's plantation country, it also owned and controlled most of the country's railway, media, telegraph and electricity installations, in fact anything that had a remote connection to the smooth operation of their business. Soon the people refered to United Fruit as *El Pulpo*, the octopus, and the company's controlling influence in Guatemalan politics was an accepted fact of life: it was a 'banana republic'.

The Arbenz government, elected in 1950, did no more than request the unused land of large estates, to be compensated by the declared tax value of that land. In the case of United Fruit, who used less than 20% of their holdings at any one time, the company was offered almost three times what they had paid for the land. Yet, like other large landowners, United Fruit objected on principle and set the propaganda machine in motion in America. Eventually, 'Operation Success' was initiated on 18 June 1954, which ended in the collapse of the Arbenz government, and the puppet government of Colonel Carlos Castillo Armas was installed.

GETTING TO ESQUIPULAS AND ONWARDS TO HONDURAS
Direct buses for Esquipulas (4–5 hrs) leave Guatemala City from near the Zona 1 bus terminal (see p. 78). There are also direct buses between here and Puerto Barrios in the mornings.

From Esquipulas, minibuses regularly shuttle between town and the border post at Agua Caliente (20 min), for crossing into Honduras. They leave from the main street, where the buses from the capital arrive and leave, daily until around 4 pm. If you need a visa, you can get it at the consulate in Guatemala City (see p. 64) or at the one in the **Hotel Payaqui**, in Esquipulas. The fee to enter Honduras is around $1. The Guatemalan exit fee hovers around $1. Moneychangers are always waiting for custom at the border, and on the Honduran side there are regular minibuses leaving for the nearest town of Nueva Ocotepeque. If you are heading for the ruins of Copán, it is better to cross at the other border, further north.

WHERE TO STAY AND EAT
There are plenty of places to stay, most of them very close to the basilica. The telephone code for Esquipulas is 0431.

MODERATE
The smartest hotel, with pool and restaurant, is the **Posada Cristo Negro**, tel 482, on the entrance road to town.

INEXPENSIVE
On the main street where the buses stop, the hotel **Payaqui**, tel 143, is simpler, but also has a pool and a reasonable restaurant. **Casa Norman** is a small place with good rooms. The hotel **Paris**, just off the main street, the other side of the church, is clean. There are many other places in the same price range as the París.

Apart from the restaurant attached to the Payaqui hotel, there are few places to recommend. The food is generally nothing special and prices are high. There are plenty of snack bars and restaurants to choose from around the main street.

Excursion to Copán in Honduras

There are plenty of agencies offering one-day tours to Copán in Honduras. However, considering it takes around 6 hours each way, it hardly seems worth doing. It is also much cheaper and quite easy to travel independently. If you're just making a side trip, allow yourself at least 3 days, so you can explore the ruins in peace on the second day.

From Guatemala City, there are direct buses to the town of Chiquimula (3–4 hrs) with the **Rutas Orientales** company, leaving daily. If you want to be sure of making the connections as far as Copán in one day, you should set off no later than 8 am. In Chiquimula, change for a bus heading for the Honduran border post of El Florido, with the **Empresa Vilma**, whose office is next to the market. Last buses in either direction leave at 4.30 pm, and the journey takes around 2 hours.

Crossing the border is usually quick, and if you're only visiting the ruins, you can get a 72-hour permit, which does not affect your Guatemalan tourist card or visa, and has no bearing on normal Honduran entry requirements for your nationality. (In other words, it is as if you never crossed the border, officials removing the permit from your passport when you return.)

If planning to continue travelling in Honduras, many nationalities, including Canadians and Americans, but not the British, need to have obtained a visa before crossing this border, obtainable at the Honduran Consulate in Guatemala City (16 Calle 8–27, Zona 10, tel 373921; Mon–Fri). You need to leave your passport at the Consulate between 10 am and noon, and collect it the next day between noon and 1.30 pm. All visas are for 30 days, renewable once only, for another 30 days at one of the many immigration offices scattered around Honduras.

The standard entry fee is about $1, payable in local currency, the lempira. The Guatemalan exit and entry fee is usually $1. There are plenty of moneychangers at the border, and once across, minibuses take you the 40-minute journey to the small town of Copán Ruinas, next to the Maya site. For a full description and accommodation details, see p. 270 of the Honduras chapter.

Quiriguá

Past the El Rancho and Río Hondo junctions, the small turning right for Quiriguá is about 190 km from Guatemala City, along the Atlantic Highway. Virtually all traffic thunders past the turning, including the buses for Puerto Barrios, and in spite of its significance, the site is rarely visited.

Quiriguá

Located on an island of forest in a sea of banana plantations, Quiriguá was briefly a major city-state. Originally, it must have been a satellite of the great city of Copán, just 50 km away. But in 724, Quiriguá's ruler, Cauac Sky, began aggressive moves towards independence. By 738, he had succeeded in taking Copán's lord prisoner, and instituted his own emblem glyph for Quiriguá, an honour only granted to Maya centres of political importance. From that date onwards, huge stelae were regularly erected, and elaborately carved with portraits of rulers, celebrating their achievements, and also important events in the Maya calendar. Nine of these great monuments remain, and they are the reason for

155

Quiriguá's significance today, the highly ornate and detailed sculptures being second only to Copán. The tallest of these is almost 9 m high, dwarfing its human visitors.

The Maya were obsessed with time, and their development of arithmetic and astrology was the most sophisticated of all ancient peoples. They were concerned not only with the dating of events in their own history, but most especially with locating themselves in the universal balance created by the Gods. Thus they used the calender to work out precise times in the ancient past as well, and on stelae F and D there are references to dates 90 million and 400 million years ago. Apart from the stelae, there are some monstrous carved stones, known as zoomorphs, which depict surreal creatures of the Underworld, usually entangled with one of the lords of Quiriguá. Some look like toads, others like crouched jaguars, but it is impossible to make sense of these carvings, and nobody knows what their purpose was.

The city's glory days did not endure, and the last known date carved on the site is 810. Soon afterwards, the city fell from power. Why this happened is an unsolved mystery, but the timing fits in with the general disintegration of Classic Maya civilization, which flourished from around AD 300–900. By the time the Spanish arrived, this site had been abandoned for almost a thousand years, and its remains were not significantly disturbed until United Fruit developed the land for its banana plantations.

GETTING THERE AND WHERE TO STAY

If you do not have your own transport, the most convenient way to visit is en route to Puerto Barrios or the Petén jungle, though the 4 km walk from the main road is hardly an inviting prospect if you are carrying much luggage. From the capital to Quiriguá is about 4 hours by bus, and if you're lucky, there are motorbikes and pick-ups to ferry visitors and plantation workers up and down the connecting dirt road. The site is open daily, 8–6, and there is a small fee (insect repellent is a good idea here). The nearest accommodation is the basic but clean **Hotel Royal**, in the village of Quiriguá. Doubles with private bath cost around US$8, and meals are available here.

To get to Quiriguá village, ask to be dropped off at the village of **Los Amates**, where regular buses make the short journey away from the highway. From here you can walk to the ruins by following the railway tracks to a dirt road, which heads off to the right, through the banana plantations. Pick-up trucks regularly pass by, so you could always try hitching the 3 km distance. To continue travelling to the Atlantic coast, just flag down the relevant bus on the Highway.

Puerto Barrios

In spite of the fact that the country's largest port is just next to Puerto Barrios (in Santo Tomás de Castilla) the town has a very slow, tropical atmosphere to it. Unlike Puerto San José, the Atlantic counterpart has little of the seaside garishness of streets crammed with shops and entertainment, and there is no beach here you would want to spend time on. Instead you find yourself in a pleasantly dilapidated place of tarmac and dirt roads, peeling wooden buildings, and a mixture of black and mestizo inhabitants. The Caribbean, rather than Central America, already feels close here, and Mayas stick out a mile.

Near the waterfront, warehouses and truck depots mix with dingy brothels and a few sleazy bars, but it doesn't add up to anything much, the air too hot and humid for people to get raucous. But at least there are some people on the streets at night, a welcome contrast after the silence of most Guatemalan evenings; and while there is nothing much to do except eat or drink, a night spent here on the way to Livingston or Belize is no great hardship. (Having said that, there is no need to stay here if travelling to Livingston, since there is an afternoon boat leaving daily at 5 pm.) There is a **Lloyds Bank** on 7 Calle, as well as a few others, and a **GUATEL** office on 8 Avenida. The **post office** is on the corner of 3 Avenida and 7 Calle. Note that it is very difficult to change travellers' cheques in this town.

GETTING TO PUERTO BARRIOS
From Guatemala City, the **Litegua** bus company runs an excellent service to Puerto Barrios, which takes 6 hours. At 10 am daily, there is a 'special', which only takes 5 hours, and there are a few more, later in the day. In Puerto Barrios, buses leave from 6 Avenida, at the junction of 9 and 10 Calles.

Buses also leave from the Zona 1 bus terminal, by the train station. There are some direct buses between Esquipulas and Puerto Barrios, and if you go to any of the major road junctions on the Atlantic Highway, you can always flag down a bus there.

Train buffs might want to take the railway, with connections on Tuesday, Thursday and Saturday. The train leaves at 7 am, and can take anything up to 12 hours, though it is supposed to take only 8. Remember that the journey is mostly through desert landscape, it can get very hot, and there are no services on the train. Leaving Puerto Barrios on Wednesday, Friday and Sunday, the train departs at 6 am.

ONWARDS TO BELIZE
Boats for **Punta Gorda** in Belize leave from the dock at the end of 11 Calle, on Tuesday and Friday, at 7.30 am. You must buy your ticket and complete immigration formalities the day before travelling, and both offices close at 5 pm. The ticket office is the same as for the Livingston boats, and the immigration office is two doors down on 9 Calle near the waterfront. The Guatemalan exit fee is around $1 here. The fare is just over $2, one way, and the journey takes around $2\frac{1}{2}$ hrs, not stopping in Livingston. Charters will cost at least $35 each.

Immigration procedures in Punta Gorda are quite informal: your luggage is checked on the pier. One-month permits are issued, renewable for up to 6 months. You will be asked about sufficient funds for your stay, and must have a return flight ticket to your country of residence.

WHERE TO STAY
Undoubtedly the nicest place to stay, though overpriced, is the **Hotel El Norte,** on the seafront, at the end of 7 Calle. A large wooden building, you get the best of the Caribbean atmosphere here. Doubles from $11. Closer to the ferry dock, and cheaper, is **Caribeña**, 4 Avenida, between 10 and 11 Calles. **El Dorado**, 13 Calle, between 6 and 7 Avenida, charges the same; and so does the **Europa**, 8 Avenida, between 8 and 9 Calle. If you prefer to be near the bustle and noise of the town's market, there are plenty of cheap places there, such as the **Pensión Xelajú** on 8 Avenida. Note that streets are rarely marked here, and even the locals don't seem to know which street is where, so ask for locations by their name, rather than by address.

157

EATING OUT
The **Hotel El Norte** has a good and expensive restaurant, and with views of the sea on two sides, you almost feel as if you are in a cruise-ship dining room. More authentic seafood cooking, at much cheaper prices, can be had in the restaurants further up 7 Calle. If you wander along the avenidas running close to the ferry dock and the ticket office, you will find some reasonable places as well. For cheap, *comedor* food, head for the centre of town and the railway tracks. **Triángulo** is one of the better places in this range. Around here and down 9 Calle you will also find bars, pool halls and the rest.

Livingston

Once you leave Puerto Barrios, you are heading for a different world, a world where history and culture are tied to the legacy of the African slave trade, a place where the predominantly black inhabitants speak a boisterous dialect of Spanish, Garifuna and English—almost impossible for any outsider to understand. Music is everywhere, but instead of marimba or salsa, you hear reggae. If you're very lucky, you might even hear some of the older people singing their sad and beautiful Garifuna songs, the African drumming and chorus singing conjuring up images of distant places and their painful past. The young people prefer West Indian music, and saunter down the muddy streets in the obligatory red, green and gold hats, dreadlocks spilling down their backs.

Livingston is a two-street place, only accessible by boat, and its mostly wooden houses cling to the muddy rise that seperates the mouth of the River Dulce from the Atlantic beach. If it was not for the steady flow of tourists, there would be very little here, and even at the best of times there is not much to do. The beach is narrow, and littered with quite a bit of rubbish, so sunbathing is not much of an option either. The reason for coming here is, in fact, simply the novelty value in the Guatemalan context, and also because it is the setting-off point for a gorgeous river trip up the Río Dulce, which can be a stepping stone to continued travel into the Petén jungle.

Christmas is one of two times when things really get going: large numbers of, mainly young, travellers come to join in the reggae 'jump-ups' in the beach discos, and listen to the spontaneous concerts of Garifuna singing outside people's homes. If you're travelling alone, then this is definitely one of the best places to be for Christmas, though you will miss the Catholic processions and Masses of the rest of the country. Another excellent time to be here is on 15 May, which is the anniversary of the Garifuna arriving in Guatemala. The first landing of Garifuna boats is re-enacted on the beach, and there is plenty of singing and partying.

History
The black settlements along the Guatemalan Bay of Amatique are a relatively recent phenomenon, part of a migration that took place in the late 18th century. The people are descendants of African slaves and Carib Indians, who originally lived on the island of St Vincent, in the Eastern Caribbean. A group of them was left stranded on the Honduran island of Roatán by the British in 1795, as punishment for staging an uprising. Happily, many survived and gradually they drifted to the mainland, settling in communities along much of Central America's Caribbean coastline, from Nicaragua to Belize. Guatemala's

share of the Atlantic coast being so small, there is only one major black settlement, and there are many more in Belize and Honduras. They call themselves Garifuna, and have alway been a very independent people, keeping their history alive in a tradition of song and story-telling, and speaking their own hybrid language. Livingston is one of the most isolated communities culturally, not just because it is waterbound, but also because it is the only one of its kind in a country of *ladinos* and Indians. The Belizean and Honduran communties are much larger, and more a part of their country, though certainly distinct, even there. (For a more detailed account of the Garifuna history, see p. 276 of the Honduran chapter.)

Long before Livingston was founded, there was an important Maya port at the mouth of the River Dulce, refered to as Nito. An aspect of Maya culture that is rarely considered is their ocean-going trade and expert seamanship, and as many as 4000 canoes are estimated to have been operating before the Spanish Conquest. In 1502, Columbus and his crew became the first Europeans to encounter an Indian merchant canoe, and Columbus' 14-year-old son excitedly wrote that the canoe was 'as long as a galley and eight feet wide, all made of one tree.' By 1524, Nito had been captured and Spanish settlers moved here, the location of the Maya site since lost. The Spanish settlement was a failure, however, because the newcomers had no idea how to live off the surrounding jungle. Not until much later did Livingston briefly enjoy some importance as a port for the coffee trade, coming direct from the Verapaz highlands via a railway (now defunct) to Lake Izabal and then down the River Dulce.

GETTING TO LIVINGSTON

Boats for Livingston leave daily at 10 and 5 from the dock at the end of 11 Calle in Puerto Barrios, and tickets are sold a short walk away, at the end of 9 Calle, near the waterfront. To be sure of getting on the ferry, arrive an hour early, but at least half an hour before departure. If you miss the boat ($1 one-way), there are always boatmen waiting for custom, who will charge $15–25 per person. The trip normally takes one hour, but on the small *lanchas* it can take longer, and you and your luggage can get very wet.

WHERE TO STAY

EXPENSIVE

There is one 'luxury' hotel, the **Tucán Dugu**. For reservations call tel 347813 or 345242 in Guatemala City. Many of the rooms have ocean views, and there is a nice pool, with a nearby bar. The layout is bad, resulting in long walks down endless corridors and pathways, and the hotel is hardly luxurious.

INEXPENSIVE

A favourite for many is the **Casa Rosada**, a 5-minute walk from the dock, taking the first left turn, which offers thatched cabins on the waterfront. **Caribe**, on the same path, but nearer the dock, is a decent guest house. Also along here and with a good waterfront bar is the **Hotel el Viajero**, with the same prices as the Caribe.

Heading up the main street from the dock, a lovely two-storey wooden building houses the **Río Dulce**, which is a popular budget hotel because of the balcony where you can string a hammock and watch the world go by. Very good value is the **Minerva**, near the centre, on a side street (ask for directions). The second high street, turning left towards the church and cemetery, has one of Livingston's most extraordinary guest houses, the **African Place**. Built by an eccentric Spaniard with a taste for Moorish architecture, the place is a collection of white, concrete buildings, busy with turrets and bizarre decorations. It looks much better than it is—or more interesting, at least—and should be avoided if at all possible. Many are the bad experiences with the abrasive owner, and only the restaurant is worth checking. At the end of the street and down the bank, there is another guest house on the beach. This is the **Flamingo**, which is run by a German woman who has rather excessively fortified the guest house in a walled compound.

EATING OUT AND NIGHTLIFE

One of the best places for breakfast and cheap meals is **Dinis**, on the main street heading towards the cemetery. Also recommended is the **Café Margoth**. Towards the end of the other street is **Cuevas**, with excellent cooking, and nearby is the **Cafetín Lyly**, which is a good *comedor*. **El Malecón**, near the docks, is a large restaurant under a cool verandah and finally, you can eat at the **Tucán Dugu**, where prices are predictably high; only the pool and bar are worth trying really.

The most popular bar is the **Labuga**, on the street towards the cemetery, where there is often live music too. Down on the beach, there are a couple of shack bars, and beyond the **Marimba Beach Bar**, heading out of town, is the main **reggae disco**. Opposite the GUATEL office, you will also find the **Disco Raymondo**, which is a dark and sweaty place.

USEFUL INFORMATION

There is no bank in Livingston, but you can change cash at the **Koo Wong shop**, on the main street. For phone calls, there is a **GUATEL** office near the dock.

Boats for Puerto Barrios leave from the dock at 5 am and 2 pm, daily. Buy your ticket at least one hour early to be sure of getting on, which is usually a battle.

If you don't want to spend lots of money hiring someone to take you up the River Dulce, you can catch the **mail boat** on Tuesdays and Fridays, leaving around 9 am. This will take you as far as Fronteras, and the suspension bridge, where the Petén road heads north. The return journey by mail boat is on the same days. Unfortunately, the schedule changes all the time, and sometimes the boat does not turn up at all, so expect to be flexible. The other drawback of using the mail boat is that you cannot stop off along the way. But at least you will be paying only $8, which is a fraction of the usual cost.

Excursions from Livingston

Siete Altares

About an hour's walk from Livingston along the beach, there is a pretty spot for freshwater swimming during the rainy season: a waterfall here forms a number of beautiful pools in a cascade of several levels. To get there, just follow the beach past the disco, until you come to a river emptying into the sea. If you're lucky there will be someone to ferry you across, but otherwise you can wade or swim across. On the other side the beach soon thins out, and a path leads off to the left, finally reaching the pools. The only drawback about this place is that it is notorious for robbers, and you should never walk this way on your own.

Río Dulce

By far the most popular excursion is a canoe trip up the River Dulce, and you will find plenty of boatmen offering trips down by the dock. The price for going all the way to Lake Izabal can be as high as $60 one-way, so you need to bargain hard, and preferably share the cost with others. If you're only going on a day trip as far as the nature reserve at El Golfete, the price should obviously be much less. As always, agree exactly where you want to go and how much for, before setting off.

Almost as soon as you leave Livingston behind, you enter a gorgeous jungle environment, with all kinds of tropical birds flitting across the emerald waters. The banks either side rise steeply as the river washes through a long gorge, with huge trees and a profusion of vines and plants that hang over the river's edge. If you look carefully, you will see long-legged, white herons, standing motionless as they wait for prey, and perhaps even an iguana sunning itself on a rock.

The best part of the river is this gorge that stretches a number of kilometres between the mouth and a section known as El Golfete, where the waters widen considerably to create a lake. About half way along, there is a hot spring that bubbles directly into the river, and makes for a steaming natural jacuzzi. You have to swim to it from the boat, so ask to stop here if that is what you would like to do. Further along, the area around El Golfete has been designated the **Biotopo Chocón Machacas**, which is intended to help protect the rare manatee, or sea cow, as well as the jungle flora and fauna. There is a landing jetty for boats, and trails to wander around in the forest, though you are unlikely to see any wildlife other than butterflies and birds during the daytime, and it is more fun to explore the many canals by boat. If on a day-trip from Livingston, this is as far as it is worth going.

Into the Jungle

If you plan to continue onwards to the Petén Highway for buses to the jungle or back to the capital, then you should hire a boat to take you as far as the **Castillo de San Felipe**, which is a tiny fort, built by the Spanish to protect Lake Izabal from British pirates, who regularly came to raid trading posts here. Without stopping along the way, the ride takes about 2 hours, and very close to the fort is the inexpensive **Hotel Umberto**, which also offers meals, across the mud road. The only problem with this place is that it's a long walk to the Highway if there is no one to give you a lift.

More convenient, but pretty horrible, are the *pensiones* in the village of **El Relleno**, directly by the suspension bridge. (If you do find yourself having to spend a night here, **Comedor Mary's** is the best for fried fish.) This is where all buses either for the Petén or the capital stop, as well as local buses to nearby towns, such as Morales. If your destination is anywhere along the Atlantic Highway, the fastest option from here is to take a local bus to the Ruidosa road junction, and change there. If you arrive at El Relleno and wish to travel downriver to Livingston, you can find boatmen under the bridge. They know you are more or less dependent on their service, so you will have to bargain hard.

Luxury Resorts on Lake Izabal
Hiding along the shores of the lake are a number of luxurious resort hotels, most of them only accessible by boat. The clientele are mainly rich Guatemalans and American yachting enthusiasts who come here to enjoy exclusive holidays and weekends. Fishing, water-skiing, and sailing charters around Lake Izabal, down the Río Dulce, or as far as the Belizean Cayes, can all be arranged from here, and this elite group of hotels make up the only place in Guatemala where tropical luxury is genuinely laid on, with great food, and sporting entertainment if you want it. To reach any of them, just take a water taxi from below the suspension bridge at Fronteras. This should only cost around $5, but can be as much as $20, depending on your bargaining skills.

One of the nicest places, just past the Castillo de San Felipe, is **Izabal Tropical** (no pool), which charges from $50 for doubles and $56 for triples. Another favourite is the **Catamarán**, which has the best swimming pool and tennis courts, and charges from $36 for doubles and $42 for triples. Two more resort-style places, in the same price category as the Izabal Tropical are **Turicentro Marimonte**, and **Del Río**, both with their own pools. The only place not recommended is **Mario's Marina**.

Of the various yacht **marinas** dotted around, **Susanna's Laguna** is best for meals, and **Mañana Marina** does good breakfasts and has the best bar. **Bar Hotel California** can be reached on foot from Fronteras, and is also worth checking.

THE PETÉN

From the air the Petén jungle, which makes up a third of Guatemala, looks like one green blanket, stretching endlessly into the horizon. On the ground, however, the landscape is surprisingly hilly, and the many rises were favourite places for the Mayas to build their city-states. Look at any map, and you will see it peppered with the names of ancient ruins, many still unexcavated, and many more inaccessible to the traveller without a helicopter or time for many days of jungle hiking.

The land is mostly still covered by thick ancient forest, cut by many rivers and also lakes and swamps. The wildlife is one of the most varied and profuse in Central America, which has a lot to do with the relatively recent incursion of modern man. In spite of the fact that 20% of the jungle has been destroyed in the last decade alone, the impact appears minimal, compared to neighbouring Mexico or Honduras. Here there are jaguars, magueys, snakes, tapirs, howler

Piedras Negras   monkeys, anteaters, armadillos, crocodiles, tropical birds, and an infinite number of creepy-crawlies, from scorpions to bird-eating spiders—though, most likely, you will only see monkeys, birds and insects. It is always a good idea to shake out your clothes and shoes before putting them on, and insect repellent is essential.

It was in this region, the Yucatán peninsula, of which the Guatemalan Petén is a sizeable part, that Maya civilization developed into its highest form. The largest and most elaborate architecture flowered here, with huge pyramids rising above the jungle, and finely decorated plazas, ball courts, residential structures, temples, and much more. The greatest of these cities was Tikal, where successive rulers enjoyed not only political and economic power, but also fostered the arts and sciences, in particular writing and astrology. Other major sites include El Mirador, El Ceibal, Altar de Sacrificios, Yaxchilán and Piedras Negras, but there were hundreds of other settlements, usually along important trading routes or near permanent sources of drinking water.

The Maya Golden Age was during the period AD 250–900, and to many it is a mystery how they could have built cities and developed such a sophisticated society in this inhospitable region. Food supply is difficult, since agricultural farming can only be limited. Hunting and gathering in the forest can sustain a nomadic existence, but is incapable of sustaining centres like Tikal, which possibly had up to 40,000 inhabitants. The current explanation of this enigma is that the Maya were great traders, and their cities grew up in this region because of their monopoly on trade between the Mexican Gulf and the Caribbean. In their time, a lot of merchandise travelled either in ocean-going canoes, or across the Yucatán along the riverways that once existed but have long since disappeared. Thus they would have charged high taxes along their trade routes, and had the contacts to import most of their food supplies, as well as anything else they needed. Their centres of habitation were also spread out over a far greater area than previously realized, with distant satellite communities engaged in maize production solely for the central core where the elite lived.

The three most accessible archaeological ruins are Tikal, Uaxactún, and El Ceibal. The first two are virtually neighbours, and can be visited from the modern town of Flores, or you can stay the night at Tikal itself. El Ceibal needs more time and effort to reach, since you first need to take a bus to the town of Sayaxché, in the southern Petén. Travel in the entire region is by dirt roads that disintegrate into turgid soup during the rainy season from May to October, making travel virtually impossible.

Only Tikal can easily be visited at any time of year, thanks to the airport in nearby Flores, which has regular, daily flights to and from Guatemala City. Also, the road connecting Flores to Tikal is the only surfaced one in the Petén. Expect prices to be high, but do come to Tikal. You will not see another place like it and all other Guatemalan ruins pale besides this one for size, for splendour, for the jungle setting, and the magical combination of ancient architecture, mysterious rainforest and abundant wildlife.

Overland to Flores

The journey overland, from Guatemala City to the jungle capital of Flores (488 km), is famous among travellers for being one of the most harrowing experiences you could possibly inflict on yourself. What is theoretically a 14-hour bus ride takes more like 24 hours, and never less than 16. Even hardened travellers of Latin America are surprised by the seemingly endless torture of this journey, which really comes into its own after crossing the River Dulce, where the tarmac road becomes mud and the bus drivers struggle to negotiate the giant furrows in the road. Whenever it rains, great lakes form across the road, disguising its true depth until it's too late. Matters are not helped by the view out of the window, which is an endlessly monotonous stretch of forest, slashed by the red gash of what calls itself a road. None of the jungle's magic reveals itself to fuel your anticipation.

Approximately 10 to 12 hours after leaving the capital, you arrive at **Poptún**, the fastest growing town in the Petén, though you would never guess it from the miserable collection of mud-stained, concrete houses. It is, however, an excellent place to break the journey, being close to the **Finca Ixobel**, a beautiful jungle farm on the outskirts of town (3 km). It used to be run by an American couple, who lovingly built this place and offered delicious home-grown food and comfortable shelter to weary travellers. (Sadly, the husband was murdered in unclear circumstances and his wife fled the country, leaving the farm to be run by friends.) The business is still running, and there are not many other places in Guatemala where you can combine beautiful surroundings with such pleasant accommodation and delicious meals.

Many visitors turn their overnight stopover into a couple of days, since there is much more to do other than relax and eat well: there is an extensive traveller's library with plenty of books to read, there are horses to rent for jungle excursions, or you can hire a guide to take you hiking, and there are ponds for swimming. Accommodation comes in three varieties. In the main house, there are a few rooms, which are $3 for one and $6 for two, sharing the bathroom (the only snag is the lack of privacy due the absence of a ceiling covering top-floor rooms, just the roof, high above). There are outhouses, which are dormitories, and there are treehouses, both of which cost $2 per person. You can also camp on the meadows surrounding the farm. Meals are not cheap, but certainly worth it. If arriving by bus, ask to be dropped off at the entrance to the farm, which is on the main road. On leaving, you unfortunately have a 3 km walk into Poptún, though you might be able to hitch from the main road. The farm also runs a *pensión* in Poptún itself, as part of the **Restaurante Ixobel**, on the main street. Other accommodation cannot be recommended.

Heading for Flores, buses leave Poptún at 8, 10.30, 11 am, 1, 2 and 3.30 pm. In order to have any hope of a seat, you should take one of the first two buses, which actually originate in Poptún. The journey can take up to 9 hours.

Heading for Guatemala City, buses leave at 2.30, 5, 9 am and 2.30 pm, and the second bus is the only local one.

Flores

Flores comes as quite a surprise: like an overheaped plate of food, this tiny town piles onto an island on the edge of Lake Petén Itzá (which is about 32 km long and 5 km wide). Narrow streets and pastel-coloured, stone houses squeeze together around a colonial church and square at its elevated centre, where the view is refreshingly open, across rusty roofs and the glistening lake, to the jungle all around. To circle the island takes less than twenty minutes and the reason you come here is not the town or its attractive setting, but to see the glorious Maya city of Tikal, 65 km from here.

Although nothing remains to bear witness, the island was probably once the capital of the Itzá, named Tayasal. They were a people who originally came from the Mexican Yucatán, and the city of Chichén Itzá still has their name. They were extremely independent and able to resist the Spanish for over 170 years, though a steady flow of soldiers and missionaries bothered them all that time. The first to arrive here was Hernán Cortés himself, in 1524. He was on his way to a campaign in Honduras, and since the Itzá king received him willingly, he did not stop for bloodshed, and only left his lame horse. Almost one hundred years later, two Spanish priests arrived to find that a statue of the horse was being worshipped as the god of rain and storms, and had to flee for their lives after they smashed it.

Other groups of missionaries arrived with soldiers, and one such group, in 1623, was promptly defeated and sacrificed. Finally, in 1697, the Spanish attacked Tayasal via a war galley, and slaughtered every Indian they could find, while the rest swam to the mainland, never to be seen again. The Maya king was taken to the capital, and paraded in chains.

GETTING TO FLORES

By Air
Apart from the overland route, either by bus or four-wheel drive, you can fly from Guatemala City. At least four flights daily shuttle between the capital and Flores, leaving early in the morning (around 7 am) and returning in the late afternoon (around 4 pm). The flight takes about an hour, and costs around $106 return. From both ends, you can either turn up at the airport and buy direct from the airlines, or go via any travel agent. Flores is usually a stop-over for flights on their way to Belize City, so you can easily visit Tikal on your journey to or from that country.

The only honest **travel agent** for flight tickets from the Petén is in the **Hotel Petén** in Flores. The **Hotel San Juan**, on the mainland, near the causeway connecting Flores, also sells tickets and offers a free bus ride to the airport, but watch out for hidden extras, and you might be sold a seat that does not exist.

In Antigua and Guatemala City, travel agents can not only arrange flights and transport to the airport, but also 1 to 3-day **tours to Tikal**, inclusive of accommodation and guides. However, a 2-day tour can cost as much as $350 plus extras, so if you have the time and initiative you can save yourself a lot of money by travelling independently.

By Road
Other than the route already described, you can also get a bus from Sayaxché, if coming from the southern Petén, via the back road from Cobán. Buses between Flores and Sayaxché are run by the **Pinita** company, and leave at 6 am and 1, in both directions. The journey takes 4–6 hours, and most buses arrive and leave from outside the Hotel San Juan.

WHERE TO STAY AND EAT
The nicest place to stay is in Flores itself, which is generally more expensive than staying on the mainland, where modern Santa Elena and San Benito sprawl. A mud causeway connects the island, so access is easy, though very messy after rains.

In Flores

MODERATE
The best hotel on the island is the **Hotel Petén**, tel 0500–692, fax 0500662, which has a good restaurant and clean rooms with fans. Try to get a room with a lakeside view. With a

pleasant waterfront terrace and bar, the **Hotel Savanna** is also a good choice. Rooms with fans and dinner included go for $20 for two, secure parking available. On the waterfront near the causeway, the **Hotel La Jungla** is a very friendly place.

INEXPENSIVE

Next door to La Jungla is the **Hotel El Itzá**, which is nothing special. Also on the lakeside, with a cosy patio for eating and drinking, is the guest house **El Tucán**, though the rooms are not that nice. Other establishments are opening fast.

Other than the hotel restaurants, there are quite a few places to eat and drink. The top restaurant is the **Palacio Maya**, with a good choice of seafood and other dishes for around $5. **La Jungla**, not to be confused with the hotel, is small and cosy, with good food at medium prices. Next door is a good *comedor*, the **S'Quina**. If you feel like trying traditional Maya cooking, such as stewed venison, armadillo, wild turkey, or fish, then head for **La Mesa de los Mayas**.

On the Mainland: Santa Elena

EXPENSIVE

Not far from the causeway to Flores, the **Hotel Del Patio Tikal** is a two-storey building set around a cool courtyard, which also shades the restaurant. Tel 501229, or fax 502–2–374313 in Guatemala City.

MODERATE

A very pleasant choice is the **Hotel Maya International**, which is a collection of wooden bungalows and a restaurant, built directly over the water, with views of Flores. Tel 501276, fax 500032.

INEXPENSIVE

The **Hotel San Juan**, tel 500041, profits from the fact that buses virtually empty passengers into its lobby, but does not in fact deserve the custom it gets. There is a restaurant attached. Two cheapies are the **Don Quijote**, which offers bare rooms and communal baths; and the **Hotel Jade**, which is better than it looks and good value for money.

Near El Remate, on the lakeshore, halfway to Tikal

LUXURY

The most exclusive hotel in the region is the new **Camino Real**, which is a sister hotel to the one in the capital, with all the same services and prices too (book via the hotel in the capital, see p. 85). Discreetly built into the jungle along the lake, this is the place to come for tropical luxury. You will need to hire a taxi from the airport or arrange to be picked up by the hotel's own vehicle.

INEXPENSIVE

On the branch road leading to the Camino Real, you will find the **campsite El Mirador del Duende**, which styles itself an 'eco-campsite', and is very basic. Either sling a hammock under cabins provided, or pitch a tent. Washing is in the lake, and the toilet is a hole in the ground. Further along the road is the **Gringo Perdido** guest house and campsite, which gets mixed reports. However, it has a restaurant, and also hires out canoes, mountain bikes and horses. **Agua y Tierra**, nearby, hires out 500cc scramblers for around $20, plus the cost of a full tank. These are excellent for making your own way to the ruins of Uaxactún, 24 km beyond Tikal.

If you do not wish to pay for an expensive taxi from the airport, you could wait for one of the minibuses heading for Tikal, on the main road. If they have space they will take you and drop you at El Remate, from where you will have to walk 3 km to reach El Gringo Perdido; or try hitchhiking from the airport.

USEFUL INFORMATION

Tour Agents

For the most impartial advice on reputable **tours, guides, boat, car or bike rental** firms, see the INGUAT representative at the airport, from Tuesdays to Sundays. Alternatively, see the staff at the Hotel Petén, or failing that, the man at the Hotel San Juan, though he is not above ripping you off. A short walk from the San Juan, there is also a tour agency, **Yaxhá Outdoor Life Tours**, which can help with adventurous trips into the jungle. But remember that the only time jungle expeditions are a realistic prospect is during the dry season, from November to April, and even then the weather might go against you.

Money Matters

There is a **bank** in Flores, and you can also change money at the Hotel San Juan; but the shop **Brenda**, opposite the Hotel Jade around the corner, gives a much better rate.

Telecommunications

There is a **GUATEL** office in Santa Elena, or you can pay a lot to use the hotel phones.

Boat Hire

Canoes for exploring Lake Petén Itzá can be rented from **El Relleno**, halfway along the causeway. A double canoe costs $2 per hour. **Boat tours** of the lake are easily arranged with the boatmen who congregate by the causeway, and a trip around the whole lake, taking in the lakeside **Petencito zoo** and a swimming stop, should not cost more than $10.

Tikal

You hear so much about the ruined city of Tikal before you get there, see images of the famous Temple of the Giant Jaguar on so many tourist posters, that you think you know what to expect. But all preconceptions are forgotten as soon as you enter the twilight jungle to walk to the Central Plaza, especially if you use one of the smaller paths, rather than the main gravel one. High above your head, the swaying branches are home to spider and howler monkeys, who occasionally like to pelt visitors with nuts, though they usually miss. Green parakeets squawk above the canopy of trees, while toucans hide from sight, only the chattering 'tock' of their giant bills hinting at their presence. Most exhilarating of all is the lucky sight of a pair of macaws, majestically spreading their red, blue and green wings, but making a very undignified racket, their screams audible far and wide across the forest.

Tikal

Before you know it, you stumble out into your first grassy clearing and come face to face with a pyramid, its damp limestone walls blackened with age and lichen. It seems oddly out of place, a monument in the middle of nowhere. But then the path leads on to the heart of Tikal and opens out onto the green carpet of the **Great Plaza**, where **Temple I** and **Temple II**, more beautifully known as Temple of the Giant Jaguar and Temple of the Masks, tower over you. Their pinnacle tops jab the pale blue sky at 58 m and 50 m respectively, and the giant stairways up their immense bulk can be a daunting prospect. But the effort of climbing Temple II is greatly rewarded by the view from its temple platform. Up here, you find yourself standing above the jungle canopy, looking out across a sea of forest as far as the eye can see, while nearby, the peaks of other pyramids rise up from the depths. One of the very best views of the Great Plaza and its famous pair, is from the **North Acropolis**, which lines one side of the square.

Incredible to imagine that the Maya had no metal tools to create these huge monuments, nor pack animals either—only generations of slave labour sweated here. For over one thousand years the ceremonial centre of Tikal was built and rebuilt to become one of the greatest Maya cities there ever was. There were settlements here as early as 600 BC, but the Golden Age of monumental building was from AD 250–900, an age referred to as the Classic Period by archaeologists. This period is sub-divided into the Early Classic (AD 250–550) and the Late Classic (AD 550–900), and what you see today is almost all from that later period, the rest buried underfoot. The great temples, for example, were built around AD 700, while the North Acropolis dates from AD 550 onwards, though the earliest constructions date from 200 BC.

An interesting feature of Maya rebuilding was that the accompanying stelae—the monumental sculptures that recorded the all-important dates of royal lineages, wars and construction dates—were ritually 'sacrificed', when a particular building had fulfilled its ordained purpose. Usually the stela carried an elaborate portrait of the ruler associated with the building in question, and the Mayas took special care to smash his face, for what reason is uncertain. The ruined or defaced sculpture would then be 'buried' under masonry near an altar, or bricked into a disused building. This is the reason why so many of the stelae at Tikal are damaged or defaced, though vandals and looters have also done much damage.

At its height, central Tikal is estimated to have had 10,000 to 40,000 permanent residents, though most recent thinking favours the lower estimate. However, if you consider that Tikal's territory actually encompassed 40 square kilometres, the subject population of Tikal's rulers may have been much greater. Central Tikal covers an area of 16 square kilometres, where over 3000 buildings of all types have been recorded so far. Added to these there are over 200 stelae and attendant altars, so the day visitor-tour cannot hope to see more than a fraction of what makes up this site. Of course the undisputed highlight of any visit is the magnificent Great Plaza, but there are two other temples worth exploring for bird's-eye views of the jungle and surrounding monuments, and those are **Temple III**, just west of the Great Plaza, and most especially **Temple IV**.

The latter is the highest structure ever built by a Native American civilization, towering a breathtaking 96 m from the ground.

Built around AD 741, this temple has not been cleared of the forest that has invaded its steps and walls, and to reach its summit, you have to clamber up ladders and over trees, unsuitable for vertigo sufferers (as are all the pyramids). A large number of toucans congregate around here, and you have a good chance of coming almost face to face with one as you climb the ladders. Another building you should be sure to visit is the Temple of the Inscriptions, some way from the centre, which is covered in mysterious hiero-glyphics.

GETTING TO TIKAL

Transport to Tikal is by minibus, and most of the hotels run their own service. The journey is expensive at $6 return, and takes one hour. On entry to the National Park of Tikal, you will be charged an extra $6. In theory, this is a daily fee, but in practice, those staying overnight in Tikal itself only pay once, on entry.

A Guide to the Site

For a detailed description of the site, an excellent map, as well as historical and archaeological guidance on Tikal, you cannot do better than buy William R. Coe's handbook. *Tikal: A Handbook of the Ancient Maya Ruins* (about $10). This should be on sale at the site, but to be certain, you should buy it before arrival, and best read it before exploring the ruins too. This excellent book will tell you all you need to know in a readable style, and the map is very helpful. In Guatemala City, the book is available at the Popol Vuh Museum, and all the bookshops in Antigua sell it. You should also be able to buy it in England and the United States.

Without this handbook and its map, you will need a guide if you are not on an organized tour, not just to explain the site, but also to help you explore, since it's easy to

get lost. Official guides wait around the entrance path to the site, and especially around the Great Plaza. As elsewhere, you need to bargain out the price before setting off, and it helps if you know which parts you especially want to see.

USEFUL INFORMATION

The entrance fee to the National Park of Tikal is now $6, and the ruins themselves are open daily from 6 to 6, though you can usually stay a little longer to watch the sunset and listen to the grunting howler monkeys. There are no toilets by the ruins, only by the car park, some distance away.

There is a small **museum** near the car park (Mon–Fri, 9–5, Sat and Sun, 9–4, nominal fee), which is worth visiting to see fading black and white photographs taken by Alfred P. Maudsley in the 1880s. These will give you an excellent idea of how much work has been necessary to clear the jungle from the ruins, most of which has been done by the Tikal Project, which got under way in the 1950s. There is also a fine collection of Maya vases and pottery found at the site, as well as jade jewellery and carved bones taken from royal tombs. For the best preserved stelae, see the **Stelae Museum** next to the **visitor's centre**, where you will also find a selection of brochures and books.

Clothing for the jungle should cover your legs and arms to protect against the incessant mosquitoes and scratchy foliage, and you should certainly bring repellent. A hat and binoculars are useful, and it is best to wear comfortable, flat shoes, suitable for jungle paths and climbing the pyramids. If you plan to be here in the evenings, you will need a torch, as there is no lighting. Remember also that it can get chilly at night, and frequently rains.

WHERE TO STAY

In spite of the expense and bad value for money, you should try to spend at least one night next to the ruins, so that you can explore them in peace when most other tourists have left, and also experience them during their most magical times, at dawn and dusk. During peak seasons, such as Christmas, New Year and Easter, you can expect the hotels to be fully booked up. To reserve a room, you will have to go via a travel agent, and even then you cannot be certain that your reservation will be honoured. The only way you can be guaranteed a room is if you are flying in on an organized tour, otherwise you just have to try your luck on arrival. Prices change constantly here, so those stated can only be a general guideline.

EXPENSIVE

There is a choice of three hotels: the **Tikal Inn** is expensive and dirty, with *cabaña* style rooms around a small swimming pool. The **Jaguar Inn** offers a few simple rooms. It does have the best restaurant though. **Jungle Lodge**, nearest the ruins, offers bungalows with private baths. Limited cheaper accommodation in old buildings and dormitory rooms is also available, which is always worth asking about. This place is your best choice, even though there is sometimes no water, the service is bad, and the restaurant is totally lacking. Their minibus usually meets incoming flights, and will take you straight to Tikal, avoiding Flores.

INEXPENSIVE

There is a **campsite**, which charges $6 for you to pitch your tent or sling a hammock under leaky shelters (mosquito nets are essential). Shower and toilet facilities are available, but there is often no water.

EATING OUT
The cheapest option is to bring your own picnic and something to drink, though sodas are sold at strategic places around the ruins. The restaurant in the visitor's centre is outrageously expensive and not very good, and you are much better off at the restaurant of the Jaguar Inn. There are a number of *comedores* scattered along the entrance road to the site, but the very best is right next to the campsite and car park, a friendly place to be in the evenings too.

Uaxactún

During the dry season, buses occasionally drive the extra 24 km north, to Uaxactún, and hired jeeps can also be used. Or you could take a guide and walk to the site from Tikal, which takes about 6 hours, so you would have to camp overnight before returning—an excellent introduction to the delights and discomforts of jungle hiking. Tikal's closest neighbour, this is a small and undramatic site by comparison: the pyramids and other structures are much lower and also unrestored, though if they were cleared, it would be easy to see that this was a large Maya centre as well. There is much more of a 'lost world' feeling here, and you are unlikely to see any other tourists, since it does take time and effort to get here. The site is significant today, because of Sylvanus G. Morley's excavations and research here that have considerably advanced our understanding of Maya writing.

El Ceibal and Other Maya Sites

El Ceibal is a site that is primarily interesting for its beautiful jungle setting, on the banks of the Río de la Pasión. The stone used here was very hard, so although the temples are not impressive for size, they do retain some excellently preserved carving. El Ceibal was probably taken over by Mexican peoples in the Late Classic Period (AD 550–900), and you will notice that some of the sculptural style has a strong Mexican influence.

To reach the site, your best option is to hire a boat from the town of Sayaxché. If you can find a group of people it will be much cheaper, since the boatmen charge around $30 for the round trip. Set off early to give yourself plenty of time, as it takes 2 hours on the boat, and then 45 minutes' walking to reach the site. Bring your own food and drink, and do not forget the insect repellent.

Sayaxché

Sayaxché is a thriving jungle town on the Río de la Pasión, which is a good base for the adventurous traveller with plenty of time (and money). From here you can organize journeys of any length and distance, into the jungle, down the rivers or to visit specific sites. Of course any excursion to a Maya site involves a jungle trip, of which the one to El Ceibal is the easiest.

Although hunting has been outlawed, the fishing is still very good here, and one of the best places to do this is **Lake Petexbatún**, 48 km south of Sayaxché. There are also a couple of small Maya sites here, of which **Dos Pilas** is the only one with guards and the best place to camp. You will need to bring all necessary equipment, most of which you can hire in Sayaxché, and all food and drink. Spare a thought for the guards too, who will be much more helpful and willing to share fires and advice if you bring enough food to share with them.

You can reach Lake Petexbatún by boat (plus a 12 km walk), and you will certainly need to hire someone who can also act as guide. For the best advice about trips to and around the lake see Julián Mariona Morán, at the Hotel La Montana, in Sayaxché. Or talk to Julio Godoy at the Hotel Guayacán, who is a well-known expert on the region. One general rule about hiring a guide is that you are expected to provide his food and drink, as well as his fee. To avoid arguments, try to be as detailed as possible in the arrangements about what exactly you will do and how long it will take. The guide who asks to be paid in full before departure is a dubious prospect, and you should never pay more than half before the end of your journey. Expect a general fee of $30–40 per day.

GETTING TO SAXAYCHE
The easiest route is from Flores and **Pinita** buses leave daily at 6 and 1 from both directions. The town lies 56 km southwest of Flores, and the journey along the mud road takes 4–6 hrs, but do not even think of it during the rainy season. Boats ferry arriving passengers across the river to Sayaxché.

WHERE TO STAY
INEXPENSIVE
A long-standing favourite is the **Hotel Guayacán**, known as Hotel Godoy after its owner, which is not far from the ferry landing. Meals are also offered in the restaurant. Cheaper is the **Hotel la Montaña**, also with restaurant. Last choice should be the **Hotel Mayapan** for simple rooms. The best place to eat is the Hotel la Montaña.

Remote Maya Sites

North of Flores
Two significant sites lie in this direction: **El Mirador** and **Río Azul**. Of these, the former is the more important, and was in fact a huge city in its day, as significant as Tikal before it was eclipsed by it. To reach El Mirador, which lies just 5 km from the Mexican border, you need to hire a four-wheel-drive or hitch to Carmelita (35 km), and there enquire about a guide and mule to take you on the two-day trek to the ruins. Camping equipment, food and water must all be brought with you, and you should check with the INGUAT official in Flores whether you need permission from the authorities to travel this way. Río Azul does not merit a special expedition unless you have a specialist interest. The round trip takes up to 3 tough days by four-wheel-drive.

East of Flores
Yaxhá lies 48 km away, on the shores of Lake Yaxhá. This is believed to be a huge site, as yet unrestored, though INGUAT has plans to develop it as a new tourist attraction. One

of the few things known about this site is its unusually late period of habitation, probably between the 12th century and 14th century, long after the Classic Maya civilization had collapsed. To reach the site is relatively easy, since you can catch any bus heading for the Belizean border, and ask to be dropped off at the turning for Yaxhá. From there you will have to walk up to three hours, along a clear track (turn left when the track reaches the lake). Camping equipment, food and water are all necessary, since you will have to stay the night. Alternatively, you could try reaching the site by four-wheel-drive, and by the time you get to Guatemala, there might even be tours going here, so it is worth checking with the INGUAT official.

Northwest of Sayaxché
Reaching the site of **Yaxchilán** is one of the most adventurous undertakings. Located on the banks of the Usumacinta river, marking the border between Guatemala and Mexico, you will have to travel over 100 km by boat, first along the Río de la Pasión, and then on the Usumacinta itself. The journey as far as the ruins will take at least two or three days one-way, and can take much longer if you decide to travel on trading boats. Commercial river traffic only goes as far as Benemérito anyway, and from there you must hire a boat. The best option is to hire a boat from Sayaxché, which will take you all the way to Yaxchilán. Either way, you will need plenty of time and money, but the site itself is beautifully located on the river bank, and certainly an interesting place to visit. If you do not wish to organize your own trip, you could always go on a tour with one of the expedition agencies working out of Guatemala City.

Onwards to Mexico
If you plan to travel into Mexico via the river town of **Benemérito**, you must get your Guatemalan exit stamp at the airport in Flores first. The Mexican immigration post is outside Benemérito, which all buses pass, leaving daily for Palenque in the early mornings. A much easier option for travelling to Mexico from the Petén is to get a direct bus from Flores to El Naranjo (Guatemalan exit stamp available here), and from there boats take you to La Palma in Mexico.

Onwards to Belize
There are daily buses leaving Flores for the border town, **Melchor de Mencos**, leaving at 5, 7, 10, 11 am, and 3pm. The mud road is really awful, and the journey of about 80 km can take quite a few hours. On the Belizean side, the small town of Benque Viejo is a few kilometres from the border, and is best passed by as soon as possible. Buses for Belize City leave the border regularly, and all pass through San Ignacio, which is the first town from the border where you will find pleasant accommodation (see p. 212, Belize Chapter).

Part V
BELIZE

Fewer than 200,000 people live in this tiny country; the majority are black or creole, their language a lilting English and their preferred music Caribbean reggae. Even the Indians speak English to a West Indian tune, and Spanish is only the second language, in spite of a sizeable number of mestizos.

Most of the population lives on the coast, leaving the interior of swampy plains, rainforest and jungle covering the mountains almost uninhabited. As a result, the species of wildlife and tropical flora are some of the richest and most diverse in all of Central America. The endangered jaguar and the scarlet macaw are just two of many rare animals that thrive in Belize and, in this part of the world, only Costa Rica can rival the variety of birds. There are even areas that have never been explored by outsiders—thick tropical forests hiding innumerable Maya ruins in their twilight world.

About 300 km long, the country looks like a large bite out of Guatemala, by which it is traditionally claimed, and whose maps pointedly include Belize in its national territory. However, the wild Maya Mountains stand as a bulwark against Guatemala's pretensions and make up almost the entire western border of a country that is never more than 109 km wide. Mexico and Guatemala mark the northern and southern borders respectively, while the east consists of a 288 km Caribbean coastline with hundreds of islands scattered along its entirety—outcrops of the largest barrier reef in the northern hemisphere.

The islands, or cayes, as they are known, provide the main focus for travellers to Belize. Life here is even more laid back than on the mainland, and refreshing sea breezes make dozing in a hammock or sunbathing highly pleasurable. In the surrounding sea a magical world lies just off the beaches, and the diving and snorkelling are excellent. The

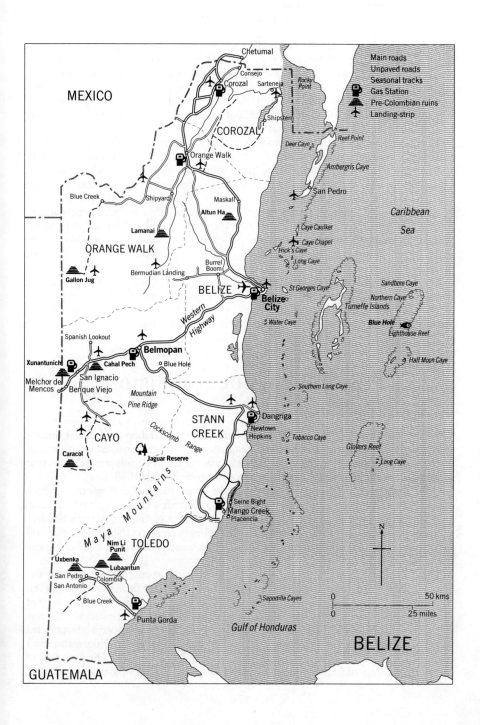

MEXICO

Chetumal

Consejo

Corozal

Sarteneja

Rocky
Point

COROZAL

Shipstern

Reef Point

Deer Caye

Orange Walk

Blue Creek

Shipyard

Maskall

Altun Ha

Ambergris Caye

San Pedro

Lamanai

ORANGE WALK

Bermudian Landing

Burrel
Boom

Caribbean
Sea

Caye Caulker

Caye Chapel

Hick's Cave

Long Caye

Gallon Jug

BELIZE

**Belize
City**

St Georges Caye

Sandbore Caye

Northern Caye

Turneffe Islands

Blue Hole

Lighthouse Reef

Water Caye

Spanish Lookout

Western   Highway

Half Moon Caye

Belmopan

Xunantunich

Cahal Pech

Blue Hole

Southern Long Caye

Melchor del
Mencos

San Ignacio

Benque Viejo

Mountain
Pine Ridge

Cockscomb   Range

**STANN
CREEK**

Dangriga

Newtown
Hopkins

Tobacco Caye

Glovers Reef

CAYO

Jaguar Reserve

Caracol

Long Caye

M a y a   M o u n t a i n s

Seine Bight

Mango Creek

Placencia

**Nim Li
Punit**

TOLEDO

Uxbenka

Lubaantun

San Pedro

Colombia

San Antonio

Blue Creek

Sapodilla Cayes

Punta Gorda

BELIZE

Gulf of Honduras

N

0   50 kms

0   25 miles

GUATEMALA

Main roads
Unpaved roads
Seasonal tracks
Gas Station
Pre-Colombian ruins
Landing-strip

most developed resort island is Ambergris Caye, but there are plenty of hideaway places too, both exclusive and cheap, so it is easy to escape the crowds.

A favourite saying among travellers is that 'the best thing about Belize is underwater', but this is simply not true. The tropical forests of the interior are equally exciting, especially if you travel along any of the rivers, where you will most likely see giant iguanas sunning themselves on the shore, brilliant kingfishers and gorgeous butterflies, sleeping bats, and lizards that can walk on water.

The great variety of wildlife, both in the sea and on land, as well as the friendly people, make Belize a very enjoyable country to visit. To the south, the remote districts of Toledo and Stann Creek combine some of the best features: tropical forests and rich wildlife; Maya villages and ancient ruins in the highlands; and some of the finest mainland beaches. More accessible, the western Cayo district hides jungle lodges along the Rivers Mopan and Macal, while also being home to the Mountain Pine Ridge, a region of pine forests, meadows and waterfalls, ideal for hiking and camping. Northern Belize is mostly flat and the least interesting for the visitor, though there are some significant Maya ruins in the region. But if it is sun, sea and surf you want, you can hardly beat the Belizean cayes.

It is not just the country's natural heritage that is exceptional—Belize is also distinguished by a government founded on parliamentary democracy, with a very good record on peace and human rights. The economy is reasonably stable too, tourism providing a major boost to income from agriculture and fishing.

Post-Independence History

Buccaneers and Pirates

The history of Belize, formerly British Honduras, is unique among the Central American countries. It was ignored by Spanish conquistadors, who only passed by on their way from Mexico to Panama, and the coast was left to be settled by British seafarers, the first of whom were shipwrecked on the treacherous Barrier Reef in 1638.

In the early days, the region was known as the Honduran Bay Settlement, and only consisted of a tiny patch around Belize City and St George's Caye, which was an ideal base for maritime bandits. The Barrier Reef provided protection from heavy Spanish galleons, who were unable to pass through the shallow waters, yet the pirates could still swoop on the seasonal migration of colonial ships weighed down by gold and other treasures.

The British government, eager to crack the Spanish monopoly on trade in the Americas and West Indies, actively encouraged piracy at that time. Some were even commissioned by the British government, such as the buccaneers and privateers. One of the most famous buccaneers was Sir Henry Morgan, whose most spectacular feat was capturing Panama in 1670, and holding it to ransom for 780 pieces of eight. His reward was to be named lieutenant governor of Jamaica. Privateers, unlike Sir Henry who was a soldier of fortune loyal to his regent, were simply hired to rob trading vessels of competing nations such as Spain, and their reward was to keep whatever bounty they found. Finally, at the bottom of the criminal scale were the pirates, who served no one but themselves and robbed any boat they could. Among the many legendary figures is Edward 'Blackbeard' Teach, who apparently was so fearsome that Spanish ships would give up their cargo without so much as a fight.

Creole Society

From the early pirate camps developed a society that was not characterized by a blending of Spanish and Indian blood, but of mainly British and African, with a limited amount of Indian. It was a society that eventually developed its own governmental institutions, far removed from the 'strongman politics' that grew up elsewhere in Central America. No plantation elite developed here, with a country enslaved to bananas, coffee or sugar, rather a society that lived from logging and the sea. The Baymen, as they were called, constructed an early form of democratic rule, where they elected governing magistrates at public meetings. For over 200 years the Honduran Bay Settlement survived even though it was entirely surrounded by hostile Spanish forces, and did not become a British Colony until 1862. Not only does the racial and political heritage differ from that in the rest of Central America—the social and economic history does too.

Slavery was officially abolished in 1838, and multiculturalism flourished throughout the 19th century, though certainly not without tension. Not all blacks who came to the Honduran Bay Settlement were slaves in the first place. For example, 500 black members of the 5th West India Regiment arrived in 1817, after their regiment was disbanded and they were given the option of land grants here. Most became free woodcutters in the emergent logwood and mahogany trade. Other blacks arrived as free survivors from shipwrecked slaving vessels or were simply given their freedom by captains who had fallen out with their contractors.

The racial melting pot was not just one of white and black, however. At least 8000 mestizo and Indian refugees remained after the end of the War of the Races in the Yucatán, in 1874, while almost twenty years earlier, 1000 East Indian Sepoys arrived after being deported by the British. The Sepoys had been responsible for a bloody uprising against British rule in India, killing many colonials in New Delhi and elsewhere. Once the British had granted the territory Colony status, they also began an immigration incentive programme for Chinese farm workers. By that time the logging trade was already going into decline, and new labour was needed to develop agriculture. Unfortunately, less than half of the 474 Chinese arrivals in 1865 remained three years later; they had either died from tropical diseases or returned to their own country. A small number of Lebanese mercantile families also settled in British Honduras, as did German-speaking Protestant Mennonites, emigrating from Canada and Mexico.

A Controversial Territory

At first Belize consisted solely of Belize City and St George's Caye, but soon the settlement spread. One reason for the expansion was that the logging trade required large tracts of forest to search for mahogany. The Spanish were always keen to assert that the British settlers had no territorial rights, and could not found permanent towns and villages. However, the 1783 Treaty of Versailles established the first outline for the

Baymen's territory. According to that agreement, the northern border was the River Hondo, the southern one the Belize River, and the western border Petén Itzá. But only three years later Belizean loggers were operating as far south as the Sibun River, and the country's present-day outline was established from this time onwards, even if the Spanish and British authorities both tried to deny it.

The 1783 Treaty had been signed by the Spanish on condition that the British government did not establish a colonial government in the region, and also gave up its claim to the Mosquito Coast. But the Baymen, with their tradition of self-rule, were never easily persuaded to curtail their operations according to British foreign policy, and thus this early territorial agreement was soon ignored. It was a thorn in the Spanish colonial side, and forces from the Mexican Yucatán repeatedly threatened the Baymen.

Finally, in 1798, a huge Spanish fleet of 32 ships, 500 seamen and 2000 soldiers set sail to rout Belize City once and for all. But as luck would have it, three ships of the West India Regiment came to the aid of the ragged flotilla of Baymen boats, in addition to 171 slaves who agreed to fight in return for their freedom, and their combined forces actually succeeded in repelling the enemy fleet. It was the last time the Spanish tried to remove the settlers by force, and the Battle of St George's Caye is still celebrated as a national holiday in modern Belize.

Once Mexico and the Central American region had gained independence from Spain, in 1821, the United Provinces of Central America were founded, from which British Honduras remained apart. However, in 1839, the union disintegrated, Guatemala claimed it had inherited sovereign rights over Belize from Spain, thus initiating a conflict that is still simmering at present. The British, in turn, declared the territory to be under the law of England and instituted a governor general to rule the country. As far as the Baymen were concerned, it was a necessary evil, but British rule always sat uneasily with a society that was founded on personal freedom and home rule.

The conflict between Britain and Guatemala continued until the Treaty of 1859, when Guatemala officially recognized British sovereignty over British Honduras—now known as Belize. The agreement was signed on condition that the British would build a road connecting the Petén with the Caribbean coast of Belize, but this part of the bargain was never kept, and thus successive Guatemalan governments have declared the 1859 and later 1863 Treaties invalid. To this day Guatemala claims the entire territory of Belize, occasionally hotting up the argument with some military threats, and this is the principal reason why the British armed forces remain in independent Belize, and why the country did not gain full independence until 1981. A new treaty of recognition was signed in 1991, but it is unlikely to hold since many Guatemalans oppose it and the next president could revoke it.

Independence and Democracy

British Honduras officially became known as Belize in June 1973, and instituted its own Belizean dollar in 1974, but did not become a fully independent member of the Commonwealth of Nations until 21 September 1981, with George Cadle Price elected as the first prime minister. He is the leader of the People's United Party (PUP), founded in 1950, and has been the country's premier on many occasions, most recently elected in 1989, when his party narrowly won the last elections with a majority of just two seats. Elections must be held at least every five years, and there is universal suffrage for all over the age of 18.

The system of government in Belize is a parliamentary democracy based on the British model, and the prime minister rules the country with an elected cabinet of ministers and ministers of state. The Queen is still the titular head of state, but she is represented by a governor general who is always a Belizean and takes his cue for appointing members to the cabinet from the Belizean prime minister.

General Information

Ze-haad pikini go da maakit two time'
Children who don't listen go to market twice: listen to advice.

Creole proverb

Getting to Belize

By Air
International airlines with regular connections from North America to Belize are American Airlines (tel 800 624 6262), Belize Trans Air (tel 305 261 3069), Continental (tel 800 0856), Pan Am (tel 800 1111), Taca (tel 800 535 8780), and Tan-Sahsa (tel 800 327 1225). The most frequent flights are from Miami, but there are also daily direct flights from Houston and Los Angeles, and regular flights from New Orleans.

There are no direct flights from Europe. The best option is to fly to Miami on British Airways, Continental, Pan Am, KLM, Eastern or Virgin Atlantic (cheapest), and then on to Belize. The cheapest option of all is to fly to Cancún in Mexico, via the US, and then catch a bus southwards to Belize. There are also flights between Cancún and Belize run by Tropic Air. Prices are much the same as to neighbouring Guatemala, so you should expect to pay around US$350 roundtrip from Miami, and around £600 from Europe. On leaving Belize, you will be charged BZ$20 departure tax, unless you have been in the country for less than 24 hours. There are also frequent direct services to Belize from all the Central American countries, except Nicaragua. The one international airport, **Philip Goldson Airport**, is 16 km outside Belize City.

Without prior notice, you can only arrive by **private aircraft** at the international airport. If you are coming from Cuba or Guatemala, the latest requirements can be obtained from the airport officials. Belizean airspace is open during daylight hours, and pilots must file a flight plan. Landing fees are around BZ$9.75 for a 6000 lb aircraft, and BZ$1.60 for every additional 100 lb.

By Boat
Ships occasionally sail to Belize from New Orleans and Florida ports, but flying will be easier to arrange and cheaper. The only scheduled ferry service arriving in Belize is the

ferry between Puerto Barrios in Guatemala (see p. 157) and Punta Gorda in southern Belize. The ferry leaves on Tuesdays and Fridays, in either direction, and the journey takes about 2½ hours. For up-to-date information in Punta Gorda itself, contact **Indita Maya**, tel (07) 2065.

Arriving by **private yacht**, you are expected to report to the police or immigration officials immediately. You do not require any special permits, but you will have to present the vessel's official document; clearance from the last port of call; four copies of the crew and passenger manifesto; and four copies of stores used or a list of cargo on board. If there is no cargo, then you just need an imballast manifesto.

By Train

There is no railway in Belize, and none leading to its borders.

By Bus

There are cheap long-distance buses from the United States, through Mexico, to Belize. This is, however, a very long and arduous trip. From Texas the journey takes up to 6 days; from California, more like 2 weeks.

From Mexico, there is a frequent, daily service of direct buses between Chetumal and Belize City, run by the **Batty** and **Venus** bus companies. The first bus leaves Chetumal at 4 am, last one at 6 pm. The journey takes about 4 hours.

Arriving overland from Guatemala, there is one road connection from Flores, in the Petén jungle, crossing into Belize at Benque Viejo (see p. 173). The **Novelo** bus company runs daily direct buses from the border to Belize City, between 4 and 11 am, and a **Batty** bus leaves at 1 pm. The journey takes 3 hours from the border. Arriving at any other time, just take a taxi from the border to Benque Viejo, 2 kilometres away. From here there are buses leaving for nearby San Ignacio, where there are regular buses to the capital, until around 6, though services are always limited on Sundays. San Ignacio is the best place to stay the night, if you don't wish to travel further.

By Car

Arriving by car, you will need your driver's licence and registration document, and third party liability insurance is mandatory. You can buy it at the border. You will also be asked to show sufficient funds for your stay. In theory you are supposed to have US$50 per day; in practice US$1000 per month should be acceptable. Drivers without an International Driver's Licence will have to apply for a temporary Belizean driver's permit from the Chief Licensing Officer, in Belize City, valid for 90 days. On leaving the country you will be charged a BZ$5 exit fee for the car.

Embassies and Consulates

As these offices are not directly responsible for tourism, you can expect very limited information on anything other than official entry requirements and investment opportunities.
In the UK: Belize High Commission, 19a Cavendish Square, London W1M 9AD, tel (071) 499 9728, fax (071) 491 4139.

In the US: Belize Embassy, 3400 International Drive, NW, Suite 25, Washington, DC 20008, tel (202) 363 4505, fax (202) 362 7468. Belize Mission to the United Nations, 820 Second Avenue, New York, NY 10017, tel (212) 599 0233.
In Canada: Belize High Commission, 112 Kent Street, Suite 2005, Place de Ville, Tower B, Ottawa, Ontario K1P 5P2, tel (613) 232 7389.

Tourist Offices

In the UK: There is only limited information available from the High Commission, and you can probably find out more by going to your local travel agent. Your best option could well be to phone or fax the Belize Tourist Board in Belize (tel 02 77213, fax 02 77490) requesting the latest brochures.
In the US and Canada: There are a very large number of tour operators specializing in Belize in the United States, and some in Canada. A full list is available from the Belizean Tourist Board, in their brochure entitled *Belize: The Adventure Coast*. **Belize Tourist Board**, 415 Seventh Avenue, New York, NY 10001, tel (212) 268 8798, fax (212) 695 3018. You can call toll-free from continental US and Canada on 800–624–0686.

Maps

Detailed maps of Belize are difficult to get hold of, and the tourist map sold by the Tourist Board is the best you will get in the country itself. Only the main roads and highways are marked, but there are street maps of most of the major towns. Petrol stations are only indicated in the towns.

A trip to your local map shop is highly recommended, as they may have more detailed maps. In England, the best place to go is **Stanfords International Map Centre**, 12–14 Long Acre, London WC2P 9LP, tel (071) 837 1321. Also worth trying in England is the Overseas Surveys Directorate, which has published maps of Belize to a scale of 1:250 000 and 1:50 000.

Passports and Visas

All visitors need a valid passport to enter the country, and are given permission to stay for one month, with extensions possible for up to six months in total. Extensions are available from the **Immigration Office**, 115 Barrack Road, Belize City, tel (02) 77237 (open Mon–Thurs 8.30–11.30 and 1–4, closing at 3.30 on Fri). Or you could try any police station. You will also be asked to show sufficient funds for your stay and, unless arriving in private transport, an onward flight ticket. As a general rule, $50 per day is considered sufficient funds by the officials. If you have less, you can always bluff, and hope they do not ask you to prove it, which they often do not. Alternatively, showing a credit card would help.

Nationals from the United States, Great Britain and Commonwealth countries do not need visas. Nor do people from Belgium, Denmark, France, Finland, Greece, Iceland, Italy, Liechtenstein, Luxembourg, Mexico, Netherlands, Norway, Panama, Spain, Sweden, Switzerland, Tunisia, Turkey or Uruguay. If you do need a visa, you must apply for it before arrival in Belize.

Customs

You cannot bring any fruit or vegetables into Belize, but otherwise there are no unusual restrictions. Electrical goods may incur duties, refundable on leaving the country. Leaving the country by air, there is an exit fee of BZ$20. Leaving by land, the exit fee is BZ$2. If arriving by air, you must have a return ticket in order to enter the country. You may be asked where you intend to stay and what you intend to do. However, if you have no fixed plans this will not cause any problems.

On Arrival

Fishaman neva say e fish 'tink.
Self-criticism is rare.

Creole proverb

Tourist Offices

There are many tour operators offering everything from sightseeing tours to sailing charters, and a full list is available from the Belize Tourist Board. The office sells maps of the country, and also a few special interest books. Free brochures are available on everything from nature reserves and Maya sites to the country's government structure. The staff can help with hotel and tour reservations. The office is open Mon–Thurs, 8–noon and 1–5; Fri till 4.30.

Belize Tourist Board, 53 Regent Street, P.O. Box 325, Belize City, tel (02) 77213/73255, fax (02) 77490.

Getting Around Belize

Hurry, hurry, get deh tomorrow; tek time, get deh today.

By Air
There are local airports in almost all of the country's main towns and some cayes (reef islands), and getting around by air is easy, if not cheap. There are three airlines providing internal flights: **Maya Airways**, tel (02) 77125/72312, has the most flights; **Island Air**, tel (02) 31140; and **Tropic Air**, tel (02) 45671. Tickets can be booked at any travel agent. There are airports in Belize City (both the international and municipal airport are used for domestic flights), Corozal, Caye Chapel, Dangriga, Big Creek (for Placencia), Punta Gorda and Ambergris Caye.

Flights to and from the municipal airport in Belize City are always cheaper than to the international one. Sample return airfares from the Belize City municipal airport are: Ambergris Caye, BZ$70; Corozal, BZ$75; Caye Chapel, BZ$54; Dangriga, BZ$81; Big Creek, BZ$141; Punta Gorda, BZ$188. Flights connecting Ambergris Caye with Caye Chapel are around BZ$30 one-way, though at the time of writing, the only resort on Caye Chapel was closed for refurbishment. Children under 12 only get a 30% discount on their tickets.

There are also many airstrips by smaller and remote settlements, and it is easy to charter small aircraft. Ask about reputable companies at the Tourist Board in Belize City, or go direct to either of the airports.

By Train
There is no railway in Belize.

By Bus
Getting around Belize by bus is easy. There are regular daily services (greatly reduced on Sundays) to all corners of the country, and fares are cheap. As elsewhere in Central America, the buses tend to be old American school buses, rather uncomfortable for tall people. The main highways are all paved, except the Southern Highway beyond Dangriga, which makes travel in southern Belize slow. Apart from local buses operating out of the major towns, four companies have carved out their specific regions, all with their main terminals in Belize City: **Batty Bus Line** serves western Belize and northern Belize; **Venus Bus Line** also runs a service to the north; **Novelo Bus Service** runs west to the Guatemalan border; and **Z-Line Buses** serve southern Belize.

By Car
Having your own transport in Belize is very worthwhile, since the roads are generally excellent, and even in the more rustic south, the dirt roads are well maintained. It will make it much easier to visit places away from the main highway. Local buses do serve outlying areas, but not very often, and not usually when it will suit you. None of the Maya sites are served by commercial buses, but most have roads leading to them. (See above for entry requirements for bringing your own car.)

The only region where a high-clearance vehicle, and possibly four-wheel-drive, is recommended, is in southern Belize. However, the dirt road leading to the remote Maya site of Caracol also requires a tough, four-wheel-drive vehicle, and even then, you can only use it during the dry season from November to May. You also need permission to enter the Mountain Pine Ridge area from the local Forestry Commission.

Traffic drives on the right, but there is one important rule to remember: when you want to turn left, both traffic behind you and oncoming vehicles have right of way, and the custom is to move to the side of the road, allowing traffic in both directions to pass before turning left. There is only one traffic light in the entire country, on a bridge in San Ignacio, and residents are petitioning to have it removed. There are few petrol stations outside the main towns, so always keep an eye on the tank.

In southern Belize, road signs are almost non-existent and it is easy to get lost. Dirt roads can go on for a very long time before they end at a logging camp, so a road map and regular enquiries from the locals are essential. As a Belizean explained it: 'We know where we're going, so what do we need road signs for?' An entertaining book, published locally, is Emory King's *Driver's Guide to Beautiful Belize*, on sale in bookshops and from the Tourist Board in Belize City.

Car Hire
The best place to hire a vehicle is in Belize City, but there are other towns with local rental agencies too. You will have to reckon on around $90 a day for a jeep with unlimited mileage, so renting is not cheap. If you rent by the week, you get a better deal. The following agencies are officially recommended:

IN BELIZE CITY

Avis, Radisson Fort George Hotel Plaza, Belize City, tel (02) 78637; **Budget,** 771 Bella Vista, Belize City, tel (02) 32435, fax (02) 30237; **Crystal Auto Rental,** Northern Road, Belize City, tel (02) 31600, fax (02) 31900; **Elijah Sutherland,** 127 Neal Penn Road, Belize City, tel (02) 73582; **Gilly's Car Rental,** 31 Regent Street, Belize City, tel (02) 77613/77630; **Lewis Auto Rental,** 23 Cemetery Road, Belize City, tel (02) 74461; **National Car Rental** at Philip Goldson International Airport, tel (02) 31586; **Pancho's,** 5747 Lizarraga Avenue, Belize City, tel (02) 45554; **Smith's and Sons Auto Rental,** 125 Cemetery Road, Belize City, tel (02) 73779.

IN PUNTA GORDA

Alistair King, Texaco Service Station, Punta Gorda, tel (07) 2126.

By Bicycle

Belize is easy to explore on two wheels, since the roads are the best in Central America. Only in the south, where clouds of dust rise from the dirt road every time a vehicle thunders by is cycling less pleasant, and you will certainly need a sturdy mountain bike. Remember, however, that Belize is very hot and humid. Especially inland, away from the coastal breeze, cycling along shadeless roads can be utter torment. The only place where you will find spares is in Belize City. Not all Belizean buses have roof racks, but if they do, you should have no trouble transporting your bike.

Embassies and Consulates

Even though Belmopan is the capital, many offices prefer to stay in Belize City, which has always been the commercial and cultural heart of the country.

UK: High Commission, 34/36 Halfmoon Avenue, Belmopan, tel (08) 22146/22147.
EC: Commission of European Communities, 1 Eyre Street, Belize City, tel (02) 72785.
Costa Rica: Consulate, 8–18th Street, Belize City, tel (02) 44796.
El Salvador: Consul General, 120 New Road, Belize City, tel (02) 44318.
Honduras: Consulate, 91 North Front Street, Belize City, tel (02) 45889.
Mexico: Embassy, 20 Park Street, Belize City, tel (02) 30193/30194.
Panamá: Embassy, 79 Unity Boulevard, Belmopan, tel (08) 22714; Consulate, 5481 Princess Margaret Drive, Belize City, tel (02) 44940.
US: Embassy (Consular section), 29 Gabourel Lane, Hutson Street, Belize City, tel (02) 77161/73886.

Local Agencies

Belize Department of Archaeology, Belmopan, tel (08) 22106. It is housed in the National Assembly complex.

Money Matters

The Belizean currency is the Belize dollar, whose value is fixed at BZ$2 to US$1. US dollar travellers' cheques or cash are the best currency to bring with you, though sterling can also be changed. Barclays Bank is represented in Belize City and Belmopan, and you can use your normal chequebook to buy Belize dollars there. Branches of the Belize Bank are in all the major towns, and their business hours, along with other banks, are Mon–Thurs 8–1, Fri 8–1 and 3–6.

Wiring money from abroad is best done to Barclays Bank in Belize City, or by using the American Express office. As always, having to wire money can be a tedious and time-consuming business in Central America, and should be avoided if possible. Credit cards are widely accepted, and certainly necessary when hiring a vehicle. American Express and Visa are the best known here, but others should also be acceptable.

Post Offices

There are post offices in the main towns only, and the rates are fixed at BZ$0.60 for letters to the US, and BZ$0.75 for letters to Europe, taking roughly a week to ten days in both cases. Their business hours are Mon–Fri, 8–noon and 1–5. If you want to send a parcel, you will have to use a cardboard box and take it open to the parcel office in Church Street, Belize City, where it will be checked by customs before you can close it with string.

Receiving post is straightforward: just have it mailed to **Poste Restante**, The Main Post Office, Belize City, Belize. Letters will be kept for up to three months before being sent back. Remember to take your passport for identification. Alternatively, holders of American Express cards or travellers' cheques could use their office as a postal address: **American Express**, Belize Global Travel, 41 Albert Street, Belize City, Belize.

Telecommunications

Phoning to and from Belize is easy and international calls from here are the cheapest in Central America. Public payphones are very rare, and your best option is to use the phones in hotels and restaurants, which usually charge a flat fee. For example, a local call of three minutes officially costs no more than BZ$0.25; long-distance calls within Belize cost around BZ$0.60 for three minutes. International calls cost around BZ$10 for three minutes to North America, and BZ$20 to Europe.

Belize Telecommunications (BTL) has offices in all the major towns, normally in the same building as the post office. In Belize City, their office is at 1 Church Street, open daily, 8 am–9 pm. If you wish to make an international call, you will be asked for a BZ$30 deposit. Direct dialling is possible, and collect calls can be made to the United States, Great Britain, Australia and France. To make a collect call, dial the operator in the country you are calling.

Telephone codes around Belize are: Belize City: 02; Belmopan: 08; Benque Viejo: 093; Caye Caulker: 02; Corozal: 04; Dangriga: 05; Orange Walk: 03; Punta Gorda: 07; San Ignacio: 092; San Pedro/Ambergris Caye: 026.

The **emergency number** for the police, fire department or ambulance is 90.

Police and Military

Belize is the happy exception to the Central American rule: its defence forces are not known for human rights abuses or a high level of corruption. Politically motivated killings or disappearances are unknown here, though Central American refugees and non-English-speaking Belizeans have occasionally suffered abuse from the authorities. Belize even has its own Human Rights Commission, founded in 1987, which has been responsible for such projects as incorporating human rights into police training courses.

Small rudda control big ship.
Size isn't everything.

Creole proverb

The country's civilian police force is made up of just 500 people, and called the Belize Police Force (BPF). The Belize Defence Forces (BDF) were founded in 1980, a year before independence, its army not much larger than the police force. The BDF is trained and, to a large extent, financed by Britain, the United States and Canada. British military officers command them; however, the Belizean government has a programme for replacing the foreign commanding officers.

There are also still about 2000 British soldiers stationed in Belize, traditionally to protect the country from Guatemala's claim on its territory. However, Guatemala formally recognized Belize in 1991, and the British have at last agreed to honour their promise of building a road from Guatemala City to Belize City (basically the Petén road, via Flores and Benque Viejo), which they made in 1859. Thus one of the region's most futile disputes should be over, and possibly the British troops will eventually withdraw altogether. On the other hand, if you read the Guatemalan press you will see that recognition of Belize may only be temporary.

Medical Matters

Chemists stock most drugs and toiletries you might need, including contraceptives, suntan lotion and mosquito repellent. Outside Belize City, you are unlikely to find tampons, but sanitary towels are always available. See your embassy or consulate for a list of recommended doctors. If you require outpatient attention at a hospital, it's free. The **Belize City Hospital** is on Eve Street. If in the south or west of the country, you could always try the British military bases for medical help, which they often provide for the locals. There are camps outside Punta Gorda and San Ignacio.

Public Holidays and Opening Hours

New Year's Day
9 March—Baron Bliss Day
Good Friday
Easter Saturday
Easter Sunday
Easter Monday
1 May—Labour Day
24 May—Commonwealth Day
10 September—St George's Caye Day
21 September—Independence Day
12 October—Columbus Day
13 October—Pan-American Day

19 November—Garifuna Settlement Day
25 December—Christmas Day
26 December—Boxing Day

There are very few museums in Belize, so always check information for an individual institution in the relevant town. Normal business hours are Monday–Friday, 8–5. Commerce and industry hours are Monday–Friday, 8–noon and 1–5. Very few businesses are open on Sundays. Most nature reserves and archaeological sites are open to the public daily, from 8–5, though regulations vary, since you can camp in some reserves, and some Maya sites just have a local guard, but no official hours. Details are given in the guide text.

Festivals

Belize is not blessed with many festivals, but its Caribbean culture ensures there is no lack of entertainment, with parties and discos almost every weekend. Reggae music predominates, but Latin American music is also popular.

The main national celebrations are Independence Day (21 September), Columbus Day (12 October) and Garifuna Settlement Day (19 November). The latter is one of the most interesting times to be in Belize because there is a good chance of seeing some traditional Garifuna dancing if you head for Dangriga or any of the Garifuna villages further south. The Garifuna are descendants of African slaves and Carib Indians, and their festivals are rich with African songs and drum rhythms, the dancing a mesmerizing mixture of African and Caribbean.

Markets

Interesting markets are not a feature of Belize, though you may enjoy a stroll around the fish and vegetable market in Belize City, newly housed in the extension of North Front Street, past the post office. You will find all sorts of tropical food here and the vendors are always willing to explain their uses. On the other hand you may be horrified by the writhing sea animals, and the stench can be overwhelming. Trading is finished by noon, so you need to get there early.

Shopping

> *Gati gati no wanti, an wanti wanti no gati.*
> If you've got it, you don't want it, and if you want it, you can't have it.
>
> *Creole proverb*

Belize is not the place for handicrafts, though plenty of trinkets are made of sea creatures, shells, wood, and coconuts. As you browse through jewellery made of tortoiseshell or black coral, it is worth remembering that the former comes from an endangered species, and the latter is banned from export. It is also illegal to import black coral into the United States.

The quality of weaving and embroidery is very primitive compared to Guatemalan standards. The few remaining Maya settlements in southern Belize have entirely lost their artisan knowledge, and are only now trying to relearn it, in order to benefit from tourism. But what you find will be expensive—and Belizean Mayas do not seem to appreciate the art of bargaining either. The best buys are probably the wood carvings.

The Media

Belize has a large number of publications for such a small country. There are five weekly newspapers, but their reporting is dominated by school functions and personality profiles, with little useful political coverage. *The Reporter* is a business paper, with a heavy bias towards the conservative United Democratic Party (UDP), presently the country's main opposition. *Amandala*, although basically a sports paper, has the most varied political coverage. *The Beacon* is another mouthpiece for the UDP, and so is the *People's Pulse*. The *Belize Times* serves the interests of the reigning People's United Party (PUP), which is also conservative, though its origins lie in the social democratic tradition.

The left-wing periodical *Spearhead*, published by the research foundation SPEAR, concentrates on long-term issues concerning community development, education and social welfare. *Belize Studies* is published three times a year, and is a forum for Belizean and international research on the country. *Belize Currents*, published by Emory King in Belize City features local creative writing. Finally, an excellent source of tourist information and local issues is the monthly *Belize Review*, subtitled 'News, Views and Ecotourism'. Unfortunately, it only seems to be available in Belize City; you can buy it direct from their offices at 7 Church Street, Belize City.

There are two national radio stations: Belize Radio One broadcasts in English and Spanish; and Radio Krem is a newly established station, under the same ownership as the Amandala paper. National television programming is still in the early stages, and most of what you see are pirated programmes from the United States. A local company, Great Belize Productions, is trying to redress the balance with documentaries and features on local life and culture.

The only towns with cinemas are Belize City, San Ignacio, and Orange Walk, predictably dominated by the latest US releases.

Where to Stay

Belize has an enormous variety of tropical luxury hotels, though service standards are occasionally lax. To meet tourists' highest expectations, the **Belize Tourism Industry Association** is trying to establish training courses for hotel and catering staff, but this programme is in its infancy.

There are hotels and guest houses to suit all pockets, though it has to be said that Belize is expensive compared to the rest of Central America. The cheapest price range for one person, per night, is BZ$15–BZ$25, which can be a shock for travellers coming from neighbouring Guatemala. Moderately priced hotels charge anything from BZ$50 to BZ$100, and expensive resort hotels begin at BZ$100. International reservation procedures are observed by Belizean hotels.

Added to these prices is a 5% government hotel tax, and some places charge up to 15% service tax on top of that. Always make sure you know whether the price quoted includes these two taxes or not, as many places do not openly display their charges.

There are no youth hostels in Belize, and camping is forbidden in almost all parts of the country. Two exceptions to this rule are the Cockscomb Basin Wildlife Reserve and Mountain Pine Ridge, though both are difficult to reach without your own transport, and there is no food available in either place. Both sites are administered by the Audubon Society in Belize City, which can provide up-to-date information and help for organizing visits.

Commercial renting of holiday homes is common in all the touristic areas, especially on the cayes. Contact the Belize Tourist Board, 53 Regent Street, Belize City, tel (02) 77213 for information on long-term lets. Outside the main tourist season, from May to November, you should have no trouble finding a self-catering apartment or beach house, even if you haven't booked in advance.

Eating Out

In spite of Belize's Caribbean character, the food is not as good or as exotic as you might expect. Burgers and chips predominate, with Chinese food a close second. Even these are not normally very exciting, and meals are expensive for what you get. Between March and July lobster is not officially available, to protect them during their breeding season, though unscrupulous restaurants and tour operators often ignore this ban. Unfortunately you will also find turtle steaks on some menus, even though the animal is a threatened species. There is plenty of legal seafood, however, and it is best eaten on the cayes, where dishes include shark, snapper, wahoo, conch and shrimps.

Creole cooking rarely finds its way onto any restaurant menu, though one item you sometimes see is *fried jacks*. This delicious alternative to toast consists of hot slices of deep-fried dough smeared with jam. Another local dish is rice and beans, normally served with stewed meat of some kind, or fried fish. If you happen to be in southern or western Belize during Easter, you may be lucky enough to find delicious iguana, which tastes a bit like tender chicken, and is eaten especially at that time.

Drink

There is just one kind of beer available in the entire country, and that is the nationally brewed **Belikin** beer, a very mediocre variety. Only the top hotels will serve imported beers, and those will usually be American and overpriced. The best local alcohol is the rum.

Fizzy drinks and canned fruit juices are standard, though you can usually find delicious, freshly made juices as well. One of the most refreshing is made from watermelon, but many other tropical fruits are used. The strangest drink is sickly sweet seaweed, mixed with milk and cinnamon, which is certainly an acquired taste but worth trying at least once. Drinking water from the taps is not recommended, although it is claimed that the water in Belize City is safe.

Itineraries

Most visitors head straight for the reef islands (cayes), but the country has plenty to offer besides its spectacular reef.

The Cayes and the Barrier Reef

The Belizean Barrier Reef is unquestionably the country's star attraction. Situated very close to the mainland (from 1 km to 25 km away), the reef is a great underwater wall, whose unique underwater formations include the **Great Blue Hole**, which is an eerie sinkhole descending into the seabed. The main dive resort is **San Pedro**, on Ambergris Caye. There are also remote, offshore resort hotels such as on **Caye Chapel, Glovers Reef and Turneffe Islands**. For a less commercial location than San Pedro, and a relaxed atmosphere, head for **Caye Caulker**.

The West: Cayo District

Cayo District is the most accessible area for hiking and jungle excursions, the heart of which is the friendly town of **San Ignacio** , quickly reached in 3 hours from Belize City. Based here, or in one of the jungle lodges nearby, you can explore some of the best the country's tropical interior has to offer. An excellent way to spot animals is to take a canoe trip along the **Rivers Mopan or Macal**, where you will also have the best chance of seeing the astonishing variety of birds that live here.

Apart from the rainforest, there is also the **Mountain Pine Ridge**, with an almost alpine atmosphere. Camping is permitted and, properly equipped and provisioned, this is a rewarding hiking area. Many of the jungle lodges also offer tours on horseback to this area.

There are a number of Maya ruins to visit, and most spectacular of all is the huge ceremonial centre of **Caracol**, hidden deep in the jungle near the Guatemalan border.

The South: Toledo and Stann Creek Districts

The southernmost region of Toledo District is home to the majority of the country's Maya Indian communities, and a programme is being developed which will allow visitors to stay in some of their villages. Expect to find very simple accommodation and facilities: sometimes just a hammock in the thatched home of an Indian family. In some villages a special guest house has been built by the community, and each guest is fed by a different family each mealtime. Visits can be arranged in **Punta Gorda**.

Stann Creek District, with the town of Dangriga as its regional centre, is home to the **Cockscomb Basin Wildlife Reserve**, the only jaguar reserve in the world and an ancient tropical forest that even has areas never yet explored. Hidden deep in the reserve is also the country's highest mountain, the Victoria Peak, rising 1120 m from sea level. The other attraction of Stann Creek is the string of Garifuna villages lining the coastline. Heading south from Dangriga, villages such as Hopkins, Seine Bight, and Placencia are traditional fishing communities of people who still cherish their unique heritage as descendants of slaves and Carib Indians. The beaches are endless stretches of white sand. The best place to stay is **Placencia**.

The North: Orange Walk and Corozal Districts

The Belizean north reveals its few attractions only grudgingly. For the most part inaccessible, unless you're travelling by chartered aircraft or four-wheel-drive, you need plenty of time and money to visit most of the Maya sites or nature reserves located here. The prize destination is the luxury resort at **Gallon Jug**, where wealthy birdwatchers stay in lodges built on the main plaza of a Maya site—great if you can afford it. Or there are the ruins of **Lamanai and Altun Ha**, both significant Maya sites, best reached with an organized tour.

The **Baboon Sanctuary** at Bermudian Landing is one of the few places of interest accessible by public transport (from Belize City). Butterfly buffs will certainly want to visit the **Shipstern Nature Reserve and Butterfly Breeding Centre**, in the far north of the country, a few kilometres from Sarteneja.

Belize City

Belize City is no longer the dangerous place travellers warn each other about. In fact, its dilapidated wooden buildings and putrid canals have something magnetic about them, and a handful of colonial buildings add a dash of faded glamour. Built on reclaimed swamp, many houses stand raised off the ground on short wooden posts, allowing just enough space for chickens to scratch the dirt. Their back doors look onto the canals that are more like ditches, while the main streets are lined by modern concrete architecture, billboards and neon signs jostling for position over unhurried pedestrians. There is just one large waterway, Haulover Creek, and a humpy swing bridge is at the hub of people and traffic, soon a familiar marker for all visitors. Most boat traffic to and from the sea passes by the bridge, and local captains are always tempting passers-by to hop on and visit the coastal cayes, just a short distance from the city.

It takes no more than half an hour to walk from end to end of the city centre, and its cracked pavements and dirt roads, its ancient beggars and wanna-be studs—seedy details in themselves—are somehow not sleazy at all. The city is too small to be intimidating, and street crime is not a major problem, though unlit side streets should be avoided at night. Generally the city is relaxed, and women alone need take no more than the obvious precautions: such as not wearing jewellery, walking briskly and never making eye contact.

The atmosphere is more reminiscent of a Caribbean town than a major city. Uniquely in Central America too, the voices around you speak the languid English of creoles, and the hustlers somehow seem less frightening because of it. Certainly drugs are offered to tourists on the streets, and crack is a serious problem, but if you ignore the pushers you will not generally be pursued.

History

A quarter of the country's population live here, and the city has been the political, cultural and economic centre of Belize for over three centuries. The fact that it is no

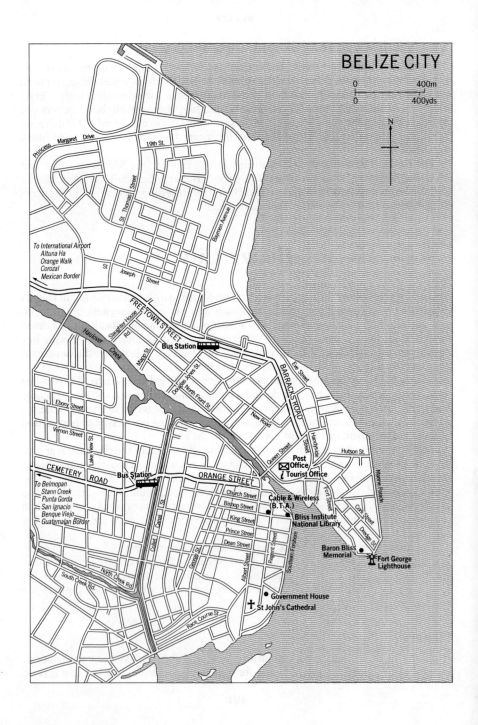

longer the official capital has done nothing to lessen its leading role, which is underlined by the reluctance of foreign embassies to move out to Belmopan, the country's capital for over thirty years now. The first people to settle here permanently were British pirates and loggers: the pirates hiding amongst the many islands of the Barrier Reef, the loggers basing themselves at Belize Point, on the mainland. The loggers called themselves Baymen, since they had operations stretching along the whole Bay of Honduras, searching out mahogany trees for Europe's gentry, and it was from their camps that Belize City grew.

The settlers used broken bottles and wood chips to fill the swampy land, and by the late 18th century, the city was a thriving frontier town: a rough place, where the families of the Baymen awaited their periodic return from the bush. The tough and dangerous work of logging was done by African slaves, and by the end of the 18th century, 75% of the country's population was made up by them, hence the predominantly black and creole population of Belize today, whose ancestors were emancipated from slavery in 1834.

The city's most glorious moment came in 1798, when the Baymen, helped by their slaves and the British navy, resoundingly defeated the Spanish naval assault that was to have established the Spanish Crown's claim to the region. The famous Battle of St George's Caye was fought in the waters off Belize City, and centered around the island which has given the battle its name. In spite of this, it took the British another 73 years to make their territorial claim official, and the country did not become a Crown Colony until 1871. It was known as British Honduras and Belize City was the capital. The city lost its political status in 1961 after Hurricane Hattie pushed a huge tidal wave through the city, destroying most of its wooden buildings and claiming many lives, and it was decided to move the capital 50 miles inland. The new capital, Belmopan, was carved out of the bush. However, all but the civil servants working in the new government offices have chosen to stay in Belize City so in practice it is still the capital of the country.

GETTING TO BELIZE CITY

By Air
Philip Goldson Airport, 16 km outside Belize City is the country's only international airport. A bus shuttle to the city leaves from outside the airport at 6, 8, 10.30 am, noon, 2.30, 4 and 6 pm everyday. Coming from Belize City, there are numerous pick-up points: Pound Yard Bridge, the corner of Cemetery Road and Central American Boulevard, the corner of Central American Boulevard and Vernon Street, and the bus stop by Palotti High School. Departure times from the first stop are at 5.30, 7.15, 8.30, 11.15 am, 1.45, 3.30 and 5.30 pm. You will need the **exact fare**, which is BZ$2, one-way. For more information on the international airport shuttle, tel 73977/77811, in Belize City. If you hire a taxi, expect to pay no more than BZ$30, and always agree on a price before departure.

There are daily flights from the following Central American cities: San Pedro Sula, Tegucigalpa, San Salvador, San José and Panamá, Flores, Guatemala City; and Cancún in Mexico.

The **Municipal Airport** lies a few kilometres north of Belize City. Taxis should cost about BZ$5, or you can walk (20 mins). Domestic flights from here include Corozal, Punta Gorda, San Pedro, Caye Chapel and Dangriga.

If you don't wish to go to the main representatives of the airlines, you can always buy tickets via any of the travel agents along Regent or Albert Street.

Aerovías, Mopan Hotel, 55 Regent Street, tel 77351.
Belize TransAir, Albert Street, just past King Street, heading south.
Continental, Albert Street, by the Hindu temple, south of Dean Street.
Eastern, 26 Queen Street, tel 78646.
Maya Airways, 6 Fort Street, tel 77215.
Taca, 41 Albert Street, tel 77185/77363
Tan-Sahsa, Valencia Building, on the corner of Queen Street and New Road, tel 77080.
Tropic Air have their office at the municipal airport, tel 45671.

By Boat
There are regular boats between Belize City and the cayes (see Cayes section p. 201 for details).

By Train
There is no railway in Belize.

By Bus
There are four main bus companies connecting Belize City with the rest of the country. They all have their main terminals here.

Batty Bus Line covers western and northern Belize, and has its terminal at 54 East Collet Canal, tel 72025/77146. For Belize City to Chetumal, stopping in Orange Walk and Corozal on the way, buses leave at 4, 5, 6, 6.15, 7, 8, 9, 10 and 11 am. The Northern Highway is the country's best road, and the journey only takes 3 hrs to Mexico, 2½ hrs to Corozal. Services to San Ignacio, via the capital, Belmopan, leave daily at 6.30, 8, 9 and 10 am. On Sundays all buses leave half an hour later. **Venus Bus Line** also runs a service to the north, and its terminal is on Magazine Road, tel 73354/77390. Buses to the Mexican border and all towns along the way leave every hour between 4 and 10 am and in the afternoons from noon to 7.

Novelo Bus Service goes to the Guatemalan border, passing Belmopan and San Ignacio. The terminal is at 19 West Collet Canal, tel 77372. Buses leave from noon to 7 pm.

Z-Line Buses run to southern Belize, calling at Belmopan, Dangriga, Big Creek and Punta Gorda. Their buses leave from the same terminal as Venus buses. Buses for Dangriga leave at 10 am, 3, and 4 pm. On Sundays buses leave at 2 and 3 pm. A direct bus for Punta Gorda leaves at 10.30 am, leaving 30 mins earlier on Sundays. It is worth getting the direct bus, unless you want to break the journey in Dangriga, as the journey takes up to 10 hrs, due to the unpaved road south of Dangriga.

GETTING AROUND BELIZE CITY
You can easily walk around the centre and find everything you will want to see. You only need transport to get to the international and municipal airports, and the bus terminals.

Taxis are plentiful on the main streets. Official taxis have green numberplates, and a journey within the city should cost no more than BZ$4. There are no meters, so always agree on a price before departure.

TOURIST INFORMATION

The **Belize Tourist Board** is at 53 Regent Street, P.O. Box 325, Belize City, (tel (02) 77213/73255, fax (02) 77490; Mon–Fri, 8–noon and 1–5.) The office is on the first floor. The staff are very helpful and there are a great variety of free brochures on everything from car rentals to tours. A few interesting books and some maps are also available here.

ORIENTATION

Belize City is such a small place that the main thoroughfares are never far away, and even if you lose your bearings, the noise from the commercial streets or sight of the sea will guide you back on course.

WHAT TO SEE

As you walk along the seafront, with the waves lapping at the crumbling sidewalk, you sense how easily houses can be washed away—something that has happened on a number of occasions, most notably during Hurricane Hattie. As a result the central city is a mix of old and new, with wooden colonial houses, raised slightly off the ground, breaking up the streetlines of modern concrete homes. There are no grand palm-fringed boulevards here. Instead you have a handful of main streets that cut through a tangle of quiet back streets, and after a day of wandering around, the city quickly becomes familiar.

The heart of the city is divided into a northside and a southside by Haulover Creek, with the **Swing Bridge** the main crossing point. The southern part of town is the oldest sector, with just two main streets: **Regent Street** and **Albert Street**. Both streets are lined by shops and offices and, before you know it, you find yourself at the far end, where **Government House** and **St John's Cathedral** mark the beginning of a rather grand residential quarter, where many gardens are met directly by the sea. Government House is a fine colonial wooden building, painted white and set in an attractive tropical garden. The cathedral is a small redbrick church, built in 1812, and looks rather provincial by comparison. It is the oldest Anglican church in Central America, and the kings of the Mosquito Coast were once crowned here by the British. The Mosquito Indians formed an alliance with them between 1815 and 1845, in the hope of avoiding Spanish colonial rule in their territory, which stretched along the Caribbean coast from Honduras to Nicaragua. Thus their 'kingdom' was under British protection and the Spanish risked the ire of the British Navy if they tried to encroach.

Near the Swing Bridge are the main BTL office, as well as the **Bliss Institute** (Mon–Fri, 8.30–noon and 2–8, Sat 8.30–noon), on the Southern Foreshore, which is the city's main cultural centre and library. Occasionally there are exhibitions here of local art or national features, such as the flora and fauna or the latest Maya finds, and it is always worth having a look.

On the north side of town, **Queen Street** makes up the main thoroughfare, also lined by shops and bars, with the **main post office** at the intersection with North Front Street and the Swing Bridge. Around the eastern tip are a number of beautiful colonial houses, as well as the market, where each morning traders sell the morning catch. A fine example of colonial architecture is at no. 4, Fort Street, which is now a popular hotel and bar/restaurant. Another attractive building houses the US embassy, on Hutson Street. If you follow Fort Street to the end, you come out onto the seashore, where the **Fort George Lighthouse** stands above the **Baron Bliss tomb**. An eccentric Englishman, with a Portuguese title, he loved the deep-sea fishing here so much that he bequeathed his fortune to the local authorities. He died on 9 March 1926, and that day is now a public holiday, celebrated as Baron Bliss Day. Following Marine Parade along the seashore, you soon reach the ugly glass box of the Fort George Hotel, which is rapidly losing its position as the city's top hotel to the nearby Villa Hotel.

WHERE TO STAY
Belize City is not a cheap place to stay in comparison with other Central American cities. Most of the up-market hotels are in the northside of the city, while moderate and inexpensive hotels are located in the southside. The telephone and fax code for Belize City is 02. The international code for Belize is 501. All hotels are subject to a 5% government tax.

Northside

LUXURY
The top-priced hotel in the centre is the **Fort George Hotel**, 2 Marine Parade, tel 77400/45600, fax 43820. All services, such as restaurant, valet service and swimming pool are provided. Across the street is the **Villa Hotel**, 13 Cork Street, tel 45751/45755, fax 30276, which is much nicer because of the smaller scale and more personal atmosphere, and is better value for money. It also has a pool and restaurant. All rooms have air-conditioning and TV. Both these hotels add a 15% tax to bills.

EXPENSIVE
Hotel Chateau Caribbean, at 6 Marine Parade, tel 30800, fax 30900, is housed in a wooden colonial building, looking out to sea, and the restaurant is excellent. Also in an attractive colonial mansion is the **Fort Street Guest House**, 4 Fort Street, tel 45638, fax 78808. There are just six rooms, all with fans, and communal bathroom. Apart from the bar/restaurant, there is also a spacious lounge and a small library.

Newly opened, but more than walking distance from the centre, is the **Ramada Royal Reef**. Part of the American chain, the hotel is on the seafront, at Newtown Barracks, tel 31591, fax 31649. Out of town altogether, and only suitable if you have your own transport, is the brand new **Belize Biltmore Plaza**, 3 miles up the Northern Highway, tel 32302. Check with the tourist office or contact direct for the prices of these new hotels.

MODERATE
Popular with Americans is **Mom's Triangle Inn**, 11 Handyside Street, tel 45073, fax 31975. Air-conditioning is available for a daily supplement of US$10, and secure parking is also available. (As always in Central America, it is best not to leave your vehicle unattended in cities.) Downstairs is a mediocre restaurant serving bland fast food, whose main advantage is its useful travellers' notice board.

INEXPENSIVE

One of the friendliest budget hotels in the city is **North Front Street Guest House**, 124 North Front Street, tel 77595, which is safe and conveniently located for catching boats to Caye Caulker. Cheapest of the lot, but still clean, safe, and friendly, is **Marin's Travel Lodge**, 6 Craig Street, tel 45166.

Southside

EXPENSIVE

Centrally located and very pleasant is the **Bellevue Hotel**, 5 Southern Foreshore, tel 77051/77052, fax 73253. All rooms have air-conditioning and TV, and there's also a popular bar/restaurant. The hotel also maintains an extension on nearby St George's Caye, where wooden cottages offer guests a choice of self-catering beach holidays, or all the facilities of a hotel. At the far end of Regent Street, the **Mopan Hotel**, 55 Regent Street, tel 77351/77356, has the advantage of a quiet location, but is otherwise a grubby place, that has seen better days; overpriced for what you get. Nearby, the **Glenn Thorn Manor**, 27 Barrack Road, tel 44212, is a friendly and extraordinary place, squeezed into a colonial house, with every room a different colour, from pink to green. Fridge and kitchen are available to long-term guests. Somewhat claustrophobic, but conveniently located, is **El Centro**, 4 Bishop Street, tel 72413, fax 74553. An immaculate hotel, but rather overpriced, is the **Orchidia Guest House and Café**, 56 Regent Street, tel 74266, fax 77600. Prices include a continental breakfast.

MODERATE

Friendly and good value is the **Sea Side Guest House**, 3 Prince Street, tel 78339. Just around the corner from the Bellevue Hotel, this place is close to the waterside and the hub of Regent Street.

EATING OUT

The most generally available, cheap food, is usually Chinese, and there are plenty of places to choose from, especially around Queen Street. Otherwise, you will find delicious meals in some of the hotel restaurants, notably at the **Chateau Caribbean**, which serves the most authentic Chinese food, and the **Villa Hotel**, which offers Lebanese dishes. Note that many restaurants close on Sundays.

Northside

A good place for breakfast, and meeting other travellers, is at **Mom's Triangle Inn**, 11 Handyside Street. Pricey, but in beautiful surroundings of polished mahogany, the restaurant at **Four Fort Street Guest House** makes delicious fruit drinks and tropical cocktails, and their Sunday brunches are renowned. The **Nile** restaurant, at 49 Eve Street, is a simple place serving Middle Eastern food. On the corner of Queen Street and Handyside Street, the **Shangri-La** serves a mixture of Chinese and international dishes. For an up-market international menu head for **The Grill**, on Barracks Road, near the Ramada Hotel, where you can expect to pay around US$30 for a meal for two.

Southside

The best creole meals are to be had at **Macy's**, 18 Bishop Street. Also good, and cheaper, is **Caribbean**, at 36 Regent Street. **G.G.'s Patio**, 2 King Street, has a pleasant little courtyard, but its menu is dominated by mediocre hamburgers. Also on King Street, **Mexican Corner** has cheap and good Mexican food; and **Pizza House** offers filling meals for big appetites. The restaurant at the **Orchidia Guest House** (see above) is pricey, but the menu is varied and tasty.

ENTERTAINMENT AND NIGHTLIFE

Belize City has the busiest nightlife in the country, which is not to say there is that much choice. Most places do not get going before 11 pm, and stay open till the early hours of the morning. You should note that drugs are a serious problem (crack, cocaine, grass), and you will most likely be offered them. Penalties are heavy and usually involve a prison sentence.

The best bars are generally in the larger hotels, though these are not very exciting places, the clientele tending to be middle-aged businessmen. A popular, rowdy bar is the **Hard Rock Café**, on the corner of Queen Street and Handyside Street. Another drinking spot favoured by travellers and locals is the **Marlin Restaurant and Bar**, at 11 Regent Street.

Big Apple, 67 North Front Street, is a dark and sweaty disco with a young crowd. The **Hard Rock Café** is best for music on Thursday nights, and occasionally has live bands. **Legends**, 30 Queen Street, is best on Saturday nights. **Lindbergh's Landing**, 162a Newtown Barracks (near the Ramada Hotel), is where young professionals go for a romantic dinner and dance, from 8 onwards, where the atmosphere is respectable and no one gets too loud. **Miami Nites I**, on the corner of Cemetery Road and American Boulevard, and **Miami Nites II**, on Orange Street, near the Batty bus terminal, are nothing flash, but wildly Belizean: vibrant atmosphere and energetic dancing till you drop.

There are two cinemas in the city, the Majestic on Queen Street and the Palace on Albert Street, usually showing imported American films.

SHOPPING

Cottage Industries, 26 Albert Street, and Di Creole, 7 Graboural Lane, both have a good selection of Belizean handicrafts. The best buy is probably wood carvings out of *zericote* wood. It is sometimes better, and always cheaper, to buy these from the street hawkers—best of all is to buy them direct from the woodcarver, if you can track one down.

USEFUL INFORMATION

Emergencies
Police: The main police station is on Queen Street, near the Swing Bridge, tel 77210.
Medical: The Belize City Hospital, Eve Street, tel 77251. Also check with your embassy or consulate for recommended doctors.

Belize Audubon Society:
29 Regent Street, P.O. Box 1001, Belize City, tel (02) 77369.

Tour Agencies
A full list of Belizean tour agencies (including diving), as well as ones operating from the US and Canada, is available from the Tourist Board.

Money Matters
The most efficient place for exchanging money is Belize Bank, on the small park south of the Swing Bridge. Barclays Bank and Bank of Novia Scotia are both on Albert Street. It is possible to change up to US$100 travellers' cheques directly into US dollars, but you must prove that you are about to leave the country with an airline ticket. The major banks will also change money. Street vendors are not recommended since sharp practice is very common and you do not get a better deal than with the banks.

The **American Express** office is at Belize Global Travel, 41 Albert Street, tel 77363/77185. Open Mon–Fri, 8–noon and 1–4.30; Sat, 8–noon.

Books
The largest bookshop is the Belize Bookshop, opposite the Mopan Hotel, and there's also a newsagent that sells foreign papers on North Front Street, by the Swing Bridge. The major hotels should also sell *Time* and *Newsweek*. If you can't find the useful what's-on magazine *Belize Review*, you can buy it at their office at 7 Church Street.

Post Offices
The main post office is on the corner of Queen Street, just north of the Swing Bridge. The *poste restante* is on the ground floor. The parcel office is on Church Street.

Telecommunications
Belize Telecommunications Ltd. (BTL) is on Church Street, open daily, 8 am–9 pm. Fax services are also offered by the large stationers on Queen Street.

Boats to the Cayes
Catch boats to Caye Caulker from the Shell Station on North Front Street, right by the Swing Bridge. They leave daily between 7.30 and 10 am. For Ambergris Caye head for the Bellevue Hotel pier, at 5 Southern Foreshore, where a boat leaves at 4 pm, Mon–Fri, and at 1 pm on Saturdays.

Day Trips from Belize City

Two places best visited from the city are the Belize Zoo, 48 km along the Western Highway, and the Community Baboon Sanctuary, 40 km northwest of Belize City. An important Maya site, unfortunately not accessible by public transport, is Altun Ha, 50 km north of the city. If you would like a taster of what the cayes are like, there is a string of tiny islands, with St George's Caye in the north and English Caye in the south, easily visited from the city in a day.

The Belize Zoo

The New Belize Zoo (BZ$10) is a pioneering place that has endeavoured to show captive animals in as natural a way as possible. Large areas of bush, forest and riversides have been fenced in to house a great variety of indigenous species of the cat family, including jaguars, puma, ocelot and maguey. Tropical birds, such as toucans, vultures, and parrots are to be found, as well as crocodiles, and forest animals such as tapirs.

Nature trails take you around all the sights, giving you a good chance to spot wild animals in a controlled environment.

Across the road, a **Tropical Education Centre** opened in 1990, located on the former property of an American, Dora Weyer, who lived in Belize for thirty years, working in support of the country's natural environment. 140 acres of wilderness, with educational trails, a visitor's centre (including a dormitory) with a small library, and lecture rooms for slide shows, are all part of the services offered here. Any bus heading for Belmopan passes the entrance to the zoo, but you must ask to be dropped off there.

The Community Baboon Sanctuary

The **Community Baboon Sanctuary** is equally pioneering, since it is one of the first conservation projects in Belize that runs with the cooperation of the local population. The sanctuary covers an area of 18 square miles on the properties of over 60 different owners. The local farmers living here have agreed to protect significant areas of forest on their land in order to sustain the troop of black howler monkeys (known locally as baboons) who live here. Administered by the Belize Audubon Society, you can find a useful booklet on the sanctuary at their offices (29 Regent Street, Belize City, tel (02) 77369). A system of trails leads visitors through the area, and there is also a visitor's centre and museum in the village of Bermudian Landing. Guides must be hired for walks along the reserve trails.

Accommodation is available in the homes of local people; see the reserve manager, Fallet Young, or contact the Audubon Society (at the above address). Alternatively, you are allowed to camp here, but remember to bring your own food and drink. To reach Bermudian Landing, follow the Northern Highway as far as the Burrel Boom turn-off, from where it is only a short drive. (You could catch any bus heading north as far as the turn-off, and then try to hitch, but there is little traffic passing this way.) Alternatively check with the tourist office for direct buses from Belize City to the village of Bermudian Landing.

Altun Ha

Altun Ha (8–5, small fee), meaning Water of the Rock, is a small but attractive site. Close to the sea, it was an important trading post during the Classic Period (AD 250–900), and merchants came by sea and land from distant parts of the Maya empire. Extensive archaeological excavations have produced some of the country's most exciting finds, such as the beautifully carved head of the Maya Sun God, Kinisch Ahau. This is one of the largest Maya jade carvings ever found, weighing almost ten pounds and nearly six inches high. It is now kept in a bank vault in Belize City.

To get there, the easiest option is to either go on a tour, or drive your own vehicle. Many of the larger hotels organize tours, or you could enquire at the tourist board. Accommodation nearby is either very simple, with locals in Maskall village, or very luxurious, at **Maruba Resort,** tel (03) 22199, near Maskall village. (You could also get any bus heading north, as far as Sand Hill, and then try to hitch. Traffic is scarce, however, and this is a very uncertain option.)

Nearby Cayes

Only 14 km northeast from the city, **St George's Caye** is the site of the famous battle and was the country's first official capital from 1650 to 1784. Even though virtually nothing remains to bear witness to the historic battle, it is a popular weekend picnic spot, and home to two resort hotels: **St George's Lodge**, tel (02) 44190, fax (02) 30461; and the newly opened annexe of the Bellevue Hotel.

English Caye, and neighbouring **Goff's Caye**, are about 16 km southeast of Belize City, and lie along the main entrance lane for ships coming in from the Caribbean. The sandy beaches here make these two a favourite weekend spot, and this is the most likely time you will find day charters leaving from the city's piers. For an organized day trip, enquire at the larger hotels.

THE CAYES

Snorkelling or diving, all you can hear is your own breathing, all you can feel is the water washing over your body, but what you see is electrifying: monstrous coral that look like brains; orange branches that can cut like a knife; countless tentacles sway in the currents; while all around flit a kaleidoscope of fish, so close you think you could reach out and touch them. Shoals of tiny fluorescent neon tetras open up to let you pass, while barracuda just stare indifferently and orange starfish ignore you altogether, slowly wending their way across the seabed. Few other natural environments will allow you to feel so close to its inhabitants.

296 km long, the Belize Barrier Reef is a giant wall of limestone and coral that has taken millennia to form, harbouring some of the most extraordinary plants and animals on the planet. The hundreds of islands (cayes) and atolls are just the crest of this underwater wonderland, and make for excellent bases from which to explore. Traditionally inhabited by fishermen, the atmosphere on the islands is relaxed, and even the most commercial places are tempered by Caribbean ease. The best time to be here is from April to June, when the sea tends to be calm. The hurricane season is from June to November, and although Belize is rarely hit, this is the time when rough weather might be a problem.

Taking a boat trip, you often find yourself being followed by dolphins dancing in the waves and, if you are really lucky, you might even see a giant turtle. Out on the reef, you can reasonably expect to see conch and starfishes, as well as countless tropical fish, such as barracuda, jacks, parrotfish, angelfish, and grunts, while the deeper waters are favoured by the harmless nurse sharks—to name but a fraction. Naturally, the fishing is excellent, and the most common catches include grouper, snapper and jewfish. To find out more about the sea creatures here, see *A Guide to Corals and Fishes of Florida, The Bahamas, and Caribbean* (Seahawk Press), by I. and J. Greenberg.

The most developed diving resort is San Pedro, on Ambergris Caye, with a full range of hotel accommodation, from budget to luxury, and offering any kind of watersport you could wish for. Neighbouring Caye Caulker has no airport, and is a much less commercial place, favoured by young and budget travellers. The other main groups of islands, such as Turneffe Islands (protective mangroves here make for great fish variety),

Lighthouse Reef and Glover Reef (interesting for underwater limestone formations, especially the Great Blue Hole), all have their own character, and you can visit them, either on a day charter, or by staying in the up-market resorts that hide there. Diving and fishing tours are offered by most of the hotels, ranging from day trips, to 'live-aboard' excursions lasting as long as you wish. Diving certification courses are available in San Pedro and Caye Caulker, as well as at the top resort hotels.

Diving Equipment

Almost all equipment can be hired locally, though the experienced diver should note that firms often only provide cylinder and air without a back-pack or harness. They do provide weightbelt and weights. The best kind of clothing for diving in these parts is a lightweight, lycra body suit, and if snorkelling, you might want to bring surf shoes to protect against cuts from coral.

Safety Precautions and Diving Code

It is unsafe to fly directly after a dive, because the change in pressure can induce the 'bends'. As a general rule, you should not fly for a period of 24 hrs after a dive that required a decompression stop, and not for 12 hrs after a dive that did not. When snorkelling, it is worth wearing shorts and a T-shirt, because you can get very badly sunburnt without feeling it while in the water.

There are no official rules for divers, but there is a voluntary code, which is designed to protect the reef. Please avoid:

1. Walking on or damaging the coral.
2. Collecting shells or coral.
3. Using spearguns or supporting speargun-fishing operations.
4. Diving near working fishermen.
5. Hand-feeding fish.
6. Allowing anchors to drag over the coral.

Ambergris Caye

Ambergris is the largest of the reef islands. Located 58 km north of Belize City, and a spectacular short plane ride away, it is the country's most visited attraction. San Pedro, the only town on any of the cayes, caters to the tourist who wants to be entertained and most of its 2000 residents are involved in some aspect of the travel trade, with the result that the place is somewhat touristy—trinket and beachwear shops crowding into every space available. San Pedro was originally a tiny fishing community of wooden houses and, in spite of the dizzy speed of development, there is still a very intimate feeling to the place. It has to be admitted that San Pedro's charm is limited but if you are here to explore the reef, you will find the widest range of opportunities, and a very helpful tourist centre.

Restaurants and bars are expensive, and unfortunately the prices are not often matched by the service. However, the hotels do their best to offer every kind of diversion a tropical holiday can provide, from beach games, to sailing, windsurfing, diving, snorkelling and deep-sea fishing. There is never a shortage of things to do and open-air bars provide the main focus for socializing in the evenings.

One of the country's best-known reserves is just off the island: the **Hol Chan Marine Reserve** is an area of particularly beautiful corals, as well as plenty of fish, easily explored by snorkelling. Unfortunately, the daily groups of tourists that are brought here have taken their toll, and it is ironically one of the most damaged areas of the entire reef. Great stumps of dead, white coral testify to thoughtless visitors, who touched the coral and thereby helped to destroy it.

GETTING TO AMBERGRIS CAYE

By Air
The fastest way to reach the island is to fly from the international or municipal airports in Belize City. If coming from Mexico, you can also fly directly from Corozal, in northern Belize. Flights are daily and frequent, so you should have no trouble making a connection without prior bookings. You can walk to most hotels in less than ten minutes from the airport. The more distant and exclusive resort hotels will come and pick you up on arrival.

By Boat
From Belize City there is a regular ferry service leaving from the pier in front of the Bellevue Hotel, 5 Southern Foreshore. It departs Mon–Fri at 4 pm; Sat at 1 pm; and no service on Sun. The fare is around US$10.

From Caye Caulker, you can always find someone to take you to San Pedro if you ask around near the main pier. The fare should not be more than US$8 per person.

Boats to Caye Caulker and Belize City leave from the Texaco pier in San Pedro, Mon–Fri at 7 am and 2 pm, Sat at 8 am and 2 pm. Alternatively, hire someone to take you, but this will prove expensive.

TOURIST INFORMATION
The most efficient and friendly place to get advice on anything from travel arrangements, hotels or diving excursions, is the **San Pedro Tourist Centre**, tel and fax 2434. This is a privately-run office, mainly catering to wholesalers from the US, but the staff are also the best source of information for the general tourist. The telephone code for San Pedro is 26.

WHERE TO STAY
Being the country's top tourist resort, prices tend to increase regularly and vary according to season. Always ask for the latest price list, not forgetting three crucial questions: Which currency is being quoted? Are prices per person or not? Are the two taxes included? Unlike the rest of the country, prices often relate to each individual, which can come as a nasty surprise to couples. The following is just a selection of the best choices, and there are many more places to stay. Prices have been listed in detail to indicate that they do not fall into the categories normally used in the book and are often substantially higher. If you cannot get hold of a particular hotel, you can always book via the San Pedro Tourist Office, tel and fax (26) 2434.

In San Pedro

Around the southern end of San Pedro, there are quite a few very pleasant hotels. Virtually next to the airport is the **Sunbreeze Beach Hotel**, P.O. Box 14, tel 2191, fax 2346. Motel-type accommodation, with air-conditioning, is offered around a small garden and private beach. Singles US$80–US$90, doubles US$90–US$105, triples US$120–125, plus 15% tax. About five minutes walk from the town, the **La Joya Caribe Hotel**, tel 2050, fax 2316, is moderately priced, and of a good but unpretentious standard. The beach is lovely and lined by palm trees, and the restaurant is recommended whether you stay here or not. Beach *cabañas* are US$65 for single or double occupancy, US$72 with air-conditioning. The **Royal Palm Inn**, P.O. Box 18, tel 2148, fax 2329, is a small hotel on the beach, rather crowded by other buildings. There's a choice of rooms or private apartments: rooms are US$55 singles, US$70 doubles, US$80 triples. Apartments are US$90, US$110, US$120 respectively, and meals are extra. The **Victoria House**, P.O. Box 22, tel 2067, fax 2429, is a luxurious place, expensive but good, and you have a choice of beach *cabaña*, suite, or rooms around a lovely private beach, within walking distance of San Pedro. All prices are per person plus 15% tax: rooms are US$85 singles, US$50 doubles, US$37 triples. Beach *cabañas* are US$110 single, US$65 double, US$37 triple. The suite is US$110.

Closest to 'downtown' San Pedro, the top hotel is **Ramon's Village Resort**, tel 2071/2213, fax 2214, which has a collection of beach *cabañas* that look rustic on the outside, but inside are first-class, with fans or air-conditioning. There is a private beach, as well as a pool, bar and restaurant. Prices are US$110–US$225 per person, depending on the standard required.

At the northern end of town, there is the **Paradise Resort Hotel**, tel 2083, which also has *cabañas* around a private beach, plus restaurant and bar, and prices are in the medium range. **Rock's Inn**, tel 2326, fax 2358, is a short walk along the beach from San Pedro. A small, comfortable and expensive hotel, that also offers apartments, it suffers from being squashed between other buildings, and its beach is nothing special.

There are some **less expensive** hotels in San Pedro: just around the corner from the beachfront, the **San Pedrano**, tel 2054/2093, is excellent value for money and friendly too. Singles US$20–US$25, doubles US$25–US$30, triples US$30–US$37. Self-catering apartments are also available at US$375–US$425 per week. **Martha's Hotel**, tel 2053, fax 2589, is the best of the budget hotels, and offers private bathrooms with all rooms. Singles are US$15–US$25, doubles US$27.50–US$35, and triples US$37.50–US$46. **Rubie's Hotel**, tel 2063, is right on the beach, nearest the airport. There is only one shower for all rooms, but the place is friendly and has a pleasant beachfront; US$12.50 per person. The **Barrier Reef Hotel**, tel 2075, has a very popular bar and expensive restaurant. All rooms have private baths, fans or air-conditioning. Singles are US$30–US$48, doubles US$30–US$65, triples US$75. The **Coral Beach Hotel**, tel 2013, offers simple rooms with private bath, fan or air-conditioning, but is too expensive for what you get. Singles are US$55, doubles US$90, plus 15% tax. Right on the beach, and operated by the same people who run the ferry to Belize City, the **Conch Shell Hotel** is by the Texaco pier. It is overpriced at singles US$20–US$50, doubles US$30–US$50.

North of San Pedro: Accessible by Boat Only

If you want to be exclusive, then the following options may be for you. Farthest away of all (10 mins by boat), is **Journey's End Caribbean Club**, tel 2173, fax 2028. Described by the manager as 'Club Med without the hassle', this is a self-contained resort hotel, which unfortunately has no proper beach. Guests have free use of surfers and Hobie Cats, and there is a dive shop on site. The pool is the most elegant on the island, and sports a great poolside bar, the stools actually in the water. Accommodation ranges from *cabañas*, to poolside rooms, to mangrove-lagoon-facing rooms. TVs in all but the *cabañas*. Singles US$137–US$152, doubles US$184–US$199, triples US$231–US$246. Air-conditioning is US$15 extra per day.

The nearest neighbour is **The Belizean**, tel 2138, fax 2635, which offers 21 rooms in individual stone cottages with beautiful interiors of polished tropical woods and also a stunning luxury suite complete with sunken bathtub. Of all the hotels along here, this is the most luxurious and quiet, with an attractive beach, as well as a pool. The only drawback is that there are no watersport facilities, which the hotel arranges via the commercial operators in San Pedro. Singles US$135–US$185, doubles US$170–US$220, triples US$195–US$255, suite US$300–US$375, plus 15% tax. All rooms have air-conditioning, TV, video, fridge and phone. Meals are extra.

A short walk further south, **Captain Morgan's Retreat**, tel 2567, fax 2616, has rustic *cabañas* with fans only, on a private beach. There is a restaurant, and all watersports can be arranged. Singles are US$125, doubles US$100, plus 15% tax.

Finally, **El Pescador**, tel and fax 2398, is a family-run hotel in a traditional, wooden colonial building. Right on the beach, the rooms are nothing fancy, but all have private bathrooms, and a restaurant provides the meals. The hotel caters almost exclusively to deep-sea-fishing enthusiasts, though others are always welcome. Singles are US$100, doubles US$160, plus 20% tax, all meals included.

WHERE TO EAT AND DRINK

Apart from the numerous hotel restaurants, **Elvie's Kitchen** is one of the most popular eating places, and **Fido's**, on the beach, is the best place for breakfast, as well as other meals such as burgers or pizza. Wherever you go, however, you will find meals very expensive.

There are three bars worth looking out for. The first is the **Sandals Bar**, at the end of the main street. Best at night is the **Tackle Box**, on the main beach, though they tend to charge an entrance fee after a certain hour. There is a water enclosure, where three giant turtles, three sharks, and various other creatures are crammed into a depressingly small area. This spectacle is a popular tourist attraction—if you feel strongly enough about the cruelty of keeping creatures in such conditions, why not write a letter of protest to The Director of Tourism, Belize Tourist Bureau, 53 Regent Street, PO Box 325, Belize City.

The bar at **Fido's** is also a popular hangout. The main disco in town is the waterfront **Big Daddy's**, which raves to the sound of reggae each night.

SPORTS AND ACTIVITIES

Dive shops and charter boats: There are a great number of these in San Pedro, and you can find out about many more by contacting the tourist office. In Belize City, you could also visit **Personalised Services**, Musa Building, 91 North Front Street, tel

77593/77594, fax 75200. This office will have all the latest information on live-aboard yachts and tours. They can also plan and arrange any trip, as well as provide any service to do with the sea. Most of the hotels can make arrangements for you too.

Bottom Time Dive Shop, tel 2348, rents out all types of diving equipment, and offers tours and courses. **Manta IV**, tel 2371, is a very popular motor yacht for live-aboard diving tours and day trips. **Out Island Divers**, tel 2151, is a specialist operator for dive tours to the atolls, especially the Great Blue Hole. For example, they offer a day trip to Lighthouse Reef, flying you out from San Pedro, so you get the most time diving. **San Pedro Water Sports**, tel 2013, runs the 50-ft *Offshore Express* motor yacht, for live-aboard diving tours. **The Dive Shop**, tel 2437, in the Holiday Hotel, rents out diving equipment and offers tours and courses.

Courses to become a certified scuba diver cost in the region of US$300. Half-day introductory courses, which involve an actual dive, only cost US$50. Much cheaper and just as rewarding is snorkelling, and snorkel equipment can be hired for around US$5.

USEFUL INFORMATION

For **exchange** there are two banks in San Pedro, and you can generally also change cash or travellers' cheques in shops and hotels. The **post office** is in the same building as the Atlantic Bank.

The Island Photos shop are specialists in underwater photography and hire out equipment at good rates.

Caye Caulker

Caye Caulker lies just south of Ambergris, 35 km from Belize City, and is a fraction of the size. Many of the roughly 1000 inhabitants still retain their traditional industry, which is lobster fishing, and tourism remains firmly in second place. The island is therefore much more relaxed and less touristy, and has long been favoured by young budget travellers, who come here to hang out with the locals, preferably in the **Pirates Bar**, which is one of the best nightspots in the whole country. There is no airstrip, though there are continuous arguments about finishing the half-built construction site, and facilities are not geared to the big-spending visitor. What you will find here is a tiny community of wooden houses on stilts, two sandy streets with hardly any vehicles, beaches, and friendly places to stay. Most accommodation is rustic, but there are a few medium-range hotels as well. Note that from December to February the sandflies can drive you crazy here, coming out whenever the breeze dies down. Insect repellent helps, but they are persistent critters. Mosquitoes are always around, as elsewhere on the cayes.

GETTING TO CAYE CAULKER

Getting here is easy: from Belize City there are daily morning boats leaving from Haulover Creek by the Shell station. From Ambergris there is the ferry from the Texaco pier, and if you ask around by the Tackle Box bar, you will always find someone to take you. Alternatively, if arriving by air at Belize City, you could fly on to Caye Chapel, and phone Caye Caulker from there for someone to pick you up by boat.

TOURIST INFORMATION

There is no official tourist information on the island, though the **Aberdeen Restaurant** is a good place to find out about snorkelling and diving trips, contact individuals, or rent equipment.

WHERE TO STAY

The more up-market places tend to be at the southern end of the village, located on the beach, while the inexpensive hotels are at the northern end, near the main pier. None of the accommodation prices rise above the moderate category used throughout this guide. If staying long-term, you can always find houses or apartments to rent, such as **M. & N. Apartments**, tel (022) 2111, located behind the grubby Hotel Martinez.

The **Anchorage**, a short walk beyond the southern edge of the village, on a lovely beach, is the nicest place to stay in your own *cabaña*. **Shirley's Guest House**, tel (022) 2145, furthest away from the village, is also good, very clean and quiet. **Tom's Hotel**, tel (022) 2102, closest to the village and also on the beach, has moderately priced huts with private bathrooms, and the rooms are good value too.

The **Tropical Paradise Hotel**, tel (022) 2124, is at the southern end of the village, and offers simple *cabañas* and there's a restaurant attached. **Vega's Far Inn**, tel (022) 2142, is just past the police station, in the middle of the village, facing the beach. All rooms share the bathroom. A private hut with bathroom is also available and you may also be allowed to camp on the hotel property.

At the northern end of the village, the **Reef Hotel**, tel (022) 2196, and **Rainbow Hotel**, (022) 2123, are both popular—all rooms with private bath. A favourite budget hotel is the **Rivas Guest House**, above the Aberdeen Restaurant, tel (022) 2127. **The Split Beach Resort** has pleasant beach huts facing the sea and mangroves. It is named after the split where Hurricane Hattie cut the island in two pieces.

EATING OUT

A popular place for travellers is the **Aberdeen Restaurant**, which offers local and Chinese meals, and there are a couple of private houses near here, offering breakfast in the morning or snacks. Just walk by and see what's on offer. Most of the restaurants are at the other end of the village, though, along the main street leading to the Tropical Paradise Hotel. New places are opening all the time, and you are bound to find something to your taste.

Apart from the nightly scene at the **Pirates Bar**, the favourite bar to spend time is the **Reef Bar**, by the main pier. Drugs and theft are sometimes a problem on Caye Caulker, so be careful. Belize City is not far away and there are crack addicts here too.

SPORTS AND ACTIVITIES

Snorkelling day trips to the reef cost around US$12.50, which includes the Hol Chan Marine Reserve and a stop in San Pedro. If just going to the reef off Caye Caulker, you can expect to pay around US$8, plus US$2.50 for renting gear. For scuba diving trips and equipment rental, contact **Belize Diving Services**, tel 2143, near the football pitch.

Charlie at the Aberdeen Restaurant is trustworthy and a good sailor, though he normally uses a motorized skiff for snorkel trips. The Rastafarian Zarmusa is also highly recommended, and sails people to all parts of the Barrier Reef. His sailing practices are unorthodox, but you will certainly have lots of fun if your nerves can take it. Amado Perez, and his sailboat *Miss Conduct*, offers both day trips and sailing tours in a more conventional style. Tours cost around US$50 per person, per day, and include three meals daily, and all equipment, which is excellent value. His father, Ernan Perez, also offers charter services and does regular runs to Belize City, on his speedboat *Chispa*.

Other Cayes

All except Caye Chapel are accessible by charter boat only, and but for the few resort hotels, are generally uninhabited. There are only seven atoll reefs in the entire Caribbean, and three are in Belizean waters. For the diver or fisherman, these far-flung specks in the Caribbean Sea are the highlight of any tour. Turneffe Islands, Lighthouse Reef and Glover's Reef are atolls, peeking out from two great underwater ridges. At the centre of each you find an aquamarine lagoon, with calm water over pristine sand, while all around the seaward rim you find innumerable ledges and great walls encrusted with coral and teeming with marine life.

Live-aboard dive tours are the best way to reach these places, and although expensive, prices are still cheaper than elsewhere in the Caribbean, and the diving is often more exciting. Contact **Personalised Services** (see p. 205 for address) for a rundown on all the latest options.

Caye Chapel

This tiny, privately-owned island, just south of Caye Caulker is given over to luxury tourism, with a resort hotel and all the trappings you would expect (**Pyramid Island Resort**, tel (02) 44409, fax (02) 32405). The bar is a popular weekend destination. Get there either by plane or charter boat from Caye Caulker or Belize City. If you plan to stay here, check first with the Tourist Board, as the hotel's future is uncertain.

Turneffe Islands

About 40 km east of Belize City, this is the largest of the atolls, comprising over 200 little cayes covered in mangroves that form a great oblong shape, 48 km long. The eastern shore has a great vertical reef descending into the sea with giant horizontal ridges that make for fascinating diving. The only resort hotel is **Turneffe Island Lodge**, P.O. Box 480, Belize City, fax (03) 0276. A budget option is the **Turneffe Flats**, which you can contact via 56 Eve Street, Belize City, tel (02) 45634.

Lighthouse Reef

About 113 km east of Belize City, this is the most distant atoll, situated on a separate ridge, with six cayes surrounding a shallow lagoon. Sandbore Caye, at the northern end, has a lighthouse and is home to a keeper and his family, while Half Moon Caye, to the south, has another lighthouse and is home to the **Half Moon Caye Natural Monument**. Made up by the entire caye of just 45 acres, it was established in 1982, and is administered by the Audubon Society. Two separate ecosystems, of dense vegetation and open palm tree clusters, provide a home to countless bird species, among them the red-footed booby and great frigatebird with a seven-foot wing span. Lizards are also found here, with odd names like 'bamboo chicken' and 'wish willy'. And if you're lucky, you might see the magnificent loggerhead and hawksbill turtles, both endangered species. Visitors must register with the lighthouse keeper, who is a mine of information and sells maps of the area. Camping is permitted, but you must bring all your own food and water, and pets are not allowed.

For divers, **The Great Blue Hole**, just off Half Moon Caye, is a 'once in a lifetime' treat. Located at the heart of Lighthouse Reef, this is a huge circular hole about 305 m wide and 145 m deep and was formed millions of years ago, when an earthquake caused the roof of an underground cave to collapse. Stalactites give vivid evidence of the catastrophe: those formed before the earthquake hang at a slight angle, while the ones formed afterwards hang straight down. The 'Half Moon Wall' is also one of the most spectacular diving sites to be found, with lots of fish and a patchwork of corals of all shapes and sizes.

There is now a resort hotel nearby, the **Lighthouse Reef Resort**, on Northern Two Caye, P.O. Box 26, Belize City. You can book via the Tourist Board or Personalised Services.

Glover's Reef

Southeast of Belize City, this atoll is nearer Dangriga, in southern Belize, and the least visited of the lot. This is not a reflection on the diving opportunities, however, and about 64 km of reef await to be explored. Snorkelling as well as diving is excellent, and some say you find the greatest variety of marine life here. Most exciting of all, you may see the harmless Great Whale Sharks, especially between April and June, and you will definitely see dolphins, who play around here all the year round.

Two medium-priced resort hotels are located on the atoll, both on South Water Caye. The cheaper is **Blue Marlin Lodge**, P.O. Box 21, Dangriga, tel (05) 22243, fax (05) 22296. **Leslie Cottages**, tel (05) 22004, offers just two rooms in pleasant cottages.

Bluefield Range

A string of tiny inlands running parallel to the mainland, between Belize City and Dangriga, this is a remote area, where fishermen are better catered for than divers. There is just one place to stay, and that is on a working fishing camp called **Ricardo's Beach Huts**, contactable via 59 North Front Street, P.O. Box 55, Belize City, tel (02) 44970; VHF Channel 68.

Tobacco Reef

Located just off the mainland by Dangriga, two of the cayes—Tobacco Caye and Water Caye—are sparsely populated and offer one of the cheapest offshore diving and snorkelling bases. Both are easy to reach from Dangriga, and you can find out about lifts with local fishermen just by asking around. You should not have to pay more than US$12.50 for the journey, whereas chartering a boat to take you will cost nearer US$100. A good place to make enquiries is at the **Hub Guest House**, by the central bus stop in Dangriga. Simple lodgings on the cayes cost around US$15–US$25 per person.

Commercial accommodation is all on Tobacco Caye. **Fairweather & Friends** offers simple lodgings, and you can contact them via P.O. Box 240, Belize City. **Island Camps** is a campsite only, and you can contact them via 51 Regent Street, Belize City, tel (02) 72109. Finally, **Reef End Lodge** can be contacted via P.O. Box 10, Dangriga.

THE WEST: CAYO DISTRICT

The western Cayo District is a place where black orchids (just one of 250 species) sprout from tropical pines, and waterfalls, pools and streams provide delicious swimming after a long day's hiking or horse-riding. Here the lowland savannah west of Belize City gradually gives way to a hilly landscape covered by humid forests which hide a number of Maya ceremonial centres. Many of these sites are small and easily reached, but there are also the magnificent remains of **Caracol**, deep in the Mountain Pine Ridge, which are possibly more important than the famous ruins of Tikal in nearby Guatemala. The forest has hardly been cleared by the archaeologists, and huge buttress roots support towering trees festooned with epiphytes, parasitic plants that cling to their branches.

The slightly higher altitude of the region, rising to 1120 m, makes the country's heat more bearable, yet even here the temperatures can be limb-deadeningly hot. In **San Ignacio**, the district's friendly heart, the streets are often empty during mid-afternoons while the locals take their long siestas. It has a larger Spanish-speaking mestizo population than the rest of Belize, many of them originally refugees from Guatemala, but others descendants of the original loggers who used to search out valuable mahogany for export to Europe and North America. The atmosphere in San Ignacio is relaxed, yet the evening nightlife can be as lively as in Belize City or the most popular cayes. Quite a few English and Americans have made their home here, not to mention the British army base close by, so there are more bars and nightclubs than you would expect. By contrast, the country's official capital, Belmopan, has no nightlife at all and very little happening in the day.

Cayo is also the perfect place to escape into nature, staying at one of the many jungle lodges that hide in the forest along the Rivers Mopan and Macal. No other part of the country will give you such a good chance to glimpse the huge variety of Belizean birds, such as kiskadees, blue-crowned motmots, or vermilion flycatchers. If you're lucky, you might even see a jaguar, tapir or howler monkey drinking from the rivers at dawn and dusk. Certainly the sounds of the forest will become familiar, the lone 'tock' of the toucan easy to distinguish.

Belmopan

The bus left the paved road and followed a gravel track to a parking area
beside a tree... 'You looking at it', the bus driver said when I asked where
the town centre might be.

R. Wright, *Time Among the Maya*

Situated 80 km west of Belize City, Belmopan is a kind of Brasília gone wrong:
government buildings and a few hotels stand in what looks like an overgrown building
site, and the visitor imagines there must be some mistake. This can't be a capital city, and
to all intents and purposes it isn't, because nobody wants to live here, and almost nobody
works here, except the civil servants, who have no choice, many commuting from Belize
City.

Few tourists visit unless they have official business at the two embassies (see p. 184 for
addresses). Anyone who does go to Belmopan may like to visit the archaeological vault in
the Department of Archaeology on the Government Plaza. Guided tours are given on
Mondays, Wednesdays, and Fridays, and you should make an appointment two days
prior to arrival, by phoning (08) 22106. There are plenty of precious pottery objects and
artefacts of obsidian and jade, and recent excavations in Caracol have unearthed a wealth
of new treasures, including a priceless jade mask, that would make an impressive display
in a proper museum. As it is, many objects are locked away for safekeeping.

There is one time in the year when it is worth making a visit to Belmopan, and that is
for the country's largest fair, the **National Agricultural Show Weekend**, held every
April. This is an interesting event, not just for the party atmosphere, but also for seeing
the range of agricultural stands, including beautiful horses, and exhibitions from many
aspects of Belizean life and culture. If you haven't tasted creole cooking yet, you will find
stands selling traditional fried chicken, as well as seaweed milk or plantain dishes. At
night, the country's favourite bands come to play here, and large crowds dance the night
away in huge tents. If you go—be careful. Theft and rape are common at this time, and it
is not a good idea to go alone in the evenings.

GETTING TO BELMOPAN
The journey takes about an hour from Belize City, taking any bus heading west,
including buses for Dangriga, which all go via the capital. From Belmopan to San
Ignacio takes another 45 mins, to the border a further 20 mins. Heading south, to
Dangriga, takes around two hours along the Hummingbird Highway, as the dirt road is
prosaicly named. Wherever you are coming from or heading to, you will end up at the
main bus terminal, which is the busiest spot in town.

WHERE TO STAY
Staying in Belmopan is expensive and not recommended. However, there are three
places if you have no choice: **Circle A Lodge**, 35–37 Halfmoon Avenue, tel (08) 22296,
is the cheapest; the **Bull Frog Inn**, 25 Halfmoon Avenue, tel (08) 22111, fax (08) 23155,
is slightly more expensive; and finally, the **Belmopan Convention Hotel**, 2 Bliss
Parade, tel (08) 22130, fax (08) 23066, is the top address.

The nicest place to stay near Belmopan, is the American-run **Banana Bank Ranch**, tel (08) 23180, fax (08) 22366. Here you can rent out horses, eat good food, and make trips on the Belize river, which runs past the ranch. Phone them for exact directions if coming in your own vehicle, or take a taxi from Belmopan.

San Ignacio

San Ignacio—always called Cayo—is a small town, 37 km west of Belmopan, and just under 15 km from the Guatemalan border. On first glance it is not very attractive, with a ragged collection of wooden buildings and rusty corrugated roofs mixing with rain-washed concrete buildings. But the people are friendly, and its location at the confluence of the Mopan and Macal rivers makes it an excellent base for exploring inland Belize. You could easily spend a week here, discovering something new each day.

GETTING TO SAN IGNACIO
Getting to San Ignacio is an easy journey from Belize City with the regular **Batty** or **Novelo** buses that ply this route daily. Coming from Dangriga, you need to change buses in Belmopan.

TOURIST INFORMATION
There is no official tourist office in San Ignacio, but Bob Jones, who runs **Eva's Bar and Restaurant** on Burns Avenue, is an excellent source of information, and holds brochures and price lists for most of the surrounding lodges, as well as official taxi fares. Whether you want to book a tour or need a doctor, he can point you in the right direction.

WHERE TO STAY
There are plenty of places to stay, in town or in one of the lodges in the surrounding countryside.

In San Ignacio

EXPENSIVE
The top hotel in town, which is nothing special, is the **San Ignacio Hotel**, P.O. Box 33, tel (092) 2034/2125/2220, fax 2134. The location, perched on the steep hill above the town centre, makes for great views, and the pool is a popular place for evening drinks.

MODERATE
A bit further up the road is the **Piache Hotel**, tel (092) 2032, which has a very attractive garden and equally good hilltop views. Rooms are simple and have private baths.

INEXPENSIVE
In the town centre hotels are very affordable and the **Central Hotel**, 24 Burns Avenue, tel (092) 2253, is the best value. Rooms are clean, all have fans, and there are two bathrooms. The **Jaguar Hotel**, opposite, is horrible, though the restaurant is worth trying. Much better is the **Venus Hotel**, 29 Burns Avenue, tel (092) 2186, which has clean, simple rooms with fans. The **Hi-Et Hotel**, 12 West Street, is a pleasant family

house, offering rooms with shared bathroom. Last choice is the **Hotel Belmoral**, 17 Burns Avenue, tel (092) 2024, which is loud and grubby.

Campsites around San Ignacio

If you follow the dirt road past the bus depot, you shortly see a sign to the **Cosmos Campsite**. About a 20-minute walk from town, this is a pleasant site on the banks of the River Mopan, where you can pitch your own tent or rent one for the night. Showers, toilets and cooking facilities are available, or you can eat vegetarian meals in the main thatched house. US$2.50 to stay the night, another US$2.50 to rent a tent. Halfway between town and the Cosmos Campsite is **Midas Campsite**, which has thatched huts by the river (nice beach), and also provides bathroom facilities, though no meals. If in your own transport, you might prefer the remoter **Black Rock Campsite**, which is on the River Macal, reached by the same mud track that turns off the main road for DuPlooy's (see below).

Jungle lodges near San Ignacio

All of these are relatively expensive, and few can be reached by public transport, which makes them great hideaways, but not necessarily convenient without your own vehicle. (If you decide to take a taxi, remember to check the official rate at Eva's Restaurant first.) However, most lodges will send someone to pick you up if you make it as far as San Ignacio, and all arrange tours and excursions (expensive) to the surrounding countryside and Maya ruins. If you book in advance, Chaa Creek and DuPlooy's might even be persuaded to pick you up from the airport, in Belize City.

LUXURY

Chaa Creek Cottages, P.O. Box 53, San Ignacio, Belize, tel (092) 2037, fax 2501, is the most exclusive lodge, with 16 rooms in beautiful stone cottages overlooking the River Macal. A short distance upriver is **DuPlooy's**, tel (092) 2188, fax 2057, which is less exclusive, but extremely beautiful, with a very friendly, family-run atmosphere. The best feature is the bar, which is on a high platform, with great views of the surrounding jungle and river below. Full board is in the luxury category but bed and breakfast is cheaper. Children under 6 years are charged at around 15% the adult fee. A 15% tax is added.

EXPENSIVE

Nabitunich Lodge, San Lorenzo Farm, tel (093) 2309, is halfway between San Ignacio and the Maya ruins of Xunantunich. In fact, on a clear day you can see the tip of the main pyramid rising above the jungle. This is one of the easiest lodges to reach by public transport, close to the Mopan river, just off the main road to Benque Viejo. Excellent value for money, even though 18% tax is added. **El Indio Perdido**, Callar Creek, tel (092) 2460, is 2 kms off the main road, just before you reach Nabitunich Lodge. The location, right on the Mopan river, is lovely, but without your own transport you are marooned here, and taxis cost around US$30 from San Ignacio. Check at Eva's Bar whether the place is open, as it is rather erratic.

    Windy Hill Cottages, tel and fax (092) 2017, on the main road to Benque Viejo, about 2 kms outside town, has the advantage of a pool and easy access, but is neither near the river nor in the forest. 15% tax added. **Maya Mountain Lodge**, Cristo Rey Road, P.O. Box 46, San Ignacio, tel (092) 2164, fax 2029, close to town, promises more than it comes up with and charges an outrageous 20% tax on all bills. **Las Casitas**, 22 Surrey Street, San Ignacio, tel (092) 2475, is just outside town, on the Macal river, and cannot be recommended.

MODERATE

Finally, a popular lodge, close to the ruins of Xunantunich, is **Rancho Los Amigos**. To get there take any bus heading for Benque Viejo, and get off at the village of San José Succotz.

EATING OUT AND NIGHTLIFE

One of the most popular meeting places in town is **Eva's Restaurant**, run by Bob Jones, an Englishman who decided to stay on after serving here in the British Army. Meals, including breakfast, are simple and filling, and prices are reasonable. Across the street is the **Jaguar**, which is occasionally good. Also on Burns Avenue is **Serendib**, which serves good curries and creole dishes, worth the slightly higher prices. The restaurant of the **San Ignacio Hotel** is highly recommended, and not as expensive as you might expect. Make sure you try the fruit juices here. There are also a few ice-cream parlours and snack shacks, which you will easily find around the centre of town.

Other than Eva's, which closes early, there are three bars/nightclubs. The **Blue Angel**, in the centre of town, is always packed at weekends, and is the most popular place. Up on the hill, the **Cahal Pech**, is a large thatched venue, which regularly has live music. This is a good place for dancing as it is open to the night breeze. On Sundays, when things are pretty dead around here, the most lively place is the **Central American Art Centre**, opposite the bus depot. There is nothing noticeably arty here, but there is usually a local band playing.

SPORTS AND ACTIVITIES

Bicycle rental: mountain bikes are available outside Eva's. However the quality is bad, and the bikes are useless for excursions outside town. Check to see if things have improved.

Float Belize, tel (092) 2188, also contactable via Eva's Bar, rents out canoes and also offers tours on the rivers. An exciting option would be spending a few days heading downstream on the River Mopan, which becomes the River Belize, teeming with wildlife, including crocodiles. To reach Belize City takes about a week, camping on the riverbank at night.

Mountain Equestrian Trails, mile 8, Mountain Pine Ridge Road, Central Farm, fax (092) 2060, attn: Jim and Marguerite Bevis, is worth visiting if in your own transport. This is an excellent base for horse-riding tours to Caracol and the surrounding reserve. Expensive at US$45 per person for half a day; a full day costs US$65.

Tours to Caracol, the only way to get there, are reliably run by Philip Burns, tel (092) 2076 or ask Bob Jones, who uses four-wheel-drives. He also does day trips to Tikal in Guatemala, or anywhere else you care to visit. Fees for Caracol are around US$50 per person, which is expensive but definitely worth it.

Camping in Mountain Pine Ridge: The only place you can legally camp in the Mountain Pine Ridge is at the entrance or the forestry station of St Augustine. Ask at

Eva's Bar about how to get there and applying for permission to enter the reserve. You will have to bring all your own food and drink, as there is none on sale at St Augustine. Hikers will find this the best base for exploring the reserve, though good maps (and possibly a compass) are essential, since you are very much on your own here. The most detailed maps are available at Edward Stanfords Ltd, in London, or directly from the Survey Department at the Ministry of Natural Resources, in Belmopan, which is also much cheaper. The most useful sheets are numbers 24, 28 and 29.

USEFUL INFORMATION
There is a **bank** and **BTL** office (Mon–Fri, 8–noon and 1–4; Sat, 8–noon) on Burns Avenue, and the **post office** is above the police station, by the suspension bridge.

Car rental is from **Godsman Ellis**, Buena Vista Road, tel (092) 2109, and **Three Flags Auto Rental**, in Santa Elena, tel (092) 72060.

Around San Ignacio

Branch Mouth

This is the point where the River Macal joins the Mopan, eventually to become the River Belize. It is a delightful, quiet spot, 30-minutes' walk outside San Ignacio. At weekends, it is popular for picnics and swimming. To get there, just walk along the dirt road that also passes the Cosmos Campsite. Diagonally across the river, you can see the thatched roof of **Las Casitas** (see above).

Cahal Pech

Its name meaning 'the place of ticks', this was an important site as early as 200 BC. Archaeologists believe it was the exclusive home of Maya nobles in the later, Classic period. Excavation work has only been carried out in recent years, but already many artefacts have been found here. The most intriguing of all is a large stone bench that still retains much of its original red colouring, as well as ancient graffiti. Perhaps it was a sleeping platform, but specialists are undecided.

Situated on the hillside above San Ignacio, you can walk here in 20 minutes. Follow the road straight up to the thatched Cahal Pech bar, next to the radio station. Opposite the bar, turn left, and then first right, along a dirt road leading into the forest, where the site hides.

Xunantunich (daily, 8–5, small fee)

Pronounced 'shoo-nan-too-nitch', this is a small Classic Maya site, with one of Belize's largest ancient pyramids, **El Castillo**, affording great views across the jungle canopy. About 40 m high, it was believed to be the highest building in Belize until the temples of Caracol were discovered. Only two plazas remain clearly visible, dotted by a few stelae, and the remaining buildings are badly eroded, the surrounding jungle creeping ever closer. However, the location and the path leading to the site are very beautiful, and even when jungle mists obscure the view, the atmosphere is quite magical.

To get there, take any bus heading for Benque Viejo, and ask to be dropped off at the ferry, by the Maya village of Succotz. Here a hand-drawn ferry (free) takes vehicles and pedestrians over the Mopan river, from where a steep track leads 1 km through the forest and up to the ruins. Unfortunately, this track is notorious for robbers, so it's best not to go alone. Also, make sure you don't miss the last ferry crossing back at about 5.

Caracol

The journey to Caracol can only be attempted during the dry season, from January to May. It is a long trip and you should take along a packed picnic and water. Setting off early, the four-wheel-drive takes you east, towards Belmopan, and then turns south, onto a dirt road leading to the Mountain Pine Ridge Reserve. Soon you're winding through the hills, until you reach Augustine, a small collection of wooden buildings among the trees, where the families of the foresters live. The pine forest could almost be in North America, but look closely, and you will see orchids growing from niches in the trees. Once past the reserve entrance, the road takes you through forests festooned with bromeliads, getting ever thicker and moister, until you find yourself surrounded by tall rainforest, hung with creeping vines and sprouting palms. The shadowy light filters through the canopy above, and the mud road is increasingly difficult.

Approaching the great city itself—which is estimated to cover a total area of 80 square kilometres, including its satellite communities—the jungle becomes especially beautiful, with huge buttress roots folding around giant trees. At the entrance, you pass **Canaa Temple** (Temple of the Sky), its huge limestone staircase gleaming white once more. This pyramid now holds claim to being the highest building in Belize, rising 42 m above the forest floor.

An archaeological team from Florida University works here every dry season, and members voluntarily take time out to show visitors around (a donation to the University

Jade object shaped like an ear flare (Pomona, Belize)

216

project is appreciated). Caracol was only rediscovered in 1936, when chicle (gum) gatherers stumbled upon the site, and archaeological work is still in the very early stages; the Caracol Project was begun in 1985. Being shown around the temple structures, stelae, ball courts, tombs and living quarters by dedicated and enthusiastic professionals is a highly educative experience.

It is believed that at the height of its era as many as 300,000 people lived in the city and its surrounding territory—which is more than the entire population of Belize today— though others argue for lower estimates of around 180,000 people. What is known for sure is that the site was occupied from Pre-Classic to Classic times, and in AD 563 its rulers defeated nearby Tikal, rising to great power and influence, which is reflected in increased building after this period. Magnificent tombs have been uncovered here, and as recently as 1991, the second largest jade mask found in Belize was retrieved from one of the temples. Eventually, Caracol may well emerge as the most important Maya city in the Guatemala and Belize region, overshadowing Tikal as the major tourist attraction, just as it once defeated its neighbour in war.

About 13 km south of Caracol, an outstanding natural phenomenon is the **Chiquibul Cave System**, which is the longest in Central America, and has the largest cave room in the Western Hemisphere. Unfortunately, however, these caves are inaccessible to all but the expert caver and guide.

On the return journey, the driver should be willing to stop for a swim at the **Río On**. This is a gorgeous place for a cool swim, where the river flows over limestone rocks to form a succession of pools, their waters fragrant with the scent of pine. If you head for the top pool, you will also find a natural jacuzzi, where boulders squeeze the water into a churning tub, just big enough for four people.

If you don't have the time or money to visit Caracol, you can still visit the reserve, by taking a shorter **Mountain Pine Ridge Tour**, which will take in the **1000 ft Falls** and the **Río On** pools, and possibly the **Río Frío Cave**. This costs around US$17.50 each, for a group of five people, and Bob Jones can help you arrange it.

Macal River Trip

This is an excellent excursion by canoe, taking in a few swimming stops, as well as an optional visit to the **Panti Medicine Trail** (US$5), next to Chaa Creek Cottages, where you stop for lunch. Along the way you'll see a tremendous variety of birds, such as egrets, pygmy kingfishers, toucans, cormorants, herons, kiskadees, kite hawks and vultures. Most startling are the huge iguanas sunning themselves on rocks or branches, their prehistoric-looking spikes giving them a terrifying appearance. Specimens of 4 ft and over are quite common. You will also pass a colony of tiny fruit bats, sleeping upside down on the roof of a limestone ridge, overhanging the water.

The Panti Medicine Trail, named after a local Maya healer, is an interesting opportunity to learn about the forest's medicinal qualities, and a marked trail tells you about which plants take care of what, ranging from contraception, headaches and upset stomachs, to malaria or headlice.

The best person to take you on this trip is the Rastafarian Tony, who charges US$12.50 per person, and does most of the work paddling you in his canoe, though it helps if you offer to paddle too. He's immensely knowledgeable about the river's wildlife, and you won't see half the birds and animals without his expert eyes and ears to point them out. Contact him via Eva's restaurant.

Onwards from San Ignacio

The last town before the Guatemalan border is Benque Viejo. There is nothing to see here, and if coming from Guatemala, you should try to make it as far as San Ignacio. The only place remotely worth visiting is the local art centre, where you can buy hand-painted T-shirts. If you do get stuck here, the best place to stay is the inexpensive **Hotel Maya**, 11 George Street, tel (093) 2116. Buses connect Benque Viejo with San Ignacio regularly, but you can always find a taxi too.

If heading for Guatemala, your best bet is to catch a bus that leaves San Ignacio and goes all the way to the border, a few kilometres beyond Benque Viejo. The border operates between 6 am and midnight, and if you intend to catch a bus to Flores from the border town of Melchor de Mencos, you are strongly advised to get here early in the day. If there are no buses leaving when you arrive in Guatemala, there are always minivans and taxis awaiting charters, but the prices will be outrageous, and it would be worth staying the night, and waiting for the next bus.

THE SOUTH:
STANN CREEK AND TOLEDO DISTRICT

If western Belize is interesting for its tropical landscape and wildlife, then southern Belize is interesting for its diversity of people and cultures. As you head south on the unpaved Hummingbird Highway, you cross over the furthest outcrops of the western highlands before heading out into the open plains. Here you are surrounded by huge citrus plantations and row upon row of orange trees stretch into the distance. From here onwards the traveller follows a route between the contours of the western Maya Mountains and the coast.

Almost no one lives beside the Southern Highway and so there is a tantalizing sense of emptiness. You wonder if there are any people here at all. Yet the intensely farmed countryside tells you villages cannot be far, and small tracks lead off towards the jungle-covered mountains or the sea, inviting you to break your journey and discover what might be at the end of the road. Independent transport is essential if you want to make these kind of detours, since no public buses leave the highway. If you can overcome this inconvenience, you will find few tourists and a pleasing sense of discovering rarely visited places.

The first town on the coastal plain is Dangriga, 'capital' of the Garifuna people and the country's second largest town. Descendants of African slaves and Carib Indians, the Garifuna are part of the same group that inhabit many settlements along the Gulf of Honduras, in Belize, Guatemala, Honduras and Nicaragua. To the outsider they look indistinguishable from other Belizeans. Their culture and original language, however, are quite different and, particularly in the small fishing villages further south, the people are as likely to use a traditional healer as a modern doctor.

Beyond Dangriga, the pace of life really slows down. Tracks lead off the dirt highway to coastal Garifuna settlements such as the traditional fishing village of Hopkins. Further south, you will find the most beautiful mainland beaches on the thin peninsula that culminates in the lovely village of **Placencia**, which is rapidly becoming a popular holiday resort. Here you can walk for ages and ages along white sand lapped gently by the sea, and the chances are you will meet nobody along the way. Shrubs and the occasional cluster of palm trees line the shore, and there are plenty of places to play out your Robinson Crusoe fantasies.

South of Dangriga, you find yourself in the country's remote Toledo District, where Mopan and Kekchi Mayas live in traditional villages embraced by the thick forests near the Guatemalan border. Their homes are made to the ancient designs of their forebears: square or oblong wood constructions, sometimes raised slightly off the ground, and covered by a thatched roof made of palm leaves. The strong Maya heritage of the region can also be seen at three small but interesting sites: **Lubaantun, Nim Li Punit** and **Uxbenka**.

Out on the coast, the small town of **Punta Gorda** is the main centre of population, where Garifuna mix with Creoles, while surrounding areas are settled by East Indians, descendants of American Confederates, German Mennonites, and other foreigners. In fact, walking down the street in Punta Gorda, you are as likely to meet a Rastafarian sauntering to his reggae music as a dungaree-clad Mennonite, an East Indian worker or a Kekchi Indian farmer.

Although the south has this varied cultural mix, it is sparsely populated and substantial areas are still untouched by human hand. This is especially true of the Maya Mountains which trace the border with Guatemala and, with a bit of initiative, you can find yourself deep in the ancient forests that cover the region. An ideal introduction to this kind of environment is in the **Cockscomb Range**, where you will find the world's only jaguar reserve and the country's highest mountain, Victoria Peak. Solitary mahogany and ceiba trees tower above the jungle canopy, while marked trails take you through the hidden world below.

Dangriga

If you could head straight along the coast, the distance from Belize City to seaside Dangriga would only be around 58 km. In fact, if you have the time, you might consider hiring a boat, which would take you through two interesting inland lagoons, before cruising out to sea and into Dangriga harbour. Taking this route, you might even spy the rare sea cow (manatee), which hides around Gales Point, and is said to have inspired the myth of mermaids. There is a small luxury hotel here for those who want the best chance to see this legendary animal.

By road, the 168 km journey from Belize City takes three hours, first taking you west to Belmopan, before heading southeast to Dangriga, which is a town of fewer than 9000 residents. On the way, you pass one of the country's national parks: **The Blue Hole National Park** (daily, 8–4) where you can swim either in the River Sibun or the Blue Hole itself. This is a karst sinkhole, filled with water from the river to form a perfect swimming pool. If you are feeling energetic, you could also hike to **St Herman's Cave** from here. Unfortunately, this park has a bad reputation for mugging and rape, so it is best not to go alone, and you should also remember to lock your car.

In spite of the fact that Dangriga is the administrative centre of Stann Creek district, the atmosphere is provincial; the mostly wooden houses sit in a haze of dusty heat, the inhabitants moving slowly under the shade of huge umbrellas. The town was almost completely destroyed by Hurricane Hattie, and the place still has a somewhat ragged appearance, even after thirty years. From here you can take a boat to nearby Tobacco Reef or Hopkins village, along the coast. The only time when the town springs to life is during Garifuna Settlement Day on 19 November. At this time you will find plenty of street parties and dancing, singing and heavy drinking. Highlight of the festivities is the re-enactment of the Garifuna settlers arriving by boat from Honduras in 1823. However, many Garifuna had already come to Belize prior to this date, brought in as free labourers for the logging trade.

In fact, the Garifuna heritage has much more to do with freedom than slavery, although their roots lie with Nigerian slaves who were shipwrecked in the early 17th century on the Caribbean island of St Vincent. It was there that their ancestors mixed with the surviving Carib Indians and became known as the Black Caribs, evolving their own unique language which still survives today. Their descendants were never again enslaved, and even though the British tried to subdue them, they were not entirely successful. Eventually they did manage to beat the Black Caribs militarily, in 1796, and decided to get rid of them once and for all by leaving them on the Honduran island of Roatán. From there the Garifuna, as they called themselves, migrated to the Honduran mainland, working as labourers and even soldiers for the Spanish.

For the casual observer it is almost impossible to distinguish the Garifuna from other Belizean blacks, since their dress and appearance is the same, and they only speak their language among themselves. Many of the younger generation do not speak their traditional language at all, and in many ways, the Garifuna culture in Belize is something that is being revived for tourism, unlike in Honduras, where their numbers are far greater and communities are self-contained and close-knit, outsiders rarely settling among them.

GETTING TO AND FROM DANGRIGA

If at all possible, it is highly recommended that you have your own transport for southern Belize, since there are few buses, and journeys are long because of the unpaved roads. (Car rental is available in Punta Gorda.) There is almost no public transport to the coastal villages or inland regions, and you will find it very difficult to visit any of the Maya ruins or other interesting places. You could always try hitchhiking, but there are very few vehicles on the country roads, and a better, if more expensive, option would be to go on one of the organized tours that leave from Dangriga, Placencia or Punta Gorda.

By Air

Since the bus journey is only 3 hours long it hardly seems worth flying. However, there are daily flights from Belize City to Dangriga, which is a stopover on the way to Mango Creek (Independence) and Punta Gorda. If you wish to book flight tickets from Dangriga, you can do it at the Pelican Beach Resort hotel.

By Sea

Coming from Belize City, you could hire someone to take you south, which will be very expensive but a novel way to travel. Get advice from the tourist office before striking a deal with the local boatmen, and remember never to pay the full fee before the journey is completed.

By Bus

There are regular daily buses run by **Z-Line**, between Belize City and Dangriga (3 hrs). Coming from San Ignacio, you need to change buses in Belmopan, where all buses from Belize City pass by. Coming from the south, there are direct buses from Punta Gorda, also run by **Z-Line**. The bus depot is by the bridge over the North Stann Creek, in front of the **Hub Guest House**. The ticket office is opposite, in the Tropic Zone Club on St Vincent Street, and if you want to be sure of getting on the bus, you should buy your ticket in advance.

There is also a direct bus connecting Placencia with Dangriga, on Mondays, Wednesdays, Fridays and Saturdays. The bus leaves Dangriga at 2.30, and the journey can take up to 3 hrs. Coming from Placencia, the bus goes on the same days, but leaves at 5 am.

TOURIST INFORMATION

The local tourist information office is located in **B. J.'s Gift Shop**, tel (05) 22266, on the corner of Commercial Street and Lemon Street. This is an interesting little place to visit, which sells tourist maps and booklets, as well as various locally made handicrafts such as drums.

WHERE TO STAY

If you choose to travel from Belize City via the lagoons, you will pass by the luxury hotel **Manatee Lodge**, Gales Point Caye, P.O. Box 170, Belmopan, tel (08) 23321, fax (08) 23334; alternatively, the hotel will arrange transport for you if you book accommodation in advance.

EXPENSIVE

The **Pelican Beach Resort**, P.O. Box 14, Dangriga, tel (05) 22044, fax (05) 22570, is the top hotel, which isn't saying much. Located on the seafront, on the northern edge of town, the colonial-style house is clean and very quiet. They offer boat charters for up to 8 people costing around US$135 per day; van rentals for 4 people are US$135, for 5–10 people US$150. The hotel also rents out holiday cottages on Southwater Caye. At the lower end of this price category, the **Bonefish Hotel**, 15 Mahogany Road, tel (05) 22165/22447, is a friendly, small hotel with excellent meals in the restaurant. All rooms have private bathrooms and TV. Tours also arranged.

MODERATE

Soffie's Hotel, 970 Chatuye Street, tel (05) 22789, is a friendly and clean place, with meals available, just south of the Creek mouth. Facing the sea, across the road, is the **Río Mar Inn**, 977 Southern Foreshore, tel (05) 22201, also with restaurant.

INEXPENSIVE
Right by the bus stop is the basic **Hub Guest House**, 573a South Riverside, P.O. Box 56, tel (05) 22397. The outdoor restaurant is a good place for a snack or breakfast. All rooms should have fans. **Cameleon Hotel** and **Tropical Hotel** are cheap and bang in the middle of town, on Commercial Street, but not recommended for single women.

South of Dangriga
The new **Sittee River Lodge**, 19 High Sand, Sittee River Village, tel (05) 22006, located 35 km south of Dangriga, is ideal for nature and fishing enthusiasts and the price category is moderate. Equipment for fishing, camping and snorkelling is available on site, and there are also tours you can join, if you would prefer. All rooms with bath, or you can camp, for which daily rates are US$5, US$15 if hiring camping equipment.

EATING OUT
The best meals are to be had at the **Bonefish Hotel**, or the **Pelican Beach Resort**, though the latter is about 10 minutes' walk from the town centre, and more expensive. In the centre, most people prefer the filling meals offered by **Burger King**, on Commercial Street, whose name has nothing to do with the restaurant chain. The snacks at the **Hub Guest House** are worth trying, and there are a few indifferent Chinese restaurants too.

ENTERTAINMENT AND NIGHTLIFE
The entertainment options are rather limited, apart from getting wrecked in the local pool bars—take a walk along St Vincent and Commercial Streets, and you will easily find these places.

USEFUL INFORMATION

Money Matters
There is a Barclays Bank and Novia Scotia Bank (Mon–Fri, 8.30–noon; Fridays 3–6 as well) on Commercial Street, north of the river.

Tour Agents
Rosado's Tours, 35 Lemon Street, tel (05) 22119, is the place to go for car and van tours, as well as boat charters to the cayes for snorkelling and fishing. An all-day fishing trip costs around US$50 per person for a group of four. **Lester Eiley**, 25 Oak Street, tel (05) 22113, works as a tour guide, and offers boat charters.

Post office
This is at Caney Street, south of the river.

Taxis
Tino's Taxi Service, 127 Commerce Street, tel (05) 22438.

Art Centre
Dangriga Art Centre, 174 St Vincent Street, is recommended for local handicrafts and Belizean music.

Around Dangriga

To reach Tobacco Caye, either contact your hotel before arrival, so they can pick you up, or ask around for lifts with local fishermen. The tourist office or guest houses in Dangriga should be able to help. The same goes for boat lifts for the short journey to Hopkins village, south along the coast. Whichever way you arrive in Hopkins, you will find a photogenic fishing village of thatched houses on the beach, and you can even stay the night, in the **Sandy Beach Lodge**, tel (05) 22023, which offers local-style accommodation and interesting home cooking.

Placencia

Placencia is the kind of place you come to see for a few days, and end up staying a few months. This is the real thing: white sandy beaches, palm trees fringing the shoreline, and windswept houses on stilts hiding in the shade. The village is small and the people say 'hello' to each other when passing. 'All right', they say, with a creole lilt, and you feel like you've landed in Caribbean heaven. Great mounds of conch shells pile up by the village path like rubbish, their pinkness gleaming in the sun. In fact, there is such an abundance of these lovely shells that they are just tossed away or used for building fill.

San Pedro, on Ambergris Caye, must have once been like this, and the people of Placencia village are very aware of how much they have to lose. Originally a fishing village, many inhabitants still make a good living this way, and are loath to sell themselves or their land to tourism. One can only hope that they keep that attitude. You will not, therefore, find a resort with people eager to fulfil your every wish, but you will find a beautiful place, friendly locals, and accommodation ranging from luxurious hideaway to simple rooms.

GETTING TO PLACENCIA

By Air
Flights to Independence, which is in fact the same place as Mango Creek, can stop off here, coming either from Punta Gorda or northern towns. If there are no boatmen at the airstrip, you can phone the post office in Placencia, tel (06) 2946, and a boat will come and collect you. The fare should not be more than BZ$30 (US$15). If you have booked accommodation in advance, your hotel will send someone to pick you up.

By Bus
From Belize City, you need to take a bus to Dangriga, and change there for a direct bus to Placencia (75 km), which leaves at 2.30, Mondays, Wednesdays, Fridays and Saturdays. Coming from northern or western Belize, you can change buses for Dangriga in Belmopan. The bus departs from Placencia at 6 am, on the same days.

Coming from Punta Gorda, in the south, you can take any bus heading north, and get off at Mango Creek. Here you should walk to the waterside, and ask around for a boatman to take you to Placencia. The journey takes about 25 mins, and you should not have to pay more than BZ$30 (US$15), whether there is one passenger or three.

TOURIST INFORMATION

There is no official tourist office, but then there are few things you will need to know. The handful of resort hotels offer their guests every kind of land or sea tour, while other visitors will always find a group to join if they make themselves known to Janice, who runs the **post office**. Located in a wooden shack, just past the village pier, she can coordinate snorkelling trips or visits inland. The village **telephone** is here as well, and the code for Placencia is 06.

WHERE TO STAY

Up-market Beach Hotels

As in San Pedro on Ambergris Caye, accommodation prices outstrip the usual categories used in the guide, especially at the top end of the market. Prices have therefore been listed as a general guideline.

Furthest away from the village (30 mins walk) is **Rum Point Inn**, tel and fax (06) 22017. It is also the most expensive. There are five concrete *cabañas* that look like they have just landed from outer space, while the main house is a more traditional wooden structure, with a good bar and library. Singles are US$140, doubles US$165, plus US$50 for an extra person, all meals included. A short walk further south (15 mins walk from the village) is **Kitty's Place**, P.O. Box 528, Belize City, tel and fax (06) 22027, which is a delightful small hotel, with a choice of rooms, either in the main house, in beach *cabañas*, or two-room apartments. The bar and restaurant are a great place to socialize, and there is a good library too. This is also the only place with a **Dive Shop** with a diving instructor, and **bicycle rental**. (Diving certification courses cost around US$325.) The cheapest rooms are around US$25 singles, US$35 doubles, sharing the bathroom; while the two-person apartment is around US$75. 15% tax is added to bills.

The **Turtle Inn**, tel (06) 22069, is a beautiful spot, with six thatched cottages looking out to sea. Total capacity is twenty people, so this is the place if you want peace and quiet; and personal service from the friendly proprietors is assured. Meals are served family-style at one table. There is a bar and lending library. Prices include all meals: singles US$72, doubles US$123, plus US$35 for an extra person. A fully equipped beach house for two people is US$400 per week. Finally there is the **Cove Resort**, just outside the village, which has six rundown beach *cabañas* that sleep up to three people each. It is outrageously overpriced at US$75 per person, all meals included.

In the Village

EXPENSIVE

Beautiful beach *cabañas* are for rent via **Jene's Restaurant**, which go for around US$50 per person, per day. Janice, from the post office, also rents out beach *cabañas*, with great views of the lagoon, at the same price. **Sonny's Resort**, tel (06) 23103, in the middle of the village, has a mediocre restaurant and unhelpful staff.

MODERATE

The best hotel in Placencia is the **Sea Spray Hotel**, tel (06) 23148, which is a pleasant wooden building, raised slightly off the beach. Rooms are clean and simple, and there's a small bar on the beach.

Next to the best bar, at the southern end of the village, is the **Paradise Vacation Hotel**, tel and fax (06) 23179, which is plain and friendly.

INEXPENSIVE

Ran's Travel Lodge, tel (06) 22027, is a good budget choice. There are also plenty of families renting out rooms, and one of the best is **Conrad and Lydia's Rooms**. Conrad can also take you on boat trips. There are five basic rooms, sharing the bathroom.

EATING OUT

The best restaurant in the village is **Jene's**, which offers delicious meals and good drinks. Right on the beach, the **Kingfisher** (6–midnight only) offers tasty seafood at reasonable prices, while the **Tentacles Bar/Restaurant** is good but pricey, more popular for drinking than eating. The **Stone Crab** is also excellent and good value for money, while **Sonny's** is not. Home cooking is offered by **Jaimie's** and **B.J.'s**.

ENTERTAINMENT AND NIGHTLIFE

While all the restaurants in the village double up as drinking spots, some of the nicest places to drink are the beachside bars of the hotels outside the village. The **Turtle Inn** bar is recommended, and **Kitty's Place** is very popular. The only disco is the **Cozy Corner Disco**, which is right on the beach, in the village, blasting reggae music out to sea.

SPORTS AND ACTIVITIES

You will see many signs for tours and charters around the village so you have plenty of choices. A snorkelling trip to the reef generally costs US$15 per person, gear included, for a group of six. Sailing charters are around US$35 per person, for a group of four.

USEFUL INFORMATION

The nearest **bank** is in Mango Creek, and only open on Friday mornings, 9–noon. No need to worry, however, since most hotels and shops in Placencia should change travellers' cheques or cash.

Flight tickets can be booked at **Sonny's** restaurant, who can arrange transportation to the airstrip as well. Mango Creek also has the nearest **immigration office**, at the police station, where you can get extensions for your visitor's permit, or an exit stamp.

If you're self-catering, the **market store** is at the entrance to the village, on the dirt road, and the only place to buy groceries.

Around Placencia

Cockscomb Basin Jaguar Reserve

An interesting inland excursion is to visit the **Cockscomb Basin Jaguar Reserve**. It can be reached by a one-hour bus journey from Placencia, to the village of Maya Centre, on the way to Dangriga. By the time you read this, there should also be a shuttle bus from Maya Centre to take you into the reserve—otherwise you have a hot 8 km walk ahead of you, which takes 2 hours (remember that you have to be back at Maya Centre by 3, if you want to catch the bus back to Placencia). Tours to the reserve are also offered (US$25 per person), which is an expensive option, but perhaps more convenient.

Covering an area of 100,000 acres, the reserve is a wonderful place for hiking, and although you are unlikely to catch sight of the elusive jaguars and other cats, you will certainly see many bird species, even the endangered scarlet macaw. Beautiful trails, none longer than 3 km, have been cut into the forest, and there is a clear river to cool off in afterwards. A visitor's centre with a small exhibition can provide further information, and if you contact the Audubon Society (address on p. 198) in advance, you can also arrange to stay at the campsite or cabins here. There are no provisions available, so you should bring all your own food and drink. If you plan to hike as far as Victoria Peak, you must obtain a permit before arrival from the Audubon Society. Remember also that you will need a good map for this tough hike, and it would probably be a good idea to hire a guide to come with you, since this is a remote and uninhabited region.

Punta Gorda

Punta Gorda, or P.G., as it is generally known, is a quiet little town at the end of the Southern Highway, with just over 3000 inhabitants. A handful of roads, lined by dilapidated buildings, give the place a pleasant atmosphere of a forgotten film set, and nothing happens very quickly here. Most days the heat is freshened by a sea breeze, but to be in a room without a fan is almost unbearable. Being so far from the rest of Belize, P.G. never gets many visitors, and those that do pass this way are usually on their way somewhere else, only stepping off the ferry from Guatemala and onto a bus heading north. It is nevertheless a useful base from which to see interesting destinations inland, most of them relating to the Maya heritage, past and present.

In an effort to vitalize the tourist trade, and more importantly, help the Maya (and Garifuna) population share in the profits, a highly innovative programme is being developed, which should be fully operational by 1992. The **Toledo Eco-Tourism Association** plans to help six villages in the region, one of which is Garifuna, build guest houses, so that tourists can get the best out of visiting their traditional communities. The idea is that guests will sleep in the village guest house, but eat each meal with a different family, thus getting an excellent opportunity to meet the local inhabitants and learn about their culture. Local guides will also be provided to take a maximum of four people at a time along trails in the surrounding jungle. Profits from this project will go into a central fund, helping to improve the living standards and opportunities of the communities. To find out more, contact Chet Schmidt at **Nature's Way Guest House**, 65 Front Street, tel (07) 2119.

In the meantime, there is also a private project being run by Alfredo Villoria, called the **Indigenous Experience**. It is an unfortunate aspect of increased tourism opportunities that two competing operations are under way. This threatens to split local communities since they cannot belong to both. The idea behind this programme is to bring foreigners and Mayas together, but the project is potentially damaging. The Indian households who have been chosen as suitable hosts are paid directly by the guests, thus giving them a lucrative income over others in the village, which will undoubtedly lead to bitter friction and undermine traditional communal systems. Not only that, but chosen families do not necessarily have the resources to host foreigners, whose expectations of bathroom facilities may not match the hole in the ground they are bound to find. Nor does a family always have space for an extra person, resulting in a member of the family having to give up their sleeping place for the guest. This is wrong, and also potentially embarassing for the visitor, who would not wish to impose to such an extent. To find out more, you can contact Alfredo Villoria, who will put you in touch with a host family on payment of a registration fee, either at his **visitor's centre** at the Punta Gorda dock (daily except Thursday and Sunday, 8–noon); or via P.O. Box 73, Punta Gorda.

Whichever programme you choose to use, the experience of staying in a Mopan or Kekchi Maya village is a memorable one. An extraordinary aspect of meeting these people is that they speak English—if you have just arrived from Guatemala, you will find it very odd to hear soft, Belizean creole coming from an Indian mouth. In fact, a 'traditional' Maya community in Belize is very different from its Guatemalan equivalent. Here, many of the communities developed from refugees fleeing from persecution or slavery in Guatemala, and although their traditional architecture and cooking remains, their language and dress have often been lost. Only in recent years has there been any effort to regain old traditions. The children go to English-speaking schools, and many never learn their Maya language. Equally, the famous Maya weaving and embroidery is not to be found here. Instead, the most rewarding thing about visiting these villages is meeting modern, Belizean Mayas, who have a unique knowledge of the surrounding forest flora and fauna, which they are happy to share with you.

GETTING TO AND FROM PUNTA GORDA

By Air
There are six daily flights from Belize City, which stop at all main towns along the southern coast.

By Bus
Since Punta Gorda is the end of the line for the Southern Highway, you really cannot miss the place. It is 171 km from Dangriga, a hot and dusty journey along unpaved roads which takes 6 hours. Coming from Belize City, you can travel by comfortable Pullman bus with the **James Bus Line**, leaving Mondays, Wednesdays, Fridays and Saturdays, at 9 am. In the other direction, buses leave at 6 am on Sundays and Thursdays, and 1 pm on Tuesdays and Fridays. Phone (07) 2056 for information and booking tickets.

By Sea: to and from Guatemala
For information on the ferry service from Puerto Barrios, Guatemala see p. 157. Leaving Belize, the ferry goes on Tuesdays and Fridays, between 2 and 3, but supposedly at 2.30. Try to buy your ticket (US$5.50) as early as possible on the day, or you have little chance of getting on the boat. The ticket office is at 24 Middle Street. Remember to take your passport for buying the ticket, and get your exit stamp at the police station (on Front Street) before you leave. The journey to Puerto Barrios takes around $2\frac{1}{2}$ hrs.

TOURIST INFORMATION

There is a small information booth at the town dock, run by the friendly Alfredo Villoria, who can advise you on tours or regional buses, and also keeps a selection of brochures. Another excellent source of information and organizer of all kinds of tours is Chet Schmidt, at **Nature's Way Guest House**, 65 Front Street, which also happens to be the nicest place to stay. Get there by walking south along Main Street, until you come to a small sign pointing left for the guest house.

WHERE TO STAY

MODERATE

Nature's Way Guest House, 65 Front Street, tel (07) 2119, is a beautiful house, cooled by sea breezes, with meals cooked to order. All rooms share the bathroom. At the other end of town, the new **Charleston Inn**, on the corner of Main Street and North Street, has clean rooms, with fan and private bathroom. Close by, **Mahung's Hotel**, tel (07) 2044, offers good rooms around the back of the hotel only. **St Charles Inn**, 23 King Street, tel (07) 2149, is very respectable, but rather expensive for the town. The **Lux Drive Inn**, 43 Front Street, and the **Mira Mar**, 95 Front Street, are overpriced and unpleasant.

The only up-market hotel is the **Safe Haven Lodge**, 2 Prince Street, tel and fax (07) 2113.

EATING OUT

The best place for creole cooking is **Lucille's**, on Main Street. Get there early, since you usually have to wait a long time, which goes for all the eating houses in town. Another good creole restaurant is **Scheibers**, on Front Street, and surprisingly, so is the **Airport Café** (Mon–Sat, 8–6).

Bobby's Restaurant Bar, on Main Street, is best for soups, and if you feel like a Chinese meal, head for the **Kowloon** restaurant.

USEFUL INFORMATION

The **airport** is right in the town, so everything is within a short walking distance. **Pennel & Son**, 50 Main Street, is an agent for Tropic Air and Maya Airways. The **bus terminal** is located opposite the army barracks in the southern part of town, on West Street. Local buses leave from the municipal park, at the junction of Main Street and Queen Street. **Cars** can be rented from Texaco service station, tel (07) 2126.

There are a couple of **tour agencies**: **Briceno Taxi and Tour Services**, 6 Cemetery Lane and, for tours and boat charters, **Julio and Placida Requena**, 12 Front Street, tel (07) 2070.

The **Belize Bank** is located on Main Street, near the municipal park.

Around Punta Gorda

Maya Ruins and Villages

Nearest to Punta Gorda is the Kekchi village of **San Pedro Columbia**, which you can reach by local bus, either direct to the village or by taking a bus to San Antonio and getting off at the appropriate junction. The second option involves a 3-km walk. Located about 20 km northwest of Punta Gorda, the village is on a clearing in the forest, close to the emerald waters of the broad River Columbia. Houses are a variation on the pole and thatch design, and the people live from slash and burn agriculture, only venturing to town on market days.

The surrounding landscape, in the foothills of the Maya Mountains, is very attractive, and a walk of around 45 minutes will take you to the most important ruins in the region: **Lubaantun**. Two major pyramids remain, their most significant feature that they were built without the use of mortar. Unfortunately, an English adventurer used dynamite to explore them early this century, so they look like a giant has given them a good kick, causing them to cave in and tilt at odd angles. Stones litter the site, and looting has done its worst here. The site's name, meaning 'Place of Fallen Stones' is sadly apt. However, the location is beautiful, and certainly worth making an effort to see.

An unresolved controversy originated here: the mysterious **Crystal Skull** was discovered by the North American F. A. Mitchell Hedges, in 1926. He found the skull—which is perfectly shaped, yet has no trace of tool marks on it—on his daughter's birthday. Some believe it was a hoax for her benefit—his daughter, however, insists otherwise, and still owns the skull today.

San Antonio village, about 5 km west of San Pedro Columbia, has a direct bus service from P.G., and also has a hotel, which makes a good base from which to visit the **Uxbenka** ruins. Inhabited by Mopan Maya, this is a modern village, with a stone church built by resident American missionaries. The community has strong ties to its traditions, however, and the best time to see this is on 5 August, on San Luis Rey Day. The Maya ruins are about 5 km away, just off the dirt track leading to Santa Cruz village. Situated on a small hilltop, the site was not officially discovered until 1984, and what you find is a small, unexcavated ceremonial centre, with good views over the surrounding jungle.

About 1 km further along the road, a small track leads off to the left to **New Falls**, which is an excellent place for a swim and picnic. The river broadens out into a wide pool under some waterfalls, embraced by thick jungle on both sides (if you reach St Elena village, you have gone too far).

The only place to stay in San Antonio is the basic **Bol's Hilltop Hotel**. Meals must be ordered in advance, and this is the only place to serve food in the village. If you would like to hire a guide for exploring the region, you could not do better than Matilde Kaal, who, in spite of his name, is male, and extremely knowledgeable and friendly. You will find his home by asking around in the nearby settlement of Crique Lagarto.

The Maya site of **Nim Li Punit** is not conveniently accessible by public transport, but if you have your own, the place is worth visiting for the terrific views across the coastal plain and nearby highlands. Its name means 'Big Hat', and it was only discovered in 1976, hiding on a small hilltop above some Indian homesteads. The best preserved details are the stelae, of which no fewer than 25 have been found, indicating that this was an important ceremonial centre. The site is near Indian Creek settlement, off the Southern Highway, 40 km north of P.G.

Blue Creek

At the junction for San Pedro Columbia, where **Roy's Coolspot** offers snacks and cold drinks, there is a turning for Blue Creek, which is a beautiful place for swimming, huge trees shading the deep green water (unfortunately, you need your own transport to get here). Heading up the right-hand side of the river on foot, you soon come to a lovely natural pool, perfect for tranquil swimming without any currents.

Dem Dats Doin

Finally, for anyone interested in integrated farm systems, a visit to Dem Dats Doin is a must. Run by a Hawaiian couple, Alfredo and Yvonne Villoria, their farm is a delightful place, full of innovative and simple technology that anyone could use to create a self-sufficient, tropical farm. There are also a huge number of fruit trees grown, and a tour (US$5) around the farm is not only educative, but beautiful as well. To get there, follow the road to San Pedro Columbia, and turn right where a wrecked car is parked, with the farm's name painted on its side. There is also one room available for overnight stays, moderately priced. To book the room or a tour, contact Alfredo at his information booth in P.G., or via P.O. Box 73, Punta Gorda, Toledo District, Belize.

NORTHERN BELIZE

Much of northern Belize is flat and swampy, dotted by lagoons and marshes that make an ideal habitat for aquatic birds, but not for spectacular views (unless you're a birdwatcher, of course). The coastal lagoons stretch endlessly and are for the most part uninhabited—fishermen are the only regular visitors. The exception to this is near the Mexican border, where the town of Corozal nestles in a bay surrounded by small ancient and modern settlements. Only the western reaches of Orange Walk differ from the general description. Here the landscape becomes hilly and is covered by thick tropical forests which are some of the least accessible and least explored in the country. Exploring the region without your own transport is difficult, though if you have the time and money there are some worthwhile sites, such as the ancient ruins of Lamanai, and the Shipstern and Crooked Tree reserves.

Historically, northern Belize has often been a refuge for people fleeing from violence elsewhere. Some of the earliest refugees were the Santa Cruz Maya of the Mexican Yucatán who came to Belize in 1901. They were a group of Mayas who had allied themselves with the British after defeat in the Caste Wars of 1847, during which the Spanish had violently put down an Indian uprising. After their defeat, the Santa Cruz Maya were among a larger group, who formed separate and independent Maya states in the Mexican region of Quintana Roo. However, the Mexican authorities could not allow independent Indian states in their country, and so they mounted another attack in 1901, which resulted in final and bloody victory. Thus the Santa Cruz Maya fled to the lands of their former allies, to what was then British Honduras, and their descendants remain until this day.

Other groups that have come to the region include German Mennonite communities, who settled in Shipyard and Blue Creek; and Nicaraguan and Salvadorean refugees, squatting in various remote parts, including around the Maya site of Lamanai. The Spanish language predominates here, unlike in the rest of the country, and the closer you get to the Mexican border, the more likely you are to meet people who speak no English at all, being mestizos not creoles.

The paved Northern Highway cuts straight through the region, and travel from Belize City to Mexican Chetumal is just a matter of four hours. The only significant town on the way is Orange Walk, which was once at the centre of a lucrative sugar-cane industry, but has now become severely impoverished. In response, farmers have turned to marijuana cultivation, and Belize has become a signigicant drug exporter, as well as a stopover for cocaine aircraft on the way to North America.

Along the Northern Highway

Crooked Tree Wildlife Sanctuary

Located about 53 km northwest of Belize City, this reserve is the first point of interest beyond the close environs of the city. Established in 1984 and administered by the Audubon Society, the sanctuary's landscape is predominantly wetlands, which are the ideal home for all kinds of resident and migratory birds. In particular during the dry season, the place is a safe haven for thousands of birds, including many types of heron, two species of duck, egrets, kingfishers, ospreys, hawks, and many, many more, the largest of which is the Jaribu stork. The best time to see birds here is from November to May, and a visitor's centre in the village of Crooked Tree offers further information.

Orange Walk

86 km north of Belize City, the town of Orange Walk is a scruffy place that holds no attraction for the tourist in itself, but is a starting point for visits to the Maya site of **Lamanai**. Originally a timber camp, the town became an important centre for sugar-cane and citrus production. It is now a depressed area, where a significant proportion of local agriculture is now the illicit cultivation of marijuana, popularly known as 'Belize Breeze'. A rough town, Orange Walk was also the scene of gory battles in the 19th century, when the local Indian population regularly attacked settlers. The last battle was in 1872, and the ruins of Fort Cairns and Mundy are a legacy of the time when Orange Walk was frequently besieged and needed military protection.

WHERE TO STAY
Jane's Guest Houses in Bakers Street and Market Lane are recommended for budget travellers; **Baron's Hotel** tel (03) 22518, is more expensive.

Lamanai

The ruins of Lamanai (8–5, small fee) are located about 20 km southwest of Orange Walk, on the shores of the New River Lagoon. An important site, it is estimated that in the 6th century, it was home to around 20,000 people. The earliest inhabitants came here in 1500 BC and this site has one of the longest records of occupation, long before it became a Maya ceremonial centre. The earliest stone architecture appeared in the 9th century BC, and the largest Pre-Classic structure in the Maya territory is to be found here, a pyramid rising 33 m above the surrounding savannah, whose earliest building phase dates back to 100 BC. The site's name is the original Maya one, and means 'Submerged Crocodile', and images of crocodiles appear frequently amongst the carvings found here.

Maya descendants were living here as late as the 16th century and the Spanish duly built a mission church to Christianize them. The results were poor, however, and the Indians burnt the place down in 1640. In the 19th century the British built a sugar mill nearby but this failed too, when the manager died of a fever and the ruins have been left in peace, the surrounding area sparsely populated, until this day. As you wander around this unspoilt site you will find abundant wildlife, especially birds and butterflies.

GETTING TO LAMANAI
To reach Lamanai, your best bet is to go on a tour from Orange Walk (Mr Godoy, tel (03) 22969) or Belize City (such as Gilly's Inland Tours, tel (02) 77630). Otherwise you must make your way to the villages of Guinea Grass or Shipyard (closer), from where you can hire a boatman to take you south along the New River. There are no facilities there, though the resident archaeology camp has a small museum showing artefacts found here.

Río Bravo Conservation Area

The north's most exotic resort hotel is the **Chan Chich Lodge**, built in the middle of a Maya plaza in a remote jungle bordering Guatemala (contact via 1 King Street, Belize City, tel (02) 75634, or P.O. Box 37, Belize City). This is a private reserve, administered by the Programme for Belize, and the lodge is a superb place to discover the colourful flora and fauna of tropical forests while enjoying the comforts of rustic luxury. To get there you have to charter a plane to Gallon Jug airstrip, or during the dry season, tough vehicles can get there via Orange Walk, San Felipe and Blue Creek.

Shipstern Reserve

This reserve is in a remote region northeast of Orange Walk, near the village of Sarteneja, about an hour's drive from the town along a dirt road. There is an efficient visitor's centre where you can arrange for a guided tour around the reserve which covers 31 square miles and a variety of habitats, ranging from the shallow Shipstern Lagoon to savannah and forests. One of the most interesting trails is the 'Chiclero Botanical Trail', where you can learn about the uses for many of the trees. Almost all the species of animal found in Belize are found in this region, including the jaguar. Over 60 kinds of reptiles and amphibians have been recorded, and a staggering 220 species of birds. A special attraction is also the nearby **Butterfly Breeding Centre**. Visit on a sunny day, and you will have the best chance to see some of the 200 species of butterflies.

Corozal

Of all the northern settlements, this is the most pleasant to visit, facing out to the turquoise seas of Corozal Bay, 134 km north of Belize City and 14 km from the Mexican border. Corozal was badly damaged by Hurricane Janet in 1955, however, and so it does have a somewhat empty feeling to it. Like Orange Walk, the town has suffered from the decline of the sugar industry, and employment is scarce. Bored youths hang around street corners and there isn't very much to do for the visitor either. It is a good spot to break the journey to or from Mexico. There are also flights to Ambergris Caye from here.

GETTING TO COROZAL

By Air

Corozal's landing strip is set amongst fields but a cab or two are always ready to meet arrivals. For flight tickets from Corozal contact **Menzies Travel**, Ranchito village, tel (04) 22725, and they will send someone to pick you up free of charge.

By Bus

Batty buses stop at 4 Park Street North, and Venus buses stop at 7th Avenue. You should have no problem travelling to and from Corozal by public transport, as all buses between Belize City and Chetumal stop here.

WHERE TO STAY

EXPENSIVE

The top place to stay is the attractive **Tony's Inn**, at South End, tel (04) 22829, fax (04) 22829, which is right by the sea. Rooms have either a fan or air-conditioning and TV.

Outside Corozal, near the village of Consejo, you will find the reasonably up-market **Adventure Inn**, P.O. Box 35, Corozal Town, tel (04) 22187, fax (04) 22243. Overlooking the bay the hotel is made up of a main lodge and 14 cabins, and all watersports, especially fishing, are catered for.

MODERATE

Hotel Maya, South End, tel (04) 22082, is clean and simple. Rooms with fan and private bath are available.

INEXPENSIVE

Capri, on the corner of 14th Avenue and 4th Avenue is loud and grubby, and the best budget choice is **Nestor's Hotel**, 123 5th Avenue, tel (04) 22354, which also has a restaurant.

Part VI

HONDURAS

Honduras is the largest Central American republic after Nicaragua—a bit smaller than England and about the same size as the American state of Ohio. In the south a narrow corridor leads towards the Pacific Gulf of Fonseca, squeezed tight by the borders of El Salvador and Nicaragua, while the country's main body blossoms out towards a substantial share of the Atlantic coast, bordered by Guatemala to the northwest, and Nicaragua to the northeast. It has a rugged highland interior, occasionally covered in rare cloud forest, which softens into verdant hills towards its western border. There are windswept plateaus to the east and narrow coastal plains along both seashores. To the extreme northeast, the landscape is different again, being covered by the moist Mosquitia rainforest, one of Central America's least explored regions. All in all the countryside offers great variety, and in many parts the traveller can enjoy it without ever feeling crowded by people. Not only are there few tourists, but also few inhabitants. In fact, the population of Honduras, about 4.9 million, is smaller than El Salvador's, even though it's about five times the size.

Ninety per cent of the population is mestizo, with only a small indigenous population, mostly living in the Mosquitia. But there is a sizeable black population, who live all along the north coast of Honduras and on the Bay Islands. Many of these are Garifuna, living in small communities by the Caribbean Sea, where they still retain much of their Afro-Indian heritage in their religion and culture. On the Bay Islands, you also find a unique people, who are descendants of pirates, slaves, Indians and Spanish colonists. They are known as the islanders, and they speak the lilting English of the Caribbean. On the island of Utila, in particular, there are still many whites, keeping their blue-eyed,

234

blond features to this day, even if their English is getting a bit rough. Everyone also speaks Spanish on the islands, and the schools here are all bilingual.

Until war depressed the Nicaraguan economy even lower, Honduras was the poorest country in Central America, with low income levels and high unemployment. Over half the population live by the land, and coffee, shrimps and bananas (Honduras is the world's fourth largest banana exporter) are the main exports, while beef and cattle are growing in importance. The department of Olancho is the main cattle-raising area. It is cowboy country where you will see men with their faces hidden by outsized hats, their feet in heeled leather boots, and pistols tucked into their trouser belts, riding beautifully saddled horses.

For travellers, Honduras has traditionally held little attraction because it is so desperately poor, and there is no large Indian population with colourful markets and festivals. Neither is the landscape as beautiful as neighbouring Guatemala, nor as accessible, and touristic facilities are in their infancy everywhere except on the Bay Islands. Yet Honduras does have a special character of its own, and while its treasures are not so easily found, there is the attraction of travelling in a country where tourism has made little impact on the local way of life, and where there is the additional bonus of relative safety, since no guerrillas are active here. The Honduran military does make its presence felt with regular road blocks, but is not generally concerned with foreign visitors, and while there is a substantial American presence, you would never know it, since you rarely see US army personnel.

The capital, Tegucigalpa, is also one of the more pleasant Central American cities, with an unexpected stylishness and attractive 19th-century architecture, while coastal La Ceiba has all the energy and spirit of a small Caribbean port. For those who make the effort, Honduras certainly holds some unforeseen treats, especially along its north coast and on the Bay Islands.

Post-Independence History

Early Years of Independence

Honduras won its independence from Spain in 1821, after which it became a member of the United Provinces of Central America in 1823 along with Nicaragua, Costa Rica, El Salvador and Guatemala. Most Central Americans, however, had never fought for independence, and a significant number didn't even want it. As a result the union was split right from the start. It didn't take long for fighting to break out, and the Honduran pro-union forces were defeated in 1838, a year before the Central American experiment dissolved into the countries we know today. The defeated Honduran general, Francisco Morazán, died a few years later, but he is still regarded as a hero, and the capital's most opulent boulevard is named after him.

For Honduras, the collapse of the federation meant a return to relative insignificance. Even in pre-Conquest times, the territory had never been encompassed by the great Maya civilization (except for the area around Copán), instead, its remote interior was home to a number of tribes, most notably the Lencas. When the Spanish arrived, the

Lenca chief, Lempira, tried to expel the invaders, but was defeated and killed in 1537. Today the country's currency bears his name, but the majority of his and other tribes have long since dwindled.

At the time of the Spanish Conquest, the estimated Indian population was as high as 450,000, but almost a quarter of them were killed in the early stages of armed colonization. Up to 150,000 were enslaved and sold to distant parts of the empire, from Guatemala to Peru, and large numbers died from Old World diseases like smallpox. Today there are believed to be fewer than 80,000 Indians surviving, of which the largest tribe, the Lencas (around 50,000), have mixed with mestizos and are now regarded as *ladinos*. Of the remaining five tribal groups, the Miskito Indians form the largest, ethnically intact society, which has been able to retain many of its traditions due to the inaccessibility of the Mosquitia jungle.

After Independence, Honduras remained on the sidelines of the region's political and economic development. Few settlers had come to Honduras, and those that stayed were largely living by subsistence farming in remote areas, where no roads reached. Because of the difficult terrain, coffee did not become the country's first major export, and therefore it didn't develop a powerful landed oligarchy either, who might have shaped the country's political development, as it did elsewhere. Instead, bananas grown along the northern coast became the main export, which, in the absence of powerful landowners or a cohesive government, rapidly came under foreign control. Central government was so weak in Honduras that civil wars were a regular occurrence in the 19th century. Just in the years from 1821 to 1876, no fewer than 85 different presidents ruled Honduras.

The Original Banana Republic

The country lagged behind its neighbours in economic and political development, and vital infrastructures, such as a road and railway network, central banking and a national currency, did not emerge. The country did not have its own national bank or currency until 1953, which is only one year before it granted female suffrage, the last to do so in all of Latin America.

There was no national capital to invest in the country, and so the lucrative banana industry was sold to foreigners, who gained huge land concessions and much more besides. The idea was that the foreign investors would develop the country in return for favourable concessions, such as exemption from customs duties, mineral rights to the land, and the right to build and control railways, canals, ports, finance centres and export houses. Unfortunately, the mainly American investors only developed these things as much as they were necessary for the smooth running of their plantations and exporting the crops, and not for the general use and benefit of the country. Honduras had sold itself out, to become the archetypal 'banana republic'.

Two companies emerged as the country's dominant powers: **Cuyamel**, based around the Tela area, and **United Fruit**, based around the La Ceiba area. Between them they directed a booming banana industry, so that its share in total exports went from 11% in 1892, to 66% in 1913. By 1918, 75% of banana lands were owned by just three companies, and with the government concessions on top of that, they just about owned all of northern Honduras. Political control was inevitable, and the director of the

Cuyamel company is supposed to have said, 'In Honduras a mule costs more than a deputy.' Each of the two giant companies backed a different political party: Cuyamel financed and used the Liberal Party, while United Fruit did the same with the National Party. Virtually no governmental decision could be taken without recourse to the fruit companies.

The 1929 Wall Street Crash rather spoilt the party for the banana kings, and the effect on Honduras was devastating. Unemployment and wage cuts became the norm, and the civilian government had to give way to dictatorship in order to keep control. It was a development common throughout the region, and in Honduras, the dictator Tiburcio Carias Andino ruled for 16 years, from 1932 to 1948. In the meantime, Cuyamel had sold out to United Fruit, ending the eternal economic and political division in the country, and paving the way for United Fruit's almost total monopoly of the country's remaining banana industry. Naturally its traditional ally, the National Party, became the ruling force in government, its officials on company payrolls and the national budgets financed by the company. Thus the country remained undeveloped apart from the banana industry—to the extent that its capital city, Tegucigalpa, had no connecting road to the coast until the 1950s.

The Emergence of the Military

After the Second World War the country's economy gradually diversified. A broader agricultural sector developed, including coffee, cattle farming, sugar, and cotton, which in turn stimulated a home-grown mercantile and business community. During the 1950s power shifted away from the banana companies towards other business interests and the military. US influence remained dominant, though it changed with the times as well, becoming concentrated in military aid programmes. A 1954 military treaty signed with the US gave it unlimited access to Honduran raw and semi-processed materials in return for military aid. The Honduran government was staunchly anti-communist, which made the country a perfect ally for US foreign policy in Central America.

The Honduran military gradually emerged as the strongest centralized institution in the country, expanding their role as referee to the national parties into a political power in their own right. The first military coup came in 1956, when the Nationalist president, Julio Lozano Díaz, tried to stay on after his term of office was over, and from then onwards, the military took on the role of governmental arbiter, if not always ruler in its own right.

1957 saw an important change made to the Honduran constitution, whereby the high command of the military came under the control of the Chief of the Armed Forces, independent of any civilian government. What is more, the Chief of the Armed Forces also had the right to disobey presidential orders if he considered them unconstitutional. Thus the military's role as an independent political power was secured.

Honduras may be notable for its backwardness but in recent years it has also been notable in Central America for its relative peace and lack of revolutionary movements. This seems surprising considering the level of deprivation in the country. In the 1970s 2% of Honduran landowners held 44% of the land, and by the late 1980s there had not been much change, with 4% still owning 56%. Recent statistics, for 1989, indicate that up to 77% of the rural population lives in 'absolute poverty', meaning they are unable to afford food for minimum nutritional requirements. Yet Honduras has not suffered the same political violence as neighbouring Guatemala, El Salvador or Nicaragua.

The traditional bone of contention in Latin America is agrarian land reform. In neighbouring countries the rich oligarchies took over most available land during Liberal reforms at the turn of the century but Honduran governments didn't need to abolish public and communal lands as there was no coffee boom to swallow up all available land and leave huge numbers of people landless. When the diversification of agro-exports after the Second World War led to unemployment on the banana plantations, the government (who still owned 52% of national territory as late as 1952) was able to hand out parcels of public land for subsistence farming without antagonizing the landowners. Thus the traditional division between the landless poor and the elite was avoided. Although only 22% of the landless Honduran population benefited from agrarian reform, it is considerably more than elsewhere.

Another reason for the relative peace in Honduras is that the military developed independently of elite patronage (the Honduran upper classes being too disparate and poor). This meant that military intervention in national politics was less identified with one particular sector of society, and thus didn't fuel the usual political antagonism between the landless peasants and the business and agricultural elite.

The Football War of 1969

Honduras was therefore an ideal channel for US foreign policy as well as multinational interests—even if the military coup of 1963 did prove a little unpalatable. The only period of unrest came in 1969, when the so-called **Football War** with El Salvador threatened to unbalance the country's peaceful tradition. On the surface the war, which only lasted 100 hours, was sparked off by rivalry concerning which country would go to the 1970 World Cup. Both countries lost in the play-offs that took place on the rival's soil, and allegations of foul play at both occasions sent tensions to fever pitch, erupting into violence against Honduran fans in El Salvador. Honduras retaliated by expelling 100,000 Salvadorean immigrants.

This was a serious matter, and lay at the root of the war. At the time, 20% of the Honduran rural population was Salvadorean, originally brought in by the fruit companies as labour, but large numbers were also arriving because of land shortages in their country. El Salvador is a fraction of the size of Honduras, yet its population is larger and most land is firmly in the hands of a few families. Antagonism against the Salvadorean immigrants was high in Honduras in the late 1960s, when land shortages were first an issue there but, more importantly, Honduras was suffering economically from Salvadorean competition, and its government was only too keen to divert people's anger to an external issue to avoid criticism. However, the Salvadorean army was far superior to the Honduran one, and defeated its neighbour's forces. Only a threatened trade boycott from the Organization of American States (OAS) forced the Salvadorean army to retreat, but there has been a border dispute with Honduras ever since. In spite of US-inspired assistance against leftist Salvadorean guerrilla forces, Salvadorean refugees in Honduras are treated with suspicion, and are generally encouraged to return to their own country, occasionally by force.

United States Satellite

After the 1979 Nicaraguan Revolution, the Carter administration chose Honduras as its most important ally in Central America. It was to be the bulwark against revolutionary movements in Central America, and the US/Honduran military relationship became ever closer. Pressure for a civilian government from its powerful ally resulted in free elections in 1981, and the country was held up as an example of democracy in the region. When Reagan took office, the Honduran connection in Central America was seen as vital to US interests, to help clean up its 'back yard', and use it as a base for counter-insurgency programmes against Nicaragua and El Salvador. US economic aid to Honduras doubled in 1980, and military aid almost doubled as well. In fact, over the next six years, military aid went from US$4 million to an incredible US$88.2 million, and US military personnel in Honduras went from less than 30 to 11,000 stationed permanently in the country after 1985. An extensive assistance programme was developed, and thirteen strategic air bases have so far been built with the help of the United States military. Over the same period, 40,000 Contras became stationed in southern Honduras, from where they mounted attacks into Nicaraguan territory, while an estimated 22,000 Hondurans were displaced from the Nicaraguan border region, making them refugees in their own country.

Since the departure of Reagan and the failure of the Nicaraguan Revolution, American operations in Honduras have been cut back drastically, and US military aid has gone from US$41.2 million in 1988 to half that amount in 1990. Instead, aid has been channelled into economic and social development, which was estimated at a total of US$188.3 millions for 1990. One of the organizations active here is the American Peace Corps, which has its largest operation in this country. Thus Honduras is still referred to as the 'Pentagon Republic', and although more peaceful than its neighbours, it is also poorer and less developed.

The semblance of democracy continues in spite of the fact that the military conducts its affairs independently of government control, and also has the right of veto over cabinet appointments. The latest president is the Nationalist Party's Rafael Leonardo Callejas, who won the elections in 1989, and took office in January 1990. However, in spite of the fact that voting is compulsory, abstention was estimated at over 23% of the electorate, showing that not all Hondurans are willing to take part in the charade of free elections.

General Information

Getting to Honduras

By Air
There are five international airlines that serve this country, all with connections to North America, so if you're coming from Europe, you must change in the US. Miami, Houston, New Orleans, and Los Angeles have the best connections. Three Central American

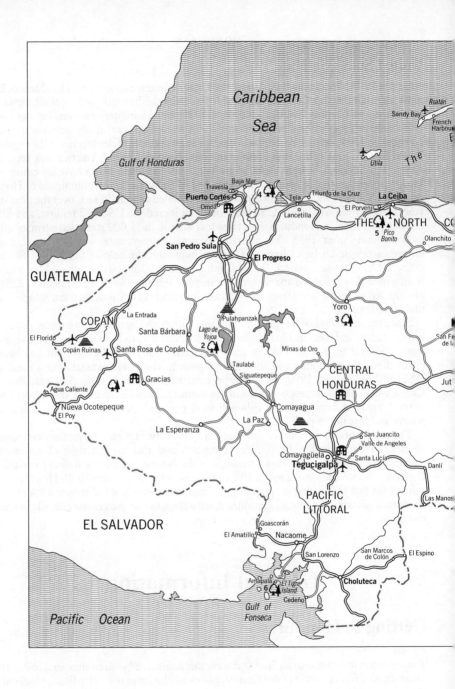

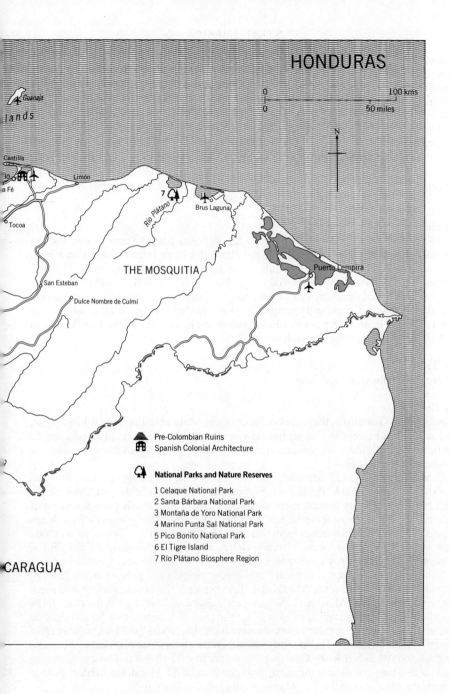

HONDURAS

0   100 kms

0   50 miles

N

Guanaja

lands

Castilla

lo

a Fé

Tocoa

Limón

Río Plátano

Brus Laguna

THE MOSQUITIA

San Esteban

Dulce Nombre de Culmí

Puerto Lempira

7

CARAGUA

🔺 Pre-Colombian Ruins
🏛 Spanish Colonial Architecture

🌳 National Parks and Nature Reserves

1 Celaque National Park
2 Santa Bárbara National Park
3 Montaña de Yoro National Park
4 Marino Punta Sal National Park
5 Pico Bonito National Park
6 El Tigre Island
7 Río Plátano Biosphere Region

airlines fly to Honduras from the US: Tan-Sahsa (national airline), Lacsa, and Taca. American Airlines and Continental are the main North American carriers. The two main airports are in Tegucigalpa (Toncontín) and San Pedro Sula (Ramón Villeda Morales), of which the latter is the more convenient if you intend to travel along the north coast, and many consider it much safer than the antiquated airport by the capital. There are also international airports on the Bay Island of Roatán and outside the city of La Ceiba.

Arriving by air you must have an onward or return ticket to enter the country. Alternatively, you could argue that you intend to leave Honduras by land, but this may cause problems. On leaving the country, the airport exit tax is US$10, and there may be inspection charges for luggage as well. On arrival, the entry fee is around US$2. A taxi into the capital should not cost more than US$3.

By Boat

Trading boats occasionally travel between the Belizean port of Punta Gorda and the Honduran port of Puerto Cortés, and sometimes boats go from Guatemalan Puerto Barrios as well. However, it is very difficult to find out who is sailing when. The best maritime connection is by motorized canoe from Mango Creek in Belize to Puerto Cortés. The 7-hour journey can be very wet in rough seas. Belizean exit stamps are available in Mango Creek, and you must get your Honduran entry stamp as soon as you arrive. It is easier and safer to enter Honduras by land, since ships have been known to sink owing to overloading or rough seas.

By Train

There is no railway to Honduras.

By Bus

Coming from Guatemala, there are border crossings at Agua Caliente, near Esquipulas, and at El Florido, east of Chiquimula. If you plan to visit the ruins of Copán, the El Florido crossing is the more convenient, and since many tourists pass this way, it also has less hassle (see p. 155).

Crossing from or to El Salvador, you are almost guaranteed aggravation. The two main border posts are at El Poy in the northwest, and El Amatillo in the east. Buses run to both borders from San Salvador, but since northern El Salvador is often the scene of fighting, the eastern border is probably more peaceful. It is also closer to the Honduran capital (130 km). Regular buses leave from the Honduran side for Tegucigalpa, dropping you at the terminal by the Mercado Belén, a short distance from the city centre. Take a taxi, and don't pay more than US$1.

Coming from Nicaragua, there are two border posts: El Espino, near the town of Somoto, and Las Manos, north of Ocotal. The former is the easier crossing, and there are regular buses from Managua to Somoto, and minibuses from there to the border. On the Honduran side, you will need to head for the town of Choluteca via San Marcos de Colón (2 hrs), where regular buses connect with the capital (143 km), a journey of around 3 hours. Once in Tegucigalpa, you will either arrive at the terminal by Mercado Belén, or on Avenida 6, in the Comayagüela part of town. Either way, best catch a taxi to your chosen hotel, remembering not to pay more than US$1. Honduran borders close at 6, with the exception of the Las Manos border, which closes at 4.

By Car

Much the same advice as for bus journeys applies. Coming from Guatemala, the easiest border post is at El Florido. Coming from El Salvador, best head for the eastern border at El Amatillo, and coming from Nicaragua, best cross at El Espino. Your car will be fumigated on entry, for which you are normally charged US$2. There are also charges for official permission to drive in Honduras (US$2), and for inspection of papers (US$1); don't be surprised if other 'charges' are applied. Make sure your papers are in perfect order, including national driving licence, insurance, and proof of ownership. Permission to drive in the country will be given for one month, which you can extend for up to two months before you must pay heavy import duties. You are expected to carry warning triangles in case of a breakdown. Military and police roadblocks are frequent, especially near borders and outside major towns, so always have your papers at the ready.

Embassies and Consulates

UK: 115 Gloucester Place, London W1H 3PJ, tel (071) 486 4880 (Mon–Fri, 10–2).
US: 4301 Connecticut Avenue, NW, Washington DC 20008, tel (202) 906 7700. Honduras also has representation in Los Angeles, San Francisco, Houston, New Orleans, Miami, and New York.
Canada: Embassy: 151 Slater Street, Suite 300–A, Ottawa, Ontario K1P 5H3, tel (613) 233 8900. Consulates: 1500 Stanley Street, Suite 330, Montréal, Québec H3A 1R3, tel (514) 849 4053; 104–535 West Georgia Street, Vancouver, British Columbia V6B 1Z6, tel (604) 685 7711.

Tourist Offices

Outside of Honduras, the consulates and embassies are your only source of information, and they are not really equipped to answer your questions. However, a brand new tourist office has opened in the capital, Tegucigalpa (see p. 244 for address).

Passports and Visas

Honduras has a very bad reputation for difficult border procedures. Visitors report being turned away for no apparent reason; having to pay unexpected 'fees'; and only being given entry for a few days. Try to stay calm, and remember that there is absolutely nothing you can do about it. Do not attempt bribery unless you know what you're doing. A last option, if you cannot get permission to enter the country, is a military escort through the country and out at another border. This can be very expensive, since you must bear the costs. Having said this, Honduras is waking up to the benefits of tourist dollars, and border officials are becoming less obnoxious.

All visitors need a valid passport, and visas are needed by North Americans, Australians and New Zealanders. If you need a visa and don't get it in your own country, the most efficient place is at the Honduran Consulate in Guatemala City, though there are Honduran Consulates in all Central American countries, listed in this guide under the 'Tourist Information' sections for each country. British and Canadian subjects do not need visas. Honduran entry requirements change frequently, however, and it is vital that you check with the relevant embassy before leaving your country. Visas are generally valid for two months. Visitor's permits (US$1), given to all others at the border, are valid for one month, and can be renewed for up to two months at immigration offices in Tegucigalpa (Dirección General de Migración, Calle Jérez, Tegucigalpa—avoid coming here if possible because of unhelpful staff and overcrowding), San Pedro Sula, Comayagua, La Paz, Siguatepeque, Santa Rosa de Copán, Tela and La Ceiba. If you stay more than one month, you will also need to obtain an exit visa (small fee) from the Ministry of Foreign Affairs, Palacio de los Ministerios, Avenida Miguel Paz Barahona and Calle Los Dolores, in Tegucigalpa.

Any passport holders with stamps from Cuba will be refused entry, so will those with stamps from countries Honduras has no diplomatic relations with, which includes many Middle Eastern and Asian countries. Except for those with communist stamps, visitors can always try negotiating if an official takes against a particular entry.

Customs

You cannot bring any communist or left-wing literature into Honduras. Otherwise there are no restrictions and no duties, other than the standard one for alcohol and tobacco: one bottle of spirits or two bottles of wine, and one carton of 200 cigarettes. If arriving from El Salvador or Nicaragua you can expect to have your luggage searched thoroughly.

On Arrival

Tourist Offices

A new tourist office has opened in the capital, where you will find helpful staff able to answer most queries. **National Tourist Office**, Centro Guanacaste, Barrio Guanacaste, Tegucigalpa, tel 22 6618/22 7752, fax 22 21 02 (Mon–Fri, 7.30–3.30). Do remember, though, that organized tourism is in its infancy. Maps and brochures are still very limited, and almost none are in English.

Around the rest of the country, official tourist offices are scarce, and are only to be found in San Pedro Sula, Ocotepeque, Copán and the airport on Roatán. More often than not, local travel agencies are the best source of information.

Orientation

The country's towns and cities can be confusing at first, not because of their size, but because streets are rarely signed and the locals tend to know their way around by landmarks rather than street names. When asking for directions it is therefore most useful if you simply say what building or office you are looking for, rather than its address.

As a general rule, Honduran street names are defined by a city's division into north, south, east and west. For example, 2 Avenida N.O. means the address is in the northwestern sector of the city (*oeste* = west, *este* = east). This is important, since the streets can be very long, and the same number can occur, depending on whether it is at the western or eastern end of a street.

Maps

Since Honduras has traditionally been ignored by travellers, there are few maps. In fact the **Honduras Tourist Map** is the best you are easily going to get, which also has street plans for Tegucigalpa, San Pedro Sula and La Ceiba. The **Texaco Map** is also useful, but rarely on sale anywhere. If you plan to explore the interior for some time, by whatever means, it would be worth making the effort to buy the 1:1 000 000 map of Honduras, available from the **Instituto Geográfico Nacional**. This map is very useful and shows many dirt roads not marked elsewhere.

To buy it can be somewhat time-consuming: take your passport to the Instituto Geográfico Nacional (Mon–Fri, 7.30–noon and 12.30–3.30), at the southeastern end of Comayagüela district. Here you must choose the relevant map and get an invoice. Having done that, you must return to the city centre, to pay for the map at window 21 in the **Palacio del Distrito Central**, on the main square. Now all that is left is to return to the institute, where you can have the map in return for the slips you received on paying. It may be possible, and a lot easier, to buy the Institute's map at the shop under **Hotel Honduras Maya**. Hikers might also find the 1:50 000 topographical maps of Honduras useful, for which the same buying procedure applies. If you're coming from England, why not check at **Stanford's International Map Centre**, 12 Long Acre, London WC2E 9LP, tel 071 836 1321, who might also sell these maps.

Getting Around Honduras

By Air
There are plenty of local airports, though many of them are not in public use. Some are military, others private or simply abandoned. The most common connections are between Tegucigalpa and San Pedro Sula (30 mins, around US$20 one-way), and to the Bay Islands from the coastal town of La Ceiba (about 30 mins, and prices ranging from US$10 to US$20 one-way). The northeastern coastal town of Trujillo and the remote Mosquitia town of Puerto Lempira also have airstrips with regular flights. Apart from the national airline of Tan-Sahsa, there are a few private airlines, such as Aeroservicios, Isleña, Sammy and Sosa, which offer commercial routes as well as charters.

By Train
The Honduran railway is solely made up of the old banana railway and the only passenger route is from San Pedro Sula to Tela, via the port of Puerto Cortés. You will not be using the train if you are in a hurry, but the four-hour journey between Puerto

Cortés and Tela is one of the great Latin American train rides, old steel carriages clanking you through endless tropical plantations of banana and African palms.

By Bus

Bus services are not as frequent or cheap as in Guatemala, but are still the best way of getting around Honduras. Remember always to have your papers easily available, since military and police checkpoints are frequent. Men and women will be asked to line up separately outside the bus, and must then present their papers while the bus and its contents are searched. This is nothing to worry about. What they are looking for is arms and illegal Central American immigrants.

A variety of minibuses, old American school buses and occasional Pullmans cover all major roads, including the back route from Trujillo to Tegucigalpa, via San Esteban and Juticalpa. The best paved road is between San Pedro Sula and the capital, and although the major roads are generally paved, keep in mind that the country's interior is extremely underdeveloped, and road building has only been taking place in the last 30 years. Thus it is much easier to travel around the edges of Honduras than cross the interior. Distance is not always indicative of time needed for a journey. All bus terminals are listed in the text.

By Car

Given the nature of Honduran roads and the frequency of military and police checkpoints, driving your own vehicle in Honduras can be more trouble than it's worth. On the other hand, you have a much better chance of exploring remote areas, which may have dirt roads but no public transport, as well as the towns and villages off the main highways. This goes particularly for eastern Honduras, except the Mosquitia, which remains closed to roads. Wherever you go, always remember to keep your vehicle locked, and if possible, always park in a guarded compound.

The Honduran Tourist Map is the best road map, and shows all major petrol stations, of which there are very few in country areas. Four-wheel drive is not necessary, unless you plan to go off the beaten track. Remember that dirt roads disintegrate after rain and Honduras gets lots of it, especially along the north coast, where the best months to travel are April to June. For the rest of the country, the driest months are November to May.

Car Hire

The best places to hire a car are Tegucigalpa and San Pedro Sula. You will need a valid driver's licence, a deposit or credit card, and to be over 25 years old.

IN THE CAPITAL

Budget, International Airport, tel 33 5170; **Molinari**, International Airport, tel 33 1307; **Avis**, Hotel Honduras Maya, tel 32 0088; **Blitz**, Hotel La Ronda, tel 33 9272/34 2732; **Margus**, Col. Rubén Darío, Frente Campo Scout, tel 32 8735.

In the Comayagüela district: **National**, Col. Prado, Fente Valentín Flores, tel 33 2653; **Toyota**, Col. Prado, contiguo Valentín Flores, tel 33 5210.

IN SAN PEDRO SULA

Budget, International Airport, tel 56 2467; **Maya**, International Airport, tel 56 2463; also at 3 Avenida 7–8 Calle, N.O., tel 52 2670/52 2671; **American**, 3 Avenida 3–4 Calle

N.O., tel 52 7626/56 2337; **National**, Hotel Copantl, tel 53 2108; **Toyota**, 4 Avenida 2–3 Calle N.O., tel 57 2644/57 2666.

By Bicycle

Bicycle journeys are not ideal in a country with many mountains and bad roads. Not many people use cycles either, so you will find yourself quite a novelty, and spare parts will be almost impossible to find. Motorcyclists are much better off, and the dirt roads are ideal for cross-country bikes.

If you come well equipped, however, including camping gear, the country offers many areas where you could explore off the beaten track. The western region of Copán is especially beautiful, while in the northeast, you will find great plateaus dotted with isolated villages. A note of warning: do not stray too close to the Nicaraguan or El Salvadorean border regions, since you will almost certainly be treated with great suspicion. Remember also that Honduras is a very poor 'cowboy country', and bandits are not uncommon.

Embassies and Consulates

These are all in the capital of Tegucigalpa, mostly in the eastern district of Colonia Palmira. Those marked by an asterisk (*) are best reached by taxi.
UK: Edificio Palmira, Third Floor, tel 32 0612/320618 (opposite Hotel Honduras Maya, Mon–Fri, 8–noon and 2–5).
Belize: Colonia 15 de Septiembre, 1703, tel 33 1423 (must call to make appointment).
Canada: Edificio El Castaño, Sixth Floor, Boulevard Morazán, tel 31 4538.
Costa Rica:(*) Colonia El Triángulo, Subida Lomas del Guijarro, tel 32 1768.
El Salvador: Colonia San Carlos, #219 2 Avenue, tel 32 5045/32 1344.
Guatemala:(*) Colonia Las Minitas, 4 Calle, #2421 (corner of Avenida Juan Lindo and 1 Avenida) tel 32 5018/32 9704.
Mexico: Colonia Palmira, Calle Brasil, tel 32 6471.
Nicaragua:(*) Colonia Lomas del Tepeyac, Bloque M-1, tel 32 4290/32 9025.
Panamá: Edificio Palmira, Second Floor, tel 32 5441 (opposite Hotel Honduras Maya).
US: Colonia Palmira, Edificio Embajada Americana, Avenida La Paz, tel 32 3120/32 3124 (Mon–Fri, 8–11 am).

Local Agencies

Corporación Hondureña de Desarrollo Forestal (COHDEFOR), Carretera al Norte, Comayagüela, tel 22 8810/22 2449. This organization is in charge of the country's National Parks and Reserves, and should have the latest information on facilities and access. The country's parks and reserves were only established in the last twenty years, and are generally no more than areas marked on the map, very difficult to reach or explore.

Money Matters

The Honduran currency is the **lempira** which is made up of 100 **centavos**. There are notes to the value of 1, 2, 5, 10, 20, 50 and 100 lempiras, and the last two should be avoided, since few will want to change them for you. Note that the size of coins does not imply their value, so that the 20 centavo is much smaller than the 10 centavo coin.

There are banks in all major towns, and their hours of business are generally Mon–Fri, 9–3. The most common banks are Banco Central de Honduras, Banco Atlántida, Banco de Honduras and Banco de Londres y Montreal, which is affiliated to Lloyds International, and the best option for wiring money from abroad. There is also a thriving black market for money exchange in the country's two cities, and you will get a faster and better deal with the moneychangers there. In Tegucigalpa, moneychangers hang out on the commercial, pedestrian streets leading to the main square. In San Pedro Sula you will also find them in the pedestrian shopping areas around the main square. Elsewhere you will rarely find moneychangers on the street, but the up-market hotels and shops always change US travellers' cheques or cash, and few will turn you down if you offer to pay for a transaction in US dollars. Visa, Mastercard and American Express are commonly accepted in the top hotels and commercial outlets, and can also be used for cash advances in most banks.

Post Offices

There are post offices in the major towns, and their opening hours are generally Mon–Fri, 7 am–8 pm, and Saturdays 8–noon. To receive mail by poste restante, best have it sent to the *lista de correos* in Tegucigalpa. It is advisable to have letters addressed to you by your surname only, without initials or titles, which will avoid any possible confusion. The address for the main post office is: **Lista de Correos**, Correo Central, Avenida Miguel Paz Barahona, Tegucigalpa, Honduras. Remember to bring your passport to collect mail, for which there will also be a small fee. **American Express** card holders can also use the main office in the capital to receive mail, located at the top of Avenida República de Chile, opposite the Hotel Honduras Maya.

Faxes can be sent and received quite cheaply at the main post offices in the larger towns, and certainly in the capital (fax 37 9715) and San Pedro Sula (fax 52 4923).

Telecommunications

Honduras is one of the few Central American countries from which you can make collect calls to Britain, as well as Italy, Spain, the United States and Canada. The HONDUTEL telephone system is excellent, and the company has offices in almost every large town. Direct international dialling is possible and there are also USA Direct booths at the phone offices in Tegucigalpa and San Pedro Sula. The code for the international operator is 197. There are no area telephone codes for Honduran numbers, just six digits. The emergency number for the police is 199, fire department 198.

Police and Military

The Honduran police force, believed to have around 4500 members, is under the jurisdiction of the army. In fact, it is a branch of the armed forces, called the Fuerzas de Seguridad Pública (FUSEP), which was formed in 1946, and is controlled by army officers. Their duties include not only normal policing, but also counterinsurgency operations with their special unit, known as the Cobras.

The military began as the strongmen of the fruit companies, and did not become a professional national armed force until the US signed the Bilateral Military Assistance Treaty in 1954. During the 1980s, the US government's choice of Honduras as its main ally in the region led to a huge increase in the country's military, from a few thousand members in the 1970s, to around 30,000 in 1990. You will see them regularly at road-blocks near major towns and border regions, checking documents and searching for weapons. In general, Western visitors have nothing to worry about on these occasions.

Medical Matters

Drugs and medicines are expensive, and many items are not available, so if there is anything you absolutely must have, bring it with you, including tampons, contraceptives and contact lens solutions. Medical care is limited, and if you need urgent hospital treatment, try to have it done in Tegucigalpa. The best two hospitals there are **La Policlínica**, 3 Avenida 7–8 Calle, Comayagüela, tel 37 3503; and **Viera**, 5 Calle 11–12 Avenida, tel 38 0736. Contact your embassy for a list of recommended doctors. Malaria pills are only necessary if you're heading for the Mosquitia region. Water is not safe to drink in Honduras.

Public Holidays and Opening Hours

New Year's Day
14 April—Day of the Americas
Easter Week—Thurs–Sun
1 May—Labour Day
15 September—Independence Day
3 October—Francisco Morazán Day
12 October—Discovery of America Day
21 October—Army Day
25 December—Christmas

In general, commercial business hours are Monday–Friday, 9–noon and 2–6; Saturday, 8–noon. Along the north coast, the lunch break is often extended by shops closing half an hour earlier, and opening half an hour later. There are very few museums and no standard opening times for them.

Festivals

Honduras is an almost 100% mestizo country, so the annual calendar is peppered with Catholic festivals, but none that match those of Guatemala for interest. The only region where you will find festivals worth visiting is along the north coast, where the black musical culture makes for energetic events. The most important is the National Carnival in La Ceiba, usually during the third week of May, when bands come from all over Central America, performing in the streets at all-night parties. Otherwise one of the liveliest festivals is the one in Santa Rosa de Copán, held in the last week of August.

Markets and Shopping

There are few interesting markets in Honduras, since there is no significant indigenous population producing craftworks. However, the country is renowned for its cigars, best bought at the factory in Santa Rosa de Copán. If you have time to head off the beaten track, you could visit the Indian market at Tutule (Thurs and Sun), southwest of La Paz. Standard items you will find in the tourist shops are leather goods, wood carvings, ceramics and paintings of the picturesque red-tiled villages of rural Honduras. Straw hats and baskets are a good buy. A 7% government tax is added to all commercial transactions.

The Media

The Honduran media is generally regarded as dismal and hobbled by censorship. It is also overdependent on US news services and television programming, so that little local reporting is included. The most liberal newspaper, and controversial because it occasionally dares to criticize the government and military, is *Tiempo*, published in San Pedro Sula. *La Tribuna* is based in Tegucigalpa, and reflects the views of the Liberal Party. Two conservative papers, reflecting the views of the National Party and the military, are *La Prensa* and *El Heraldo*, which are both owned by the same family. There's also an English language paper, *Tegucigalpa This Week*, available at the top hotels in Tegucigalpa, useful for finding out what's going on culturally in that city. Magazines are popular, and some of the most interesting are *Presente*, *Tragaluz*, and *Prisma*.

The government publishes *La Gaceta*, which carries all the latest decrees and speeches. A good monthly bulletin with at least some analysis of the news is *Boletín Informativo*, published by the Honduras Documentation Centre (CEDOH).

The radio is the most important form of communication, and there are no less than 152 stations. The two largest stations are HRN, The Voice of Honduras, and Radio América. The government also has its own station, called Radio Honduras. Apart from these, there are a great many evangelical and Catholic stations. There are six television channels, all privately owned, but only one is broadcast nationally.

Cinemas are to be found in most Honduran towns and are very popular, cheap entertainment. Films are generally American releases with Spanish subtitles, but don't expect the presentation quality to be too good.

Where to Stay

Accommodation in Honduras is slightly more expensive than in Guatemala, but the standard is about the same. The only place where you will find top-class hotels is in the capital, and there are first-class hotels in San Pedro Sula, La Ceiba and Copán Ruinas, as well as on the Bay islands of Roatán and Guanaja. For the rest of the country, you will find perfectly decent hotels in all the towns, and basic accommodation, if any, in the smaller settlements. The 7% government tax is always added to hotel bills, plus service charges. If you travel in remote regions of the interior, you will find little commercial accommodation, and there are no facilities for campers. Sleeping rough or in your vehicle is not safe in these areas and your only chance of shelter is to contact the local police station or mayor (*alcalde*), who might recommend a private family.

Youth hostels are non-existent, but cheap guest houses can always be found. The only places where you will find private holiday rentals is on the Bay Islands, mostly on Utila and Roatán.

Eating Out

Honduran cuisine is disappointing, except for the coconut bread and seafood dishes along the north coast. For the rest, you will find eggs, rice, pasta and beans the standard ingredients of all meals. Usually the best item on the menu is the *comida corriente*, which is the meal of the day, and served at breakfast, lunch and supper. This is normally a meal of meat, bean paste, rice, fried plantain, fried egg, and a slice of cheese. A particular ingredient of Honduran meals is thick cream, which is served up with most meals, but does not generally improve things. In the cities, hamburgers and pizzas predominate, and the best national dish you will find is *pinchos*, which are meat skewers, served with salad, similar to shish kebabs. A delicious snack is *anafre*, which is a hot bean paste, covered with melted cheese, and served with tortilla chips.

Other common Honduran dishes include *sopa de mondongo*, which is tripe soup; *tajadas*, which are fried plantain served with grated cabbage; and *baleadas*, which are tortillas filled with mashed vegetables and sometimes meat. *Pupusas* are normally pork-filled tortillas, and best avoided for the insanitary meat.

Drink

There are four national beers in Honduras. The best is *Port Royal*, which is a Pilsner type of beer. *Imperial*, sold mainly around Tegucigalpa, is just as good, and some say better. *Salva Vida* is a refreshing light beer, but *Nacional* is a dog's piss of a beer, best not bothered with. Rum is good and cheap, such as *Flor de Caña* and *Matusalem*. And for hardened drinkers, there's always the local *aguardiente*, made from fermented sugar cane.

Since the water is not safe in Honduras, be careful about *licuados* and freshly made fruit juices, though they can be delicious. Fizzy drinks are available anywhere, and coffee is better here than in many other Central American countries.

Itineraries

Western Honduras: Copán

Western Honduras is scenically the most beautiful part of the country, but the greatest draw are the Maya ruins of Copán, just a short distance from the Guatemalan border and unlike any other Maya site. There is also plenty of scope for hiking, and unlike in other Central American countries, you will probably find yourself the only one doing it, and quite a novelty to the local people, who are friendly and helpful.

The North Coast

Next to western Honduras, the north coast, from Puerto Cortés to Trujillo, is the most interesting journey you can easily make. The train ride from Puerto Cortés to Tela is a must for train buffs, whereas the beaches outside the towns of Tela and Trujillo are not only attractive, but also have interesting Garifuna villages on them.

The northern littoral gets very heavy rainfall for most of the year, but the months of May and June are generally quite dry, and the best time to come here.

The Bay Islands

The Bay Isands are a world apart, not just physically, but also culturally, since they were occupied by the British from the 17th–19th centuries.

Roatán is the largest of the three islands, and boasts one of the most beautiful beaches in the Caribbean. Guanaja, the most easterly island, claims to be the most beautiful and caters mainly to the luxury tourist. Utila, on the other hand, is the smallest and least developed island, most popular with budget travellers.

Central Honduras: The Capital and Beyond

The capital, Tegucigalpa, is located in south-central Honduras, and is a surprisingly pleasant city. There are no particular attractions as such, but the atmosphere is relaxed, and this is a good place to enjoy some of the comforts of city life.

The main artery throught the region is the highway connecting Tegucigalpa to the country's second city, San Pedro Sula, in the northwest. Along this route, there are several small towns of interest, such as Comayagua and Siguatepeque, as well as Lake Yojoa.

Eastern Honduras

Eastern Honduras is a remote and wild region, where banditry is not uncommon, and large areas along the Nicaraguan border still bear the burden of former Contra camps. There is, however, an interesting back road you can travel, connecting coastal Trujillo and Tegucigalpa, via San Esteban and Juticalpa.

The northeast of the country is a region of almost impenetrable jungle, known as the Mosquitia, and to visit it you need a lot of money, time and initiative. However, it is easier and cheaper to reach than Amazonia, and can offer the adventurous traveller unexplored rivers and forests, rich in wildlife.

The Pacific Littoral

This is the poorest region of the country, where environmental destruction from deforestation and pollution is at its worst, and the standard of living is very low. The only place worth visiting is Tigre Island, in the Gulf of Fonseca. Sitting in the shadow of a small volcano, its small settlement of Amapala is like an abandoned film set.

THE CAPITAL AND BEYOND

Central Honduras is an extensive mountainous region, where peaks over 2000 m are not uncommon. No towns or cities have sprung up and there are very few dirt roads connecting its remote villages with the outside world. This is where rural Honduras is still at its most underdeveloped: transport by oxcart and mule is the order of the day and the people are used to walking long distances. If you wanted to explore this area, you too would have to walk, and you would need your own four-wheel-drive transport to get there in the first place. For toughened hikers, central Honduras offers great potential. Access is difficult, facilities are non-existent, but the rural inhabitants are friendly, and you have the chance to travel where very few outsiders ever reach. With good maps and all your own provisions and camping equipment, you could have a very adventurous time here.

Only around the edges of this rugged area have population centres developed, almost exclusively along the great gash in the landscape that forms a corridor from San Pedro Sula, in the northwest, to the capital, Tegucigalpa, in the south. These are the county's two most important cities, and they are connected by a major highway, along which there are a number of worthwhile places to visit, such as Lake Yojoa and the former colonial capital, Comayagua. Public transport is regular and frequent along this road, and Tegucigalpa has buses heading for many parts of the country, including some interesting destinations nearby.

Tegucigalpa

Capital of Honduras since 1880, Tegucigalpa originally sprung up as a mining settlement. The Spanish colonists, who came this way from Guatemala, found silver in the surrounding mountains, and a small number of settlers moved here to exploit it. In fact, the city's name means 'silver hill', and originates from two Indian words joined together (*tegus* = hill, *galpa* = silver). All around the city there are small mining towns and villages perched on the steep mountainsides to the north and east. However, the mineral deposits were not very large, and even in colonial times the area was neglected for the richer pickings in Mexico and South America. Tegucigalpa, or Tegus, as it is universally called, thus grew very slowly, and only became a city of over one million people in recent decades.

Its location is attractive, squeezed between the banks of the River Choluteca and the slopes of mount El Picacho. The city's streets are often steep and narrow, and for once you do not find a colonial grid system, but a characterful tangle of twisting alleys, lined by crumbling old buildings, which gives Tegus an almost Italian flavour. The centre is tightly packed around the **Parque Central**, which is closed to traffic and always a lively place, bustling with shoeshine men and vendors. As a whole, Tegus is a pleasant city to spend a day or two, with few sights or things to do, but plenty of good places to stay and eat.

Across the river, the city also encompasses the town of Comayagüela. It is a sleazy district, whose regular grid of streets cover a small, flat plain. This is where most buses

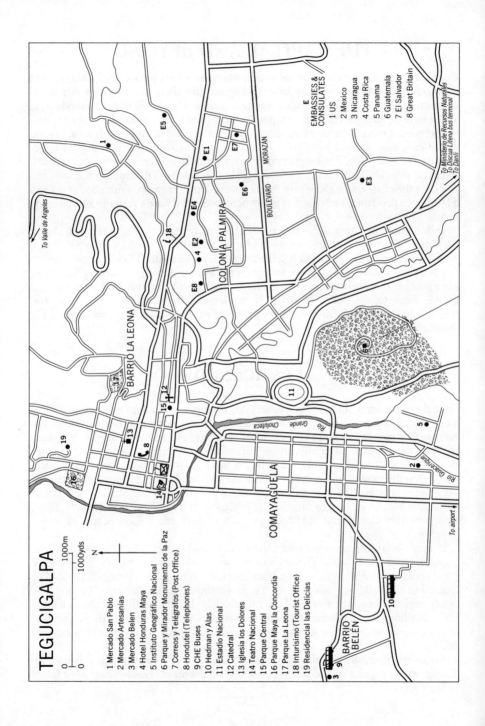

TEGUCIGALPA

0   1000m
0   1000yds

N

1 Mercado San Pablo
2 Mercado Artesanías
3 Mercado Belén
4 Hotel Honduras Maya
5 Instituto Geográfico Nacional
6 Parque y Mirador Monumento de la Paz
7 Correos y Telégrafos (Post Office)
8 Hondutel (Telephones)
9 CHE Buses
10 Hedman y Alas
11 Estadio Nacional
12 Catedral
13 Iglesia los Dolores
14 Teatro Nacional
15 Parque Central
16 Parque Maya la Concordia
17 Parque La Leona
18 Inturismo (Tourist Office)
19 Residencial las Delicias

E
EMBASSIES &
CONSULATES
1 US
2 Mexico
3 Nicaragua
4 Costa Rica
5 Panama
6 Guatemala
7 El Salvador
8 Great Britain

To Valle de Angeles

BARRIO LA LEONA

COLONIA PALMIRA

MORAZÁN

BOULEVARD

To Ministerio de Recursos Naturales
To Discua Litena bus terminal
To Danlí

Río Grande Choluteca

COMAYAGÜELA

Río Guacerique

To airport

BARRIO
BELÉN

will drop you; and if you're coming from the airport, you will have to pass through here before you reach the old part of the city. It is a notoriously rough area, and although there are plenty of cheap hotels (which often double up as brothels), it is not recommended that you stay there, as it is dangerous at night.

GETTING TO TEGUCIGALPA

By Air
The international airport, Toncontín, is 6½ km from the centre of the city. Buses run between the airport and the centre regularly. The taxi fare should not be more than US$3. There are **international** flights from all Central American capitals, Mexico City and San Andrés Island. Regular **internal** flights run between Tegucigalpa and San Pedro Sula, La Ceiba, Mosquitia and the Bay island of Roatán.

American Airlines, Edificio Palmira, tel 32 1414 (opposite Hotel Honduras Maya).
British Airways, Edificio Sempe, Boulevard Comunidad Europea, tel 33 5101.
Continental, International Airport Toncontín, tel 33 7676.
KLM, Edificio CICSA, Avenida República de Chile, tel 32 3876/32 3885.
Pan Am, Barrio La Plazuela, Edificio San Miguel, tel 37 0158.
Taca, Edificio Interamericana, Boulevard Morazán, tel 31 2479/31 2483.
Tan-Sahsa, Centro Comercial, Los Castaños Shopping Centre, 2nd floor, Boulevard Morazán, tel 37 8674.

By Bus
Most of the bus terminals are in the Comayagüela district, and the easiest way to get into the centre is by taxi. One or two are in the outer suburbs, and these are also best reached by taxi. The main terminals for destinations around the country are listed below. Bus tickets must be bought before boarding the bus, and are only valid for a specific time. If you want to be sure of getting your chosen bus, allow plenty of time to buy the ticket.

To San Pedro Sula and all towns along the Northern Highway: The best company, with daily buses at 6.30, 9, 9.45 am, 1, 3, 4.15, and 5.30 pm, is **Hedman Alas**, 11 Avenida 13–14 Calle, Comayagüela, tel 37 7143. Other companies, with regular departures, include **Sáenz**, 12 Calle 7–8 Avenida, Comayagüela, first buses at 2 and 5 am, last bus at 6 pm; **El Rey**, 6 Avenida and 9 Calle, Comayagüela, buses every hour between 6 and 6; and **Norteños**, 12 Calle 6–7 Avenida, Comayagüela, first buses at 3 and 4 am, last bus at 6.15 pm.

The journey takes around 4 hrs to San Pedro Sula (242 km); just over 2 hrs to Siguatepeque (114 km); and 2 hrs to Comayagua (86 km). If you are travelling to any of the towns along the highway, you will be dropped off at the relevant road junction, where there are normally plenty of taxis waiting to ferry you into the town centre. The distance into Comayagua or Siguatepeque is no more than 2 km, so the fare should be less than US$1.

To Santa Bárbara: Transportes Junqueños run a service from the corner of 12 Calle and 8 Avenida, Comayagüela, on Tuesdays, Thursdays and Saturdays, leaving any time between 6 and 7 am. This journey of around 200 km takes over 5 hrs.

To the coastal towns of Puerto Cortés, Tela and La Ceiba: These towns are all easily reached from San Pedro Sula, so your best option is to go there, and either change buses or stay the night before travelling onwards.

To La Esperanza and Santa Rosa de Copán: Your best option is to travel to the pleasant town of La Esperanza, stay overnight, and continue the next day. Otherwise this is a very long journey of 389 km, which takes around 8 hrs because of the road. If you follow the first choice, **Empresa Joelito**, 4 Calle 8–9 Avenida, Comayagüela, has one bus per day to La Esperanza; check the time. If you decide to travel direct to Santa Rosa de Copán, the **Sultana** company, on the corner of Avenida 8 and 12 Calle, offers one departure per day, at 3.45 am.

To Juticalpa, with connections to coastal Trujillo: Empresa Aurora, 8 Calle 6–7 Avenida, Comayagüela, has buses leaving daily, on the hour, between 5 and 4. The journey of 169 km takes around 3 hrs. The total distance from Tegus to Trujillo, via San Francisco and San Esteban, is 429 km, and the onward bus journey, from Juticalpa to Trujillo takes around 6 hrs. If there is no bus to Trujillo (they only go every other day), then take one to Tocoa instead.

To Danlí: Buses for Danlí are run by **Discua Litena**, which has its own terminal in the southeastern Colonia Kennedy suburb, next to the Mercado Jacaleapa. Take a taxi to reach it. The journey of 96 km takes 2 hrs, and buses leave daily between 6 am and 6.30 pm.

To Choluteca and the Nicaraguan border: Mi Esperanza, 6 Avenida 24–25 Calle, Comayagüela, runs regular, daily buses to Choluteca (143 km, 3 hrs) between 4 am and 5.30 pm. The first bus of the day goes all the way to the border post of El Espino (200 km, 5 hrs).

To Amapala/Tigre Island: Dilapidated **CHE** buses run from the Mercado Belén, Comayagüela, leaving at 11 am daily. The journey of 125 km takes 4 hrs, with a motor-boat connection to the island that adds around 20 mins. If nobody else is travelling to the island when you arrive, an 'express' boat fare will cost you US$4 per person.

To Nacaome and the Salvadorean border: Regular, daily buses leave from the Mercado Belén, Comayagüela, between 7.30 and 5.30. The buses will be signed for El Amatillo (130 km), which is the border post, and the journey takes around 3 hrs.

GETTING AROUND TEGUCIGALPA

Like almost all Central American capitals, the traffic and pollution in the city is awful. Around central Tegus, you are unlikely to need transport, since this compact area can easily be explored on foot. However, if you need to go to surrounding districts, you will find **buses** heading in almost every direction (including the airport) from or near the Parque Central. There is no centralized information on the public transport system, but people will always be happy to advise you on the best connection. You will find a tourist information booth on the main square, open at weekends, which should also be able to advise. Another place where many buses pass is by the central market.

Taxis are plentiful and not very expensive—any destination around the city should not cost more than US$1. Journeys to outlying areas, such as the airport, should not cost more than US$3. Honduran cab drivers have an irritating habit of honking at foreigners. Try not to let this bother you; they just want your custom, and they do it to everyone. Naturally, you should fix the price before departure to avoid arguments later.

TOURIST INFORMATION
Instituto Hondureño de Turismo, Centro Guanacaste, Barrio Guanacaste, tel 22 6618/22 7752 (Mon–Fri, 7.30–3.30). The office is near the American Embassy. If you don't wish to walk from the city centre, there should be buses heading this way along Avenida Máximo Jérez, two blocks north of the central square. You will find helpful staff, though limited printed matter in English. There are tourist information booths at the international airport and on Parque Central, open at weekends.

ORIENTATION
Streets are often not marked, or are confusingly known by two different names. The locals respond to this by referring always to landmarks. Rather than asking for a particular street, ask for the place you are looking for, be it a café, museum or office. This advice goes for all Honduran towns.

WHAT TO SEE
The City Centre
Downtown Tegus is cupped in the arms of the narrow rivers Choluteca and Chiquito that curve around the base of El Picacho mountain. Within their embrace, the city centre's streets are tightly packed, spilling up the mountain, in a tangle of spaghetti loops that make for exhausting walking, but offer terrific views, as well as some of the most attractive architecture. The city has never been destroyed by earthquakes or disasters, and so you find large numbers of town houses dating from the last century and before. Most are tattered images of their former elegance, but nevertheless you can imagine how they must have looked, and tightly squeezed together on steep streets they almost have a European character about them.

Wandering around this elevated, northern part is the best introduction to the city, and ideally you should head for the **Parque La Leona**, where you'll be treated to views of most of the city. From up here, you can see the busy centre below, and looking south, an oddly out-of-place Grecian temple sits on a small hill. It is a peace monument, and you can see it from most parts of the city. Looking southwest, you see the grimy streets of Comayagüela district, lined by the River Choluteca on one side, and the dusty hills of shantytowns on the other. To the east, if you could see around the mountain, you would see the rise of Colonia Palmira, where embassies mix with the fortified villas of the country's wealthy, and the grand Boulevard Morazán is lined with fancy shops and restaurants. If the steep walk up to Parque La Leona is too much, you can always catch a bus, and marvel at the way the driver manages to get around the steep hairpin bends.

Down below, everything radiates from the **Parque Central**, whose centre is closed to traffic, giving a welcome break from the fumes. The **cathedral**, which was built in the late 18th century is nothing special architecturally although it does have a precious, colonial altar. The other large building, this side of the square, is the **City Hall**.

Two of the most important streets in the centre are **Calle Bolívar**, which runs south from the main square, towards the River Choluteca, and **Avenida Paz Barahona**, which crosses the centre from west to east, marking the northern border of the main square. The former is a short street, which leads to the **Puente Mallol**, crossing the river for the Comayagüela district. If you head down this way, you pass the attractive **La Merced** church (unfortunately next to the highly unattractive concrete of the **Congress building**), and soon come to the somewhat ridiculous pink **Presidential Palace**, set close to the river. Built in 1919, it is in the tradition of tasteless imitations of medieval castles.

Following the Avenida Paz Barahona west, you pass the **post office**, as well as the **Ministerial Palace**, whose colonial courtyard you can visit on production of your passport (Mon–Fri, 8–3.30). A short distance further, you reach one of the city's most elegant little squares, the **Parque Herrera**, fronted by the newly restored **Teatro Manuel Bonilla**, gleaming in neo-Classical splendour. Shows here are rare, but if you get the chance, you should have a look inside, just for the decor. If you follow 2 Avenida, heading north for about five blocks, you reach yet another popular square, the **Parque Concordia**, on the banks of the River Choluteca, which has plenty of stone benches under cooling trees. There are also small, decorative, if romanticized, imitation Maya temples and sculptures.

Heading east along Avenida Paz Barahona, you find yourself in a less hectic part of town, where residential housing mixes with fewer shops. The most important building is the **San Francisco** church, which was originally built in 1592, and is the city's oldest. The earliest worshippers were mining settlers, who paid for this church from the wealth they found in the local silver. An interesting cultural meeting place is right next door, the **Café Paradiso**, where local artists come for coffee, and where you'll find a variety of books and the occasional exhibition. If you continue to the end of the street, and then turn right, you find yourself on the Avenida República de Chile, which crosses the River Chiquito, and leads to the city's showpiece, the Boulevard Morazán. If you cross the river, and take the first left, you quickly find yourself climbing up to the tall **Hotel Honduras Maya**, perched on a hill and a useful marker, visible around the city. Its terrace offers a good place for a quiet drink with views across the city.

Northwest of the central park, there is another interesting square, with the city's most unusual church on it. To get there, walk two blocks north, and turn left down the Avenida Máximo Jérez, where you will soon come to the pink dome of **Los Dolores** church. Built in the early 18th century, its Baroque architecture somehow manages to have a Moorish flavour. It is the liveliest church in the city, since the surrounding stallholders and assorted customers and beggars are constantly wandering in and out.

Finally, if you continue west along Avenida Máximo Jérez, and take the second right, along 3 Avenida, a ten-minute walk will get you to the country's best museum: the **Museo Nacional** (Wed–Sun, 8.30–3.30, small fee). Housed in the grand Villa Roy, this is the former home of president Julio Lozano Diaz, who is distinguished by having provoked the country's first military coup in 1956. His widow generously donated the lovely mansion, painted an unmistakable baby blue, to the nation in 1981. The most interesting exposition is on the indigenous people of Honduras, showing their tribal costumes and traditional tools and artefacts.

South to Comayagüela

Comayagüela was once a town in its own right, but has long since been swallowed up by the city. It is mainly flat, its streets forming an oblong shape between the River Choluteca and the impoverished shanties clinging to the western hills. This is now the down-market commercial end of the capital, where shops of all kinds mix with scruffy hotels and raucous bars, and the endless flow of traffic chokes pedestrians at every turn. All this frantic activity can have its own fascination, and one of the busiest spots is the **Mercado San Isidro**. Located just across the river, along 6 Avenida, the market encompasses several blocks and is a huge, filthy mass of market stalls and rotting vegetables, scrawny dogs, and smooth operators looking for a deal. The merchandise is generally tacky and modern. But you may enjoy the chaos here. Otherwise there is nothing to draw you to this part of town, unless you need to visit the geographic institute, or are heading to or from one of the bus depots.

The Eastern District: Boulevard Morazán and Colonia Palmira

If you follow the Avenida República de Chile across the River Chiquito, you find yourself walking past some up-market restaurants, before coming to the beginning of **Boulevard Morazán**. This is the city's grandest road, its pretensions to American style fully displayed with one neon sign after another. Fast-food restaurants mix with pricier establishments, and the newest, glossiest shopping malls are here. The Boulevard is on a gentle rise, heading east from the city centre, and to walk from one end to the other takes half an hour. If there is anything you need to buy, you should be able to find it in the **Los Castaños Shopping Centre**, also popular at night, when teenagers hang out in front of the ice-cream parlours, music blaring from their cars. In the evenings, Boulevard Morazán is not only the best place for good meals, but also for bars and a few discos.

With the Boulevard as its southern border, and the spacious Avenida la Paz as the northern border, Colonia Palmira is the city's most exclusive neighbourhood. There are no particular sights around here, and it is an eerily quiet part of town, but pleasant enough to wander through on your way to some of the embassies here. The most prominent is the US Embassy, which is at the base of Avenida la Paz. The fastest way to reach this road from the city centre is to follow the Avenida Paz Barahona east, turning left at its end, and right onto Avenida Juan Gutenberg. This large road crosses the River Chiquito, passing the **tourist office** by the bridge, and then becoming the Avenida la Paz.

WHERE TO STAY

The choice of accommodation in Tegus is not particularly wide, and if you're on a really tight budget you will have to stay in Comayagüela, which can be dangerous at night. However, there are a number of medium-priced hotels scattered around the centre, so you should be able to find something reasonable. The most pleasant part to stay in is the eastern half of the city centre, which is the quietest.

LUXURY
The city's top hotel is the **Honduras Maya**, Avenida República de Chile, Colonia Palmira, tel 32 3191, fax 32 7629. Located on a hill overlooking the city, you get great

views from here. Children under 12 years stay for free. The government tax is added to all bills.

EXPENSIVE

The next best hotel, where all rooms include air-conditioning, TV, and private bath, is the **Hotel Plaza**, Avenida Miguel Paz Barahona, tel 37 2111, fax 37 2119. The **Hotel Prado**, Avenida Cervantes, tel 37 0121, fax 37 2221, offers the same level of service, but is overpriced. **Hotel La Ronda**, Avenida Jérez 1104, tel 37 8151, fax 37 1454, is reasonable, and also offers apartments. Tax is added to all room prices in this category.

MODERATE

Hotel Istmania, 5 Avenida 7–8 Calle, tel 37 1638, fax 37 1446, is opposite the police station. Rooms are slightly grubby, but otherwise all right.

INEXPENSIVE

The best in this range, which is clean and safe, as well as close to the British Embassy, is **Excelsior**, Avenida República de Chile. Also excellent value is **Hotel Marichal**, Calle los Dolores, tel 37 0069. Not far away, the **Hotel Iberia**, Peatonal los Dolores, tel 37 9267, is a newish place and very clean. A favourite among travellers is the **Hotel Boston**, Avenida Jérez, tel 37 9411, which is in an attractive old building. Rooms are clean, and there's also a communal TV room. The new annexe of the **Granada**, tel 22 0597, has secure parking and good rooms. It is just a short walk from the old Granada Hotel, on Avenida Juan Gutenberg 1401, which cannot be recommended.

EATING OUT

Around the city centre, you will be hard pressed to find anything other than fast food restaurants. **Pizza Hut** is just off the main square, and you will also find plenty of 'chicken shacks' and the like. A pleasant, open-air snack place is the **Burger House**, on Callejón de Olvido, south of the main square. For vegetarian meals try **Al Natural** on Avenida Miguel de Cervantes, behind the cathedral. It is in a quiet courtyard and serves delicious food during the day. Further west, on the same street, you'll also find the **Restaurante Vegetariano**. For meat-based Honduran dishes, the best place in the centre is **El Patio**, Calle Ministerio de Hacienda 162. Apart from the arty **Café Paradiso**, on the eastern end of Avenida Miguel Paz Barahona, an excellent café/restaurant is the **Marbella**, near the corner of Avenida Miguel Cervantes and Calle Salvador Mendieta. As the name implies, this is a Spanish place, and you could almost think you were in Spain, with old men sitting around discussing the latest news over their *anís*.

For proper evening meals, you are best off heading along Avenida República de Chile and up Boulevard Morazán. Two excellent, if pricey, restaurants on Avenida República de Chile are the **Hungry Fisherman** and **El Arriero**, while the **Café Allegro** is a favourite café among visitors to the city. For the best steaks in Honduras, try **Restaurante El Novillero**, also on Avenida República de Chile. At the top end of Boulevard Morazán, there is another **El Patio**, where the *pinchos* are great. You will also find Chinese, Swiss, French and Italian restaurants on the Boulevard, as well as fast food places, like **McDonald's**. There are a number of grimy bars around the centre of town, but the better places are along Boulevard Morazán.

ENTERTAINMENT AND NIGHTLIFE

There is not much to choose from here. The **Hotel Honduras Maya** is a quietly exclusive place, where you will also find the casino, which only allows foreign guests, who must show their passports to enter. There are just two discos worth recommending: **Sueños**, on Boulevard Morazán, and **Tropical Port**, on Boulevard Juan Pablo II. Otherwise, nightlife consists of wandering along the Boulevard Morazán, sampling the latest music bars, or drinking in one of the up-market restaurants, such as the **Hungry Fisherman**, which has a popular bar.

There are several **cinemas** showing recent American films: Alfa and Omega, Av. La Paz; Plaza, Centro Comercial Plaza Miraflores; Regis Real and Opera, Centro Comercial Centroamérica, Blvd. Miraflores. Also Lido and Palace, Clamer and Variedades in the centre.

SHOPPING

Café Allegro, Avenida República de Chile sells Honduran ceramics and handicrafts; also try Carmen Honduras Quality Art and Handicrafts just south of Hotel Maya. Amano on Avenida de la Paz has good-quality artefacts.

USEFUL INFORMATION

Emergencies

Police: 5 Avenida 7–8 Calle, opposite the Hotel Istmania; emergency tel 199.
Medical: see p. 249 for recommended hospitals, or your embassy for a list of doctors.

Tour Agencies

If without your own transport or on limited time, you might prefer to join tours to the most popular destinations around the capital—or the country in general. The following agencies are officially recommended: **Copán Tours**, Edificio Maya, tel 32 6769 (by the Hotel Honduras Maya); **Explore Honduras**, Edificio Medcast, no. 206, 2nd floor, Boulevard Morazán, tel 31 1003, fax 32 9800; **Gloria Tours**, Casa Colonial, 2nd floor, tel 38 2232 (on the main square); and **Trek Honduras**, Pasaje Fiallos Soto, no. 227, 2nd floor, tel 37 4876.

Money Matters

Since the black market is legal and the most convenient, it hardly seems necessary to go to a bank. However, there are plenty of banks in the city. **Banco de Londres y Montreal** is on the corner of 4 Calle and 5 Avenida.

The **American Express** office is at Trans Mundo Tours in the Edificio Palmira, opposite the Hotel Honduras Maya, tel 32 0072.

Books

The best place for English language books and press is **Book Village**, 2nd floor, Los Castaños Shopping Centre, Boulevard Morazán, tel 33 4858; for Central American literature and other publications, have a look in the **Café Paradiso**, at the eastern end of Avenida Miguel Paz Barahona.

Post Office

The central post office is west of the main square, on Avenida Miguel Paz Barahona.

Telecommunications
The HONDUTEL office (open 24 hrs) is on Avenida Cristóbal Colón, running parallel to Avenida Miguel Paz Barahona, one block north. The building is on the corner with Calle el Telégrafo.

Excursions from Tegus

Some of the easiest excursions are to the surrounding mining towns and villages such as **Santa Lucía, Ojojona** and **Valle de Angeles.** Just north of the city is the country's most accessible national park, the **Parque Nacional La Tigra**. Further afield, to the east, you find the town of **Danlí** and the attractive village of **Yuscarán**.

The old mining centre of **Minas de Oro** is a remote base for hiking trips. It is a long bus ride, so this is not a day-trip destination.

Santa Lucía, Valle de Angeles and Ojojona

Santa Lucía (14 km) and Valle de Angeles (25 km) are two picturesque former mining villages, northeast of the capital. You will not only have terrific views across the wooded slopes of the surrounding hillsides, but also find the typical Honduran rural scene of whitewashed houses and red-tiled roofs. Cobbled streets lead to tiny main squares, where squat colonial churches rise above the village. The bus ride is beautiful too. Buses for Santa Lucía leave from the Mercado San Pablo, reached by taking any El Sitio bus from the central square. To reach Valle de Angeles, you can either walk to the main road from the other village, and a bus will pass to take you further. Or you can go directly from Tegus, by taking a bus from Avenida Domenicana, which is in the Barrio San Felipe, after the Bolívar monument, at the top of Avenida La Paz.

Ojojona (25 km) lies southwest of the city, and is best visited on Sundays, which is market day. Here you will not only find an attractive colonial village, but also a museum of art (Tues–Sun, 8–4), which shows contemporary as well as early Honduran work, particularly landscapes. The views are terrific, and on a clear day, you can see all the way to the Pacific Ocean and the Gulf of Fonseca. The visit is worth it for the bus journey alone. Buses leave from the Comayagüela district, at 4 Calle 6–7 Avenida.

La Tigra National Park

The first of the country's national parks, La Tigra was established in 1979, and encompasses a mountainous area, covered by rare cloud forest. The highest peak in the area is 2290 m. The area survived the ravages of deforestation as the land is generally too steep and high to be useful for agriculture. Situated northeast of the capital, the main entrance to the park is at the abandoned mining camp of **El Rosario**, which is reached by a branch road from the village of San Juancito, 40 km from the city, owing to the circuitous road. Even if you don't intend to walk in the park, you should consider coming to El Rosario, just for the creepy atmosphere: wooden houses creaking in the wind, with birds the only residents. The mines around here were abandoned in 1954, the homes and civic buildings left to rot.

There is simple accommodation in San Juancito, but then it's an exhausting, uphill walk to El Rosario, and when you get there, there are few facilities and no well-marked trails, though a couple of park guardians can give limited advice. This is a great pity, since the forest is beautiful and hides plenty of exotic plants and animals, as well as eerie old mining shafts. However, if you have the time and money, it would be worth either going on a tour, or hiring your own four-wheel-drive vehicle to visit this area. If you plan to hike through the forest, there are old mule trails, left over from the 1950s, and one of the most popular leads from El Rosario to Jutiapa and back, which takes around six hours. The best topographic map for exploring La Tigra is available from the Geographic Institute in Tegus. You could also make enquiries at the official organization responsible for all the national parks: Dirección General de Recursos Naturales Renovables (RENARE), Boulevard Comunidad Europea 1534, Comayagüela. Bring your own food and drink if you plan to spend any length of time in the park.

Without your own transport, it is very difficult to visit the park, since the bus schedule does not allow for a return journey the same day. Buses leave for San Juancito at 10 am daily, from the Mercado San Pablo, a journey of 90 minutes.

Danlí and Yuscarán

Travelling east of Tegus, the road soon winds up the familiar pine-clad hills. The occasional scars of forest fires are not enough to spoil pretty views of picture-postcard villages. Danlí (96 km from Tegus) is a pleasant town with lovely scenery around it and a decent place to have lunch is the **Rancho Típico**, opposite the local brothel, known as 'disco'. Once a year the town bursts into activity for the **Fiesta del Maíz**, which is normally held during the third week of August. At this time there are street parties and plenty of food and boisterous drinking.

If you do decide to stay, the best hotel is the inexpensive **Hotel Ebenezer**, tel 93 2655. Two other hotels worth trying are: **Hotel La Esperanza**, tel 93 2106, which offers rooms with private bath, and **Hotel Apollo**. Buses to Danlí leave from the Colonia Kennedy bus terminal, in Tegus (see p. 256).

If you have your own transport, you should not miss the pretty mining village of **Yuscarán**, reached by a branch road, heading south from the main highway before you reach Jacaleapa and Danlí. The surrounding landscape is ideal for hiking and walking. There is only simple accommodation available here, and if you wish to explore the surrounding area, you should bring camping equipment.

Minas de Oro

The former mining village of Minas de Oro is a remote hiking base. Armed with topographic maps, camping equipment and provisions, this is a region worth exploring. Beautiful villages hide in the highland countryside, with ancient mule tracks leading through forests and over mountains. Accommodation in the village is basic, and you can expect meals to consist of little more than eggs and beans.

The village is situated north of the capital, and reached by taking the road northeast to Juticalpa, and then turning north at Talanga, where a rough road takes you through Cedros, to Minas de Oro. You can also get here on public transport from Tegus or

Comayagua. Coming from the capital, **Transportes Díaz-Donavil** buses leave from the corner of 10 Avenida and 4 Calle, Comayagüela, at 6.30 and 1. The journey takes 3–4 hours.

NORTH FROM TEGUS

There are a number of places worth visiting along the 170-km stretch of the Northern Highway from Tegus to Lake Yojoa.

Comayagua

The first town of significance that you come to is Comayagua. Founded in 1537, it was the capital of the Spanish authorities in Honduras until 1880. There are a number of attractive colonial churches, and a few 16th- and 17th-century houses remain as well. Today, however, Comayagua is a provincial town, whose most significant feature is that it is virtually next door to the largest American military base in the country: Soto Cano Airbase, formally known as Palmerola.

The most important building is the **cathedral** on the main square, which has simple, but beautiful, white stucco on its frontage. Note the Latin flavour to the designs, mixing tropical palm fronds with traditional vine patterns. If you look closely, you will also see a number of pagan images that crept into the Indian labourers' masonry. In all, it can rightly claim to be one of the most beautiful churches in the country, built at the turn of the 17th century. The clock tower holds an ancient clock, made by the Moors for the Alhambra, but donated to Comayagua by Philip II in 1582. It is over 800 years old and still works. Just off the main square is the **Colonial and Ecclesiastical Museum** (Mon–Fri, 8–4, small fee), where you can view documents and exhibits of the town's glory days.

La Merced, near the market, is a plain little church. A skilfully carved **bishop's chair** stands neglected by the entrance, just as the whole building is neglected. There is nothing to show that this was once the town's cathedral, the first in the country. The **market**, in the surrounding streets, is unusually large for such a small town, and offers any kind of fruit, vegetable, junk or utensil, you could possibly want to buy. Another attractive church is **San Francisco**, at the other end of town, set back from a leafy square, and still retaining much of its colonial beauty. Nearby, you will also find the **Archaeological Museum** (8–noon and 1–4, small fee) which is worth visiting for the exhibits that cover both indigenous and imported cultures, such as the Maya and the Garifuna.

Services in town include a HONDUTEL office, post office, and plenty of banks.

WHERE TO STAY
There are a few good guest houses here, all in the inexpensive category. First choice is **Hotel Quan**, 8 Calle N.O. 3–4 Avenida. This is on the edge of town, within five minutes' walking distance of the main square, and offers clean rooms with fan and

private bath. **Hotel American Inn,** near the market, is also good value, where rooms can include air-conditioning, TV and fridge. In the unlikely event that these two are full, you could also try the **Emperador,** or the **Motel Puma.**

The local bus terminal is some way from the centre, so your best option is to take a cheap taxi straight to your chosen accommodation.

EATING OUT
A rather expensive but good restaurant is the **Yadis'Ma,** near the main square, which offers a varied menu, ranging from spaghetti to *pinchos.* Around the main square, you will find a few restaurants, of which **Garfield's Pizzeria** is the best of a poor selection. Otherwise, try looking around the market area, and especially on the main boulevard leading into Comayagua, where you will find a few steak houses.

Onwards from Comayagua

You will easily find a taxi to take you out to the bus terminal, either in the main square or the large boulevard connecting the town to the main highway. Unless you want to visit the surrounding towns or villages, the fastest way to travel onwards is to make for the main highway and get on a fast bus heading for Tegus or San Pedro Sula.

There are local bus services to Minas de Oro (hiking), La Paz (connections to the Indian market in Tutule, which takes place Thursdays and Sundays), La Libertad (pleasant coffee-growing town), and Siguatepeque. If you want to travel west to La Esperanza (Sunday market, hiking), you need to change at Siguatepeque. There is no tourist information here, but guest-house staff should at least be able to tell you when and where local buses leave.

Siguatepeque

A small highland town, a short drive from Comayagua, Siguatepeque is an important centre for forestry research. It always has a refreshing breeze, which keeps it pleasantly cool. The central park has some beautiful mature trees in it, and the surrounding streets have a surprising variety of shops and restaurants. The town does not merit an overnight stay, although it does make a quiet and convenient base for exploring the surrounding countryside, west of the highway. In particular the region around La Esperanza is beautiful, though travel can be rough, since most roads are, as yet, unpaved. Accommo-dation in the region is basic but (especially if you have your own vehicle) it would be worth spending some time here, walking amongst the lush hills and quiet forests. The region is traditionally home to Lenca Indians, whose villages dot the landscape, and are worth visiting.

If you decide to stay in Siguatepeque, the best place is the inexpensive **Boarding House Central,** on the main square, which also has a good restaurant. Services in town are limited, but there are some banks.

Northeast to Santa Bárbara

Instead of continuing north on the main highway, you could turn west shortly after Siguatepeque, and head for **Santa Bárbara**. An unspoilt colonial town, the drive to get there takes you over the undulating landscape west of Lake Yojoa, passing quiet villages rarely visited by outsiders. The Department of Santa Bárbara is renowned for *artesanía*, much of which is made from the *junco* palm, and you can buy baskets and Panama hats.

Another excellent reason for coming to Santa Bárbara is to explore the **Parque Nacional de Santa Bárbara**, which is home to one of the country's highest mountains, of 2836 m. Strangely, maps do not give it a name. It is located between the town and Lake Yojoa, and although there are no facilities, the landscape of forests and streams is ideal walking country. If you plan to hike here, it would be a good idea to get the relevant topographic map, which will show most dirt roads and mule trails.

There are a number of simple guest houses in Santa Bárbara, and public services such a banks, post office and telephones are available. As you can imagine, restaurants are basic. To get here by public transport, you can either get the infrequent buses from the capital (see p. 255), or you can get one of seven daily **Catisba** buses from San Pedro Sula, which leave from 6 Avenida 8–9 Calle. Coming from this northern city, the journey is less than 3 hours.

Lake Yojoa and Pulhapanzac Falls

Continuing on the main highway after Siguatepeque, you reach the small village of **Taulabé** after about 38 km. Next to it, about 1 km south, is an interesting cave formation, where stalactites and other ancient shapes can be found. Lights and a walkway make it possible to explore quite safely, and guards are also present. Soon after Taulabé you come to the shores of Yojoa, the largest highland lake in the country (almost 25 km long and around 10 km wide), bordered by towering mountains to the west, and marshy lowlands to the east. It is along this flat eastern shore that the highway threads its way to San Pedro Sula, a further 87 km to the north. The setting is impressive, yet the lake itself is difficult to explore since there are almost no facilities for doing so, and the marshy earth doesn't allow for walks along the beach. The only places where you can hire boats is at the hotels at the southern and northern tip of the lake. On the southern shore is the inexpensive **Los Remos**, and on the northern shore, on the road to El Mochito, is **Agua Azul**, tel 53 4750, which is slightly more expensive. Between these two points the highway occasionally meanders within sight of the lake, and all along here you will find cheap *comedores* serving the local fish, especially bass and carp.

Just north of the lake are the **Pulhapanzac Falls** (small fee), which are a very popular weekend spot for the people of San Pedro Sula (so avoid weekends). Almost 50 m high, water from the River Lindo gushes into a gorgeous pool, which is especially impressive during the rainy season. Thick jungle vegetation frames the falls, the damp atmosphere perfect for all manner of ferns and vines. Don't forget your swimming gear, or you will miss an opportunity for wonderful cool bathing.

The falls can be reached by bus from San Pedro Sula, taking a bus for El Mochito. Check with the local tourist office for bus schedules. Alternatively, there are plenty of tours offered from San Pedro Sula, and this is the easiest option if not the cheapest.

COPÁN

Torchbearer, sculpture at Copán

Western Honduras is one of the most beautiful areas of the country the landscape is a vigorous green, hills and mountains are cut by many streams, and plenty of forest is still standing. It is also a region where there are a significant number of Indian inhabitants, members of the Lenca and Chortie tribes. They live in the small villages and hamlets away from the larger settlements, and the only time you are likely to meet them is on market days or by hiking in the countryside. The men are easily recognizable by their white linen trousers and beautiful handmade shirts of the same colour.

Of the two western districts, Copán and Ocotepeque, Copán is the more interesting, and its regional centre of Santa Rosa de Copán is the prettiest of colonial Honduran towns. Perched on a steep hill overlooking the surrounding countryside, it is the centre of a fertile agricultural and cattle-raising region. To the southeast lies the historic town of Gracias from where you can hike up the country's highest mountain, the Montaña de Celaque (2849 m).

Close to the western border post with Guatemala stands the country's only Maya city, the famous ruins of Copán. If you're coming to Honduras from Guatemala, they make an impressive first destination, but they should certainly be part of any journey to Honduras. The site is not only unique for its architectural layout, but also for the famous hieroglyphic stairway and the large number of finely carved stelae, an art form that reached its zenith here, one of the last Maya cities to emerge as a major centre of power.

Santa Rosa de Copán

Santa Rosa de Copán is the largest town (pop. 28 870) in western Honduras, 200 km northwest of Tegus, and 147 km southwest of San Pedro Sula (from where it is most

267

easily reached, along the paved Western Highway). A colonial town perched on a hill overlooking beautiful countryside, its steep cobbled streets are attractive though it's by no means as beautiful as some guidebooks suggest. The main square is lined by crumbling municipal buildings and a damp church. The people are friendly and the only drawback is the large number of Honduran soldiers who seem to be based here. The town is worth visiting at any time of year, but especially during its annual festival in the last week of August.

Santa Rosa lies in a rich tobacco-growing area, and the cigars sold in the local factory are some of the best in the country. It is located in the centre of town, on the Calle Real Centenario, where you can buy cigars direct, or just go on a tour of the factory, if the staff happen to feel like showing you around. Very fine *sombreros de junco* (Panama hats) are also made and sold in the town.

Services include banks, HONDUTEL, and a post office.

GETTING THERE
If arriving by bus, you will find yourself at the bottom of a steep hill, outside town. But there are always taxis to the centre, which people normally share, so the price is very cheap. Apart from the fast buses to San Pedro Sula or the border town of Nueva Ocotepeque, which pass every hour throughout the day, there are also numerous local buses that leave from here. Check their times either at the terminal or with your hotel proprietor. For example, there are regular buses to the eastern town of Gracias, a few direct buses to Copán Ruinas, and limited services to small villages, such as Dulce Nombre, Lepaera and Corquín.

WHERE TO STAY
INEXPENSIVE
The options are limited, but the best hotel is the **Elvir**, on the same street as the cigar factory, where rooms are around a quiet, modern courtyard, and there's also a good restaurant. The **Copán**, 3 Avenida N.E. and 4 Calle N.E. is also a good choice. The **Hotel Maya**, 1 Calle N.O. and 3 Avenida N.E. is cheap, but the rooms are damp and the beds terrible. None of the others have much to recommend them, though there are a number of budget *hospedajes*; if you're short of money try the **Hospedaje Calle Real** on Real Centenario and 6 Avenida, which also offers meals.

EATING OUT
Again the choices are very limited. The best restaurant is in the **Hotel Elvir**, but a cheaper, good alternative is the **Aries** restaurant, just off the main square, near the cathedral. There are a number of other places along this street, south of the main square, and a few cafeterias on the square itself.

Around Santa Rosa de Copán

Gracias
Described by some as a dusty 'cowboy' town, and others as a 'splendid place to visit', the most notable things about Gracias today are its location and the Sunday market.

Historically, however, the town has played an important role: firstly, as the base from which Spanish forces defeated and killed the Lenca chief Lempira, in 1537; and secondly, as the brief administrative home of the Audiencia de los Confines, the Spanish judiciary that covered the entire isthmus. Nestling between two rivers at the foot of Mount Celaque, it is an ideal base for exploring the countryside on foot. If you're not feeling very energetic, you could walk (or hire a taxi) to some **hot springs** (*aguas calientes*), about an hour and a half's walk away. More strenuous and adventurous hikes can be made to surrounding villages, such as La Iguala and El Nispero (camping only, or stay with locals), while climbing Mount Celaque is extremely hard work. This last trail is, however, an exciting day trip, which takes you through moist cloud forest as you go higher up the mountain. Ideally, you would hire horses at Villa Verde, 30 minutes below the visitor's centre of the Celaque National Park. You should certainly hire a guide, since the trail is not clear all the way, and it's easy to get lost in the forest.

For advice on hiking in the surrounding area, but especially about the Celaque National Park, contact the staff of the local COHDEFOR (forestry commission) office, near the main square in Gracias. To reach the visitor's centre from Gracias takes about two hours on foot, but there is also a road leading to it. You will find that the centre is frequently closed, and not particularly useful. But even if you don't plan to hike any further, the setting is beautiful, with great views. Serious hikers should also invest in the topographic maps of the area, unfortunately only available in Tegus.

Accommodation in Gracias is predictably basic. The best choices are the *hospedajes* **Iris** and **Erick**, and the **San Antonio** isn't bad either. Services in the town include a bank and a HONDUTEL office, as well as a post office and petrol station. Leaving Gracias is easiest if you head back to Santa Rosa de Copán, but it is also possible to travel onwards to La Esperanza and the highway to Tegus. The road between Gracias and Siguatepeque was supposed to be paved by 1991, but work is still in progress.

Dulce Nombre

A small village north of Santa Rosa de Copán, this is the starting point for trails across the Sierra Gallinero mountains, eventually leading you to the road for Copán Ruinas. However, this area is not well mapped, nor easy walking, so only suitable if you are well prepared and physically fit. There is no commercial accommodation on the route, so you will need camping equipment.

Towards Two Borders

You can cross both the Guatemalan and the Salvadorean borders from the town of **Nueva Ocotepeque**. Buses to the town leave from Santa Rosa de Copán at 6 and 9 am, daily, and the journey takes about 3 hours. If you miss these two, there are also buses coming from San Pedro Sula, heading for the border, but these are often full and you may not get a seat. Whatever you do, don't make the mistake of taking a bus to San Marcos Ocotepeque, which is a different town. Whichever way you arrive, you will find the road from Santa Rosa southwards very beautiful, climbing over passes and snaking its way through pine-clad countryside.

Nueva Ocotepeque really is a dusty cowboy town, busy with moneychangers and shops selling all manner of contraband. There is certainly no reason to stay here, unless you arrive too late to cross either of the borders. In that case, you might as well stay at the **Hotel Ocotepeque,** run by the Impala bus company, which operates between here and San Pedro Sula. Minibuses head both to Agua Caliente (Guatemala) and El Poy (El Salvador), leaving from the main street. Although things can appear somewhat hectic here, you will have no trouble finding the relevant transport, since you will be approached by touts as soon as you arrive. In general, the Guatemalan border crossing here has a bad reputation, rarely giving travellers more than one month on their tourist cards, even though you are allowed up to three. If this is a problem for you, you should cross by Copán Ruinas, where officials always give you three months if you ask for it. Crossing the Salvadorean border here is not ideal either, as the northern region of El Salvador is always plagued by armed conflict.

Copán Ruinas

The small town of Copán Ruinas, just 14 km from the Guatemalan border, is a peaceful little place, which lives off tourism to the nearby ruins. Some of the streets are cobbled, others are just dirt, and the main square is generally empty, except for the odd tourist or horseman clattering by. Located on the edge of a fertile river valley, the surrounding countryside can be explored on horseback, or you can go for pleasant walks along the river or over the nearby hills. Getting to know the Maya city of Copán could easily fill a couple of days in itself. The ruins are about one kilometre outside of town, so within easy walking distance, and there is a good choice of accommodation.

The Ruins of Copán

Visiting Copán (daily, 8–4) is a pleasure, not only for its intrinsic architectural beauty, but also for the landscape it is set in. The site is characterized by wide open spaces, huge ancient trees, and cooling forest around the edges, which makes any visit a discovery of nature as well. As you arrive at the entrance gate, you are greeted by four squawking macaws, their feathers a brilliant blue, red and yellow. They are reasonably tame, but their beaks can peck very hard. While exploring the ancient buildings, you may come upon a number of other tropical animals, generally shy and harmless, but in particular butterflies and birds. If you enjoy this aspect of the site, you could follow the marked 'nature trail', to which you will see signs on the way to the entrance. You will need insect repellent for this short walk, which is also useful while visiting the ruins

Copán

themselves.

The first building you come to on arrival at the Copán site, is the large **visitors' centre**, where you must buy your ticket for a small fee, and where you can ask for a guide. The exhibition of the city's design and special features is well worth spending time at, since it will give you a good introduction to what you are about to see. Facilities at the centre include toilets, a souvenir shop and a cafeteria. Across the road, there's also a small snack place, which is good and cheaper.

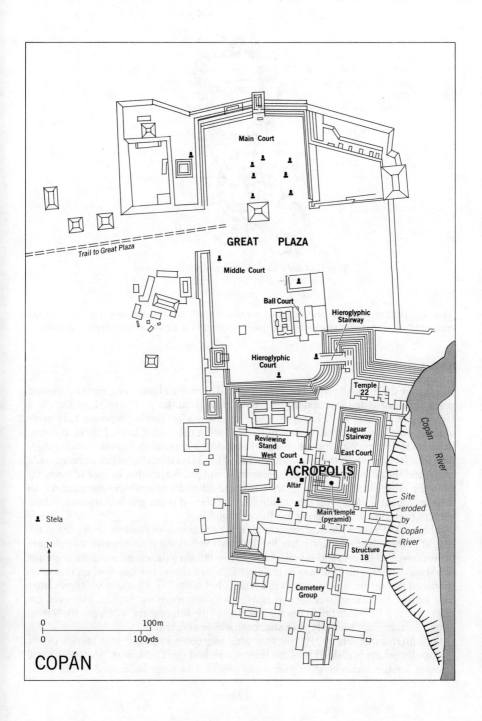

Main Court

Stela

GREAT PLAZA

Trail to Great Plaza

Middle Court

Ball Court

Hieroglyphic Stairway

Hieroglyphic Court

Temple 22

Jaguar Stairway

Reviewing Stand

West Court

East Court

ACROPOLIS

Altar

Main temple (pyramid)

Structure 18

Cemetery Group

Copán River

Site eroded by Copán River

Stela

N

0   100m
0   100yds

COPÁN

Stone head and torso of the Young Maize God (Copán)

The description below is intended as an orientation around the site and it is highly recommended that you study the specialist booklets for more archaeological details.

The Site

By the time the Spanish arrived here, the city had been abandoned for almost a thousand years. The last dated inscription the Maya left is from the year AD 800, so the city's Golden Age was over while Europe's Charlemagne was just coming to power. Like many of the major Maya centres, Copán flowered during the Late Classic Period, the time from AD 550 to AD 900, though human habitation was certainly present much earlier than this. Its location, at the southern reaches of the Maya domain, was on a crucial trade route, and thus it became a powerful economic and political centre, in spite of being far from the other sites. Obsidian, jade, cacao and quetzal feathers were the mainstay of their merchant trading, and they controlled the flow of these goods from their inland sources to destinations all along the Bay of Honduras.

The mark of a site's political importance is the use of its own emblem glyph, and in the case of Copán, the first known date for this is AD 564. From then onwards it must have been a powerful centre, and is believed to have controlled the entire southern region of the Maya empire, with Quiriguá its main satellite. For almost two hundred years, Copán remained the uncontested power in this region, but in AD 737, Quiriguá's leader, Cauac Sky, mounted a successful challenge, and Copán's hegemony was broken. However, the city recovered for a short time towards the end of the 8th century, when the site's most famous feature, the **hieroglyphic staircase** was completed.

On entering the site today, the first area you come to is the part known as the **Acropolis**, which is divided into the West Court and the East Court. Much work still remains for the archaeologists, and many precious carvings lie around in discarded

272

heaps, but the most impressive aspects of this area are the altar at the base of the central pyramid, and the stairways decorated with large carvings of animals and mythical figures. If you climb up the eastern edge of the East Court, you will see the Copán river, and the ancient ramparts that used to protect the city from its waters. They were diverted in this century to stop erosion, which was already quite advanced. Following the wall north, you come to the great steps of **temple 22**, which rises from the river bed in huge blocks of beautiful symmetry. This marks the division between the Acropolis and the **Great Plaza**, and if you walk around the temple's bulk, you come out onto the vast expanse of Copán's central area.

It is here that you get a full sense of the site's horizontal nature, the grassy plaza so large that the 20-foot stelae look small by comparison. Unlike the towering pyramids of Tikal, Copán's temple platforms are broad rather than high, and what impresses here are not the buildings themselves but the sculptural art that decorates them. Unique in the Maya world is the magnificent **hieroglyphic stairway** on temple 22. Every one of the 63 steps is decorated with intricate carvings that make up a huge hieroglyphic text, which is made up of around 2500 glyphs, still mostly undeciphered to this day. It's a shame that the stairway has to be covered as protection from the elements, but standing at its base, the beautiful craftsmanship is as impressive as ever.

Just north of the stairway, you find another unique feature, which is the **ball court**, the most perfectly restored example in the Maya world. Here the Maya sportsmen would play in deadly rivalry, knowing that some of them would be sacrificed at the end. The game was a tough one, played with a solid rubber ball that could not be touched by hands, feet or heads, but had to be propelled by hard bounces off the body. If you look at depictions of the game, you see that the players wore heavy protective clothing.

Finally, wandering around the Great Plaza itself, you can marvel at the most sophisticated carving found on any Maya stelae. Around twenty of these were erected here between Early and Late Classic times, as well as fourteen altars. They were carved in a

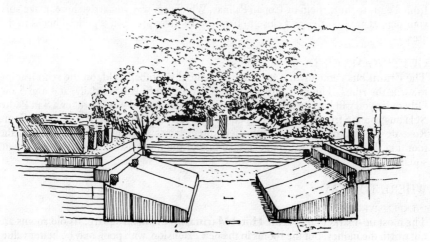

The Ball Court at Copán

greenish volcanic stone found nearby, which is much harder than the usual sandstone, and thus the carving has survived better here than elsewhere. What makes them so special is the three-dimensional nature of the carving, which stands out from the stone, almost creating separate sculptures. The faces of the Maya lords are extraordinarily detailed, their costumes and headdresses intricately formed, down to the finest feather. To some the carving may have a certain rococo excess to it, so elaborate are the designs. But on the other hand, the portraiture is so fine that you actually get a sense of what these rulers might have looked like. Their faces seem like those of real people. When the British diplomat and explorer John Lloyd Stephens saw them in 1839, he was so impressed he bought the entire site for US$50. No doubt he planned to ship the best parts back to England, but happily he never did.

TOURIST INFORMATION
Specific information about the ruins and possible excursions in the surrounding area is available from the visitors' centre at the site. There are also a number of leaflets and publications on sale there. Another excellent source of information, in the town, is the proprietors of the **Tunkul Bar**, Mike and René. If you have a special interest, you might consider hiring Mike to guide you around the site (expensive).

GETTING THERE
Getting to Copán is easy. If coming from Guatemala, it is the first place you reach. If coming from inland Honduras, the best connection is from San Pedro Sula, from where you can either catch a direct **Etumi** bus (4–5 hrs, see p. 279), or any bus to La Entrada, and change there for a minibus to Copán Ruinas. The latter is not recommended, however, since the minibuses are frighteningly overloaded. By the time you read this, the road connecting the central highway from Tegus with Santa Rosa de Copán may be entirely paved, in which case you could easily travel this way, though it would still take a whole day, and there are no direct buses. Alternatively you could charter a small aircraft from Tegus to the airfield by Copán Ruinas. Whichever way you arrive here, make sure your papers are in order and close to hand, since there are always police checks in the area.

GETTING AROUND
The **Etumi** bus company has its office opposite the football field, on the road leading towards the ruins. The only direct buses to San Pedro Sula leave daily, at 4 and 5 am. Otherwise you will have to take a minibus to La Entrada, and wait there for a San Pedro Sula bus coming from Nueva Ocotepeque. You can also change here for a bus to Santa Rosa de Copán, or take one of the few direct buses, leaving Copán Ruinas in the morning. If heading for Guatemala, take one of the minibuses leaving from the main square.

WHERE TO STAY
INEXPENSIVE
The most up-market hotel is the **Hotel Marina**, off the main square. Its old rooms are not worth the money, but the rooms in the new extension, with pool, may be better value, though certainly more expensive. There is also a good restaurant here. **Hotel Maya**, on

the main square, is pleasant and cool, and has a restaurant. All rooms have a private bath. **Hotelito Brisas de Copán** is one of the best budget hotels and also offers rooms with a fan and private bath. **Los Gemelos**, near the football field, is a favourite budget hotel with communal bathrooms. **Hotelito Peña**, at the entrance of town, coming from the Guatemalan border, is very stuffy. **Pensión Honduras** is friendly, clean and basic. **Pensión/Restaurante Paty** is clean and basic, and the restaurant is recommended.

EATING OUT

Apart from the hotel restaurants, there are a few good places to eat. Very popular is the *comedor* **Llama del Bosque**, near the main square, but the tastiest meals are to be had at the **Tunkul Bar**, which is also the best place to socialize in the evenings. It has a friendly atmosphere, and the views, service and music are good. Ask here if you are interested in renting horses, or adventurous tours to the remote Mosquitia jungles, in eastern Honduras. René does personal tours to the region, charging around US$500 per person, for a week's trip, if there are at least five people. **Hotel Paty** restaurant is good for *comida corriente*, and **Burger Zotz** is reasonable for hamburgers. In the evenings, there are also women selling freshly grilled *pinchos* on the main square, which make a delicious snack.

USEFUL INFORMATION

Museum: Located on the main square the municipal museum is worth visiting for the fine examples of Maya pottery, ceramics, and jewellery. The place is small, but does a good job of presenting some of the best stelae and a glyph bench found at Copán, as well as a complete burial chamber, which gives you a graphic idea of how people were buried in Maya times. (Daily, 8–noon and 1–4, small fee.)
Exchange: There is a bank in town, but you can also change money at the **Marina** Hotel, and possibly at the **Tunkul bar**.
Post office: This is located on the main square, next to the museum.
Petrol station: There is one opposite the ruins.
Guatemalan border crossing: Crossing to or from Guatemala at El Florido is easy. Minibuses regularly ply the route between the border and Copán Ruinas, departing when full up. The fare should be no more than US$1. If you do not need a visa for Guatemala, you will receive a tourist card for US$5, payable in US dollars or local currency. There are plenty of moneychangers here and the border closes at 6.

THE NORTH COAST AND EASTERN HONDURAS

The Caribbean coast is a heady mix of tropical beaches and sweaty towns, where you can find either the peaceful relaxation of endless sand melting into the sea, or energetic *salsa* music in the bars. The most densely populated area of the country, the predominantly black culture ensures a more casual atmosphere than Latin reserve usually allows, yet the slow pace of life along the coast means that things never get hectic. By contrast, northeastern Honduras is the least populated region of the country due to the tangled jungles of the Mosquitia. Traditionally an impenetrable place hiding the homes of forest Indians, recent decades have seen inroads along its coast and waterways, where prospectors and squatters rub shoulders with former members of the Contras. It's a wild place, where adventurous travellers can still find rare animals like the jaguar, float along hidden rivers, or find their fortune in gunslinging prospecting camps.

The coastal landscape is reasonably flat along its entire length. In places, however, the countryside rises steeply behind a narrow plain, reaching heights of a couple of thousand metres in the Nombre de Dios Mountains that rise parallel to the central coast. This makes for dramatic views from the coastal highway, especially near the city of La Ceiba, where the highest peaks are, and also behind the town of Trujillo, where rainforest clings to steep hills close to the sea. The beaches are generally of a fine white sand, often stretching for miles and miles, with only small fishing villages occasionally breaking the horizon of palm trees leaning towards the ocean. East of Trujillo, the landscape flattens out into swampy marshes that soon become the Mosquitia rainforest, where mangroves often crowd right up to the beaches. You could find some really deserted beaches along here by boat, but otherwise you're unlikely to see the eastern reaches of the coast.

Travelling overland you are bound to pass through the country's second city, San Pedro Sula, which lies just inland at the western end of the coast. A city choking with traffic and industry, you'll soon be taking a bus to the first coastal town, which is the small port of Puerto Cortés, a has-been sort of a place that nevertheless manages to keep some charm in its dilapidated streets and buildings. Travelling east, ideally by rickety train, you soon come to Tela, a sleepy seaside town that was once home to the big bosses of the United Fruit Company, but now dozes in tropical torpor close to some excellent beaches. Almost at the centre of the coast, the city of La Ceiba is a jumping-off point for the Bay Islands, but also deserves a visit in its own right for some of the best nightlife in the country. Few travellers venture further east than La Ceiba, since the road gets bumpy and the journey to Trujillo takes a few hours. But it's time well spent, because what you find is a relaxed town on a perfect sandy bay, as well as some great seafood cooked directly on the beach.

The Garifuna Heritage

Unlike elsewhere in Honduras, the population here is strongly influenced by the blacks who live all along the coast. Many are Garifuna, while others are descendants of imported slaves, who used to work the huge banana plantations. The two groups are visually almost indistinguishable, but their culture is certainly different. The Garifuna of Honduras are the largest society of all those that live along the coast, from Belize to Nicaragua, and unlike in the rest of Central America, their culture and language is still a living part of daily life, not a tourist attraction or historical remembrance. The reason for this is easy to find, since the Honduran coast was the first mainland area settled by these people, and all the other communities sprang from here, distant offshoots of the original settlement. 80% of all Garifuna still live in Honduras, where they make up around 2.5% of the national population.

Their origins date back to 1635, when British slaving vessels from Nigeria sank off the island of St Vincent, in the eastern Caribbean. The survivors managed to swim to the island, where they escaped slavery, to live freely with the local Carib Indians. Relations between the two peoples weren't entirely peaceful, but they nevertheless intermarried, and soon a new race emerged, known as the Black Caribs or Garifuna. Within a few generations, the Garifuna came to dominate racially and culturally, forming a new society with its own language and customs. Meanwhile, St Vincent was being fought over by the British and French, and their forces regularly clashed with the fiercely independent Garifuna. The island was claimed by the British, but in effect for most of the 18th century half of it was under Garifuna control, who numbered around 5000 people by 1800.

Encouraged by the French, the Garifuna regularly attacked British garrisons on St Vincent, until things finally came to a head in 1795, when a major battle was fought, which the Garifuna lost. Forced to surrender completely, the British punishment was harsh: deportation to Roatán, where many starved or died of disease. The deportation was also tactical, since the British hoped the Garifuna would repel any Spanish claims to the island. But the Garifuna handed Roatán to the Spanish, based on the coast of Honduras, and in return they were shipped to the mainland, where they thrived once more, as free labourers and fishermen. The first settlement was in Trujillo, where the Spanish had built a fort. However, small groups of Garifuna soon dispersed along the entire Bay of Honduras, many becoming expert smugglers on the Belize coast, where they traded contraband with the British. They also found work in the burgeoning logging trade, and in the 19th and early 20th century, in the banana plantations. But primarily, they were fishermen and sailors, and even today many Garifuna men work in sea-related trades.

Their traditional homes are always villages by the sea, their houses made of wood and palm thatch, and their diet characterized by seafood, coconuts, and the tropical fruit that grows on the coast. The language they speak among themselves is a mixture of Arawak, French, Yoruba, Swahili and Bantu. But they also speak Spanish, and many of the younger people are losing their own language altogether, as they emigrate inland, or even to the United States (an estimated 25,000 Garifuna now live in New York and Los Angeles). In the villages, children are taught in Garifuna as well as Spanish, but as soon as they leave for secondary school, they speak only Spanish. The Garifuna's long association with the Spanish has also made them nominal Catholics, though Afro-Indian rites form a significant part of their religious customs, and the shaman is still the most respected member of any community, next to the local healer, or *curandero*.

For the visitor, the Garifuna villages appear little different to any other local fishing community, and the people, though friendly, are certainly not interested in being tourist attractions, ready to display their culture to all and sundry. They keep to their own, and it would only be by chance that you would witness a village festival, where the inhabitants sing their traditional songs. One reason for this is that festivals have no fixed dates, but occur when there is a birth or death, or an important spiritual event occurs, such as someone becoming a healer.

The tourist board has only discovered the potential of this ethnic minority in the last decade or so, concentrating on Garifuna singing and dancing, and the most likely way you will see this performed is by professional groups in the cities. The Garifuna villages meanwhile, remain quiet, small communities, often located on beautiful beaches. The best bases from which to visit the villages are Tela and Trujillo.

San Pedro Sula

San Pedro Sula sits on the edge of the broad Ulúa river valley, and is the country's second largest city. It is also the country's economic heart—an important centre for business, trade and industry. It is reputedly the fastest growing city in Central America, with a population of 319,740. Not particularly attractive, with little colonial architecture, the city nevertheless has a pleasant atmosphere, with neither the pollution or hectic streetlife of the capital. The climate is hot and sticky, so nobody rushes too much, and the central park is a small, but relaxed space to stroll among the vendors. Good accommodation is limited, but not that expensive. Nice places to eat and drink are few, and you will find the best options around the main square.

Travelling around Honduras, you will inevitably pass through the city at some stage, since it is an important transportation centre, from which buses leave to many different destinations. There is no particular reason to stay here, though if you do, a day trip you could easily make from here is to Pulhapanza Falls (see p. 266). The one time of year when staying over is worth it is during the **Semana Sampedrana** festival, which takes place at the end of June. At this time, the city erupts into singing and dancing, as well as horseracing and an agricultural fair.

GETTING TO SAN PEDRO SULA

By Air
The international airport, Ramón Villeda Morales, is 13 km east of the city, on the road to the former banana centre of La Lima. There is a tourist information booth located here, but otherwise there are few facilities. Connections via this airport can be made to a number of internal and international destinations, such as Tegus and La Ceiba, and Belize City (around US$76 one-way), Guatemala City (around US$80 one-way), San Salvador, San Jose, Miami, Dallas, Los Angeles and New York. The best way to reach the airport or travel into the city is by taxi, and the fare should not be more than US$3.

American Airlines, 16 Avenida and 2 Calle N.O., tel 58 0518.
Continental, Gran Hotel Sula, Plaza Central, tel 57 8708.
Lacsa, 8 Avenida 1–2 Calle S.O., tel 52 5893.
Taca, 1 Calle and 9 Avenida, tel 53 2646.
Tan-Sahsa, 5 Calle 1–2 Avenida N.O., tel 53 1681.

By Train
There is a rail link between San Pedro Sula and coastal Puerto Cortés, with one train daily in either direction. Departure from San Pedro Sula is at 6.30 am; departure from Puerto Cortés is at 3.30 pm. The most interesting part of the journey, however, is between Puerto Cortés and Tela, so you might as well save your ride till then—and anyway the buses are faster. The train station is east of the central park, on 1 Avenida.

By Bus
There are many bus companies operating out of the city, and there are direct

connections to the capital and all destinations along the way, also to the west, such as Copán Ruinas, north to Puerto Cortés, Tela and La Ceiba, and east to Yoro.

To Tegucigalpa and all destinations along the Highway: Hedman Alas buses leave from 3 Calle 7–8 Avenida N.O., and depart regularly, between 6.30 and 5.30, daily. **Transportes Sáenz** has buses leaving as early as 2 am, and the last departure is at 5.30 pm, from 9 Calle 7–8 Avenida S.O. **Norteño** buses are at 6 Calle 6–7 Avenida S.O., with the first bus at 3 am, and the last one at 6.15 pm. **El Rey**, at 7 Avenida 5–6 Calle S.O. runs buses all day, the last one leaving at 7 pm.

To Pulhapanzac Falls (about 80 km): The **Mochito** bus leaves from the corner of 5 Calle S.E. and 1 Avenida S.E., and the journey takes around $1\frac{1}{2}$ hrs. Make sure you check the return journey times, or you might get stuck.

To Puerto Cortés (58 km): The best service is run by **Impala**, at 2 Avenida 4–5 Calle S.O., and the journey takes around 1 hr. Buses leave regularly between 6 am and 7 pm.

To El Progreso (28 km), Tela (96 km) and La Ceiba (197 km): Tupsa buses leave from 2 Avenida 5–6 Calle S.O. between 5.30 am and 6 pm. If heading for the eastern town of Yoro, you need to change in El Progreso.

To Nueva Ocotepeque (248 km) for Guatemalan and Salvadorean borders: Impala buses leave from 2 Avenida 4–5 Calle S.O., with the first departure at 3.30 am and the last at 3 pm. The journey takes around 6 hrs direct. These buses also pass by Santa Rosa de Copán (147 km). If only travelling to Santa Rosa de Copán, you could also travel by **Copanecos** buses, which leave frequently from 5 Avenida 5–6 Calle S.O., last departure at 5.15 pm. **Torito** also runs this route, leaving from 7 Avenida and 8 Calle S.O.

To Copán Ruinas (159 km): Etumi buses leave from 6 Calle 6–7 Avenida S.O., one at 11 am and one at 1 pm, and the journey takes around 5 hrs. Note that the bus parks in a parking lot, and there is no recognizable terminal as such. Alternatively, take any bus as far as La Entrada, and change there for one of the minibuses to Copán Ruinas.

To Santa Bárbara (about 130 km): Catisba buses leave from 6 Avenida 8–9 Calle S.O., and the journey takes around 3 hrs.

GETTING AROUND
The bus terminals are spread all over the city, but most are within a short walk of the centre. If you have too much luggage to walk, you can always take a taxi, which should not charge more than US$1 for the fare.

TOURIST INFORMATION
The local **tourist office** is at 4 Calle 3–4 Avenida N.O., Edificio Inmosa no. 21, third floor, tel 52 3023/3095. (Mon–Fri, 8–4). The staff are friendly, even if they have very few brochures and little information to offer. You can buy the tourist map of Honduras here, with street plans of San Pedro Sula, Tegus, and La Ceiba.

WHERE TO STAY

LUXURY

Copantl Sula, tel 53 2108, fax 57 3890, outside the city centre, on the Carretera Chamelecón in the suburb of Colonia Las Mesetas, claims to be the country's best hotel. Tax is added.

EXPENSIVE

The **Gran Hotel Sula**, tel 52 9999, fax 52 7000, on the main square, is the top hotel in town, with pool and restaurant. The place is hardly luxurious, but certainly up to international standards, and rooms have TV, air-conditioning and phone.

MODERATE

The **Hotel Bolívar**, 2 Calle and 2 Avenida N.O., tel 53 3218/1811, fax 53 4823, is a small and attractive hotel, in spite of its age. Certainly it has the most beautiful pool, as well as a good restaurant and secure parking. All rooms have TV, air-conditioning and phone, and are excellent value for money. **Hotel Ambassador**, 5 Avenida and 7 Calle S.O., tel 57 6824, is a modern building, with clean rooms and a restaurant. All rooms have private bath, air-conditioning or fan.

INEXPENSIVE

Hotel Roma, 8 Calle 6–7 Avenida, Barrio Lempira, is one of the best budget hotels, rooms with private bath and fan available. A friendly and clean hotel with a roof terrace is the **Hotel París**, 2 Avenida 3–4 Calle S.O., located near the Impala bus terminal. The **San Juan**, 6 Calle and 6 Avenida S.O. is clean and offers doubles with private bath and fan. **Hotel San Pedro**, 3 Calle S.O. 1–2 Avenida, tel 53 2655, has a good restaurant, but the rooms have nasty metal camping beds. **Hotel Castillo**, 8 Calle 5–6 Avenida S.O. is a dingy last choice.

EATING OUT

As always, the main hotels have some of the best restaurants, but there are plenty of others to choose from as well. For steaks and Honduran dishes try **Don Udos**, in the Hotel Los Andes, Avenida Circunvalación, Barrio Los Andes. For more of the same kind of meals, check **Pat's Steak House**, 17 Avenida and 5 Calle S.O., **La Estancia**, 2 Calle 9–10 Avenida N.O., **Vicente**, 4 Avenida 2–3 Calle S.O., and **El Mandarín**, 17–18 Avenida and 4 Calle N.O. A popular place for cheap meals and open-air bar is the **Pincho Palace**, 2 Calle and 4 Avenida. If you enjoy *licuados*, then be sure to try the ones at **Fruitlandia** in the pedestrian passage off the main square, just past the **Cafetería Madrid**, which is also a good place for simple meals with a Spanish touch.

For Chinese food, three of the best are **China Town**, 7 Avenida and 5 Calle S.O., **Taiwan**, 5 Avenida 2–3 Calle N.O., and **Lucky**, 3–4 Avenida and 2 Calle N.O. Fast food is available from **Pizza Hut**, at 16 Avenida and 1 Calle N.O., **Chicken Shack**, 17 Avenida and 4 Calle S.O., **Skandia**, in the Hotel Gran Sula, and **Popeyes**, on the road leading out towards Puerto Cortés.

ENTERTAINMENT AND NIGHTLIFE

Nightlife is limited in this city, but two recommended **discos** are **Confettis** and **Henry's**, which are both on the Avenida Circunvalación, in the Barrio Los Andes. If you have your own transport, it would be worth driving all around the western side of the city on the Avenida Circunvalación, since you will find a number of music bars along here.

The Centro Cultural Sampedrano, 3 Calle N.O., No. 20, has theatrical events and an art gallery. There are five cinemas.

SHOPPING
There is a large artisan market six blocks northwest of Central Park where you can buy Honduran handicrafts.

USEFUL INFORMATION
Money Matters
All the major banks are represented near the main square, and the **black market** is in the pedestrian passage leading off it. The top hotels also change traveller's cheques. The **American Express** office is at **Agencia de Viajes Trans Mundo**, 6 Avenida S.O., no. 15, tel 54 1140.

Books
The Book Store, 3 Avenida 2–3 Calle S.O., just off the main square.

Post Office and Telecommunications
The post office is at 9 Calle 3–4 Avenida S.O. HONDUTEL is at 4 Calle and 4 Avenida S.O., opposite the Banco de Londres y Montreal.

Car hire
The international airport, tel 56 2467, has offices for **Budget, Molinari** and **Maya**. **National** has an office in the Hotel Copantl, tel 53 2108. **American** is at 3 Avenida 3–4 Calle N.O., tel 52 7626/2337 and **Toyota** at 4 Avenida 2–3 Calle N.O., tel 57 2644.

Consulates
Belize: Bellavista suburb, 4 Calle and 33 Avenida, no. 415, tel 53 2305. Mon–Fri, 7–11.30 am.
UK: 4 Avenida and 4 Calle N.O., 29th floor, tel 52 3452. Mon–Fri, 7.30–11.30 am.
Guatemala: 8 Calle 5–6 Avenida N.O., no. 38, tel 53 3560. Mon–Fri, 8–2.
El Salvador: Edificio Rivera y Cía, no. 218, 5th floor, tel 53 4604. Mon–Fri, 8–3.

Immigration
The immigration office is at 4 Avenida 2–3 Calle S.O.

East from San Pedro Sula

The town of **Yoro**, just over 100 km east of the city, is a useful base for excursions to the little visited **Parque Nacional de Montaña de Yoro**. In particular if you have your own vehicle, this would be a rewarding excursion, and you will find yourself in one of the country's largest remaining cloud forests. The highest point here is 2378 m, so expect to do some tough walking and bring your own provisions. For more information on the park and its trails, check the COHDEFOR (Forestry Commission) office in Yoro. If arriving by public transport, you can get a bus from El Progreso, and you will find accommodation cheap and simple.

There are also plenty of remote villages to visit around here, some inhabited by Xicaque Indians. If you don't feel like returning to San Pedro Sula, you could continue east from Yoro, via San José and Olanchito, where roads lead towards the coastal highway, to La Ceiba or Trujillo. If you try this by public transport, be prepared to spend a few days, since buses along this stretch are sporadic, and same-day connections are not always possible.

Puerto Cortés

Puerto Cortés may be the country's largest port, but it is a dusty forgotten place. In its heyday, Puerto Cortés turned over millions of banana shipments from the surrounding plantations. Huge container ships still come here today, filling up with fruit, and also with Honduran export goods manufactured in the industrial zone nearby. But wandering around the dock area and the main square, it is hard to get a sense of the town's importance. Dilapidated hotels seem overlarge for present-day needs, while the wooden shacks along the railway and docks stand crooked and peeling. The bars are grimy, darkened places, where only the whores and dockworkers spend much time, sipping warm beers or dozing in chairs. Yet this kind of place has its own special atmosphere. Tourists rarely stay for long, so the locals are always pleased to meet someone who cares to remain a while. Being a port, it is a man's town, but women are not threatened here, since the place is far too small to be very dangerous.

The main reason for coming here is to catch a morning train to the coastal town of Tela, or to see the annual festival, which takes place during the third week of August. The highlight of this event is the *Noche Veneciana*, when there are street parties, deafening fireworks and colourful gondolas.

There are a couple of excursions you can go on. Municipal buses leave from the main square, heading to coastal settlements to the west and east, where sandy beaches await the weekend crowds, empty for the rest of the time. Heading west, a 30-minute bus ride takes you to **Omoa**, and an ancient Spanish fort (Mon–Fri, 8–noon, Sat–Sun, 9–5, small fee). Built in the mid-18th century, it played an important role in defending the coast against pirates, and its walls are immensely thick, still in perfect condition today. In this century, the fort was used as a prison, and a depressing place it must have been, its cavernous cells damp, dark places, which you are free to explore if you don't mind bats. Further along the road are some popular beaches. Heading east from Puerto Cortés, a favoured destination is the Garifuna village of **Travesía**, which looks onto a beautiful beach. To get there, catch a bus from the main square.

WHERE TO STAY
The best place to stay near the centre is **Mr. Ggeerr's**, tel 55 0444, which charges around US$10 for a double. The hotel is four blocks east of the main square, on 2 Avenida. If you have your own transport and prefer something more up-market, there are a couple of hotels near the beach: **Hotel Costa Azul**, zona Puerto Cortés,

tel 55 2260 and **Hotel Costa Mar**, Barrio La Coca Cola, tel 55 1367. Of the inexpensive hotels in town, the **Tuek-San** on the main square is the most sanitary, though still run down. Other options are positively sleazy.

EATING OUT
The **Tuek-San** has a good Chinese restaurant, and another popular place is the **Café Vienna**, next door. Service is a bit slow, but then there is nothing to be in a hurry about. If you wander along 3 Avenida, heading west from the main square, you will find snack places, and soon be in the red-light district. Another place to find cheap restaurants and bars is along the railway tracks, one block south of 2 Avenida. One of the best bars is the open-air one, opposite the Texaco station, on the corner of the main square.

By Train to Tela

This train journey, in scantily welded metal wagons, is an education in Third World economics. As your ears are pounded by squealing wheels on the track, with no window panes to protect you, the train goes past plantations of bananas, African palm, rice paddies and cattle farms. At one stage you see a palm-oil processing plant, which really seems like a Victorian nightmare—rusty pipes blast sudden jets of white steam, while workers sweat away, their faces covered in masks to protect them from the noxious fumes. Inside the train, the impoverished families of plantation workers crowd onto the seats, baskets and children piled high in the gangway. The train is divided into three different classes: first-class compartments have covered seats, second class offers wooden benches, while third class is the cattle wagon. You have to change trains at La Punta, and the entire journey takes four hours. If at all possible, bring ear plugs with you, since the noise really can be excruciating.

The train leaves daily at 7 am. There is no train station as such, but the place where passengers embark is on the part of the track three blocks west of the main square. The train just stops for a while, and people get on, before it moves off again. There is no departing whistle, so don't hang around. Tickets are bought on board and cost a fraction of a US dollar.

Tela

Tela is the kind of place that grows on you. On first impression this small town looks a bit grubby, with its dilapidated concrete and wooden buildings, but the palm-fringed beach with white sand is picturesque, there is a friendly daily market, and the few places where people socialize are quietly pleasant. In fact, over the years, a number of travellers have made their home here, captivated by the slow rhythm of tropical life in a town where nothing much happens. The beaches are some of the best along the north coast, and you should make time for Tela just so you can walk along the endless shores to the east and west. The only time Tela wakes from its tropical torpor is during the annual festival held on 13 June.

If you walk along the beach for an hour, heading east, you pass quiet lagoons until you reach the village of La Ensenada. From here, you leave the sea for a short while, to follow a dirt road to the Garifuna settlement of **El Triunfo**, stretching out along a perfect beach. Palm trees bend lopsided towards the sea, driftwood and marine debris sprinkles the white sand, and fishermen sit mending nets in the shade, or working on their ocean-going canoes. It's a lovely place, and if you asked around, you could probably find someone to rent you a small house here. The villagers are reserved but friendly, and the children will soon come up to you and offer to plait your hair in Afro-style, or sell you fresh coconut bread. You'll also find a few places on the beach that sell fried fish and drinks. Local buses connect between here and Tela, so there's no need to walk back.

Heading west along the beach, you soon come to **Telamar**, which is the former headquarters of the United Fruit Company. The large wooden beach houses were once the exclusive homes of American managers. Those were the days when Tela was an important town at the heart of the banana industry. Now the place has been turned into a holiday complex, complete with pool and restaurant. The white, sandy beach continues as far as the eye can see, gradually curving out to the Punta Sal peninsula.

If you're feeling energetic, you could walk the three hours to the Garifuna village of **Miami** on the peninsula. Rarely visited, since it is not accessible by road, this is another fishing village set along a gorgeous beach. If you don't make it that far, there are two other villages, San Juan and Tornabé, along the way, and the beach is great throughout. There are buses back to Tela from the first two villages. This whole area has been designated the **Parque Nacional Marino Punta Sal**, and if you're lucky, you might see all manner of wildlife among the different habitats here, though you would have to head inland. The area is very swampy, so bring insect repellent. If interested in the park, visit the **Recursos Naturales office** in Tela for more information. There is not much shade along the beach, so protection from the sun is essential.

Finally, another park, much easier to visit, is the **Botanical Gardens of Lancetilla**, just outside Tela. The best way to get there is to hire a taxi from the main square, and make sure it takes you all the way to the reception, which is some way from the entrance (weekdays 7.30–3.30 and weekends 8.30–4). There's a restaurant here, and guided tours are available, which are very informative about the hundreds of tropical plants you'll see. Originally it was a research station of the United Fruit Company, but now it has developed into one of Central America's foremost botanical gardens.

GETTING TO TELA

You will arrive at the **bus terminal** right by the market, on the high street. The journey to La Ceiba (101 km) takes 2 hrs along the paved coastal highway. If heading back to Puerto Cortés, the train leaves daily at 1.30 pm. The buses for nearby villages also leave from the market. For further travel information see the Agencia de Viajes Tela, tel 48 2152, located on the main street.

WHERE TO STAY ON THE BEACH

EXPENSIVE

The fanciest place to stay is the **Villas Telamar**, tel 48 2196, fax 48 2984, right on the beach, west of central Tela. You have a choice of bungalows on stilts, and rooms or apartments close to the pool and restaurant. Apartments are around US$80; beach villas range from US$96–US$292, depending on how many bedrooms, all prices per day and plus tax.

MODERATE

The other places are on the beach near the centre of town. The **Puerto Rico**, tel 48 2413, is very popular, and also has a restaurant. **Atlántico**, tel 48 2202, has overpriced, dark rooms.

INEXPENSIVE

Excellent value is the **Marazul**, on the corner of 4 Avenida, where a double with private bath and fan costs around US$5. Finally, the most popular budget hotel is **Sarah's Boarding House**, which is also by a favourite beach bar.

WHERE TO STAY IN TOWN

INEXPENSIVE

Good value for money is the **Gran Hotel Presidente**, in front of the Municipal Building, tel 48 2821, fax 48 2992. Friendly and efficient service, with clean, bright rooms. The **Hotel Tela**, tel 48 2150, on the main street, looks nice from the outside, but is run down inside; the restaurant is worth trying. **Gina's Boarding House**, one block south from the post office, and then left, is a respectable little place with a pretty courtyard, but overpriced.

EATING OUT

If you walk along the high street of Tela, you will come across a number of restaurants and bars, and once you pass the market, at the eastern end of town, you find yourself in the red-light district, where the bars get decidedly sleazy, most notably the **Alameda** and **Hollywood**. For a more salubrious bar and excellent seafood meals, try the **Sherwood**. Situated on the beach, not far from the Hotel Marazul, this is the best place to watch the sunsets. Another good place for meals, but especially breakfast, is **Luces del Norte**, run by a lanky Canadian. It's located on the street leading to the beachside Puerto Rico hotel. Finally, a popular beach bar with gringos, complete with pool table, is **El Tiburón Playero**, just a short walk from the market, in front of Sarah's Boarding House.

La Ceiba

Third largest city of Honduras, La Ceiba has a great atmosphere, in spite of its filthy streets and polluted canals. You're as likely to see horses and carts as modern vehicles, which somehow softens the sense of being in a city. It's a port, with all the trappings of sleazy bars, pool halls and bordellos. Yet the place still retains something of its Caribbean location, and the people are relaxed and friendly. An added bonus is a handful of good restaurants and open-air bars. Most travellers just use La Ceiba as a stepping stone to the Bay Islands, but if you enjoy the hustle and bustle of a tropical town, you should give yourself at least a day to stay over.

The best time of year to be here is for the **annual music festival**, during the third week of May. At this time you get a lively sense of the country's rich heritage of Latin and Afro-Caribbean music, and bands come from all over to perform in the streets and at popular venues. Each *barrio* organizes its own street party, all competing to have the best and loudest music, lots of dancing, and lots of food and drink. It's the closest you'll get to a Caribbean carnival in Central America.

If you have your own transport, you could explore the beaches beyond the city. You need to get some distance away to avoid the pollution, but an interesting beach to the west is at **Porvenir**, which gets crowded with millions of crabs in July and August. To the east, the village of **Corozal** is by a lovely beach. Heading inland, dirt roads lead into the beautiful Nombre de Dios mountain range that rises behind the city. On a clear day, wherever you are in La Ceiba, you can see the dramatic contours of Pico Bonito (2435 m), towering above the **Parque Nacional Pico Bonito**. The easiest way to visit this area is to take the road leading through the park, which connects La Ceiba with San José and Olanchito, the other side of the range. This way you can stop off wherever you feel like it, and make short walks into the forest. Near the village of Los Mangos, you'll also find a dramatic 80 m waterfall. Like most Honduran National Parks, Pico Bonito is not well developed yet. Most parts are inaccessible to any but expert hikers and climbers. Contact the COHDEFOR office (tel 42 0800) for the latest on park developments. The office is outside town, in the Barrio Buenos Aires.

GETTING TO AND FROM LA CEIBA

By Air
The Aeropuerto Golosón is about 10 km outside town, so it's best to take a taxi to get there. Arriving here by air, the taxis are much cheaper if you walk to the main highway, where many await passengers. The fare should be less than US$1. If coming from Tela and heading straight for the islands, you could ask to be dropped off at the airport, since the bus drives right past it. There are so many flights that you are bound to get a ticket there and then.

There are at least six flights daily to Roatán, between 7 and 4, and at least four daily to Guanaja and Utila. **Isleña Airlines**, tel 43 0179/2739, has its office on the main square, next to Taca. Fares to the islands are between US$10 and US$20 one-way.

By Bus
The **bus terminal** is located about a kilometre outside town, on the road to the airport. Taxis are the best way to arrive and leave, though remember the fare should be less than US$1. There are regular daily buses to Tela, Trujillo, San Pedro Sula, Tegucigalpa, Olanchito, and local villages around La Ceiba.

By Boat to the Bay Islands
The service is so erratic that it is hardly worth bothering with, and it is almost impossible to find out when a boat will sail. The official place to enquire is the **Capitanía del Puerto**. There are also boats to ports on the Mosquitia, though the same applies: you will need lots of time, patience, and you still might not get a passage.

TOURIST INFORMATION
There is no official tourist information office in the city, but the **Caribbean Travel Agency**, Avenida San Isidro, tel 43 1360, has very efficient staff, who speak excellent English, and can help with all travel enquiries, whether for tours or flights to the islands. Ask for Ann Crichton.

WHERE TO STAY

MODERATE

The **Gran Hotel París**, tel 43 2371, fax 43 2391, on the main square, is the largest hotel in the city. However, it lives off its reputation as the top hotel, and has certainly seen better days. The only advantage now is the pool. Tax is added. **El Colonial**, Avenida 14 de Julio 6–7 Calle, tel 43 1953, fax 43 1955, is a spotless hotel of much higher standard. All rooms have air-conditioning, TV and private bath. Tax is added. **Hotel Iberia**, Avenida San Isidro 5–6 Calle, tel 43 0401, is excellent value for large, clean rooms, with air-conditioning and private bath. **Gran Hotel Ceiba**, 5 Calle and Avenida San Isidro, tel 43 2737, is a popular hotel with restaurant and bar.

INEXPENSIVE

The best choice is **La Isla**, tel 43 2835, which is at the eastern end of 4 Calle, the other side of the Estero canal. It's about ten minutes walk from the centre of town, but the location is very quiet, and you won't find a nicer place in this price range. There are many budget hotels along the railway track and near the market, but the rooms are really horrible.

EATING OUT AND NIGHTLIFE

Other than the restaurants in the hotels, the top eating venue in the city is **Ricardo's**, Avenida 14 Julio, near the cathedral. It has a rather pretentious atmosphere, but the food is good and expensive. Just around the corner, behind the cathedral, is a recommended Chinese restaurant, called the **Palace**. If you enjoy pizzas, you should definitely try **Pizzeria Italiana**, on the Avenida la República, which follows the railway track through the city. These could well be the best pizzas in the country. For Honduran meals, including the delicious *anafre* (fried been paste), make for **La Carreta**, on 4 Calle and 2 Avenida, near the canal. The restaurant is open-air, so always pleasantly cool.

Other than these, there are many fast-food and snack-type restaurants, along the railway, around the market, and on the streets leading to and along the seafront. This is also where you will find the bars, which make no concessions to foreign tastes. **Cric Cric Burgers** is one of the nicest places to drink, and there are three around the city centre, one very close to the seafront. They are open-air, have music and cold beers, and stay open until 3 am. If you want something more energetic, try the **Black and White Disco**, which is off 4 Calle, the other side of the canal.

USEFUL INFORMATION

Exchange: There are plenty of banks between the main square and the market, especially on Avenida San Isidro.

HONDUTEL and the **post office** are next door to each other, one block east of the market, towards the Estero canal.

Trujillo

A small town 196 km east of La Ceiba, this is a tranquil place located on a gorgeous bay of white sandy beaches. It's the last town before the inaccessible Mosquitia jungles, so not often visited, and remains an insider's tip for those who really want to relax for a while.

This is the end of the road, and it feels like it too, though it wasn't always like that. Once Trujillo was an important colonial town, in fact it was the first in Honduras, founded in 1525. Columbus was one of the first arrivals, in 1502, when he and his crew celebrated the first Christian Mass in Central America here, more than 20 years before the spot was settled. The Spanish colonists soon built tough fortifications here to protect their shipments of gold from Olancho. But pirates regularly attacked the ships, and the Spanish had to build three forts to fight them off with heavy cannon fire. In the 19th century, the American soldier of fortune William Walker also passed this way. He was a notorious adventurer, and had plans to seize power in the entire region. Unfortunately for him, he was captured by the authorities, who executed him in Trujillo in 1860, where his remains were buried in the local cemetery.

The ruined forts and cannons strewn at odd angles are the only reminders of Trujillo's colonial past. The most dramatic thing nowadays is the view. The magnificent bay curves in a perfect arc, with modern Puerto Castilla at its northerly point. Looking inland, you see dense forests clinging to steep hills and mountains. An excursion worth doing while you're here is to the Garifuna village of **Santa Fé**, accessible by bus from Trujillo. As always, the village is situated on a beautiful beach. It takes about two hours to walk back along the beach.

GETTING TO TRUJILLO
There are buses from San Pedro Sula, Tela and La Ceiba. There is also public transport to San Esteban and Juticalpa.

WHERE TO STAY
MODERATE
The best place to stay is the **Villas Brinkley**, tel 44 4444, fax 44 4045, which is situated high above the town, with bird's-eye views of the entire Trujillo Bay. Rooms are built around a pool, restaurant and sunny courtyard. The hotel also offers tours to the Mosquitia and surrounding area. In the town itself, the largest hotel is the overpriced **El Colonial**, which offers double rooms with private bath.

INEXPENSIVE
Much better value for what you get is **El Emperador**, which has rooms with private bath and fan. **Hotel Trujillo** is also good value, and charges the same prices as El Emperador.

EATING OUT
There is excellent fried fish to be had at **Belsy's**, which is right on the beach, and is also the best bar, owned by a friendly Englishman. Walking along the beach, you will find many other restaurants and bars as well. Once you've eaten on the beach you won't want to eat anywhere else, but if you feel like a change, the best restaurant in town is the **Granada**. The pizzas at the **Pantry** are not very good. Even if you're not staying at the **Villas Brinkley**, you could still eat at the restaurant there, and enjoy the great views. It takes about 20 mins to walk up the steep hill, but it is worth it.

The Back Road to the Capital

An alternative to returning to Tegucigalpa along the coast is to travel south, through eastern Honduras, via the towns of San Esteban, San Francisco de la Paz, and Juticalpa (429 km). This can easily be done in one day (around 10 hrs), and offers an interesting tour of the country's remoter areas. The route leading south from Trujillo is by good dirt road, and although the drive is long and hard, it is one of the most scenic the country has to offer. As you leave the humid greenery of the Caribbean, you slowly climb up into the mountains, past dwellings made of wattle and thatch, animals wandering in the road, and *campesinos* going about their daily chores. The forest is damp cloud forest at first, sadly burnt down almost everywhere here, and later you come into rocky pine country. The largest settlement you pass in this region is San Esteban, a poor place of mud houses and dirt roads, situated on a large highland plain. After about 6 hours you reach the town of Juticalpa, a busy market town, with little to justify a stopover, and then another 3 hours by paved highway takes you to Tegus, and back to 'civilization'.

Large minibuses leave Trujillo for Juticalpa every other day at 4 am, departing just off the main square. Alternatively, go to the nearby town of Tocoa, where more frequent services operate to Juticalpa. The bus will drop you at the main bus terminal in Juticalpa, where you must change for transport to the capital. From Juticalpa, there are also buses to distant places in eastern Honduras, such as Catacamas and Dulce Nombre de Culmí. A dirt road is being built from Dulce Nombre de Culmí to connect with the only road in the Mosquitia jungle, serving the settlements of Ahuasbila, Leimus and coastal Puerto Lempira. However, there is no public transport, and you will have to hitchhike if heading into the jungle this way. There is also no accommodation, except with local people. If you wish to try this route, make sure it is during the months of March to May, when there is less chance of roads being washed out by rain.

Olancho and the Mosquitia

Eastern Honduras is the least visited part of the country, by virtue of the fact that most of the region is inaccessible, or has no commercial accommodation. You will see on the map that the eastern department of Olancho has very few roads, and most of those are not paved. In your own four-wheel transport with camping gear, you could get well off the beaten track here, and the landscape of windswept plateaus, mountains, and occasional pine forests is certainly impressive. It's a lonely, rather barren area, and very sparsely populated, but if you enjoy the kind of atmosphere that generates, you will not be disappointed.

To the northeast, there are no roads at all (except the one connecting Puerto Lempira with Leimus and Ahuasbila on the Río Coco), since the country is covered by impenetrable jungles, known as the Mosquitia. Traditionally this area was inhabited by Miskito Indians and other tribes, but in recent decades the Contra War with Nicaragua has resulted in both soldiers and refugees living here, and they are still present in spite of repatriation programmes. Gold and mineral prospectors, as well as landless squatters, have made inroads along the coast and up rivers, and life has a rough, frontier character to it, where death comes easily. Diseases such as malaria and dysentery are common, so if you do choose to travel here, be sure to take the appropriate medicines, as well as mosquito repellent and a torch for when there is no electricity. There is also a heavy military presence, in particular in Mocorón, southwest of Puerto Lempira, so make sure your papers are in good order.

Probably the most rewarding area to visit in the Mosquitia is the **Río Plátano Reserve**, west of Brus Laguna. This is a beautiful jungle area, which can be visited by *cayuco*, travelling up the River Plátano, and camping in the forest. There are tours to this area, which is undoubtedly the best way to visit if you have no experience in planning jungle journeys. Contact René at the Tunkul Bar in Copán Ruinas, or the recommended tour agencies listed in the capital (see p. 261), or **Cambio C.A.**, Apdo. Postal no. 2, Trujillo, tel 44 4044, fax 44 4045. The last specializes in adventurous 'ecotours' in northeastern Honduras. For example, there are trips to remote beaches east of Trujillo, or a week's tour along the River Patuca, which runs through the Mosquitia jungles. For the jungle tour, prices are US$650 per person if there is a group of seven to twelve people, US$975 per person if there are only two to three people.

Travel in the Mosquitia is by air or along the rivers, and the only towns with basic hotels are Puerto Lempira and Brus Laguna, both accessible by air from the capital or La Ceiba. In other settlements you must ask around for people who rent out rooms, who are often missionaries or relief workers. There are also weekly sailings to Brus Laguna and Puerto Lempira from La Ceiba. Check with the port authorities there to find out if any boats are leaving, and expect to spend a day or two getting there. Whichever way you choose to travel in the Mosquitia, it will be expensive and time-consuming, and not for the faint-hearted—if you come here you are going to be roughing it. The best time to visit the region is during the 'dry season', from March to May.

THE BAY ISLANDS

There are three important islands strewn off the mainland coast, at a distance of around 48 km. The closest and smallest is Utila. Northeast lies Roatán, the largest island, and east of that, lies petite Guanaja. Together they make up the major tourist attraction of Honduras, and although they are still less well known than other Caribbean islands, more and more people are discovering their attractions, in particular the spectacular diving.

Each island has its own distinct character: Utila is a small, swampy island, favoured by budget travellers, who find cheaper prices here, while the diving can match the rest of the region. Roatán, on the other hand, is a long, mountainous island, which offers not only the best beaches, but also dramatic drives on dirt roads, tropical forests, and settlements with a good selection of hotels, restaurants and diving facilities. Its neighbour, Guanaja, is different again: a small, mountainous island, covered in steaming forest that hides exotic waterfalls and pools. There are lovely beaches here too, hidden away around the coast, accessible only by boat. Some of the most exclusive hotels are located here, and the island caters primarily to up-market tourism.

The inhabitants of the Bay Islands are an extraordinary mix of race and culture, being descendants of English and Dutch pirates, black slaves and Garifuna from St Vincent, as well as a smattering of Spanish colonists. The result is a population that is bilingual in English and Spanish, and a culture that is more reminiscent of the West Indies than mainland Central America. In fact, the *isleños*, as they are called, often prefer to think of themselves as English, rather than Honduran, and they certainly regard the mainland as a foreign place. They live close to the sea, usually in wooden houses on stilts to escape the sandflies and mosquitoes that infest the beaches whenever the wind dies down. Insect repellent is always essential here.

Historically the islands have played an important role throughout the colonial era. Columbus was the first to arrive here from the Old World, landing on Guanaja in 1502, when he set a precedent for times to come by capturing an ocean-going Maya canoe. In those days, the islands were inhabited by Maya Indians, but their population was soon reduced by slavery, war and disease, and none remain today. They were replaced by African slaves, who worked on the fruit plantations, and settlements of British, Dutch and French pirates, who made an excellent living raiding Spanish galleons bound for Europe with gold and other precious goods. The war between Britain and Spain, in 1625, gave the pirates a good opportunity to establish themselves while the colonial authorities were busy in battles of their own, and the famous pirate, Henry Morgan, was based at Port Royal, on Roatán. The king even rewarded him for his attacks on the Spanish fleet, but the British never held on to the islands for very long, finally ceding them to the Honduran government in 1859.

GETTING TO THE BAY ISLANDS

By Air

The fastest and most convenient way to reach any of the islands is by air. Roatán has an international airport, and incoming flights to Tegucigalpa and San Pedro Sula often have connections to the islands. Otherwise the standard place to fly from is the coastal city of La Ceiba, where the Honduran airlines Isleña and Sosa make frequent trips back and forth on a daily basis. You don't usually need to book tickets in advance, but to be sure, buy the day before travelling.

Flights from La Ceiba to **Utila** leave at 6 and 4 daily, with Isleña, and there are more departures with Sosa. Flights to **Guanaja** also leave at 6 and 4, daily. Flights to **Roatán** leave daily at 7, 8, 10 am, 12 noon, 2, and 4. Journey times are around 30 minutes. The cheapest ticket is to Utila at US$21 return. Return flights to Roatán are US$33, to Guanaja US$41. Please note, however, that prices are bound to increase as the islands become ever more popular tourist destinations.

By Boat

There are boats between the mainland and the islands, but their schedules are so erratic that it is not worth your time to pursue this form of transport. If you cannot afford the flight ticket, you will probably not like the prices on the islands either, which are some of the highest you'll find in Honduras. However, there are plans to establish a regular ferry service, and the best place to enquire about it is at the **Caribbean Travel Agency**, Avenida San Isidro, La Ceiba, tel and fax 43 1360.

DIVING OFF THE BAY ISLANDS

Equipment

Almost all equipment can be hired locally, though the experienced diver should note that firms often only provide cylinder and air without a backpack or harness. They do provide weightbelt and weights. The best kind of clothing for diving in these parts is a light-weight, lycra body suit, and if snorkelling, you might want to bring surf shoes to protect against cuts from coral.

Safety Precautions and Diving Code

See p. 202.

Utila

Utila is the closest island to the mainland but the least attractive physically. A small, flat island, there is just one narrow beach, and the rest of the shoreline is swamp, making sunbathing an unattractive proposition, especially because of the maddening sandflies. It is therefore not the island itself you come here for, but the cheap accommodation and diving facilities, and the beauty of the underwater world all around. The atmosphere on the island is also very friendly, and there are a number of good bars, popular with easy-going travellers on a tight budget. There is a disco every Saturday night, and regular weekend beach parties on the island's only beach.

Planes land on a dirt airstrip, from where you can easily walk into the main settlement on the island. There is just one sandy road, that stretches for almost five kilometres, and makes up the main drag of life on Utila. Here you will find mostly wooden buildings on stilts, built over the swampy land all about you. Facilities on the island include banks and a post office.

WHERE TO STAY

EXPENSIVE

Trudy's Hotel, tel 45 3195, is the most up-market place to stay on the island. For the price, however, you can do better on Roatán, which has a more attractive landscape.

MODERATE

Captain Spencer, tel 45 3162, whose charges are in the middle of this price bracket, is the only other 'fancy' place to stay.

INEXPENSIVE

The most popular budget place to stay is **Cross Creek**, which also offers four-person bungalows. Note that electricity on the island is cut from midnight to 6 am, often making nights unbearably hot because the fans cannot work. There are quite a few other cheap places to stay and you should have no trouble finding a house to rent if planning to stay for longer periods.

EATING OUT
Orma's Restaurant and **Manhattan Restaurant** are recommended for good cheap food. **Irman's Restaurant** has good seafood.

ACTIVITIES
There are ever more diving facilities on the island, and it is possible to get your diving certification here, costing around US$250. The Dutchman at Cross Creek takes people diving, but there are others who are reputed to be safer. The best option is to ask around. You can also take boat and snorkelling trips to small cayes off the Utila coast. However long you plan to stay, remember to bring plenty of sunscreen and insect repellent.

Roatán

Roatán is the largest of the Bay Islands, 54 km long but never more than 5 km wide, with a mountainous interior, rising up to 240 m above sea level. Most of the population live along the southern shoreline, with the small town of **Coxen Hole** as capital. The tiny international airport is just outside town, a 20-minute walk away, or a short taxi ride, which should cost no more than US$1. It is the nicest town on the island, with the widest choice of hotels and restaurants, as well as providing facilities such as a supermarket, banks, post office and travel agents.

By far the best beaches are by the village of **West End**, and unless you're staying in a secluded resort hotel, this is the ideal place to stay. Access is easy, since minibuses regularly connect between Coxen Hole and West End during the day. Just before you reach the village of West End, you pass **Sandy Bay**, which is a misnomer, since there are no beaches here, but there is the excellent hotel of **Anthony's Key Resort**, with its adjacent dolphin enclosure, worth visiting in its own right.

At West End you will find one of the loveliest beaches in the Caribbean, namely **West Bay**. The beach is uninhabited and everything you could possibly wish for: fine white sand slopes gently into turquoise waters, while the shore line is fringed by shading palm trees. It is possible to swim to the reef from here, so worth bringing snorkel equipment. Access is either by motorboat from West End village (ask at **Foster's**), which costs around US$3 return. Or you can walk for 40 minutes along the beach, a beautiful way to get there.

Heading along the island's only road, east, you come to the small town of **French Harbour**, a 20-minute bus ride from Coxen Hole. This is an important shrimp port, but has nothing to recommend it to the visitor. Dirty and dilapidated, the only two havens are the **French Harbour Hotel**, which has great views of the sea and harbour, and the **Buccaneer Hotel**, which has an attractive waterside location. Further east still, along a bumpy dirt road that twists along the high eastern ridges of the island, you eventually come to the port of **Oak Ridge**. The views along the way are spectacular, and often you can see both the northern and southern shore of the island and admire the changing colours of the sea. The coast is often very jagged, with many small bays and lagoons only accessible by boat, steep hills rising up behind them.

Oak Ridge itself is a festering little place, its waters shining with the rainbow colours of floating petrol. Its stilted wooden houses, built over the water, are picturesque enough, but the attraction is the journey there and not the destination. There is one good hotel located on a small caye beyond the harbour, and the diving is said to be excellent this side of the island. Minibuses reach all the way to Oak Ridge, but it's faster to hitchhike, preferably in an open pick-up, so that you can get the best of the great views from the road.

TOURIST INFORMATION
There is no official tourist office, but there is some information at the airport, and the travel agents in Coxen Hole should be able to advise you as well. Should you wish to try your luck with boats leaving Roatán, contact the port authorities in Coxen Hole, near the main square. There is supposed to be a boat leaving for La Ceiba every Sunday, which charges around US$8. There are banks here, as well as a post office and plenty of shops.

WHERE TO STAY AND EATING OUT
All the main settlements offer a variety of accommodation, and there are also some very exclusive hide-away hotels dotted around the island's coastline. Most hotels have restaurants attached, and there are usually places to eat and drink in the towns and villages. Prices have been listed in detail as they are often higher than our categories, but please remember they can only be a general guide, with increases regular on this popular island.

In West End
The largest hotel is the fairly simple **Lost Paradise Inn**, tel 45 1306, fax 45 1388, which has beach cabins or rooms in the main building, with fan and private bath, and a good restaurant attached. Doubles go for US$20. A resort-style hotel, 10 minutes' walk from the village is the **Seagrape Plantation Resort**, tel 45 1428, which is very friendly, with private cabins and a restaurant. But there is no beach here, only very sharp coral. Rooms with meals included cost US$50 singles, US$40 doubles, and US$35 triple, all prices per person and plus tax. Rooms only cost US$20 singles, US$30 doubles, US$40 triples. Beautiful wooden beach cabins are rented out by **Foster's and Vivian's**, with prices starting as low as US$4 each, and going up to US$20 each, depending on location and facilities. They also run a glass-bottomed boat that heads for the reef daily at 10 am and 2 pm.

One of the most popular inexpensive hotels by the village is **Robert's Hill Hotel**, which charges US$4 for singles and US$6 for doubles. The **Islandia** is not good value, with stuffy rooms and no fans, US$8 for two. **Rooms** are also rented out by various local families, and some of the best are with Mrs Zoe Jeffrey, who lives behind the local church, near the beach. Double rooms with private bath cost US$8 for two.

The most popular place to socialize is **Foster's**, which is built out over the water, and not only offers a bar and restaurant, but also hammocks to laze away the evenings in. If you want to eat at the **Lost Paradise** you have to book in advance if you're not a guest. On the beach, an overpriced but tasty pizza and pasta place is the **New York Bar**, while if you feel like *comedor*-type meals, head for **Chino's**, in the middle of the village.

In Sandy Bay

Very close to West End, this is a small settlement where you will find the glamorous **Anthony's Key Resort**, tel 45 1003, fax 45 1140, which charges US$110 for singles, and US$100 per person for doubles, plus tax. The resort hotel is entirely self-contained, wooden cabins built discreetly into the lush hillside overlooking a small bay. There are also cabins on a small island in the bay, just a stone's throw from the mainland. Facilities for diving and watersports are excellent, and an added attraction is the neighbouring dolphin enclosure, where visitors get to swim with these friendly mammals. A scientific research station, this is a good place to learn something about dolphins, and the conditions for the animals is as decent as the staff can make it.

In Coxen Hole

The only place worth recommending here is the **Caye View Hotel**, tel 45 1202, which is overpriced at singles for US$17–US$23, doubles US$26–US$29. Next door is the cheaper **El Paso**, which is simple and reasonable at US$6 for singles and US$8 for doubles. The restaurant at the Caye View Hotel is all right, and there are a few small snack places along the high street.

In French Harbour

On the way to French Harbour, about 12 km east of Coxen Hole, the island's most exclusive resort hotel hides on a private 15-acre island just off the mainland. Any facility you could wish for is provided here. It is appropriately called **Fantasy Island Beach Resort**, tel 45 1191, fax 45 1268, and singles are US$80, doubles US$60 and triples US$50, all prices per person, plus tax.

A friendly, American-owned hotel, catering mainly to yachtsmen who anchor at French Harbour, is the **French Harbour Yacht Club**, tel 45 1478, fax 45 1459. Singles are US$23–US$30, doubles are US$28–US$35, triples are US$31–US$38, plus tax. On the waterfront is the **Buccaneer**, tel 45 1032, fax 45 1036, which offers very well-kept rooms but no beach, though its waterside location is quite attractive. Singles are around US$25, doubles US$37. Not far from here you will also find the **Dixon Plaza**, tel 45 1317, which charges US$12–US$18 for singles and US$18–US$22 for doubles. There is a good restaurant attached, and this is your only choice unless you want rock-bottom grubbiness.

In Oak Ridge

While there is no place to stay in the port itself, not that you would want to, there is an attractive resort hotel located on a caye outside the harbour, looking out to sea. The **Reef House Resort Hotel**, tel 45 2297/2142, charges US$65 per person, all meals included, plus tax. If you want to be somewhere very quiet, with diving facilities available if required, this is a good place to come. Accommodation is in simple *cabañas*, and a small pool has been formed by blocking off the sea, right in front of the hotel. You are very much marooned here, and there are no other places to eat or drink or socialize.

ACTIVITIES

If you're not staying at one of the resort hotels the best place for diving certification courses is at West End village. A four-day course costs US$300. A resort course, which gives non-certified divers a chance to find out what scuba diving is all about, costs US$50, and includes one dive. A regular dive for certified divers costs US$21, a night dive US$26 plus batteries. Pay a visit to **Roatán Divers**, tel 45 1255, at the entrance of West End village.

Guanaja

Guanaja holds a special place among the Bay Islands, not only for its historic importance, but also for the variety it has to offer as an island. The locals boast that theirs is the most beautiful island of all, and it's difficult to argue with them. Not only are there secluded bays and inlets around the coast, but inland you find humid tropical jungle as well as pine groves, a dramatic hilly landscape and some beautiful waterfalls near the northern shore. There are no roads on the island, and the only way to get around is on foot or horseback, or more commonly, by boat. The capital of the island is known as **Bonacca**, and has the interesting feature of being built over the water, with swaying pontoons connecting house boats. It likes to advertise itself as the 'Venice of Honduras' but the floating houses and resident boats are much more like a floating gypsy camp, with quite a few foreign 'yachties' and maritime wanderers, who have washed up here permanently. Unfortunately, cheap accommodation is hard to find, and if you really want to stay here on a tight budget, you should try renting a room with a local family. Just ask around. Facilities on the island include banks and little else, though you should be able to get all you need at your hotel.

WHERE TO STAY
Most of the resort hotels are tucked away around the island, and only accessible by boat. If you book with them, they should be able to collect you from the airport. The top resort, in terms of price, is the **Posada del Sol**, tel 45 4311, which offers everything from tennis courts and a swimming pool, to certification diving courses, private beach and excursions. Rooms are in a beautiful house, built like a Spanish villa. Singles are US$132, doubles US$264, plus tax. More rustic, but just as beautiful in its own way, is the **Bayman Bay Club**, tel 43 0457, which offers wooden cottages set among the seaside forest, which rises above a gorgeous beach nearby. All diving activities are catered for here. Singles are US$115, doubles US$230, plus tax.

Other than these two star attractions, there are a number of other hotels, only slightly cheaper. **Alexander**, tel 45 4326, offers spacious accommodation for US$100 singles, US$125 doubles. **El Rosario**, tel 45 4240, charges US$90 singles, and US$100 doubles. **Casa sobre El Mar**, tel 45 4180, has rooms for US$75 singles, and US$150 doubles. And finally, **Miller** is the cheapest hotel, at US$60 for singles and US$70 for doubles.

EATING AND DRINKING OUT
The only place you will find bars and restaurants outside the main hotels is in Bonacca. **Harbour Light** and **The Nest** are recommended and **Glenda's** has good, cheap meals.

THE PACIFIC LITTORAL

Southern Honduras looks like a crumpled piece of parchment: brown, treeless hills crease a barren landscape—the legacy of unrestricted deforestation and the excessive use of pesticides. Near the coast, the landscape becomes flat and is covered in thorny shrubs. Even prior to 20th-century destruction, this was not a very fertile land, but today it is one of the poorest areas in the country. Cattle farming and agriculture form the mainstay of the local economy, but many people have left for the capital, and the area is severely underpopulated.

The climate is oppressively hot, and temperatures of 35–40 degrees Celcius are not uncommon, with winds sweeping blinding clouds of dust across the countryside. The coolest period is from June to September, when the rainy season turns the roads to sludge, but at least there is less dust.

For the traveller this area of Honduras has the least to offer, and most only pass this way when heading for the Salvadorean or Nicaraguan borders, at either end of the Pan-American Highway. The only large town is **Choluteca**, which has its origins in the 16th-century first colonial settlement here, while coastal **San Lorenzo** has the country's main Pacific port. There is one place which is worth visiting, however, and that is the island of **El Tigre**, set in the peaceful waters of the Gulf of Fonseca. There are also a few attractive beaches which are best visited on day trips from Choluteca, since there is no acceptable accommodation available in the villages there.

Public transport from Tegus to the two international borders is frequent, and there is also a daily connection to Tigre Island, though it is not possible to return the same day. The only decent accommodation is in Choluteca, and if you stay anywhere else, you will only find basic refuge, ranging from straw mats on the ground to ancient beds in disused hotels. Tigre Island no longer has any functioning hotels, but a few people rent out rooms. For information on transport to the region see p. 256, where the capital's bus terminals are listed.

Choluteca and Around

Capital of the southeastern department by the same name, Choluteca is one of the oldest colonial towns in the country. The first Spanish settlement here was established in 1535, though the town was not officially founded until 1825. Some 18th- and 19th-century architecture still remains—one of the most attractive buildings being the former church on the Plaza de la Merced, which is now the **Casa de Cultura**. Choluteca's importance today is as a cattle-farming centre, but historically it has always held strategic importance in Honduran claims to the Gulf of Fonseca. Both Nicaragua and El Salvador have made claims on the region over the centuries.

An interesting time to be here is from November to February, when thousands of migratory birds pass this way, filling the streets with deafening noise. For the rest of the year, white doves roost in the trees, popular with local hunters. The only other time of year the town gets any excitement is during its annual festival, starting on 8 December.

If you decide to stay here, there are a few excursions you can go on. The most popular take you to the Pacific beaches of **Cedeño** and **Punto Ratón**, accessible by bus from Choluteca, with journeys taking around two hours. The latter is less convenient to reach,

297

but the beach is the more attractive. In either case, you should try to avoid having to stay overnight, since shelter is very primitive and outrageously expensive. There are some shacks offering food and drink, but you may prefer to bring your own provisions. Another place worth visiting is **San Marcos de Colón**, on the road to the Nicaraguan border. High up in the mountains, the views of the Gulf of Fonseca are terrific, and the old colonial town itself is attractive as well.

WHERE TO STAY

INEXPENSIVE
In Choluteca itself, the best place to stay is the **Hotel Pierre**, Avenida Valle and Calle Williams, tel 82 0525. Just outside town, on the road to Guasaule, is the **Hotel Camino Real**, tel 82 0630. And on the Pan-American Highway, in the Barrio Los Mangos, is the **Hotel La Fuente**, tel 82 0263, which has a swimming pool attached. There are also quite a few budget hotels, so you should have no trouble finding somewhere to stay here. Facilities in town include banks, a post office and travel agents. Places to eat and drink are ranged around the main square and near the market.

Towards the Nicaraguan Border

The only functioning border crossing in this region is via El Espino, northeast of Choluteca. Direct buses go there from Tegus, as well as from Choluteca. Usually transport between Choluteca and the border is by minibus or shared taxi. The border is open 8–4, daily.

El Tigre Island

Once **Amapala** on Tigre Island was a thriving port, and if you look at the 2-lempira note, you will see its picture, which is still true to the view you find today, even if many of the buildings are abandoned. San Lorenzo's port has taken all life and sustenance away from here and there are hardly any people left, except for the Honduran Marines, who are stationed outside town. The locals make a meagre living from fishing, or working on the mainland, but many have left altogether, abandoning their homes to rot quickly.

Along with Choluteca, Amapala was one of the first colonial settlements, reached by Spanish expeditioners in 1522, who were making their way up from Panamá looking for gold or Indians to enslave. The island is just a short distance from the mainland, and its extinct volcano rises 783 m above the Gulf of Fonseca, offering great views from its cone, which is easily climbed. There is just one dirt road that threads around the base of the mountain, and in a vehicle—if there were any—it would take no more than half an hour to encircle the island.

It is the atmosphere that makes this forgotten place so magnetic. Crumbling colonial buildings line the seafront, weeds growing through their decaying walls, while more recent houses of wood or concrete are hardly less dilapidated, ragged curtains fluttering through broken windows. The mud and cobbled streets are strangely quiet, and silent inhabitants stare as you walk by. Only a few children and the odd stray pig make any noise at all, and a sense of emptiness sits oppressively on Amapala.

You can escape the ghostly atmosphere by walking out to the beach (**Playa Grande**), which is not beautiful, being narrow and of black volcanic sand, but at least the stillness here is natural, and the sunsets can be spectacularly orange and red. A small shack sells beers, but there is nowhere to stay here, except with a local family that rents out a small house. Not far away is the **Sirena Cave**, where the adventurer Francis Drake is said to have left hidden treasure in 1578. Nobody has found anything yet.

GETTING TO EL TIGRE

Just one ancient bus a day leaves the capital for Amapala on El Tigre Island. **CHE** buses leave from the Mercado Belén at 11 am daily, and the journey takes around 4 hours to Coyolito, on the island of Zacate Grande, connected by causeway with the mainland. From Coyolito, you continue by motorboat for a short journey of less than half an hour. The return journey starts daily at the unpalatable hours of 2–3 am, when boats take you to the mainland, for the bus that leaves for Tegus at 4 am. If you miss this bus, a few morning buses leave for San Lorenzo, from where there are more frequent services to the capital. If you are unfortunate enough to be the only passenger needing a boat ride, you will be charged at least US$5.

WHERE TO STAY

Accommodation in Amapala has now been reduced to one defunct hotel by the pier, which nevertheless still rents out the remaining beds, and the greatly preferable private room available from **Mrs Marianna Andrades**, whose house is also on the waterfront, a short walk to the right of the pier. The hotel offers a bed with no sheets, in a room with blown-out windows, and the washing facilities constitute a bucket of water. However long you choose to stay, insect repellent is absolutely essential, in particular during the night.

EATING OUT

As you might expect, facilities are minimal (though there is still a bank on the main square). A popular kiosk selling snacks and beers is right by the pier, and otherwise there are one or two places around the main square. In any case, you will not find much more than hamburgers, eggs and beans to eat.

Towards the Salvadorean Border

The main highway leading south from the capital climbs over a mountainous region, and then descends onto the Pacific plain, where the first large town is **Nacaome**, reached by turning west at Jícaro Galán. This is also the direction to take for the Salvadorean border post of **El Amatillo**, which closes at 5 daily. Direct buses leave from Tegus. See p. 256 for the location of the bus terminal and departure times.

Part VII
EL SALVADOR

CUIDADO CON EL CYCLISTO
PODRIA SER SU HERMANO

"TAKE CARE OF THE CYCLIST, HE MAY BE YOUR BROTHER"

Tucked into the underbelly of Central America El Salvador is the isthmus's smallest and most troubled nation. It's a country full of surprises; blessed with astonishing beauty but cursed by a decade of violence. The 11-year civil war, which came to a halt in 1991, left 75,000 dead and made the country seem synonymous with death squads, roadside executions and military governments. However, following the UN-sponsored peace agreement, El Salvador is once again a viable destination. If the peace holds then this tiny country, covering just 21,000 square kilometres, will offer new and interesting possibilities for visitors to Central America.

The first thing to strike visitors to El Salvador is the country's delicate beauty. For those expecting to see bomb craters and burnt-out cars, a landscape of supreme fertility is perhaps a little shocking. A string of volcanoes run through the length of the country, forming a spiky backbone and creating a series of high, lush green valleys. Scattered among them are a handful of crater lakes ringed by steep, forested hills and harbouring the ingredients of an excellent crab soup. The country's other scenic attributes include beaches that offer the best surf on the isthmus, and huge pine forests in the dry mountains of the north.

El Salvador is also the most densely populated nation in Central America, packing in a population of just over five million. People squeeze into the markets, fill the streets and cram the buses, often spilling out of the doors and overflowing onto the roofs. But these are no ordinary people and, wherever you go, meeting them is one of the great delights of travelling here. Their enthusiasm and energy are all the more astonishing given the circumstances. Jumbling together a handful of English words, Salvadoreans greet outsiders with tremendous warmth. And compared to most Central Americans they're

300

tremendously courteous, offering help and assistance at every turn—a blessing for women travellers, many of whom find El Salvador the easiest country to explore.

For the moment El Salvador remains battered and bruised; a long history of earthquakes, the most recent in 1986, has reduced most colonial architecture to dust, while the civil war left much of the country's infrastructure cracked and crumbling. The country's volcanic soils are ideal for the growth of coffee, which is still the basis of the economy, although El Salvador is also the most industrialized country on the isthmus, supplying Central America with a wide range of basic goods, from clothing to machetes. The economy was badly hit by civil strife and went into decline in the 1980s. This, combined with the desperate human rights situation, persuaded millions of Salvadoreans to leave the country in search of work.

El Salvador doesn't have much to offer in the way of luxury and has few conventional sights, but it does have an unmistakable charm, and if you're tired of Guatemala's tourist overkill then El Salvador is the ideal antidote.

Post-Independence History

In less than two hundred years El Salvador has transformed itself from a forgotten colonial backwater into the most industrialized and war-torn nation on the isthmus. Sadly, repression lies at the very heart of the nation's history and for most of this century Salvadoreans have been sliding towards civil war.

Under colonial rule El Salvador languished in provincial obscurity. With virtually no mineral wealth it attracted only a handful of Spanish settlers, and it wasn't until the early 19th century and the eve of Independence that the country began to rank alongside its larger neighbours, as cattle farming and indigo production boosted the economy and San Salvador emerged as the second city of the colonial captaincy.

The Rocky Road to Independence

Salvadoreans are proud of their country's role in the struggle for Central American independence, even though they were tossed around by the larger players, only settling into nationhood once the grand schemes had foundered. Nevertheless it was here that Spanish rule in Central America faced its first challenge. In 1811, an unsuccessful revolt was led by a local priest, José Matías Delgado, who remains a national hero. A second revolt was staged in 1814, but it wasn't until 1839 that El Salvador, having been first claimed by Mexico and then embraced by the United Provinces of Central America, finally emerged as an independent republic.

The country's early years set a pattern that was repeated through its history. The first government, headed by the commander of the Salvadorean army, was installed by the Guatemalans. All of the early administrations faced small uprisings and by the end of the century two presidents had been assassinated and five ousted in military coups, as Honduras and Guatemala fought for control of the republic. By the early 20th century things had begun to settle; the Conservative Party emerged as a dominant political force, leaving the country free to develop a solid economic foundation based on the export of coffee. Huge tracts of land were cleared and planted, and thousands of rural peasants thrown off their farms and forced to work on the plantations. Meanwhile the strength of the conservatives ensured that the benefits of the coffee boom reached only a handful of families. It was during this period that the Salvadorean oligarchy took shape, monopolizing the nation's greatest resource and gaining a political and economic stranglehold on the country.

Recession, Dictatorship and Repression

In the 1930s Salvadorean history slipped into the realms of magic realism thanks to the bizarre rule of General Maximiliano Hernández Martínez. This classic Latin American despot combined extremes of eccentricity and brutality. El Salvador's fortunes had taken a serious downturn in 1931, as world recession sent coffee prices plummeting, and the country's increasingly organized working classes responded with a series of demonstrations and strikes, prompting the general to assume control in a military coup.

His approach to government was enlightened but eccentric, relying heavily on the advice of mystics and spiritualists, who used magical formulas to address the nation's problems. A typically odd gesture was his response to a smallpox epidemic, when he had coloured lights strung up in the streets of the capital in the belief that they would halt the spread of the disease. However, his approach to the growing tide of unrest was not so endearing. Revolutionary rumblings had accompanied the onset of recession and matters came to a head in January 1932 when, as the Irazú volcano erupted, rural peasants attacked villages and cities, aiming at the interests of local oligarchs, military outposts and telegraph offices. The official response was swift and unrestrained. Troops were sent into the countryside with orders to slaughter agricultural peasants. They killed until they ran out of bullets, focusing their attention on the country's indigenous population and leaving an estimated 30,000 dead.

Commonly known as the *matanza*, the killing, the massacre forced the Salvadorean opposition deep underground and is regarded as one of the great shaping moments in Salvadorean history, ultimately giving birth to one of the continent's most enduring civil wars and the most tenacious of armed resistance movements.

Postwar developments

Martínez was finally ousted in 1944, but his rule had firmly established the army as a political force and locked it into an alliance with the landowning elite. Throughout the 1950s and 1960s the military was never far from office, either occupying the presidency or whispering in the ears of those who did.

Nevertheless this was a period of economic boom, with enormous expansion in cotton production during the 1950s, and in light industry during the 1960s, largely thanks to the creation of the Central American common market. The boost to revenue enabled the government to make considerable improvements in health, education and housing, easing the pressure for reform. Meanwhile the so-called Fourteen Families, a tight-knit group of wealthy landowners and industrialists, remained unchallenged, dominating the economy without having to dirty their hands in the political arena.

Towards the end of the 1950s the mood changed as Salvadoreans began to shake off the fear which had smothered opposition since the massacre of 1932. Throughout the 1960s the rural opposition developed a fresh momentum and trade unions gained new ground in the modern industrial economy of San Salvador.

The 1970s: Fraud, Protest and Mounting Tension

The 1970s got off to a bad start as the growing tide of political unrest pushed the oligarchy towards extreme measures, paving the way for all-out conflict. In 1969 a futile war with Honduras, the so-called Football War, cost the government more than US$20 million and resulted in around 100,000 Salvadoreans being forced out of Honduras, arriving home to find little prospect of work. Conditions in the countryside were also difficult and by the mid-1970s the demand for change had risen to a clamour. The government responded with increasing severity, repressing protests by students, workers and peasants, and resorting to electoral fraud to win elections in 1972 and 1977. Towards the end of the decade, guerrilla forces began small-scale operations and opposition leaders abandoned all faith in the electoral process. The oligarchy resorted to desperate measures and death squads took a heavy toll among students, labour leaders and peasant organizations.

The 1980s: Civil War

For El Salvador the 1980s was a decade of terror. Once unleashed, the crisis, which had been brewing for 50 years, plumbed unpredictable depths. During eleven years of war the nation suffered some of the most horrifying abuses of human rights. At least 75,000 Salvadoreans died in the conflict, many of them civilians caught in the crossfire; many others were tortured to death by the infamous right-wing death squads. Around 25% of the population were displaced and much of the country left in ruins.

At the end of the 1970s the political situation became increasingly polarized, as the army began to take matters into its own hands and the opposition was inspired by the success of the revolution in Nicaragua. In October 1979 the army staged a military coup and installed a coalition government in a final bid to create some acceptable middle ground. But when the new government began to propose radical measures, including land reform, the army withdrew its support and staged another coup in early 1980, eventually handing the presidency to José Napoleón Duarte of the Christian Democrats. The coup prompted an uprising in San Salvador, which met with brutal repression by the armed forces and tipped the country into civil war.

The opposition responded with a consolidated armed resistance. The Farabundo Martí National Liberation Front (FMLN), a coalition of five different guerrilla movements, declared all-out war on the government, the army and the oligarchy. In its early stages the war appeared to be moving swiftly for the insurgents and by January 1981 the FMLN had launched a 'final offensive' bringing its forces within 15 miles of San Salvador. But early hopes of a Nicaraguan-style takeover were soon dashed. The US government, terrified of the domino effect, pumped military aid into El Salvador throughout the 1980s, to the tune of a million dollars a day, ensuring that the Christian Democrats remained in power.

It was an embarrassing war for the US, but despite repeated atrocities by the army and

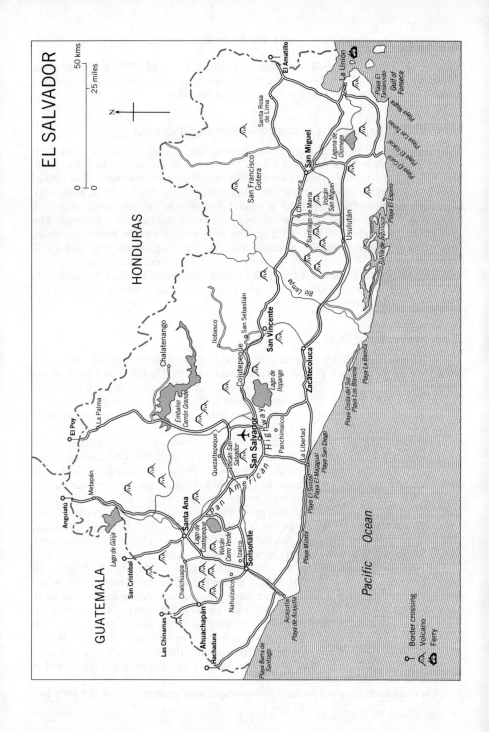

associated death squads (often off-duty soldiers), the US government felt unable to turn its back on the Salvadorean army. Prominent victims of the repression included Archbishop Romero, shot while saying Mass, a group of US nuns and, more recently, six Jesuit priests and their housekeeper who were slaughtered in November 1989. Meanwhile, in the countryside the army responded to the success of the FMLN by terrorizing the local population; this was done by destroying villages, massacring civilians, blanket-bombing and setting fire to forests and crops.

Throughout the conflict, the FMLN managed to control as much as a third of the country, mainly in the north and east. Receiving arms from Cuba and Nicaragua, the group, which has a huge following among the poor and strong links with the trade unions, was regarded as the strongest guerrilla army on the continent. However, despite several large FMLN offensives—the most recent in November 1989 when they gained control of a large section of the capital—the guerrillas failed to break the stalemate and by the end of the decade the two armies appeared to be locked in a war of attrition, which both sides gradually realized they could never win.

Duarte, who had long since become an impotent figurehead, gave up the presidency in 1989 and died of cancer in early 1990. In the elections that followed his resignation the right-wing ARENA party came to power and the FMLN responded by proposing a cease-fire and pushing for peace talks.

1992: Peace?

A UN-sponsored peace agreement was signed by both sides at the end of 1991, formally ending eleven years of fighting. The peace talks, spread over two years, are intended to enable the FMLN to give up the armed struggle and become an active political party, with many of its former fighters forming a new national police force. The agreement also calls for a large reduction in the size of the armed forces and an effective procedure for investigating and prosecuting human rights cases. It remains to be seen if the right-wing will allow this to go ahead, but for the moment the fighting has stopped and both sides wait with bated breath.

General Information

Getting to El Salvador

By Air
From Europe. El Salvador's unenviable reputation has persuaded European airlines to stay away, although strong links with the US ensures daily flights to several North American cities. Return airfares from Europe to San Salvador go for around £550, flying with either American Airlines, via Miami, or Continental, via Houston.

From the US there is a lot more choice with daily flights from Washington, Miami, New Orleans, Los Angeles, San Francisco, New York, Houston, and obviously connections to Canada. **Within Central America** daily flights connect San Salvador with all of the other capitals, as well as Mexico City and a handful of destinations in South America and the Caribbean.

El Salvador's international airport at Cuascatlán is one of the newest, finest and least used in Central America, situated 36 km southwest of the capital, near the town of Comalapa. The old airport at Ilopango, on the eastern edge of the capital, has now been taken over by the military and is highly fortified, although domestic flights still leave from here. There is no bus service from San Salvador to the international airport but pick-ups run a shuttle to and from Comalapa, which is served by regular buses from the capital, or you can take a taxi to or from San Salvador for around US$10–20.

A 10% tax is charged on all plane tickets sold in El Salvador; the departure tax is around US$10 and you have to pay an additional US$5 to get through immigration.

By Bus
A swift and comfortable international bus service connects El Salvador and Guatemala. To and from Honduras you'll have to rely on ramshackle local services.

From Guatemala the route between Guatemala City and San Salvador is covered by former Greyhound buses, serving out retirement in Central America. The service uses the Pan-American Highway and the San Cristóbal border crossing, taking a mere five hours, with departures every hour from 5–5. The route is covered by several companies, the best of which is **Melva y Pezzarossi**, whose office in Guatemala City is at 4a Avenida 1–20, Zona 9, while the others are all within a block or two. In San Salvador all direct buses for Guatemala City leave from the Terminal del Occidente.

You can of course travel between San Salvador and Guatemala on local buses, providing you've plenty of time and energy. These run from San Salvador and Santa Ana to the borders at San Cristóbal, Las Chinamas and Hachadura; the last is also served by buses from Sonsonate. On the Guatemalan side there are frequent buses from all of these borders to the Zona 4 terminal in Guatemala City.

A less direct option is the border crossing at Anguiatú, right up in the northwest corner of El Salvador, which is served by hourly buses from Santa Ana.

From Honduras you have two options: El Poy, which is in the mountains north of San Salvador, and El Amatillo, at the eastern end of the country, which is where the Pan-American Highway crosses into Honduras on its way to Nicaragua. Bus 119 connects the El Amatillo border with the Terminal del Oriente in San Salvador and there are departures in both directions every couple of hours, with the last leaving around 2 pm. The journey from El Poy to San Salvador takes about four hours and is very beautiful, dropping through forested hills with magnificent views of the Cerrón Grande lake and the San Salvador valley, picked out by the perfect cone of the San Salvador volcano. The El Amatillo route is served by a regular flow of buses from San Miguel and from the Terminal del Oriente in San Salvador, as well as minibuses from Santa Rosa de Lima, the last of which leaves at around 6 pm. On the Honduran side there are regular buses between the border and the Mercado Zonal Belén in Tegucigalpa, a journey of around 4 hours.

To and from Nicaragua
If you're heading for Nicaragua then you want to cross the border as early as possible and take the first bus to Choluteca, Honduras, which is about 3 hours from the border and from where you can get a direct bus to San Marcos de Colón, for the El Espino border crossing into Nicaragua, or to Somotillo if you're heading directly to Chinandega and

León in Nicaragua. Either way you need to get an early start to reach Nicaragua the same day. Connections in Choluteca are few and far between and you are likely to end up spending the night in San Marcos.

For the more adventurous there's even a direct route from El Salvador to Nicaragua, by boat across the Gulf of Fonseca. This route used to be served by a couple of roll-on/roll-off ferries but the revolution in Nicaragua prompted the Salvadoreans to sever all links with their 'commie' neighbours. Now that Central America's ideological battle lines are a little more blurred an irregular ferry service is again operating between La Unión in El Salvador and Potosí in Nicaragua. There are boats three or four times a week and immigration offices in both Potosí and La Unión.

Consulates

UK: Flat 9, 3rd floor, Welbeck House, 62 Welbeck Street, London W1, tel (071) 486 8182.
US: 2308 California Street, NW, Washington, DC 20008, tel (202) 265 3480.

Passports and Visas

British citizens do not need visas to enter El Salvador and can simply turn up at the border with a valid passport, as can the Belgians, Spanish, Germans and Italians. Citizens of Canada, USA, Australia and New Zealand do need visas. Outside Central America it should only take 48 hours to obtain one, but Salvadorean embassies in Central America have established a complex assault course involving telexing San Salvador, which can take 2 weeks or more. If you need a visa, make sure that you get hold of one before you leave home, unless you want to spend a couple of weeks in the Salvadorean consulate in Guatemala City.

Once you arrive at the border, the length of stay that you're initially granted depends greatly on the mood of the immigration official and the current situation inside the country. Two weeks seems to be a fairly standard first offering. Obtaining an extension is normally fairly easy and can be done at the immigration office in any of the main towns.

On Arrival

Tourist Office, Maps and Orientation

Basic road maps are available from bookshops and from the Tourist Office, which is at No. 619 Calle Rubén Darío, while for a more detailed map you'll have to visit the Instituto Geográfico Nacional at No. 59 Avenida Juan Bertis.

Salvadorean street numbers take a little getting used to. Avenidas run one way and calles the other, but they are numbered with regard to a central axis, odd numbers heading away in one direction and even numbers in the other, so that Calle 5 is six blocks from Calle 6. It all seems very confusing but you soon get the hang of it.

Getting Around El Salvador

By Air

In a country the size of El Salvador air travel is nothing short of an extravagance. However, the country's elite are always casting round for ways to dispose of their spare cash, so there is an occasional service connecting the capital with San Miguel, Santa Rosa de Lima, La Unión and Usulután. The service is operated by **Transportes Aéreos de El Salvador (TAES)**, from the Ilopango airport on the eastern edge of the capital. For information and reservations call 270120.

By Bus

El Salvador's buses are among the most efficent and overcrowded on the isthmus. Few Salvadoreans can afford their own cars and there is a never-ending flow of bus traffic racing along the country's roads. The service is astonishingly cheap and easy, providing you don't stray from the main roads. On main routes there are departures every half-hour or so, although the buses are still packed. When things start to get out of hand you can always travel on the roof, which is an exhilarating way to see the country—but watch out for those low wires!

By Car

Salvador has one of the most developed road networks in Central America. Tarmac has reached most corners of the country, although in many areas it is patchy and potholed. Traffic is heavy and driving furious on the main highways, while on smaller roads you'll meet only a pick-up or two. You can expect a fair amount of interest at military checkpoints, but if your papers are in order you've no reason to worry, although troops may prevent you from visiting areas of conflict.

If you are bringing a car into El Salvador you will have to present your licence and some proof of ownership. Initially permission to bring a car into the country is granted for between 15 and 30 days, but this can be extended to 90 days at the **Dirección General de la Renta Aduanas**, which is near the Terminal de Oriente in San Salvador.

Car Hire

Hire rates range from around US$25 a day and 25c per kilometre for a Toyota Starlet to US$60 and 60c per kilometre for an air conditioned four-wheel-drive jeep. You can usually pay in colones or dollars and it's well worth pushing for a discount.

The larger companies have offices at the airport and in the luxury hotels, but their main offices are as follows:

Avis: 43 Ave. Sur No. 137, tel 242623.
Budget: 79 Ave. Sur No. 6, Colonia La Mascota, tel 231668.
Hertz: Calle Los Andes No. 16, Colonia Miramonte, tel 268099.
Imosa: Boulevard Los Héroes and 3a Calle Poniente, Edificio Kent, tel 246082.
Dollar: Avenida Roosevelt No. 3119, tel 244385.

Embassies and consulates in San Salvador

UK: Paseo Escalón No. 4828, tel 239639.
US: 25 Avenida Norte No. 1230, tel 257100.

Costa Rica: Alameda Roosevelt No. 3107, tel 238283.
Nicaragua: 9 Calle Poniente and 8 Avenida Norte, tel 213255.
Guatemala: 15 Avenida Norte No. 135, tel 213618.
Panamá: 1a Calle Poniente No. 2506, tel 236190.
Honduras: 7 Calle Poniente and 83 Avenida Norte, tel 789524.

Money Matters

The Salvadorean **colón** is one of the more stable Central American currencies and is fairly simple to get hold of, although travellers' cheques can be a problem. You can change money (either dollars or other Central American currencies) with ease at the main land borders and at the bank in the international airport. Elsewhere dollar cash is easy to change and some of the more up-market shops, restaurants and hotels will accept payment in dollars. Banks are open Mon–Fri, 9–1 and 1.45–4, while some also open on Saturday mornings. They all close for a couple of days at the end of June and December to balance their books.

Many places, including banks and *casas de cambio*, are extremely reluctant to exchange travellers' cheques unless you have the original receipts, issued by the bank, as proof of purchase. If all else fails, you can change cheques on the streets in San Salvador, with black marketeers, who operate outside the Post Office and at the entrance to the Parque Infantil on Boulevard Juan Pablo II, which is also home to the largest concentration of *casas de cambio*. If you do use the black market, keep your wits about you and count the cash with care.

American Express, Mastercard, Diners Club and Visa are accepted at more up-market establishments, including hotels, airlines, car hire firms and the more expensive restaurants.

Leaving El Salvador, up to US$80 worth of colones can be changed back into dollars at the bank in the airport and colones can be exchanged for other Central American currencies at the land borders.

Tips of 10–15% are given in more expensive restaurants, but not to taxi drivers. Policemen sometimes expect to be bribed, particularly in connection with petty road offences. They will make it perfectly clear and you should never offer a bribe unless they ask for money.

Post Offices

Airmail letters and postcards take around two weeks to reach Europe, a little less to the US, while parcels stand a reasonable chance of getting lost along the way. Post offices are open Mon–Fri, 8.30–4. The main post office is in the Centro de Gobierno with its entrance north of Boulevard Juan Pablo II on 11 Avenida Norte, which is where you can pick up letters sent to the Poste Restante or Lista de Correos.

Telecommunications

The state phone company, ANTEL, has been badly battered by ten years of civil war, during which telegraph poles and telephone exchanges have been prime targets.

Nevertheless the service is surprisingly efficent, with international direct dialling available to most parts of the world, although you may be told that you cannot reverse the charges to the UK. Telegrams are sent from the Post Office while faxes and telexes can be sent from any of the larger ANTEL offices.

The main ANTEL office is at the corner of Calle Rubén Darío and 5 Avenida Sur and is open every day, 7 am–9 pm; in other towns the company usually occupies a good central location. To speak to the international operator, who can put through reverse-charge calls, dial 119, and for long-distance calls within El Salvador dial 110.

Police and Military

At the time of writing, the situation with regard to internal security is somewhat uncertain, with both sides in the civil war suspending their activities. In theory the country's sizeable guerrilla army will soon cease to exist, government forces will return to their barracks and the streets will be patrolled by a new national police force, incorporating members of the FMLN. Bearing this in mind, it's virtually impossible to predict the situation at the time you read this, short of saying that the country's official security forces have a long and bloody history, characterized by corruption and brutality. It seems extremely unlikely that this will change quickly and therefore travellers in El Salvador should continue to take particular care. The army has wielded virtually unrestricted power for a decade and should be treated with extreme delicacy. The same goes for all other armed men, whether policemen, guerrillas or freelance bandits. Avoid areas of conflict, city streets late at night and driving after dark. The areas to be avoided vary from week to week and before setting out to explore the country you should consult with the Tourist Office in San Salvador.

Medical Matters

In the Canal area, and to the west, tap water is safe and the risk of infection is low. In the Darién Gap the risk of infection is seriously greater; mosquitoes bear malaria.

Public Holidays and Opening Hours

Banks, government offices and shops are all closed on national holidays but nothing stops the buses. Shops and offices are generally open Mon–Fri, 8–noon and 2–6, with most shops staying open on Saturdays but very little activity on Sundays. Government offices are open Mon–Fri, 8–4, banks Mon–Fri, 9–1 and 1.45–4, and ANTEL (phone company) offices from 7 am–9 pm.

1st January:	New Year
March/April:	Holy Week
1st May:	Labour Day
June:	Corpus Christi
15th September:	Independence Day
20th October:	Revolution Day
2nd November:	All Souls' Day
5th November:	Cry of Independence Day
24th, 25th December:	Christmas

Festivals

El Salvador has a strong tradition of local fiestas. Every town and village, however small, has its own annual fiesta and almost all of them are worth a visit. However, among the most important and impressive are the following:

January:	13–24 Feria de la Caña de Azúcar, Cojutepeque
	last Saturday in the month, Verbena de Sonsonate
February:	Verbena de Ahuachapán
March/April:	Holy Week—at its best in Sonsonate
April:	Festival Reina de las Ruinas, San Vicente
May:	3rd Fiesta de las Flores, Panchimalco
July:	17–26 Fiestas Julias, Santa Ana
August:	1–6 Fiestas Agostinas, San Salvador
October:	Festival del Bálsamo, Santa Tecla
	Festival del Maíz, San Antonio Los Ranchos
November:	Feria del Canasto, Zacatecoluca
	Festival Hawaiano, Zacatecoluca
	Carnival, San Miguel

Markets

Despite the virtual eradication of El Salvador's indigenous population the country retains a strong tradition of local markets. The central market in San Salvador is well worth a visit, sprawling on for block after block and offering everything under the sun, whether it's legal or not. The best local markets are held in Ilobasco, for ceramic figures, and San Sebastián, for hammocks, while the large daily market in Cojutepeque is the most extensive and impressive.

Shopping and Artesanía

Salvadoreans are among the most industrious people in Central America and the country's various regions produce a range of local specialities, ranging from the hammocks of San Miguel and San Sebastián to the spicy sausages of Cojutepeque. Among the most popular presents are the locally made ceramics of La Palma, Ilobasco and Nahuizalco. Back in the capital you'll find that the wealth of the Salvadorean oligarchy ensures the availability of all photographic, pharmaceutical and electronic goods, although the shortage of tourists means that it's difficult to get hold of English-language books, newspapers and magazines.

The Media

The bulk of El Salvador's official media is owned and controlled by the country's right-wing oligarchs and inside the country it is extremely difficult to get a clear picture of what's happening. The largest daily paper is *La Prensa Gráfica*, which is owned by the Dutriz family and follows the army line with undying fidelity, describing the FMLN as 'terrorists'. However it is relatively moderate when compared to its main rival, *El Diaro de Hoy*, which supports the extreme right of the ruling ARENA party, regarding President Cristiani as a moderate. The paper is edited in Miami by its owner, Enrique Altamirano, a coffee and cotton baron. Both papers are tabloids and their covers are masked by full-page advertising and scantily clad ladies. The only other daily paper is *El Mundo*, which gives a slightly broader picture and limited space to opposition groups. It comes out in the afternoon.

Attempts to produce more balanced coverage of the country's affairs have generally been silenced, although new publications continue to emerge from time to time. The Catholic Archdiocese publishes a weekly paper, *Orientación*, which is vaguely aligned with the Christian Democrats, and the University of Central America publishes a weekly journal called *Proceso*, which is more progressive but remains largely academic and aloof.

Television has managed to escape outright government control and the country's four commercial channels provide comprehensive news, particularly channels 6 and 12, while many hotels offer CNN and Univision. There are two government 'information' channels.

Radio is an important medium, with an estimated 4.3 million listeners daily. The largest stations, including La Poderosa and Radiocadena are owned by members of the oligarchy but the vast majority of the music stations, blasting out *salsa*, *meringue* and US pop are local shoe-box operations with a deliciously Latin flavour. However, in true Salvadorean style, the battle lines are clearly drawn: the FMLN transmit their side of the story on Radio Farabundo Martí, while the army control Radio Cuscatlán.

Where to Stay

The size of El Salvador means there's no great need to stay in more than one or two towns, which is particularly good news when you bear in mind the shortage of good quality hotels. Top of the range accomodation is really only available in San Salvador and at the beach on the Costa del Sol. Elsewhere you'll have to make do with the crumbling majesty of the lakeside hotels or settle for the rougher, cheap hotels of the smaller towns. For budget travellers there is reasonably priced accommodation in almost every village or town but real bargains are few and far between.

Itineraries

It is possible to see much of the country in a week or two by basing yourself in San Salvador, Santa Ana and San Miguel and taking day trips out into countryside or to the beach.

Western El Salvador is relatively stable and offers some of the most accessible dramatic scenery in the form of the **Cerro Verde National Park**, which can easily be visited from **Santa Ana**, while **Lake Coatepeque** and the ruins at **Chalchuapa** are also well worth seeing. In the **central area** the sights of the capital demand a day of two and you can easily make a day trip to **the coast** at **La Libertad** or **Costa del Sol**.

The area to **the north** of the capital, around **Chalatenango** and **La Palma**, is also beautiful, dominated by pine-clad hills, but has been one of the most hotly contested regions of the country. Finally, heading **east** you can call in at the market in **Cojute-peque** and eat lunch in the spectacular setting of **San Vicente**, ending the day in **San Miguel**.

San Salvador

Blessed with a magnificent setting, but deeply divided and chronically overcrowded, San Salvador is alive with the tensions of the country's recent history. Nestling in a highland bowl and ringed by volcanic peaks and lush green hills the capital is often shrouded in a thin yellow cloud of smog, beneath which more than a million people struggle for survival.

San Salvador has grown fast and furiously in recent decades and is one of the most energetic and overpowering cities in Central America. Under colonial rule it was a small, provincial centre, of little importance, but as the country developed in the 19th century the city grew along with it. In the 1970s and 1980s, when Salvadorean politics reached crisis point and Salvadorean society became increasingly polarized, the city divided along similar lines. In 1986 the old centre, already abandoned by the rich, was badly damaged by a massive earthquake, the impact of which is still plain to see. Packed into the city are a large proportion of the country's poor and the vast majority of its wealthy elite. Their lives rarely meet, each confined to their own sections of the city, but their joint presence generates a hothouse atmosphere which is easily ignited.

In the city centre the industry and enthusiasm of Salvadoreans reaches a peak, motivated by a strange blend of ambition and desperation. All normal economic activity is replaced by informal street trading in which poverty is the shaping factor. Rambling markets, selling basic necessities such as food and clothes have their pitches beneath the ruins of the city's main buildings, the stalls shaded by torn plastic sheeting. Many of the bold 19th-century buildings have crumbled into dust, while others are now cracked, abandoned and crumbling, splattered with graffiti. The rich have abandoned the city centre, fleeing to the high ground of the western suburbs, where tree-lined avenues and plush shopping centres are watched over by a small army of private guards. Here the streets radiate the calm of California, although the high walls, barbed wire and hardware are a constant reminder that this world is under siege.

It's a city which has few tourists and even fewer conventional attractions. However, it sits firmly at the centre of this tiny country, unavoidable in every way, and is an ideal base from which to explore; it offers a significant insight into the forces which shape modern El Salvador and the way in which the country is carved up between rich and poor. You won't be charmed or delighted by San Salvador but the city does have a certain fascination and its sheer energy is always impressive.

Despite the end of the civil war, San Salvador remains one of the most dangerous cities in Central America. The centre and up-market suburbs are generally safe during the day, when the streets are crowded, although pickpockets operate everywhere and at all times. At night the streets are unsafe and then you should always travel by taxi.

The city's main **festival** is that of the Saviour, El Salvador, which takes place during the two weeks preceding 6 August and involves processions, dances and much drinking.

An image of the Saviour is carried through the streets on 5 August and there are commemorative church services the following day.

History

Modern San Salvador is the latest version of several battered cities which have stood on this site, all rocked by a turbulent combination of politics and plate tectonics. The original Spanish city was established in a neighbouring valley at La Bermuda in 1524. It was rattled by several earthquakes and eventually swept away by a rainstorm in 1541. The city was then moved to a couple of temporary locations and eventually came to rest at its existing site in 1545, only to be devastated by another earthquake two years later, after which it was rebuilt with assistance from the wealthy religious orders in Guatemala. Nevertheless the earth continued to shake and in 1854 a huge earthquake completely destroyed the city, reducing all the original colonial architecture to dust.

During the colonial era San Salvador was a forgotten corner of the empire with a rough, frontier spirit, although it grew increasingly wealthy, exporting quinine from the forests of Honduras and gold and silver from the Salvadorean mountains. Boom time came at the end of the 19th century, when coffee transformed El Salvador into a rich nation and the capital grew at a phenomenal rate, spreading out across the valley.

Today the city continues to suffer at the hands of natural and unnatural disasters. Throughout the last decade it has been rocked by both street fighting and seismic disturbances. In 1986 a huge earthquake left at least 10,000 homeless, while as recently as 1989 the city was invaded by the FMLN, whose soldiers held about a third of the town, while street battles left at least 2000 dead. Today's city has had little chance to recover from the violence and, for the vast majority of the population, survival is a bitter struggle against unemployment, repression and hunger, while the city centre remains badly damaged, the great buildings cracked and unused.

GETTING TO SAN SALVADOR

By Air
Arriving by plane you'll come into the international airport at Cuscatlán, 36 km from the city. There are no buses to the airport but taxis are plentiful and pick-up trucks run to the nearest town from where there is a regular bus service to San Salvador.

By Bus
Arriving by bus you'll either come into the Terminal del Occidente—if you're coming from Guatemala or Santa Ana—from where buses 34 and 27 will take you to the city centre, or the Terminal del Oriente—if you're coming from San Miguel, La Libertad, or the Honduran border—from where buses 27 and 42 will get you to the centre. If you're just passing through then bus 27 connects the two terminals. (For anywhere east or north of San Salvador you want a bus from the Terminal del Oriente; for anywhere west you want the Terminal del Occidente.)

TOURIST INFORMATION
Calle Rubén Darío No. 619, tel 228000, open 8–4, Mon–Fri. The staff are always delighted to see a tourist or two and are only too keen to help, although they have limited

314

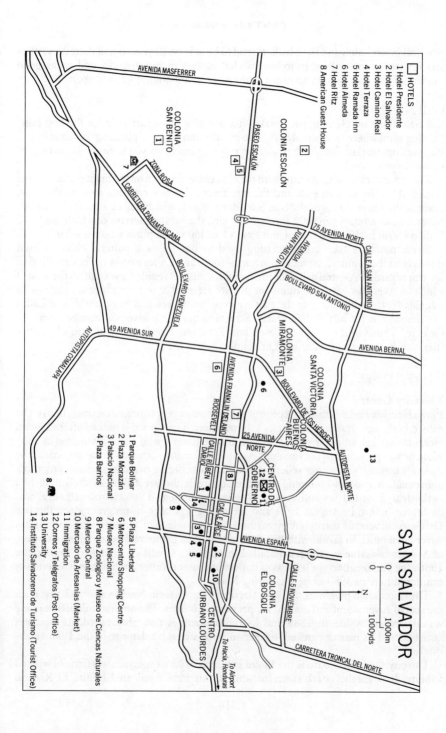

SAN SALVADOR

HOTELS

1 Hotel Presidente
2 Hotel El Salvador
3 Hotel Camino Real
4 Hotel Terraza
5 Hotel Ramada Inn
6 Hotel Almeda
7 Hotel Ritz
8 American Guest House

1 Parque Bolívar
2 Plaza Morazán
3 Palacio Nacional
4 Plaza Barrios
5 Plaza Libertad
6 Metrocentro Shopping Centre
7 Museo Nacional
8 Parque Zoológico y Museo de Ciencas Naturales
9 Mercado Central
10 Mercado de Artesanías (Market)
11 Immigration
12 Correos y Telégrafos (Post Office)
13 University
14 Instituto Salvadoreno de Turismo (Tourist Office)

AVENIDA MASFERRER

COLONIA
SAN BENITO

ZONA ROSA

PASEO ESCALÓN

COLONIA ESCALÓN

CARRETERA PANAMÉRICANA

BOULEVARD VENEZUELA

75 AVENIDA NORTE

CALLE A SAN ANTONIO

BOULEVARD SAN ANTONIO

AVENIDA BERNAL

COLONIA
MIRAMONTE

COLONIA
SANTA VICTORIA

AUTOPISTA COMALAPA

49 AVENIDA SUR

AVENIDA FRANKLIN DELANO ROOSEVELT

BOULEVARD DE LOS HÉROES

COLONIA
BUENOS
AIRES

25 AVENIDA
NORTE

CALLE RUBEN DARÍO

CALLE ARCE

AVENIDA ESPAÑA

AVENIDA PALOU

CENTRO DE
GOBIERNO

AUTOPISTA NORTE

CENTRO
URBANO LOURDES

COLONIA
EL BOSQUE

CALLE 5 NOVIEMBRE

CARRETERA TRONCAL DEL NORTE

To Hacia, Honduras

To Airport

N

0   1000m
0   1000yds

practical information and their leaflets tend to be at least 10 years out of date. Neverthe-less it's well worth calling in to have a chat as they're very friendly and speak good English. They also operate an office at the airport, although it's rarely open.

ORIENTATION
San Salvador's unrelenting pace makes it a daunting city to arrive in for the first time. Finding somewhere to stay is always a top priority and if you're planning to stay in one of the more up-market districts then you can rely on a taxi to get you from the airport or bus station to your hotel.

The city is rectangular in shape with the old centre, focused on the main plazas and the cathedral, in the eastern end, and the wealthier suburbs stretching away to the west, towards the lower slopes of the San Salvador volcano, which makes a useful landmark. Several main arteries run right through the city, the most important of which are Calle Rubén Darío in the central area and Paseo Escalón in the plush western suburbs.

Street numbers take a little getting used to but follow a pattern which is used throughout the country. Avenidas run north–south and Calles east–west, but are divided up with regard to a central axis. For the Avenidas this is Avenida Cuscatlán, to the west of which all Avenidas have odd numbers and are referred to as Norte (north), such as 24 Avenida Norte, while those to the east are even-numbered and Sur (south). For Calles the central axis is Calle Rubén Darío. Streets to the north have odd numbers and are Oriente. Those to the south are even and Poniente. Confused? Well you can either spend an hour or two mastering it or simply stick to the taxis.

WHAT TO SEE

The City Centre
Plaza Barrios ranks as the city's central square and its grey concrete expanse, flanked by ruined buildings, epitomizes the city's desperation. The square is named after General Gerardo Barrios, an old friend of Napoleon Bonaparte's, who was assassinated in 1865 while he was president of the republic. A statue of Barrios, seated on a charger, marks the square's centre. Newspaper sellers mingle with wandering preachers, musicians and a policeman or two, and looming over the square is the great bulk of the unfinished **cathedral**, boarded up and coated in wiry scaffolding. The original cathedral was destroyed by fire in August 1951 and rebuilding has been in progress since the late 1950s, continuously disrupted by earthquakes and a lack of funds, as the church has never been much in favour with the government. The cathedral houses a famous figure of *Salvador del Mundo*, which is paraded through the streets on 6 August. During the 1980s the building become a focus of opposition protests after Archbishop Romero was murdered here in 1980 as he was saying Mass.

The other main buildings on Plaza Barrios is the **Palacio Nacional**, which was once the seat of government and housed the president's offices. The original colonial building was destroyed by fire in 1889 and its replacement is now abandoned, its windows smashed and its plaster cracked, having suffered extensive damage in the 1986 earth-quake.

The city's second square is the **Plaza Libertad** with its spectacular statue of winged Liberty. It is another stark concrete square, this time dominated by the El Rosario church, a bare modern building of stained concrete, which was once the setting for Salvador's society weddings but is now splattered with opposition graffiti.

A couple of blocks north of the Plaza Barrios is the **Plaza Morazán**, site of the city's parade ground in colonial times, now converted into a car park and market. The restored Baroque façade of the **Teatro Nacional** looks out over the sprawl of traders and shoppers.

Elsewhere in the centre street trading dominates. Rows of market stalls have taken over a number of the smaller streets, snaking their way towards the main market, which is off Calle Gerardo Barrios and is a dense maze of narrow alleys and tiny stalls, where you can buy everything from a machine gun to a chicken.

The Wealthy Suburbs

Wealthy Salvadoreans, including the president and his staff, abandoned the city centre long ago and fled to the newer suburbs of the north and west. The backbone of this part of town is **Paseo Escalón**, which is lined with up-market boutiques, expensive restaurants, car showrooms, cinemas and nightclubs—a testament to the wealth of San Salvador's elite. Its main rival, **Boulevard de los Héroes**, is a slightly down-market version, dominated by the Hotel Camino Real and a string of fast-food restaurants, as well as the city's largest shopping centre, the **Metrocentro**. Other than the **Revolutionary monument** and **Museo Nacional**, both of which are in San Benito there are few real attractions in this part of town, but it is well worth taking a look, if only to witness the stark contrast with the city centre.

San Benito and the Museo Nacional

San Benito, in the southwestern side of the city, rides a low hill and is topped by the Revolutionary monument, which depicts a massive, muscle-bound figure reaching for the sky, more in the style of revolutionary Nicaragua or the former Soviet Union. Below the monument is the Museo Nacional (open every day except Monday, 9–noon and 2–5), which offers a quick summary of Salvadorean history. It opens with some interesting pieces of pottery from the country's main archaeological sights, including Tazumal and Chalchuapa. Many of these clearly show the influence of the Olmecs and the Maya. However, once it leaves the pre-Columbian era, the museum gets a little thin, with a very brief summary of colonial times and a display in which the industrial revolution is explained with a typewriter, a film projector and a diver's helmet. In true Salvadorean style there's a large display of guns and then a final section on El Salvador's indigenous culture, which includes dance masks and traditional weaving.

WHERE TO STAY

LUXURY AND EXPENSIVE

The finest hotel in the city is the **Camino Real**, tel 233344, fax 235660, which has a good central location at the southern end of the Boulevard de los Héroes. It meets all the highest standards and is the traditional haunt of the international press corps. Other up-market establishments include the **Hotel Presidente**, tel 243044, fax 234912, in Colonia San Benito, which is another excellent modern hotel, set in the calm and safety of one of the city's most exclusive neighbourhoods, and the **Hotel El Salvador**, tel 24222, 11 Calle Poniente and 89 Avenida Norte, which was formerly the Sheraton. It changed its name and lost a lot of business after it received some unwanted guests when it was stormed by the FMLN during their 1989 offensive. The guerrillas found the hotel full of US military advisers, whom they held hostage for several days.

MODERATE

Among the best of the mid-range hotels is the **Hotel Alameda**, tel 239999, fax 239811, which is good and central at 43 Avenida Sur and Alameda Roosevelt, with air-conditioned rooms and a swimming pool. Similarly equipped are the **Ramada Inn**, tel 239233, fax 791889, 85 Avenida Sur and Calle Juan José Cañas and the **Hotel Ritz Continental**, tel 220033, 7a Avenida Sur—just south of Calle Rubén Darío—which is a little more run down but is situated in the heart of the city, surrounded by the bustle of street markets.

INEXPENSIVE

At the very top of the budget range is the **American Guest House**, tel 710224, 17 Avenida Norte No. 119—just north of Calle Arce—where some rooms have the luxury of a private bathroom and all have the benefit of a good restaurant and an excellent central location. If that's full then you could try the **American Guest House Anexo**, which is run by the same family—although the two branches rarely speak to each other these days—or you might try the **Family Guest House**, tel 221902, which is around the corner on 1a Calle Poniente. While for those on a tighter budget the **Hotel Nuevo Panamerican**, tel 222959, 8a Avenida Sur No. 113, is good and central, while the **Hotel San Carlos**, tel 224808, Calle Concepción No. 121, is rougher and even cheaper.

EATING OUT

The centre of San Salvador is monopolized by the city's poor and there are few good places to eat other than the cheap *comedores* in the market, where stews and steaks are washed down with sweet black coffee. Those restaurants that there are specialize in a bland repertoire of pizza, fried chicken and hamburgers, although there are also a few stalls and cafés offering traditional Salvadorean *pupusas*. Most of the main streets have a branch of **Pollo Campero**—El Salvador's answer to Kentucky Fried Chicken—while there are also a couple of **McDonald's** and several branches of **Biggest**—a local version. In the more sophisticated surroundings of the city's western suburbs cheap food is available at the **Rancho Alegre**—just behind the Metrocentro at the southern end of Boulevard de los Héroes—where the city's middle-class office workers feast on fast food lunches, including Japanese fish and Mexican *chile*.

For something a little more up-market there are a handful of mid-range restaurants on Calle Lamatepec, behind the Hotel Camino Real, where you'll find **La Hola Betos**, an excellent Italian place, **Metroconchas** and a couple of reasonable Chinese restaurants. If you're looking for the city's finest cuisine then stick to the Californian calm of Paseo Escalón where you'll find the best in seafood at **Siete Mares**, steaks at **Diligencia**, Spanish at **El Bodegón**, Argentinian at **La Pampa Argentina**, Mexican at **Señor Pico** and Chinese at **Asia** or **Abordo**.

ENTERTAINMENT AND NIGHTLIFE

By any standards San Salvador is intimidating at night. Few people venture out into the dimly lit city streets and drunks staggering home are watched closely by armed men, while army jeeps, their windows blacked out, move slowly through the back streets.

In the city centre the throb of commerce dies with the setting sun and within an hour or two of dusk the streets are virtually deserted. For those who can afford it there are a few rough bars, but for the most part the city's poor take their pleasures at home. There are, however, several cinemas, and elsewhere in the city the rich drink and dance regardless.

In the heart of the city there are only two night spots. By far the better is the **Café Teatro**, which is down the side of the Teatro Nacional, on 2a Avenida Sur and provides a focus for the young, artistic and mildly left-wing, with live music on Friday nights. The atmosphere is distinctly sophisticated, with members of the audience taking the microphone to sing songs of the revolution, but this is a small, local club, where most people know each other and if it's very full you may not be allowed in unless accompanied by a member. The other city-centre night spot is the **Hotel Ritz**—7a Avenida Sur, just south of Calle Rubén Darío—which has weary live dance music on Friday nights.

For really active nightlife you'll have to seek out the wealthy suburbs where the Salvadorean elite spend their ill-gotten gains. The best collection of clubs is in Colonia San Victoria at the northern end of the Boulevard de los Héroes, where you can dance to modern rock music at the **Malibu** and to the more Latin rhythms of *salsa*, *samba* and *meringue* at **Villa Fiesta** and **Altamar**. All three offer food, drink and fiesta with typically Salvadorean enthusiasm and are at their best on Friday and Saturday nights. Elsewhere in the western suburbs there are several clubs on Paseo Escalón and in the really up-market district of San Benito, where the so-called 'Zona Rosa' offers a string of very expensive restaurants and clubs, although many of these are only open to members.

Cinemas

The city's cinemas offer a cheap and safe form of after-dark entertainment, with two or three showings a day.

Cine Avenida, 18 Avenida Norte.
Cine Caribe (four screens), Plaza las Américas.
Cine Universal, 8 Avenida Norte and 3 Calle Oriente.
Cine Central, 1 Avenida Norte and 3a Calle Poniente.
Cine Libertad, Plaza Libertad.
Cine España (three screens), Avenida España and 3 Calle Poniente.
Cine Majestic, Boulevard Juan Pablo II and Avenida España.

USEFUL INFORMATION

Money

Most banks in San Salvador, of which there are several on Calle Rubén Darío, are open 9–1 and 1.45–3.30 and operate *casas de gambio*. However, few of them will change traveller's cheques and even fewer if you don't happen to have receipts for the cheques as proof of purchase. If all else, fails you can always change money with the black-market changers on Boulevard Juan Pablo II, between 7a and 9a Avenidas, outside the Parque

Infantil, where you will also find a string of *casas de gambio*, open 9–1 and 2–4, Mon–Fri; again, it can be difficult to change cheques unless you have the receipts, except on the street that is. If you do end up changing money on the street then exercise extreme caution as sharks and false currency abound.

The agent for **American Express** in San Salvador is the El Salvador Travel Service, on the ground floor of the Centro Comercial La Mascota at the junction of Calle Mascota and the Pan American Highway (where it enters the city from the southeast).

Post Office
Centro de Gobierno—entrance on 11 Avenida Norte, north of Boulevard Juan Pablo II—open 8–5, Mon–Fri and 8–noon on Sat.

Telecommunications
The main office of the phone company, ANTEL, is at the junction of Calle Rubén Darío and 5 Avenida Sur and is open daily from 5 am–10 pm for international phone calls, faxes and telexes. For local calls there are pay-phones dotted throughout the city.

Immigration and Visa Extensions
Ministry of the Interior in the Centro de Gobierno at the junction of Boulevard Juan Pablo II and 15 Avenida Norte. Open 8–4, Mon–Fri.

Around San Salvador

The San Salvador Volcano
Towering above the city, its sides covered in carefully groomed coffee plantations, is the sharp cone of the San Salvador volcano (also known as *El Boquerón*). The volcano's summit offers superb views over the central valley, with the capital mapped out beneath you. On a clear day you can see the distant peak of the **San Vicente volcano**, more than 30 km to the east, and even make out the hazy curve of the Pacific coastline. The mouth of the cone is more than 1 km in width, while deep inside is a smaller cone and mound, the result of a more recent minor eruption.

The peak is surprisingly easy to reach with buses from the capital running as far as **Santa Tecla**, a busy satellite town on the Pan-American Highway, perched in a low pass on the shoulder of the volcano. From here you can either drive or take a bus up to a small village just below the peak, from where it's only a couple of hundred yards to the radio masts which mark the summit, although it is steep uphill. Once you make it to the top you look down over the city or head on around the cone of the volcano, a circuit which takes about 40 minutes. Buses to Santa Tecla from San Salvador leave from Parque Bolívar (Calle Rubén Darío and Avenida 13 Norte), and to get to *El Boquerón* from Santa Tecla take bus 103, which leaves from the corner of 4a Avenida Sur and Calle David Hernández at around 6.30 and 10.30 am. If you're driving, make sure you get good directions in Santa Tecla.

Los Chorros
Beyond Santa Tecla the Pan-American Highway drops into a narrow forested gorge and tucked in on the left (about 6 km beyond Santa Tecla) is the Los Chorros 'Turicentro', a

set of natural swimming pools fed by fresh clear water gushing from the side of the volcano. At the weekend thousands of Salvadoreans come here to cool off, but during the week you may well have the entire place to yourself. Buses to Los Chorros—number 79—run from the Terminal del Occidente in San Salvador, with departures every 20 minutes or so, and you can pick these up as they pass through Santa Tecla.

Parque Balboa and La Puerta del Diablo

Over on the other side of the city, to the east, a road climbs high into the hills, crossing a steep ridge before dropping towards the ocean and passing the Parque Balboa and La Puerta del Diablo—the devil's door—one of the city's great beauty spots.

The park is a narrow strip of gardens and wooded walkways, straddling a ridge some 1200 m above sea level which looks out across the city. It is one of a network of government-run 'Turicentros', all of which are popular with Salvadoreans, who come here for romantic strolls and family picnics. It's a pleasant place to spend an hour or two escaping the claustrophobia of the city. Beyond the park the road continues to the Puerta del Diablo, which is made up of a pair of craggy rocks framing a superb view of the valley. If you scramble up above the rocks again it's possible to see as far as the **San Vicente volcano**, while below you, towards the Pacific, is the colonial village of **Panchimalco**. But be warned that it can be dangerous to go to the park or the Puerta del Diablo alone as muggings do occasionally take place up here.

To get to the park take bus number 12 from beside the central market in San Salvador—Avenida 29 Agosto and 12 Calle Poniente.

Panchimalco

Over the ridge the road drops steeply into a deep-cut valley, where much of the land is so inaccessible that it remains coated in dense tropical forest. Nestling in amongst the trees, some 600 m beneath the Puerta del Diablo, is the colonial village of Panchimalco, a quiet outpost of rural calm, just 20 minutes from the capital. The village is most famous for its colonial church, **El Chulo**, the front of which is elaborately decorated with eight figures of the saints and an ornately carved wooden door. In front of the church is a dusty plaza, shaded by a massive ceiba tree. This forms the centre of village life, with chickens pecking at the feet of passers-by. From here there are excellent views down the valley, over the treetops towards the coast or back up to the craggy outcrop of the Puerta del Diablo.

The village is also famous for its handwoven *pañuelas*, which are simple headscarfs made in the village and still occasionally worn by the older women, while some local people still speak the Nahuatl Indian language.

To get to Panchimalco take bus number 17 from beside the central market in San Salvador—Avenida 29 Agosto and 12 Calle Poniente.

Lake Ilopango

Ringed by low, forested hills and the holiday homes of the rich, Lake Ilopango is the largest crater lake in the country. Just 14 km to the east of San Salvador, the lake has a long and unsettled history with its water level rising and falling in response to seismic disturbances and in 1880 a sudden rise in the level was followed by the emergence of a small volcano in the centre of the lake, which rose to a height of some 40 metres and wiped out all aquatic life. These days the island remains a feature of the lake, the fish have returned and the lake is a popular weekend retreat for Salvadoreans, who come here to swim, water-ski, drink, eat and generally enjoy themselves. During the week the place has a magical atmosphere and you can laze on the beaches, water-ski, paddle around in a dugout, sample the local crab soup, or take a dip in the murky waters.

To get to the lake take bus number 15 from 2 Avenida Norte and Plaza Morazán in San Salvador, which will drop you in **Apulo**, the main village on the lake.

The Beaches

Several of the country's finest beaches, incorporating miles of clean sand and the purest Pacific surf, are within easy reach of the capital. Bearing in mind the poor quality of accommodation on the coast, you might want to consider visiting them on day trips—unless, that is, you can afford to splash out on the luxury hotels of the Costa del Sol, which are among the best in the country.

La Libertad

La Libertad was a surprise. It was hot and humid, but sitting by the sea wall under a palm roof, it was possible to catch a little breeze as the waiter brought the uncooked food around instead of a menu. There were lobsters, shrimps, oily black crayfish, fresh white fish and trays full of crabs in dressed psychedelic colours. Noisy family parties sat around sipping their well chilled beer... The occasional swimmer ventured out, ducking beneath the waves as they broke, to avoid swallowing the thick, yellow foam. Somebody said that the beach was noted for its sharks and undertow, but La Libertad was too peaceful to make it likely. Here on a Sunday afternoon one could almost believe oneself in a country like one's own.

Patrick Marnham, *So Far From God*, 1985

Bustling with seaside delights and infused with the smell of fresh fish, La Libertad is El Salvador's most popular beach resort, but also happens to be one of its busiest fishing ports. While this may seem an unfortunate combination, with fish heads floating among the bathers, it also makes La Libertad one of the most interesting places on the coast. The town is old and busy, like any other medium-sized centre, while the sea front is a beautiful sweep of black sand, flanked by rocky outcrops and dominated by a rusty pier which juts out, high above the waves. It's a base for small fishing boats, which are lowered off the pier on a winch and dropped into the swell, hooking up when they return, to be hauled out and wheeled to their post, from where they sell their catch. Wandering up and down the pier is fascinating: each boat displays a selection of weird and wonderful fish, including shark, turtle and octopus, while at the pier's end a couple of simple restaurants offers the freshest of fish meals.

Away from the pier the sea front is dominated by the Salvadorean tourist industry, which caters for large parties of happy, drunken Salvadoreans who come down from the capital at weekends. There's an abundance of fish restaurants, hotels and bars, with brave bathers chancing their luck in the surf and young children paddling in the mucky streams which run out across the sand. La Libertad may not be the ideal place for a beach holiday but there's no doubt that it's an interesting place to spend some time watching the action and feasting on fine seafood.

Bus number 102 to La Libertad leave every ten minutes or so from 4 Calle Poniente and 17 Avenida Sur in San Salvador and the trip takes just 45 minutes.

Around La Libertad

For a cleaner and quieter place to swim head out of La Libertad, either to the east or west, where the wealthy have established exclusive beach resorts, leaving La Libertad to the masses.

Heading west the best beaches are **Playa El Majagual, Playa El Sunzal**, which is said to offer some of the best surf in Central America, and **Playa El Palmar**. To the east are the **Playas San Blás** and **San Diego**, of which the latter is the better bet, although, as with all the above, much of the sea front is blocked off by large enclosed beach houses and it can be a little difficult to find a way through to the sand. The pretensions of the place are best spelled out in the name of the local sports club: 'The Jet Set Tennis Club.'

La Costa del Sol

Poking a nobbly finger along the Pacific coast to the east of La Libertad is the **Península de San Juan del Gozo**, an extremely beautiful beach which offers mile upon mile of fine white sand, swept by Pacific rollers. The area, known as the Costa del Sol, is large enough to accommodate an immensely popular workers' resort and some of the country's best hotels with plenty of space to spare. And despite the fact that it attracts the usual stream of weekend visitors and includes a squalid beachside village, this expanse of sand is well worth visiting and must rank as El Salvador's best beach.

Buses to the Costa del Sol leave every hour or so from the Terminal del Oriente in San Salvador and the trip takes between one and two hours.

WHERE TO STAY AT THE BEACH

In La Libertad the best hotels are the **Hotel Posada de Don Lito**, tel 353166, the **El Malecón de Don Lito**, tel 353201, or the **Posada de Don Rodrigo**, all of which are at the western end of the beach and even if you're only here for lunch they offer excellent food and a great view of the bay. If you're looking for something a little cheaper then try the **Motel Rick** or the **El Retiro Familiar**, both of which are also on the sea front at the western end of the beach.

Around La Libertad there are some middle-range hotels which offer reasonable accommodation at the smaller beaches, including the **Hotel Conchalio** at the Playa San Blas and the **Hotel El Pacífico** at Playa Majagual.

On the **Costa del Sol** there are a handful of rough and extremely basic hotels around the public beach where the buses turn round, although there is little to recommend them. Further on, towards the end of the peninsula are the luxurious hotels: **Tesoro Beach**, tel 340600, fax 232891, and the **Izalco Cabana Club**, tel 230764, fax 240363, both of which are superb beach hotels.

323

NORTHERN EL SALVADOR

A world of ancient pine forests, steep twisting mountains and sharp corners, northern El Salvador is the country's most embattled and impoverished region. Here the grand volcanic peaks and lush fertility of the central valleys give way to a crumpled world of angular hills, in which peasant farmers carve a patchwork of fields and small, ancient villages perch among the hills. Glimpsed from the highway these villages seem to radiate rural permanence, with cobbled streets, white walls and red-tiled roofs, but in reality they are among the most bitterly fought-over villages in all of Central America. Their streets are dominated by a massive military presence, their graffiti-ed walls painted over time and time again, the plaster shattered by gunfire.

Throughout the 1980s the area was in a state of continuous conflict, with some of the main towns and most of the countryside falling under FMLN control. Local people, caught in the crossfire, were forced to take sides and were manipulated by both the army and the guerrillas. Large numbers of local people were either killed in the fighting, fled the country, or simply massacred by the armed forces. At the time of writing, despite successful peace talks, the area remains under military occupation, with columns of government troops strung out along all main roads.

Nevertheless this is one of the most beautiful parts of the country, with a spectacular landscape and a couple of charming rural towns, unspoilt by the congestion which characterizes so much of El Salvador. Generally speaking, foreigners are not at great risk here, although it is obviously hazardous to enter the area at times of conflict. If there is any danger you'll probably find the entire area closed to outsiders, but it's usually easy enough to travel through to the border or make a side trip to Chalatenango. It is worth trying to check the situation before you travel, either through the tourist office in San Salvador or through your consulate. At all times you should stick to the main roads and never go walking in the countryside, where armed men and land mines present a very real threat.

Troncal del Norte: San Salvador to La Palma and El Poy

The Troncal del Norte is the highway which connects the capital with the Honduran border at El Poy. Leaving San Salvador it passes through desperate slums before escaping into open farmland. The first place of any interest is the ruins of **Cihuatán**, a small Maya site which has received little attention but is known to have been occupied by Pipil-speaking Indians around AD 1000. The site isn't much to look at, comprising nothing more than a series of low mounds, but it's thought to have been the Pipil capital of Cuscatlán, which was conquered by Alvarado in 1528. If you do drop by, you'll have to reconstruct the city in your mind, as nothing has been done to help you, but the archaeologists tell us that this was a substantial centre with several large temples, two main plazas and at least one ball court.

Continuing to the north the highway crosses the Río Lempa and moves into the troubled department of Chalatenango. If there is any fighting, the army will stop buses and turn back foreigners. Beyond this point the land begins to change dramatically, as the easy fertility of the central valley is replaced by a tougher, more demanding landscape. The road begins the long climb into the mountains; the slow, twisting curves become tighter and tighter, the mountains swallowing the narrow river valley, reducing the fertile ground to a thin strip on the valley floor. The road gives superb views across central El Salvador and on a clear day you can make out the perfect symmetry of the San Salvador volcano, towering above the capital, and catch glimpses of the Cerrón Grande reservoir.

The only town along the road is **La Palma**, a small mountain settlement which is famous for its crafts. The town has been fought over on countless occasions and still bears the scars, although on a clear, still morning this is a spectacular highland town, perched on a hillside and surrounded by low mountains, with wisps of mist lifting off the pine forests. With its soft, pine-scented breeze and cool, fresh climate this is perhaps the most beautiful part of El Salvador. Meanwhile the town's craftsmen still beaver away, specializing in woodcarvings, which include trucks and tanks, that can usually be bought in the village.

Beyond La Palma the highway runs another 10 km or so to the small village of **San Ignacio** and from there to the border at El Poy. If you're coming through this way either to or from Honduras then it's a good idea to make an early start if you want to make it through in a day.

If not, there's a basic *pensión* in La Palma and another, which comes strongly recommended, just before the border.

Chalatenango

Just north of the Cerrón Grande reservoir a paved road heads east to the small mountain town and departmental capital of **Chalatenango**. Despite the fact that it has also been hotly fought over and occupied by the FMLN on a number of occasions, most recently in early 1991, the town appears astonishingly normal. It is, after all, an ancient place, founded in 1791 by order of the then governor of Guatemala, a certain Baron Gararda-let, as a centre for the production of indigo. Again, if it wasn't for the war, this would be a calm highland town. It forms the focus of a simple regional economy, and retains busy, well-stocked shops, an interesting cathedral, a relaxed plaza and a bustling market. At the time of writing, Chalatenango was acting as a forward post for the army's counter-insurgency campaign and was packed with weary young conscripts and battered military equipment. As a foreigner, you can expect to be welcomed by local people but treated with a degree of suspicion by the army, who prefer to work unseen.

USEFUL INFORMATION
Bear in mind that while the security situation remains unclear this can be a dangerous and unpredictable area for travel. Army checkpoints dot the main roads and the FMLN often interfere with local transport and occasionally set up their own checkpoints.

If travelling by car then stick to the main roads, these being the Troncal del Norte and the branch road to Chalatenango, and avoid driving at night or close to military vehicles.

Travelling by bus you'll find that the service is astonishingly good, if a little packed, although most buses provide additional seating on the roof. Bus 119 from the Terminal del Oriente runs to La Palma (4 hrs) and El Poy (5 hrs), with departures every hour or so, while bus 125, also from the Terminal del Oriente, runs to Chalatenango (3 hrs).

It is possible to visit both towns as a day trip from San Salvador but if you do get stuck there are basic **hotels** in La Palma and Chalatenango. Neither are signposted so you'll have to ask someone to point you in the right direction.

WESTERN EL SALVADOR

Stretching from San Salvador to the Guatemalan border is the Salvadorean heartland, a landscape which is both delicate and daunting. It is packed with people and farmed to the limit of its capacity. The scenery is scattered with volcanic peaks and broken by ranges of low forested hills, with sweeping fertile valleys hung between distant volcanoes.

For those who live here times are tough. Despite the fact that the majority of the fighting has taken place in other areas, the west has suffered badly during the 1980s, with the local economy devastated by the civil war. At least half the population are unemployed and most towns have an exhausted appearance, rundown, battered and chronically overpopulated. Nevertheless the people, in true Salvadorean style, remain alive and alert, brushing aside their circumstances with waves of enthusiasm and industry.

The main towns are **Santa Ana** and **Sonsonate**, both buzzing with small-scale commerce. To the north of Santa Ana the hills are dry and inhospitable, sheltering a few ancient villages. To the south is the great highland area around the Cerro Verde, which is now the country's finest national park, offering unrivalled views of the Salvadorean landscape.

Heading West: the Ruins of San Andrés

Leaving San Salvador to the west, the Pan-American Highway climbs slowly through the suburbs of Santa Tecla, traffic slowing to a crawl as heavy lorries drag themselves up to the lip of the central valley, belching inky black fumes. But once the descent begins, things start to speed, the highway winding down through a forested gorge, unravelling onto a broad plain between two parallel ridges.

Out in the open ground are the ruins of **San Andrés**, a small Maya site which commands the centre of this plain and superb views of the distant hills. The site is simple, with the stark design features of the Late Classic Maya (AD 550–900). In all there are more than 200 structures here, although only a small section has been restored, including two plazas and a principal temple. If you come during the week you'll probably have the place to yourself, although you may stumble across a courting couple or two. Despite its bare simplicity the sight does have a powerful atmosphere, bolstered by its impressive setting.

The ruins are about 500 m to the north of the Pan-American Highway, along a dirt track which is marked by an inconspicuous sign. The bus from San Salvador to Santa Ana passes the entrance.

Santa Ana

The town only looked Godforsaken; in fact, it was comfortable. It was a nice combination of attributes. In every respect, Santa Ana, the most Central American of Central American towns, was a perfect place—perfect in its pious attitudes and pretty girls, perfect in its slumber, its coffee-scented heat, its jungly plaza, and in the dusty elegance of its old buildings whose whitewash at nightfall gave them a vivid phosphorescence. Even its volcano was in working order.

Paul Theroux, *The Old Patagonian Express*, 1979

Salvador's second city has a population of some 210,000, and despite being a major centre of commerce and light industry it has a bedraggled, exhausted appearance. More than ten years on it still fits Theroux's description, although much of the whitewash has now flaked from the walls, and desperate circumstances have heightened the furious bustle of commerce played out on its ramshackle streets. Around the market traffic squeezes between the traders and buses nudge their way into the terminal, splashing through muddy pools or whipping up a swirl of dust.

The town centre has a more sedate atmosphere, infused with the calm of provincial government, and boasts several impressive buildings, including a Spanish gothic **cathedral**, with intricately decorated bell towers and small trees growing out of its sides, and a grand neo-classical **theatre**. The central plaza remains very relaxed, with guards dozing outside the police station, teenagers giggling on the benches and local bureaucrats hurrying in and out of the town hall. However, for the passing tourist there isn't a great deal to do in Santa Ana, other than wandering the streets and sitting in the plaza, but it does make an ideal base for exploring this part of the country.

North to Metapán and the border with Guatemala

Heading north from Santa Ana you leave the lush security of the central valleys and move into a harsh, dry environment, which has little potential and few inhabitants. Shortly before Metapán a sudden view of **Lake Güija** provides welcome relief; this shallow lake, ringed by low hills, rubs shoulders with the Guatemalan border and has supported a strange, traditional way of life for centuries. Its shores are still heavily populated and hundreds of inexplicable stone carvings have been found on the island of Igualtepeque. The waters of the lake rose dramatically in the 17th century, destroying several nearby villages, while today they are harnessed by a hydroelectric dam.

A bizarre local tradition, which survived until a few years ago, was a Holy Week ritual in which local fishermen would catch alligators and take their bodies to the village prison. Once the head fishermen had been locked in, the entire population of the village would surround the jail, each person passing in a few *colones* in return for a slice of alligator meat, which they ate raw.

Today the lake is still fished and you can see plenty of fresh lake bass and live crabs on sale in the markets at Metapán and Santa Ana, and if you're very lucky you might track down a bowl of locally made crab soup.

A few kilometres to the north of the lake is **Metapán** itself, a small and traditional town of cobbled streets and red-tiled roofs, with a large local market. Metapán was founded in the 17th century by survivors of the flood at Lake Güija and now acts as the commercial hub of northwestern El Salvador. The town has two great attractions: the **market**, which spreads out across several blocks and has a calm, rural atmosphere, with horses and donkeys tethered on its outskirts and fish still twitching in their baskets; and the **Iglesia de La Parroquia**, which is one of the country's finest local colonial churches, breaking with traditional earthquake-proof design to incorporate an unusually narrow façade and a single bell tower. According to parish records the church was begun around 1700 and took just under 50 years to complete, although it was later added to in 1803. Its main altar is magnificent, faced with a sheet of *plata repousada* (beaten silver) from local silver mines, while eight smaller altars flank the nave.

To the northeast of Metapán the land rises to an immense forested peak known as **Montecristo**, which is part of a national park marking the three-way border between El Salvador, Guatemala and Honduras. The reserve supports the last vestiges of Salvador's cloud forest and was declared a national park in the early 1970s. It is extremely difficult to get to and even with your own four-wheel-drive vehicle you should allow a couple of hours for the drive from Metapán. Little has been done to develop the reserve for visitors although there are plans to open an information centre and a network of trails at **Los Planes**, where there is already an orchid garden and camp site.

Lake Coatepeque

Sunk deep in the base of a huge volcanic crater, with steep forested sides, Lake Coatepeque is the most breathtaking of El Salvador's many crater lakes. Just 13 km to the south of Santa Ana the lake is on the edge of the Cerro Verde National Park, overshadowed by the sharp peaks of the Cerro Verde, Santa Ana and Izalco volcanoes.

With its clear blue waters, fed by natural hot springs, the lake is a popular Salvadorean resort and much of its shoreline is now monopolized by the holiday homes of the country's elite, with high brick walls restricting public access to the few scruffy beaches. At weekends and holidays the place is often packed, but whoever else is there the setting remains stunningly beautiful and you can dine in the faded splendour of the **Hotel del Lago**, where the rainbow bass or *guapote* is considered something of a delicacy and the crab soup, made from the lake's very own crabs, has almost legendary status. The best places to stay or swim are either at the **Hotel del Lago**, tel 782873, a crumbling structure which dates from 1924 and looks as though it hasn't been touched since or the more modern **Hotel Torremolinos**, tel 411859. If you're on a tight budget you might try the **Balneario Los Obreros**, a workers, resort (officially you need permission from the Ministry of Labour in San Salvador, 2a Avenida Sur and Calle 3 Oriente, but during the week they may let you in regardless).

The Cerro Verde National Park

Punching up through the middle of western Salvador is a monumental block of high ground in which a cluster of hills rise to the cones of the Santa Ana, Izalco and Cerro

Verde volcanoes, dominating the landscape, providing absolutely superb views and forming the country's only developed national park.

A paved road enters the park, branching off the road from Santa Ana to Sonsonate, passing to the east of Lake Coatepeque. Some 14 km inside the park there is a car park, from where a series of trails take you through the forest and up the peaks, and a road continues to the **Hotel Cerro Verde**, which is just below the peak of the same name. Cerro Verde is certainly the easiest of the peaks to climb, as you can either walk or drive straight up the road, but the other peaks are perhaps more challenging.

The Izalco Volcano

Rising to the south of Cerro Verde is the bare, black cone of the Izalco volcano, its sides streaked by lava flows. The cone began life on 23 February 1770, when a small hole in the ground started puffing out steam and ash. Within a year or two it had grown to such a height and developed such ferocity that it became known as the lighthouse of the Pacific, visible for hundreds of miles (today the cone is 1910 m high). When John Lloyd Stephens climbed it in 1839 it was clearly still a dramatic sight:

> The crater had three orifices, one of which was inactive; another emitted
> constantly a rich blue smoke; and after a report, deep in the huge throat of
> a third appeared a light blue vapour, and then a mass of thick black smoke,
> whirling and struggling out in enormous wreaths, and rising in a dark
> majestic column, lighted for a moment by a sheet of flame; and when the
> smoke dispersed, the atmosphere was darkened by a shower of stones and
> ashes.

In the early 1960s the scene was so extraordinary that the Salvadorean tourist board decided to build a luxury hotel on top of the neighbouring Cerro Verde, giving visitors a bird's-eye view of the action. However, in 1966, just as the hotel was nearing completion, the volcano decided it was not willing to perform and suddenly went quiet, erupting for the last time in October that year.

Today the Izalco volcano is still an awe-inspiring sight. It can be climbed in a couple of hours, although it is hard going on the upper slopes where the lava slips away beneath your feet. The path starts just below the Cerro Verde car park and there's a sign to point you in the right direction. If you can't face the walk there are excellent views of Izalco from the top of Cerro Verde.

The Santa Ana Volcano

Within the Cerro Verde national park the best hike takes you up the Santa Ana volcano (2365 m), the highest peak in El Salvador, which is old enough to support mature trees and still offers fantastic views. The cone has erupted four times, each producing a cone inside the one before, the deepest of which contains an emerald green lake, while another emits sulphurous fumes. In eruption this too was a formidable sight. In 1524 the conquistador Pedro de Alvarado described it as *'una de las bocas del infierno'*, one of the mouths of hell—a sight which must have sent shivers down his spine considering he was almost certainly heading in that direction.

To walk up the Santa Ana volcano follow the trail from the Cerro Verde car park. It takes around half an hour to reach the crater and then about another hour to walk around it.

Chalchuapa and the Ruins of Tazumal

A few kilometres to the west of Santa Ana is the ancient town of Chalchuapa, with its cobbled streets and crumbling plaster walls. The town has several impressive colonial churches and made its way into the Central American history books when General Justo Rufino Barrios, president of Guatemala, was killed there in a battle in 1885. The area was bitterly fought over long before then and is thought to have been occupied by Lenca Indians in the 11th century, who were later ousted by the Pokomanes, who themselves were superseded by Nahuatl or Pipil Indians migrating from the north.

Between them these various groups left a scattering of ruins in and around the town, the largest of which are at **Tazumal** on the eastern edge of the town. The site is El Salvador's most important pre-Columbian site and was first inhabited around 5000 BC. The structures that are visible today, which include a large central pyramid and several lower platforms, all restored in slate grey concrete, date from AD 300–1200 during the Maya period, when the site was occupied by Pipil-speaking Indians.

Beside the ruins is a small museum which explains the history of the site with some faded black and white pictures of the early excavations. Among the artefacts are a collections of ceramics which were unearthed during the excavations, some of which are thought to have come from Guatemala and Honduras, proving that there were well-established trade links in the region during Maya times. The site and museum are open daily 9 am-noon and 1-5.30 and admission is free.

Sonsonate and Around

On the southern side of the Cerro Verde National Park the great volcanic uplands drop down onto the coastal plain, an area rich in fertility where cattle farming and coffee are the main sources of income. The town of **Sonsonate** lies at the heart of the region, its streets packed with traders and traffic, the roar of ill-tuned buses drowning the cries of ever-optimistic salesmen. The town is a battered and impoverished city, where the majority of the population are bound up in an informal economy of street trading. However, this is a town of impeccable colonial pedigree, founded by Pedro de Alvarado in 1524, directly after he had conquered the area. Four large convents were built here and several important churches, including the **Parroquial**, which is the most imposing, **Nuestra Señora del Pilar**, built in the colonial baroque style with a superb façade, topped by a statue of the Virgin, and the **cathedral**, which sprouts some 17 cupolas, one of which is covered with white porcelain and all of which are different sizes, designed to distribute weight and minimize earthquake damage.

Sonsonate's other claim to fame is as the site of El Salvador's best Holy Week celebrations, when religious devotion and fiesta fill the streets to bursting, so if you happen to be in the country for Holy Week this is certainly the place to head for, although finding somewhere to stay may be difficult as the celebrations attract people from all across the country.

Nearby Villages

Sonsonate serves as a regional centre for trade and transport but the land to the east and west is dotted with small villages, many of which are worth a visit.

On the western edge of Sonsonate is **San Antonio del Monte**, which has an early colonial church that is lacking in charm but contains an image of San Antonio which is said to have miraculous powers and draws pilgrims from all over the country. Sundays are particularly busy and if you're in a hurry you can hire a 'praying woman' to put in a prayer on your behalf. If you're suffering a particular sorrow they'll even cry for you—for a fee, of course.

Further west still, up in the coffee-coated foothills of Cerro Verde, is the village of **Nahuizalco**, one of the last outposts of Salvador's indigenous culture, where a handful of old folk still wear traditional *huipiles*, white blouses, and *faldas*, hand-woven skirts. Local cloth is woven with a dark blue and green background and a grey-figured design although its use is certainly dying out. The ideal time to visit Nahuizalco is for the Sunday market, when you can see the work of local craftsmen, who specialize in wickerwork. Their baskets, chairs and hats are always on sale in the village, as is locally made pottery and cloth, offered alongside piles of potatoes and squawking chickens.

One last village of note is **Izalco**, a relaxed little place to the east of Sonsonate, which was founded in 1523 when the Spaniards merged the neighbouring Indian villages of Dolores and Asunción. Until recently the village still had its own Indian chief and Indian court, although these days its most notable feature is the massive Spanish bell which stands next to the ruins of an old church, destroyed by an earthquake in 1773, and declares '*María Asunción me llamo, cien quintales peso, el que no crea, que me levante en peso*' (I am called María Asunción, I weigh 100 quintales [2240 pounds], if you do not believe it then lift me up).

La Costa del Bálsamo

El Salvador's western coastline is a jumble of rocky outcrops and sandy bays, interrupted by the modern port at Acajutla. This section of coastline is known as '*la Costa del Bálsamo*'—the balsam coast—as in colonial times it was planted with balsam trees, which proved a valuable source of income. In Europe the end product became known as balsam of Peru as it was shipped south to Panamá and then sent home to Spain on ships carrying Peruvian gold. The trees are still grown and tapped there although the industry has shrunk significantly, replaced by modern commercial agriculture.

A good paved road runs from Sonsonate to **Acajutla**, with a branch road running off to the purpose-built port facility. The main road reaches the sea at Acajutla's beach, a rough, popular spot with a row of sleazy hotels, restaurants and brothels, which run behind the beach as far as the army base. It's hardly paradise on the Pacific although it does have the appealing tropical ease of a downbeat port town and at weekends it fills with Salvadoreans in search of sun, sand and sin.

If you're looking for something a little more savoury then you can either head west to the beach at **Barra de Santiago**, which is a couple of kilometres off the main highway to the border with Guatemala, or east along the road to La Libertad, which passes behind a string of scrappy villages and beautiful black sand beaches, including **Playa Sihuapi-lapa**, **Playa Mizata** and **Playa El Zunzal**, a favourite with the international surfing set.

WHERE TO STAY IN WESTERN EL SALVADOR
Despite its importance **Santa Ana** doesn't have any particularly good hotels so unless you're looking for budget accommodation you'd do best to visit the town as a day trip from San Salvador. If you do end up here the best hotel in town is the **Nuevo Hotel Roosevelt** on 8a Avenida Sur, which is at the top end of the inexpensive range, closely followed by the **Hotel Libertad**, in the corner of the main plaza. For something a little cheaper try the **Hotel Livingstone** or the **Hotelito Monterrey**, both on 10a Avenida Sur.

If you want to soak up some scenery then there are a couple of crumbling hotels on the shores of **Lake Coatepeque** (their details listed below) and there's a simple government-run hotel on the peak of the **Cerro Verde**. This establishment, built for views of the erupting Izalco volcano, missed the action when the volcano dried up but still offers some of the best views in the country. However, it's often closed so check with the tourist board in San Salvador or phone the hotel direct on 281903.

Elsewhere there are basic hotels in **Metapán**, **Sonsonate**, where the **Hotel Orbe**, 4a Calle Oriente is actually surprisingly good, and **Acajutla**, where your best bet is the **Motel Acajutla**.

GETTING AROUND WESTERN EL SALVADOR
Buses to Santa Ana leave every 10 minutes or so from the Terminal del Occidente in San Salvador.

To get to **Lake Coatepeque** from Santa Ana take bus 220, or if you're coming from San Salvador take any bus heading for Santa Ana and change at La Congo.

From Santa Ana there are buses every half-hour or so to **Chalchuapa** and **Metapán**, $1\frac{1}{2}$ hrs, bus No. 211.

Lake Coatepeque, 1 hr, bus No. 220.

Cerro Verde, bus No. 248—daily at 10.30 am and 3.30 pm—although it often doesn't run so you may have to rely on the 209B which will drop you at the entrance.

Sonsonate, bus No. 216 or 209B—the latter route offers better views.

From Sonsonate terminal there are regular buses to San Salvador, No. 205; Acajutla, No. 207 and the Guatemalan border, No. 429B.

EASTERN EL SALVADOR

El Salvador's eastern end, bitten into by the Gulf of Fonseca, is rougher and wilder—a region of sweeping volcanic vistas with a uniquely sophisticated rural charm. Battered by a decade of conflict the area still manages to welcome visitors with astonishing openness and hospitality. Its main focus is the provincial capital of **San Miguel**, while its geographical features follow a familiar Salvadorean pattern. The northern highlands drop off into a more manageable fertile strip, separated from the coast by a handful of sharp volcanic peaks, dwarfed by the huge cone of the Chaparrastique volcano. In many ways the area mirrors the eastern half of the country, but the land here is subtly different; it's bolder, wider and a great deal less populated.

As you head east the big divide comes at **Río Lempa**, where the country shakes off the claustrophobic desperation of the capital and moves into a world of surprising calm and self-sufficiency. Despite a decade of conflict people have managed to salvage an astonishing degree of normality and whether or not you like the beaches, towns, villages and mountains you can't fail to be impressed by the warmth of the people.

Among the more interesting towns in the east are **Cojutepeque**, with its sprawling market and **San Vicente**, set in a lush volcanic valley, while **San Miguel** makes an ideal base for exploring the far eastern end of the country. The finest scenery is to found along the volcanic ridge separating the Pan-American and coastal highways, while the best beaches are **El Tamarindo** and **Cuco**, both being within easy reach of San Miguel.

Cojutepeque and Around

Escaping San Salvador to the east the Pan-American Highway swings around to the north of Lake Ilopango, climbing high above its shores and offering superb glimpses of the water below, the shoreline ringed by steep forested hills.

The first place of any size or importance is the market town of **Cojutepeque**, which straddles the highway. Pausing buses are besieged by a swarm of traders, all screeching bargain prices at passengers and thrusting up bunches of onions, oranges or ice creams, as well as handfuls of hot food. At first sight their fury combines with the grit of the highway to give the town a dusty, desperate appearance, but if you walk a block or so to the south the **market** has a more dignified bustle, spreading out into every available side street. The village is a local commercial centre and its daily market is among the most energetic and extensive outside San Salvador. Between the piles of tomatoes, beans and potatoes you'll be able to find a good selection of local *artesanía*, including hammocks and pottery, as well the local delicacies of smoked meats and spicy sausages, while you might even bump into a wandering preacher, street musician or snake charmer.

Cojutepeque's other star attraction is the **Virgin of Fátima**, a tiny plaster figure, reputed to have healing powers, whose shrine attracts a steady stream of Salvadorean tourists and pilgrims. In true Salvadorean style the shrine sits on top of the **Cerro de Las Pavas**, the hill of the Turkeys, to the south of the town, sharing the view with a small army base. The main market street takes you directly to the foot of the hill, from where it's a breathless fifteen minutes to the top. The shrine is in a small grotto just below the summit and is surrounded by a typically Latin American array of offerings, including thousands of notes of thanks, acknowledging the Virgin's miraculous powers, bunches of rotting flowers and a collection of lighted candles, while an old tape recorder keeps up a steady flow of religious music, the guard getting up from time to time to rewind the tape.

If you happen to be in the area on 13 May, the Virgin's feast day, annual celebrations are held and the grotto is the scene of fervent religious activity, with thousands of devout pilgrims making the trip from all over El Salvador, along with a few devotees from the neighbouring republics.

The Cerro de las Pavas is also famous for its views across Lake Ilopango and the Santa Ana, San Salvador and San Miguel volcanoes. However, as is the case with so much in El Salvador, the army have claimed the summit as a site of strategic importance and it is now ringed by barbed wire and heavily armed teenagers. If you ask politely they might let you take a look, otherwise you'll have to make do with rummaging around below the peak and glimpsing the view between the trees.

Ilobasco and San Sebastián

Scattered in the mountains to the north of Cojutepeque are several small villages which are traditional centres for the production of *artesanía*, providing a large proportion of the goods that are bought and sold in the Cojutepeque market. It's a troubled and impoverished region, which has been swept through by both the FMLN and the army but remains true to tradition, inhabited by subsistence farmers, potters, weavers and wood-carvers.

The most famous of these villages are **Ilobasco** and **San Sebastián**. The former is famous for its ceramic plaques depicting family groups, religious figures, fruit and animals, all displayed in bold, garish colours. Whether you're after lurid pottery or not, the Sunday **market** here is certainly worth a visit, although it's smaller and quieter than the market in Cojutepeque, as is the town's fair on 19 September. But if you'd rather shop for textiles and hammocks then try **San Sebastián**, another relaxed rural community, where locals weave delicate fabrics that are similar to those made in Guatemala.

San Vicente

Clustered around its brilliant white cathedral and phallic clock-tower San Vicente sits beautifully at the foot of the Chinchontepec volcano, surrounded by a sea of sugar cane. As you drop down from the highway it seems to nestle perfectly into the landscape—an archetypal Latin American colonial town, neat and compact, slotted into an enormous landscape. Behind it terraced cane fields rise up the sides of the volcano, eventually giving way to dense forests and steep fields of lava.

This was one of the first areas to be colonized by the Spanish, who recognized its fertility and began planting sugar cane and indigo, pressing the local Indians to work for them. The town was founded on 26 December 1635, by 15 Spanish families. They had originally settled in the surrounding countryside but decided to unite for their own protection, in the face of growing Indian resistance. The town then became a traditional seat of conservative power and served as the Salvadorean capital from 1834 to 1839, during the unrest surrounding the rise and fall of the Central American federation. Meanwhile its inhabitants have faced several Indian uprisings and a number of serious earthquakes, most recently in December 1936. During the 1980s the area was bitterly fought over as the FMLN tried to press south from their mountain strongholds and the army still maintains a strong presence here, with dismembered military vehicles littering the streets around the barracks. Nevertheless San Vicente is still one of the most pleasant and picturesque of Salvador's provincial towns, with a strong colonial atmosphere, cobbled streets, a fine plaza and a couple of interesting churches. On the plaza itself is the large 18th-century **cathedral**, which is bare but big. A couple of blocks to the east is the tiny colonial church of **El Pilar**, with its classic squat, earthquake-proof façade. The only other structure of note is the clock-tower, dominating the plaza like the skeleton of a concrete Eiffel tower.

San Miguel and Around

Heading west from San Vicente the highway leaves the picturesque comforts of the Salvadorean heartland and moves into a much larger, bolder landscape. Twenty kilometres beyond San Vicente the twisting hills open out into the vast expanse of the Lempa valley, laid out beneath you as the road drops towards the river, the perfect cone of the Chaparrastique volcano rising in the distance to announce the positioning of San Miguel. In happier days the Pan-American Highway crossed the river on a bridge, an engineering achievement which was the pride of the Salvadorean government. Always keen to upset the elite, the FMLN destroyed the bridge in 1983, although the hydro-electric dam just above it is still in operation, guarded by a formidable section of the Salvadorean army. If you're interested to see what the bridge looked like, take a look at a 50-coln note, on which it's shown in its full glory. For the moment you'll have to make do with crossing the river on a shaky temporary structure.

San Miguel

Overshadowed by the charred cone of the Chaparrastique volcano El Salvador's third city is a bustling provincial capital, alive with commercial activity but with none of the tension of the capital. The city is by no means remarkable, lacking the provincial charm of San Vicente, but it is pleasant and makes an ideal base from which to explore the eastern end of the country.

San Miguel was founded in 1530 by Luis de Moscoso, acting on the orders of that arch conquistador Don Pedro de Alvarado. Under colonial rule it was a substantial regional centre with two large convents and its own bishop, but in 1655 a volcanic eruption swept away the entire city—although legend has it that one part of the church did survive, a wooden image of Lucifer, refused by the fire.

Today the volcano continues to smoke and rumble, erupting as recently as 1976, and the oldest building in town is the 18th-century cathedral, which was built by Indian labourers to replace the earlier one lost to the lava. In the 1980s much of the town received a severe battering, including the barracks, which has come under heavy attack on several occasions. However, the town appears to have weathered the storm and is in a better state than most.

The High Village of Santiago de María;
Usulután and the Coastal Highway

Some of the best day trips from San Miguel take you south to the coast, where there are a couple of excellent beaches. The most interesting way to get there is the least direct, travelling via the volcanic highlands to the west of the **Chaparrastique volcano**. Several stunning routes cross the high ridge, twisting through some of the country's finest coffee plantations. The routes through the villages of **Chinameca** and **Jucuapa** are relatively remote, with no regular bus service, so unless you're driving (and even then you may need four-wheel-drive) by far the easiest route is through **Santiago de María**. The road branches off the Pan-American Highway to the west of San Miguel and things really start to get interesting up above Santiago, where the road snakes between several sharp volcanic peaks, cutting through a narrow, gusty pass before dropping sharply towards the coast, with dramatic views of the scarred sides of the the Chaparrastique volcano. Along the way the land on either side of the road is given over to carefully groomed coffee plantations, the olive green bushes shaded by arching banana plants.

The road meets the coastal highway at the town of **Usulután**, a busy commercial centre with an enormous straggling market, where you can watch snake charmers and listen to travelling salesmen hustling everything from Peruvian shampoo to a foolproof cure for tapeworm. Despite its distinctly modern appearance, the town has been the departmental capital since 1865, although apart from the market its only other attractions are a bold town hall and clock-tower. Nevertheless it's an interesting place to spend an hour or two before heading on down the highway.

Heading west from Usulután the coastal highway runs through an intensely farmed area, although occasional lava flows, black and barren, cut through the rice fields, stretching back up the slopes of the volcano. If you're looking for sea and sand then a dirt track branches off to the south to the remote beach at **El Espino**, although there's no bus service along this route so if you're dependant on public transport you will have to stick to the beaches further west.

Beyond the turning to El Espino the highway passes the **Laguna Jocotal**, a beautiful shallow lagoon ringed by a swampy shoreline of reed beds and matted water plants, which abounds with fish and bird life. Some 56 species of waterbirds have been seen here, including muscovy ducks, shovellers, herons, grebes, gallinules and two varieties of tree duck. The place has a magical quality about it. A small army of fishermen work the lake, fishing for an hour or two at dawn or dusk in small two-man canoes, and if you offer them a dollar or two they'll gladly take you on a tour of their territory and may even teach you to cast a net.

A rough dirt track connects the highway with the lagoon, a distance of around a kilometre, passing through a desperate, scrappy village. Officially the lake is a national nature reserve, administered by the Ministry of Agriculture, but little is done to protect it and there's certainly no warden or official information, beyond a large sign announcing the rules and regulations. (For more information contact the ministry in the Colonia Santo Lucas, Calle A, San Salvador.)

The Eastern Beaches and the Port of La Unión

The coastline at Salvador's eastern end offers a variety of beautiful beaches, ranging from miles of clear sand, pounded by the surf, to small sandy bays where the sea laps gently ashore. The former is to be found at **El Cuco**, which is the closest beach to San Miguel and a favourite weekend spot with locals. If you come during the week you'll have the place to yourself, with miles of empty sand and an endless supply of Pacific rollers. The only let-down is the scruffy village behind the beach, although once you reach the sand it's easy to forget all that as you watch tiny fishing boats battling their way out to sea, tossed into the air by breaking waves.

Heading further west along the coastal highway you pass **Intipuca**, a small town which makes no bones about its links to the US, announcing its existence in English, 'Welcome to Intipuca City'. A couple of kilometres further west is a turning for the beach at **El Tamarindo**. The road to it runs via **Playa Icacal**, where the surf is still strong, thundering ashore to a series of rocky points and small sandy bays, and **Playa del Tuna**, while Tamarindo itself is just around the point inside Gulf of Fonseca, where the sea is gentle and the sand clean.

The coastal highway and the Pan-American Highway eventually meet just outside the port of **La Unión**, a sweaty, seedy spot on the shores of the Gulf of Fonseca. The port still ranks as one of the country's main shipping terminals, but to the visitor it's simply a tough fishing town, as the commercial port is a couple of kilometres away in a sealed compound. There's not much to do here, other than watch the fighting boats and gaze out across the glassy Gulf of Fonseca, but if you're heading for Nicaragua you may be able to cut out Honduras and get a lift on a boat to Potosí. (There are immigration offices in La Unión and Potosí.)

Northwards: Morazán, Santa Rosa de Lima and El Amatillo

Throughout the 1980s the rugged hills to the north of San Miguel were 'bandit country', almost entirely occupied by the FMLN. At the time of writing the departmental capital of **San Francisco Morazán** (also known as San Francisco Gotera) was occupied by the army and the area remains tense.

If you're travelling directly from San Miguel to the border at El Amatillo there's no need to go all the way to San Francisco. The Pan-American Highway takes an extended loop to the south, passing the port of La Unión and running behind the Gulf of Fonseca, although a shorter route, known as the Ruta Militar, runs through the small red-roofed town of **Santa Rosa de Lima**, which is both interesting and traditional, making it an ideal spot to break the journey. The town has a busy market, said to attract traders from throughout El Salvador and across the border in Honduras, but its biggest attraction is fish soup. Cooked from a secret recipe invented in 1969 by Señora María Eufemia, Santa Rosa's fish soup, still concocted and served by the same family, is on offer in an unmarked restaurant known as **La Pema**, a block or so to the west of the plaza. Washed down with cool coconut milk the soup is famous throughout the country and is undoubtedly El Salvador's greatest culinary delight, making it well worth stopping for.

Buses to San Francisco Morazán and Santa Rosa de Lima leave every half-hour or so from the terminal in San Miguel, those to the latter continuing to the border at **El Amatillo** (about an hour from San Miguel). There is also a regular shuttle of minibuses between Santa Rosa and the border. The border itself is relatively straight-forward with the Honduran and Salvadorean border posts on opposite sides of a bridge and clusters of moneychangers eager to exchange any combination of Central American currencies.

WHERE TO STAY AND EAT IN EASTERN EL SALVADOR
Heading east it is easy enough to reach San Miguel in a day, perhaps stopping off in Cojutepeque and San Vicente along the way, but if you're particularly taken by the charms of San Vicente then you can always spend the night in the **Hotel Central Park**, right on the plaza, giving you a superb view of town life from the second-floor balcony. It's a simple budget hotel, so don't expect any luxuries, let alone hot water. For such things you'll have to press on to San Miguel, although even there the selection is fairly limited. The best hotel in town is the **China House**, tel 610568, on the highway just at the entrance to town, but even this is only at the upper end of the budget range. For something a little cheaper try the **Hispanoamericano**, 6A Avenida Norte B.

When it comes to eating in San Miguel **El Gran Tejano** is a good spot for macho meat dishes, and there are plenty of cheap *comedores* around the bus terminal.

The best hotels in the east are to be found at the beach. At **El Cuco** the **Hotel Trópico Club**, tel 611288, which is a couple of kilometres to the east of the village, is the best, while the **Hotel Tortuga** follows a close second. There are also several cheaper places, including the **Palmera** and **Cocolinda**, in the village itself. At **El Tamarindo** there's little luxury on offer but you'll still find plenty of basic beachside accommodation. At weekends, however, both beaches get crowded.

Elsewhere in Eastern Salvador, including La Unión, Santa Rosa de Lima and Usulután you'll always find a cheap *pensión* and plenty of simple places to eat, but certainly nothing to write home about, other than the fish soup at Santa Rosa.

GETTING AROUND EASTERN EL SALVADOR
All buses to eastern El Salvador leave from the Terminal del Oriente in San Salvador. To all the main towns there are departures every half-hour between 6 am and 6 pm. The bus numbers from San Salvador are as follows:

Cojutepeque, 113
Ilobasco, 111
San Sebastián, 110 (or 19C from San Vicente)
San Vicente, 110 (1 hr 30 mins)
San Miguel, 301 (around 4 hrs).
Local routes from the terminal in San Miguel include:
Usulután, 373, via the coast,

Santa Rosa de Lima, 330
El Amatillo, 330
Chinameca, 333
La Unión, 324
El Tamarindo, 385, or the 383 from La Unión to Tamarindo
Intipuca, 320
El Cuco, 320.

If you're travelling by car then you can either head east on the Pan-American or the coastal highways, which join just outside La Unión. Both are well used and in a reasonable state of repair so it's really a question of deciding what you want to see along the way.

Part VIII
NICARAGUA

Cathedral at Léon

The largest and most infamous of the Central American republics, Nicaragua occupies a pivotal position on the isthmus and lies at the heart of the region's political instability. Despite a population of just three million and meagre resources it has featured in international headlines for more than a decade. In the wake of the 1979 Sandinista revolution Nicaragua became a disastrous obsession for President Reagan, when the unpopularity of his Contra heroes led to a bungled attempt by Colonel Oliver North to find alternative funds for their campaign.

Nicaragua has been transformed by the revolution, which has made Nicaraguans the most educated, informed and inquiring people in Central American. Empowered by a new sense of hope and participation, they have an astonishing sense of their position on the world stage, so don't be surprised if fellow bus passengers ask you to justify your country's stance on Central America or want to discuss the ramifications of the Aids epidemic. The revolution has done much to break down hierarchies and Nicaraguans are refreshingly informal—always joking, talking and questioning—making this an interesting, exciting and entertaining country, although at times people do appear exhausted and somewhat disheartened. They live, after all, in a deeply troubled country, scarred by two decades of destruction in which earthquakes, hurricanes, wars and trade embargoes have dragged them down into poverty and hardship.

Nevertheless Central America's beauty defies political boundaries. The majority of the population live along the Pacific coast, in the narrow fertile lowlands. Here the great colonial centres of Granada and León are still packed with architectural wonders, although the modern capital of Managua is largely in ruins, its chaotic remains sprawled across the shores of Lake Managua. Outside the cities this part of the country is heavily

339

farmed, with huge cotton and rice fields stretching from the sea to the great volcanic peaks. To the south the landscape is dominated by the huge expanse of Lake Nicaragua, one of the few place in the world where you can be eaten by freshwater sharks. To the east are vast tracts of empty land, ending in the wilds of the Caribbean coast.

Nicaragua is a country which reveals itself subtlely and unexpectedly. The scenery is not as dramatic as that of Guatemala, nor the culture as obvious and unusual, but this is still a fascinating country with an astonishing history. Despite the difficulties of getting around and the uncertainty of the political situation Nicaragua is a viable, if demanding destination. For those who have the time and energy to explore Nicaragua and get to know its people, this tiny country often reveals itself as the most enchanting country in the isthmus.

Post-Independence History

The link between politics and violence was established early in Nicaragua. Independence from Spain came as something of a shock to Nicaragua and Nicaraguans immediately set about using their new-found freedom to settle old scores and establish new battle lines. Full independence came in 1839 and the republic promptly divided into two factions: the Liberals, based in León, sought a radical French-style revolution, while the Conservatives, with their capital in Granada, were keen to maintain colonial structures. The two sides rapidly consolidated their positions and fighting became commonplace, the grand political struggle being often used as an excuse to settle old family feuds and local disputes.

William Walker

Among the first of many US citizens who tried to plant the Stars and Stripes in Nicaragua was William Walker, the 5-foot-five self-proclaimed 'grey eyed man of destiny'. With typical heavy-handedness and more than a touch of eccentricity. Walker was to set the tone for US intervention in the region and as such he casts a long, dark shadow.

Born in Nashville, Tennessee in 1824, Walker led a chequered career, trying his luck as a doctor, lawyer and journalist before taking a small army to conquer northern Mexico, parts of which he declared independent before being driven out by the Mexican army. Not being one to learn from his mistakes, he gathered another force and with the backing of US millionaire Cornelius Vanderbilt set sail for Nicaragua, where Vanderbilt owned the Nicaraguan Steamship Company. Arriving in June 1855, Walker sided with the Liberals, tipping the balance in a bloody civil war and winning a series of bold victories against the Granada-based Conservatives. Storming up from San Juan del Sur, Walker's ragtag army managed to capture Rivas and then sail across Lake Nicaragua to take Granada. Within a year he had declared himself President, made English the official language and reimposed slavery, much to the surprise of his Liberal associates.

However, by the end of 1856 Walker's position had begun to weaken. Having alienated all his former allies, including Cornelius Vanderbilt, he was driven from

340

Granada, torching the city before he left, and eventually faced defeat at Rivas, where his troops confronted an army of liberation moving up from Costa Rica. Walker himself managed to slip away, but four years later he was captured by the British in Honduras, handed over to the local authorities, and shot at dawn on a nearby beach.

Thirty Years of Peace

If one thing unites Nicaraguans it is their hatred of US intervention and Walker brought them together as never before. Traditional rivalry between Granada and León was eased by the relocation of the capital at Managua and for some 36 years the country enjoyed a rare spell of peace and prosperity under Conservative rule. The coffee boom, already sweeping through much of Central America, reached Nicaragua in the late 1860s, bringing a wave of European immigrants, while a parallel boom in bananas led to the development of the Caribbean coast.

Meanwhile US businessmen retained their interest in Nicaragua, which was seen as the ideal site for a canal between the oceans. During 1849 thousands of US citizens had signed up with Vanderbilt's Steamship Company and crossed the isthmus here on their way to dig for gold in California. Steamers ran up the San Juan river and across Lake Nicaragua, with stagecoaches covering the final stretch between the lake and the Pacific. In 1880 a private US company surveyed the route and in 1889 work actually began on a canal, although by then a more ambitious French team had begun to dig in Panamá.

José Zelaya: the Liberals Return and the US Invades

Typical of so many Latin American despots, José Zelaya, who in 1893 became the country's first Liberal president for more than 30 years, presented two faces to the world. On the one hand he was the thoughtful man of the people, separating the church and state, abolishing the death penalty and expanding the provision of education and health care; on the other his manner was that of a cruel, iron-fisted tyrant.

Zelaya's greatest mistake was to offer Japan and Germany the right to build a canal in Nicaragua, which outraged the US government. In 1909 US companies in Bluefields financed a rebellion and the country once again descended into civil war, forcing Zelaya to resign. In 1912 the US responded by sending in 3000 marines to protect US property, but the troops went a step or two further and ended the conflict by bombarding Masaya and ensuring a Conservative victory.

After the war the US tightened its grip on Nicaragua, taking control of the country's banks, railways, customs and shipping and manipulating presidential elections to estab-lish a puppet government. Meanwhile the marines stayed on, adding insult to injury and enraging a large section of the population.

Sandino

Throughout Nicaragua a large floppy hat is the most potent of political symbols, daubed on walls, splashed across T-shirts and even heading up the front page of *La Barricada*. Here the outsized sombrero has come to represent Augusto Sandino, one of the greatest figures in Nicaraguan history, who founded a movement which took 80 years to reach fruition and eventually changed the country beyond recognition.

Born into a middle-class family in 1895, César Augusto Sandino led a normal provincial existence until 1920, when he was forced to flee the country after killing a man during a quarrel. Ending up in Mexico, he worked in the booming oil fields, becoming involved with communist-inspired unions. Here his horizons were thrust wide open and he embarked on an unusual course of revolutionary education, studying yoga, ancient history, politics and spiritualism. In 1926 news of a revolt against Nicaragua's Conservative government inspired him to return home, taking with him just US$2000 and a pistol.

Back in Nicaragua, Sandino worked among gold-miners in the north, hustling support for the revolt and using his savings to buy guns and ammunition. He launched his first raid against a government post on the Caribbean coast and within a few months was commanding a band of more than 100 men. They based themselves in the high mountains near San Rafael del Norte and engaged government forces in a series of open battles. Elsewhere in the country other Liberal leaders fought their own campaigns, and as the uprising spread, the US government sent 2000 marines to bolster government forces. Cowed by the prospect of taking on the marines, the Liberals were soon persuaded to lay down their arms in exchange for money and land.

Sandino, however, refused, declaring that he would fight on until the last marine had left, and moving deep into the mountains to wage an extended guerrilla war. In 1928 the US staged an election in Nicaragua, although their candidate only survived for a year before the pressure for change proved irresistible and a Liberal candidate was elected. The US senate responded by voting to withdraw the marines, and once they'd left, Sandino's troops came down from the mountains.

342

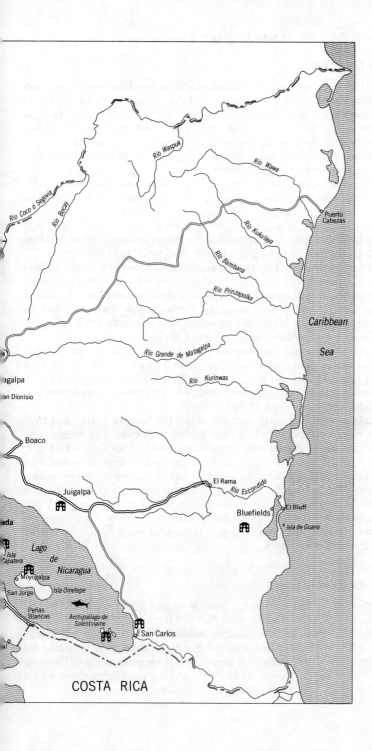

The Somoza Dynasty

In the wake of the US departure tensions ran high and Sandino's demobilized forces still resented the presence of the National Guard, which had been created by the US to support their presence. Nevertheless on 21 February 1935, Sandino came to Managua to sign a peace treaty. As he left the meeting his car was ambushed by soldiers and Sandino was shot dead. At the time the head of the National Guard, General Anastasio Somoza denied any knowledge of the killing, although he later admitted that he had ordered it, with the complicity of the US government.

The killing of Sandino cleared the way for a Somoza takeover and later that year the general staged a coup and siezed power, founding a dynasty which was to include two generations of his family and dominate Nicaraguan politics for the next forty years. Somoza had spent his youth in the US, first at business school and then selling second-hand cars in Philadelphia, but returned to Nicaragua to join the army, building up a considerable power base by serving as a liaison officer with the US forces.

Once he had taken control, Somoza ran the country as a personal fiefdom, making money through trade, politics and corruption, and creaming off a percentage in everything from coffee exports to earthquake relief. Anastasio alone amassed US$120 million in just ten years. The National Guard remained the key to his power base and all opposition was stifled at source. Meanwhile he repaid his US benefactors by allowing them to build military bases in Managua and Puerto Cabezas.

However, Somoza was fast accumulating enemies and in 1956, at a reception celebrating his nomination as presidential candidate, Somoza was shot four times by a disaffected young tailor. Hitting the ground with an almighty thud he is said to have uttered: 'I'm a gonner', before taking his last breath, while his assassin was beaten and shot, his body riddled with more than 30 bullet holes.

But it was to take more than a single assassin to end the Somoza dynasty and Luis Somoza Debayle wasted no time in taking over his father's empire. Opposition continued to grow and, despite several attempts to legitimize his rule, Luis was forced to rely on repression. In 1959 the National Guard cut down four protesting students and even the US began to call for a change of tactics, insisting that he install a puppet president. Waiting in the wings was yet another Somoza, Anastasio Somoza Debayle, who had taken command of the National Guard while his brother ran the country. As Luis's grip loosened, Anastasio pushed for control, insisting that they resort to the strong-arm tactics of their father. In 1967 Anastasio took over the presidency and a couple of months later his brother died of a heart attack.

The Sandinista Revolution

In Nicaragua's universities and unions the Sandino legacy lived on, fuelled by the corruption and incompetence of Somoza rule. By 1969 the young revolutionaries had regained their confidence and a group of radicals, including Carlos Fonseca and Tomás Borge, formed the FSLN (Sandinista National Liberation Front) to fight against the regime. The organization's early years were cramped by the imprisonment of Fonseca, who was one of its great driving forces, but in 1970 the hijack of an airliner secured his release and the movement began its most important decade.

In December 1972 it received an unwelcome boost when a massive earthquake rocked Managua, reducing the city to dust and killing 10,000 people. International assistance flooded in but Somoza was unable to resist the temptation and seized millions of dollars, siphoning the money into his pet companies. The suffering and disgust engendered by this swelled support for the Sandinistas and over the next few years the movement grew rapidly, staging a series of bold raids, including storming a Somoza Christmas party and holding the guests to ransom. Somoza responded by imposing martial law, and by 1977 the FSLN was launching all-out attacks on National Guard bases. In February 1978 the movement could claim some 2000 members; a year later their forces were strong enough to take control of Estelí and León.

In March 1979 the FSLN leadership formed itself into a National Directorship and made a final bid for power. As guerrillas fought street battles in the small towns a provisional government was formed in Costa Rica. León was the first city to be fully liberated, closely followed by Estelí, Matagalpa and Masaya; on 19 July the FSLN took Managua, although only after Somoza had ordered his air force to bomb the city.

Somoza and his family managed to escape in a private jet and he found refuge in Paraguay, which was under the control of the great strongman Stroessner. However, a couple of years later Somoza was killed in a bazooka attack on his car. While this was probably the work of the Sandinistas, it was also rumoured that Somoza had overstayed his welcome and was beginning to threaten Stroessner's position.

The Sandinista Government and The Contra War

Ten years in the mountains had hardly prepared the Sandinista directorate for running a small and bankrupt country and victory came as a bit of a shock. In the early years ideology dominated, with Sandinista leaders stepping out of helicopters to hand bewildered peasants the deeds to their land and dashing back to Managua to greet the world's leading left-wingers.

Nevertheless the new government tried hard to create a mixed economy and to raise the standard of living throughout the country. A huge campaign reduced illiteracy from 50 to 13%, and great strides were made in the provision of housing and health care. The economy fared less well, with collective farms proving unproductive, and once Ronald Reagan was in the White House the country faced the added burden of a US trade embargo. Nicaraguan trade had always been firmly linked to the US, and the embargo left the country without spare parts for its buses or tarmac to fill its potholes, forcing the government to rely heavily on support from Cuba and the Soviet Union, and to expand its horizons, exporting sugar, coffee, cotton and bananas as far afield as Germany and Japan.

In 1984, under heavy international pressure, the Sandinistas held elections. Winning some 61% of the vote, Daniel Ortega was re-elected as President. President Reagan refused to accept the regime's legitimacy and remained preoccupied by the idea that Nicaragua was an ideal Soviet missile base. The Contras declared all-out war and conditions in Nicaragua declined sharply, with food shortages and unemployment becoming commonplace.

The Contra War

Described by Ronald Reagan as the moral equivalent of the founding fathers, the Contras were formed in 1982 from a motley collection of former National Guardsmen, embittered peasants and ambitious mercenaries. Despite massive US assistance they never managed to control any Nicaraguan territory although they did present a major obstacle to the success of the revolution, sapping its meagre resources. Blundering into Nicaragua from their bases in Honduras and Costa Rica, Reagan's anti-communist heroes fought a low-intensity war, raiding farms and villages along the borders and forcing the government to spend a third of its budget on the conflict. By the time it came to an end the war had cost more than 60,000 lives and devastated the Nicaraguan economy.

The irritation caused by the war was added to by an Indian uprising along the Caribbean coast, also funded by the US, and by the work of the CIA. US navy special forces also got involved, planting mines in the harbour at Corinto and blowing up a couple of oil storage depots. Meanwhile, back in Washington an over-zealous Colonel Oliver North pushed things a little too far with his arms for hostages deal, and by the end of the 1980s the Contras had lost all credibility.

The 1990 Elections

As Nicaraguans went to the polls in February 1990 the Sandinistas were quietly confident, with all observers predicting that they would win at least 60% of the vote. The following day they awoke with a bump to discover that Violeta Chamorro's UNO (United Nicaraguan Opposition) alliance had pushed them into second place.

Central America's answer to Cory Aquino, Violeta Chamorro fits a very modern mould. Her husband, Pedro, editor and owner of *La Prensa*, was murdered by the National Guard shortly before the revolution and Violeta herself served in the first Sandinista government as a respresentative of the middle classes. Nevertheless the basis of Chamorro's election victory appears to have been the desire for a change. Ten years of conflict and hardship had left most Nicaraguans exhausted and disillusioned. Few could face the prospect of more shortages, deaths and unemployment, and with US backing they felt Chamorro could at least end the war, while her free-market policies could even revitalize the economy.

Since her election Chamorro has been able to offer little clear direction, struggling to hold together her piecemeal alliance and stumbling from one crisis to another. Price subsidies have been removed, conscription ended and land returned to its original owners, but for most people the situation has deteriorated rapidly. More than half the population is now unemployed and social programmes have been severely cut back, while prices, crime and homelessness have risen dramatically. However, it is on the world stage that Nicaragua's new president has managed to make an impact, hugging President Bush when they first met, prompting a small scuffle between their respective bodyguards, and touring Europe in search of ever elusive foreign aid.

Back at home the war refuses to end and an assortment of former Contras, dubbing themselves the re-Contras, have taken to the hills to harrass the civilian population, steal from buses and attack government forces. In response a group of former Sandinistas, known as the re-Compas (from *compañero*) have also taken matters into their own hands, vowing to defeat the re-Contras. For the moment all this shows little sign of erupting into a full-scale conflict, but the presence of large numbers of well-armed and deeply divided individuals is sure to maintain a degree of tension. For the average Nicaraguan, life is as hard as ever; with the revolution finally defeated, the country appears to be collapsing into an economic and ideological vacuum.

General Information

Getting to Nicaragua

By Air

Direct flights **from Europe** to Managua are offered by Iberia, KLM and Aeroflot, with a return fare costing between £500 and £600. Direct flights **from the US** leave from San Francisco, Miami and New York, amongst others, and are provided by a range of North and South American airlines. You should expect to pay around US$600 for a scheduled return fare from Miami and double that from New York or Canada.

Flying in **from other Central American cities** there's at least one flight every day from Panamá City, San José, San Salvador, Guatemala City, Mexico City and a couple of times a week from Belize City. There are also regular flights to all South American capitals and a number of destinations in the Caribbean, including Havana.

Nicaragua's international airport is on the southern edge of Managua and there is a US$10 departure tax on all international flights.

By Bus

International buses operated by the **Ticabus** connect Managua with San José and Panamá City three times a week. The Ticabus office in Managua is in the Barrio Martha Quezada, tel 26094. A similar service is also provided by the **Sirca** bus company, whose office is just north of the Shell Centro América. Local buses also operate to all the border crossings and you can easily make it from Managua across the border into Costa Rica or Honduras in a day. The border crossing points are open daily 8–4.30.

Embassies and Consulates

UK: 8 Gloucester Road, London SW7, tel 071–584 3231.
US: 1627 New Hampshire Ave, Washington DC 20009, tel (202) 9396570.

Passports and Visas

Citizens of Canada, Great Britain and most West European countries do not require visas and are issued with 90-day tourist cards at the border. If you arrive by air you may be asked to produce an onward ticket. US citizens require visas, which are normally valid for one month and must be obtained from a Nicaraguan consul outside the country. Visas and tourist cards can be extended at the immigration office in Managua (on the Pista de la Resistencia, 1 km west of Zumen).

On Arrival

Tourist Offices

The state tourist board, **Inturismo**, has offices in Managua, a block west of the Hotel Intercontinental, and Estelí. They're very friendly and can offer some help and information, but are often stumped by surprisingly simple queries.

Maps

Good maps of Nicaragua have been hard to come by for more than ten years now. Military secrecy and widespread shortages appeared to shut down the map-making industry, although just recently a simple tourist map, showing Managua on the back, was published by Inturismo. It's available from their offices in Estelí and Managua and some bookshops.

Getting Around Nicaragua

Despite the introduction of the free market Nicaragua's transport system remains the most dilapidated, overcrowded, uncomfortable and ineffecent in all of Central America. However, there are some signs that things are getting better, and by the time you arrive, it may even be possible to get a seat on a bus.

By Air

Nicaragua's main cities are all within a couple of hundred kilometres of each other, making air travel largely impractical. The only routes on which it makes any sense at all are those to Puerto Cabezas, Bluefields and the Corn Islands on the Caribbean coast. Here a rough service is operated by **Aeronica**, with three weekly flights to each destination, although you need to book well in advance and cancellations are common. At the time of writing, flights to the Corn Islands have been suspended because the airstrip has reverted to sand dunes. Private charter companies, based at the international airport, also fly to more remote destinations, although they offer no scheduled service. There is a US$1.50 tax on all internal flights.

By Bus

Nicaragua's bus system is the worst in Central America. A decade of unrest and trade embargoes has left the country with a strange selection of East European trucks, Soviet jeeps, ancient US buses and more modern Brazilian versions, all of which show signs of inventive repair and adaptation. They offer an interesting reflection on Nicaragua's international political alliances but as a way of getting from A to B they leave a lot to be desired. Schedules are vague, and when buses do turn up, there's a desperate scramble for seats, with young street children climbing aboard and selling spaces. Empty seats are almost unheard of and even the roof space can become cramped. But if you do decide to use public transport there's really nothing that can be done to avoid the crush, so it's best to just get there early, pitch in and fight for a seat—but beware of pickpockets.

By Train

If you've plenty of time and patience then Nicaragua's trains are cheaper and less crowded than its buses. Train travel is certainly eventful and you can travel in a seat or an open box car. Passengers scramble all over the train accompanied by a range of livestock.

Speeds rarely exceed 45 kph. The principal lines connect Managua with León and Granada, with three trains a day in either direction, taking around three hours.

Car Hire

Rates are as high as in Europe and the US. Bearing in mind conditions on public transport, hiring will save you a lot of time and bother, although in remote areas, particularly the northern highlands, beware of banditry. Hire companies are all in Managua—addresses are listed in the Managua section—and you'll need an international driver's licence. Watch out for buried extras such as insurance and mileage.

By Taxi

Within the major cities taxis are certainly a lot easier, safer and quicker than buses, and even the most dedicated user of public transport may resort to taxis when confronted by Managua. Taxis tend to be readily available, hooting eagerly at waiting foreigners, although supplies dwindle during rush hour and rainfall. At any time you may have to share a taxi as drivers pick up any number of people heading roughly in the same direction. Many unofficial 'private' drivers also operate as part-time taxi drivers, but whether it's official or not, fix the fare beforehand. Taxis can also be used for trips between towns or you might even consider hiring one for a day or two, to save you getting lost in a hired car. They can be arranged through the tourist office in Managua and taxi drivers also advertise in the 'services' section of *El Nuevo Diario*.

Embassies and Consulates

Costa Rica: Pista Benjamin Zeledón, nr Plaza España (to south).
France: Km 12 Carretera del Sur, tel 26210/27011.
Guatemala: Just after Km 11 on Masaya Road.
Honduras: Carretera del Sur, Km 15, Colonie Barcelona.
UK: El Reparto, 'Los Robles', Primera Etapa, Entrade Principal de la Carretera a Masaya, Cuarte Cesa a la man derecha, tel 70034.
US: Km 41/2 Carretera del Sur, tel 23881.

Money Matters

The Nicaraguan córdoba is a notoriously unstable currency, even by Latin American standards and dollar cash is often in use alongside the córdoba. Cash is king and here, more than anywhere else in Central America, you'll need dollar cash to get hold of local currency. Black-market operators change money in the streets of Managua (particularly around the Plaza España) and at all overland border crossings. If you only have traveller's cheques then there is only one place where you can change them: the Banco Nacional de Desarrollo in the Plaza España, Managua, open 8–12.30 and 1.30–4 Mon–Fri.

Communications

All communications are operated by TELCOR, a state-owned corporation with offices in the centre of every town. Since there are no coins there are no public phones; so unless you call from your hotel, all calls have to be made from TELCOR offices, which are normally very efficient and can arrange collect calls to anywhere in the world. To contact the international operator dial 116.

Mail is also handled by TELCOR and takes 10–15 days to reach Europe, although oddly enough it can take as long as 30 days to reach the US. If you're sending a package, its contents have to be inspected by customs at the central office. **Faxes** and **telegrams** are also sent from TELCOR offices. To send a telegram from a private phone, call 117.

Police and Military

The desperate economic situation in Nicaragua has led to a upsurge in crime. For the most part this is confined to petty theft and pickpocketing is common, particularly on crowded buses and in the streets of Managua. A more sinister trend is the increase in armed robbery, particularly on the back roads. The areas to avoid are the highlands to the north and east of Estelí. You should also take particular care in Managua at night and bear in mind that it is a dark, desperate city, in which taxi travel is advisable.

Opening Hours

Generally speaking businesses are open 8–noon, 2.30–6, Mon–Fri, banks 8.30–noon, 2–4, Mon–Fri, and some 8.30–11 on Saturday mornings.

Media

In a country obsessed by political debate it's hardly surprising that there are several excellent and deeply ideological **newspapers**. The two most infamous are *Barricada*, which is the official Sandinista paper but has now modified its header, dropping the masked gunman, and *La Prensa*, which backs Chamorro's UNO alliance and was formerly edited by her husband. Both provide excellent, opinionated coverage. Weekly publications include *Semana Cómica*, offering 'humour, marxism, sex and violence', the conservative *La Crónica*, and the communist party's *Avance*.

If you're taking a wander through the air waves, you'll also find hundreds of **radio stations**, large and small, offering everything from evangelical sermons to red hot *salsa*. When it comes to **TV** there are just two channels, Channel 6 and Channel 2, both of which are run by the state and offer a blend of education, soap opera, news and current affairs. Weekday programmes run from noon to 11, while at weekends the cartoons start at 9 am and the late movie runs into the small hours.

Public Holidays

Jan: 1, New Year's Day. **Mar/Apr**: Holy Thursday, Good Friday. **May**: 1, Labour Day. **July**: 19, Revolution of 1979. **Sept**: 14, Battle of San Jacinto; 15, Independence Day. **Nov**: 2, All Souls (*Diá de los Muertos*). **Dec**: 7 and 8, Immaculate Conception (*Purísma*); 25, Christmas Day.

Itineraries

Despite the fact that it's the largest country in Central America the best of Nicaragua can easily be seen in a week or two. Managua makes an unfortunate but unavoidable base. However, the other two main towns, León and Granada, are both less than an hour away and among the most interesting cities on the isthmus. Outside this narrow heartland you can choose between the northern highlands, centred on Estelí, with its cool, fresh climate and wide-open views, Lake Nicaragua, dotted with islands and unusual cultures, the Pacific beaches and the Caribbean coast. Each of these demands at least a couple of days, although if you decide to head out east, it's worth taking a little longer, bearing in mind the time it takes to get there.

Managua

If you stand on a rise in the centre of Managua, you can see the rain squalls crossing the lake like columns of smoke; the edge of the storm marked against the far shore. Another squall chases along a mile or so behind. On a clear day you can count twenty-one volcanoes on the opposite shore. After a good lunch you can count twenty-five.

Patrick Marnham, *So Far From God*

Marnham's description of Managua has, perhaps, one obvious flaw—having located himself at its centre he then completely ignores the city. But after a couple of days here you soon learn that it's an understandable omission. Managua is a city that isn't; whichever way you turn, it somehow slips through your fingers. The city centre is open and empty, most of the original buildings cracked and abandoned, while activity is focused on a handful of sprawling markets and bus terminals, strung out in the suburbs. The bizarre and shattered layout defies description, with open fields scattered across the city and temporary shantytowns flanking the abandoned centre. The cathedral is burnt out and roofless, the former Bank of Managua now home to a handful of impoverished families.

Managua is a miracle of survival. The capital was moved here from León in 1858, in an attempt to bridge the gulf between Conservative Granada and Liberal León. Since then it has taken several severe batterings: the first earthquake struck in 1931, destroying three-quarters of the city. A huge fire swept the city in 1936 and a second earthquake, in 1972, killed more than 12,000. Finally the 1979 revolution smashed up many of the remaining buildings. Since then little has been done to repair the damage and the centre is something of a ghost town, although the government does still operate from here. In the last decade a massive influx of refugees and migrants has added to the city's problems, with thousands of poor families setting themselves up on empty waste ground and scraping an existence on the edge of a non-existent economy.

This is a city of disaster and desperation. The wealthier suburbs just manage to appear normal, their streets still pitted and cracked. Low-lying and sprawling aimlessly, Managua is an eternal confusion. A shantytown gives way to an open field, then a ruined church, a stadium, a bus terminal, a four-lane highway. It's an extremely difficult city to get to grips with, saved only by the warmth and energy of its people. In the huge suburban markets, thick with bus fumes and mud, Managua is at its most extraordinary: sharp-witted and alive, desperate and exhausted.

GETTING AROUND MANAGUA
If you'd like to sample the smell and sensation of Managua's bus system, which is certainly an unforgettable experience, then here are some of the main routes, all of which pass in front of the Hotel Intercontinental. But bear in mind that pickpocketing is particularly common on crowded buses.

118: Israel Lewites market, Plaza España, Hotel Intercontinental, Mercado Oriental, Mercado Iván Montenegro.

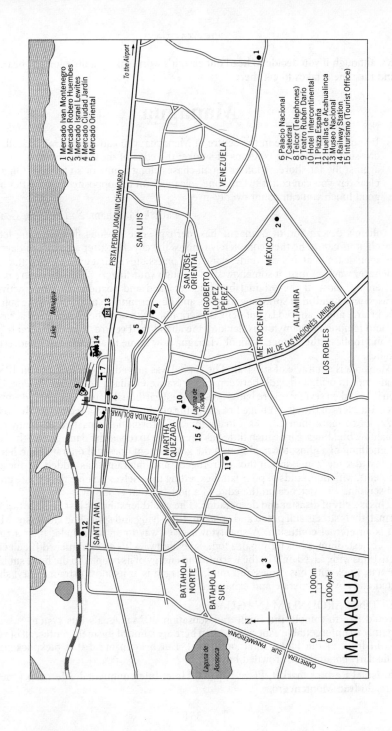

MANAGUA

1 Mercado Ivan Montenegro
2 Mercado Robero Huembes
3 Mercado Israel Lewites
4 Mercado Ciudad Jardin
5 Mercado Oriental

6 Palacio Nacional
7 Catedral
8 Telcor (Telephones)
9 Teatro Rubén Darío
10 Hotel Intercontinental
11 Plaza España
12 Huellas de Acahualinca
13 Museo Nacional
14 Railway Station
15 Inturismo (Tourist Office)

Lake Managua

To the Airport

PISTA PEDRO JOAQUIN CHAMORRO

SAN LUIS

VENEZUELA

MÉXICO

SAN JOSÉ
ORIENTAL

RIGOBERTO
LÓPEZ
PÉREZ

METROCENTRO

ALTAMIRA

AV. DE LAS NACIONES UNIDAS

LOS ROBLES

Laguna de
Tiscapa

AVENIDA BOLIVAR

MARTHA
QUEZADA

SANTA ANA

BATAHOLA
NORTE

BATAHOLA
SUR

CARRETERA
SUR PANAMERICANA

Laguna de
Asososca

N

0   1000m
0   1000yds

119: Plaza España to the Mercado Huembes.
119: Hotel Intercontinental to the Mercado Oriental.
105: Metrocentro, airport.

Car hire is also a viable option (the main companies are listed below), although you're still saddled with the problem of finding your way around. The main car hire companies are: **Budget** main office in **Hotel Intercontinental**, tel 23531; **Hertz**, main office, tel 666461; **Tur-nica**, near Plaza España, tel 661387.

Alternatively you could **hire a bicycle**, from 'Bikes not Bombs' in the Mercado Periférico, opposite the Cementerio Oriental, although as ever the same problems present themselves, with the added danger of Nicaraguan drivers.

USEFUL INFORMATION

Airlines
Most airline offices, including **Aeronica, Tan/Sasha, Iberia** and **Aeroflot** are in the Plaza España. For the addresses of others, look in the phone book.

Banks
The only bank which certainly changes traveller's cheques and cash is the **Banco Nacional de Desarrollo** in the Plaza España, which is open 8–12.30 and 1.30–4, Mon–Fri.

Embassies and Consulates
UK: tel 70034, right turning to the north of Metrocentro, although all consular affairs are handled by the consulate in San José, Costa Rica.
US: tel 23881, Apartado 327, Carretera Sur.
Costa Rica: Pista Benjamín Zeledón, south of the Plaza España.
Guatemala: Km 11 Carretera Masaya.
Honduras: Km 15 Carretera del Sur, Colonia Barcelona.

Post Office and Telephones
The main TELCOR office is a block to the west of the Plaza de la Revolución. Opening hours for international phone calls, 7 am–10.30 pm every day; post, 7–7 Mon–Fri, 7–3 Saturday; fax 8–noon and 1–5 Mon–Fri, 8–1 Saturday.

Tourist Office
On a small street a block west of the Intercontinental, the tourist office is open 8–12 and 1–5, Mon–Fri and is reasonably helpful.

ORIENTATION
Of all the Central American capitals Managua is the most confusing: distances are enormous, street signs virtually non-existent and the city's focal points very spread out. It's a city in which taxis are a godsend.

Locals use four all-important directions: north is *al lago*—towards the lake; south, *al sur* or *montaña*—to the south of the mountains; east, *arriba*—up; and west, *abajo*—down. In the city centre the most important landmarks are the Hotel Intercontinental, a strange pyramidal structure which can be seen throughout the city centre, and the

Cathedral, which is down by the lakeshore. The old city centre stretches between these two points, as does Avenida Bolívar.

Elsewhere it's the main markets and bus terminals, that are the focal points. In the west is the Israel Lewites terminal, used by buses heading to the León area, Rivas and San Juan del Sur. To the southeast is the Roberto Huembes terminal, serving Masaya, Granada, Estelí and Matagalpa, and further east the Iván Montenegro terminal, also known as Oscar Benavides, from where buses run to the Atlantic coast. If you're planning to arrive or depart by train the station is about 200 metres east of the Cathedral, while the airport is on the lakeshore to the east.

WHAT TO SEE
Managua's troubled history has left the city with few tourist attractions and those that remain are relatively simple. Sadly some of the Sandinista museums have recently been closed down by the UNO government and many of the city's finest murals painted over. Nevertheless this is a fascinating city, its streets and markets unlike any other, and exploring it is a bizarre revelation as you come to see how it fits together in a totally unique way.

The City Centre
The most striking thing about the centre of Managua is that most of the activity takes place elsewhere. Shattered and largely abandoned, the city centre reveals a great deal about the country's troubled history.

The main focal point is the **Palacio Nacional**, a great neoclassical rectangle which embraces a leafy courtyard. Just a block south of the lake, the palace still houses the main government offices and a mural above the entrance depicts the Mexican and Nicaraguan revolutions. The building looks out on the **Plaza de la Revolución**, which was the scene of enormous celebrations following the fall of Managua to the Sandinistas in June 1979, when an estimated 100,000 people turned out to welcome the guerrillas into office. The plaza is flanked by the **Cathedral**, which is cracked, roofless and burnt, having been badly damaged by the 1972 earthquake, its clock still stuck at 12.32—the moment the ground began to shake. Plans are afoot to build a new Cathedral on a huge field in the southwest of the city, near the Metrocentro, although the Church is having trouble raising the cash. For the moment Nicaragua's right-wing bishop, Cardinal Miguel Obando y Bravo, delivers his Mass in the church of Las Sierritas on the edge of Managua. Opposite the Cathedral, on the other side of the plaza, is a small shaded park which houses the **tomb of Carlos Fonseca**, one of the most famous founding fathers of the FSLN, who was killed in 1976. When Fonseca was interned here, an eternal flame was lit to over his grave, but in 1990 the newly elected UNO government had it put out.

Between the Plaza de la Revolución and the lakeshore is the **Rubén Darío Theatre**, the nation's cultural flagship, a huge and faceless building with seating for over a thousand. During the day you can take a look inside, where there is a gallery of modern art and a coffee bar. Alongside the theatre is a large open-air grandstand used for sporting events and political rallies, which seems to be inspired by Soviet-style concrete architecture.

To take in what used to be the heart of Managua walk back up towards the Hotel Intercontinental, alongside Avenida Bolívar. In the middle of the main road behind the Palacio Nacional, a huge black statue of a man reaches for the sky, clutching a pickaxe in one hand and an AK-47 sub-machine gun in the other. An inscription below the statue, somewhat pre-glasnost, reads: 'Only the workers and peasants will go to the end'.

Walking up through the centre of town is a strange experience. Among the ruins are shanty homes, small parks, brand new office blocks, basketball pitches and government offices. This part of town has never really recovered from the earthquake and has none of the city bustle that you might expect. Nevertheless there are some impressive new buildings, including the national bank and the Olaf Palme convention centre, an all-modern 1200-seater, alongside which is the National Assembly.

Museo Nacional

By no means one of the world's greatest museums, Nicaragua's national museum is small and homely, offering a brief insight into the country's natural history, geography, archaeology and anthropology. The exhibition opens with a gathering of stuffed birds, animals, butterflies, beetles and fish, including a young shark from Lake Nicaragua. From there it moves on through the country's volcanic structure to a small but interesting archaeological section, which includes pottery and totem poles from the country's most important sites, including the islands of Zapatera and Omotepe. Things are finally brought to a close with a couple of colonial cannons and a display featuring Nicaraguan crafts such as hat-weaving, pottery, saddle-making and gourd-carving. (The museum is on the lakeshore just east of the train station and is open 9–5, Mon–Fri.)

Las Huellas de Acahualinca

Said to be Nicaragua's most important archaeological site the Acahualinca footprints, said to have been made in lakeside mud by Indians fleeing a volcanic eruption, have been carbon dated to 6000 years ago. The site is now carefully preserved, although the most remarkable thing is that footprints then looked pretty much as they do today. Adjacent to the site is a small museum displaying ancient pottery fragments found nearby. (The museum is beside the railway tracks in the Barrio Santa Ana, west of the National Palace and open 8–3, daily.)

Museo de la Alfabetización

Following the 1979 revolution Nicaragua's army of 95,000 young idealists set out once again to conquer an evil force. This second battle, staged in 1980, was against illiteracy and its success is charted in a small museum near the Parque Las Palmas. Photographs, books, graphs and teaching materials all tell the story of the campaign which reduced illiteracy from 53% to 13% in just 6 months. But be warned: the government of Violeta Chamorro is in the habit of closing down museums which celebrate Sandinista rule, so this too may face the chop.

The City's Markets

At times it seems as though the only place where anything happens in Managua is in the markets, and certainly it's here that the city comes alive. The largest and most chaotic of the city's markets is the **Mercado Oriental**, a great sprawl of shacks and stalls, packed with intrigue, bad smells and commercial bustle. The market is a black-marketeer's dream, a maze of tiny alleys, blind corners and dodgy dealers, where you can buy anything from sandpaper to snakes.

Further out, on the edge of town, are several large commercial markets, which double up as bus terminals, only adding to the congestion. The largest is the **Huembes market**, where you'll find a good selection is craftwork (although if you're after this sort of thing then the selection is wider and the quality higher in Masaya). The other markets, **Israel Lewites** and **Iván Montenegro**, offer more in the way of food and clothing.

The Church of Santa María de los Angeles
Throughout the 1980s one of Managua's most prolific forms of cultural expression was the political mural. Across the city, spare wall space was covered with the bold colours and strident message of the Sandinista revolution and the history of Nicaragua was spelled out in graphic terms, moving from pre-Columbian paradise through gringo-inspired hell to the success of the Sandinista struggle. Sadly the new UNO government has done all it can to eradicate this message, including whitewashing most of the city's street art. However, in the impoverished *barrio* of Riguero, one last mural survives inside the church of Santa María de los Angeles. Christ, Columbus and the revolution are all swept into a set of murals, which leap from the wall, alive with enthusiasm and confidence. It's a fascinating testament, both to the revolution and to the force of liberation theology in Nicaragua, which has deeply divided the country's clergy.

The church is not particularly easy to find, but if you ask around in the *barrio*, someone will point you in the right direction. Opening times are equally uncertain but there's usually a cleaner or priest in attendence.

WHERE TO STAY
EXPENSIVE
The best hotel in town is the **Hotel Camino Real**, tel 31381, on the road to the airport, which offers two restaurants, a gym, a pool, tennis courts and even a barber's shop. Just next door the **Hotel Mercedes**, tel 32111, offers almost as much, or if you'd like to be in the centre of town then the **Hotel Intercontinental**, tel 23531, one of Managua's great landmarks, could hardly be more central and has a panoramic view across the city centre.

MODERATE
Managua's mid-range hotels have a long tradition of serving a pack of freelance journalists so don't be surprised if there's a typewriter on the dressing table. The **Casa de Huéspedes Fielder**, tel 666622, is among the best, situated just west of the Barrio Martha Quezada. For something a little more luxurious, including a pool, try the **D'Lido**, tel 666145 while back towards the centre the **Hotel Magut**, tel 22166, a block west of the Intercontinental, is good value.

INEXPENSIVE
A steady flow of impoverished young idealists has given Managua a handful of classic budget hotels. Three of the best are the **Pensión Santos**, which has tiny rooms around a nice open courtyard, with hammocks and food on offer, the **Pensión Mesa** and the smaller family-run **Hospedaje Quintana**. All three are basic, cheap and on the same street in the Barrio Martha Quezada, which is just to the west of the Hotel Intercontinental.

EATING OUT
Buried among Managua's *barrios* are a respectable selection of cafés and restaurants, offering a vaguely cosmopolitan variety.

EXPENSIVE

For a touch of European flavour your best bet is **La Marseillaise** (in Los Robles, west of the carretera Massaya), which is one of the city's finest eating houses, serving up French cuisine with a splash of Central American spice. Other top establishments include **El Panorama** (at km 6.5 on the Carretera Sur), the neighbouring **Lobster Inn**—serving seafood, in case you hadn't guessed, or **Mirador Tiscapa**, which overlooks the lagoon and is popular at weekends, when locals come here to dine and dance. For a traditional macho meat meal the ideal venues are **Los Ranchos** (Carretera Sur km 3) or **Los Gauchos** (Carretera Massaya km 2.5), which is a favourite with Managua's high-profile business boys.

MODERATE

If you're looking for more moderately priced food then the selection is even more interesting. Home cooked pasta and vegetarian dishes are available from **El Tucán** (Carretera Sur km 7.5) and excellent seafood from **Los Arrieros** (two blocks south of the train station). For really exotic local food, including iguana and snake, head for **Walpa Tara** (three blocks east of the Montoya statue). Oriental food, lovingly prepared by a Thai chef, is available at **The Plaza** (in Parque de las Madres).

INEXPENSIVE

For really cheap food try your luck in any of the suburban markets or among the cafés and *comedores* of the Barrio Martha Quezada. Here the **Pensión Santos** offers good, filling food, the **Bambú** serves up vegetarian specials and you can drink and dance at the **Gallo Pinto**.

Cooling Off Around Managua

In the countryside around Managua are a couple of small lakes and pools which provide the city's inhabitants with the opportunity to cool off at weekends. **Jiloa**, a small circular lagoon just 18 km to the northwest is the most popular. Here Managuans come to sail and swim in the warm waters, said to have miraculous healing powers. The lagoon is just off the new road to León, a small road branching north just beyond Ciudad Sandino and at weekends there are special buses, from the Parque Piedrecitas, Carretera Sur km 6, in Managua.

Alternatively you can take a dip at the **El Trapiche** tourist park, where a pool has been formed in the Tipitapa river and there's a small floating restaurant and bar, built from the remains of an old plane. El Trapiche is on the old Tipitapa–Managua road.

The Pacific Beaches: Pochomil, Masachapa and Montelimar

The closest beach to Managua is **Pochomil**, where hoards of city dwellers indulge themselves at weekends. There's plenty of surf, food, music and beer, with bars open well into the small hours and Holy Week is one long party here. If you'd like something a little quieter then head a few kilometres north to **Masachapa**, a small fishing village which has several small hotels but tends to be a little more relaxed. Buses to Pochomil and Masachapa run from the Israel Lewites market.

Last, but by no means least, is the resort at **Montelimar**. An old favourite with Somoza and the oligarchy, this is the country's number one resort, complete with a luxury hotel, golf course, tennis courts, airport, casino and prices to match. Package tourists are flown in direct from Miami to enjoy the perfect faceless beach holiday, but if you're overwhelmed by the fury of Managua, this an excellent place to spend some money. Buses don't run to Montelimar but you can arrange a three or four-day package with the travel agent in the Intercontinental in Managua, or with any other major travel agent.

NORTHERN NICARAGUA

Squeezed in along the northern Pacific coast is a belt of extremely fertile country which is focused on the colonial city of León, one of the most beautiful cities in Central America. León alone demands a couple of days', attention, but if you're keen to explore, it also makes an ideal base for trips along the coast to the port of Corinto or even as far afield as Potosí on the Gulf of Fonseca.

León

Occupying an uncertain position somewhere between colonial splendour and revolutionary fervour Nicaragua's second city is a wealth of contradictions. The city's magnificent colonial architecture is perhaps the most impressive in Central America, while spare wall space is claimed by bold revolutionary murals, in which the colours and images shout out at passers-by. The city's private life is equally diverse, incorporating both impoverished desperation and middle-class ease. Torn plastic sheets protect market stalls from the midday sun, but behind the city's battered walls and lace curtains is a glimpsed world of cool courtyards and polished rocking chairs. Any residue of colonial pomposity is punctured by the strong student presence and the city is relaxed and approachable.

As the unchallenged centre of culture and left-wing politics, León occupies a pivotal position in Nicaraguan society, having served as the capital for more than 300 years. The city was originally founded, in 1524, on the shores of Lake Managua, but a massive earthquake soon reduced it to dust, persuading the colonial authorities to move the settlement 20 km to the west. Here León flourished, serving as the religious and cultural centre, although never approaching the wealth of Granada, which remained the centre of trade and commerce. Following independence the two cities became locked in bitter rivalry, dispatching raiding parties to settle old scores and disrupt trade. By 1858 the authorities decided to act and León's supremacy was finally ended as the capital moved to neutral Managua. Since then the city has remained prosperous, situated in the midst of the country's finest farmland and halfway between the capital and the main port, although during the revolution it took a pounding as young Sandinistas fought house-to-house battles with the National Guard.

GETTING TO LEÓN

Two roads connect Managua and León: N28, the old road, passes through La Paz Centro and is preferred by most traffic, while N12 takes a slightly more direct route, passing the turning to Puerto Sandino. Buses from the Israel Lewites terminal run to León every hour from 5 am to 6 pm and there are also a couple of trains a day, which are cheap, slow and laden with character.

GETTING AROUND LEÓN

León's bus terminal is on the northeastern edge of the city, a couple of kilometres from the plaza. Horse-drawn carriages run a shuttle service to the train station and market, from where you can easily walk to any of the hotels. The city is small enough to be explored on foot, although finding your way around the city is a little tricky as street signs are scarce, and the easiest way to locate yourself is by using a map and steering between the major landmarks.

WHAT TO SEE

Any tour of León has to start in the **Parque Central**, which is dominated by the massive **Cathedral**, regarded by many as Central America's finest colonial building. Legend has it that the Cathedral was intended for Peru, but that two sets of plans were somehow switched on their way across the Atlantic. Building began in 1746 and took more than a hundred years to complete, but it has since managed to survive an onslaught of eathquakes and cannon fire. The exterior has a certain muscle-bound solidity to it, with two low bell towers and a great barrel-shaped body, while beneath the main structure a labyrinth of tunnels is said to connect the Cathedral with other churches. The entrance is guarded by a pair of magnificent lions and inside the walls are dotted with powerful religious painting and carvings of the saints. A small crypt, reached by some steps, contains the **tomb of Rubén Darío**, watched over by a tearful lion. In 1992 the entire building was carefully restored as part of a public works programme intended to ease the city's unemployment problem.

The centre of the Parque Central is marked by a rather limp statue of Máximo Jérez, a Liberal general who headed the government following the dispatch of William Walker. The sides of the plaza are occupied by cafés, shops, the post office and a cinema. The northwest corner is dominated by an extended mural, telling the history of Nicaragua with a handful of relics lying in the desert and culminating with a smiling child flying a kite.

Elsewhere the streets of León have a generous scattering of fantastic colonial architecture and wherever you wander you're sure to stumble on strange studded doorways and crumbling arches. However there are a few churches which warrant specific mention.

La Merced, dating from 1615, is one of the oldest of León's churches, built shortly after León was relocated. The building is small but superbly decorated, with a square clock tower, set to one side, a magnificent ornate altar and a large statue of the Virgin which is paraded through the streets on 24 September, giving the entire town an excuse to indulge in a couple of days of drink and dance.

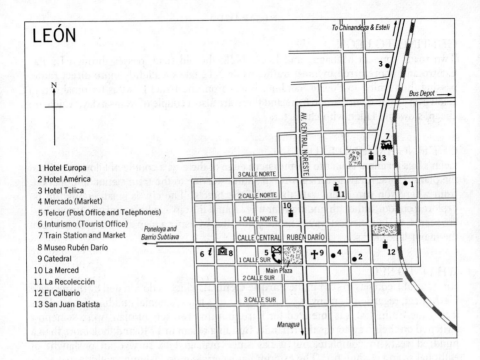

LEÓN

To Chinandega & Esteli

N

Bus Depot →

1 Hotel Europa
2 Hotel América
3 Hotel Telica
4 Mercado (Market)
5 Telcor (Post Office and Telephones)
6 Inturismo (Tourist Office)
7 Train Station and Market
8 Museo Rubén Darío
9 Catedral
10 La Merced
11 La Recolección
12 El Calbario
13 San Juan Batista

AV. CENTRAL NORESTE

Poneloya and
Barrio Subtiava

3 CALLE NORTE
2 CALLE NORTE
1 CALLE NORTE
CALLE CENTRAL   RUBÉN DARÍO
1 CALLE SUR
2 CALLE SUR
Main Plaza
3 CALLE SUR

Managua

The church with the best views is **El Calvario**, which is out on the eastern side of town, near the railway track, and looks out across the rooftops. The church confronts visitors with three gruesome images of the crucifixion, carved into the façade, a theme which is continued inside, where a lifesize figure of Christ on the cross, looking relaxed and blissful, is flanked by the two villains, contorted in agony.

Last, but by no means least, is **La Recolección**, the city's most beautiful church, with an amazingly ornate façade carved with twisting vines and coats of arms, and a beautiful patched clock tower, yellowed, cracked and stained by years of exposure to the elements.

On your way between La Recolección and the plaza take a look at the enormous mural on Avenida 1 Poniente in which Central American politics is depicted as a game of snakes and ladders; the ladders represent Sandinista reforms, with peasants climbing high on land reform and education, while the snakes, threatening to drag them down, are sprouting from the soldier's helmet, marked CIA.

With such a distinguished history León also has a couple of museums. The **Rubén Darío museum** (9–noon and 2–5, Tues–Sat and Sunday mornings) celebrates the life and times of the nation's most famous poet, who spent his childhood here, reaffirming León's claim to be Nicaragua's cultural capital. A second museum, the **Galería de Héroes y Mártires**, spells out the city's revolutionary credentials and chronicles León's

360

struggle against the Somoza dynasty, following its development from student protests to armed uprising.

A Short Walk in the Countryside; El Fortín and Subtiava

After treading the city streets for a while, head out into the countryside for fine view of the city and a slice of revolutionary history. Leaving the plaza along the street which runs downhill from the Cathedral you walk past the hospital and an old **Somoza jail**, now serving as an advertising hoarding and inhabited by a couple of impoverished families. Further down the hill are the ruins of the **Iglesia San Sebastián**, while across the river and up the hill is the **Iglesia Guadalupe**, from where there are good views back across the city. Here you want to head down the right-hand side of the church and then around to the right of the enormous graveyard. A dirt track runs out into the countryside and you want to branch off to the right for a couple of kilometres. The small **Fortín de Acosasca**, perched on a low hilltop, soon comes into view, and it's well worth scrambling up to the fort, which is now abandoned, its eerie rooms musty with damp and daubed with political graffiti. The site offers an unrivalled view of León, with church spires poking high above the rooftops and the city neatly framed by the surrounding fields, against a dramatic volcanic backdrop. Behind the fort is León's municipal rubbish dump, where the poor pick through the garbage as bulldozers shunt it from one corner to another. To head back into León, take the road directly in front of the fort, which brings you into the **Subtiava suburb**, an ancient section of the city which contains one of the oldest churches in Nicaragua, the **Iglesia San Juan de Bautista de Subtiava**, which was built in 1530 and where Bartolomé de las Casas preached during the early years of colonial rule. Around the corner in the **Casa de la Cultura** you'll find a small collection of pre-Columbian idols found in the area.

WHERE TO STAY

Hotels are in surprisingly short supply in León; the best is the moderately priced **Hotel Europa**, tel 2596, which is beside the railway track on 2 Calle Norte in the east of the city. It has a small restaurant and air-conditioned rooms, as well as cheaper ones with electric fans. Budget accommodation is hard to come by; the **Hotel América**, a couple of blocks behind the Cathedral, is overpriced, making the **Hotel Telica**, also on the tracks, a couple of blocks north of the station, the best bet.

EATING OUT

Despite the fact that there are plenty of restaurants in León, getting a good meal is not as easy as it might at first appear. If money is no object then sample the delights of **El Jordán**, on the corner of 1 Calle Norte and Avenida 14 July, or **El Sacuanjoche** on Calle Rubén Darío, which are the city's most exclusive eating establishments. For something a little more reasonable try the vaguely Chinese food at **Dragón de Oro** or **Los Angeles**. If you're looking for a good spot to down a beer or two then the **Cueva de León** offers excellent colonial ambiance, while the **Café El Sesteo** in the corner of the plaza is the ideal place from which to watch León going about its business.

Around León

Poneloya

When things get too hot to handle, the people of León spend their weekends in Poneloya, which is the nearest beach. Before the revolution the resort was dominated by the second homes of León's wealthy families but most are now abandoned and the emphasis has shifted to the seafood restaurants and bars clustered behind the sand. During the week you may well have the place to yourself, at other times the beach is swamped by raucous Nicaraguans determined to have a good time.

Buses to Poneloya run from the El Silo terminal in the Barrio Subtiava, which is a short taxi ride from the centre of León. If you set out early, the beach makes a good day trip, if not there's always the **Hotel Lacayo**—a roughish spot at the best of times.

León Viejo and the Momotombo Volcano

Nicaragua's first and last capitals have suffered an identical fate. Built by the fertile shores of Lake Managua, the founders of both cities could not have predicted that they would soon be destroyed by huge earthquakes. The destruction is still plain to see in Managua but is a touch elusive at **León Viejo**, the nation's original capital, which was founded in 1524. Fortunately the site was later buried under a layer of volcanic ash, thanks to the eruption of the nearby Momotombo volcano, preserving it for the arrival of 20th-century archaeologists.

The ruins of the original city are spread across a couple of fields beside a dusty modern village, but there's really not that much to see beyond a series of low walls sketching the outline of a few churches and the governor's house. Perhaps the best feature of the site is a hill which gives excellent views across Lake Managua and the sinister, black cone of the Momotombo volcano, at the base of which is a plant generating electricity from the heat in the soil.

GETTING THERE
Take a bus, taxi or drive to La Paz Centro—there are regular buses from the terminal in León—and from there another bus—from the northern edge of the town—to León Viejo itself. The service on this last section is a little sporadic, so set off early.

Chinandega and Corinto

Just 40 km to the west of León is the busy market town of **Chinandega**, which lies at the heart of Nicaragua's cotton industry. Huge cotton plantations surround the town and in September and October light aircraft skim the plants, depositing clouds of insecticide. Chinandega itself is unremarkable, although it does have a busy market and a pool in the plaza is home to a bored and fat alligator.

Nearby attractions include the village of **El Viejo**, which is 6 km to the north and has a beautiful little colonial church with a delicately crafted silver altar. To the south is **Corinto**, the country's main port, which lies on an island, connected to the mainland by a narrow causeway. The docks are out of bounds, protected by a high fence to prevent gringo saboteurs. Nevertheless the town has a unique atmosphere, with a hint of sleazy decay creeping in among the shipping agents and wooden boarding houses. The original colonial port of **El Realejo** was a few kilometres to the south and its ruins can be reached along a road which branches off the Chinandega–Corinto road and is signposted.

Buses to Chinandega run every 20 minutes or so from León and there is an equally frequent onward service to Corinto. To get to El Viejo you have to catch a bus from behind the church in the centre of Chinandega.

The Cosegüina Peninsula and the Gulf of Fonseca

Jutting out into the Gulf of Fonseca, at Nicaragua's northwestern tip, is the **Cosegüina Peninsula**, a stumpy thumb of land which is dominated by the volcano of the same name. The volcano erupted massively in 1835, blowing itself apart and reducing its height from around 3000 m to just under 100 m. The remains of the peak can be climbed from the village of **Potosí**, but it's an extremely difficult hike. You'll certainly need a machete to clear the path, and plenty of water. If you do make it to the top, there's a superb view of the Gulf of Fonseca, its glassy waters scattered with islands, and the crater itself contains a beautiful turquoise lake.

Very basic accommodation is available in Potosí, which is served by buses from Chinandega and you can either swim in the sea or bask in some steamy hot springs in the centre of the village.

If you'd rather visit a more accessible beach then head for the village of **Jiquillo**, a quiet seaside spot which is popular at weekends. Again basic accommodation is available and buses run from Chinandega. Buses to both Potosí and Jiquillo leave the terminal in Chinandega every couple of hours.

THE NORTHERN HIGHLANDS

Estelí and Around

Estelí, regarded as the cradle of the revolution, is frankly disappointing. It's a modern town, bombed and battered during the struggle against Somoza, and there are only a few buildings with more than one storey. Nevertheless it's a town which holds an important place in the nation's heart and is steeped in Sandinista history. During 1978 and 1979 the locals staged three grand insurrections here, before eventually ousting the National Guard, after which Somoza had the town bombed from the air.

Estelí is in the midst of a high, dry plateau, where stony ground supports oak and walnut trees, and local people work enormous tobacco plantations, making this Nicaragua's prime cigar city. The main sites are simple revolutionary memorabilia. A couple of good murals still survive in the plaza, one showing Daniel Ortega at the head of a cavalry charge, and there are also a couple of interesting pre-Columbian carvings on display beneath the trees. Around the corner is the **Galería de Héroes y Mártires**, where pictures of the town's fallen are displayed alongside a few photographs of the revolution and some old firearms used by the Sandinistas.

If you're spending the night here then it's well worth taking a wander in the surrounding countryside, particularly to the **Salto de Estanzuela**, a spectacular waterfall which is an ideal place to take a swim. The falls are about 5 km west of Estelí, reached down a road which branches off the Pan-American Highway just before you reach Estelí—if you're coming from Managua, that is.

Somoto, Ocotal and the Border Crossings

Heading on towards the border with Honduras the highway splits; left to Somoto and the El Espino border crossing and right to Ocotal and the Las Manos crossing. Officially the Pan-American Highway takes the former route, running past the small dusty town of **Somoto** and if you're heading for El Salvador this is the most direct road. If, on the other hand, you're making for Tegucigalpa or just looking for somewhere decent to stay the night, then Somoto is a pleasant hill town with cobbled streets and red-tiled roofs. And if you've a day or two to spare then the remote villages of **Ciudad Antigua**, **Jalapa** and **Madriz**, previously off-limits because of the war, are once again safe to visit, away in an isolated world of colonial heritage and superb mountain scenery.

GETTING THERE
Three or four daily buses connect Estelí with the capital, running to the Huembes market in Managua. From Estelí there are hourly buses to Somoto and Ocotal and from there to each of the borders, both of which are open 8–5, although if you're coming from Honduras make sure you get to the border a little before 5 pm if you're planning to catch a bus to Somoto or Ocotal. Buses to Ciudad Antigua, Jalapa and Madriz all run a couple of times a day from the small bus terminal in Ocotal.

WHERE TO STAY
Estelí has an astonishing number of hotels, although the vast majority are in the budget range, originally catering for the young foreign-aid workers who came here during the 1980s. The best hotel in town is the **Hotel El Mesón**, a block to the north of the plaza, while there is an abundance of cheap hotels, several of them on the main street, including the **Hotel Nicarao**, which is probably the best, the **Hospedaje Bolivia**, **Pensión La Florida**, **Hospedaje San Francisco**, which is also one of the better ones, and the **Pensión Juárez**.

If you end up in Somoto for the the the night then the **Hotel Panamericano**, a simple budget hotel with an English-speaking owner, is very good value. In Ocotal the selection is less appetizing but includes the **Hospedaje Peralta**, **Pensión Castillo** and the **Hotel Portal**, which is the best of a bad bunch. There is no accommodation at either of the border crossings.

Matagalpa and Around

Ringed by fresh green mountains, cloud forest and coffee plantations, Matagalpa is Nicaragua's largest mountain town. At a height of 675 m, it is blessed with a refreshingly cool climate, while the surrounding hills are ideal for the cultivation of coffee, ensuring a healthy local economy.

The area was originally inhabited by Chorotegan Indians who fought bitterly against Spanish rule and in its early years Matagalpa was a fortified colonial outpost, from which troops set out to pacify the locals. Later, during the brief reign of William Walker, Matagalpa served as a centre of resistance, opposition forces gathering here before launching an attack on the imposters. The town really boomed in the 1950s and 60s as European immigrants arrived to establish large coffee plantations in the hills. However, in the 1980s these same hills again provided a safe haven for armed opposition and the Contra war had a profound impact here, filling the town with soldiers and refugees. Today many refugees remain, afraid to return to their remote mountain villages, and the town is once again bustling, serving as an important centre of trade and transport.

The main attraction of Matagalpa is the surrounding countryside although the town itself is worth visiting. Calle Central is the main thoroughfare, connecting the small **Parque Darío**, where a sculpture of the great poet sits hand-on-chin, to the stern 19th-century **Cathedral**, which rises above the town. A block west of the Parque Darío is the **Carlos Fonseca Museum**, which holds a collection of photographs telling the story of the great man's life. Fonseca was born here on 23 June 1936, although it was in Managua as a student that he developed a taste for revolutionary politics and became one of the founding members of the FSLN. Fonseca was shot dead in 1976 but is still regarded as one of the founding fathers of the Sandinista revolution, described by fellow revolutionary Tomás Borge as 'one of the dead who never dies'. (The museum is open daily from 10–5, with an often extended lunch break.)

Jinotega and the High Mountain Villages

To the north of Matagalpa a tightly coiled road makes its way over the mountains, moving into a world of cloud forest, pine trees, brilliant green pasture, breathtaking views and terrifying hairpin bends. As it crosses the ridge, high above Matagalpa, a track cuts off to the left to a superb mountain hotel, the **Selva Negra**, which sits on the ridge, swept by cloud and cool breezes and surrounded by dense forest and well-groomed coffee plantations. The hotel is sandwiched between a couple of artificial lakes and offers hiking, horse riding and superb food, with the Bavarian menu inspired by its German owners.

Dropping down on the other side of the ridge the road eventually reaches **Jinotega**, 'the misty city' which sits at the bottom of a steep-sided mountain bowl. Nearly twice as high as Matagalpa, Jinotega is a rougher, poorer city, still surrounded by desperate refugee camps and bearing the scars of a decade of conflict. There's little to detain you here, although the highland scenery is stunning.

If you're not keen on returning by the same route then there are several back roads which head further north from here, high up among the rocky peaks and pine trees, through villages where cattle farming is the dominant industry and the cowboy is king. From Jinotega the place to make for is **San Rafael del Norte**, from where two roads cut down towards Estelí and the Pan-American Highway, either via **La Concordia** or through **Yalí**, which is a longer but more impressive route. The roads are rough and progress is slow, but the sheer majesty of the mountains makes it all worth while.

GETTING THERE
From Managua the Pan-American Highway skirts around the eastern shores of Lake Managua before climbing towards the mountains, splitting at Sébaco in the foothills, where the right branch heads up to Matagalpa and Jinotega. Hourly buses to both towns run from the Huembes market in Managua and there are also less frequent connections from Estelí to Matagalpa. Buses also run hourly between Matagalpa and Jinotega. Beyond there are a couple of buses a day to San Rafael del Norte and Yalí, with connections to Estelí, and sometimes a bus that runs all the way through, although you need to be in Jinotega at dawn to be sure of getting to Estelí.

WHERE TO STAY AND EAT
The finest hotel in Matagalpa is the **Hotel Ideal**, tel 2483, which is up above the Cathedral and has the luxury of air-conditioning and maid service. Next in line is **Hotel Bermúdez**, a good, clean, budget hotel near Parque Darío, while there are a couple of other reasonable budget places on Parque Darío itself.

The best restaurant in town is the **Don Diego**, although good food is also available in the Hotel Ideal. For something a little cheaper try one of the *comedores* on the lower end of Calle Central, which are very popular with the locals.

Perched on the ridge above Matagalpa (on the road to Jinotega) is the **Hotel Selva Negra**, tel Managua 6664000, an excellent luxury hotel surrounded by dense forest and man-made lakes. This probably ranks as one of the top hotels in the country and is certainly a good place to enjoy the cool of the mountains and explore the forest.

In Jinotega the best accommodation is offered by **El Tico**, a small, simple, budget hotel which also has the best restaurant in town. There are a couple of simple basic *pensiones* in the centre of town. You'll also find similar accommodation in Yalí and San Rafael del Norte, although I'd recommend pressing on to Estelí for the night.

SOUTHERN NICARAGUA

Traditionally the stronghold of right-wing conservatism, southern Nicaragua is firmly focused on the ancient city of **Granada**, which was for years the nation's natural capital, serving, in a roundabout way, as its key Caribbean port. The city sits at the western end of **Lake Nicaragua**, a massive expanse of water, populated by freshwater sharks and scattered with tiny islands. The other main cities in the south, both less than an hour or so from Granada, are **Masaya**, which is overshadowed by the volcano of the same name—Nicaragua's most important national park—and **Rivas**, gateway to Costa Rica, from where you can reach the beach at **San Juan del Sur**. Southern Nicaragua is both interesting and extremely beautiful and demands a few days of exploration, for which Granada makes the ideal base. If you're keen to see the lake and its islands, you'll need to spend at least a week in the area.

Granada

Nicaragua's third city rivals the splendours of liberal León. Smaller, wealthier and a great deal better preserved, Granada boasts colonial architecture, a network of narrow cobbled streets, pompous airs, red-tiled roofs and a lakeside setting. Founded in 1524, this is one of the classic Spanish colonial cities with a large open plaza and a scattering of magnificent churches.

For more than two hundred years Granada was Nicaragua's main Atlantic port, with ships running up and down the San Juan river and crossing the lake to reach it. The city soon became the principal trading centre, serving as one of the great commercial capitals of Central America. Its wealth was a constant temptation to Dutch and English pirates, who followed in the wake of the Spanish galleons, sneaking up the river and sacking the city on a number of occasions. Among those who set a torch to Granada were Sir Francis Drake and Henry Morgan. More recently the greatest pirate of them all, William Walker, set fire to the city after he discovered that the Nicaraguans weren't enjoying his presidency. In his own account of events Walker's fond reminiscences include 'the mouldering dead at Granada'.

But over the years much of the city has refused to burn and the great buildings of the centre remain largely intact. Today Granada has an air of normality rare in Nicaragua, and the desperate decay which is so typical of León and Managua is confined to the poorer *barrios* on the outskirts. The city is smaller and quieter than its rivals but there's little doubt that it is also a great deal more prosperous.

GETTING TO GRANADA
A steady flow of buses connects Managua and Granada, with departures every 20 minutes or so. In Managua the buses leave from the Huembes market, in Granada from the terminal on the northwestern side of town.

Three trains a day also link Granada with the capital, although progress is slow. Both the buses and trains pass through Masaya.

WHAT TO SEE
Arriving in the centre of Granada the most striking building is the **Cathedral**, although compared to some of the smaller churches it's of recent vintage and has little architectural merit. The original structure was reduced to dust in 1857, when it was blown up by Walker's men, but rebuilding began in 1860, taking some 50 years to complete. The finished building is by no means remarkable but does contain some interesting paintings and sculptures, including a famous statue of the Virgin which was made in Seville.

Outside the Cathedral the city's plaza is a beautiful open expanse, L-shaped and elongated, with a marvellous, stately 18th-century atmosphere. The small central plaza is thick with trees, clustered around a bandstand, while a huge open street branches off towards the lake. All around are low arches running down the sides of the plaza, beneath which are shops, hotels, a cinema and the post office. There's always plenty of activity, with a surplus of shoeshine boys hustling for business and horse-drawn carriages resting in the shade.

Other points of interest include the **Iglesia San Francisco**, which was built in honour of the city's founder, Hernández de Córdoba. Earlier versions were destroyed by fire in 1665 and 1685, after which the church became a military fortress. Towards the end of the 19th century it was destroyed by William Walker's men, but the existing structure still contains a 16th-century image of the Virgen Rosario. Attached to the church is a beautiful convent with a palm-shaded courtyard and the fascinating **Exposición Estatuaria Zapatera**, a collection of 28 bizarre pre-Columbian stone carvings. The carvings, which look something like stone totem poles, date from AD 800–1200 and depict contorted figures which are half-man/half-animal, including a jaguar, a crocodile and a snake. The carvings were originally found on Zapatera island in Lake Nicaragua and moved to the convent in 1970.

Granada is dotted with interesting architecture and wherever you go you're sure to come across an ornate façade or unusual colonial doorway, but there are one or two places that are well worth including in your wanderings. The **Iglesia de La Merced**, three blocks west of the plaza, has a wonderfully ornate façade, engraved with 6 August 1781, although in actual fact the building was erected in 1534 and the date only refers to the clock tower. The entire structure was badly damaged by William Walker's boys in 1854. If the doors are open, it's well worth climbing the clock tower, which brings you up above the church's five cupolas, giving superb views across Granada's red roofs and the surrounding countryside.

Further afield the churches of **Xalteva**, which was rebuilt in 1854, and **Guadalupe**, which dates from 1626, but has suffered much modification and fortification, are both worth a visit, as is the semi-fortified dock and the city's **cemetery**, where the ornate headstone and grand family tombs are a testimony to the pretension of Granada's great families.

WHERE TO STAY AND EATING OUT

A great hotel in Granada is the **Hotel Alhambra**, which is still only moderately priced but occupies a corner of the plaza and indulges in all the pompous grandeur of the city. Air-conditioned rooms are available, although nights are rarely uncomfortably hot in Granada, and the hotel has an excellent restaurant overlooking the plaza. A little more ritzy is the **Hotel Granada**, which is a modern tourist complex complete with disco and conference room, while budget travellers tend to stick to the **Hospedaje Cabrera**, which is good value, situated on the main road to the lake, or its opposite number the **Hospedaje Vargas**. For a cheap meal in Granada there are plenty to reasonable places along the main street to the west of the plaza.

Around Granada

Literally the biggest attraction in the Granada area is **Lake Nicaragua** and its waters do offer some interesting excursions. Along the shore from Granada itself is the Granada Tourist Centre, a typically Central American resort-style complex which includes bars, restaurants and beaches, while 4 km from the entrance to the centre is **Puerto Asese**, where boats can be rented by the hour or even chartered for more extensive tours of the lake.

On the waters of the lake the most interesting features are the islands. Ringing the Asese peninsula are **Las Isletas de Granada**, 354 tiny islands which are thought to have been great slabs of lava thrown out by the **Mombacho volcano**. The islands support an abundance of plant and bird life and there's even a community here, with its own small restaurant. Further out in the lake are the islands of **Zapatera** and **El Muerto**, both of which are sparsely populated and have yielded a range of strange archaeological finds, many of which are on display in Granada.

Masaya and Around

Halfway between Managua and Granada, Masaya has always been in the thick of things and was one of the most bitterly fought over cities during the revolution. Before the arrival of the Spanish this was the home of the Dirianes Indians and pre-Columbian influences are still strong. The festival of San Jerónimo, held in late September, is closely followed by the Torovenado carnival, in which local people mimic anybody who has put their backs up. (Sadly both fiestas attract large numbers of hard-drinking weirdos, who can be boringly insistent when it come to tourists, particularly women.)

These days Masaya isn't much to look at, although there are some crumbling colonial façades, the best of which are the **Iglesia de San Juan**, which contains some interesting wooden images, the **Iglesia de Nuestra Señora de la Asunción**, which dominates the plaza, and the old market, which is now used as a bus garage. Nevertheless the city is still deeply traditional, with a large indigenous population and a very strong craft tradition. Hammock-making, pottery, weaving and woodcarving have been practised here for centuries and today Masaya is the country's leading crafts centre. For those on a **shopping** spree—and this is certainly the best place to shop in Nicaragua—the new market on the eastern edge of the town has an astonishing range of *artesanía*, offering everything from juggling balls to rocking chairs. For a more official version but smaller selection you could also try the National Artisans Centre, a government-run outlet which has a smart shop overlooking the Masaya lagoon, and is worth visiting for the view alone.

The Masaya Volcano and National Park

Looming above Masaya, wrapped in a tangle of tropical forest and occasionally lost in low cloud, is the Masaya volcano, Nicaragua's most important national park. The park covers some 54 square kilometres and an excellent paved road (leaving the main road from Managua shortly before it reaches Masaya) reaches all the way to the summit, where you can gaze down into the murky depths of the crater as sulphurous clouds are carried off in the wind.

Halfway to the peak is a restaurant and small museum, easily the best in the country, which tells the story of the volcano and shows how radically it has changed shape over the years, as well as offering a brief lesson in plate tectonics and Nicaragua's natural history. The volcano has never failed to impress those who've passed by; the local Indians called it *Popogatepe*, the mountain that burns, and the first Spaniards to see it in eruption described it as the *Boca del Infierno*, the mouth of hell. When Pedrarias Davila wrote home to the king of Spain he spoke of 'a giant mouth of fire which never ceases to rage'.

Since then the lava has opened a second crater, which began to flow in 1852. Today the volcano is dormant but by no means inactive.

The national park is open daily from 7 am to 5 pm and any bus running between Managaua and Masaya will drop you at the entrance, from where it's 2 km to the museum and 7 km to the peak, although with luck you should be able to hitch it.

San Carlos and the Solentiname Islands

Life at the eastern end of Lake Nicaragua is firmly centred on San Carlos, an unfortunate trading post and port which is mostly visited by people who are heading elsewhere. Travellers on their way up or down the **Río San Juan** have often paused here, including pirates on their way to sack Granada, who would destroy a fort or two in San Carlos just to get themselves in the mood. Over the years the town has been occupied by the British, Spanish and French, as well as being attacked by both the Sandinistas and the Contras. Today it's a humble but bustling market town, with boats heading off down the river or nipping across into Costa Rica. There's little to detain you here, but you may well get stuck overnight on your way to the Solentiname Islands. For really adventurous travellers this is also the starting point of any trip down the Río San Juan. Boats regularly run to the village of **El Castillo**, where you'll find the remains of an old Spanish fort and a basic hotel, but traffic beyond there is extremely scarce. (At the time of writing, the border with Costa Rica at Los Chiles was closed to foreigners.)

PRACTICAL INFORMATION
You can either get to San Carlos by ferry from Granada (leaving from the main wharf at 2 on Monday and Thursday, returning at 2 Tuesday and Friday and taking 12–14 hrs), or by bus from Managua—a mere 12 hours. There are plenty of basic budget hotels in San Carlos, the best of a bad bunch being the **Hotel San Carlos**.

The Solentiname Islands

Solentiname—
little archipelago in the lake,
and place where the poet
gives flavour to his poems.
In the measureless silence
only the sound of birds can be heard:
the quack, quack of grubby ducks,
the cry of the flycatchers,
the bugle call of the grackle,
and the uproar of the waterfowl
when the chocalla flies in to its chicks;
the lapping of the waves against the stony shores
which begin and end each island,
where the tortoises come to enjoy the warm sun.

From *Life in Solentiname* by Donald Guevara

At the southern end of Lake Nicaragua is a cluster of 38 islands known as the Solentiname archipelago. The islands vary in size, some supporting 50 or 60 families, others just a tight pocket of forest which rises straight out of the water, inhabited by birds and monkeys. It is a place of astonishing beauty and tremendous peace. At night the boom of howler monkeys echoes in the silence; by day the only things that disturb the ducks and parakeets are the sudden rain squalls, dropping off the volcanic peaks in Costa Rica and sweeping across the lake, churning its surface and darkening the sky.

For centuries the islands supported a small and impoverished peasant population but towards the end of the 1970s the presence of a radical young priest changed all this, creating a self-aware, purposeful community which became a centre for poets and painters. Ernesto Cardenal first came to the islands in 1966 to set up a small Catholic community, and was deeply committed to both liberation theology and poetry. Gradually gaining the respect of the islanders, he led them in support of the revolution and in the development of their own artistic skills, as well as attracting a number of artists from outside. In 1977 the community suffered a severe setback when it was attacked by the National Guard, in reprisal for an attack on the barracks in San Carlos. But by the time Cardenal left, to become arts minister in the new Sandinista government, the islands had become Nicaragua's most important centre for poetry and painting. Sadly the hardship of the 1980s and the demise of the Sandinista government have led to a decline in the number of artists living and working here, but a small artistic community still survives and the islands have retained their magic; calm, fertile and overwhelmingly beautiful.

PRACTICAL INFORMATION

There isn't actually that much to do on the islands but being here is deeply relaxing and the church on Mancarrón is well worth a visit, painted with delicate and simple murals. You can swim, sunbathe, walk or borrow a canoe and paddle between the islands. Boats to the islands run from San Carlos every couple of days, and certainly on Friday and Tuesday, when they meet the ferry from Granada. Once you reach the islands you'll probably end up on either Mancarrón, the largest and most populated, or San Fernando. The official hotel is currently closed, but may have opened by the time you read this. If not there are several local people who put up passing travellers. Either way, conditions are basic.

Rivas and Around

The so-called isthmus of Rivas is the gateway to Costa Rica, a narrow wedge of land between Lake Nicaragua and the Pacific. To many this has always been the most obvious site for a canal between the oceans and there are still vague plans for a sea-level canal here, with funding rumoured to be available from Japan.

Throughout its history Rivas has served as a crucial crossroads and it saw a lot of action towards the end of the 19th century. Destroyed by earthquake in 1844, the city was reawakened by the 1849 goldrush, when thousands of North Americans, bitten by gold fever, passed through on the long journey from the east coast of the US to California. The route, pioneered by US millionaire Cornelius Vanderbilt's Accessory Transit Company, took them up the San Juan river and across the lake to the little port at

La Virgen, and then by coach to San Juan del Sur, where it was back on a steamer for the journey north. A decade later, in 1855, William Walker fought his final battle here, charging into town to take on an army of Costa Rican volunteers, who had come north to liberate their neighbours. Walker's men were routed when a teenage drummer boy set fire to the building they were holed up in, forcing them to flee but destroying a large section of the city.

Today Rivas is a great deal calmer, although the Pan-American Highway sweeps through its northern suburbs. For the passing tourist the main attractions are in the surrounding area, but you might want to head into town for a bite to eat or to take a look at the small regional museum (open Tuesday to Saturday, 9–4), which is in an old *hacienda* beside the bus terminal and has some interesting stone carvings found on the islands in Lake Nicaragua. Buses to Rivas run from Granada and Managua (from the Huembes terminal) and if you do get stuck here there are plenty of simple hotels in the centre of town.

Puerto San Jorge and the Island of Ometepe

A good paved road heads north from Rivas to the lakeshore, passing the Cruz de España, an awkward-looking monument which marks the spot where the Indian chief Nicarao first encountered the Spanish conquistador Captain Gil González in 1522. The lake-shore itself is occupied by the little village of San Jorge, looking out on the twin peaks of Ometepe island, the largest in the lake, which was home to a sophisticated culture long before the arrival of the Spanish. The larger of the peaks is the perfectly conical **Concepción volcano**, rising out of the water to a height of some 1610 m, while its neighbour is the **Maderas volcano**, a mere 1394 m, which has a magnificent lagoon perched just below its summit. The two peaks, which are both wrapped in dense forest, giving way to streaks of black lava near the summit, were once independent islands, but thanks to a steady flow of lava they are now connected by a narrow band of volcanic rock forming an 8-shaped island. A single road runs around the base of the volcanoes, connecting the two villages of **Moyogalpa**, which faces San Jorge, and **Alta Gracia**. Both are small, scruffy places, typical of the Nicaraguan countryside but blessed with lakeside locations. The plaza in Alta Gracia is scattered with strange pre-Columbian stone carvings found on the island. There are a couple of basic **hotels** and **restaurants** in Moyogalpa and a single welcoming *pensión*, the **Hospedaje Castillo**, in Alta Gracia. Once you arrive you should be able to arrange horse-riding (try the *pensión* in Moyo-galpa), fishing and hiking trips, including visits to archaeological sites, but be warned that both the volcanoes are extremely hard going.

PRACTICAL INFORMATION
The only way to get to the island is by boat. Ferries run from San Jorge to Moyogalpa at 11 am, 12 and 4.30 pm, returning at 6.30, 7 am and 1.30 pm. Buses run a regular shuttle service between Rivas and San Jorge and on the island itself a bus service connects the two villages.

San Juan del Sur

A final stopping point on the route to Costa Rica, San Juan is one of Nicaragua's finest beaches. This small seaside town has managed to avoid the ravages of war and has attracted a sizeable community of foreigners, many of whom have opened hotels and restaurants. There's a small port here and a handful of fishing boats operate offshore, but for the most part this is a relaxed resort, nestling in a broad horseshoe bay with Pacific rollers gently running ashore. Behind the beach a couple of simple restaurants offer superb fresh fish and some of the best sunsets in Central America. If Nicaragua has worn you down, this is the ideal place to recover.

PRACTICAL INFORMATION
Buses from Rivas run a regular service to San Juan del Sur, a journey of less than an hour. There is an impressive range of **accommodation** on offer in San Juan del Sur. Top of the pile is the **Hotel Barlovento**, an impressive luxury hotel which is perched on a hill behind the town and offers air-conditioned rooms as well as superb views from its excellent restaurant. Most of the other places are in the inexpensive range; among the best are **Joxi**, tel 0466348, run by a former Norwegian seaman, and **Casa Quebec**, while the **Hotel Estrella**, right down by the sea, does a good line in faded splendour, complete with an impressive dark wood bar.

THE CARIBBEAN COAST

A world apart and a law unto itself, Nicaragua's Caribbean coast is only tenuously connected to the rest of the country. Here in the soggy lowlands of the east you'll find a distinct language, economy and culture. Cooled by Caribbean breezes and barely touched by the Sandinista government the coast is sparsely populated, relaxed and deeply tropical, enthused with ease and energy. Here the exotic culture of rum and reggae sits easily with an economy based on bananas and lobsters, while the remoteness of the area has protected it from the plague of drugs and violence which has saturated most of Central America's Caribbean cities.

Much of the area is uninhabitable, covered by dense tropical forest and a network of slow, swampy rivers. The largest towns are Bluefields and Puerto Cabezas, reached only by boat or plane, where the majority of the people are English-speaking blacks, the descendants of slaves. Scattered along the coast are hundreds of small fishing villages inhabited by indigenous Indians from the Miskito, Rama and Sumu groups.

The fate of the Caribbean coast has been very different to that of the rest of the country. In the early days Dutch and English pirates made their mark here, sheltering in the well-shielded bays, and the area later became a British protectorate, ruled over by the Miskito kings, who were crowned in Belize City Cathedral. In this century the Caribbean coast has fought bitterly against intervention from Managua. In 1926 Bluefields was the centre of a US-sponsored uprising and during the early 1980s groups of Miskito Indians took up arms against the Sandinistas, once again armed and financed by the US. However they later settled their difference with the government and the entire Atlantic coast was granted a degree of autonomy.

The other great shaping force here was hurricane Joan, which swept the entire coast in 1988, carrying away buildings, picking clean much of the rainforest and leaving millions of bare stumps; coasting the sea is a mat of splintered timber and shattered housing. Much of the damage has not been repaired and Bluefields still bears the scars.

Bluefields

At the heart of Nicaragua's Caribbean coast Bluefields is something of a cultural cocktail, testifying to the presence of indigenous Indians, Dutch pirates, black Africans, English and Spanish colonial authorities, as well as the damage done by hurricane Joan and the tug of war between the Sandinistas and the Contras. The city is named after the Dutch pirate Abraham Blaauwvelt, who landed here in the 17th century, although the name is clearly influenced by the British, who later established a trading post here as part of their 'Mosquito Coast' protectorate, bringing in thousands of black African slaves to work on sugar and banana plantations.

The town was badly buffeted by hurricane Joan in 1988, which carried off many of the larger buildings. The Caribbean coast has never been favoured by Nicaragua's central government and rebuilding has been a slow process, with the Moravian church still half built. Nevertheless Bluefields has a distinctive atmosphere, its wooden buildings and second-floor balconies giving a Midwestern flavour, while the mood on the streets is distinctly Caribbean, exotic and open. It's a scruffy, rough town, spread out along several small bays, the shoreline marked by boat yards and rusting hulks. But when the sun breaks through and the mud dries, Bluefields does have an unmistakable charm with street sellers offering everything from turtles' eggs to banana patties. Carnival, held during the last week in May, is particularly wild here, incorporating that old English favourite the *Palo de Mayo* (maypole), while during the San Jerónimo festival, held in October, young men dress as old hags and chase girls through the streets, beating them with rolled-up newspapers.

GETTING THERE
The Caribbean coast is the most inaccessible part of the entire country, but can be reached by either land or air. **Aeronica** fly five times a week from Managua to Bluefields, with some flights continuing to the Corn Islands. Flights leave Managua at 6 am and seats must be from Aeronica at the airport: reservations, tel 666785, tickets, tel 666098.

If you decide you'd rather travel overland, prepare yourself for an epic journey. The first place you have to head for is Rama, where road meets river on the Río Escondido and from where you have to take a boat to Bluefields. Buses to Rama, taking a mere 8 hrs, leave during the morning from the Iván Montenegro market in Managua (last bus at 12 noon). You can either take a regular bus and stay the night in Rama, where there are a couple of simple hotels, or take the legendary *Bluefields Express*, which leaves Managua at around 1 am on Tuesday, Thursday, Saturday and Sunday. Tickets can be bought at the terminal during the afternoon and you can spend the night on the bus—get there early to ensure a good seat. The bus arrives in Rama in time for the 11 am sailing of the *Bluefields Express*, a superb river-boat, which chugs down to Bluefields in about 5 hours, passing some amazing hurricane-damaged forest and a couple of huge rusting ships, beached on the river-bed. The boat runs from Bluefields to Rama on the same days—Tuesday, Thursday, Saturday and Sunday—leaving at 4 am. There's no doubt that it's a gruelling trip, but for those who enjoy traditional travel this is a journey to remember.

WHERE TO STAY
The best hotel in Bluefields is the **South Atlantic Hotel**, tel 242, which offers an excellent restaurant, air-conditioned rooms and 'refreshing and sanitary baths'. Otherwise you'll have to settle for a reasonable selection of simple budget hotels, the best of which are the **Hotel Hollywood** and the **Hotel Costa Sur**, although there are plenty of cheaper places.

WHERE TO EAT AND NIGHTLIFE
When it come to eating, you'll find an excellent selection of seafood, including lobster and shrimps, as well as some good Caribbean food featuring coconut and plantains. The restaurant in the **South Atlantic Hotel** is good, as is **Chez Marcel**, although for something a little cheaper try the **Tropical bar**. Once you've eaten you can head for the cinema or sample the rum and reggae at one of a number of small clubs—known locally as ranches—although they only really get going at weekends.

Around Bluefields

Guarding the mouth of Bluefields bay is **El Bluff**, a spit of land which takes the brunt of the Atlantic rollers and is home to Nicaragua's deep-sea fishing fleet. The musclebound fishing boats were provided by the former Soviet Union and have numbers rather than names. Their base appears to be in terminal decline, having been hit badly by the US trade embargo. A former generation of fishing boats lies rusting in the harbour with many boats rolled over on their sides or half submerged in the Atlantic swell, giving the whole place an air of East European decay.

In days gone by El Bluff was the site of the nearest beach to Bluefields but the two were separated by Hurricane Joan and these days you'll have to persuade the boatman to drop you at the beach. Speedboats run every 20 minutes or so from the market wharf in Bluefields to El Bluff, taking around 15 minutes to cover the distance.

Elsewhere in the Bluefields bay the only point of interest is **Rama Cay**, where the bulk of the Rama Indians live. Boats from the market wharf run to the Cay several times a day, or you can always hire a watertaxi. If you've got a day or two to spare, you might consider a trip to the Pearl Lagoon, a massive marine lagoon which is ringed by Indian villages. The lagoon is a couple of hours away by boat, but the journey is superb, taking you through pristine jungle, much of which escaped the ravages of the hurricane. At the lagoon itself the boatman will point you in the right direction and arrange basic accommodation for a night or two.

The Corn Islands

Fringed by sandy beaches and coral reefs, the Corn Islands are one of Nicaragua's many unrealized assets. Over the years the islands have been put to an assortment of uses:

17th-century pirates sheltered here; early this century the US used the islands as a naval base; Somoza used them as an upmarket resort and prison; and the Sandinistas planned to turn them into a luxury tourist attraction. The islanders have a profound indifference to all this and their relaxed lifestyle makes Bluefields seem positively hectic, although they were badly hit by Hurricane Joan in 1988. Nothing has come of all the great schemes and these days the airstrip is so potholed that pilots often refuse to land. The larger of the two islands has a population of just 4000, with a deep dedication to the joys of rum and reggae. Life here is easy-going in the extreme, with lobsters, turtles, coconuts and a trickle of tourists keeping the islanders alive.

If you can get there, the Corn Islands are a superb spot to unwind. The beaches are ideal for swimming and snorkelling and there are a couple of simple hotels serving up traditional Caribbean meals of fish and coconut. There are three flights a week from Managua to the larger of the two islands, stopping off in Bluefields, although the schedule is often disrupted. Boats also run a couple of times a week between the islands and from Bluefields to the larger island.

Puerto Cabezas

Isolated and inaccessible, even by the standards of the Caribbean coast, Puerto Cabezas is a tough frontier town, seldom visited by tourists and surrounded by war-torn forests, Indian villages and empty coastline. For centuries this region has been dominated by the Miskito Indians, Nicaragua's largest indigenous groups, who have fought bitterly against outside interference. During the 17th century the British lent their support to the Miskitos in the struggle against Spanish rule, while more recently US money and guns encouraged the Miskitos to wage war on the Sandinistas. The area suffered heavily during the war and even today Puerto Cabezas is a ravaged town, with a weary, battered appearance. There's little to lure tourists all this way, although the coastline is beautiful, dotted with Miskito villages, and with a cluster of coral islands, the Miskito Cays, lying offshore.

If you are tempted by this remote outpost then set aside plenty of time and expect to organize all excursions and accommodation once you arrive. There are a couple of basic hotels in Puerto Cabezas and several flights a week from Managua, although if you've more time than money it is sometimes possible to hitch a ride on a supply truck from Matagalpa, a journey of at least two days.

Part IX

COSTA RICA

'*Pura vida*'—pure life—is Costa Rica's commonest catchphrase, used by people of all ages whether raising glasses or greeting each other in the street. And there can be little doubt that by Central American standards life in Costa Rica does have a certain purity. The air here is cleaner, the forests greener, the pace relaxed and the people healthier. Costa Rica's calm speaks loudly in this part of the world and the people have a gentle, compromising approach and reserved formality.

Costa Rican politics seems strangely out of place on the isthmus. Since 1949 it has had no army, although there is a formidable police force, and the country can claim four decades of stable democratic government. Costa Ricans enjoy excellent schools and hospitals and have developed a deep respect for peace, human rights and the environment.

Peace and stability has given the Costa Ricans a rare opportunity to preserve what is best within their country. This is the second smallest of the Central American nations but with a population of little more than three million the Costa Ricans have been able to set aside nearly 20% of the land in a superb network of national parks. The parks cover an amazing range of environments, all alive with the overwhelming fertility of the tropics and offering a unique opportunity to see Latin American wildlife. Protected areas include several steaming volcanic peaks, a collection of magnificent and undisturbed tropical forests, lakes, islands, dry grassland, superb beaches, mountains and pre-Columbian ruins. Most are teeming with birds, animals and fish. Costa Rica is home to some 750 species of birds, more than are found in the entire US, while resident animals include jaguars, crocodiles, tapirs, peccaries, otters, four types of monkeys, armadillos and many, many more. In the Tortuguero National Park, on the Caribbean coast, you can watch massive sea turtles drag themselves ashore to deposit their eggs, and nimble spider-monkeys crash through the trees. Up in the mountains, in the Cerro Chirripó National Park, a clear day gives you a view which takes in both the Pacific and the Atlantic oceans.

If this is your first port of call in Central America then Costa Rica provides a gentle introduction to the area, while if you're coming in from elsewhere in the isthmus, it makes a fascinating comparison. While it may not be as wild as many other Latin America countries, Costa Rica has certainly managed to seduce many outsiders with its easy-going charms, natural wonders and astonishing beauty.

Post-Independence History

Costa Rica was Central America's late developer. Under colonial rule it was a poor, forgotten backwater with a tiny population of rugged farmers and four small towns. In 1821, when the captain general of Guatemala announced Central America's Independence, Costa Rica was still committed to Spanish rule, but accepted Independence by default.

Costa Rica's early years as a republic were unsettled as Mexico, Guatemala and Nicaragua all tried to assert control. The four main towns, San José, Alajuela, Heredia and Cartago, operated as independent city states, between which a serious dispute soon arose over whether they should join General Iturbide's Mexican republic or the United Provinces of Central America, with the conservative leaders of Cartago and Heredia ranked against the liberal and progressive leaders of San José and Alajuela. In 1823 the dispute erupted into open hostility, with a victory for San José and Alajuela ensuring that the Costa Rica joined the ill-fated Central American Union.

Under the federation each republic elected its own head of state and in 1824 Juan Mora Fernández was elected as Costa Rica's first *jefe supremo*, a post he held until 1833. In Costa Rica these were settled times, although the rest of the isthmus was ravaged by war, prompting the people of Guanacaste to secede from Nicaragua in 1824 and unite with Costa Rica.

The Nation Finds its Feet:
Strong Men and Strong Coffee

Costa Rica's stability was largely due to the fact that each part of the country remained autonomous, but conflict became inevitable once the nation attempted to reach a collective decision. The peace was shattered in the early 1830s by a disagreement over the location of the nation's capital. As a compromise it was decided that the official capital was to be rotated between the four main cities. However, when the liberal Braulio Carrillo was elected head of state he forced the nation into unity and firmly established San José as the permanent capital. The decision was challenged by all contenders, who sent an army of 4000 against San José, although Carrillo's forces drove them back. Carrillo ruled despotically for seven years, forcing the nation to integrate and establishing an effective public administration. His heavy-handed approach was not popular and he was driven into exile in 1842, after which another brief struggle put Juan Rafael Mora, a wealthy coffee grower, into power.

While power struggles simmered, the nation was taking shape in the hills, as the introduction of coffee began to transform Costa Rica into a modern, prosperous country. When Carrillo came to power, Costa Rica was inhabited by poor small-scale farmers and had a population of just 120,000, the majority crammed into the central valley. However, in 1843, an English captain took a load of coffee to Europe to serve as ballast in his ship. Europeans were so taken by its flavour that orders flooded in. For the first time in its history Costa Rica was producing a valuable export and the government was so keen to encourage trade that they offered free land to farmers and decreed that every home-owner plant a few bushes. As the export trade developed a new breed of 'coffee barons' came to dominate the business, buying up land from smaller farmers and controlling processing and transportation. In due course these men emerged as Costa Rica's political and economic elite, wielding immense power.

As Costa Rica grew rich, the rest of Central America was becoming increasingly unstable. In 1856 the country faced its first external threat when the American adventurer William Walker, who had gained control of Nicaragua, invaded the province of Guanacaste. The invading army were met by a small Costa Rican force, which then pushed on into Nicaragua and confronted Walker's troops in Rivas. In a much celebrated victory they destroyed Walker's army after a 19-year-old drummer boy, Juan Santamaría, set fire to their headquarters, losing his life in the process. The incident helped to give Costa Ricans a firm sense of national unity and purpose; the battle is still the cause of much pride and Juan Santamaría remains a national hero.

Military Muscle: the Rule of General Tomás Guardia

In 1870 Costa Rican politics adopted a more Central American style as democratic rule was ousted by a military coup and General Tomás Guardia, a radical, iron-fisted despot, took control. Having outlawed all political parties, Guardia introduced sweeping reforms, modernizing the country rapidly. Large land-holdings were confiscated, broken up and distributed to the poor and heavy taxes were levied on the rich. Guardia used the money to develop public education; he also abolished capital punishment, and boosted the sugar and coffee industries. His approach drove much of the old liberal establishment into exile, leaving Guardia's friends and family to dominate.

In 1871 Guardia initiated the construction of the railway from San José to Puerto Limón, opening up the Caribbean coast and increasing the export of coffee. The railway introduced two new elements to Costa Rican society: Jamaican blacks, who were brought in to work on the railway but stayed to colonize the coast; and bananas, which were grown alongside the tracks and soon rivalled coffee as the country's main export. It was all part of a gradual broadening of Costa Rican society, which had remained fairly closed since Independence, dominated by a narrow elite and producing a single viable crop. Guardia's dynamism helped the nation to break out of this isolation, becoming involved in international trade and accepting waves of immigrants, who colonized new areas.

Following Guardia's death in 1882 his strength lived on in his dynasty. The presidency was taken up by his son-in-law, who was succeeded in turn by his brother-in-law, Bernardo Soto, a committed liberal who finally dismantled the Guardia legacy, but not before he had established Costa Rica's free and compulsory school system. In 1889 Soto proved the depth of his liberal pedigree and stepped down, initiating the country's first fully free election, complete with freedom of the press and frank debate of the main issues. As if to prove a point, Soto's candidate was defeated and a group of young liberals took control, headed by José Joaquín Rodríguez, who adopted a stern authoritarian approach, having his enemies flogged in public. Nevertheless he ushered in a period of relative stability and power changed hands peacefully following elections in 1902, 1906, 1910 and 1914.

Troubled Times: 1900–40

By the turn of the century Costa Rica's expanding economy and population placed the country under great strain, as immigrants and members of the new middle class sought more involvement in running the country. Successive governments continued to promote health and education and between 1860 and 1910 the population tripled, reaching 360,000. Large numbers of immigrants arrived from Spain, Germany and Italy, setting themselves up among the existing rural elite, colonizing new areas and introducing new ideas. Nevertheless the traditional oligarchy of coffee barons remained firmly entrenched while the emergence of a broader social structure, including a vastly expanded middle class, put the political system under great strain.

Additional uncertainty was caused by the country's first major economic crisis. At the turn of the century a dramatic fall in coffee prices forced the government to increase taxation and cut the government payroll. In 1917 General Federico Tinoco staged a successful military coup, but even the army was unable to assert control and three years of civil strife, strikes and uncertainty followed, until, in 1920 the US government, already in control in Panamá, insisted that Costa Rica stage democratic elections, sending a cruiser to ensure fair play.

Tinoco was ousted and in the 1920s and 1930s politics was again dominated by the elder statesmen of the liberal establishment. The situation remained deeply unstable, with the middle classes demanding economic and social change. They deeply resented the uneven concentration of power and expressed real concern over the distribution of wealth and frustration at the country's backwardness, poor housing and the general lack of transport and infrastructure. By the 1930s this discontent, fuelled by a continued fall in the price of coffee, boiled over into a series of strikes and demonstrations, culminating in a communist-led strike by 10,000 banana workers, which shut down the plantations for several months.

Socialism and Civil War: 1940–8

In 1940 the promise of real reform restored a degree of stability to Costa Rica with the landslide election of the charismatic Rafael Calderón, the first president to make social and economic reform the primary goal of his administration. In order to secure a firm power base Calderón and his successor, Teodoro Picado, formed an unusual alliance with both the church and the Communist Party, prompting considerable disquiet in the ranks of the middle classes. Nevertheless the administration did make a considerable impact on Costa Rica's development, eroding the power of the old oligarchy and setting the country on the path towards social democracy and the welfare state. The government was generous in allocating funds to health and education and in 1940 it opened a new university, while a new labour code guaranteed a minimum wage and the right to strike. When the US entered the Second World War in 1941, Costa Rica declared war on Japan. Though the country could be of little use to the allied war effort the decision was seen as an act of solidarity with the US. However, when a merchant vessel owned by the United Fruit Company was sunk in Limón harbour by a German submarine, the opposition condemned Calderón for entering the war without the means to defend the country.

Meanwhile many sectors of society began to grow uneasy with Calderón's rule, concerned about a 'personality cult', alleged corruption and the increasing numbers of communists in his government. Following the 1944 election, which was won by Picado, Calderón's appointed successor, the opposition focused around the Social Democratic Party, led by José Figueres, a dashing, handsome man, who had spent two years in exile and was a romantic symbol of resistance. The opposition staged a series of anti-government strikes and protests, which came to a head in 1946 when government forces fired into a crowd of protesters, killing two. The incident was followed by a massive lockout by merchants and managers in the cities, and was a major turning point. As the 1948 election approached, Figueres and the opposition placed little faith in the ballot box, convinced that Picado and Calderón would find some way to hold on to power. Figueres called for armed uprising and began training a small army of insurgents at La Lucha, a family ranch in the mountains south of Cartago.

The election campaign was bitterly fought. Both sides claimed that the other had rigged the voting and intimidated voters, and when the oppositon candidate was announced as the victor, the Calderón camp refused to accept the verdict and open hostilities soon broke out. José Figueres' Liberation Army blocked the Pan-American Highway to the south of San José and they were soon locked in battle with the small government army. The civil war lasted for just a month, and after much strategic manoeuvering and several medium-sized skirmishes Figueres was able to lead his troops into Cartago and command the approach to San José, forcing the Calderón camp to accept a cease-fire. The civil war, usually referred to as the War of National Liberation, is still the bloodiest episode in Costa Rica's recent past, having claimed the lives of 2000, and is regarded as a the turning point in the nation's history.

Modern Costa Rica Emerges: the Figueres Government

Figueres emerged from the civil war as the head of a new interim government and proclaimed the formation of a second republic, committed to democracy and sharply opposed to communism. A new constitution was adopted in 1949: the army was disbanded, the banks were nationalized, the civil service was revamped, women were given the vote and a whole series of autonomous institutions were created to control education, health, railways, roads and social security. In many ways the end of the civil war marks the starting point for modern Costa Rican politics, and many of the structures created in 1949 are still in place today.

Political activity has been split into two camps. The Social Democrats (now the National Liberation Party), protecting the Figueres legacy, regard the nation's welfare

381

state as a fundamental pillar of the nation's development, ensuring the even distribution of wealth and the adequate provision of education, housing and health care. The Social Christian Unity Party, representing the legacy of Rafael Calderón, has taken a mildly right-wing stance, its policy-making dominated by the economic elite.

Since the early 1950s the great majority of the population has shared in steady economic expansion, while the government has offered subsidized credit to the ambitious middle classes, merchants and industrialists. During the 1960s the government embraced the Central American Common Market, which enabled Costa Rica to expand its industrial base and lessen its dependence on coffee and bananas. However, in the wake of the political upheavals which rocked the rest of Central America in the late 1970s and 1980s, the market has contracted considerably, as has the supply of easy loans from international institutions.

The Cracks Appear: 1970–92

Towards the end of the 1970s the long-standing social pact, which provided excellent education and health care to all and had held the country together since 1948, began to show signs of cracking. The state was no longer able to pay its bills and met with increasing calls for the dismantling of the elaborate state structure. As power was switched back and forth between the two main parties, both began to respond to international pressure, with a gradual reduction in the state sector. It seems unlikely that the great social security system will ever be fully dismembered as it is seen as fundamental to the country's unique stability, although some Costa Ricans complain of living in 'an economic dictatorship', in which the cost of the state far outweighs the benefits for ordinary people and salaries are gobbled up by the highest taxes in Central America.

In recent years Costa Rica's greatest achievers have found glory outside the country and the president from 1986 to 1990, Oscar Arias, earned himself a Nobel prize for his attempts to negotiate a Central American peace plan. However he was less popular at home, unable to resolve ongoing economic worries, and in 1990 Rafael Calderón was elected, offering to fight corruption, introduce no new taxes and meet the needs of ordinary working people. The conservative policies espoused by Calderón's advisers contrasted sharply with his claim to be the 'candidate of the poor' and, prompted by the IMF, he soon introduced a severe austerity plan, including a rise in income tax and a devaluation of the currency, generating talk of a new economic crisis.

General Information

Getting to Costa Rica

By Air
From the UK. Direct flights from Europe to San José are operated by KLM and Iberia; you can also fly via the US, changing planes in New York or Houston. A return fare from London will cost from £560 to £650. A fixed date return, valid for two or three months, will cost a little less than a flexible return, which is valid from six months to a year.

From the US. There are direct flights from New York, Houston, Washington, Dallas, Los Angeles and Miami. Most major US airlines cover these routes and you should expect to pay around US$400 for a scheduled return fare from Miami and double that from New York or Canada.

Within Central America. There's at least one flight every day from Panamá City (US$130 return), Managua, San Salvador, Guatemala City, Mexico City (around US$350 return) and a couple of times a week from Belize City. There are also flights to Colombia, with daily departures to San Andrés (US$70 one way), Medellín, Cartagena and Bogotá (US$350 return), and regular flights to all the major South American cities.

San José's **Juan Santamaría International Airport** is about half an hour (25 km) from the city centre, near the town of Alajuela. There's an excellent and regular bus service to San José, which operates from 5 am to midnight. In San José these buses leave from Avenida 2, between Calles 10 and 12, which is also where they drop you when you arrive from the airport. A taxi to or from the airport will charge around US$10. There is a departure tax of US$7 on all international flights.

By Bus

International buses operated by the **Ticabus** connect San José with Managua and Panamá. Panamá City is 18–20 hours away and tickets costs US$25. The bus leaves Panamá City daily at 11 am and San José at 8 am, from the office at 9 Calle, Avenida 2–4. The Costa Rican bus company **Tracopa** also runs a daily service between San José and David, leaving from Avenida 18, Calle 2–4, in San José at 7.30 am and from the Pensión Costa Rica in David, Calle 5, at 8 am. The Ticabus to Managua leaves on Tuesday, Thursday and Saturday, from the terminal in Barrio Martha Quezada, returning on the same days. **Sirca** also operate daily buses between San José and Managua, leaving from Calle 7, Avenida 4–6, in San José and from the terminal in Altamira on Avenida Eduardo Delgado in Managua.

International buses coming from Panamá use the Paso Canoas border crossing on the Pan-American Highway and you can also do this trip on your own, using local buses, which takes a little longer but costs a little less. There are two alternative border crossings: the mountain crossing from Río Sereno in Panamá to San Vito in Costa Rica, and the crossing on the Caribbean side, from Guabito in Panamá to Sixaola in Costa Rica, both of which have reasonable bus connections on both sides.

All road traffic between Nicaragua and Costa Rica uses the Peñas Blancas border crossing on the Pan-American Highway, and although there are other remote border crossings these are currently closed to foreigners. Again, there are plenty of local buses serving this main route and no need to rely on international buses. In Costa Rica there are hourly buses to the border from Liberia, while on the Nicaraguan side local buses run to Rivas.

By Car

Driving into Costa Rica from Nicaragua or Panamá is fairly easy. A simple US$10 tax allows you to keep the car in the country for 30 days, and can be extended to six months at the customs office in San José. Cars are usually fumigated on arrival, for which you have

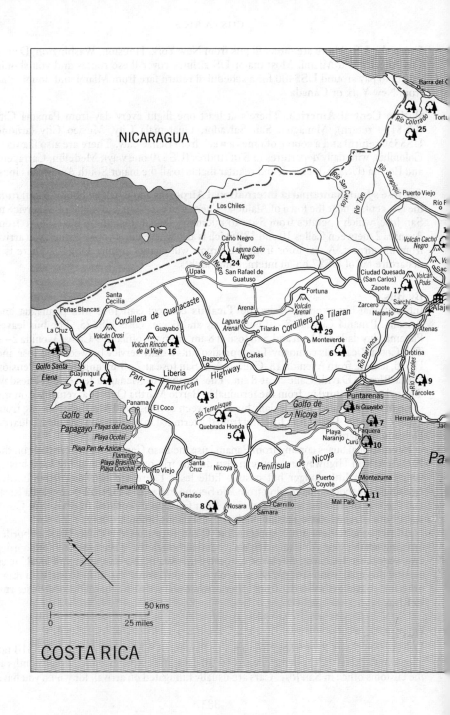

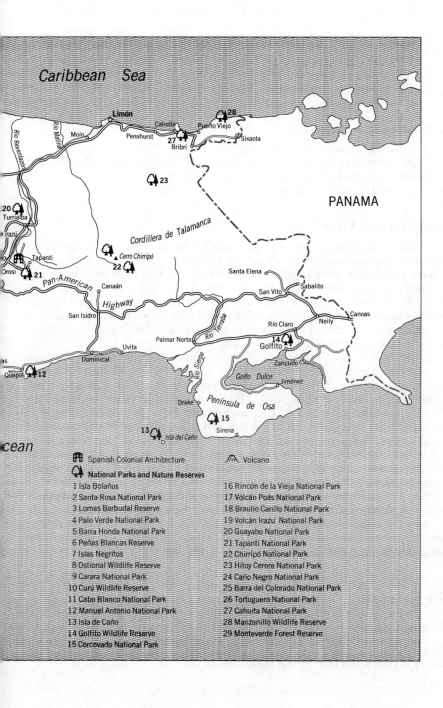

Caribbean Sea

Limón

Cahuita
Puerto Viejo 28
Penshurst 27 Sixaola
Bribrí
Moín
Río Matina
Río Reventazón

PANAMA

23

Cordillera de Talamanca

20
Turrialba
Irazú
Tapanti
Orosi 21
Pan-American
Canaán
Highway
San Isidro
Santa Elena
San Vito
Sabalito
Canoas
Neily
Río Claro
Río Terraba
Río Claro
14
Golfito
Palmar Norte
Uvita
Dominical
Quepós 12
Zancudo
Golfo Dulce
Jiménez
Drake
Península de Osa
15
Sirena
13 Isla del Caño

cean

🏛 Spanish Colonial Architecture

🌲 National Parks and Nature Reserves

1 Isla Bolaños
2 Santa Rosa National Park
3 Lomas Barbudal Reserve
4 Palo Verde National Park
5 Barra Honda National Park
6 Peñas Blancas Reserve
7 Islas Negritos
8 Ostional Wildlife Reserve
9 Carara National Park
10 Curú Wildlife Reserve
11 Cabo Blanco National Park
12 Manuel Antonio National Park
13 Isla de Caño
14 Golfito Wildlife Reserve
15 Corcovado National Park

🗻 Volcano

16 Rincón de la Vieja National Park
17 Volcán Poás National Park
18 Braulio Carillo National Park
19 Volcán Irazú National Park
20 Guayabo National Park
21 Tapanti National Park
22 Chirripó National Park
23 Hitoy Cerere National Park
24 Caño Negro National Park
25 Barra del Colorado National Park
26 Tortuguero National Park
27 Cahuita National Park
28 Manzanillo Wildlife Reserve
29 Monteverde Forest Reserve

to pay a small fee and you are obliged to buy insurance stamps for at least three months, which will cost you around US$15 for a car, US$10 for a motorbike. According to Costa Rican law seat-belts must be worn in cars and taxis and helmets worn on motorbikes. Selling a car or motorbike in Costa Rica is extremely difficult and you are required to pay duty which amounts to several times the value of the vehicle.

Embassies and Consulates

UK: Flat 1, 14 Lancaster Gate, London W2, tel 071 723 1772.
US: 1824 Connecticut Avenue, NW, Washington DC 20009, tel (202) 234 2945.
Guatemala: Avenida La Reforma 8–60, Zona 9, tel 319604.
Panamá City: Edificio Plaza Regency, Vía España, tel 642980.

Passports and Visas

Costa Rican entry requirements are not particularly strict and tourists are usually given a smooth ride through immigration and customs. Officially you are required to have a valid passport, sufficient funds and a return air ticket from Costa Rica. It's this last requirement that can cause trouble, although under normal circumstances a ticket out of any Central American country, or simply enough money to buy one, is considered adequate. Generally speaking it's rough-looking backpackers arriving by bus who are most likely to face serious hassle. Travellers arriving by land are also asked whether they are taking malaria pills, and if not they are given a supply.

Visas are not required for citizens of Britain, Australia, New Zealand and most Western European countries, while US and Canadian citizens do not even need a passport and can enter the country on a birth certificate or voter's registration card, providing it's backed up by some proof of ID. Instead of a visa you are required to pay US$2 for a 30 to 90-day tourist card, although in many cases you simply get a stamp in your passport, which in the case of British visitors is valid for 90 days. If your tourist card is valid for just 30 days, it can be extended at the immigration office in San José, at Calle 21, between Avenidas 6 and 8. To do this you will need a ticket out of the country, two photographs, your passport, a couple of days and a lot of patience. You may also be required to take a blood test for HIV.

Officially, visitors who have been in country for more than 30 days are required to have an exit visa before they can leave, although if your tourist card is valid for three months this does not seem to matter. The exit visa is valid for 30 days and is therefore an automatic extension of your visa or tourist card. It costs US$5 and is available from the Tribunales de Justicia in San José, Calle 17, Avenida 6–8.

On Arrival

Tourist Offices

The Costa Rican tourist board has an excellent information office in the Plaza de la Cultura in central San José, open Mon–Fri, 9–6.

Orientation

Finding your way around the towns and cities is easy enough as they are almost all built on a strict grid pattern and use the same numbering system. Streets, (*Calles*) run one way and avenues (*Avenidas*) the other. Number 0 is the central street or avenue and running parallel to this on one side are the even numbers, with the odd numbers moving away in the other direction. So walking a block from Calle 2 brings you to Calle 4, and Calle 3 is six blocks away on the other side of Calle 0. Addresses are given with the street or avenue that they are on and then the two streets or avenues which they are between, leaving you to look along that block. So Avenida 1, Calles 3–5, is on Avenida 1 between Calles 3 and 5. It may sound a touch confusing now, but you'll soon get the hang of it.

Maps

In San José **Jitan** produce a series of reasonable maps, including one of central San José, one of the central valley or 'Greater Metropolitan Area' and one of the country as a whole. These maps are simple but unless you're planning some hiking or detailed exploration they are adequate. The best map of the country is a 1:50,000 map produced by **International Travel Map Productions** (PO Box 2290, Vancouver, BC, V6B 3W5, Canada) and distributed in England by Bradt publications (41 Nortoft Road, Chalfont St Peter, Bucks, SL9 0LA). All of the above maps are normally available from **The Bookshop**, Avenida 1, Calle 1–3, San José. More detailed trekking maps are produced by the **Instituto Geográfico Nacional** (IGN) and are available either from their offices at the Ministry of Public Works, Avenida 20, Calle 9–11, or from the **Universal Department Store** (*láminas* department), Avenida Central, Calle 1–3, and the **Librería Lehmann**, also Avenida Central, Calle 1–3.

Getting Around Costa Rica

By Air
Costa Rica is served by an extensive network of inexpensive internal flights operated by **SANSA**, although the planes are old and the service is a touch unpredictable. Tickets can be bought from the office, tel, 330397, which is just off Paseo Colón on Calle 24 in San José and is open Mon–Fri, 8–5, and Sunday, 8–noon. All flights leave from the Santamaría airport, from a smaller terminal beside the main one, and the schedule on the main routes is as follows:

Golfito (US$25, 45 minutes) daily at 6 am, returning at 7 am.
Quepos (US$12, 20 minutes), daily at 8 am and 3 pm, returning at 8.35 am and 3.55 pm.
Tamarindo (US$25, 35 minutes), Mon, Wed and Fri at 6 am, going on to Nosara at 6.50 am and returning to San José at 7.20 am.
Sámara (US$25 and 35 minutes), Mon, Wed and Fri at 8.20 am, returning at 9.45 am.

Sansa also fly once a week to Barra del Colorado although at the time of writing the schedule had yet to be confirmed. A number of charter companies and 'air taxis' also operate in Costa Rica, most from the smaller Pavones airport to the west of San José, and if your plans include a visit to Barra del Colorado or the Corcovado National Park, you may have to use one of these. Two of the larger companies are **Aviones Taxi Aéreo**, tel 411626, and **Seeta**, tel 321474. However, even if you manage to fill the plane a short flight will still cost around US$100 per person. A couple of small operators also run flights from Golfito to Puerto Jiménez, a superb 15-minute flight which is a bargain at US$5.

By Rail
Costa Rica's railways are in decline and it now seems likely that they will close altogether within a few years. From the traveller's point of view this is a real tragedy, for the country's main railway offers one of the finest train journeys on the continent—the so-called 'jungle train', which drops from San José to Puerto Limón. In 1991 the tracks took a pounding at the hands of an earthquake and it was decided to close the first section of the track from San José to Turrialba, from where trains are still running to Siquirres and Limón. The country's other main line, from San José to Puntarenas, is less dramatic and also suffers from deteriorating rolling stock. It's a painfully slow and uncomfortable service, but is nevertheless a charming trip: the train rattles its way to the Pacific, constantly besieged by people selling food and drink.

By Bus
Undeniably the most efficient and popular method of travel in Costa Rica is the bus. Compared to other Central American countries Costa Rica's bus service is very slick, although it lacks the spontaneous vitality you find in Guatemala or Panamá. An excellent service of well-maintained modern buses connects San José with all main towns. For the most part it's punctual and reliable, although beyond the main road progress is slow and the ride rougher.

Bus tickets are usually bought on the bus, although the larger companies sometimes insist that you buy a numbered ticket before getting aboard. Bear in mind that Costa Ricans work a rigid five-day week and buses become crowded on Friday evening and Saturday, when it's worth turning up an hour or so before departure. Buses can be flagged down along the highway, but are under no obligation to stop. In most cities buses operate from modern purpose-built terminals. However in San José the situation is somewhat chaotic with bus terminals scattered across the city, and individual companies operating from street corners and vacant lots.

The main services from San José are as follows:
Alajuela (35 minutes). Departures every 20 minutes from 5 am to 12 noon from Avenida 2, Calles 3–5.
Cartago (40 minutes). Departures every half-hour from Calle 13, Avenidas 0–2, from 5.30 am to midnight—make sure you're on an 'express'.
Heredia (25 minutes). Departures every 20 minutes from Calle 1, Avenidas 7–9, from 5.30 am to 10 pm.
Puerto Limón (3 hours). Hourly departures from 5 am to 10 pm from Calle 21, Avenida 3. Details of bus services to Cahuita and Puerto Viejo are given in the text.
Puntarenas (2 hours). Fast 'express' bus service with departures every hour from Calle 12 and Avenida 4.

Monteverde. Departures from Calle 14, Avenida 11 at 2.30 am Mon–Thur and at 6.30 am Sat and Sun. Returning at 6.30 am Tues–Thur and at 3 pm Fri–Sun.

Liberia and Nicoya. Departures from San José to Liberia hourly from 7 am to 8 pm, from Calle 14, Avenidas 1–3. There are regular buses from Liberia to Nicoya and from there to the beaches on the Nicoya peninsula. Alternatively **Tracopa** run direct buses from San José to Nicoya, from Avenida 5, Calle 14 in San José, with departures at 6, 10 am, 1.30, 3 and 5 pm.

Nicaraguan border. Direct buses, at 5 and 7.45 am, from Calle 16, Avenidas 3–5 in San José, returning from the border at 3.30 and 10.30 pm, and hourly buses between Liberia and the border.

Jaco (2–3 hrs). Departures from the Coca Cola bus terminal, Calle 16, Avenidas 1–3 at 7.30 am and 3 pm, returning at 5 am and 3 pm.

Quepos. Departures from the Coca Cola terminal, Calle 16, Avenidas 1–3, at 6, 8 am, 2 and 4 pm, returning at 7, 10 am, 2 and 4 pm. This is a slow service taking around 5 hrs.

Manuel Antonio. Departures from the Coca Cola terminal, at 6 am, 12 noon and 6 pm, returning at 6 am, 12 noon and 5 pm. Journey time $3\frac{1}{2}$ hours.

San Isidro. There are hourly buses to San Isidro, run by three companies along Calle 16 next to the Coca Cola bus terminal.

Golfito (5 hrs). This route is operated by Tracopa, Avenida 11, Calles 2–4 with departures at 6.30 am and 3 pm.

Paso Canoas. This route is also operated by Tracopa, Avenida 11, Calles 2–4 with departures at 5 am, 1, 4.30 and 6 pm.

By Car

Compared to other Central American countries, driving in Costa Rica is relaxed and problem-free. Buses are fairly scarce off the main routes so a car can save you a great deal of time. The main roads are well maintained and traffic is not particularly heavy or hair-raising, although off the main roads conditions can be rough, particularly during the rainy season, when you'll need four-wheel drive and good clearance. The main routes are well signposted, but smaller roads are rarely marked. Petrol stations are well distributed; get hold of the **International Travel Map Productions** map, which marks all petrol stations.

Small tolls are charged on the main roads leaving the capital. The speed limit is 75 km/h, unless otherwise specified, and police speed traps are sometimes used. You can also get a ticket for not wearing a seat belt. Tickets are issued by the police and fines have to be paid at a bank. If you haven't paid by the time you leave, it's just possible that you will be detained at the airport. If you're involved in a serious accident, the police will confiscate your number plates, preventing you from driving until the matter is resolved. A foreign driving licence is valid for three months and all vehicles must be insured with the National Insurance Institute, INS. Hired cars are automatically covered within Costa Rica and if you drive your own car in from either of the neighbouring countries you can take out insurance at the border.

In San José parking is often difficult, particularly during the day. There are parking meters, but your best bet is one of the supervised parking lots, where you pay a little less than US$1 an hour. At night traffic lights are turned off and a flashing orange light serves to indicate that you have right of way.

Car Hire

Costa Rican car hire is expensive but there are plenty of companies, most of which have English-speaking staff. As ever, you should exercise a degree of caution when hiring: read the small print and check the car closely for damage. Cars on offer range from the most basic Nissans—March and Sunny—which rent for around US$30 a day or US$200 a week, to air-conditioned landcruisers, which go for around US$70 a day or US$450 a week. This includes free mileage but you pay an additional US$10 or so for insurance. Four or five of the largest companies have offices at the Juan Santamaría International airport, open until at least 10, so you can pick up the car when you arrive.

The main companies are:
Adna, Avenida 18, Calles 11–13, tel 337733.
American, Paseo Colón, tel 215353.
Budget, Paseo Colón and Calle 30, tel 233284, Mon–Sat 8–6, and at the Juan Santamaría airport 7 days a week from 4.30 am to midnight.
Elegante, Paseo Colón, Calle 34, tel 210066, who also have offices at the airport, in Quepos, Puntarenas, Liberia and Jaco.
Poas, Paseo Colón, Calles 34–36, tel 221956.
Pilot, Paseo Colón, tel 228715, Mon–Fri 8–6, Saturday 8–4, Sunday 8–1.
Toyota, Paseo Colón, Calles 34–36, tel 411411, and at the Gran Hotel Costa Rica, tel 229569.

By Bicycle

Costa Ricans share Central America's enthusiasm for cycling and here, as much as anywhere, cyclists will be warmly welcomed. The country is well suited to cycling, although unless you have a robust mountain bike you will have to confine yourself to the main paved roads. Most towns have small bike shops and wherever you go you will find plenty of expertise and invention when it comes to repairs.

Embassies and Consulates

All embassies and consulates are all in San José. Most are open to the public from 8–12 noon Mon–Fri. Visas generally take at least 24 hours to process (although a visa for El Salvador can take two weeks).

Colombia. Calle 5, Avenida 5, tel 210725.
El Salvador. Avenida 10, Calles 33–35, tel 249034.
United States. Pavas, west of San José, tel 203939.
United Kingdom. Paseo Colón, Calles 38–40, tel 215566.
Guatemala. Sabana Oeste, tel 316654.
Honduras. Calle 5 and Avenida 0, tel 222145.
Mexico. Avenida 7, Calles 13–15, tel 225528.
Nicaragua. Avenida 0, Calles 25–27, tel 333479.
Panamá. San Pedro, tel 253401.
Canada. Calle 3 and Avenida 0, tel 230446.

Money Matters

Costa Rica's currency, the **colón**, is divided into 100 **centavos**. At the time of writing, US$1 was worth around 125 colones. By Latin American standards the economy is stable, although the country still suffers from inflation rates of more than 20%. The current exchange rate, for both the banks and the black market, is listed in the papers.

Given the fact that the colón is regularly devalued you should avoid changing too much in one go, although bear in mind that changing money in a bank is a boring and time-consuming business. Banks charge a commission of 1% and are generally open from 9–3, Mon–Fri. In San José some keep longer hours. The black market, which is focused in the streets around the Banco Nacional in San José, is a quick and easy way to change money. It is illegal but widely tolerated. At times it is forced underground but when in business its agents will waste no time in making themselves known to you. The dealers will generally take both cash and traveller's cheques, although you should take care when doing a deal as rip-offs are common. Most of the people that you meet on the streets are in fact agents for bigger dealers and will take you to some shop or office, where the money changes hands.

Cash can be drawn on a Visa card from any branch of the Banco Nacional. Try to bring enough money for your entire trip as sending money to Costa Rica is time-consuming. It is, however, possible and American Express has to be one the quickest channels. Up-market hotels will also change cash and traveller's cheques, although they rarely offer a good rate. Outside San José the rate of exchange drops off quickly and it is generally a lot harder to change money, except in the main tourist areas.

Generally speaking, hotels, restaurants, car hire companies and travel agents will accept well-known credit cards, including American Express, Visa, Diners Club, Access/Mastercard and Citibank. However, a card is of less use at the budget end of the market and outside the main cities.

Leaving Costa Rica by air you can change up to US$100 worth of colones back into dollar cash, at the bank in the airport, providing you show your passport and air ticket.

Post Offices

Costa Rica's postal service is one of the finest in Central America. Letters to Europe and the US sometimes reach their destination within a week and the main post office in San José, at Calle 2, Avenidas 1–3, has a special section which is open until midnight. Post offices, *correos*, throughout the country are generally open 7.30–11.30 and 1.30–5.30, Mon–Fri.

Postal addresses in Costa Rica are called *apartados* and function as post boxes. If you want to receive mail while in Costa Rica, you can have it sent to the Lista de Correos, Correo Central, San José, or use the American Express mail service, providing you have either an American Express card or traveller's cheques. The service is efficient and reliable and their postal address is Tam Travel Agency, c/o American Express, Calle 1, Avenidas 0–1, Apartado 1864, San José. The office is on the fourth floor of the Edificio Alde, and open 8–5.30, Mon–Fri.

Telecommunications

Radiográfica Costarense operates phone, telex, fax and telegram services across the country. Their main office in San José is at the corner of Calle 1 and Avenida 5 (open 7 am–10 pm), although for international calls they have a much better office at Avenida 2, Calle 0–1 (open 7 am–10 pm). In small towns and villages the phone company shares an office with the post office. Pay phones are found in most town squares and scattered throughout the main towns, although demand is high and you usually have to wait your turn. Some shops and bars have phones for public use, and charge a little over the odds, although it's only a matter of a cent or two. Within Costa Rica there are no local codes and all numbers have six figures. Some small villages just have a single line and each house has an extension number, which you have to ask for when you get through.

It is possible to direct-dial international calls from Costa Rica or you can contact the international operator by dialling 116. Collect calls are easily arranged through this number and can be made from any phone in the country, including pay phones. To get through to an AT and T operator call 114.

Police and Military

Here in the so-called Switzerland of Central America the security forces are virtually non-existent by the standards of the isthmus. Since 1949 the army has been outlawed, and although certain parts of the police force are dressed and armed in a distinctly military fashion they are officially policemen. Yet things are fairly relaxed and law enforcement is a sporadic affair. Costa Ricans are proud of their freedom and they are always reluctant to accept any increase in the militarization of the police.

Crime is a serious problem in Costa Rica, particularly in San José and Puerto Limón. As in every Central American country the local criminals have a specific approach and here pickpocketing and petty theft are top of the list. Whether you're on a bus, walking the streets or camping in a tiny village, keep a close watch on your possessions or they will disappear. In general there is very little violent crime and it's your possessions that are at risk. However, this is untrue of certain sections of San José and Puerto Limón, which are dominated by the twin trades of prostitution and drug-dealing and are best avoided, particularly at night.

Medical Matters

Chemists, *farmacias*, stock a good range of international drugs and medicines, most of which are produced in the US. Condoms, contraceptive pills, tampons and sanitary towels are all available; it's always best to stock up in San José where the supply is more reliable. Malaria pills are also easy to get hold of and are given away by health officials at the borders. As ever, contact lens solution is difficult to find. San José has several excellent hospitals and private clinics, many staffed by doctors trained in the US.

Public Holidays

Banks and government offices are closed on national holidays, but public transport continues to operate. Apart from the following national holidays there are also some local holidays and fiestas which bring local banks and businesses to a halt, but compensate with plenty of drinking, dancing and bull-baiting.

New Year's Day	
19 March:	**St Joséph's Day**, patron saint of San José
11 April:	**Juan Santamaría Day**, the anniversary of the battle of Rivas
Holy week:	Public holidays on Thursday and Good Friday
1 May:	**Labour Day**
15 May:	**Farmer's Day** and San Isidro's Day; processions are staged to celebrate the end of a plague of locust in 1977
29 June:	**St Peter and St Paul**
25 July:	**Annexation of Guanacaste**, marked by celebrations in the northwest
2 August:	**Day of the Virgin of Los Angeles**, Costa Rica's patron saint
15 August:	**Assumption**, Mother's Day
15 September:	**Independence Day**
15 October:	*Dia de la Raza*—Colombus Day
25 December:	**Christmas Day**

Opening Hours

Opening hours are fairly consistent throughout the country and most people work a rigid five-day week. Banks are open 9–3, Mon–Sat, although some are open until 6. Museums and offices are usually open 8–12 and 1–4.30/5, Mon–Fri, although several museums are open on Sundays and close Mondays. Most shops are open 9–6, Mon–Sat, although some are closed on Saturdays. Public transport operates seven days a week.

Festivals, Markets, Shopping and Artesanía

Regional festivals, which take place throughout the year, offer a fantastic opportunity to see Costa Ricans letting their hair down. Every town and village has a fiesta, usually held on the **patron saint's day** and including processions, bull riding, drinking and dancing.

All the large cities have markets, although by Central American standards these are fairly tame. Some smaller farming towns have weekly markets, usually held at weekends.

Heavy restrictions on the importation of consumer goods mean that Costa Rica is a poor place to buy high-tec items. When such goods do make it into the country, they carry heavy import duties and may easily be twice as expensive as in neighbouring Panamá.

Costa Rica also suffers from a dearth of traditional *artesanía*. The most popular traditional craft is the manufacture of hand-painted ox-carts, most of which are made in the village of Sarchí and here you can buy small toy carts or simple wooden panels, painted in traditional geometric designs. Other goods include hammocks, excellent woodwork and leather goods, all of which can be bought from shops and street traders in San José. The best-quality coffee is exported but what you buy here is still delicious and extremely good value.

The Media

The Costa Rican media is a little on the weak side. The main newspapers are *La Nación*, which is prone to right-wing editorials, and *La República*. Both are simple tabloid papers offering a straightforward account of the day's news but with little international coverage or analysis. *La Nación* includes a good *Viva* supplement, with details of theatre and cinema. Other popular daily newspapers include *El Diaro*, which is unashamedly sensationalist, and *La Prensa Libre*, which comes out at midday and is only available in San José and the surrounding area. Weeklies include the *Semenario Universidad*, which is the official paper of the University and *Esta Semana*, both of which are more liberal than the daily papers but have a small circulation.

The Tico Times, Costa Rica's English-language paper, comes out on Friday and offers an excellent summary of the week's events and some good listings, although there is a total lack of international news. A sizeable proportion of this paper's readers are retired Americans living in Costa Rica and it regularly carries articles about cut-price medical care, problems with domestic staff and tax dodges. US papers, including the *New York Times*, *USA Today* and *The Miami Herald* are available in San José as are *Newsweek*, *Time* and *The Economist*.

With Costa Ricans the radio, TV and cinema are all immensely popular. There are literally hundreds of radio stations; *Radio Reloj* claims to be the most listened to, although *Radio Monumental* and *Radio Sonora* are very much in the running.

Around 90% of Costa Rican households have TV sets and there are more than a dozen local stations and foreign cable networks. **CNN**'s 24-hour news service is widely available, shown in many hotels and bars, as are **MTV** and **Turner Network Television**. Of the local channels, **Channel 7**, which was formerly owned by ABC, leads the field. The cinema is also popular in San José, although outside the capital there are very few cinemas. The bulk of the films are from the US, shown with Spanish subtitles.

Costa Rica's theatrical tradition is well developed, although again almost all activity is rooted in the capital. Not only does San José have some of the finest theatres in Central America but they are also kept very busy and complemented by a vibrant fringe element, performing in small theatres across the capital. Theatre listings are given in *La Nación*, and in English in *The Tico Times*.

Where to Stay

The most developed tourist industry in Central America offers a wide range of accommodation but it tends to be booked up, particularly during the high season from December to April. There are plenty of luxury hotels in San José, at the Pacific beaches, on the Caribbean coast and in Manuel Antonio, and a few scattered in more remote locations. Moderate and inexpensive hotels are to be found in all towns and all beaches and budget hotels in even the smallest of villages.

Hotel prices are regulated by the tourist board (who charge a 13% tax on all rooms). When you're paying cash, prices can be flexible. The cheapest of hotels, with shared bathroom and cold water, charge around US$4 and the country boasts the only three youth hostels in Central America. Mid-range places, with a private bathroom and fan, air-conditioning if you're lucky, charge anything from US$12.50 to US$30, and are often very good value. Up-market hotel prices are either in the expensive bracket, US$30–90 or the luxury US$90–130. Many of the best hotels are owned and run by retired Americans. Hotels come under a variety of names—*pensiones, hospedajes, posadas*—but these don't really reveal much.

Camping is possible in almost all national parks and if you want to see Costa Rica's wildife at its best a tent will certainly be useful. Some parks also have basic refuges and shelters, for which you will need a sheet or sleeping bag. If you plan to travel off the beaten track, in low lying areas, you'll need a mosquito net.

Eating Out

The basis of traditional Costa Rican food is *gallo pinto*, a boring mix of rice and beans, occasionally brought to life with a touch of coriander or garlic. Most local restaurants, known as *sodas*, serve standard *casados*, a plate of rice, beans and simple salad, with either meat, chicken or fish. More interesting national specialities tend to be cooked and eaten at home, although there is one traditional restaurant, the **Cocina de Leña**, in San José, that serves up delights such as *chiles rellenos*, stuffed chillies, *tamales*, maize dough stuffed with chicken or meat and *olla de carne*, a rich beef stew with yucca and plantains.

Costa Rica's answer to international cuisine includes steaks, *chao mein*, hamburgers, chicken and eggs. However, in San José there are also some excellent restaurants, serving Swiss, Mexican, German, Italian, French, and even vegetarian, food. There is some excellent seafood to be had on both coasts and some interesting Caribbean food, richly flavoured with coconut, served in the restaurants of Limón and Cahuita. Elsewhere mediocrity dominates.

The usual range of sweet soft drinks is on offer (including ginger ale, which is referred to as *gin*), although local *sodas* also do superb fruit juices and *refrescos* made from fruit and water or *batidos* made with fruit and milk. Costa Rican coffee is also excellent, but often served with sugar. *Café con leche* is a half-and-half mix of coffee and milk.

Costa Ricans also love to drink the hard stuff: *guaro*, a powerful, clear alcohol is their favourite tipple; rum and whisky are also popular. People drink at all hours and you often see drivers pause at a roadside café, down four or five beers and then head off into the night. The main beers are Bavaria, Tropical and Imperial, while locally produced wines are also available, made from a bizarre selection of tropical fruit. Anyone with taste buds will stick to imported Chilean and Spanish wines, which are available in all good restaurants.

Itineraries

San José is the unchallenged centre of transport, commerce and culture, though lacking in fine architecture, but it is certainly worth spending a few days here at some stage, exploring the central valley, visiting a museum or two and enjoying the food, theatres and cinemas—which are scarce outside the centre. The ideal way to see the country is to use the capital as a base.

In the **northwest** the main attraction is the **Pacific coast**. Parts have been heavily developed but there are literally hundreds of beaches, most of them beautiful sand crescents flanked by low hills, and many are remote and virtually untouched. Inland the northwest has some superb national parks, including the dry deciduous forest of the **Santa Rosa National Park**, the lush tropical forest and streaming hot springs of **Rincón de La Vieja** and the beautifully preserved cloud forest of the **Monteverde Reserve**. A trip to any of these reserves can easily be made on the way to or from the beach, giving you a good taste of the diversity of the northwest, from dusty dry coastline to rain-soaked mountains. Expect to spend at least a week on the round trip.

The **Caribbean** coastline also offers several unique attractions. The **jungle train**, heading from Turrialba to Puerto Limón, is the best way to introduce yourself to this part of the country—if it's still in action. **Puerto Limón** is a bustling port; sleazy but fascinating. To the north the **Tortuguero National Park** is one of the best places to watch nesting turtles, and to the south are the beaches at **Cahuita**, with its superb coral reef and adjacent national park. Again you should expect to spend at least a week in this part of the country.

The **south** falls neatly into two distinct sections. The coastal route to the **Manuel Antonio National Park** is easily accessible and includes yet more wonderful beaches, the very best in the park itself. The remainder of the southern area is more of a long haul, although the trip south, taking you high over the mountains, is fantastically dramatic. From San Isidro you can climb **Mount Chirripó**, in the national park of the same name, which is the highest peak in the country and from where you can see both coasts. Heading further south you reach the old banana town of Golfito, from where you can visit the **Osa Peninsula** and the **Corcovado National Park**, which is perhaps Costa Rica's wildest nature reserve, supporting an incredible array of tropical wildlife. However, the park is extremely remote and can only be explored on foot, demanding a lot of time and energy. A short trip to Manuel Antonio can be done in a couple of days, although to explore the far south you'll need at least 10 days.

San José

If San Salvador and Guatemala City were hosed down, all the shacks
cleared and the people rehoused in tidy bungalows, the buildings painted,
the stray dogs collared and fed, the children given shoes, the refuse picked
up and all the soldiers pensioned off, those cities would, I think, begin to
look a little like San José.

Paul Theroux, *The Old Patagonian Express*

The established focus of every type of activity in Costa Rica—power, politics, business and transport—San José is perhaps the most civilized of Central America cities. With a population of more than a million it is twice as large as any other city in Costa Rica, but has managed to avoid taking on the squalor of Managua or the aggression of San Salvador. The city feels calm, relaxed and even a touch provincial, despite laying claim to the tallest building in Central America and an abundance of exclusive shops, theatres, cinemas, hotels and restaurants. It lacks the cosmopolitan bustle and assertive street life of Panamá or Guatemala City, but is charming and safe, and easy to understand, explore and enjoy. There's little hustle here, although moneychangers are impressively

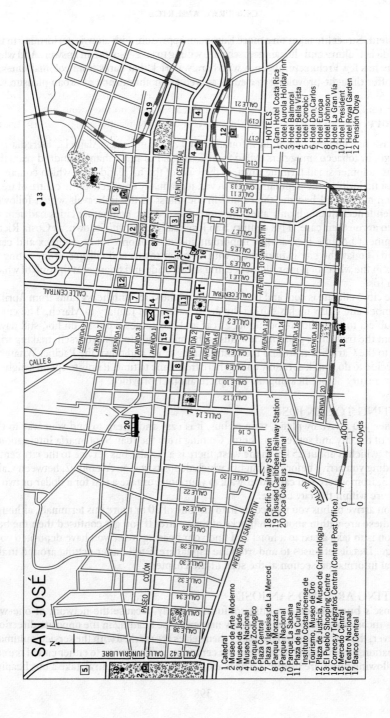

SAN JOSÉ

N

1 Catedral
2 Museo de Arte Moderno
3 Museo de Jade
4 Museo Nacional
5 Parque Zoologico
6 Plaza Central
7 Parque y Iglesias de La Merced
8 Parque Morazán
9 Parque Nacional
10 Parque La Sabana
11 Plaza de la Cultura,
   Instituto Costarricense de
   Tourismo, Museo de Oro
12 Plaza de Justicia, Museo de Criminología
13 El Pueblo Shopping Centre
14 Correos y Telégrafos Central (Central Post Office)
15 Mercado Central
16 Teatro Nacional
17 Banco Central
18 Pacific Railway Station
19 Disused Caribbean Railway Station
20 Coca Cola Bus Terminal

HOTELS
1 Gran Hotel Costa Rica
2 Hotel Aurola Holiday Inn
3 Hotel Balmoral
4 Hotel Bella Vista
5 Hotel Corobici
6 Hotel Don Carlos
7 Hotel Europa
8 Hotel Johnson
9 Hotel La Gran Via
10 Hotel President
11 Hotel Royal Garden
12 Pensión Otoya

400m
400yds

persistent. Street life takes on a more European approach, with clowns performing in the Plaza de la Cultura and shoeshiners who are willing to take 'No' for an answer. And while the city has few architectural gems, with barely a brick that dates from colonial times, it does offer thought-provoking museums as well as an abundance of urban pleasures.

History

San José has ignoble beginnings, founded in 1737, long after Alajuela, Heredia and Cartago, by tobacco smugglers exiled from Cartago. For more than a hundred years this was just another small farming town, at the base of the highland bowl which contained the vast majority of the population. However, it gradually emerged as the centre of trade and commerce and became the capital in the midst of the upheavals which followed Independence, although only after the more conservative competing cities had sent an army to argue their case. This century San José really came into its own, as Costa Rica's government became increasingly important and its economy more complex and centralized. Today the city is unrivalled, with all other towns and villages firmly acting as spokes in the wheel of power, influence, transport, trade and finance, at the hub of which is San José.

The city's climate is cool and fresh throughout the year, with heavy rains from April to December and chilly nights during the dry season, from January to March. The city is also subject to periodic air-pollution, as car and bus fumes build up on hot, still days.

From the traveller's point of view this is the only place to base yourself, making trips down to the Caribbean, around the central valley or up and down the Pacific. Whatever you decide to do, you'll certainly end up here from time to time, if only to spend a night of relative luxury before heading off to explore another province.

GETTING TO SAN JOSÉ
Whether you arrive by plane, train or bus, it is easy and cheap to find your way to the centre of the city and settle into a hotel. Coming from the Juan Santamaría International airport, which is about 25 km to the west, there is a regular bus service to the city centre (providing you arrive before midnight), which deposits you on Avenida 2, between Calle 1 and 3, from where you can either walk to your hotel or take a taxi for a dollar or two to anywhere within the city centre.

If you arrive by bus you may come in to any one of 20 or more bus terminals, although all of these are within about ten blocks of the centre. If you get confused then the best solution is to take a taxi to a hotel and find your bearings once you have deposited your luggage. Details of buses to and from the capital are listed under getting around in the general information section at the start of the chapter.

GETTING AROUND SAN JOSÉ
San José's **bus service** is a little confusing, largely because the network of one-way streets means that a bus facing one way may easily be heading in the opposite direction. However, the bus stands and the buses themselves are marked with the service's ultimate destination, and almost all leave from the central area. To get you to either end of the city the following buses are useful. To head east, along Avenida Central, take a bus heading

from Avenida 2, Calle 5–7. To head west along Paseo Colón take a bus heading for Sabanilla from Avenida 2, Calle 5–7.

A lot easier and surprisingly cheap are the city's **taxis**, of which there are hundreds, although they can be hard to find during afternoon downpours or rush hour.

TOURIST INFORMATION

The Costa Rican Tourist Board's office is in the Plaza de la Cultura, Calle 5, Avenidas 0–2, and can provide accurate information on almost any aspect of life and travel in Costa Rica. The office is open Mon–Fri, 9–6, and the staff speak excellent English.

ORIENTATION

The city is laid out on a traditional grid pattern, occasionally interrupted by a large hospital, hill or park. Avenida Central is the city's backbone, running through from the Sabana Park in the west to the elevated suburbs on the eastern outskirts. Street numbering is typical of Costa Rica: Streets or Avenues of even numbers head in one direction and odd numbers head in the other: so Calles 8 and 9, are on opposite sides of Calle 0, nine blocks apart. It's a system that makes perfect sense although it takes a little getting used to. Local people tend to identify an address by telling you that it's near a prominent landmark, such as the Pizza Hut on Paseo Colón (which is all very well if you have lived in the city all your life but virtually useless if you have just arrived).

Broadly speaking, the centre of San José is a small section to the north of Avenida 2, between Calles 16 and 21, and bordered to the north by Calle 7 or 9. Here you will find the majority of the hotels and restaurants, and close by, the bus terminals. All the main attractions are within walking distance. To the west is the more modern and expensive part of the city, centred on Paseo Colón, while to the east the main avenues climb uphill to the Bella Vista district and on to the university. The other main thoroughfare is Avenida 2, a broad and busy street, running down the side of the Cathedral, which dominates the centre of the city. One block to the north is the smaller Avenida Central, which runs right through the entire city, becoming Paseo Colón to the west.

WHAT TO SEE

San José got off to a late start, becoming the capital after independence in 1823, as a result of which it lacks colonial architecture. The few interesting buildings there are date from the late 19th and early 20th centuries, when local architects used neoclassical styles to give the city the cultural integrity that they felt was lacking. The city's streets are worth exploring for their distinctive atmosphere: a subtle blend of restrained calm and bustling commercial activity. Late into the evening the main streets are awash with pedestrians, street-sellers and moneychangers, making this a fascinating place to wander.

A good place to start is the **Parque Central** (bounded by Calle 0 and 2 and Avenidas 2 and 4), which is dominated by a concrete bandstand and forms the rough heart to the city, bustling with shoeshiners and beggars and overwhelmed by the flow of buses and taxis. To the south and east of the plaza is a sleazy area of bars and tough nightclubs, where drunks doze in the gutters and prostitutes patrol the streets by night. Across Calle Central the great bulk of the neoclassical **Cathedral** looks unimpressive from the outside, but its broad barrel-arched interior is an oasis of calm amidst the hustle of the city centre, with striking murals high above the altar and natural light flooding in from the dome.

Over on the other side of Avenida 2, is the **Cine Palace**, one of the city's grandest cinemas and the **Teatro Melico Salazar**, a bold 1920s building with fluted Classical columns and ornate little balconies. At either end of this block are two of the city's most important cafés, the **Soda Palace** and the **Perla**, both of which are open 24 hours a day and play an essential role in the city's social life, frequented by moneychangers, dodgy businessmen and all-night drinkers.

Heading east along Avenida 2 you come to the beautifully proportioned neoclassical **Teatro Nacional** (between Calles 3 and 5), which is the city's single most impressive building. The theatre was built in response to a bitter blow to national pride, dealt in 1890 when an opera company cancelled a performance here because of the lack of a suitable venue. The coffee growers responded by levying a cultural tax on their exports and had the theatre completed by 1897. The building is beautifully maintained and preserves all its original features, such as the huge mural depicting a coffee harvest and the neat folding seats. Performances were halted in 1989 as a result of earthquake damage although repair work has now been completed—see *La República* or the *Tico Times* for current listings. If you just want to take a look inside you can buy a ticket and wander around the auditorium, which is well worth seeing, or stop off for a coffee in the theatre's café, which is very civilized and serves coffee in more ways than you can imagine.

Alongside the Teatro Nacional is the **Plaza de la Cultura**, San José's answer to Carnaby Street, where young hippies sell jewellery and Costa Rican street traders offer hammocks, T-shirts and tacky souvenirs. It's also a popular spot for impromptu speeches, evangelical preachers and rock concerts. For the young and cool this is the centre of the city. Beneath the square are the **Museo de Oro** and **Tourist Information Office**, while around its sides are an assortment of fast-food restaurants and tourist shops, including the inevitable McDonald's.

From the Plaza de la Cultura head west (left as you face McDonald's) along **Avenida Central**, which is thick with pedestrians at all hours and is the city's main shopping street, lined with delis, bookshops, department stores and fast-food restaurants. Between Calles 2 and 4 you pass the **Banco Central**, which is the tallest building in Central America and where moneychangers pester passing tourists. A sculpture outside the bank's entrance depicts dry-faced *campesinos* (peasant farmers), a typically democratic Costa Rican gesture, although the figures are dwarfed by the scale of the bank.

Heading further west along Avenida Central the street moves distinctly downmarket, the radios and foreign foods replaced by cut-priced clothes. Within a block or two you are in the heart of the city's **market area**, where vegetables are sold in the streets and fish lorries, arriving fresh from the coast, mix the smell of salt water with that of rotting fruit. The covered **Mercado Central**, where you'll find everything from chile sauce to herbal medicine, occupies an entire block (between Calles 6 and 8, and Avenidas 0–1). Outside the market Calle 8 is a mass of market traders, while to the north and west the neighbourhoods become increasingly rough, dominated by light industry and a chaotic sprawl of bus terminals. To the west of Calle 16 is the **Coca Cola Bus Terminal**, which is named after the bottling plant which used to be sited here and now serves as the city's main bus terminal.

Outside the City Centre

Outside this central area the city is lower, quieter and a lot less congested. To the west Avenida Central becomes the **Paseo Colón**, a broad boulevard which cuts through a wealthy section of the city and is lined with car-hire companies, travel agents and smartish hotels. At its western end is **Sabana Park**, which was formerly the city's main airport but has been reshaped, planted with trees and landscaped, accommodating football fields, a running track, a swimming pool and a man-made lake. Beyond here the city fans out through up-market suburbs, merging with the surrounding satellite towns. Out in the other direction, to the east, the main avenues climb through the Bella Vista area towards San Pedro, where more well-to-do suburbs surround the huge university campus.

Museums and the Zoo

The Gold Museum (Museo de Oro). Buried beneath the Plaza de la Cultura, at Calle 5, Avenida 0, open Fri–Sun, 10–5, entrance free. The museum holds an astonishing collection of pre-Columbian gold, undermining any suggestion that ancient Costa Rica was a cultural backwater. The museum's first floor is a little disappointing, devoted to slick gadgets explaining early history, while the floor below shows a massive collections of glittering gold—arm bands, gold breast plates, hundreds of tiny animals, human figures, even a gold fish hook.

The Jade Museum (Museo de Jade de INS). Situated on the 11th floor of the Social Security building, at Avenida 7 and Calle 9, with fantastic views across the city centre. Open 8–3, Mon–Fri, entrance free. This is another fascinating collection and includes an interesting explanation of the various divisions in Costa Rica's pre-Columbian culture, influenced by the Maya, Aztec and Inca cultures. The jade itself is superbly lit, displayed its deep colouring, and the artefacts include pieces depicting animals and people, as well jade knives, an Olmec jade spoon, some delicate Maya glyphs and a piece of translucent jade. The exhibition ends with some outrageous phallic pottery.

The National Museum (Museo Nacional), Calle 17, Avenidas 0–2. Open Tues–Sat 8.30–5, Sun 9–5, entrance US$1. Occupying the Bellavista Fortress, which was formerly the headquarters of the Costa Rican Army, the museum is a comprehensive and frank account of the country's history. Among the exhibits are some pre-Columbian artefacts, including beautiful ceremonial stone *metates* used for preparing food during religious rituals, and a good collection of pottery and statues. The country's modern history is equally well covered, with a realistic account of the equivocal impact of bananas and coffee and an interesting portrait of contemporary Costa Rican life, with everything from industrialization to deforestation.

The Museum of Costa Rican Art (Museo de Arte Costarricense), in the Sabana Park on Calle 42, at the western end of Paseo Colón. Open Tuesday to Sunday, 10–5, entrance US$1. An interesting collection of modern Costa Rican art, dominated by rural scenes but including some stark images from the lives of the middle classes. The museum also features some excellent travelling exhibitions, usually featuring Latin American artists.

The Museum of Criminology (Museo de Criminología), in the middle building of the Supreme Court complex, Avenida 6, Calle 15. Open Mon, Wed, Fri, 1–4, entrance free. Off-beat but astonishing, this museum includes a collection of guns and knives, counterfeit money, drugs, an explanation of forensic investigation, and pictures of car crashes and dead bodies. Among the oddest exhibits is a collection of pickled heads, hearts, lungs and hands, accompanied by an explanation of the cause of death and a warning to passing schoolchildren such as 'be careful with electricity', 'don't play with guns' and, in true Catholic style 'abortion is a criminal act'.

The Museum of Natural Sciences (Museo de Ciencias Naturales), in the Colegio La Salle at the southeast corner of the Sabana Park in the MAG building—bus from beside the Cathedral on Avenida 2. Open Mon–Fri 7–3, Sat 8–12, entrance US$1. A huge collection of stuffed birds and animals from around the world, including pickled snakes, fish and toads. The whole place has a mildly eccentric air, with a stuffed swan swaying overhead, a model US space shuttle and live freshwater turtles living in a pond in the middle.

The Insect Museum (Museo de Insectos) in the Facultad de Educación, in the university in the San Pedro district—bus from Avenida 2, Calle 5–7, ask the driver to drop you at the 'Universidad'. Follow the road right into the university and the museum, which is marked by a small sign, is on your left as the road bends around to the left. Open Mon–Fri, 1–5, entrance US$1. An huge collection of butterflies, wasps, spiders, beetles and termites, which includes some interesting explanations of insect lifestyles and gruesome pictures of the victims of diseases transmitted by insects.

The Serpentarium, Avenida 1, Calle 9–11. Daily, 10–7, entrance US$2. A small, private collection of Costa Rican snakes, including the dreaded and deadly fer-de-lance and bushmaster. Enough to put you off venturing into the countryside.

The Zoo (Parque Bolívar), reached along Calle 7, off Avenida 9. Open Tues–Fri 8–3.30, weekends 9–4.30. Scruffy and a little depressing, with lions, jaguars, crocodiles, and various other birds and beasts, crammed into tiny cages.

WHERE TO STAY
San José has an astonishing number of hotels but with an equally astonishing number of tourists, particularly from December to April, it can be hard to find a room. Once you do find somewhere, bear in mind that you will probably be back in San José from time to time during your trip, so make a point of booking up for your return.

EXPENSIVE
Several of the most exclusive hotels are on the main highway between the airport and the city. The very best of these is the **Cariari Hotel and Country Club**, tel 390022, fax 392803, which has the benefit of an excellent restaurant, a casino, 10 tennis courts, an 18-hole golf course and three swimming pools. Other luxury hotels on this highway are the **Hotel Sheraton Herradura**, tel 390033, which is a kilometre or so to the west of the Cariari, and the **San José Palacio**, tel 202024, a huge modern hotel. A little cheaper and a touch less luxurious, but also out this way, is the **Hotel Irazú**, tel 324811, fax 323159. The **Hotel Corobicí**, tel 328122, fax 315834, beside the highway where it enters the

city (in the northeast corner of the Sabana Park on Calle 42), is a huge modern hotel with an excellent pool, a gym and sauna.

In the centre of the city the best hotel is the **Gran Hotel Costa Rica**, right at the heart of things, beside the Plaza de la Cultura at Avenida 2, Calle 1–3, tel 214000, fax 213501. The hotel's ground floor-café is a bustling centre of San José social life with live music and delicious food. There is also a more private rooftop restaurant. The only international hotel in the city centre is the **Aurora Holiday Inn**, a slick modern building with an indoor pool, rooftop restaurant and a no-smoking floor. The hotel is a little quieter than the Gran Hotel although just as central at Calle 5, Avenida 5, tel 337233, fax 551036. A little less luxurious, but still a good, modern hotel with an excellent central location, is the **Hotel Balmoral**, Avenida 0, Calle 11, tel 225022, fax 217826.

MODERATE

Among mid-range hotels the **Hotel Europa**, tel 221222, Calle 0, Avenidas 3–5, is perhaps the most distinguished. Despite its modern building the hotel has a sedate, old-world atmosphere, and an outdoor pool. Other hotels in this price range also tend to be in modern buildings, but there are several that are good and reasonably priced, including the **Hotel Amstel**, Calle 7, Avenida 1, tel 224622, the **Royal Garden Hotel**, Calle 0, Avenida 0–2, tel 570022, and the **Hotel Ambassador**, Paseo Colón, Calle 26–28, tel 218155. If you would rather stay in a smaller, more intimate hotel then head for the **Hotel Santo Tomás**, which is friendly, quiet and very civilized, at Avenida 7, Calles 3–5, tel 223946, fax 223950, or the **Hotel Don Carlos**, Calle 9, Avenida 5–7, tel 216707, fax 550828.

INEXPENSIVE

San José's cheaper hotels are concentrated in the central area, although some of the better ones are around Paseo Colón. Here prices are at the upper end of the budget range. The **Hotel Cactus**, has to be one of the best, at Avenida 3, Calle 28–30, tel 212928, fax 218616. More intimate is the **Petit Hotel**, just off Paseo Colón at Calle 24, Avenidas 0–2, tel 330766. For real budget accommodation you should first try the **Pensión Otoya**, tel 213925, Calle 0, Avenidas 5–7, where you'll find warmish water and laundry service. Cheaper still is the **Hotel Ticalinda**, Avenida 2, Calle 5–7 (through a tiny door, the city's classic backpacker's budget hotel, which is rough but cheap. That much cleaner is the **Toruma Youth Hostel** (Avenida 0, Calles 29–31)—cheaper with an international Youth Hostel card. Other good budget hotels include the **Hotel Johnson**, tel 237633, Calle 8, Avenidas 0–2, the **Hotel Musoc**, tel 229437, which is in a rough spot but convenient for buses at Calle 16, Avenidas 1–3, the **Hotel Capital**, tel 218497, Calle 4, Avenidas 3–5 and the **Pensión Centro Continental**, tel 331731, Calle 0, Avenidas 8–10.

EATING OUT

EXPENSIVE AND MODERATE

San José offers a wide range of international cuisine, with food from as far afield as Japan and Switzerland. Among the city's finest restaurants are the **Chalet Suizo**, Avenida 1, Calle 5–7, which serves excellent and authentic Swiss food, the **Casino Español**, Calle 7, Avenidas 0–1, where you'll find good Spanish food and **Ile de France**, Calle 7,

Avenida 0–2, which will take you through the gastronomic wonders of France. Slightly cheaper, but very popular is the **Balcón de Europa**, Avenda 7, Calle 1, where you can eat good Italian and international food. If you'd rather sample some local delights then head for **La Cocina de Leña**, which is in the Pueblo centre, on the northeastern edge of the city, and which serves up an interesting selection of traditional Costa Rican food, including tripe, tortillas and the inevitable rice and beans. San José's finest Chinese food is on offer at the **Cin-jo**, Avenida 1, Calle 5–7, while just off Paseo Colón, at the **Restaurant Beirut**, Avenida 1, Calle 32, you can eat good traditional Middle Eastern food. Good cheap vegetarian food is available from the **Soda Vishnu**, either at Calle 3, Avenidas 0–1 or Calle 14, Avenidas 0–2 and at the **Restaurant Shakti**, Avenida 8, Calle 13.

If you're just browsing around the city or in search of a good breakfast then there are three excellent and atmospheric cafés. The first of these is **Café La Perla**, a wonderful city-centre café, at the corner of Calle 0 and Avenida 2, which does superb breakfasts, milk shakes, and full-scale meals at any time of the day or night, 365 days a year. One block west, at the corner of Avenida 2 and Calle 2, is the **Soda Palace**, which is a great open café, also open 24 hours and popular with money changers—watch out for overcharging! The last of the three is the café in the **Teatro Nacional**, Avenida 2, Calles 3–5, which has to be the most sophisticated place to take tea in San José: all the classical grandeur of the theatre, including a marble floor, a majestic carved wood bar and a total of 12 different types of coffee.

INEXPENSIVE
For the cheapest food in San José try the **Mercado Central** during the day, where you can get an excellent lunch for a couple of dollars. Alternatively **Pollo Campesino**, Calle 7, Avenida 2–4, does chicken, roasted over coffee wood, while the **Restaurante San Remo**, Calle 2, Avenida 3–5, does good, cheap food, with a vaguely Italian slant. There is also an abundance of cheap, fast-food restaurants on Avenida Central, anywhere from Calle Central to Calle 11.

NIGHTLIFE AND ENTERTAINMENT
Despite its air of gentle calm San José has a fairly active **nightlife**, offering everything from fine theatre to the very sleaziest of strip joints. The city has plenty of cinemas showing modern films, and a strong theatrical tradition. Lists of what's on are given in *La Nación* and *La República* and in the English weekly *The Tico Times* and the addresses of all cinemas and theatres are listed below.

San José is also one of the few places where you can hear excellent classical music. **The National Symphony Orchestra** stages regular performances throughout the year, the details of which are listed in the papers, including a series of 12 concerts held between April and November at the **Teatro Nacional**. There are also performances by the touring orchestras and by the **National Lyric Opera Company** and **National Symphony Chorus**.

On a less sophisticated note the city has plenty of weird and wonderful **bars**. Many of the most popular are very American in their style and approach, with long dark bars, expensive beers, loud Western music and video screens. A little quieter than most is the **Key Largo**, Calle 7, Avenida 1–3, which is popular with fat American men and ladies of the night, while the **Nashville South**, Avenida 1, Calles 5–7, is frequented by more serious drinkers. For a touch of Mexican flavour try **La Esmeralda**, Avenida 2, Calle 5–7, where wandering *mariachi* will help settle your food; or **Bar México**, Avenida 13, Calle 16, which has excellent *bocas* (snacks), and equally impressive *mariachi*.

The younger crowd tend to hang out in **Promesas** and **Caballo Loco**, which are both American-style bars with loud music and video screens; the **Show Bar**, Calle 9, Avenidas 0–1, is a lot more fun, frequented by the young and beautiful. Over on the other side of Avenida 2 the bars have a distinctly local feel, frequented by the city's hard drinkers and prostitutes. Typical of these bars is the **Margot Bar**, Avenida 6, Calle 2, although there are plenty of other, similar places along Avenida 6 between Calles 2 and 0, but beyond Calle 2 they get increasingly rough. Back on the northern side of Avenida 2 there are several **strip joints**, some of which have live shows, around the junction of Calle 0 and Avenida Central, although these are sad, dull places, with none of the wild nightlife you might expect.

At weekends it's worth heading out to the **Pueblo Centre**, on the northern edge of the city's central section, where there are several small bars, lots of live music and a couple of nightclubs, which are packed with San José's middle classes on Fridays and Saturdays.

USEFUL INFORMATION

Airlines
Aeronica: Avenida 1, Calles 1–3, tel 332483.
American Airlines: Calle 42, Avenida 5, tel 551911.
Copa: Calle 1, Avenida 5, tel 237033.
Eastern: Paseo Colón, Calles 26–28, tel 225655.
Iberia: Calle 40, Paseo Colón, tel 213311.
KLM: Calle 1, Avenida 0, tel 210922.
Lacsa: Calle 1, Avenida 5, tel 233011.
Sahsa: Avenida 5, Calle 1–3, tel 215774.
Sam: Avenida 5, Calle 1–3, tel 333066.
TACA: Calle 1, Avenidas 1–3, tel 221790.

American Express
American Express; Fourth floor of the Edificio Alde, Calle 1, Avenidas 0–1, open Mon–Fri, 8–5.30.

Books, Newspapers, Maps and Magazines
The best bookshop in town is **The Bookshop**, Avenida 1, Calles 1–3 (Mon–Fri, 9–7), which sells an excellent but pricey selection of English-language books as well as some US newspapers, *Newsweek* and *The Economist*. Other shops selling English books, magazines and newspapers include **Kiosco Centro**, Avenida 1, Calles 3–5: **Kiosco Catedral**, Avenida 2, Calles 0–1: **Librería Lehmann**, Avenida 0, Calles 1–3, which also stocks detailed maps of the country. Second-hand books are available from **Book Traders**, Avenida 1, Calles 3–5, above the Pizza Hut and **Casey's**, Calle 0, Avenidas 7–9, both of which stock plenty of well-used pulp novels. US newspapers and magazines, including the *Miami Herald*, *USA Today*, *The Wall Street Journal*, *Time*, *Newsweek* and the locally published *Tico Times*, are sold by street traders in the centre of the city.

Money

Most banks change dollar cash and traveller's cheques and are open Mon–Fri, 9–3, although some keep longer hours, including the **Banco Nacional de Costa Rica**, Avenida 4, Calle 0–2 (open until 6.30 and Sat, 9–12 noon). Black-market money-changers, who operate illegally but are tolerated, can be found along Avenida 0, between Calles 2 and 4.

Medical Problems

To call an ambulance dial 215858. In a medical emergency make for the Hospital San Juan de Dios, Calle 14, Avenida 0, tel 236422, or if things are a little less urgent then try one of the private clinics such as the Clínica Bíblica, Calle 1, Avenida 14, tel 236422, where at least some of the staff will speak English.

Post Office

The main office is at Calle 2, Avenidas 1–3, and the letters section is open Mon–Fri, 7 am–12 midnight and Sat 8–12 noon, other sections 8–5 pm.

Telecommunications

These can all be sent from Radiográfica Costarense at Calle 1, Avenida 5, or at their more efficient international office at Avenida 2, Calle 1. Both offices are open 7 am–10 pm, seven days a week.

National Parks

The National Parks information office is the Parque Bolívar, reached along Calle 7, off Avenida 9 and is open Tues to Fri, 8–3.30.

Theatres

Teatro Carp, Avenida 1, Calle 29–33, San Pedro.
Teatro de la Compañía Nacional, Calle 13, Avenidas 2–6.
Teatro Angel, Avendía 0, Calles 13–15.
Teatro Laurence Olivier, Avendia 2, Calle 28.
Teatro Nacional, Avenida 2, Calles 3–5.
Teatro Melico Salazar, Avenida 2, Calle 0.
Teatro Sala de la Calle 15, Avenida 2, Calles 13–15.
Teatro Tiempo, Calle 13, Avenida 0–2.

Cinemas

The films currently showing are listed in *La Nación* and *La República*.
California, Calle 23, Avenida 1.
California, Calle 28, Avenida 1.
Capri, Avenida 0, Calles 9–11.
Central, Calle 2, Avenidas 0–2.
Colón, Calle 38, Avenidas 1–3.
Garbo, Avenida 2, Calle 28.
Magaly, Calle 23, Avenidas 0–1.
Metropolitano, Calle Central, Avenidas 6–8.
Moderno, Calle 2, Avenidas 6–8.

Omni, Calle 3, Avenidas 0–1.
Real, Calle 11, Avenidas 6–8.
Rex, Avenida 4, Calle 11.
2000, Calle 9, Avenidas 6–8.
Universal, Paseo Colón, Calles 26–28.

Travel Agents
There are plenty of travel agents in the centre of San José; among the more reputable are: **Agencia de Viajes Excai**, Avenida 1, Calles 1–3, tel 230155, **Blanco Travel Service**, Avenida Central, Calles 7–9, tel 221792, **Cosmos Tours**, Avenida 9, Calles 1–3, tel 333466, **Swiss Travel Service**, Hotel Amstel, tel 224622.

Around San José, the Central Valley

Since the arrival of the Spanish the central valley, known as the Meseta Central, has been Costa Rica's heartland. Until the middle of this century few people lived outside this area and today it still contains 50% of the population, dotted with small towns and villages as well as the four main cities of San José, Alajuela, Cartago and Heredia. The entire area is within easy reach of San José and all of the places mentioned below make excellent day trips from the capital.

Alajuela and Around

Just 23 km from the capital and with a population of 50,000 Costa Rica's second city, sedate and civilized, is an intensely proud place. Although its people shun the chaotic commercialism of San José, in the past they have sided with the capital's liberal leaders against the more conservative cities of Heredia and Cartago.

Founded in 1790 the city benefits from a slightly warmer climate than the capital and is a traditional centre for cattle farming, and sugar processing, while the hills above are packed with coffee plantations. Today the city feels distinctly well off, its streets calm, clean and well maintained, the main plaza dominated by a fairly ordinary church, which was damaged by an earthquake in 1989 and closed for much of the following year, when services were held in the open. Six blocks behind it is the **Iglesia de la Agonía**, which was built in 1935 and has an Art Deco flair to it, with delicious rounded curves and soft pastel colours, sprouting angels from every corner.

Alajuela's most famous son is the drummer boy Juan Santamaría, who lost his life in 1857 at the battle of Rivas, after he had succeeded in setting fire to William Walker's headquarters. A monument to Santamaría (who looks as though he's brandishing a bunch of flowers but is in fact holding a flaming torch) stands at Avenida 2, Calle 2. There is also the **Juan Santamaría Historical Museum**, which is devoted to the battle of Rivas and Santamaría's heroic role, at Avenida 3, Calles 0–2, open Tues to Sun 2–9 pm, entrance free.

GETTING THERE AND WHERE TO STAY
Although the city is within easy reach of San José, you may decide that you would rather stay in the relative calm of the smaller town. Alajuela's best hotel is the **Hotel Alajuela**,

tel 416595, fax 417912, on the main plaza, which has mid-range prices. There are also several cheap places around the market, but they leave a lot to be desired and when it comes to budget accommodation you are better off sticking to San José. Buses from San José to Alajuela run every 10 minutes or so from Avendia 2, Calles 10–12, returning from the bus terminal in Alajuela.

Poás volcano

Towering above Alajuela and marking out the northern rim of the central valley, the smoking cone of the Poás volcano is surprisingly accessible. A winding road struggles up through the hills, offering superb views of the central valley and taking you through a wild fertile landscape, where farmers take advantage of the rich volcanic soil to grow coffee, strawberries and flowers. Some 20 km from Alajuela and at a height of well over 2000 m the road reaches the edge of the **Poás National Park**, which covers the cone and much of the surrounding forest. From the park headquarters you have to walk just a kilometre to peer down into the cone, which is constantly oozing smoke, steam and ash. The force of previous eruptions, the most recent in 1910, has left a great gash in the mountain, exposing layers of rock and leaving the landscape alive with volcanic activity. Deep in the midst of the crater is a small green lake, swept by plumes of sulphurous steam, which emerges in clouds of greys, greens and blues.

The summit also affords panoramic views of the surrounding countryside and on a clear day you can see both oceans, although perched on the continental divide, the peak is often shrouded in cloud, mist and rain. From the crater you can walk through the forest, along a marked trail, to the **Laguna Botos**, 1 km away. The lagoon occupies an extinct cone and has a sharp turquoise colour to it, while the walk takes you through some amazing dwarf cloud forest, a dense tangle of trees and bushes, dripping with ferns, bromeliads and orchids.

The Poás National Park is open 9–2.30, providing the volcano is calm. There is no regular bus service up here but on Sunday special buses leaves the plaza in Alajuela at 9 am, and another from beside La Merced in San José, Avenida 2, Calles 10–12, at 8 am. At the top you get a couple of hours to explore and the bus returns at around 2. There's no need to book in advance as they lay on enough buses to cope with demand. There is no accommodation in the park.

Grecia, Sarchí, Naranjo, San Ramon and Zacero

Out to the west of Alajuela amidst a sea of coffee and sugar plantations are several small villages. From a distance they have a romantic simplicity, clustered tightly around white church towers, although up close they reveal a sprawling uncertainty and are largely made up of nondescript new housing. Nevertheless these are some of Costa Rica's oldest villages and they have some interesting touches.

The first in this string is **Grecia**, which is surrounded by sugar-cane fields and has a tasty-looking, chocolate-coloured church. Next comes **Sarchí**, the central valley's ultimate *artesanía* factory, where Costa Rica's famous wooden ox-carts are made. Several roadside stores sell replica carts and a wide-ranging selection of *artesanía*, much of which has little connection with Sarchí. Nevertheless the design skills of these villagers are undeniable and every wall is brought to life by a splash of paint and the traditional geometric designs.

Beyond Sarchí the main road rolls on through the coffee plantations to **Naranjo**, which is raised up on the western rim of the central valley, with good views across to Alajuela and San José. Naranjo's central plaza is its best feature, shaded with mango trees and focused on a pyramid-shaped bandstand. The village church is a bold Baroque structure, with a solid squat body separating twin towers.

From Naranjo the road splits; one branch heads to San Ramón, to join the Pan-American Highway before dropping towards the Pacific and Puntarenas, while the other turns north, into the hills. Several small villages mark out this second route and again the views are wonderful. If you're driving, press on through **San Juanillo** for a couple of kilometres, until you reach the **Soda El Mirador**, where you can stop for a cup of coffee with the entire central valley mapped out beneath you. In the foreground small villages are scattered among the coffee plantations, while way out there in the bottom of the valley is San José, with a handful of high buildings standing out above the general sprawl of the city.

Up above here the road slips out of the central valley into a land of twisting high valleys on the side of the Poás volcano. The climate is perfect for dairy farming and fields of pasture are mixed with small blocks of pine trees, giving the area an alpine atmosphere. The largest settlement in this high country is **Zacero**, a small town famous for its cheeses, pickles, jams, apricots and hedges. The town's plaza is a topiarist's wonderland, with hedges clipped into an astonishing array of shapes and figures. The centrepiece is a row of twin arches, leading up to the church, while all around the plaza are various figures, including fish, oxen, birds, monkeys, rabbits, a man on a bicycle, an elephant and even a bullfight complete with matador and audience. It may not rank as one of the great tourist sites of the globe but there's no doubt that the town has a very talented and eccentric gardener.

Beyond Zacero the road climbs the last few hundred metres to the continental divide before dropping down towards the town of **San Carlos** (also known as Ciudad Quesada). On a clear day you can see for miles, across the lowlands which stretch into Nicaragua to the north and to the Pacific in the east.

GETTING AROUND

All of the above villages are served by a regular flow of buses from Alajuela's main bus terminal and from the Coca Cola bus terminal in San José, Calle 16, Avenidas 0–3, with departures every 20 minutes as far as Naranjo and every hour or so to Zacero. Most buses heading for Zacero are going on to San Carlos. The last bus back leaves San Carlos at 6.15 pm.

Heredia and Around

At the foot of the Barva volcano **Heredia** is the smallest and most conservative of the four central valley towns. Founded in 1706 Heredia has traditionally sided with Cartago against the modern liberalism of San José and Alajuela. Today it is a relaxed and pleasant satellite town, bustling with commuters during the rush hour but a little dull in the calm of the day. Its main point of interest is the solid **church** on the plaza, designed to survive the impact of earthquakes. It dates from 1797, making it one of the oldest in the country, and has a beautiful crumbling façade. To the north of the plaza is **El Fortín**, an ancient tower that is all that remains of an old Spanish fort and has become a symbol of Heredia. Buses to Heredia leave San José from Avenida 2, Calles 10–12, and as accommodation is in short supply in Heredia it is best visited as a day trip from San José.

North of Heredia: San Pedro de Barva and the Barva Volcano

To the north of Heredia the land rises towards the Barva volcano through prime coffee country. The village of San Pedro de Barva is home to a research station belonging to the Costa Rican Coffee Institute, which is housed in a beautiful 19th-century hacienda and has a small museum of specialized coffee-processing equipment. The institute is open Mon–Sat 8–5 and buses for San Pedro Barva leave from Avenida 1, Calles 0–1 in Heredia.

Further to the north the Barva volcano itself is embraced by the **Braulio Carrillo National Park**. To reach the park you have to head through the villages of Barva, San José de la Montaña and Sacramento, from where it is about 6 km to the summit. If you are travelling by bus, it's a long haul as you have to take a bus from Heredia to San José and then another to Sacramento, so get an early start. However, once you're up there the views are well worth the trouble.

Cartago and Beyond

At the eastern end of the central valley, **Cartago** is the oldest Spanish settlement in the country. Founded in 1563 the city was the Costa Rican capital until 1821, but never grew to any great size. It has an unsettled history, wiped out by the eruption of the Irazú volcano in 1723 and badly damaged by earthquakes in 1841 and 1910.

The inhabitants of Cartago remain fiercely proud and, like all the other central valley towns, they claim that their city is more civilized and sophisticated than San José. Today's town is certainly a lot quieter than San José although most of the architecture is modern. The **Parque Central** is dominated by the ruins of **La Parroquia**, which is the site of the first church ever built in Costa Rica. The church was first built in 1575; it was destroyed by an earthquake in 1841, and before reconstruction was completed, the replacement was badly damaged by another earthquake in 1910. Inside the ruins is a beautifully landscaped garden, with a pond, several trees and scattered blocks of masonry.

The city's other great site is the 18th-century **Basílica de Nuestra Señora de Los Angeles**, which is seven blocks to the east of the Parque Central. The Basilica, which was built early this century, is a zany building, sprouting angels and domes all across its front. The virgin is the patron saint of Costa Rica and her image is attributed with miraculous powers, making this the country's most popular place of pilgrimage. The small black statue of the Virgin, known as La Negrita, appeared on a small rock at the site of the church, and whenever it was taken away it would mysteriously find its way back to the rock. The authorities eventually gave way and decided to build the church around the rock, which can be seen in the crypt, to the left of the altar, which is home to the statue. The room above the crypt is filled with tiny silver figures of hands, legs, feet, crutches, and bodies, each of which represents a miracle performed by the Virgin. The Basilica is a site of pilgrimage throughout the year although the most important day is 2 August, the anniversary of the finding of the image, when the Virgin is paraded through the streets.

GETTING THERE
Buses to Cartago run every 20 minutes from Calle 13, Avenidas 2–6 in San José, from 5.30 am to 11 pm, returning from the main bus terminal in Cartago. The journey takes around 30 minutes. Again, bearing in mind the shortage of accommodation in Cartago, it's best visited as a day trip from the capital.

Volcán Irazú
Towering above Cartago and occasionally raining down on it, is the **Irazú volcano**, a massive active peak which reaches a height of 3432 m. The sides of the peak are extremely fertile, supporting a thriving market-gardening industry, while the peak is a bitter wilderness of ash and volcanic rock, the cone spewing out steam and sulphurous gas. Irazú last erupted in 1963, covering more than 300 sq km with volcanic ash.

A paved road leads all the way to the top and you can walk along one side of the crater and in the forest below the peak, which is all part of a national park. Walking around the crater is not permitted as the rim is unstable and the gases can be overpowering, nevertheless you get an excellent view from the observation point, both of the crater and of the surrounding landscape.

GETTING THERE AND WHERE TO STAY
If you're driving, try to reach the top early, before the clouds obscure the view. The distance from Cartago to the peak is around 30 km. If you're dependant on public transport then your best bet is the Saturday and Sunday excursion bus, which leaves from the Parque Central in Cartago at 8 am. The bus goes right to the top and waits an hour or two before heading back. At other times you can take a bus as far as Tierra Blanca, from where it's another 20 km to the summit. There are some cheap hotels lower down and a campsite just below the top.

East to the Reventazón Valley
Heading east from Cartago the main road to Turrialba and the Caribbean drops towards the spectacular Reventazón valley. But before it reaches the valley the road passes the **Lankester Gardens**, a beautiful botanic garden run by the University of Costa Rica, where you can see a wide selection of tropical plants. The garden covers some 25 acres and was founded by the British botanist Charles Lankester. An hour's walk takes you on a tour of the gardens, which are laid out with small sections corresponding to regions of Costa Rica, each with examples of the appropriate vegetation, ranging from high-altitude *páramo* to tropical rainforest and including well over a thousand varieties of orchid. The gardens are open from 8.30 am to 3.30 pm.

To get there from Cartago take any bus heading for Paraíso, which leave from the south side of the Parque Central, beside the ruins of La Parroquia. Ask the driver to drop you at the Jardín Lankester as it can be a little difficult to spot. A large cement cube beside the road points the way, but it's easy to miss.

Beyond the Lankester Garden the road divides at the small town of Paraíso, one side heading right to Orosi and Cachí, the other branching left towards Turrialba and the coast. Taking the right-hand road you drop into the lush **Reventazón valley**, which is one of the country's most beautiful areas, a secret world of brilliant green hills, coffee plantations and cattle pastures, all centred on the bumbling waters of the Río Reventazón, which is popular with white-water rafters. The first village that you come to is Orosi, a loose collection of houses clustered around a charming colonial church, built in 1735, making it one of the oldest churches in Costa Rica. Inside its solid adobe walls are some interesting woodwork and religious paintings, while the adjacent monastery is home to the **Franciscan Museum**, a small collection of colonial exhibits which includes some Guatemalan silver. The museum is open 9–12, 1–5, Tues–Sun. **Buses** to Orosi leave from the southern corner of the Parque Central in Cartago, from 6 am to 5.30 pm.

In the hills above Orosi, high up on the northern slopes of the Talamanca mountains, is the **Tapantí Wildlife Reserve**, a rain-soaked slice of tropical forest and a bird-watcher's paradise. The reserve is crossed by more than a hundred small streams and rivers and with around 3 m of rain a year the forest is always rich with greenery, the trees dripping ferns, bromeliads and orchids. Two hundred species of bird have been spotted here, including hummingbirds, quetzals, toucans, parakeets, parrots and squirrel cuckoos, while the reserve contains monkeys, anteaters, otters, red brocket deer and a lot more besides. To accommodate enthusiastic twitchers the reserve is open from 6 am to 4 pm. At the entrance is a rangers' station, where you can pick up a map and booklets in Spanish. There are several trails through the forest, complete with specified areas for swimming, picnicking and fishing.

Heading on down the Reventazón valley you come to the village of **Cachí**, which has a huge modern church and a tourist centre on the shores of the Cachí reservoir, where Costa Ricans come at weekends to sail, swim, water-ski and relax.

Ujarrás is famous throughout Costa Rica as the home of the one of the earliest Spanish settlements in the country and is the site of a beautiful ruined church, which was abandoned after it suffered serious damage from floods and earthquakes. The church was originally home to the Virgin of Ujarrás, which is reputed to have been found in a nearby river by a humble fisherman. When the Welsh pirate Henry Morgan sent a force to seize Cartago in 1666, he was repelled by a small Costa Rican militia, who had appealed to the virgin for assistance and since then the statue, which is now housed in Paraíso, has been widely revered.

GETTING THERE

Getting to the **Tapantí Reserve** is easy enough if you're driving, being just 11 km from Orosi and served by an excellent road. Buses, however, go no further than Río Macho, a couple of kilometres from Orosi, and it is a long and exhausting climb so your best bet is to take a taxi from Orosi.

Buses from Cartago run to **Cachí**, but they go no further down the valley, so if you want to continue to **Ujarrás** by public transport you have to head back to Paraíso and catch a bus around the other way. If you're driving, hitching or walking you can continue around the bottom of the reservoir to the village of Ujarrás, which is about 13 km from Cachí.

Turrialba and Around

Heading east towards the coast the main highway from Cartago runs through a beautiful landscape of coffee and sugar plantations. The land here is significantly lower than the central valley and the vegetation has a wild tropical feel to it. At Juan Viñas, a small roadside town, is a huge, mucky sugar mill, surrounded by heaps of cane during the harvest when it belches black smoke.

The largest town in the area is **Turrialba**, two hours by bus from San José, a modern commercial town which is often used as a base by rafting expeditions setting off along the Río Reventazón. Here you can visit CATIE, the **Tropical Agronomic Research and Education Centre**, a project funded by a group of Latin American nations to investigate possible advances in tropical agriculture. The setting is beautiful, with hundreds of acres of experimental plantations spread out along the banks of the river. But unless you have a specific interest in this sort of thing there is little for the ordinary tourist. The centre is a few kilometres east of Turrialba and any bus heading for La Suisa, from the main terminal in Turrialba, will drop you there.

Alternatively you could set out to climb the extinct Turrialba volcano, which is just over 3000 m high. To climb the volcano take a bus to Santa Cruz (12 noon, 3.30 and 6.30 pm Mon–Fri, 11 am, 2.30 and 5 pm Saturday and 12.30 and 5.30 pm Sunday), then walk or hitch to La Central, from where it is a couple of hours' climb to the top.

The Guayabo National Monument

In the hills to the north of Turrialba is Costa Rica's most important archeological site, the Guayabo National Monument, which dwindles when compared with Tikal or Copán but is nevertheless an interesting site is an absolutely superb setting. The site is thought to have been occupied from AD 800 to 1400, with most of the construction dating from AD 1000 to 1300, after which it suffered a marked decline. Visible today are the remains of several circular stone buildings, some tombs, paved walkways and a collection of petroglyphs, or stone carvings. Some of these clearly show animals; most, however, remain a mystery, with abstract images and designs perhaps serving as some kind of calendar or map based on the night sky. The site is thought to have been a ceremonial and population centre, surrounded by 13 smaller villages and settlements, with a total population of around 2000. Archaeologists digging here have unearthed stone carving, primitive pottery and metalwork, including some gold bells and a frog made from copper and gold, most of which are on display in the National Museum in San José.

The monument is open from 8 am to 4 pm, entrance US$1, and there are some excellent trails, the best of which is the **Sendero de los Montículos**, which takes you on a tour of the site and into some of the surrounding forest, where you can see rainbow-billed toucans, broad-winged hawks and hummingbirds. At the northern end of the site is a superb *mirador* (vantage point), offering a breathtaking view across the site and out over the Reventazón valley.

WHERE TO STAY AND GETTING THERE

The best hotel in Turrialba is the **Hotel Wagelia**, which charges US$25 for a double and has a good restaurant, while for the budget conscious the **Hotel Laroche** and **Pensión Chilita** are good value at US$4. The nearest hotel to the Guayabo Monument is **Albergue de Calzada**, tel 560465, which is about 2 km from the park and has simple double rooms for US$10.

Buses to Turrialba leave hourly from Avenida Central, Calle 13, in San José between 7 am and 8 pm, returning from the main terminal in Turrialba from 5 am until 4 pm. To get to the Guayabo Monument take a bus from the Turrialba terminal, heading for Santa Teresita, at 10.30 am or 1.30 pm. The bus will drop you at the turning, from where you have to walk 4 km uphill to the monument. Buses heading back to Turrialba pass the turning at 1.15 and 4.30 pm.

NORTHERN COSTA RICA

The Northern Pacific Coast

Perched on a narrow strip of sand, **Puntarenas** is a sleepy, rusting port, which was once the country's main link with the outside world. Opened in 1814 the port was Costa Rica's only outlet to world commerce until the opening of Puerto Limón in 1880. These days Puntarenas has taken something of a back seat and all international cargo passes through a purpose-built container terminal at Caldera, 10 km to the south. The town has sunk into a slow tropical decay, kept alive by down-market tourism and a small fishing industry. It has a slow, sleazy atmosphere, but none of the wonders that are associated with life on the Pacific coast.

A few tourists, mostly working-class Costa Ricans from the capital, come here at weekend to enjoy the beach, although this is certainly one of the country's grubbiest and you would be well advised to head on north if you're looking for sea and sand. Nevertheless you might easily end up spending the night here, along the way, before catching a ferry across to the Nicoya peninsula.

The Gulf of Nicoya

One of the country's great natural harbours, the Gulf of Nicoya is a superbly protected stretch of water, dotted with tiny islands and offering perfect conditions for tourism and marine wildlife. Several travel companies offer day tours of the Gulf, skirting the shores of some of the smaller islands and stopping off on the **Isla Tortuga**, a beautiful tropical island, complete with white sand, clear waters and arching palm trees. The tours sometimes include fishing and snorkelling and are designed with luxury in mind, costing around US$70 per person. A bus picks you up from your hotel in San José and you are fed and pampered throughout the day. Tours can be booked through any of the main hotels in Puntarenas or with one of the following companies: **Calypso Tours** (tel 333617, fax 330401), **Costa Sol Tropical Cruises** (tel 200722) or **Fantasia Island Cruise** (tel 550791, fax 231013).

If your interests are more specific then you can arrange a tailor-made trip to one of the other islands, including **Devil's Island**, a former prison colony now being developed for tourism, or the islands of **Negritos, Los Pájaros** and **Guayabo**, which are all nature reserves, noted for their abundance of seabirds, including pelicans, frigatebirds and boobies. Boats can be arranged through the yacht club or from Rafael at the Hotel Río, tel 611143. Fishing charters are also available from Puntarenas, with several boats working out of the yacht club, including 'Dockside' fishing charter (tel 630107).

WHERE TO STAY
The finest hotel in Puntarenas is the **Hotel Yadran** (tel 612662), at the far end of town, which has a pool and restaurant, while beside it is the smaller **Hotel La Punta**, which is a little cheaper but also has a pool. The other luxury hotels are all on the entrance road and include the **Hotel Colonial** (tel 611833, fax 212969) and the **Portobelo** (tel 611322). In the middle range there are several hotels along the seafront, including the **Hotel Tioga** (tel 610271), the **Hotel Gran Imperial**, US$12 for a double, and the somewhat scrappy **Hotel La Hamacas**, which has bare double rooms. The very cheapest places are to be found in the centre of town around the market; the **Hotel Río** is very cheap but basic, while the **Hotels Ayi Con** and **Helen** are a little better, though still simple. Expect thin wall and noisy neighbours, particularly at weekends.

GETTING THERE
Buses to Puntarenas leave hourly from Calle 12, Avenida 9, in San José, from 6.15 am to 7 pm, returning from Calle 2, Avenida 4, on the seafront in Puntarenas. The journey takes two hours. Other buses leaving Puntarenas go to: Liberia at 5.30, 7 and 9.30 am, 12.20, 3 and 5.50 pm; to Quepos at 5 am and 2 pm; to Santa Elena and the Monteverde Reserve at 2.30 pm. Trains from San José to Puntarenas leave at 1 pm, returning from Puntarenas at 6 am, Mon–Fri, and at 6.30 am, Sat–Sun, returning at 4 pm. The journey takes at least four hours.

The Nicoya Peninsula

Across the bay from Puntarenas the Nicoya Peninsula is a dry, exposed hump of land which juts out into the Pacific and is ringed by superb, isolated beaches. There are two ways to reach the peninsula, either by ferry from Puntarenas, which gives you good access to the southern coast, or by road through Nicoya and Santa Cruz, from where you can reach any of the beaches to the west. The following section takes a tour around the peninsula, running down its southeastern end first and then covering the beaches along the western side.

The South Coast

The easiest way to reach the Nicoya peninsula is by ferry from Puntarenas. Two services cross the gulf, one carrying trucks and cars to Playa Naranjo, almost directly opposite Puntarenas, while the other, taking only passengers, heads further south to Paquera.

A rough dirt road runs down this side of the peninsula, climbing into the hills between bays and dropping down to the sweeping horseshoe beaches, where the vegetation is fresher and greener. This road comes south from Nicoya through Carmona, reaching the sea at Naranjo, where the vehicle ferry from Puntarenas makes its landfall.

The beach at **Naranjo** is a delicate sweep of black sand, dominated by the Hotel Oasis del Pacífico, which offers a day rate, giving you the use of its swimming pool and showers.

Heading south from Naranjo the road climbs through dusty hills to the **Bahía Gigante**, which is another beatiful arch of sand, flanked by low, forested hills, a large slice of which is owned by the Hotel Bahía Gigante. The road never quite makes it to the beach here, passing high above, with excellent views across the bay and of the Isla Gigante in its midst. From here the road climbs again, winding through more hills to the coastal village of **Paquera**, which is the largest settlement on this coast and where the passenger ferry from Puntarenas comes ashore. The beach, however, is a little overused and if you're here to enjoy the sun and sand then press on south. The next bay is the massive sweep of **Tambor**, which has a magnificent expanse of uninterrupted sand, stretching for several kilometres between two sets of low hills. The bay is extremely beautiful and there's just one budget hotel on the beach and a huge bar and yacht club, the Bar Bahía, on the side of a hill to the south, where you can drink, eat, windsurf, water-ski, sail and fish.

From Tambor the road heads southwest, away from the beaches, to the small town of **Cóbano**, although along the way dirt tracks branch off to two luxury hotels, La Hacienda and Tango Mar. The road also passes the **Curu Wildlife Reserve**, a small private reserve which covers a small section of undisturbed forest behind the beach and is home to 115 species of birds (including fish eagles), rattlesnakes, white-tailed deer, and mountain lion, as well as serving as a nesting site for hawksbill and Olive Ridley turtles. The reserve can only be visited by appointment with its owners, the Schutz family, made by calling 612392 a day in advance.

Cóbano is the nearest town to the peninsula's southern tip and from here the road splits, one half heading to the isolated and beautiful beach at **Malpais**, which is seldom visited by tourists but has a single hotel, and the other to the small village of **Montezuma**, which has become a site of pilgrimage for young backpackers and where tourists now outnumber the locals. Montezuma is a tiny coastal village, nestling beneath steep forested hills and facing two small bays, each of which has a gorgeous golden beach. Tourism here is big business although its impact is very low key, with small, friendly hotels, restaurants and bars, mingling quietly with a traditional fishing community. It's a beautiful and relaxing place to stay and many travellers find it hard to leave.

Montezuma's beaches are the main attraction but there are also some beautiful waterfalls, about 20 minutes from the village, (reached by following the path uphill beside the stream in the bay to the south of Montezuma) and you can visit **Cabo Blanco National Park**, which occupies the southern tip of the peninsula. The park is a beautiful slice of tropical forest, covering a series of low hills and including a couple of superb beaches. There are several trails into the forest, taking you towards the sea and giving you the chance to see an abundance of wildlife, including howler, spider and white-faced monkeys, deer, coatimundi and hundreds of species of birds. The park is open from 8–4, entrance US$1. It is 11 km from Montezuma and you can either walk there, in around 3 hours, take a taxi (from the Pensión Alfaro for US$24 return, for 6), or go by horse (horses can be hired in Montezuma but are not allowed inside the park, although they can be left at the entrance).

WHERE TO STAY

At Playa Naranjo the only hotel is the **Hotel Oasis del Pacífico** (tel 611555), an up-market beach hotel which charges just US$3 a day for the right to use the beach, pool and showers. The hotel also offers tennis courts, horse riding and a large restaurant. Further south the **Hotel Bahía Gigante** (tel 612443) is perched on a cliff in an isolated world of tropical forest, sun and sand, with superb views across the gulf, fishing, water-skiing, sailing, diving and horse riding. Prices are in the mid to upper range. In Paquera you will find the first budget accommodation along this side of the peninsula; the **Cabinas Ginana** is the best on offer, but if that's full then try the **Cabinas Rosita**. At Tambor the only hotel is the **Hotel Dos Lagartos** (tel 611122, ext 236), which is excellent value, at the top of the budget range. Between Tambor and Montezuma are two luxury hotels, each offering a very different style of holiday. The first is the **La Hacienda** (tel 612980, fax 216609), a charming and very dignified hotel surrounded by cattle pasture and set behind the beach at Bahía Ballena, from where they offer excursions to the Curu and Cabo Blanco wildlife reserves. The second hotel is **Tango Mar** (tel 231864, fax 552697), a self-contained luxury resort complex offering tennis, diving, sport fishing, horse riding, sailing, windsurfing, water-skiing, golf and volleyball. Access is by reservation only.

Montezuma has an abundance of small hotels. The best of these is the **Cabinas El Sano Banano** (tel 611122, ext 272), where a series of small cabins are scattered throughout a small section of towering forest and feeding monkeys will wake you at dawn. The hotel is in a small bay a kilometre to the north of Montezuma, reached on foot from the village and prices are in the mid-range. In the centre of the village are the **Hotel Pacífico Montezuma**, which is in the upper budget range and has air-conditioned double rooms, while solid budget accommodation is offered at the **Hotel Montezuma**, the **Cabinas Mar y Ciel** and the **Pensión Arenas**, which is among the cheapest— camping is permitted on the beach outside, for a small fee which entitles you to use the showers. In another bay to the south of Montezuma are the **Hotel Alfaro**, and the cheaper **Hotel Lucy**, while further south still, halfway to the Cabo Blanco National Park, is the **El Ancla de Oro**, which has a small restaurant and good double cabins at budget prices. Around the point, in Malpais, is **Otto's**, which has double cabins for top of the range budget prices and an excellent restaurant.

GETTING THERE

Getting around the Nicoya Peninsula is easier said that done. There are few buses and the roads are extremely rough, so hiring a car is certainly a good idea. The easiest way to reach this southern end of the peninsula is by ferry from Puntarenas. The vehicle ferry *Salinero* leaves Puntarenas (from the inland side of Puntarenas about halfway along the town) for Playa Naranjo on Monday, Tuesday, Wednesday and Friday at 7 am and 4 pm, returning at 9 am and 6 pm. The passenger ferry *Paquera* leaves Puntarenas for Paquera daily at 6 am and 3 pm, returning at 8.15 am and 4 pm. On the other side the only bus services are those which meet the ferries, going from Paquera to Montezuma and from Naranjo to Nicoya. There is no bus service between Naranjo and Paquera.

Nicoya and Around

At the geographical heart of the peninsula the town of Nicoya is sedate and provincial, but makes an ideal base from which to explore the peninsula's central section, including an inevitable string of beaches and a national park. The town's single tourist site is its tin-roofed colonial church, which is a simple crumbling structure.

To the east of Nicoya the **Barra Honda National Park** lies on the edge of the arid Tempisque valley, an area which receives less rainfall than anywhere else in Costa Rica. The park contains several low, limestone hills, formed from ancient coral reefs, beneath which is a complex network of caves, some which has never been explored. The caves are a maze of chambers with bizarre natural features and some strange inhabitants, including rats, insects, bats, blind fish and birds. Access to the caves is restricted but guides can be hired in a village nearby and park staff have the necessary equipment, although this may take some time to get together. Alternatively you can arrange a tour from San José, with **Turinsa Receptivo**, Avenida 3, Calles 3–5, tel 219185, or you can simply walk among the hills, take in the superb views across the Gulf of Nicoya, watch the iguanas and monkeys and peer into the caves. There are several trails across the hills, the largest of which reaches a height of 300 metres, although it can be heavy going in this hot, dry atmosphere.

The park is open 8–4. To get there either drive from Nicoya, taking the road towards the Tempisque ferry or take a bus heading for Quebrada Honda (from Nicoya at 10.30 am or 3.30), and get off at the entrance road, from where it is a 6 km walk to the park headquarters. Camping is permitted and drinking water is available but bring your own food.

Out to the west of Nicoya are another set of superb Pacific beaches, all reached along rough dirt roads. The most popular of these is **Playa Sámara**, a massive sweep of sand, which has several tourist hotels but more than enough sand to go around. Four or five kilometres to the south of Sámara, around the point, is **Cárrillo**, another huge horseshoe bay. Here the first beach is a beautiful corner of sand, protected from the force of the breakers and far from the hotels which dominate the other side.

Twenty kilometres or so to the north of Sámara is **Playa Nosara**, a dead straight beach, behind which is a superb stretch of dense tropical forest. The village of

Turles on sand

418

Nosara, which is a dispersed farming community, is a few kilometres from the beach in a beautifully fertile river valley. Despite the fact that the beach here has been well developed, with a couple of hotels and a new apartment block, the forest manages to mask most of this new building and gives the beach itself a remote, tropical feel. As an added bonus a large portion of the beach is protected by the **Ostional Wildlife Reserve**, as it is a crucial nesting site for Olive Ridley Turtles. The turtles come ashore here from July to December in huge numbers—there can be as many as 120,000 turtles arriving in a single weekend. Each turtle lays several hundred eggs, some of which are legally collected by local people for food. In exchange for this small harvest locals watch over the young turtles as they make a dash for the sea a couple of months later, protecting them from predatory seabirds. If you want to watch turtles, bring a torch and register your interest at the park's office, who will send you out with a guide. The parks also includes a large area of swamp and forest, so if your timing does not coincide with that of the turtles then you can walk some of the forest trails, and perhaps bump into the odd howler monkeys or coatimundi, while there is also excellent birdwatching around the mouth of the river.

WHERE TO STAY

In Nicoya the finest hotel is the **Hotel Yenny**, which has double rooms, complete with air conditioning and television, which is a bargain—at the top end of the inexpensive range. A touch more expensive, but not nearly as good is **Las Tinajas**, while the best budget deal is the very basic **Pensión Venecia**, on the main plaza.

In Sámara there are several good tourist hotels, the best of which is **Las Brisas del Pacífico**, a luxurious but intimate hotel with a good pool and restaurant, which is right on the beach. Other inexpensive hotels include the **Hotel Marbella** (tel 339980) and the **Cabinas Marta**, and there are plenty of rougher places, including the **Hotel Playa Sámara**, which has a booming disco at weekends. Around the point in Carrillo there is just one luxury hotel, the **Guanamar** (tel 200722), which offers packages of two nights and three days, including daily fishing for marlin, yellow fish and tuna.

In Nosara you have to decide between the beach and the village, which are several kilometres apart. The smarter hotels are scattered around the beach and include the **Hotel Playa Nosara**, which is perched on a cliff high above the beach, with superb views and top-range prices to match, and the **Rancho Suizo**, a small friendly hotel, surrounded by forest, with mid-range prices. For inexpensive accommodation you have to stick to the village and the **Cabinas Chortega** or **Agnel**.

GETTING AROUND

Buses from San José to Nicoya, from Avenida 5, Calle 14, leave at 6, 10 am, 1.30, 3 and 5 pm, returning from the terminal in Nicoya at 7.30, 9, 12 noon, 2.30 and 4.20 pm. To the beaches, buses from Nicoya leave for Playa Naranjo at 5 am and 1 pm; for Sámara at 3 and 8 am at weekends; returning at 7 am; for Nosara at 1 am returning at 6 am; and every hour or so to Santa Cruz.

Santa Cruz and Beaches from Playa Junquillal to Playa Panamá

Twenty kilometres to the northwest of Nicoya is the small town of **Santa Cruz**, which is of little interest in itself (although there are plenty of hotels and restaurants should you get stuck here), but provides access to yet another selection of excellent beaches.

Working up from the south the first of these is **Playa Junquillal**, a broad and exposed bay with a couple of up-market hotels. The bay used to rank as one of the great undiscovered beaches of the north although these days it has a forlorn, arid feel to it and much of the land has been cleared for development. By contrast **Tamarindo** still rates as one of the country's most beautiful beaches, a massive crescent of golden sands, swept by spectacular Pacific breakers. The surf is excellent and the fresh waters of Río Tamarindo spill into the bay, its banks protected by **The Tamarindo Wildlife Reserve**, which covers much of the estuary and offers an opportunity to explore the mangrove swamps and watch crocodiles basking in the sun. On the other side of the river the huge expanse of **Playa Grande** is another favourite nesting site for turtles, which come ashore here during the rainy season.

With all this on offer it's hardly surprising that Tamarindo is one of the most highly developed beaches in Costa Rica. Though small, the town is almost entirely made up of hotels, restaurants, surf shops and tour companies, but with sand stretching for several kilometres in either direction and few buildings rising more than a couple of stories, it all feels fairly unobtrusive. And there can be no doubt that this is one of the most spectacular and enjoyable beaches in the north, with everything from surfing to birdwatching and car hire. Tours of the estuary, horse riding and fishing trips are offered by **Papagayo Expeditions** and **Fiesta del Mar**, and surf boards can be hired from several shops.

To the north of Tamarindo another road reaches the sea at the small village of **Brasilito**, which has somehow managed to escape heavy development and remains popular with Costa Ricans. The village is a little scruffy but has one extremely friendly budget hotel and a kilometre of so to the left is **Conchal**, a spectacularly beautiful white beach, with crystal clear waters, which you may well have to yourself during the week. Heading north from Brasilito the next place of real note is **Flamingo**, a massive purpose-built resort, dominating a great finger of land, which is popular with rich US visitors and sport-fishermen. There's a large marina hidden behind the hotel and the surrounding hills are dotted with luxury villas, but this a typically antiseptic international resort. Further north the road pushes on to some slightly more interesting hotels, in **Portero bay**, behind the Flamingo resort, and finally a single hotel in the isolated **Sugar Beach Bay**.

To the north of here a third access road, served by buses from Liberia, reaches the coast at **Playa del Coco**, an extremely popular beach which has been dragged down by trashy development and overuse. Four kilometres to the south of Coco is the exclusive **Playa Ocotal**, where a luxury hotel, specializing in diving and sport-fishing, is set in a very beautiful bowl-shaped bay. To the north is the **Playa Hermosa**, another lovely beach which is overlooked by a large hotel. Further north still is the **Playa Panamá**, where the residents have been moved out to make way for impending development.

WHERE TO STAY

In Santa Cruz you will find the best lodgings at the **Hotel Diria** (tel 680080), which has a pool, a dance hall, air-conditioned double rooms and moderate prices, while the best budget deal is the **Hospedaje Avellanas**. At Playa Junquillal there are two luxury hotels: the **Hotel Villa Serena** (tel 680737), which has a pool and tennis court, and the larger

Hotel Antumalol, both of which charge high prices. The only budget accommodation is at the Hotel Junquillal.

In Tamarindo there is plenty of excellent accommodation. Among the best are the **Hotel Tamarindo Diria** (tel 680474), which has air-conditioned rooms and luxury prices, and the **Hotel Pueblo Dorado** (tel 225741). Excellent double cabins, with fridges and cookers, are available at **Cabinas Pozo Azul** (tel 680147), the **Cabinas Marielos,** and the **Cabinas Zullymar,** all at low to moderate prices. The best budget deal is the **Hotel Doly.** There are plenty of excellent restaurants in Tamarindo, including the **Coconut,** the **Stella,** which does good Italian food, and **Johan's bakery,** which serves delicious homemade pizza, croissants and cakes.

In Brasilito the only hotel is **Cabinas Mi Posada,** which is friendly and relaxed, charging budget prices. Heading towards Flamingo you pass **Villas Pacífico** (tel 680932), a sport-fishing resort which charges top prices for double cabins, while at the **Flamingo Beach Hotel** (tel 338056) prices are still in the luxury league. Beyond Flamingo there are a couple of hotels in the Portero Bay and a friendly luxury hotel at the Sugar Beach bay, the **Hotel Sugar Beach** (tel 680959), where prices are in the upper mid-range.

In Playa de Coco the best hotel is the luxurious **Flor de Itabo** (tel 670003), which is a kilometre or so from the beach, while beside the sea the **Hotel Anexo Luna Tica,** provides reasonable budget accommodation and there are plenty of cheap, roughish places, catering for weekenders from the capital. At Playa Ocotal the **Hotel Ocotal** (tel 670230) offers an expensive up-market diving package. At Playa Hermosa is the luxury **Condova resort** (tel 670267), which struggles to meet your every need, while down on the beach you'll find the **Cabinas Playa Hermosa,** a pleasant and friendly hotel with moderate prices and there are also a couple of simple budget places.

GETTING THERE
Buses to Santa Cruz from San José, leave from Calle 20, Avenida 3, at 7.30, 10.30 am (going on to Flamingo), 2 (going on to Junquillal), 4 (going on to Tamarindo) and 6 pm, returning to San José at 4.30, 6.30, 8.30 am, 1.30 pm. They leave Junquillal at 5, Tamarindo at 6.45 and Flamingo at 9.30 am. There are also hourly buses between Santa Cruz and Nicoya from 6 am to 9.30 pm and between Santa Cruz and Liberia from 5.30 am to 7.30 pm.

You can also get to Junquillal by taking a bus from Nicoya to Paraíso and then walking the last 4 kilometres, and there are buses from Santa Cruz to Tamarindo, at 10.30 am and 3.45 pm, returning at 6 am and 12 noon, and from Santa Cruz to Flamingo, passing through Brasilito, at 10.30 am and 2 pm, returning at 6 am and 5 pm. Buses run from Liberia to Playa del Coco at 5.30 am, 12.30 and 4 pm, returning at 7 am, 2 and 6 pm and from Liberia to Playa Hermosa at 11.30 am, returning at 5 pm.

The Pan-American Highway
—from San José to Nicaragua

Heading north from San José the Pan-American Highway drops out of the central valley to the west, towards Puntarenas, and then pushes up towards Nicaragua. Along the way the highway is overshadowed by two mountain ranges to the east. The first, the Cordillera Tilarán is a great block of forested hills containing the Monteverde Reserve and Lake Arenal, while to the north this range merges into the Cordillera de Guanacaste, a string of volcanic peaks which encompass two national parks and drop off into the lowlands along the border with Nicaragua. On the other side of the highway, separating it from the coast, are the low dry hills of Nicoya and Guanacaste, a parched dusty landscape which is heavily used for cattle farming, although close to the border a huge slice of dry tropical forest has been preserved in the Santa Rosa National Park. It's the variety of natural environments which provide the main attraction along this route and there are several important wildlife reserves which can be reached from the highway, offering insights into a number of very different ecological niches.

The Monteverde Reserve

The Monteverde Forest Reserve has to rate as one of the most beautiful and most popular of Costa Rica's wildlife reserves, with around 15,000 visitors a year. The reserve is a perfect example of a tropical cloud forest, a wildly fertile environment, which is kept moist and lush by a succession of cloud, mist and rain. Its trees are coated in ferns, bromeliads, orchids, mosses and lichens. You still stand a good chance of seeing some interesting birds, including the resplendent quetzal, or even the famous golden toad, which was only discovered in 1964, although the ever increasing numbers of visitors have driven the larger animals deep into the forest, beyond the reach of all but the most intrepid.

The reserve was founded by a group of forty Quakers from Fairhope, Alabama, who settled here in the 1950s, many of them recently released from jail for refusing the draft, attracted to the fact that Costa Rica had abolished its army. The original settlers were devoted to living in harmony with their environment and set aside a huge area of forest around the headwaters of the Río Guacimal, to preserve their water supply. Today this area forms the hub of the Monteverde Reserve, which is now administered by the Tropical Science Centre, while several new reserves have also been created, including the Arenal and San Ramón Forest Reserves and the Bosque Eterno de los Niños, which was bought with money raised by schoolchildren around the world. Quakers still form a large part of the community here although their numbers have been supplemented by Seventh-Day Adventist, US hippies and an assortment of Costa Ricans and Europeans attracted by the environment, lifestyle and increasing business opportunities. And while cattle farming and cheese making are still an important part of the local economy it is now tourism that accounts for the largest slice of local income.

Approaching the reserve from the Pan-American Highway is a slow process. A rough dirt track climbs into the hills for some 35 kilometres, to the village of **Santa Elena**, which is a scruffy collection of simple houses, cheap hotels and cafés. From here the road heads up through the dispersed community of Monteverde, which has no real centre, past the cheese factory (open to visitors Mon–Sat, 7.30–4 pm and Sun, 7.30–12.30 pm) and meeting house, to the reserve itself (which is 5 km from Santa Elena). The reserve is open daily from 7–4.30 pm, entrance fee US$10, boot hire US$1 (there is a lot of mud). At the entrance you can pick up a map and the reserve staff will recommend a route that suits your plans and gives you a good chance to see the forest, its inhabitants and perhaps a waterfall or two. A network of excellent trails fans out into the reserve and you can explore for anything from an hour to a week. If you really want to soak up the atmosphere then you can stay inside the reserve at a couple of shelters (U$2 per person per night): the Valle shelter (about 2 hrs' walk from the entrance) and the Alemán shelter (6–8 hrs), both of which have wood stoves, although you will need to take your own food.

Outside the main reserve there are some other spectacular sights in the surrounding hills, including the Río Negro reserve, from where you can see down across Lake Arenal to the puffing peak of the Arenal volcano. Horse riding is a popular option and a superb way to see this area, available from several people in Santa Elena (including Luigi at the Hospedaje Banco) or through any of the main hotels in Monteverde.

WHERE TO STAY
Hotels in Monteverde tend towards the rustic and although you'll find hot water and wholesome meals you should expect a little more simplicity than normal. Most of the better hotels are off the road between Santa Elena and the reserve, and for sake of clarity the list takes you from Santa Elena up towards the reserve—bear in mind that unless you have your own car you'll have to walk up to the reserve as there is no bus service. As you leave Santa Elena a small side road branches off to the left towards the **Hotel Sapo Dorado** (tel 612952), which is a small friendly hotel with superb views across the valley and full board at moderate prices. A little further up the hill, off to the right, is the **Monteverde Inn** (tel 612756), which is Canadian owned and offers full board, with a private bathroom, for moderate prices or a special budget bed and breakfast. Next comes the **Hotel Heliconía** (tel and fax 611009), a strange and small hotel. Higher still is the **Pensión Manakin** (tel 612854), which offers simple half-board at a moderate price, while next door the **Hotel Montaña Monteverde** (tel 611840), a modern, expensively priced motel. Just before you reach the cheese factory is the **Pensión Quetzal** (tel 610955), which is an easy-going and friendly place, set away from the road and owned by one of the few remaining Quaker families. Lodgings and two meals a day are available for moderate prices. Up above the cheese factory is the **Pensión Flor Mar** (tel 610909), another intimate family hotel, also owned by Quakers, which also charges moderate prices for full board and is just 2.5 km from the entrance to the reserve. Nearing the top of the village is the **Hotel Fonda Vela** (tel 612551), which is among the most luxurious hotels in Monteverde, perched above a steep slope, with superb views, and charging expensive rates. Finally just over one kilometre from the reserve is the **Hotel Villa Verde** (tel 611255), where basic rooms go for a bargain inexpensive price, including two meals and a picnic lunch.

For really cheap budget accommodation you are confined to Santa Elena, quite a hike from the park. Here the **Hospedaje Banco**, run by the irrepressible Luigi, charges inexpensive rates, as do the **Pensión El Tucán** and the **Pensión Santa Elena**. There are also several cheap restaurants in Santa Elena, while in Monteverde you will have to eat in your hotel, although in most places that is part of the deal.

GETTING THERE
Buses from San José to Santa Elena leave from Calle 12, Avenida 5 at 2.30 pm Mon–Thur and 6.30 pm Sat–Sun. From Santa Elena to San José the bus leaves at 6.30 am from Tuesday to Thursday and at 3 pm from Friday to Sunday. There is also a

bus from Santa Elena to Puntarenas at 6 am, returning at 2.30 pm, and from Santa Elena to Tilarán at 7 am, returning at 12 am.

North to Liberia

Continuing to the north of the turning for Monteverde, along the Pan-American Highway the first town of any size is Cañas, a quiet provincial centre which has been largely bypassed by the sweeping tide of Costa Rican tourism, but where you might end up spending the night. There are a couple of decent cheap hotels, the inexpensive **Hotel Cañas** (tel 690039), and the **Hotel Guillén**, while just north of Cañas is **La Pacífica Ecological Centre** (tel 690050), a huge cattle ranch which has been developed as a tourist centre with a large pool, several lakes for swimming, horse riding and moderately priced double rooms.

To the southwest of Cañas is a huge swampy wildlife reserve which covers some 19,000 hectares and is made up of the neighbouring **Palo Verde National Park** and the **Rafael Caballero Wildlife Refuge**. The area is a great expanse of marshes, islands, lagoons, mangroves, and dry and evergreen tropical forest, running along the eastern bank of the Río Tempisque. Even by Costa Rican standards this is a superb place to watch birds and animals and you have a good chance of seeing spider and white-faced monkeys, peccaries, deer, herons, storks, macaws and parrots, to mention but a few. The only place to stay within the reserve is a simple field station operated by the Organisation for Tropical Studies, who charge modate rates full board (half-price for students if you can produce a card), and you must book in advance through the OTS in San José (tel 366696), who will arrange transport from Cañas.

Another 40 kilometres to the north of Cañas is **Liberia**, the capital of Guanacaste, a prosperous and relaxed town with a population of around 20,000. Guanacaste is rich in rural traditions and if you are lucky enough to coincide with a fiesta you'll see traditional dances and hear local music that is unrivalled in Costa Rica, not to mention witness some extremely dangerous bull baiting. At other times the town is very calm indeed, although on Sundays it takes on a distinctly formal air as families promenade in the main plaza, buying food and drink from temporary stalls and sometimes dancing to a band in the cool of the evening. But beyond this interesting air of provincial formality Liberia has little to hold the passing visitor, although it does make a good place to base yourself for exploring the surrounding area, taking in a national park or two and spending a couple of days at the beach. The town has an excellent tourist office (four blocks to the left of the church—as you face it, closed Mondays), where you can get excellent information about visiting the nearby National Parks and see a small exhibition on the history of Guanacaste. The lady who runs the office is very helpful, speaks perfect English and can arrange the hire of camping equipment from the local boy scouts.

WHERE TO STAY

There are plenty of good hotels in Liberia, with the best of them clustered around the junction with the Pan-American Highway, including the **Motel El Bramadero** (tel 660371), which has air-conditioned doubles for moderate rates, and the slightly more expensive **Hotel Boyeros** (tel 660995). In the centre of town the **Hotel La Siesta** (tel 660878) has a tiny swimming pool and air-conditioned double rooms for moderate rates. The best of the budget hotels is the rough **Hotel Liberia**. Car hire is available in Liberia from the Motel El Bramadero.

GETTING THERE
Buses to Liberia leave San José from Calle 14, Avenidas 1–3, hourly from 7 am to 8 pm, returning from the purpose-built terminal on the edge of Liberia. From Liberia there are also buses to the Nicaraguan border every couple of hours, and to Santa Cruz and Nicoya every hour or so.

The Rincón de la Vieja National Park

To the northwest of Liberia is the Rincón de la Vieja National Park, a huge protected area which embraces the active Rincón volcano and a slice of the surrounding forest. Among the attractions are some bubbling mud holes, soothing natural hot springs, clear rivers, cool lakes, waterfalls and trails which run deep into the forest, giving you a chance to see armadillos, white-faced monkeys, peccaries, white-tailed deer and, of course, a wide variety of birdlife. If the volcano isn't rumbling too much, you can climb the cone in around eight hours and there is a small refuge about halfway up, where you can stay the night in order to get to the top early, and avoid the gathering cloud. But, be warned, it's a tough hike!

The entrance to the park is 27 km from Liberia and there is a rough road connecting the two. A taxi, which can take up to six, will cost you US$25, or you can take a bus to Colonia Blanca (which leaves Liberia at 2 pm, returning at 5 am), from where it is another 15 km to the park. You can either walk this last stretch, in 3–4 hours, or hire horses for the trip. At the park headquarters you'll find basic accommodation and camping is permitted, although you must bring your own food.

Alternative accommodation is available at the **Rincón Mountain Lodge** (tel 662369), which is just outside the reserve but provides a more luxurious base from which to explore it. The lodge, which is also a youth hostel, charges moderate rates—inexpensive with a youth hostel card—and can provide guides to take you into the reserve, either on foot or on horseback. Food is available at the lodge. A taxi from Liberia to the lodge will cost you around US$25 or they will come and pick you up for a similar fee.

The Santa Rosa National Park

Up in the northwest corner of Costa Rica the Santa Rosa National Park ranks as one of the country's most important historical and biological sites. With regard to the former it was in 1856 that the Santa Rosa Hacienda, which still stands inside the park and is now a museum (open 8 am to 4.30), was the site of a famous battle between the Costa Rican militia and the forces of William Walker, who had invaded from the north. The success of Costa Rica's ragged army is hailed as one of the nation's great historical events and was also one of the first issues that managed to unite Costa Ricans. These days it is fabled as a typically heroic response to the threat of external rule and dictatorship.

However, for the historically uninitiated, the main attraction has to be the dry tropical forest, which occupies the bulk of the park, and its superb beaches, which are prime nesting sights for olive ridley turtles, which come ashore in huge numbers from August to December. The forest, which is relatively open, dry and deciduous, is one of the few remaining examples of an ecosystem which used to cover Central America's coastline from Mexico to Colombia, but has almost all been swallowed up by the needs of commercial agriculture. The park also offers a quite surprising opportunity to see wildlife at close quarters since certain species, such as white-tailed deer, coatimundi, white-faced and spider monkeys, armadillos and iguanas are found here in abundance, while others, including coyote, peccaries, tapir and jaguar are sometimes seen but remain shy and elusive.

The entrance to the Santa Rosa Park is on the Pan-American Highway, about 40 minutes from Liberia, and any bus heading for La Cruz or the border will drop you here, from where it is another 7 kilometres to the park headquarters and the main campsite. Food is not officially available, although if you ask nicely they may let you pay to eat in the staff canteen, and there is no accommodation for visitors. Entrance to the park costs US$1, and you must pay another 50 cents to camp. From the campsite there are a number of short trails, to the Hacienda, through the forest and to some small lakes, where animals gather, particularly during the dry season. A dirt track also continues through the park to the beach at Playa Naranjo, which is about 11 kilometres from the park headquarters and where there are two campsites: Estero Real, at the northern end of the beach, and Aegelia, which is more popular. Passable drinking water is available here but you must bring your own food, although with a touch of luck you might be able to hitch a ride with surfers, who come in here with four-wheel-drive vehicles to check on the waves. The beach is, however, absolutely beautiful, and even in peak season there are rarely more than a dozen people here.

The Guanacaste National Park

On the east side of the Pan-American Highway is Costa Rica's newest reserve, the Guanacaste National Park, which stretches across a huge area, ranging from dry, open savannah to the rainsoaked peaks of the Orosí and Cacao volcanoes. In many ways the park is a new phase in Costa Rica's environmental protection programme as attempts are being made to reforest the low ground with dry tropical forest, reconnecting the coastal environment with the higher forests on the slopes of the volcanoes.

As yet little has been done to encourage tourism here and if you want to you visit the park you must first obtain permission and information from the park headquarters in Santa Rosa. However, there are three biological stations here, all of which have beds and food for passing strangers. The first of these is Maritza, which is 22 kilometres from the highway, reached along an entrance road about 10 kilometres north of the entrance to Santa Rosa. The second is the Mengo station, commonly known as Cacao, which is high on the side of the Cacao volcano and can only be reached on foot, either from Maritza or from the village of Quebrada Grande (which has bus connections to Liberia). If you are interested in visiting this park, you may have to be persistent but the views from Cacao are superb, with a sweeping vista across the plains to the coast and north to Lake Nicaragua, and the volcanic peaks can be climbed as day trips from either station. There is also a third biological station, perched on the northern slopes of the Orosí volcano in the Atlantic watershed, which can be reached from the village of Santa Cecilia.

La Cruz and the Border

Before it finally arrives at the Nicaraguan border the Pan-American Highway passes the small town of La Cruz, which is perched above the sea on a high cliff, and if you are driving it's well worth dropping in for the dramatic views across the Gulf of Santa Elena.

Just 19 kilometres to the north of La Cruz is the border with Nicaragua at Peñas Blancas. The border is open 6.30–11, 12.30–5.30, and 6.30–10. Buses from the border run every couple of hours to Liberia and on the other side there is a fairly regular service to Rivas.

The Central Northern Area

Costa Rica's northern lowlands are huge and sparsely populated: an enormous open landscape crossed by thousands of small rivers and streams, which push their way north, emptying into the mighty Río San Juan on the border with Nicaragua. Only in the second half of this century have farmers begun colonizing the area and it remains rough frontier country, producing rice, cattle, maize and timber. For the visitor the main attractions are on its margins, focused on the loop around Lake Arenal, where you can bathe in natural warm springs while watching the Arenal volcano spewing lava, and the jungles around Puerto Viejo, which are prime bird-watching country.

San Carlos, Fortuna, Lake Arenal and Tilaran

The main route from the central valley to the northern lowlands slips through a high mountain pass on the shoulder of the Poás volcano and passes the small town of Zacero, before dropping into San Carlos. It's an extremely beautiful road, taking you up through carefully tended coffee plantations into high cattle pastures and pine groves, and as it drops towards San Carlos the lowlands stretch out into the distance, vast and featureless.

San Carlos (which is also known as Ciudad Quesada) is a bustling and prosperous town, very much at the heart of the push north. Here transport and trade are focused and the development of the lowlands is financed and directed. It is a modern town, with little to offer the passing tourist other than a decent meal and an onward bus. It does, however, have several banks and restaurants, plenty of hotels and even a couple of cinemas.

From San Carlos a good paved road runs northwest towards the perfect cone of the Arenal volcano and small town of **Fortuna**, which is an excellent base for exploring the surrounding area. From here you can visit the hot springs at **Tabacón**, where you can either bathe in the luxury of the new tourist complex or in the more natural surroundings downriver, where a stream of warm water meanders through a meadow, surrounded by lush tropical forest. Camping is encouraged here and in the early morning monkeys feed in the overhanging trees.

Towering above you is the **Arenal volcano**, which is Costa Rica's most active volcanic peak and is continuously spouting great bursts of ash and lava. The cone's north and western sides offer the best views, which are at their most dramatic after dark, when the dull grey lava clouds become a fantastic fountain of orange fire. You can either watch the cone from the Tabacón springs and the nearby restaurant of Los Lagos, or you can take a trip up the western side of the cone in a four-wheel-drive vehicle. Such trips are arranged by the Albergue Burio in Fortuna or you can set them up on your own, which is certainly cheaper, with a taxi driver (try Marvin Santa María, tel 479150, who has a white Toyota land cruiser and can usually be found at the petrol station in Fortuna). It's not a particularly good idea to try this yourself, either by car or on foot, as the volcano has claimed the lives of several tourists over the years.

Fortuna's other attractions include a superb **waterfall**, which is signposted from the western side of town and is just a couple of hours' walk away—it's a toughish stroll, mostly uphill, but once you arrive you can scramble down to the pool below and swim beneath the cascade. One final possibility is a visit to the **Venado caves**, an extensive network of underground chambers which are entered near the village of Venado. If you have your own car you can drive to Venado, where you'll find a guide waiting eagerly to take you down, but if you're travelling under your own steam you'll have to arrange a taxi or take a tour from the Albergue Burio in Fortuna.

Heading on from Fortuna a spectacular road skirts the eastern shores of **Lake Arenal**, pushing on through Arenal village, which was built to replace an earlier version lost beneath the waters of the lake. At the northern end of the lake the largest town is **Tilarán**, from where a main road runs down to the Pan-American Highway and a rough back road heads south, through the mountains, to Santa Elena and the Monteverde Reserve. The Arenal lake is the largest hydroelectric project in Central America. Its waters used to drain to the Pacific but are now diverted to the west, irrigating new farmland. The lake offers excellent fishing for rainbow bass, known locally as *guapote*, which weigh up to 12 pounds and are caught on bass lures, deep runners and jigs, whatever they may be! (Several hotels, listed below, offer fishing on the lake.)

WHERE TO STAY

In San Carlos the finest hotel is the **Hotel Conquistador**, at the entrance to the town, while on the plaza is the **Hotel La Central** (tel 460766), which is moderately priced. The best of the budget hotels is the **Hotel Ugalde**, on Calle 2. If that's full, try the **Hotel Axel Alberton** or the **Hotel Crystal**, which are also on Calle 2.

In Fortuna the **Albergue Burio** (tel 479137), which is inexpensive, is easily the best place to stay, offering simple but clean rooms, with private bathrooms. The Albergue can also organize tours of the surrounding area and fishing on the lake. Other hotels include the **Hotel Las Colinas**, the **Hotel Central** and the **Hotel Fortuna**, all offering simple inexpensive accommodation. The best place to eat in town is the **Restaurant Jardín**, which serves good, typically Costa Rican food at bargain prices and is the heart of social life in Fortuna.

At the eastern end of the lake two up-market lodges offer accommodation, volcano watching and fishing. The **Arenal Volcano Observatory** (tel 553418, fax 554410) was built in 1978 as a geological research station and offers full board in the luxury price range, while the **Arenal Lodge** (tel 282588), also expensive, specializes exclusively in lake fishing.

In Tilarán the **Cabinas El Sueño** has double rooms for inexpensive rates, while the **Hotel Spot** is a touch more luxurious, in the moderate price bracket. The best of the budget places is **Cabinas Mary**, on the plaza.

GETTING AROUND

Buses to San Carlos leave hourly from the Coca Cola terminal in San José, returning from the main terminal in San Carlos. From San Carlos there are buses to Fortuna at 9.30 am, 1, 3.30 and 4.45 pm, and to Tilarán at 6.30 am and 3 pm. From Fortuna there are buses to San Carlos at 5, 6.30, 7.30, 10 am and 1 pm and to Tilarán at 8 am and 4 pm. From Tilarán there are buses to San José at 7, 7.45 am and 4.30 pm, and a bus to Santa Elena (Monteverde) at 12.30 pm, returning the next day at 7 am.

Los Chiles and Upala

Costa Rica's most northerly towns (rivalled only by La Cruz) are far-flung frontier settlements and you need a good reason to subject yourself to the rigour of travelling out this far. Few tourists ever make it here and of those who do most are disappointed to find that the frontier post at Los Chiles is closed to foreigners. However, there is one main attraction, beyond the raw frontier feel of the place, which is the **Caño Negro Nature Reserve**, a great swampy lagoon which is home to thousands of water birds, crocodiles and fish, as well as some impressive mammals, including otters, peccaries, jaguars and tapirs. The reserve headquarters, which are in the village of Caño Negro and where you should be able to stay, can be reached from Upala (by bus at 3.45 pm, returning at 4.30 am), or by boat from Los Chiles, along the Río Patos (at around 2 pm on Mon or Thurs, unless you want to hire your own boat for a hundred dollars or so).

WHERE TO STAY

There are basic, inexpensive hotels in Upala and Los Chiles, the best being the **Hotel Upala** in Upala and the **Hotel Carolina** in Los Chiles. Buses to both towns run from San Carlos and Upala can also be reached along a rough road from La Cruz, although if you travel this route by bus you'll have to break the journey in the village of Santa Cecilia, where there are a couple of extremely basic hotels.

Puerto Viejo and Around

The only other town of any size in the northern lowlands is Puerto Viejo, on the banks of the Río Sarapiquí, which is a small trading and transport centre. The town itself is of little interest, although there are occasionally boats heading downriver towards Barra del Colorado, if you've plenty of time to spare and a thirst for adventure. Otherwise the main attraction here is the surrounding forest, which is teeming with birds and mammals and where you will find several jungle lodges catering to the needs of growing numbers of ecotourists. Of these the most famous is **La Selva**, a research station run by the Organisation for Tropical Studies. The research station covers some 1500 hectares, merging into the massive **Braulio Carrillo National Park** and crossed by a superb network of trails. The area receives huge volumes of rainfall and there is a real abundance of animal and plant life, making this a superb place to experience the jungle first hand. Daily rates, including meals, are US$76 per person, or US$22 for students (providing you have an ISIS card), and you must book through the OTS in San José (tel 366696). Other similar biological stations include **Rara Avis** (tel 550844), a private reserve in pristine forest which contains a massive waterfall and a cable car for studying the forest canopy, and there are several smaller establishments.

GETTING THERE
Buses to Puerto Viejo leave from Avenida 9, Calle 12, in San José at 6.30, 9 am, 1, 3 and 4 pm. If you are planning to stay at Rara Avis or La Selva, you must book in advance and they will arrange transport from Puerto Viejo.

SOUTHERN COSTA RICA

Bathed in tropical downpours the rugged landscape of southern Costa Rica explodes with fertility. Remote, inaccessible and sparsely populated, the area still has a wild frontier spirit to it. The lumbering mountains to the south of San José have always hampered travel in this direction and it was not until the 1950s that a road finally crossed the mountains, bringing settlers into the valleys to the south. The coast, however, has a longer history of habitation and was developed earlier this century by the United Fruit Company, who planted huge expanses with bananas. For the traveller southern Costa Rica offers some wild and largely untouched landscapes. The national parks of the far south, particularly Chirripó and Corcovado, include some of the country's most dramatic scenery, while the Manuel Antonio National Park is smaller and a great deal more accessible, embracing a series of stunning beaches and some beautiful rainforest.

The Coastal Route

To the south of San José the Pacific coast undergoes a radical transformation as the dry hills of Nicoya give way to wildly fertile tropical forests and gentle sweeping bays are replaced by great expanses of sand, pounded by Pacific surf. Steep, forested hills rise out of the sea, and in the rainy season fierce tropical storms gather over the mountains, darkening the sky and unleashing massive downpours.

The area is easily accessible from San José and several of the beaches have been developed as weekend resorts, attracting hoards of weary city dwellers. An excellent paved road leaves the capital through **Atenas** and **Orotino**, dropping into deep river valleys and winding its way over several steep hills before it finally descends onto the narrow coastal plain.

Carara Biological Reserve

Surrounded by open cattle pasture the Carara Biological Reserve is a miracle of preservation, its tangle of dense forest rising sharply from banks of the Río Tárcoles. The reserve covers some 4700 hectares, mostly pristine primary forest, and is criss-crossed by a network of small streams and rivers. Large sections of the forest remain almost impenetrable and provide an ideal refuge for a wide range of birds and mammals, including iguanas, jaguars, ocelots, macaws, toucans, white-faced and spider monkeys, squirrels and even the odd snake, while the rivers are home to kingfishers, herons, otters and crocodiles. Most of these creatures are extremely elusive, although you may well catch a glimpse of a family of monkeys as they crash through the trees, or see the flash of a macaw's tail. Crocodiles are realtively easy to track down, and can often be seen from the highway, basking on the banks of the Río Tárcoles or lying motionless in the water, a watchful eye just above the surface. But whether or not you're lucky enough to see any wildlife, the reserve is a good place to take a look at the forest with its massive trees and musty humidity.

The reserve also contains a rare fragment of Costa Rica's pre-Columbian heritage: a number of burial mounds dating from 300 BC to AD 1500, in which archaeologists have unearthed the remains of Indian chiefs, accompanied by their slaves, wives, pottery and food—all of which was considered essential for the journey to the underworld.

Carara is 110 km from San José, on the main to Jacó, and buses heading for Jacó or Quepos pass the entrance. Camping is not allowed and a ranger is on duty 8–12 and 1–4.30 at the main entrance. From here a 3 km trail runs to the Quebrada Bonita, a small stream, and there's a second entrance towards the Río Tárcoles. Bear in mind that your chances of seeing wildlife are a lot better if you visit the reserve with a guide. Day trips from San José, usually including a swim and lunch in Jacó, are offered by **Geotur** (tel 341867) and **Otec** (tel 550554).

The Beaches: Tárcoles, Herradura and Jacó

Just south of the Carara reserve the highway reaches the coast at **Tárcoles**, a small fishing village with a scruffy stretch of sand, from where you can hire a boat to explore the swamps around the mouth of the Río Tárcoles. Beyond Tárcoles the road runs just behind the shoreline, with occasional glimpses of the sea and sweeping views of the low hills on the Nicoya Peninsula. The next beach of any interest is at **Herradura**, where you'll find another ordinary strip of black sand and a couple of simple hotels. However, the first really serious beach town is **Playa Jacó**, which is the closest beach to the capital and is popular with surfers, city dwellers and foreign tourists. It's a pleasant enough beach, shaded by palm trees and pounded by furious surf, but is well developed for tourism, with fresh building always in progress. Nevertheless it rarely feels congested; the beach is several kilometres long and the village stretches out behind in a loose gathering of small hotels, restaurants and souvenir shops. If you're in search of tropical paradise then press on to Manuel Antonio but if you just want to sample some sea and sand, or enjoy the surf, then Jacó is an easy day trip from San José.

The main activity in Jacó is surfing and boards can be hired from 'Chad' at the Cabinas Emily, or from the 'Trail Bikes' shop in the middle of the village, which also hire bicycles. There is also a bakery, a launderette and several car-hire companies, including 'Elegante' (tel 6432224), 'Ada' and 'Budget', and a couple of travel agents offering snorkelling, deep-sea fishing and excursions to Tortuga Island or Montezuma.

South of Jacó are a few more beaches: the first two, **Playa Naranjo** and **Playa Palma**, are primarily of interest to surfers, although the **Playa Esterillos Este**, has its own exclusive beach hotel and is an excellent place to escape the crowds.

431

WHERE TO STAY

If you are traveling by car then it's a good idea to get an early start, drop in at Carara and Jacó, and then press on to Manuel Antonio for the night, where you'll find the best accommodation. However, if you would prefer to take your time then there are plenty of places to stay along the way.

The nearest hotel to the Carara Reserve is the **Cabinas Carara**, in Tárcoles, which offers simple, clean budget accommodation. Further south is the resort hotel at **Punta Leona** (tel 690511), which lays claim to several private beaches and where you'll need a reservation and a fistful of dollars just to get down the drive. In Herradura there's the inexpensive **Cabinas Herradura** or the campsite, although you need to bring your own tent.

Accommodation is on quite a different scale in Jacó, where hundreds of small hotels cater for weekenders. The best hotels are the expensively priced **Hotel Jacó Beach** (tel 32567), which has air conditioning and a pool, and the **Hotel Cocal** (tel 643067), which doesn't have the luxury of air-conditioning but is a little more intimate. If you'd rather rent a bungalow, still inside a hotel-style complex with a pool, then the **Hotel Estella-mar** has double cabins, or the **Chalet Tangeri** has cabins for 4–6 people. Some of the larger chalets come complete with fridges and cookers.

Inexpensive accommodation in Jacó tends to be a little overpriced, although there are an abundance of *cabinas*-style hotels so you can always take your pick and bargain over the price, particularly during the rainy season. Right at the entrance to the villages are the **Cabinas Fragata** and the **Hotel El Jardín**. A little cheaper is the **Hotel Maryland** and back in the centre of the village among the cheapest places is **Cabinas Emily**.

To the south of Jacó there are basic surfers' hotels at **Playa Naranjo** and **Playa Esterillos** and an excellent resort hotel, the **Hotel Delfín** (tel 711640), at the Playa Esterillos Este. The hotel offers bike riding, horse riding and the exclusive use a great expanse of sandy beach.

GETTING THERE

Buses to Jacó leave from the Coca Cola terminal in San José at 7.30 am and 3.30 pm, returning at 5 am and 3 pm.

Quepos

Split down the middle Quepos is an archetypal banana town. Out on the point, catching the sea breezes and best views, is the original company compound with its sterile white walls, clean streets and neatly mown lawns. Down by the beach, hemmed in by surf and swamps, is a more realistic settlement, complete with bars, hotels, mud pools and markets. Quepos is by far the largest town along this stretch of coast, and was established by the United Fruit Company as a centre for their Pacific operations. These days the banana industry is very much in decline, although the company's residential compound still reeks of colonial discipline. The town is now bound up in the tourist boom, busy trying to attract tourists in its own right, offering sport fishing, accommodation and a handful of restaurants. If you do decide to stay here, bear in mind that Manuel Antonio is another 7 kilometres to the south, on the other side of sharp ridge, so you'll have take the bus in the mornings, and be warned that the beach at Quepos is subject to dangerous currents—as are those in Manuel Antonio, although to a lesser degree.

The Manuel Antonio National Park

Clustered around a rocky point and containing some of the most beautiful beaches in Central America, Manuel Antonio has to rate as one of Costa Rica's finest national parks. Lacking the scale and wildlife of many other areas, this set of small arched bays, backed by steep hills and towering forest, is something of a tropical paradise, with golden sand and crystal clear seas. The park covers just 682 hectares and can easily be explored in a day, although once they see it most visitors prefer to linger here, enjoying the beaches and wandering through the park at a more leisurely pace.

The entrance to the park is marked by a small stream, which swells to waist height at high tide. A map at the administration office explains the layout of the park and here you have to pay a small entrance fee. The main trail runs from the office along the back of the beach. To your left is a long sandy beach, which ends at the **Punta Catedral**, a densely forested outcrop rising sharply from the sea. A muddy trail runs around the point and although it's not an easy walk, with several steep inclines, the views of the coastline are superb. Sea birds skim the surf beneath you and monkeys bounce through the trees.

Beyond the Punta Catedral, at right angles to the first beach, is a second spectacular bay with a cresent of sand hemmed in on both sides by spectacular forest. This is as far as many visitors get, but there are several other trails which head off into the park. The **Sendero Poderoso** arches back towards the entrance and a trail marked 'mirador' takes you to a peak further to the south, from where there are superb views of the **Punta Serrucho** and the coastline beyond. The further that you go from these first beaches the more likely you are to see some wildlife, including coatimundi, monkeys and sloths, while iguanas can be seen throughout the park, basking in the sun or scurrying for cover.

Dominical and Uvita

South of Manuel Antonio the coastal highway becomes a rough dirt road, pushing through huge palm-oil plantations and passing a series of small company villages, where plantation workers are housed in colonial-style wooden homes, complete with regulation football pitches and neatly clipped hedges. The road runs through the heart of the plantations, a couple of kilometres from the sea, and access roads cut off through the trees to a couple of isolated beaches. The tarmac returns at **Dominical**, another small coastal village which is immensely popular with surfers, but dangerous for swimming. From here another rough road heads south and is passable to the beach at **Uvita**, beyond which travel is only possible in the dry season, and even then you need a good four-wheel-drive to make it as far as **Palmar Norte** (although improvements are said to be under way). A good paved road connects Dominical with San Isidro, winding up into the mountains with superb views of the coast.

WHERE TO STAY
The bulk of the up-market hotels are on the hill between Quepos and Manuel Antonio, while in Quepos itself there are plenty of good budget hotels. The best hotel in Quepos is

the air-conditioned **Hotel Kamuk** (tel 770379, fax 770171). A lot cheaper are the **Hotel El Parque**, which is excellent value, the **Hotel Mar y Luna** and the **Hotel Malinche**, both of which are similarly priced, while there are also very basic hotels.

Heading out of Quepos and up the hill towards Manuel Antonio, the first hotel that you pass is the **Plinio** (tel 770055), an excellent small hotel. Next comes the garish **Hotel Bahía**, which looks rather like a US motel and has the benefit of a jacuzzi, although you certainly pay for it. Further up the hill **La Colina** is small and simple, while higher still, and a little more expensive, is the **Hotel Lirio** (tel 770402). The most spectacular position is dominated by the luxurious **Hotel Mariposa** (tel 770355, fax 770050), which has incredible views in all directions, a pool and a good restaurant. Children under 15 are not welcome. Also high up, with fine views is the **Hotel Divisamar**, which has air-conditioned rooms, and the **Colibrí** (tel 770432), a small friendly hotel which is excellent mid-range value. If it's good food you're after then head for **El Byblos** (tel 770411, fax 770009), which has an excellent French restaurant with prices to match, although all meals are included.

Coming down the hill, towards Manuel Antonio, you pass the **Hotel Arboleda** (tel 770414), which has a small forest reserve and offers horse riding, while two other hotels offer excellent self-catering apartments. The larger is **Costa Verde** (tel 770584, fax 770560), which has double cabins, complete with a cooker and fridge, while the **Karahé** (tel 770170), has a smaller selection but similar prices.

Down at the beach, near the entrance to the park, are several cheaper hotels. The **Hotel Manuel Antonio**, which is closest to the park, offers good quality budget accommodation, right on the beach, while across the road and down a short track are the **Cabinas Espadilla**, which offers double cabins with a fridge, cooker and fan, for mid-range prices, while the **Hotel Costa Linda** (tel 770304), which claims to be a youth hostel, offers the cheapest deal in town.

Between Manuel Antonio and Dominical the only good hotel is the **Terraza del Sol** at **Playa Matapalo**, while in Dominical itself you'll find several cheap hotels catering to passing surfers, including the **Cabinas Narayit** (tel 711878), which is just behind the beach, the **Cabinas Willy** and the more up-market **Cabinas Río Mar**. To the south of the village the **Punta Dominical** juts out into the ocean and is home to a hotel of the same name (tel 255328), which has its own restaurant. The hotel is hardly convenient if you are travelling by public transport, but if you're driving it's a beautiful place to stay. Further south still there are some basic hotels in Uvita.

GETTING THERE

Buses from San José to Quepos leave from the Coca Cola bus terminal at 6, 12 noon and 6 pm, and from Quepos to San José at 6, 12 and 5 pm. Between Quepos and Manuel Antonio there are buses in both directions at 5.45, 8, 10.30 am, 1.30, 3 and 5 pm. From Quepos to Dominical and San Isidro there are buses at 5 am and 1.30 pm. To Uvita there is a bus from San Isidro at 3 pm, returning at 7 am.

It is also possible to fly from San José to Quepos with **Sansa**, who have daily flights from San José to Quepos at 9.45 am and 3 pm and from Quepos to San José at 10.20 am and 3.45 pm.

South Through the Highlands

The Pan-American Highway south of San José is perhaps the most chillingly spectacular road in the entire country. The highway runs past Cartago before winding up into the foothills of the Talamanca mountains and within an hour or so it is running along the spine of the mountains at a height of more than 3000 metres, with sheer drops on either side and astonishing views all around. On a clear day it's possible to see both the Pacific and Caribbean from up here, while at other times the swirl of heavy rain clouds mixes beautifully with wisps of thin white mist rising off the forest. This high pass, known as the Cerro de la Muerte—the hill of death—has been the main route to the south for centuries, and its name is a tribute to countless oxcart drivers who froze to death or tumbled into the valley below. These days lunatic bus and lorry drivers ensure that it remains a serious health hazard.

These jagged mountains receive enormous volumes of rainfall and their steep slopes and bitter frosts have protected them from development. Cloud forest still covers much of the land, offering an excellent opportunity for bird-watching and providing a home for the country's largest population of quetzals, while a network of fresh streams gives good trout fishing. The best place to watch birds is **Genesis 200**, a small guest house run by Canadians Steve and Paula Friedman, where you need to reserve space in advance. Accommodation is simple, although prices, which include all meals, are steep, with a mimimum stay of three days—but the bird-watching is superb. For reservations fax to 250271 or write to Apdo 10303, 1000 San José, Costa Rica. Alternatively you can try the **Cabinas Chacón** (tel 711732), a small hotel run by the Chacón family near San Gerardo de Dota, where you can either watch birds or fish for trout. The turning for San Gerardo de Dota is at kilometre 80.

San Isidro de El General

On the other side of the Cerro de la Muerte the highway unwinds into the Río General valley, a sweeping highland valley overshadowed by the Talamanca mountains and separated from the sea by a low ridge of hills. The valley has only been accessible by road since the 1950s and this is still very much frontier country, colonized by pioneer farmers who carve their fields from the forest. The small modern town of San Isidro de El General, which is the centre of trade and transport, is an odd combination of commercial bustle and provincial calm. Its appearance is unremarkable but it does offer good facilities for the visitor, including a couple of banks, a cinema, a fiesta in the second week in May and some passable restaurants, the best of which is in the Hotel Chirripó, on the plaza.

WHERE TO STAY

San Isidro has an abundance of budget accommodation, mostly catering to passing traders, although it suffers from a shortage of up-market hotels. The best hotel in the area is the **Hotel del Sur** (tel 710233), which is at Palmares, 6 km to the south of San Isidro. In town the best is the **Hotel Chirripó** (tel 710529), on the plaza, which is a clean budget hotel; alternatively you might try the **Hotel Iguazu** (tel 712571), halfway between the plaza and the highway, the **Hotel Amaneli** (tel 710352), right on the highway, or for a really cheap bed try the **Hotel El Jardín**.

GETTING THERE

Buses between San José and San Isidro are operated by three companies and run every hour or so from 5.30 to 5.30. The trip takes around three hours and in San José the buses leave from Calle 16, between Avenidas 1 and 3. In San Isidro they leave from company offices on the main highway. 'Tracopa' runs buses from San Isidro to Ciudad Neily at 4.30, 7.30 am, 12.30 and 3 pm, to San Vito at 5.30, 9, 10 am, 1, 2 and 4.30 pm, to Golfito at 9.30 am and 6 pm and to the border at Paseo Cañoas at 8.30 am, 7.30 and 9 pm. There are also buses from San Isidro to Dominical at 7 am and 3 pm, the latter going on to Uvita, and two daily buses to Puerto Jiménez on the Osa Peninsula. There are also buses from San Isidro to Quepos (for the Manuel Antonio National Park) at 7 am and 1.30 pm.

The Cerro Chirripó National Park

At the heart of the Talamanca mountains, taking in frosty peaks and musty tropical forest is the huge Chirripó National Park, which covers a beautiful, dramatic and inhospitable region including the country's highest peak, the Cerro Chirripó (3820 m). The park is dominated by a central block of high ground and its vegetation goes through a series of abrupt changes in response to the range of temperature, climate and altitude. At lower levels a rich cloud forest is home to tapirs, armadillos and quetzals, while above the treeline *páramo* vegetation of coarse grasses and stunted bushes is all that can survive the thin soils and sudden frosts. For visitors there are three basic shelters on the mountain, but you need to bring plenty of food, a warm sleeping bag and expect to spend at least two days in the mountains. However, if you can summon the energy, and you certainly do need to be reasonably fit, the Cerro Chirripó is absolutely beautiful, offering an environment that is unique in Central America and views which embrace half of Costa Rica.

The entrance to the park is in **San Gerardo de Rivas** (30 km or an hour by bus from San Isidro), which is set in the narrow Río Chirripó valley, surrounded by small plantations of coffee and bananas, laid out on land which was only recently claimed from the forest. Fields cling to the valley sides and only the most impossible slopes remain forested. (Buses for San Gerardo leave from the plaza in San Isidro at 5 am and 2 pm, returning at 7 am and 4 pm.) In San Gerardo you have to register at the park headquarters, which is open 5 am–9 pm, and pay an entrance fee of US$1. Only 40 people are allowed in the park at any one time but you can reserve a space by phoning 334160, although this is only really necessary in the dry season. In San Gerardo there are a couple of basic *pensiones* and a small shop, which sells tins of tuna, matches and dry biscuits.

Heading for the park you simply follow the road up through the village and across a couple of rivers to a sharp left hand bend in the road, where a signposted path cuts off to the right. From here the climb begins in earnest, steep, unrelenting and muddy, moving first over open pasture and then into low montane forest. In no time at all the views are stupendous and before you're swallowed by the forest you can see across the low, eroded hills which are beyond the confines of the park and have suffered at the hands of agriculture. After a couple of hours you reach the official limit of the park, which is marked by another sign, and anything from 3 to 4 hours from the start of the hike you arrive at the **Llano Bonito** peak, and then the refuge of the same name, which is very basic indeed. If you're running low on time or energy then it's a good idea to spend the night here, otherwise you can press on to the main refuge, which is a little more comfortable.

From Llano Bonito you climb for another three hours through lush cloud forest, in which the trees are loaded down with bromeliads, ferns, mosses and lichens. Here the forest is usually wrapped in a soft mist and during the afternoons there is often a steady drizzle. After you emerge from the cloud forest you move over a ridge into stunted oak forest, much of which is charred by forest fires and in another hour or so you finally emerge from the forest, into open *páramo* vegetation, and to the park's main refuges. The refuges provide an ideal base for exploring the peaks and from here you can climb the **Cerro Chirripó** in a couple of hours. Views from the peak are stupendous. To the north, in the Valle de las Morrenas, are a small set of lakes draining into the Chirripó Atlántico, while below you to the west the Lagos Chirripó are drained by the Chirripó Pacífico. Perched between the two you occupy the continental divide.

South: Buenos Aires, Palmar Norte and Palmar Sur

Heading south from San Isidro the highway runs through grand, daunting scenery. Much of this area has yet to be colonized and remains sparsely populated. Beyond **Buenos Aires** the highway swings south, into a steep-sided canyon where it is perched on a rocky shelf above the Río Térraba. The highway crosses the river between the twin towns of **Palmar Norte** and **Palmar Sur**. In the cane fields surrounding these twin towns Costa Rica's greatest archaeological mystery was unearthered in the form of an an amazing number of stone spheres, some weighing more than a ton. So far nobody has established their origin although it is generally believed that they were made by pre-Columbian tribes. Nevertheless the Dutch writer Erich von Däniken claims that they were cannon balls, fired from passing spaceships, thus accounting for their random patterning and near perfect form.

Golfito

Abandoned by the banana industry Golfito, the largest town in southern Costa Rica, is suffering a severe slump, its old port sinking into the Pacific. The town is hemmed in by steep forested hills at the back of a great, glassy bay, strung out along a narrow strip of level land which is squeezed between the water and the trees. The town is largely a product of the banana industry and became the headquarters of the United Fruit Company after they moved into the area in 1938. The company built a loading dock at Golfito, from which a network of railway tracks fanned out into the plantations. Some 15,000 people migrated from the north to work here and the area boomed for almost 40 years, until labour unrest and declining profits prompted the company to abandon the town in the late 1980s. Nevertheless the town still bears the stamp of the fruit company with its colonial-style residential compound, still known as the Zona Americana, while the rougher section to the south, which housed the labourers and railway workers, is known as the Pueblo Civil.

Golfito is still in the grip of a post-banana recession although in 1990 the government opened the 'Depósito Libre', a tax-free shopping centre. Shoppers are required to register at the *depósito* the day before they shop, to ensure that they spend at least a dollar or two in Golfito's hotels and restaurants, and unless you're looking for a new fridge or stereo then there is no particular reason to visit the *depósito*, although you can just drop in and take a look.

Golfito also provides access to several beaches to the south of the town and to the Osa Peninsula, across the gulf. The most popular of the nearby beaches is **Zancudo** (20 km away), at the mouth of the Río Colorado, but beyond there is **Pavones**, a popular surfing beach, said to have one of the longest breaks in world. There are assorted hotels at both of these beaches and a couple of privately owned nature reserves which offer the opportunity to combine a beach holiday with bird-watching. Buses run to Zancudo and Pavones, or you can hire a boat for the trip—from the yacht club. Sport-fishing is also available in Golfito, again through the yacht club (tel 750062).

The Osa Peninsula and the Corcovado National Park

Across the gulf the Osa Peninsula is Costa Rica's final frontier. The peninsula, which juts out into the Pacific is a one of the country's last great wildernesses, a mix of swamps and forest which is currently being fought over, often quite literally by gold miners, loggers and environmentalists. From the traveller's point of view the great attaction is the **Corcovado National Park**, which is perhaps the country's finest wildlife refuge. Occupying the peninsula's southwest corner, the park includes a range of low hills, swamps and a large lake, and most of the area is covered with towering primary rainforest. The area is teeming with wildlife, and is one of the last places in Latin America where you stand a reasonable chance of seeing animals such as jaguars, tapirs, peccary (wild pigs), three types of monkey, alligators, coatimundi, and a number of snakes, including the deadly fer-de-lance and bushmaster, as well as hundreds of different types of birds, including toucans and scarlet macaws.

Hiking into the Corcovado National Park

The Osa peninsula can be reached by air or boat from Golfito, or by bus from Ciudad Neily and San Isidro de El General. The main town is Puerto Jiménez, where you will find several hotels, shops, simple restaurants and the national park's headquarters. Although it is a lot easier to visit the park with a guide (arranged through a tour company in San José), it is possible to do so under your own steam. The following route is the most popular and it can be done in either direction. From Puerto Jiménez take a bus to the village of **La Palma**, from where you walk the three or four hours to the ranger station at **Los Patos**, which is up in the hills at the northeastern side of the park and where you should be able to find a spare mattress to spend the night. From Los Patos you walk south, across the heart of the park, for around eight hours, to the main ranger station at **La Sirena**, and stay the night in the dormitory there. From La Sirena you head back along the beach to the ranger station at **Carate**, from where a four-wheel-drive jeep runs to Puerto Jiménez on Monday, Thursday and Saturday (leaving Jiménez at about 9 am and Carate at around midday).

There are also ranger stations on the other side of the park, at **San Pedrillo** and **Los Planes**, although to reach these from Sirena you need a tent as the combined effects of tides and sharks make it impossible to walk along the beach in a single day. The northwestern side of the park can also be reached by taking a boat down the **Río Sierpe** from the small fishing village, which is connected to **Palmar Sur** by bus.

Ciudad Neily, San Vito and La Amistad International Park

Heading for Panamá you pass one final town: **Ciudad Neily**, a rough border-style town, where you'll find plenty and a regular flow of buses to Golfito and the border with Panamá at **Paso Cañoas**. A branch road leads into the mountains from Ciudad Neily, climbing steeply and giving superb views of the coastal plain before it rolls back into the mountains towards the town of **San Vito**. Before reaching San Vito the road passes the **Wilson Biological Garden**, a delicately cared for and wonderfully laid out tropical research station operated by the Organisation for Tropical Studies. The 25 acre garden, which was founded by Robert and Catherine Wilson in 1962, is home to an abundance of orchids, ferns, bamboos, heliconias, bromeliads and conifers, while an adjacent 145 acre forest reserve contains over 3000 plant species and some 300 species of birds. The garden is open every day and there's a small entrance fee. If you would like to stay for a while then contact the Organisation for Tropical Studies in San José, Apartado 676–2050, San Pedro, Costa Rica (tel 366696).

Six kilometres to the north of the Wilson Biological Garden the small mountain town of San Vito nestles in the hills and serves as the bustling focus for this remote region. Perhaps the most interesting and unusual thing about the town is that it has a large Italian community, and there are two good Italian restaurants; the finest pasta is to be had at the **Restaurant Mama Mia**, although if you're watching the pennies then stick to the **Restaurant Lilliana**—both are in the centre of town.

Leaving San Vito there's no need to head back to the Ciudad Neily. You can either head south to the Panamanian town of **Río Sereno**, from where there are regular buses to David (three or four buses cross the border every day but make sure that you look in at the customs post along the way to get an exit stamp), or you can also head west, back towards San José through the mountains—the route taken by most buses.

WHERE TO STAY

The best hotel in Golfito is the moderately priced **Hotel Las Gaviotas**, which is about 4 km before you reach the centre of town and has excellent air-conditioned rooms and a good restaurant, all right on the sea. In Golfito itself you'll find plenty of cheaper, inexpensive places, including the **Hotel Golfito**, on the main road, which has good double rooms, with a fan and private shower, while a little less luxurious are the **Hotel Delfina**, also on the main road, with double rooms, and the **Hotel Costa Rica Surf**, both of which are in the upper budget range. Last, but by no means least, is the **Hotel del Cerro**, which is on the main road near the old port and is good value.

In the towns around Golfito, including Puerto Jiménez, Zancudo and Pavones, you'll find a range of cheap and simple accommodation, but little in the way of luxury, with the notable exception of the **Tishkita Jungle Lodge**, a beautiful and remote hotel, near the beach at Pavones, which is surrounded by an experimental fruit farm and a large area of primary forest and offers four-day packages, including all food and transport from Golfito, although day rates are also available—to book call 553418. Across on the western side of the Osa Peninsula there are also several 'jungle lodges' offering environmental tourism. The best of these is the **Marenco Biological Station** (tel 211594), where five-day trips include transport from San José.

In Ciudad Neily the **Hotel Musoco**, in the centre of town, is a basic budget hotel, but recommended. Up in San Vito the finest accommodation is the **Hotel El Ceibo** (tel 7730025), while cheaper rooms are on offer at the **Hotel Collina** and the **Cabinas Firenze**. The best budget deal is **Hotel Colina Anexo**.

GETTING AROUND
Buses to the south are operated by Tracopa, Avenida 18, Calles 2–4, in San José. Leaving for Golfito (5 hrs) at 6.30 am and 3 pm, and for Ciudad Neily (5 hrs) at 10 am. From San Isidro there are buses to Golfito at 9 am and 6 pm, to Ciudad Neily at 4.30, 7.30 am, 12.30 and 3 pm, to San Vito at 5.30, 9, 10 am, 1, 2 and 4.30 pm, and to Puerto Jimenez at 5 am.

From Golfito there are hourly buses to Ciudad Neily, a bus to Pavones (3 hrs) at 1.45 pm, returning at 5 am, and to San José at 5 am and 1 pm. From Ciudad Neily there are hourly buses to the border with Panamá and four daily buses to San Vito. From San Vito there are buses across the border to Río Sereno at 7.30, 10.30 am and 4 pm, and buses to San José at 5, 7.30, 10 am and 3 pm.

There are also flights from San José to Golfito, with Sansa, at 6 am, returning at 6.50 am, while small private companies offer a shuttle service between Golfito and Puerto Jiménez.

THE CARIBBEAN COAST

Dominated by English-speaking blacks and the cool rhythms of reggae, rum and Caribbean beaches, Costa Rica's east coast is another world altogether, with a distinct culture, landscape, language and economy. The region is focused on the rough port city of Limón, where tropical ease rubs shoulders with a busy port.

Elsewhere the coast is sparsely populated; to the north a vast area of low-lying swamps and dense forests remains largely unexplored. There are no roads and all travel is by boat, along a narrow coastal canal, while the resident population is concentrated in a couple of small coastal villages. The south is a little more developed, with a single paved road connecting several medium-sized villages and some massive banana plantations. Nevertheless the population is still small and the pace of life relaxed.

A History of the Caribbean Coast

Until the end of the nineteenth century the Caribbean coast was considered remote and inaccessible, inhabited only by small indigenous groups who lived in the mountains to the south. However, in 1871 President Guardia, keen to open up the market for Costa Rican coffee, contracted Minor Keith, an American engineer, to build a railway from San José to the coast. The building of the railway took some 20 years, costing some US$8 million and 4000 lives. Costa Ricans were reluctant to work outside the highlands and

Keith brought in labourers from China and Italy, although as the death toll rose he turned to Jamaicans, who were thought to be immune to malaria and yellow fever. In the process of building the railway, Keith, who was described as having 'the heart of a benevolent pirate', introduced two new components to Costa Rican society: blacks and bananas. Taking advantage of several spin-offs associated with the railway, he built a wharf in Limón, in exchange for a share of the wharfage fee, and to offset the cost of building the track he planted bananas alongside it. The banana business was such an astonishing success that in 1884 Keith agreed to pay off the national debt in exchange for a 99-year lease on the existing railway and 300,000 hectares of land along the route, where he planted bananas. In 1889 Keith merged his company with a rival organisation to form the United Fruit Company, which, in due course, was to operate plantations from Guatemala to Panamá and become one of the great political powers in Central America.

The English-speaking Jamaicans who arrived with the railway stayed on once it was finished, living in and around Limón and working on the railway and in the banana plantations. Today the area is still firmly dominated by Jamaican culture and the black population have retained their own social institutions, schools and distinctive identity. However, the rest of Costa Rican society has been reluctant to accept their presence and it was not until 1952 that they were entitled to Costa Rican citizenship. Costa Rica's blacks still prefer life on the Caribbean coast and elsewhere they face thinly veiled racism.

Recently the Caribbean coast has suffered at the hands of economic decline, hurricanes and earthquakes and many argue that it has been badly neglected by the government. But despite obvious hardship, most notably in Limón where the depressed economy has paved the way for drug-dealing and street crime, the Caribbean coast remains relaxed and welcoming, offering the traveller a fresh and fascinating angle on Costa Rican culture. Limón remains a wonderful tropical port, rough and relaxed, with all the ease and atmosphere of the Caribbean. To the north the great attraction is the Tortuguero National Park, a sweeping expanse of forest and swamp, while to the south are several easy-going seaside villages, with fantastic tropical beaches and an abundance of cool Caribbean culture.

The Jungle Train

Costa Rica's 'jungle train', from San José to Puerto Limón, is the greatest train trip in Central America, dropping from the cool of the highlands to the sticky warmth of the Caribbean coast. However, like so many train trips on the isthmus the service is in sharp decline and a large part has now been closed for good, leaving only the section from Turrialba to Limón, although this was always the best part. But before you set off, check the detail with the Tourist Office in San José, just in case the service has been shut down altogether, a development which now seems inevitable.

Puerto Limón

With a population of some 60,000, Limón is the heart of the Caribbean coast. This steamy port city was established at the end of the railway tracks and is now sadly in decline. Badly damaged by the 1991 earthquake, Limón has a weary atmosphere, heavy with unemployment and street crime. Nevertheless it's a busy town with a great market, where open stalls offer superb seafood soup, while at night the bars and clubs are alive with rum and reggae. The city's main attraction is its relaxed atmosphere, which is at its best in October, when the place erupts in carnival. At other times there's little to persuade you to spend the night here, although you may well get stuck here on your way to Cahuita or Tortuguero. There are a couple of reasonable beaches, although avoid those to the south, behind which are some very dangerous slum areas.

The Tortuguero National Park

To the north of Limón the land drops into a tangle of forest, swamps and marshes, a large slice of which is protected by the Tortuguero National Park, one of the most astonishing environments in the entire country. The area takes its name from the huge numbers of turtles which nest on the beaches here from August to November, and includes a massive inland area crisscrossed by a complex network of canals and rivers.

In 1959 conservationists formed a society to protect the turtles' nesting sites and the national park was established in 1975, embracing a superb mix of coastline, inland waterways, swamps, forests and low-lying hills. Four species of turtle come ashore here, the green turtle, the leatherback, the hawksbill and the loggerhead, making full use of a sandy beach which stretches for around 80 kilometres between the mouths of the Río Colorado and the Río Matina. Inland the mix of canals and forests provides an ideal habitat for birds, animals and fish. The waterways are home to a wide range of fish and birds, including manatees, herons, storks, kingfishers, crocodiles, otters, sharks, eels, and the gar, a strange prehistoric fish which is regarded as a living fossil and has changed little in some 90 million years. Beyond the waterways the forest is inhabited by monkeys, skunks, peccaries, jaguars, racoons, cougars, tapirs, and hundreds of species of birds.

The national park is accessible from the port of **Moín**, which is a couple of kilometres north of Limón. From here boats run along a network of canals, parallel to the shore. The village of **Tortuguero**, a small, ramshackle place at the northern end of the park, provides overnight accommodation in simple budget hotels, while several tour companies have their own up-market lodges. It is possible to reach the park under your own steam, organizing a boat in Moin, although it is getting harder every year. The easiest and best way to see the park is with a tour company (such as **Costa Rica Expeditions**, Calle Central, Avenida 3, San José, tel 239975), who will organize overnight accommodation and take you on a tour of the park, including late-night turtle-watching in season.

South: Cahuita and Puerto Viejo

If chasing monkeys in mosquito-ridden jungles sounds too much like hard work then head south to the Caribbean beaches, where relaxation is a local speciality. Here the coast is already more developed and new facilities are emerging all the time, although the beaches remain astonishingly beautiful.

Heading south from Puerto Limón the road runs parallel to the coast, with dirt tracks cutting off here and there to banana plantations and cattle ranches. The coastline is clear and straight, swept by Atlantic surf and shaded by an endless line of palm trees. The first place of any size is **Cahuita**, a delightful village, steeped in the warmth and charm of Caribbean culture. The village is becoming increasingly popular with tourists, particularly backpackers, but it's hardly surprising when you consider the easy-going atmosphere and superb beaches which make this one of the best places to enjoy Caribbean food and culture. Cahuita is focused on a central crossroads and the Salón Vaz, where local people spend much of the day hanging-out, drinking beer and listening to the solid boom of reggae. Elsewhere the village is dotted with small bars and restaurants, many of which open in the mid-afternoon and are alive with music, dancing and drinking until the small hours.

Right next door to the village is the **Cahuita National Park**, which includes two beautiful sweeping beaches, separated by the **Punta Vargas**, a low-lying promontory off which is a spectacular coral reef. Behind the beaches a great swath of tropical forest and swamp is home to sloths, shy howler monkeys, spider monkeys, macaws, toucans, and much more. You can walk into the park from Cahuita although the main entrance is at Puerto Vargas, either reached on foot from Cahuita (in an hour or so), or by an entrance road a few kilometres from the entrance to Cahuita. The park is open 8–4. If you want to explore the reef, snorkelling equipment can be hired in Cahuita. Apart from the fish and coral, which are at their best off the point, the most interesting underwater site is a sunken Spanish galleon, reached by following a chain from the twin rows of metal posts which you pass on your way to Punta Vargas.

To the south of Cahuita several other beaches are being developed for tourism, all of which are accessible from **Puerto Viejo**, another relaxed seaside village. If you're heading for Panamá, there are three daily buses from Limón to Sixaola on the border.

WHERE TO STAY AND EAT

Few travellers plan a night in Limón, as you can easily make it to Cahuita in a day. However if you do get stuck in Limón then the best hotel is the **Hotel Maribú Caribe** (tel 584543), a luxury seaside hotel just outside town on the the the Portete road. More central and in the middle price range are the **Hotel Miami**, on 2 Avenida, and the **Hotel Ancón** (tel 581010), while there are plenty of budget hotels.

In Tortuguero the jungle lodges—booked through travel agents—provide the best accommodation, although budget-style lodging is provided by **Sabina's Cabinas**.

The hotels of the southern Caribbean are concentrated in Cahuita and Puerto Viejo. The former is much less formal and the hotels tend to be simple, but clean, friendly and perfectly adequate, while in Puerto Viejo, which has been developed much more recently, you can find luxury hotels complete with swimming pools, air conditioning and hot water.

In Cahuita there are several good hotels offering simple rooms with a fan and shower, although hot water is rare. The **Cabinas Palmer**, on the road between the Salón Vaz and the sea, has good double cabins in the upper budget price range, including a kitchen and private bathroom, while a short distance beyond, right on the sea, is **Cabinas Jenny**, a small Canadian-owned budget hotel, where rooms have a fan and shower. Between the Salón Vaz and the entrance to the park you'll find a couple of more up-market places in the middle price range, including the **Hotel Cahuita**, which has the only swimming pool in town, and the **Cabinas Sol y Mar**. Heading in the other direction, towards the Playa

Negra, you pass the **Surfside Cabinas**, which has simple budget accommodation and a couple of smarter, up-market places, offering real luxury, are **Cabinas Colibri Paradise**, where beautiful double cabins have hot water, kitchens, and prices to match, and the **Atlantic Lodge**, which has a pet anteater. A touch cheaper are the **Cabinas Toto** and the **Cabinas Iguana**, where cabins include a fridge, a cooker and two double beds. There are also some basic budget hotels near the Playa Negra, including **El Ancla**, a popular rasta hangout, and **Cabinas Brigitte**.

BUS TRAVEL ON THE CARIBBEAN COAST

An excellent fast bus service connects the capital with Limón. Buses leave hourly from Avenida 3 and Calle 21 from 5 am to 8 pm. The trip takes about two and a half hours.

Heading to the north local buses run every ten minutes or so to the post at Moín (from where boats run towards Tortuguero), while to the south there are buses to Cahuita, Puerto Viejo and Sixaola at 5, 8, 10 am, 1 and 4 pm.

Part X

PANAMA

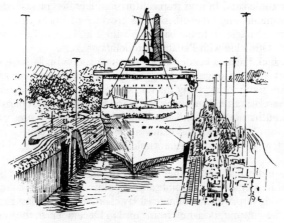

The Canal

A slither of land strung up between Colombia and Costa Rica, the tiny republic of Panamá is something of a Central American misfit. Largely ignored by international tourism, it is famous for just three things: a hat, a canal and a military leader with a face like a pineapple. Typically, none of these are entirely Panamanian: the hats are made in Ecuador; the canal belongs to the US and the general is now buried so deep beneath a Miami courtroom that his cell is referred to as 'the submarine'. P. J. O'Rourke once described the country as 'a put-up job, sleazed into existence by Teddy Roosevelt so he'd have somewhere to put the Big Ditch'.

However, it's this shaky sense of identity that makes Panamá such an exciting destination. Nothing is as simple as it might appear and the unexpected lurks around every corner. The nation is riddled with complexities—from its murky CIA-inspired beginnings to the broad racial mix, which includes Chinese, Russians, Indians, Spanish and French. Bound together in an uneasy partnership these elements have produced one of the most contradictory and cosmopolitan nations in all of Latin America. Travel in Panamá is perhaps a little more demanding (and a little more expensive, given the fact that the US dollar is the local currency), but the extra effort is well rewarded and although Panamá may be sleazy, unstable and a little dangerous it is certainly never boring.

The sight of a huge Russian freighter cutting through the jungle is astonishing and the Panamá canal ranks as the country's number one tourist attraction. In many ways Panamá is the canal, while the two great cities, Panamá City and Colón, guarding its ends and containing more than half the country's population, are wild and wonderful, mingling the energy of Latin America, the buzz of big banking and the steady pulse of

445

international shipping. Beyond this narrow central corridor Panamá has a lot more to offer. In all directions you'll find superb beaches and an array of distinct and interesting cultures. To the west, the land is dominated by commercial farming and a traditional cowboy culture which is formal and deeply hospitable. Right up along the Costa Rican border the Cordillera Central rises to a series of high, crumpled ridges, dotted with volcanic peaks and coated in lush tropical forest and coffee plantations. Towards the north coast the mountains drop off into the province of Bocas del Toro, where cool Caribbean culture mingles with the banana business and a handful of off-shore islands are a favourite destination with Panamanian holidaymakers.

East of the canal, Panamá becomes an enormous and virtually impenetrable wilderness in which the watery jungles and rugged hills are inhabited by indigenous Indians and drug-traffickers. Arching along the north coast, in the crystal waters of the Caribbean, are the San Blás islands, a string of several hundred tiny tropical islands, owned and administered by the Kuna Indians, who have managed to preserve their unique culture by fighting off all intruders. Meanwhile the south coast remains wild and virtually uninhabited, a few pioneer cattle farmers holding their own against the jungle, which still dominates.

Panamá is as individual as any other country on the continent. Its mountains may be smaller, its wildlife a little less accessible and its politics desperately compromised, but it is still packed with surprises. It can at least lay claim to the heaviest rainfall in Central America, with the downpours lasting from April to December. In the months preceding the rain the humidity can be unbearable but early in the year the weather is superb. Panamanians themselves, constantly exposed to outsiders, are deeply cosmopolitan and incredibly welcoming. It is their warmth and enthusiasm which leaves the deepest impression. Few tourists make it to Panamá: the danger of street crime and the ease of Central America's many other attractions keeping them elsewhere, but here you will certainly find adventure and uncertainty, while your expectations, if you have any, are sure to be undermined.

Post-Independence History

As the Spanish empire began to crumble, Panamá was dragged down with it. The narrow Panamanian isthmus had been a crucial trade route and Panamá City a favoured imperial port, its success ensured by restrictive trade laws. But as the empire began to collapse, trade routes opened out, bypassing Panamá. The situation became so desperate that many Panamanian merchants abandoned the cities and moved to the interior, colonizing much of western Panamá for the first time.

The Panamanians were slow to focus on the independence issue. In the end, Los Santos pre-empted Panamá City by declaring its independence in November 1821, closely followed by the rest of the country. Panamá then united with Ecuador, Venezuela, Peru and Bolivia to form the vast republic of Gran Colombia. Five years later the great liberator, Simón Bolívar, held a congress in Panamá City to discuss the future of the Americas and proposed a great union of American states. However, a hopeless lack of agreement soon lead to the break-up of Gran Colombia and prompted a disillusioned

Bolívar to declare that 'those who served the revolution ploughed the sea'. But while the other republics broke away Panamá remained tied to Colombia, making vague attempts at separation in 1830 and 1840.

Fresh Traffic: Gold-diggers and the Panamanian Railway

Panamá's flagging fortunes were eventually revived by a new wave of goods and people eager to cross the isthmus. Throughout the 19th century a steady stream of travellers heading from the the east coast of the USA to California preferred to risk the jungles of Panamá to the long and arduous land route. A regular steamship service from the US to Colón was established in 1840, although it faced hot competition from Nicaragua, and in 1848 the discovery of gold in California prompted thousands of young hopefuls to set out for the West, most of them travelling via Central America. Traffic was so heavy that a group of New York financiers began the construction of a railway across Panamá. Completed in 1855, it was an instant success, providing enormous returns for the investors and resuscitating Panamá's ailing economy. With a steady flow of fortune-hunters Panamá soon became rich and rough. At the northern end of the railway the new city of Colón began to take shape, packed with brothels, bars and cheap hotels, while in Panamá City the docks developed a similar sleazy infrastructure.

The French Canal

The railway's fortunes began to decline in 1869, with the completion of the first railway across the US, but as one trade closed down another was in the making. The US, Britain and France were all expressing an interest in building a canal between the oceans, with surveyors busily assessing the relative merits of the Nicaraguan and Panamanian routes. The lead was soon taken by a French company, formed in 1879 and headed by the charismatic Ferdinand de Lesseps, who had been responsible for the canal at Suez. Charging ahead, de Lesseps raised the money from the French public, sweeping them along with his overwhelming enthusiasm and arrogance, and work began in 1881. The plan was for a sea-level canal, but the combined impact of corruption, disease—which killed around 25,000—extravagence—prostitutes and champagne were shipped out from France—and engineering difficulties forced the company into bankruptcy in 1889. The huge dredging machines were left to rust in the jungle, while the French struggled to get to grips with an associated financial scandal, its people having forked out some US$287 million (three times the cost of the Suez canal).

The US Canal

By the turn of the century the US government had become increasingly interested in building a canal of their own. The greatest stumbling block was the Colombian government, who wanted to be cut in on the deal, but in 1903, by a stroke of good fortune and with the support of US troops, a revolutionary junta took control of Panamá. Within days a treaty was signed guaranteeing the US the right to build a canal and exercise all rights of sovereignty in the canal zone (a 16-mile strip across the country), in exchange for US$10 million and a annual payment of US$250,000. The new nation inherited a two-party system, and adopted a US-style constitution, although politics remained the exclusive preserve of the oligarchy, dominated by a few wealthy, white families.

Meanwhile the US government paid a further US$25 million in compensation to Colombia and US$40 million to the French company for their property and equipment, and began to build the canal in 1904, fired by the enthusiasm of President Roosevelt. It was one of the largest engineering projects ever undertaken and by 1913 some 65,000 men were on the payroll. Among the greatest challenges were disease, which had killed so many during the French attempt, and the famous Gaillard Cut, which was beset by endless landslides. The American design was more complex than the one adopted by the French, using three sets of locks and creating a massive lake in the centre of the country. Nevertheless on 15 August 1914 the first ship passed from ocean to ocean and the history of modern Panamá began.

Depression and the Emergence of Panamanian Nationalism

The building of the canal transformed the nation, bringing in new people from every corner of the globe, creating a prosperous middle class and linking the US and Panamá in a new and uncomfortable partnership. Throughout the 1920s Panamanians from Chiriquí to Colón developed a deep resentment of the US presence, and the US government responded by repeatedly exercising its right to intervene in order to restore order. Panamanian politics remained dominated by the white elite, until the impact of the depression led to the election of Harmodio Arias Madrid in 1932. He adopted a nationalistic, anti-US stance and negotiated a series of new agreements restricting the activities of traders in the canal zone. The election of Arias's brother Arnulfo Arias in 1940 marked the emergence of one of Panamá's most enduring and popular politicians. He too campaigned on a fiercely nationalistic platform, which included a call to expel all non-Hispanics from Panamá. In 1945, however, he was ousted and the growing power of the National Guard ensured that he remained out of office for the rest of the decade.

Canal Politics: the Rise the National Guard and Omar Torrijos

The canal remained the most explosive issue in Panamanian politics, and attempts to increase the US presence met with demonstrations and disturbances. In 1956 the nationalization of the Suez canal raised hopes in Panamá: clashes between students and US troops in 1958 left nine dead, prompting Panamanians to threaten a 'peaceful invasion' of the canal zone.

Matters came to a head in 1968, when Arnulfo Arias again won the presidential elections. But when he attempted to change the leadership of the National Guard, Arias was deposed after just ten days in office. The takeover marked a watershed in Panamanian politics. After a brief power struggle General Omar Torrijos emerged as the country's leader. Torrijos, described by his friend Graham Greene as 'a lone wolf', became one of the great figures in Panamanian history, ruling the country for 12 years in what he described as a 'dictatorship with a heart'. The early years of his rule were marked by a new labour code, the development of schools and hospitals, the establishment of agricultural cooperatives, housing reforms and the promotion of trade unions. Torrijos was also keen to encourage capitalist development in Panamá, and was responsible for the creation of the Colón Free Zone and new banking-secrecy laws, which have since made Panamá one of the great financial centres, home to millions of offshore companies and mountains of fast-moving, tax-free dollars. Torrijos also forged links with the left-wing opposition movements in Nicaragua and El Salvador as well as Castro's Cuba. His greatest achievement was the 1977 canal treaty, signed with President Carter which guaranteed that ownership of the canal would be turned over to Panamá in the year 2000.

The Rise and Fall of General Manuel Noriega

The pursuit of this dream had been the backbone of Torrijos's support, and once it had been achieved he agreed to move Panamá towards democratic rule, prompting a flowering of political activity and a breakdown of the populist alliance he had maintained throughout the 1970s. Legislative elections allowed Torrijos to retain executive power in March 1980, but the following year he was killed in a plane crash. His death lead to a brief power struggle which left a former banker, Ricardo de la Espriella, as president and General Manuel Noriega as the head of the National Guard. Elections were scheduled for 1984 and the ambitious young Noriega, who had been Torrijos's right-hand man, set about restructuring the nation's security forces into the Panamanian Defence Force, and placing them under his control. The electoral campaign was bitterly fought, and though the ballot itself passed, the following day claims of ballot-rigging prompted an eruption of violence.

The military candidate, Ardito Barletta, was finally declared the winner and he called in the IMF to help restructure the economy, instituting a severe austerity plan. Under Torrijos, Panamá had accumulated massive debts but Barletta's severe reforms were met by strikes and protests. In August 1985 Noriega declared that the country had become 'totally anarchic', and took control.

Noriega, an illegitimate boy from the slums of Panamá City, had clawed his way up through the ranks of the army. For the next four years he ran the country as a personal

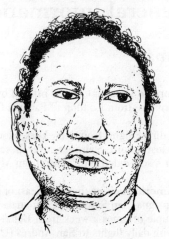

General Noriega

449

fiefdom, forging deep links with both drug-dealers and the CIA and operating a huge empire trading in intelligence, drugs, guns and contraband hi-tech goods, which he shipped to Eastern Europe and Cuba. As his power expanded, Noriega became increasingly brazen, prompting mounting resistance from the US. In an attempt to legitimize his rule Noriega held elections in May 1989, which were monitored by thousands of outside observers including the former US President Jimmy Carter. All accused Noriega of blatant fraud. Although the opposition candidate, Guillermo Endara, had apparently won two-thirds of the votes, Noriega declared himself president, locking Panamá on a collision course with the US.

On 20 December 1989 a force of 26,000 US troops, equipped with Sheridan tanks and helicopter gunships, invaded Panamá, taking on a force they had trained, supplied and paid for. Fighting raged for a full 14 hours and sniper fire continued for several days, leaving around 4000 dead, and making 15,000 homeless. A huge section of Panamá City, around the National Guard headquarters in El Chorillo, was completely destroyed. During the invasion Noriega took refuge in the Vatican mission in Panamá City, where US troops eventually flushed him out by playing loud rock music!

The invasion sunk Panamá into anarchy and economic depression, from which it has yet to recover. A new government, headed by Guillermo Endara, the winner of the 1989 elections, was installed by the US. Endara, a massive man, is generally regarded as a member of the old, white oligarchy, who have repeatedly failed to meet the needs of ordinary Panamanians. He remains in power today, deeply unpopular and highly ineffective, but a favourite with the US. So far he has failed to revitalize Panamá's battered economy. The only growth industry has been street crime, although the government has now disbanded the army, which should make future invasions a great deal smoother.

General Information

Getting to Panamá

By Air
Direct flights from Europe to Panamá City are offered by KLM and Iberia, or you can fly via the US. A return fare from London to Panamá City will cost from £560 to £650.

From the US there are direct flights from New York, Houston, Washington, Dallas, Los Angeles and Miami. Most major US airlines cover these routes. You should expect to pay around US$400 for a scheduled return fare from Miami and double that from New York or Canada.

From other Central American cities there's at least one flight every day from San José (US$130 return), Managua, San Salvador, Guatemala City, Mexico City (around US$300 return) and a couple of times a week from Belize City. Panamá is also well connected to Colombia, with daily flights to San Andrés (US$70 one way—this is the cheapest way to get into Colombia), Medellín, Cartagena and Bogotá (US$350 return).

There are also regular flights to all South American capitals and a number of destinations in the Caribbean, including Kingston and Havana.

Panamá City's Tocumen airport is 17 miles (27 km) east of the city centre. A minibus will take you from the airport to your hotel for US$8 per person or you can take a bus from the main road outside the terminal. Buses heading for 'Calle 12' will take you through the centre of town. Taxis charge around US$8 for a trip to the airport or you can pick up the bus—marked 'Tocumen'—from 'Calle 12', which costs just 30 cents. There is a departure tax of US$15 on international flights.

By Bus

International buses operated by the **Ticabus** connect Panamá City with San José, Costa Rica, an 18–20 hour journey, which costs US$25. Buses leave Panamá City daily at 11 am (from the **Ticabus** office, Calle 17, just up from Avenida 17, beneath the Hotel Ideal), and you need to buy a ticket in advance. From San José the bus leaves at 8 pm from 9 Calle, Avenida 2–4. The Costa Rican company **Tracopa** also runs a daily bus between San José and David, leaving from Avenida 18 Calle, 2–4 in San José, at 7.30 am, and from the Pensión Costa Rica in David, Calle 5, at 8 am.

This trip can also be done using local buses, which takes a little longer, costs a little less and leaves you free to travel at your own speed. Coming from San José, several daily buses run to the southern border with Panamá (7 hrs). From there there are hourly buses to David (2 hrs), and finally from David to Panamá City (6–8 hrs) there are express buses every hour or so. Two other less popular crossing points are the mountain crossing from Río Sereno in Panamá to San Vito in Costa Rica and the crossing on the Caribbean side, from Guabito in Panamá to Sixaola in Costa Rica. Both have reasonable bus connections on either side.

By Car

Driving from Costa Rica to Panamá is fairly straightforward, taking you along the Pan-American Highway, which is well paved and well used. The one drawback, as ever, is the bureaucracy; cars and motorbikes crossing the border are given a three-day entrance stamp, while their passengers get 30. The car's permission must be extended at the customs department in David or Panamá City. To leave the country you'll need to obtain the correct papers from the customs office in Ancón, near the Albrook airforce base. Bear in mind that it's extremely difficult to sell a car in Panamá, and that if you do you'll have to pay large import duties.

Panamanian Consulates

UK: 24 Tudor Street, London EC4, tel 071 353 4792, 10–12, 2–4.
US: New York, 1270 Avenue of the Americas, NY 10020, tel 246 3771.
Canada: Toronto, 65 Colfood Heights, Weston, Ontario M9P 318.
Australia: Sydney, 28–34 O'Connell Street, Sydney 2000, tel 231 6638.
Mexico City: Cincinnati No. 40, Colónia Nápoles, tel 563 9206.
Guatemala: Guatemala City, Edificio Maya, Vía 5, Zona 4, tel 325001.

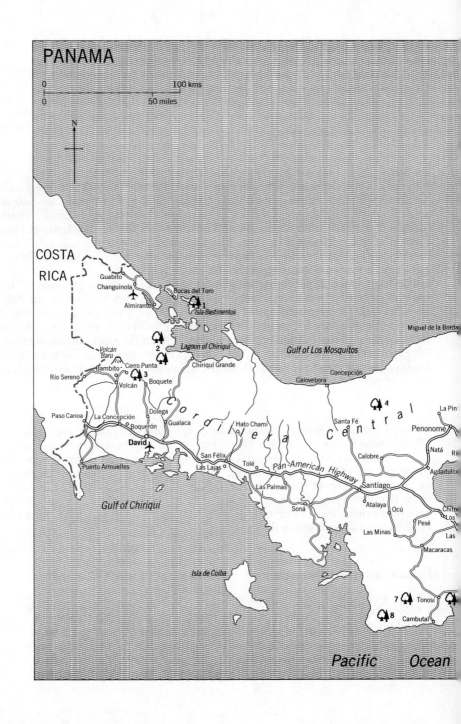

PANAMA

0 ———————— 100 kms
0 ———————— 50 miles

N

**COSTA
RICA**

Guabito
Changuinola
Almirante ✈
Bocas del Toro
Isla Bastimentos **1**

2
Lagoon of Chiriquí

*Volcán
Barú*
Bambito · Cerro Punta
Río Sereno
Volcán **3**
Boquete

Chiriquí Grande

Gulf of Los Mosquitos

Miguel de la Borda

Concepción
Calovebora

Paso Canoa
La Concepción
Boquerón
Dolega
Gualaca
Hato Chamí
David ✈

4
La Pin
Santa Fé
Penonomé

Cordillera central

Natá
Ri

Puerto Armuelles

San Félix
Las Lajas
Tolé
Pan-American Highway
Las Palmas
Santiago
Calobre
Aguadulce

Gulf of Chiriquí

Soná
Atalaya
Ocú
Chitr
Pesé
Los

Las Minas
Las

Macaracas

Isla de Coiba

7
Tonosí
8
Cambutal

Pacific   Ocean

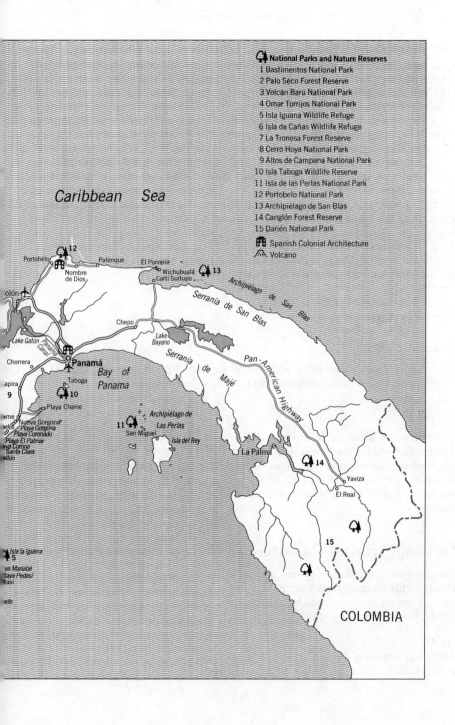

National Parks and Nature Reserves

1 Bastimentos National Park
2 Palo Seco Forest Reserve
3 Volcán Barú National Park
4 Omar Torrijos National Park
5 Isla Iguana Wildlife Refuge
6 Isla de Cañas Wildlife Refuge
7 La Tronosa Forest Reserve
8 Cerro Hoya National Park
9 Altos de Campana National Park
10 Isla Taboga Wildlife Reserve
11 Isla de las Perlas National Park
12 Portobelo National Park
13 Archipiélago de San Blas
14 Canglón Forest Reserve
15 Darién National Park

Spanish Colonial Architecture
Volcano

Caribbean Sea

Portobelo
Palenque
El Porvenir
Nombre
de Dios
Wichubualá
Cartí Suitupo
13
olón
Archipiélago de San Blas
Serranía de San Blas
Chepo
Lake Gatún
Panama Canal
Lake Bayano
Serranía de Majé
Chorrera
Panamá
Pan-American Highway
apira
9
Taboga
Bay of Panama
10
Playa Chame
me
Nueva Gorgona
rios
Playa Gorgona
Playa Coronado
Playa El Palmar
ya Corona
Santa Clara
allón
Archipiélago de Las Perlas
11
San Miguel
Isla del Rey
La Palma
14
Yaviza
El Real
Isla la Iguana
5
ya Mariabé
Playa Pedasí
así
ado
15

COLOMBIA

Passports and Visas

Panamanian entry requirements are surprisingly strict. Not only are you required to have a valid passport but also sufficent funds (at least US$20 a day and a minimum of US$200) and an onward air ticket. It's this last requirement that can cause trouble. Generally speaking, those arriving by air are not closely questioned. The two border points that seem to be most strict are those at Paso Canoas and Puerto Obaldía, although if you have enough money and explain your overland plans in passable Spanish, you should be able to get across the border.

Tourist cards are issued on arrival to citizens of Great Britain—officially they cost US$2, but they usually seem to be issued free. Citizens of other West European countries, Canada, the US, Australia and New Zealand require tourist visas, which are valid for 30 days and can be obtained from Panamanian consuls for US$10, or free if you're from the US. Visas and tourist cards can be extended for up to 60 days at the immigration department in Panamá City (28E Calle and Avenida Cuba) or David. Tourists who stay in the country for more than 30 days must obtain a document called *Paz y Salvo* from the **Ministerio de Hacienda y Tesoro** (Avenida Perú and Calle 35E) and an exit visa from the immigration department.

On Arrival

Tourist Offices

The country's only tourist office is in the Atlapa Conference Centre in Panamá City. They can only offer basic information and can be called on tel 267000.

Maps

The best maps are available in Panamá City from the Instituto Geográfico Nacional Tommy Guardia on Vía Simón Bolívar, open 8.30–4, Mon–Fri. To get there take any bus marked '*Bolívar*' from the Plaza Santa Ana. Ideal for hiking are the institute's 1:50,000 scale maps of the country. Simple tourist maps of the country are sold by street vendors and at the Casa Zaldo department store, on Avenida Central, beside the Plaza Santa Ana.

Getting Around Panamá

Panamá's internal transport system is as varied as the country itself, ranging from the hourly flights shuttling from Panamá City to Colón to the battered jeeps which plough through the mudpools of the Darién. All the main population centres are served by a regular bus service, although transport is rough and unpredictable in the east.

By Air
All the main towns in Panamá are connected to the capital by a good internal air service, with departures from the Paitilla airport in Panamá City. Tickets can be bought from

travel agents in the city, or direct from the airline office at the airport. Details of the main routes, provided by Aeroperlas (tel 694555) from Panamá City, are:

Colón (15 minutes, US$42 return), hourly, 7–6.30, Mon–Fri.
Contadora (15 minutes, US$40 return), 2 daily flights, 9.20 am and 6.30 pm, and four flights at weekends.
David (55 minutes, US$80 return), one flight a day.
Changuinola (1 hour), one daily flight, 6 am, with two on Monday and Friday.
Bocos del Toro (55 minutes), one daily flight at 8.30 am.
San Miguel (15 minutes), one flight at 6 am on Monday and Friday.
Additional services on the route between Panamá City and David are provided by **Alas Chiricanas** (tel 646468), who also fly from Changuinola to Bocas del Toro and from David to Changuinola. **Ansa** (tel 267891) fly daily at 5 am to El Porvenir in the San Blás Islands (US$50 return) and **Parsa** (tel 263883) provide flights to the Darién, with at least one weekly flight to La Palma, El Real, Yaviza and Puerto Obaldía.

By Train
Tragically Panamá's railways are in a state of terminal decline. The most interesting route, from Panamá City to Colón, which runs parallel to the canal, suspended its passenger services following the invasion. It's just possible that the service will be resumed, but the situation doesn't look hopeful. The two remaining routes are banana trains, built by the United Fruit Company and operated by its successors. The first runs from Puerto Armuelles to Concepción, a distance of just 30 km. The second, from Almirante to Changuinola, with two daily trips in either direction, rolls through a sea of banana plantations. Both services are painfully slow.

By Bus
The quickest, cheapest and most popular form of travel in Panamá is the bus, which offers an interesting glimpse of Panamanian lives and landscapes. The majority of bus services, excluding those for Colón, depart from or near the Avenida B terminal in Panamá City. Other cities usually have a central point for bus departures and there are purpose-built terminals in Santiago, David and Colón. The best services link the capital with David and Colón, with fast, efficient buses leaving every hour or so. The David route is the only service in the country for which you buy a ticket in advance, although you can also pay on the bus. On the Colón route you get the option of an air-conditioned *express* or a *corriente*, which stops along the way. Smaller buses and minibuses, known as *chivas* ('goats'), run on all other routes. Off the Pan-American Highway roads deteriorate rapidly and the pace of travel soon slows; the roughest roads are in the Darién, where torrential downpours play havoc with schedules.

Buses can be flagged down along the highway, but are under no obligation to stop. They tend to be less inclined to do so on the Pan-American Highway but almost always stop on smaller roads.

The main services depart from the Avenida B bus terminal in Panamá City, unless otherwise stated:

Penonomé and Aguadulce. Every 30 minutes, 5 am–9 pm (2–3 hrs).
Chame and San Carlos. Every hour, 5 am–8 pm (2 hrs).

El Valle. Every 2 hours, 5–4 (2 hrs 30 mins).

Chitré and Los Santos. Every hour, 5–8 (4 hrs). Most buses stop in Chitré, from where you can take a local minibus to Los Santos.

Chepo and Yaviza. Twice daily, journey time to Yaviza being 10–13 hrs.

Santiago. Departures with *Expreso Veragüense* from just north of the main Avenida B terminal. Every half hour 5–7 (4 hrs).

David. An express service from a separate terminal beside the main Avenida B terminal in Panamá City, returning from the terminal in David. Departures in both directions on the hour, 7–1 pm and at 2.30, 4, 7 pm and an express service at midnight. The regular buses take around 8 hrs, and the express has been known to do it in 6.

Colón. Departures from Avenida Central, Calle B in Panamá City—returning from the terminal in Colón on Avenida Bolívar. Departures every 20 minutes with either an air-conditioned *express*, which takes 1 hr 30 mins, or the regular *corriente*, which takes 2 hrs.

By Car

Driving is certainly a practical option in Panamá; the roads are reasonable, car hire is easy and distances are relatively short. The main highways, from the capital to David and Colón, are well maintained, although outside these narrow confines tarmac is often patchy. If you're only planning to visit the main towns then an ordinary car is fine, although if you want to explore the Darién or root out remote beaches then four-wheel-drive is essential. In the rainy season driving in the Darién is extremely difficult and roads are often impassable. Whatever your plans, it is a good idea to carry a spare tyre and a can of petrol.

Traffic is generally heavy on the Pan-American Highway and the main road to Colón. Here, and in Panamá City, you'd be well advised to give way to local traffic, particularly buses and trucks, which have a serious contempt for private cars and a deep disregard for safety. On smaller roads traffic is a great deal slower and in remote areas drivers are immensely considerate, stopping to help anyone who appears to be in trouble. Parking meters are in operation in some parts of the capital from 8–6. It's unwise to leave a car on the street at night so you should plan to stay in a hotel with secure parking.

Car Hire

Car hire is relatively cheap, but you do need to exercise a degree of caution—read the small print and check the car closely for damages, or you may end up paying for them. If you are involved in an accident, obtain a police report and contact the hire company within 24 hours or your insurance may be rendered invalid. Most car-hire companies have offices in Panamá City on Calle 55, just off Vía España; some have additional offices in Balboa, at the airport or in the main hotels. The cars on offer range from the most basic Nissans—March and Sunny—for around US$30 a day or US$200 a week, to air-conditioned Toyotas and BMW jeeps, for US$70–80 a day or US$500 a week. Insurance is an extra US$10. It's worth dropping in to Calle 55, where the concentration of rental companies gives you the chance to find the right car at the best price—it's often worth bargaining as competition is fierce.

The main companies are:

Alpha, Tocumen airport, tel 384248/389214.
Avis, Calle 55, El Cangrejo, tel 640722/640938; at the Tocumen airport, tel 384069; and in Colón, tel 417161.
Budget, Calle 55, El Cangrejo, tel 638777.
Discount, Calle 55, El Cangrejo, tel 219052.
Hertz, Calle 55, El Cangrejo, tel 636511; at the Tocumen airport, tel, 384081; at the Hotel Soloy in Panamá City, tel 271133 in David, tel 756828; and in Colón, tel, 413272.
International, Calle 55, El Cangrejo, tel 644540/648643.

By Bicycle
Panamá is good cycling country, with a well developed road network and little traffic away from the main highways. Take a tough mountain bike to handle the potholes and a good tool kit, although every town has a small bicycle repair shop and you'll doubtless find the Panamanian people full of support and assistance. Even if you haven't brought your own wheels, you can take a bike tour around the Canal Zone with **Reisa Tours** of Panamá City, tel 254728.

Embassies and Consulates

All embassies and consulates are located in Panamá City, generally at the western end of the city, with the notable exception of the French embassy, which is at the tip of the Casco Viejo looking out over the mouth of the canal. Most are open to the public from 8–12 noon, Mon–Fri, and visas generally take at least 24 hours to process.

Colombia: Calle Manuel Ma. Icaza, tel 233535.
Costa Rica: Calle Gerardo Ortega, tel 642937.
El Salvador: Vía España, Edificio Citibank, 4th floor, tel 233020.
US: Avenida Balboa and Calle 40, tel 271777.
UK: Urbana Marbella, Calle 53, Torre Swiss Bank, tel 690866.
Guatemala: Calle 55, El Cangrejo, Edificio Adir, 6th floor, tel 633475.
Honduras: Avenida Justo Arosemena, Calle 31, Edificio Tapia, tel 258200.
Mexico: Edificio Bank of America, 5th floor, Calle 50, tel 635021.
Nicaragua: Avenida Federico Boyd and Calle 50, tel 646721.
Canada: Calle Manuel Ma. Icaza tel 647014.

Money Matters

Panamá's currency is the US dollar (US$), although its Panamanian equivalent, the Balboa (B/.), is also in circulation, but only in coin form: 50c, a beautifully solid coin known as a peso, 25c, 10c, 5c and 1c. US coins are also in circulation. Both dollar and balboa, words and coins, are interchangable, even in slot machines and pay phones.

The presence of the dollar is regarded locally as one of the great insults to Panamanian dignity. However, the fiscal link with the US protects Panamá from the scourge of inflation and has provided a sound basis for the creation of international centres for banking and money-laundering. From a traveller's point of view it is a mixed blessing. While you're denied the pleasure of an new and exotic currency, this is the easiest place to obtain US dollars in Central America. Traveller's cheques can be changed into cash with ease at banks and some hotels, although a high incidence of fraud has made banks reluctant to change more than a couple of hundred dollars' worth.

Banks open from 8 to 1.30, Mon–Fri, some until 4 and a few on Saturday mornings, including the Banco General. Money should be changed and traveller's cheques cashed in the main cities—Panamá City, Colón or David—as things can be very slow elsewhere. Cash can be drawn on a Visa card from branches of Chase Manhattan Bank in Panamá City. Sending money to Panamá is fairly straightforward. However, after the 1989 invasion several banks closed down their Panamanian operations, so before you have the money sent make sure the branch is still in business. Generally speaking, hotels, restaurants, car-hire companies and travel agents will accept well-known credit cards, including American Express, Visa, Diners Club, Access/Mastercard and Citibank. These are of little use at the budget end of the market or outside the main cities, where cash rules.

Post Offices

Post offices, *Correos*, are open from 7 to 5.45, Mon–Sat. Letters should always be sent airmail, although this is usually done automatically. Mail can take anything up to four weeks to reach the US, six weeks to Europe. Parcels can be sent from any post office, but if they weigh more than 2 kilos then it's a fairly complicated process. In Panamá City parcels weighing more than 2 kilos must be sent from the parcel office in the El Dorado shopping centre—if you've got a heavy package it's a lot easier to split it up into smaller parcels and send them from the main post office in the Plaza Catedral.

Mail can be sent to 'Lista de Correos, Correo Central, Calle 6 y Avenida Central, Panamá, Republic of Panamá, Central America', the main office in the Plaza Catedral. Letters from Europe normally arrive within about three weeks, while those from the US should arrive within a fortnight. Alternatively, and a lot better in my opinion, is the service offered by American Express, which is open to anyone who has an American Express card or traveller's cheques. Letters should be sent to 'American Express, Edificio Banco Unión, 12 Piso, Vía España, Panamá, Republic of Panamá'. The office is in fact just to the south of Vía España, and open 8–4, Mon–Fri.

Telecommunications

Panamá has a superb network of public phones. However, Panamanians love to talk, so even the most remote payphones have a constant queue of people waiting to use them. The phone company, INTEL, has the benefit of modern US equipment and lines are generally very clear. For internal calls there are no codes and all numbers have six figures. Most payphones take 5c, 10c and 25c coins and shops also have phones for local calls.

Most long-distance calls must be made through the operator. Dial 106 for the international operator, who will speak good English. Calls can be made from any phone. To call from a payphone you'll need a small sack of coins. It's a lot easier to use an INTEL office, where you can pay afterwards, or reverse the charges. Some hotels will let you make international calls but their prices are often inflated. Collect calls can be made with astonishing ease, again through the international operator. Telegrams, telexs and faxes can also be sent from INTEL offices. In Panamá City there's an INTEL office in Calle 42, just off Vía España and a 24-hour office in Balboa, just off the entrance road, open 8–12 and 1–4.30, Mon–Fri.

Police and Military

Since the US invasion the status of Panamá's security has been somewhat uncertain. Until 1989 the police, army and navy were united in the Panamanian Defence Force (PDF), under the direct control of General Noriega. According to George Bush the entire operation was riddled with corruption and following the invasion the PDF was disbanded, leaving Panamá without a police force.

Somewhat belatedly the new government created the Public Force, *Fuerza Pública*, which is now responsible for law and order. However, since the invasion Panamá has suffered a 300% increase in crime, most notably in Panamá City and Colón, where armed robbery, muggings and assaults have become increasingly common. Today the criminal forces in Panamá are better armed, more numerous and more highly motivated than the country's police force, which is inexperienced and severely restricted by its US overseers—no longer free to exercise the traditional forms of rough justice. In August 1990 Vice-President Guillermo Ford declared: 'One of the most serious problems our country faces is the almost total lack of public security. I issue a call to the members of the public force, who should behave like men, not like pansies.'

For the traveller the important thing is that although the police are polite and helpful they have failed to make the streets safe. Muggings are depressingly common in the two main cities and particularly in Colón. The centre of Panamá City is fairly safe during the day, Colón a lot less so—and you should try to avoid wearing jewellery or carrying luggage in the streets. At night both cities are undeniably dangerous. The safest place for your money is in your hotel room and at night you'd be well advised to travel by taxi. Sadly, whatever precautions you take, there is a considerable chance that you'll be robbed. If you bear in mind that muggers are often armed, it's wise simply to hand over the cash.

Personal Safety

Panamanians are no more macho than Guatemalans or Hondurans but the lawless situation in some parts of the country, and particularly in Panamá City and Colón, does make it a dangerous country for women travellers. Avoid Colón if possible, and do not walk in Panamá City at night.

Medical Matters

Chemists, *farmacias*, stock a good range of internationally produced drugs, including condoms, contraceptive pills, tampons, sanitary towels and malaria pills. You may find it hard to find contact lens solution, so bring your own. Panamá City has several excellent hospitals, with the very best US-trained doctors.

Public Holidays

Banks and government offices are closed on national holidays, though public transport continues to operate. There are also countless local holidays, fiestas and saints' days, which bring local banks and businesses to a halt but are a riot of drinking, dancing and furious celebration.

1 January	**New Year's Day**
9–12 February	**Holy Week**—religious processions clog the streets as images of Christ are paraded by the faithful
1 May	**Labour Day**—union and left-wing marchers take to the streets
15 August	**Foundation of Panamá City**—only in the city
12 October	**National Revolution Day**
1 November	**All Saints' Day**
3 November	**Independence Day**—from Colombia—military parades and nationalist sentiments
4 November	**Flag Day**
10 November	**First call of Independence**
28 November	**Independence Day**—from Spain
8 December	**Mother's Day**

Opening hours

Banks are open 8–1.30, Mon–Fri, although some are open until 4 and on Saturday mornings. Museums and offices are usually open 8–12 and 1–4.30/5, Mon–Fri, although several museums open on Sundays and close Mondays. Most shops open 9–6, Mon–Sat. Public transport operates on a standard seven-day week.

Markets and Festivals

All the large cities have markets, where you buy anything from a duck to a duvet, and Panamá City and Colón are two of the great trading cities of the Americas. The only large weekly market is in El Valle on Sundays.

Regional festivals, which take place throughout the year, offer a fantastic opportunity to see Panamanians at their best: wild, explosive and tremendously hospitable. Every town and village has a fiesta; the people of Los Santos and Chitré pride themselves on their ability to celebrate for days and the rodeos of Chiriquí are certainly just as wild.

March
20th: **Portobelo**—Patron saint's day, involving the famous black Christ.
15th–24th: **David**—international industrial, agricultural and commercial fair. Cattle shows, folklore, parades and, of course, drink and dance.
April
11th–21st: **Boquete**—Coffee and Flower Festival, includes reckless partying.
May
1st: **Labour Day**—Celebrated with a fiesta on the island of Bastimentos in the province of Bocas del Toro; includes dancing around the maypole.

5th: **Sona**—southwest of Santiago—Festival of San Isidro with traditional dancing, fireworks and endless drinking.
June
2nd: **Los Santos**—Corpus Christi religious festival. Folklore and dancing, including the great Montezuma devil dance.
24th: **Chitré and Aguadulce**—Festival of John the Baptist. Processions and popular dancing.
July
16th: **Taboga Island**—Patron saint's day (the Holy Virgin of Mount Carmel); includes a procession of flower-covered boats, boat races, water-skiing, dancing, feasting and drinking.
19th: **Las Tablas**—Pollera festival.
August
15th: **Panamá City**—Foundation of the city.
19th: **Bocas del Toro**—Banana festival, a wild Caribbean carnival; rum, reggae and dancing 'til dawn.
September
27th–29th: **Bocas del Toro**—*Festival del Mar.*
November
1st: **Los Santos**—Festival of the city's founding.
5th: **Colón**—*Festival de los Congos*; drink, dance, drugs and danger.

Shopping and Artesanía

For some four hundred years Panamá has been one of the great shopping centres of the Americas and despite recent political upheavals the country remains a vibrant trading centre, dealing in everything from women's underwear to cocaine.

Modern consumer goods are more readily available here than anywhere else in Central America. The Colón Free Zone offers some bargains, ranging from perfume to sports clothes and including the full range of consumer goods, all at tax-free prices. Bulk buying is the norm and officially goods have to be picked up from the customs office in the Tocumen airport, but if you want to buy a shirt or a pair of shoes you'll get them cheaply here and should be able to walk out with them.

Panamá is also a centre of the Central American **clothing** industry and shops along Panamá City's Avenida Central sell a wide selection, made in Panamá and around the world, at amazingly cheap prices. Turnover is high and sales techniques are aggressive. The capital's shops also offer French perfumes, Cuban cigars, stereos, jewellery, toys, leather goods, TVs, cars and just about anything else you can think of. As they say in Panamá, 'shop Avenida Central and you shop the world'.

Traditional Panamanian goods and souvenirs are, however, few and far between, although there is some regional *artesanía*. The world-famous **Panama hats** are in fact made in Ecuador: Panamanians themselves much prefer US-style baseball caps. However, the hats are imported for the benefit of tourists and are available at tourist shops in the capital. More traditionally Panamanian are the hand-woven straw hats, decorated with black patterned bands, which are made in the Azuero peninsula and can be bought in the markets in Chitré and David. Also manufactured on the Azuero peninsula, in the village of Arena just north of Chitré, is traditional Panamanian **pottery**, decorated with simple abstract designs. The pots can be bought from shops in Arena and from the market in Chitré. Panamá's indigenous groups also produce some interesting **artesanía**. In the province of Chiriquí the Guayami Indians make beautiful, brightly coloured dresses and patterned collars. On the Caribbean coast the Kuna Indians are famous for their *molas*—embroidered clothes—which they wear as skirts, and **gold jewellery**. These are sold throughout the country, but it's well worth travelling to the islands to meet the people themselves and buy direct.

The Media

Prior to the US invasion Panamá's media was closely controlled by the army, who set up their own newspapers and shut down those they didn't endorse. But since the fall of Noriega the independent press has flourished. Six daily newspapers are now available, ranging from those offering serious political comment to blood and guts reportage. The most important anti-government paper of the 1980s, *La Prensa*, is back in business and provides some of the best coverage and comment, including a good *Revista* section, with listings of films, theatre and exhibitions. The paper is owned by Roberto Eisenman, one of the country's most powerful businessmen, who runs a small empire of department stores, banks and insurance firms. The other serious broadsheet is *La Estrella de Panamá*, which began printing in 1849, and has traditionally backed the party in power, although US sources have complained that it is now adopting an anti-American stance. It also offers good coverage of national and international events. Two more sensationalist tabloid papers, *El Siglo* and *El Extra*, also adopt an opposition line. Both specialize in crime and scandal—and Panamá has plenty of both—but they do spare the odd column for political comment. Other papers include *El Panamá América*, *Crítica Libre*, which includes Colombian news, *La República*, a very popular tabloid, and *El Policio*, the sleaziest of the lot.

Panamanian TV tends to be dominated by Mexican and Venezuelan soap operas, although there is also some good news reporting. The oldest station, TV4, was a strong supporter of the Torrijos regime and is fiercely anti-communist. TV2, founded in 1962, is dominated by sport; TV13 is mostly a movie channel, and Channel 11 is an educational channel operated by the University of Panamá and owned by the ministries of Planning and Education. You can watch English-language TV on SCN TV (channels 8 and 10), which is part of the American forces broadcasting network, or on cable TV, which was set up in Panamá in 1987.

As in all Central American countries there's an abundance of radio stations, offering everything from evangelical sermons to the the cool rhythms of Caribbean reggae. Radio is immensely popular and you'll be sure to hear it in bars, buses, shops and restaurants. All political parties operate their own radio stations, as do most religious sects and the US forces, who broadcast on AM and FM (91.5).

Music and Cinema

Influenced by the easy rhythms of Caribbean reggae, the complexities of Colombian *salsa* and the pulse of modern American music, Panamanians have diverse musical tastes.

As you travel through the country you'll be sure to hear the full range, as well as Panamanian *típica*, a wild yelping music which originates in the countryside and is particularly strong on the Azuero peninsula.

Film-going is also a popular pastime among Panamanians and there are plenty of good cinemas in Panamá City which show recent releases, while a couple of cinemas in Casco Viejo specialise in porn and violence. Most films are shown in English, with Spanish subtitles. Outside Panamá City cinemas are thin on the ground: David has two, Chitré one and there's a strange *minicine* in Chiriquí Grande. There is an indigenous film industry but their turnout is limited.

Where to Stay

Across the board Panamanians generally offer warm hospitality and at the top end of the market you'll find high standards of efficiency and cleanliness although, generally speaking, hotels in Panamá are more expensive than elswhere in the isthmus. Luxury hotels are to be found in abundance in Panamá City, Colón, Chame, San Carlos, El Valle and David. Elsewhere you'll have to make do with more basic lodging. (When choosing a cheaper place, particularly in Colón and Panamá City, pay close attention to the problem of security.) Even the very smallest of villages have cheap hotels and where there isn't a hotel local people will always be able to find you somewhere to stay. If you plan to travel in the Darién you'll need a hammock—or tent in the rainy season—and a mosquito net, particularly during the rainy season. There are no youth hostels in Panamá and camping is only really necessary or possible when hiking, although you can also camp on the San Blás islands.

Prices

Hotel prices are officially regulated by the Panamanian tourist board (who charge a 10% tax on all rooms), although when you're paying cash, as you almost always will be, things are often more flexible. Hotels come under a variety of names—*pensiones*, *hospedajes*, *posadas*—but these don't really reveal much. Phone numbers are listed in the text, where available, so that you can phone ahead. The Panamanian tourist industry is currently very depressed and you should have no need to book, except during a major fiesta, or at the weekends, when Panamanians all head for the beach.

LUXURY
Top-of-the-range hotels are confined to Panamá City and the Pearl Islands and offer full resort facilities and superb accommodation.

EXPENSIVE
Panamá City is awash with expensive hotels, catering to the flow of business travellers who spend a night or two in town. As a result of this many hotels are somewhat cold, designed to meet the needs of those on the move. Elsewhere these hotels offer all the luxury you might require, complete with air conditioning and fine international cuisine.

MODERATE
Mid-range hotels, spread evenly across the country, cater to middle-class locals and

Central American businessmen. They tend to be smaller hotels and offer a more intimate atmosphere. Rooms with a private bathroom and fan, or air conditioning if you're lucky, are often very good value.

INEXPENSIVE

In every town and village there is some basic accommodation on offer, with shared bathrooms and cold water. The standard varies enormously and you'd be well advised to take a look at a room before committing yourself.

Eating and Drinking

Few people come to Panamá for the food. There are some excellent up-market French and Italian restaurants in the capital but the typical menu is a vague international offering. Most people eat in simple cafés where the food is warm, filling and nondescript, while there is less food sold on the streets than in the poorer countries such as Guatemala and El Salvador. Steak and fish are good, particularly *corvina*, lobster and shrimp, although oddly shrimp is never particularly cheap, despite the fact that it is one of Panamá's main exports. Chicken, chips, rice, beans, hamburgers and *chao mein* are all common and generally unremarkable. Yucca, a delicious root crop that's either boiled or fried, often takes the place of potatoes and rice.

In amongst the normal bland offerings there are some interesting traditional Panamanian dishes, despite the fact that most Panamanians have never heard of them. *Ropa vieja*, old clothes, is shredded beef fried with onions, garlic and tomatoes. *Sopa borracha* is a sponge cake made with rum and garnished with raisins and prunes. *Sancocho* is a traditional stew of chicken, yucca, potatoes, plantain and plenty more. On the Caribbean side you might also come across some delicious coconut and fish dishes, but again the international chicken and hamburger menu dominates. Superb tropical fruit is also available throughout the country, though rarely on offer in restaurants.

Panamanians pride themselves on their ability to consume massive quantities of alcohol and there's a wide range available. Locally produced beers include Panamá, Atlas, Soberana, Balboa (*para hombres*, for men), and Löwenbrau. Imported US beers are also available, sold in supermarkets and some bars. Whisky, rum, and *seco*, a local speciality, are made in Panamá, but brands of spirits from around the world are also available. The usual array of soft drinks is on offer, with the addition of Malta, a rich dark drink made from barley. *Refrescos*, made with fruit juice and water, are excellent and thirst quenching, as are *jugos*, fruit juices. Coffee is generally mediocre but the milk is fresh and good.

Suggested Itineraries

Much of Panamá can be seen with ease from Panamá City, where you'll find the country's best food and accommodation, so it's worth staying in the capital for a while. If you're in Panamá for a couple of weeks then you might want to spend a week in Panamá City, taking various day trips in the central area, and then a week or so exploring western Panamá. Among the places that can be reached from the capital the **Canal** has to be the impressive attraction, although the two main cities are both astonishing and exciting, if somewhat intimidating.

On the Caribbean side you can easily visit Colón as a day trip and even head northeast to Portobelo and the beautiful Caribbean island of Isla Grande, where you'll want to stay overnight. On the Pacific side the island of Taboga and those of the Pearl Islands archipelago can all be reached from the Balboa and offer a slightly different experience.

The country to the east of Panamá City, the Darién, is difficult to explore, with few passable roads and a scattered population, and though fascinating it demands a great deal of time and patience, remaining off-limits to all but the most adventurous. **Travel to the west** is a lot easier. It is well worth taking a week or so to explore the area between Panamá City and the Costa Rican border. The Pacific beaches around San Carlos are beautiful as is the mountain town of El Valle, which offers a release from the heat of the lowlands and is an ideal place to spend the night after a day on the beach. Further west the Azuero peninsula is a fascinating and formal area, with deep rural tradition and superb fiestas.

Further west still is David, from where you can visit the highlands of Chiriquí, with their volcanic peaks and spectacular high forests.

Finally, in **the northwestern corner** of the country, is the province of Bocas del Toro, a remote outpost with some gorgeous islands, dominated by Caribbean culture.

Panamá City

Panamá City is the unchallenged centre of Panamanian business, culture and politics. Fanning out behind the broad sweep of the Bahía de Panamá, the city embraces sharp contradictions. At its eastern end is the banking district, a great forest of glass-sided office blocks topped with exclusive apartments. Here international bankers, drug-smugglers and money-launderers escape the grime of the streets and can be sure to catch sea breezes and satellite signals. At the other end of town is Casco Viejo, the old Spanish capital, which has changed little in the last hundred years—a secretive maze of cobbled streets, blind alleys and colonial plazas. Like New Orleans or old Havana, its faded colonial splendour and urban decay are alive with the ease and energy of the tropics. Between these two poles the city's main streets shuttle traffic from the cramped slums, congested commercial centres and the plush banking district. Further east low-lying residential suburbs and shopping centres sprawl out towards the airport, engulfing the ruins of Panamá Viejo, the site of the first Spanish city.

To the uninitiated Panamá City is undoubtedly intimidating, although once you've been here for a couple of days, and seen a little of the warmth which lies beneath the crazy swirl, you'll find it a lot easier to relax. The pace is furious and the harsh economic climate, aided by government incompetence, has produced a worrying crime wave. During the day the main streets are safe enough but at night you should travel by taxi whenever possible. Certain parts are particularly dangerous, most notably the district of El Chorrillo, which should be avoided at all times.

Amidst all this hustle and fuss Panamá City is an amazing and invigorating place; its people are among the sharpest, quickest and shrewdest in Central America. It's well worth spending at least a couple of days looking around. Take in the shabby colonial elegance of Casco Viejo or the bold skyscrapers and slick boutiques of the banking district, perhaps visit a museum or travel out to the crumbling ruins of Panamá Viejo, which have lain empty since they were sacked by the famous Welsh pirate Henry Morgan. The city is also quite firmly at the centre of things and from here you can make short trips to most parts of the country, including the canal, Colón, Portobelo, Isla Grande, the San Blás Islands, Contadora and Taboga, or even as far afield as Chitré and Los Santos, stopping off at the beach along the way.

History

Situated at one of the world's great crossroads, Panamá City is built on shifting sands, its prosperity entirely dependent on through traffic. The city was founded by the Spanish in 1519 at the site now known as 'Panamá Viejo, a few kilometres east of the modern city. In those days the city was used to store gold and silver from South America before it was transported across the isthmus for shipment to Spain. It was always a tempting target and in 1671 the Welsh pirate Henry Morgan sacked the city, after which the settlement was moved to its modern position which was thought to be easier to defend. The entire colonial city was rebuilt in what is now Casco Viejo, hemmed in by a thick defensive wall.

For the next two hundred years the decline and fall of the Spanish empire reduced the city to a small provincial centre, and following independence from Spain it was ruled from the distant Colombian capital of Bogotá. However new life arrived in the early 19th century as ambitious travellers crossed the isthmus here on their way to or from California. The 1849 gold rush created a small boom and the completion of the railway to Colón in 1855 established the city as a busy port and trading post. In due course the railway was replaced by the canal and Panamá City became an important international staging post, supplying the unsavoury needs of the world's merchant seamen.

Since then the city has mushroomed, its development fuelled by the canal and its spin-offs, the latest of which has been the financial services business. The tight-knit streets to the north of Casco Viejo were the first real development, connecting the city with the canal in the early years of this century, and reaching to the edge of the Canal Zone. However, the gap between the city and the clean streets of Balboa, the head-quarters of the Canal Commission, is growing increasingly stark as the old city slips deeper into urban decay, its inhabitants impoverished and unemployed. Meanwhile the city's money is moving east into and beyond the banking district, where more modern development has sprawled wildly in recent decades, the bold concrete architecture clearly inspired by the US.

GETTING TO PANAMÁ CITY

Arriving can be daunting. You'll probably have heard all sorts of scary stories about crime and violence, and the bustle of the streets can be overwhelming at first. So whether you arrive by bus or plane, take a taxi straight to a hotel.

By Air

International flights come into the Tocumen airport, 27 km east of the city centre. The minibus service will take you to any hotel for US$8 per person, a taxi will cost at least US$20, and a bus which passes on the highway outside the terminal—any bus marked

'Calle 12', will take you through the centre of town to the Plaza Santa Ana. It takes anything from 40 minutes to an hour to get to the city centre, depending on which method you choose.

Domestic flights land at Paitilla airport, right beside the centre of town. Buses for 'Vía España' and Calle 12 (Casco Viejo) pass the airport on Avenida 6 Sur. Coming from Calle 12 any bus marked 'Atlapa' will pass Paitilla airport.

By Bus

Arriving by bus, you'll probably end up at the Avenida B terminal on the edge of Casco Viejo. Again it's a good idea to take a taxi to your hotel, which won't cost any more than a few dollars. Travellers from Colón end up at Calle B, just off Avenida Central, which is well served by buses and taxis.

Airlines

Domestic services are listed under 'Getting Around'.

Aeronica (tel 644144), Calle 52 and Vía España.
Copa (tel 272522), Avenida Justo Arosema and Calle 39.
Eastern, Calle 53, tel 696022 and at the airport, tel 384266.
Iberia, Calle 43 and Avenida Balboa, tel 273966.
KLM, Calle 53 Urbano Obarrio, tel 646255.
Lacsa, Avenida Justo Arosemena, tel, 270257.
Sahsa, Calle 37 and Vía España, tel 271571.
Sam, Calle 42, tel 691222.
TACA, Calle B, El Cangrejo, tel 696066.

GETTING AROUND PANAMÁ CITY

By Bus

The streets of Panamá City are ruled by bus drivers, who race through town in superbly painted machines, belching black smoke and driving with unrivalled aggression. The service is astonishingly cheap, with a flat fare of 15 cts. Buses run from 6 am to around 11 pm, although they become increasingly scarce as the evening wears on.

Routes are spelled out on the windscreens of the buses. The hub of the network is 'Calle 12' in the Plaza Santa Ana, from where you can get a bus to almost any part of the city. For the most part you'll probably want to travel the between Casco Viejo and Vía España. Buses running towards Casco Viejo come along Vía España, and down Avenida Central to Calle 12, where they loop around Calle 11 before heading back east, past the bus terminal on Avenida B, and then onto Avenida Perú and back towards Vía España. It's an easy route to use and you can pick up a bus anywhere along it. (Avoid buses marked 'El Chorrillo', which turn off Avenida Central before they reach Calle 12.)

Buses to the airport, marked 'Tocumen' and to 'Panamá Viejo' can also be picked up at Calle 12. Buses for Balboa and places inside the Canal Zone leave from the Plaza 5 de Mayo on Avenida Central.

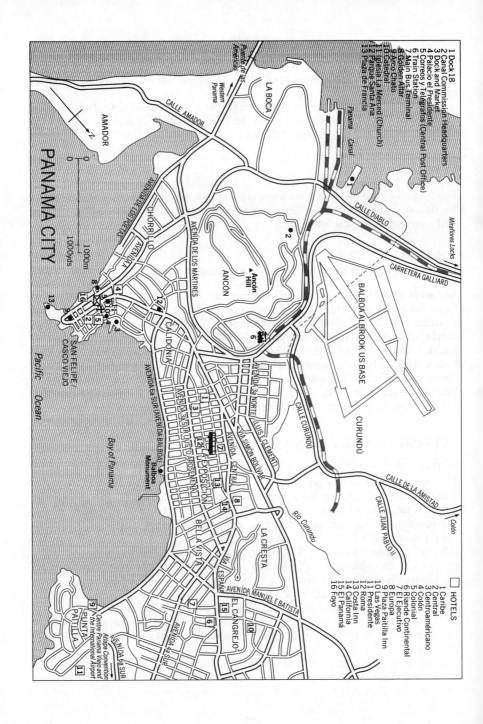

PANAMA CITY

1 Dock 18
2 Canal Commission Headquarters
3 Dock and Market
4 Palacio el Presidente
5 Correos y Telégrafos (Central Post Office)
6 Train Station
7 Main Bus Terminal
8 Golden Altar
9 Arco Chato
10 Catedral
11 Iglesia La Merced (Church)
12 Parque Santa Ana
13 Plaza de Francia

☐ HOTELS
1 Caribe
2 Central
3 Centroaméricano
4 Colón
5 Colonial
6 Riande Continental
7 El Ejecutivo
8 Europa
9 Plaza Paitilla Inn
10 Las Vegas
11 Presidente
12 Roma
13 Costa Inn
14 California
15 El Panamá
16 Foyo

By Taxi
Taxis are plentiful, except during the rush hour or a downpour. Fares are reasonable but agree a fare before you set off.

Long-distance Bus Terminals
When it comes to leaving the city the majority of long-distance buses leave from the Avenida B bus terminal, which is behind a block of flats at the junction of Avenida B and Calle 18. The one exception is buses to Colón, which leave from Avenida Central, Calle B. The main services are listed in the General Information section.

TOURIST INFORMATION OFFICE
The Panamanian tourist board's information office (open 8.30–4.30, Mon–Fri) is in the Atlapa Conference Centre in the west of the city. To get there take any bus heading for 'Atlapa' or 'Panamá Viejo', or you can call them on 267000, extension 279.

ORIENTATION
Panamá City is laid out in a chaotic fashion, sprawling around the back of the bay. The western end of the city is Casco Viejo, a small block of streets laid out on a strict grid. Heading east from here are three main avenues; Avenida Central and Avenida Perú, which go through the heart of the city, and Avenida Balboa, which runs along the seafront. All three connect the old city with the banking district, which is centred on Vía España. Further east the city is open and sprawling. The only sound points of reference are districts and the grand avenues of Vía España, Boyd Roosevelt, Avenida Balboa and Eloy Alfaro.

Making sense of the city is made particularly hard by the fact that several streets have more than one name, or at least a name and a number. A good map of the city is available from the Casa Zaldo department store in the Plaza Santa Ana.

BOOKS AND MAPS
The best English-language bookshop is **Argosy**, on Vía Argentina, just off Vía España. Some English books and maps of Panamá are also sold at the **Casa Zaldo** on the Plaza Santa Ana in Casco Viejo.

WHAT TO SEE
Life on the streets of Panamá City ranges from the hard-sell hustlers of Avenida Central through the chaotic stench of the fish market to the smooth smoked-glass of Vía España. The city's scrambled, cosmopolitan culture, embracing rich and poor, old and new, has a unique flavour and it's only by exploring its main districts that you can grasp the city's extraordinary diversity.

Casco Viejo—The Old City
The city's western tip is dominated by the San Felipe and Santa Ana districts: a tight, claustrophobic community which mixes urban decay and faded colonial splendour. The area is a complex network of narrow streets and old-style mansions, with cracked balconies and chipped plaster. The atmosphere on the streets blends the traditional Spanish with the rough street culture of the surrounding slums. Old men chat in the

plaza, children play in the streets and prostitutes wander from bar to bar, weary, overworked and underpayed.

The Spanish city was moved here in 1671, after pirates destroyed the original settlement of Panamá Viejo. Immediately after the raid the settlers relocated to the safety of Ancón hill, which looms above Casco Viejo, moving down onto the the lower ground once they had fortified the peninsula with a thick city wall. Only a couple of small sections of the wall survive today but the original structure was so costly that when the King of Spain received the bill he is said to have been amazed that he couldn't see it.

The new city was never intended to match the splendour of the earlier version, for the Spanish empire was in decline and the authorities were more concerned with defending themselves from attack. The heart of the old city, the San Felipe district, measures just eight blocks by four, and was separated by the city wall from the slums of Santa Ana, which grew throughout the 18th century, where blacks, mulattos and the poor lived. Crammed inside the city were the homes of merchants, priests and soldiers, interspersed with churches, plazas, a theatre and a cathedral.

Casco Viejo's architecture has been left virtually untouched during the last hundred years. The great changes which have swept through Panamá have left their mark elsewhere, with the development of the Canal Zone and the banking district; the only noticeable change in the old city has been a steady slide into urban decay as the rich have moved out into the more spacious suburbs. However, in 1972 local conservationists initiated the Casco Viejo Restoration Project to revitalize the area through the active participation of local people. As yet little has been done and much of the housing continues to crumble.

Exploring Casco Viejo
Casco Viejo's architectural gems are packed into a tiny area and can easily be seen in a morning. The gateway to the old city is the **Plaza Santa Ana**, which is surrounded by bars, cafés and porn cinemas. Traffic from all over Panamá City is funnelled towards this point, where buses tip out their passengers before looping around to head back into the modern city.

To reach the centre of Casco Viejo walk south from the Plaza Santa Ana, along Avenida Central. Between Calle 9 and 10 you pass **Iglesia de La Merced**, which dates from 1680. The building's crumbling façade is original, although the interior, which was damaged by fire, has been modernized. The chapel plays an important role in the old city's religious life and is home to a painting of Our Lady of the Assumption, the area's patron saint.

Heading on down Avenida Central, the narrow street opens out into the **Plaza Catedral**, the heart of the old city. In colonial times this was the hub of religious and secular authority, although these days it's the centre of a small, impoverished community. **The Metropolitan Cathedral**, which dominates the plaza, was built between 1688 and 1796, and is undoubtedly the city's finest piece of religious architecture with its barrel-shaped interior and solid twin towers, the domes of which are covered in mother of pearl. The cathedral's bells were taken from the original cathedral in Panamá Viejo; in 1882 an earthquake sent one of them crashing through the cathedral's roof. Opposite is the **Hotel Central**, a fantastic old building straight from the pages of a Graham Greene novel, with wooden balconies and a great interior courtyard. It was once the city's grandest establishment but these days, although its bar is still at the centre of social life in Casco Viejo, it has become a scruffy budget hotel. On the plaza's western side is the **Palacio Municipal**, which was built in 1910 to replace the old colonial city hall (in which independence from Spain was signed in 1821 as well as separation from Colombia in 1903). Beside the Palace is the **Post Office**, another grand, imperial structure with a complex history. The building dates from 1874, when it was the Grand Hotel. In 1881 it became the headquarters for Ferdinand de Lesseps' ill-fated Canal Company and in 1904 ownership was transferred to the US government, who used it as the first headquarters of the Panamá Canal Commission. When the commission moved to Balboa the building was bought by the Panamanian government, who remodelled it and installed the Post Office. Opposite, on the eastern side of the plaza, is the old Archbishop's Palace.

Also on the Plaza Catedral is the **Museo Nacional**, on the second floor of the **Palacio Municipal**, where Panamá's history is examined in three sections: colonial; provincial—as a province of Colombia; and, rather sadly now, as an independent nation. There are plenty of interesting documents and artefacts, including the copies of the treaties with which Panamá sold itself to the US. Open Tuesday to Saturday, 10–4, and Sunday, 3–6.

Behind the Archbishop's Palace, on the seafront, is the **President's Palace**, which ranks as one of the best kept in Casco Viejo. Its neoclassical structure, built in 1921 to replace an earlier structure dating from 1673, is also known as the *Palacio de las Garzas* or Palace of the Herons, after the birds that have lived in its fountain since 1922. The palace serves as the president's official residence. His home is in the city's clean and spacious suburbs and his motorcade, accompanied by a mass of security, can sometimes be seen blasting its way through the streets. Sadly the area around the building is off limits to members of the public, guarded by crack, teenage troops.

Heading out towards the tip of the peninsula, along Avenida B, you come to the **Plaza Bolívar**, a small, shady plaza centred on a statue of the liberator. Along the southern side of the plaza is the **Instituto Bolívar**, which was formerly part of the convent of San Francisco and is where Bolívar proposed a United States of South America during the Bolívarian Congress of 1826. Today the institute is used as a school and the neighbouring San Francisco church is closed, awaiting repairs. On the northern side of Plaza Bolívar is the **Hotel Colonial**, another impressive old-style hotel which is now run-down and sleazy.

To the west of the Plaza Bolívar is the **National Theatre**, which forms a single unit with the Palacio Nacional, built by the architect Ruggieri in 1908 and restored in 1974. The theatre is considered the heart of the nation's cultural life and concerts and plays are staged here. If the doors are open take a look inside at the murals by Robert Lewis which decorate the main hall. Alongside the theatre is the **Palacio Nacional**, which was completed in 1931, combining a Renaissance lower level with a neoclassical upper floor. In 1955 a third level was added, breaking the building's harmony.

Heading on out along first Avenida, towards the sea, you pass the ruins of the **National Guard's Sports Club**. The site was originally home to Panamá City's most prestigious social club, the Club Unión, which is now housed in the plush residential suburbs. The building was completely destroyed during the US invasion, despite the fact that it was empty at the time. Its walls, still riddled with bullet holes, bear graffiti celebrating Panamanian nationalism and declaring *ni un paso atrás!*—not one step back!

The tip of Casco Viejo is marked by the **Plaza de Francia**, centred around a column honouring the French engineers and their failed attempt to build a canal. The plaza is home to the **Palace of Justice**, the **French Embassy** and **Las Bóvedas**, a series of caverns under the old city wall, which were built in the 18th century to house the Chiriquí Garrison and later used as dungeons. More recently they've been converted to a string of up-market art galleries and a smart restaurant, which is an excellent spot for lunch.

Back towards the old city, on Avenida A, is the **Iglesia Santo Domingo**, part of a convent dating from 1749, which was one of the city's most impressive buildings until it was destroyed by fire in 1761. Among the ruins is the **Arco Chato** or flat arch, which has an astonishing lack of support. According to Panamanian folk history the decision to locate the canal in Panamá was largely based on a comparison between the arch, which testified to the stability of Panamanian soil, and a Nicaraguan postage stamp which showed an erupting volcano. Next door is the **Museum of Colonial Religious Art** (open Tues–Sat, 10–3.30; Sun, 3–5.30), which has a small collection of stern colonial paintings, all brooding and dark.

Four blocks further north, also on Avenida A, are the ruins of a Jesuit convent which housed the Jesuit university until 1767 and was destroyed by fire in 1781. A hundred yards further on is the beautiful Iglesia de San José, which dates from 1677 and houses the city's most famous and impressive gold altar. The altar's history is surrounded by uncertainty but experts now agree that it was originally crafted by creole artists in Panamá Viejo and moved to Casco Viejo sometime in the early 17th century. During the sacking of Panamá Viejo the San José monks saved the altar by painting it black, convincing the pirates that it was made of wood. Further north is the **Plaza Herrera**, which is dominated by a large equestrian statue of Herrera and borders on the rough slum of **El Chorrillo**, which was largely destroyed during the US invasion and is now extremely dangerous.

From Casco Viejo to the Banking District

On the shoreline to the west of Casco Viejo the district of Santa Ana was just outside the city walls in colonial days, when it housed blacks, mulattos and the poor. Today it is a rough residential and commercial area, containing the chaotic energy of the **Mercado Central**. The market is a small two-storey building crammed with fruit and vegetable stalls, but trading spills out into the surrounding streets, where fish is on sale within minutes of being landed, fishmongers up to their elbows in blood. The area is tough and unhealthy, with a flock of vultures feasting on piles of rubbish, but well worth a visit, alive with the bustle of street traders. Calle 13, a narrow alley crowded with stalls, is aptly known as *Sale si puedes*, leave if you can, and in colonial times it was monopolized by gold traders, whose ferocious persistence gave the street its name.

Today Panamá's most tenacious traders are at work on Avenida Central, the heart of the city's down-market **commercial district**. The avenue is lined with cut-price clothes shops so pedestrians have to struggle through a sea of salesmen and bus fumes. At the bottom of the hill is the **Plaza 5 de Mayo**, one of the city's great gathering places, a stage for political demonstrations and a bus terminal. On the other side of Avenida Central, opposite the plaza, is the **Reina Torres de Arauz Anthropological Museum** (open Tues–Sat, 10–3.30; Sun, 3–5.30). The museum houses some fantastic pre-Columbian gold, and gives some insight into Panamá's early history and the country's various indigenous groups.

Between the Plaza 5 de Mayo and the banking district the city's middle section is a little undecided, lacking the architectural interest of Casco Viejo or the wealth of Vía España. Nevertheless it's a busy area with an abundance of hotels, shops and restaurants. Two main Avenues, Central and Perú, cut through this central district. Along the shore is Avenida Balboa, Panamá's equivalent of Central Park, popular with joggers and courting couples. The avenue's most important landmark is the Balboa monument, which juts out onto the rocks and depicts Balboa standing on top of the globe, supported by four struggling figures who are supposed to represent the four nations of the world. Behind the monument, facing out to sea, is the **Saint Thomas Hospital**, flanked by the **American and British embassies**.

Also in this general area are a couple of small but interesting museums. The **Museum of Natural Sciences**, (Mon–Fri, 9–4), on Avenida Cuba between Calles 29 and 30, has a musty collection of stuffed animals, butterflies and birds, including the quetzal and a white grouse all the way from Alaska, and an exhibition of Panamanian geology. Alternatively there's the **Afro-Antillean Museum** (Tuesday to Saturday, 10–4; Sunday, 3–6), at the corner of Calle 24 and Avenida Justo Arosemena, which holds a collection of photographs, art and domestic objects from Panamá's West Indian community, focusing on their contribution to the building of the canal. Be warned that the museum is in a rough neighbourhood.

Vía España and the Banking District

Panamá's remarkable banking district, centred on the grand Vía España, is Central America's greatest imitation of a North American city. No longer cramped and crumbling, this section of the city is affluent and international, designed to meet the needs of wealthy car-driving consumers. At the northern end of España, looking strangely out of place, is the **Iglesia El Carmen**, with its sharp Gothic arches. From here the avenue is lined with skyscrapers and office blocks. The shops sell expensive international fashions, the cinemas show the latest from Hollywood and the restaurants offer food from every corner of the globe.

This splendour is rooted in Panamá's shady role as a financial centre. At least 110 international banks have offices here, lured by offers of anonymity and tax-free trading, while free and easy legislation has also resulted in some 100,000 companies and 10% of the world's merchant shipping fleet being registered in Panamá. This may not be what you've come to Central America for, but Panamá's banking district, just 4 kilometres from the impoverished streets of Casco Viejo, offers a daunting range of creature comforts, including hotels, restaurants, nightclubs and cinemas.

Beyond the banking district the city spreads out into the suburbs. To the south is the exclusive **Punta Paitilla**, with its huge skyscrapers, airport and expensive shopping centres. To the north, on Via Bolívar, is the campus of Panamá University, where some 30,000 students are enrolled each year. Heading further east you pass the **Hotel**

473

Intercontinental and the **Atlapa Conference Centre**, before reaching the ruins of Panamá Viejo.

Panamá Viejo

About 7 kilometres northeast of the present centre, strung out along the shore and ringed by slums, are the ruins of the original Spanish capital. Panamá's first governor, Pedro Arias de Avila, founded the city here on 15 August 1519 and it grew quickly, functioning as an important centre of trade and commerce and marking the southern end of the Camino Real. Here, huge volumes of gold looted from Latin America were transferred from boats to mule trains, in order to be transported across the isthmus to Portobelo. In 1671 the Welsh pirate Henry Morgan, who had crossed the isthmus using the Chagras River and had already destroyed the forts at Portobelo and San Lorenzo, stormed the battlements and destroyed much of the city, looting its riches. It is said that he needed 175 mules to carry off the stolen gold. Once Morgan had departed, the surviving Spaniards decided to move the city south to the site of Casco Viejo, which they thought would be easier to defend.

The ruins themselves are not particularly impressive and it requires a leap of the imagination to re-create the colonial city. Arriving from the modern city the first ruins that you see are a handful of decaying walls, the largest of which are the remains of the **Convento de las Monjas de la Concepción**, founded in 1598. About 500 metres beyond is the site of the city's main plaza, dominated by the bell-tower of the **Cathedral**. This crumbling structure, which replaced an earlier wooden cathedral, has become a popular symbol in Panamá, appearing on anything from T-shirts to buses. The tower was rebuilt in 1644, just seven years before the arrival of Morgan. Also on the plaza are the ruins of the **Casa del Cabildo**—the town hall, which was destroyed by an earthquake in 1612.

Just off the plaza are several more ruins, daubed with graffiti and interspaced with football pitches. They include the **Casa del Obispo**, the bishop's palace, and the **Convento de Santo Domingo**, and further north the **Convento de San José**, which contained the beautiful gold altar, which is now housed in the Church of San José in Casco Viejo. A kilometre or so further east is **Puente del Rey**, the king's bridge, across which every last ounce of gold began its journey to Portobelo.

To get to the ruins from the centre of town take any bus marked 'Panamá Viejo' from Calle 12 or anywhere along Vía España or Avenida Balboa. Be warned that the ruins are in a roughish area and muggings here are not unheard of, despite the presence of a police station.

WHERE TO STAY

Panamá City offers a complete range of accommodation, from the luxury of the Hotel Panamá to some astonishingly cheap places in Casco Viejo. Conveniently the hotels are clustered into concentrations of similarly priced establishments. High and moderately priced hotels have their own restaurants and are in relatively safe parts of town, so there's no need to worry about wandering the streets at night. There are plenty of cheap restaurants in Casco Viejo, where all the inexpensive hotels are grouped.

LUXURY AND EXPENSIVE

Several superb hotels compete at the luxury end of the market. The **Hotel Panamá**, tel 695000, just north of Vía España, is rated by many as the city's finest, catering to every whim with a massive pool, squash courts, three indoor tennis courts, jacuzzis, ballroom, nightclub and a lot more besides. To the south on Vía España the **Plaza Paitilla Inn**, tel 691122, fax 231470, can certainly claim one of the best locations, right on the seafront. The top floor of the building, which is an 18th-floor circular tower, is occupied by the Belvedere restaurant and offers superb views in the city. Out towards the ruins of Panamá Viejo the **Marriott Caesar Park Hotel**, tel 264077, on the Vía Israel opposite the Atlapa Conference Centre, is a more standard top-quality international hotel a couple of kilometres from the centre but with good sea views from most rooms.

MODERATE

At the top of the moderate range is the **Hotel Costa del Sol**, tel 237111, at the junction of Calle 55 and Avenida Federico Boyd, which is good value but still has the benefit of a pool, tennis court and sauna. The bulk of the moderately priced hotels are found to the east the city's middle section, between Vía España and Casco Viejo, generally located just off Avenida Perú. They are all very similar, located in tall, purpose-built buildings with casinos, hot water, cable TV and air conditioning. Among the best value is the **Hotel California**, tel 637844, at the corner of Vía España and Calle 43, just west of the junction of Avenidas Perú and Central. If that's full then the **Hotel Europa**, tel 636369, which has a pool, and the **Hotel Bella Vista**, tel 644029, are both on the same street. Back on Avenida Perú, at the corner of Calle 39, is the **Hotel Costa Inn**, tel 271522, which has the added benefit of protected car parking. Further down Avenida Perú is another small cluster of similar hotels, including the **Hotel Soloy**, tel 271133, on Avenida Perú and Calle 30, and the **Hotel Roma**, tel 273844, which also has a pool and plenty of safe parking space, although if it's too expensive then try the **Hotel Centroamericano**, tel 274555.

INEXPENSIVE

The cheapest budget hotels are all located in Casco Viejo. Although the area is a little rough it is also one of the most interesting and atmospheric parts of the city and perhaps the easiest place to meet people. The best of the really cheap places is undoubtedly the **Hotel Foyo**, a popular backpackers' hotel on Calle 6a, behind the Post Office. If that's full then try the **Hotel Panamá** opposite, which is a little cheaper and a little rougher. If you'd like to stay right on the Plaza Catedral then the **Hotel Central** reeks of faded colonial splendour, or in the same vein is the **Hotel Colonial**, on the Plaza Bolívar, which is a little run down. Finally there is the **Hotel Colón**, at Calle 12 Oeste and Calle B, which is probably the best hotel in this part of town, complete with air conditioning.

EATING OUT

Although traditional Panamanian food is rarely included on the menu, Panamá City's finest restaurants offer superb food from around the globe, lovingly prepared by committed ex-patriots. The best restaurants are in the northeastern parts of the city, having relocated here recently to escape the decay of Casco Viejo, while back in the old city you'll find plenty of good, basic restaurants, serving food at bargain prices.

EXPENSIVE AND MODERATE

The **Bar Restaurant Lesseps**, tel 285537, at the junction of Avenida Central and Calle 46 Oeste, is among the city's best restaurants. The menu is dominated by seafood, including *corvina*, lobster, clams, shrimp and *ceviche*. They also serve good Panamanian steaks, chicken dishes and traditional French food, including *escargots*. The restaurant is named after Ferdinand de Lesseps, the Frenchman who masterminded the failed French attempt at digging a canal. The cuisine is predominantly French, the owner Swiss and the decor decidedly Panamanian, the walls telling the story of the canal. Another top-of-the-range French restaurant is the **Casco Viejo**, tel 642644, which recently abandoned its namesake and moved to Mansión Dante, an ancient dark-wood building reeking of colonial splendour on Calle 50 in the banking district. The food is more specifically French here, prepared with patriotic devotion by Finet Pascal and the decor celebrates France and the sea. Other European establishments include the **Marbella**, tel 230749, on Avenida Balboa at the junction with Calle 36, which serves excellent Spanish seafood, including *amejas*, mussels and a *cazuela de mariscos*, seafood casserole. The **Taberna Bavaria**, tel 231187, on Avenida Frederico Boyd, offers traditional German food, including *sauerkraut* and *bratwurst*. Alternatively you can feast on excellent *raclette* and veal at the **Rincón Suizo**, tel 231660, in Calle Eusebio Morales, which is owned and run by a Swiss couple.

For oriental food try the **Korea House**, tel 692028, just off the Vía España beside the Arias theatre. The proprietor, Mr. Moon Yeung-On, offers a range of Japanese and Korean food, including excellent Sushi. Opposite the Korea House is **Russian Tea Room**, tel 638541, which is equally authentic, owned by a Russian couple whose specialities include caviar and stuffed cabbage, all washed down with traditional Russian cocktails, live Russian music and dancing. On Wednesdays they serve a buffet tea from 3–6.

The only restaurant bold enough to offer genuine Panamanian food is **El Tapiche**, tel 639999, on Vía Argentina, where house specialities include *mondongo*, a dish of seasoned tripe, and the inevitable *gallo pinto*, rice and beans. Also on Vía Argentina are **La Casa de las Costallitas**, which specializes in massive meals of meat and ribs, and the **Pizzeria Paparucchis**, tel 232869, which does excellent pizza and salads. As an antidote to slabs of Panamanian beef then head for the restaurant **Vegetariano Mireya**, tel 694353, Calle Ricardo Arias, which produces a great selection of vegetarian dishes.

INEXPENSIVE

For something a little cheaper try **Mejicanta**, a small, friendly and traditional Mexican restaurant at the junction of Avenida Justo Arosemena, or the **Café Delirys**, at Calle 45 and Avenida Venezuela, which serves a typically Panamanian menu of steak, chicken and seafood. The atmosphere is similarly Panamanian, full of noise and activity, drawing a young, busy crowd. For sheer entertainment the inevitable destination is **La Cascada**, on the seafront at the junction of Avenida 6 Sur and Calle 25, perhaps the city's most famous seafood restaurant. The massive menu includes some crazy claims and the oddest bits of advice, and you eat surrounded by huge plants, several fish tanks and a waterfall. The portions are dauntingly large but the prices surprisingly reasonable.

Good cheap food is available in Casco Viejo, where many cafés serve simple but substantial meals for a few dollars. The best of these is the **Café Coca-Cola**, in the Plaza Santa Ana on Calle 12, which, despite its name, claims to be the oldest restaurant in the city. The café is at the heart of the old city, providing an oasis of air-conditioned civilization. Local businessmen do deals here throughout the day and it offers a fascinating slice of Casco Viejo life. The menu is good and varied, including delicious **corvina**, but watch out for 'Tenderloin steak served on horseback'. The café is open from 7 am–11 pm. Also on the Plaza Santa Ana are the **Santa Ana**, a basic and bustling restaurant that's open 24 hours, and the **Café Jamie**. Back towards the centre of Casco Viejo is **La Victora**, a cheap Chinese place on Avenida Central between Calles 8 and 9.

ENTERTAINMENT AND NIGHTLIFE

There's no doubt that Panamá City is a dangerous place at night, but given the passionate enthusiam of Panamanians, it can also be a lot of fun. If you do decide to venture out late take a taxi and avoid the rougher end of town, particularly Santa Ana, Calidonia and El Chorrillo.

If you simply want to go out for a drink then two of the city's up-market restaurants have popular bars. The **Pavo Real**, tel 263559, Calle 51 in the Bella Vista district, has a pub, complete with darts board. Wednesday night is jazz night, with a live band, and there's a happy hour from 5–7, Mon–Fri. The bar at **Las Tinajas**, also in Calle 51, has a cabaret at around 9 pm on Tuesday, Thursday, Friday and Saturday. Three good discos are **Disco 200**, on Vía Brasil, **Magic**, on Calle 50 and **Bacchus** on Vía España, particularly good on Thursdays—ladies night, although all are packed on Friday and Saturday. If you want to see a wild Panamanian show, a mixture of brothel floor-show and broadway, there are several clubs which offer 'continuous cabaret and striptease'. The most famous of these are the **Costa Brava**, which is in the Edificio Torremolinos on Vía España, and **Le Palace**, on Calle 52 opposite the Hotel Executive.

SPORTS AND ACTIVITIES

Swimming pool: if your hotel doesn't have its own pool then try the Ciudad Olímpica, Calle 31 between Avenidas 1 and 2 sur, where you can cool off in a huge public pool. You'll need a photocopy of your passport to get in. The pool is open 8–12 and 1–4, Tues–Sun.

Cockfighting: principally a rural pastime, cockfighting does have a devoted urban following. Fights are held on Saturday and Sunday evenings at the Club Gallistico on Vía España, tel 6337.

Horse racing: races are staged at the Presidente Ramón racetrack at Juan Díaz, most weekends during the season, which runs from March to September.

Golf: Panamá's imperial connections have endowed the city with a golf course. The Panamá Golf Club, tel 667777, which is in the Canal Zone near the summit gardens, welcomes non-members and you can hire a set of clubs.

USEFUL INFORMATION

American Express

The company's office is on the 12th floor of the Banco Unión building, on Avenida Arosemena, between Calles 42 and 43. The office cannot change cheques but there is an

American Express Bank in Calle 42 (Manuel Maricas), just off Vía España, open Mon–Fri, 8–1.

Cinemas
Films showing in the capital are listed in the 'revista' section of *La Prensa*. The names of cinemas—*cines*—are given, their addresses being:

Alhambra, (six screens) Vía España.
Armador, Plaza Santa Ana.
Arte, Calle 35 between Avenidas 1 and 2 Sur.
Brasil, Vía España and Vía Brasil.
El Dorado, Plaza Santa Ana.
España, Vía España, Obarrio.
Majestic, Calle D, El Cangrejo.
Plaza, Vía España.

Health
The city's best hospital is the **Paitilla Medical Centre** in Paitilla, tel 690333. For cheaper treatment try the Santo Tomás hospital on Avenida Balboa. The **Farmacia Arrocha** on Vía España is open 24 hrs.

Police
Police stations are scattered throughout the city. In Casco Viejo the main office is on Calle 11 and Avenida B. In an emergency dial 104.

Travel agents
The following agents offer both international flights and tours within Panamá. Somebody in the office will always speak English. **Chadwick Travel Service**, tel 522741, inside the YMCA in Balboa. **Mario Tours**, tel 256566, Avenida Justo Arosemena. **Happy Tours**, tel 645004. **Magic Tours**, tel 325836. **Reisa Tours**, tel 254728. **Agencias Giscombe**, tel 640100.

Money Matters
Many banks are reluctant to change traveller's cheques and even those that will can rarely be persuaded to change more than a couple of hundred dollars'. The following banks do change cheques: the **Banco General**, on Vía Argentina, just off Vía España, and at the junction of Avenida Central and Calle 17, open Mon–Fri, 8.30–3 and Sat, 9–12. The **American Express Bank**, in Calle 42 (Manuel Maricas), just off Vía España, open Mon–Fri, 8–1. You can draw money on a Visa card at the **Chase Manhattan Bank** on Calle 47 and Avenida Aquilino de la Guardia.

Telecommunications
The Panamanian phone company, INTEL, has an office on Calle 42, just off Vía España, open Mon–Fri, 8–noon and 1–4.30 and an office in Balboa which is open

478

24 hrs. The main Post Office is in the Plaza Catedral in Casco Viejo. There's also an office on Calle 55, south of Vía España. Both are open from 7 to 5.45.

Taboga

Panamá's 'Island of Flowers', Isla Taboga, lies just 20 km offshore and is immensely popular with Panamanians, particularly at weekends and early in July, when it lives up to its nickname. The island is said to have been used as a base for pirates and it was from here that Pizarro set out for Peru in 1524, although these days it's devoted to fishing and tourism. Taboga's steep sides are covered with tropical forest and rise sharply out of the water. There's just one village and a couple of good beaches, both within easy reach, while on the northern side of the island is a huge pelican colony. Cars are still a rarity here and the village is a picturesque network of tiny street and holiday homes. On 16 July the island celebrates the fiesta of the Virgin of Carmen with a water-born pageant, each boat covered in the island's celebrated flowers.

The boat trip from Balboa to Taboga, which takes about an hour, takes you beneath the Puente de las Américas and through the shipping lanes which approach the entrance to the canal. The water becomes gradually clearer, pelicans waft across the bay and flying fish shoot out from beneath the boat's bows. It leaves from dock 18 in Balboa (from Mon–Fri at 8.30 am and 4 pm, returning at 10 am and 5.30 pm and on Saturday and Sunday from Balboa at 8, 11 am, and 4 pm, returning at 10 am, 3 and 5 pm). Take along your passport. You may have to produce it if the port authorities suspect you of sneaking ashore from a Russian freighter.

There are two simple hotels on the island; the **Hotel Taboga** (US$30 a double) and the **Hotel Chu** (US$20).

Contadora and the Pearl Islands

Further out in the bay is the **Pearl Island Archipelago**, a cluster of 227 small islands set in the crystal-clear waters of the Pacific. The most popular of these is **Contadora**, which is dominated by the **Caesar Park Contadora Hotel**, tel 504033, a huge 150-bed resort, with a casino, a nine-hole golf course, diving, snorkelling, sport-fishing, wind-surfing and sailing. The hotel is a scattering of low buildings and covers 220 of Contadora's 750 acres, the remainder being occupied by exclusive holiday homes. The hotel has attracted a formidable selection of guests, including Jimmy Carter, John Wayne, Patricia Hearst and Julio Iglesias. If you'd like to join their ranks then there are daily flights (US$40 return) to the island and almost every travel agent in Panamá City offers a one, two or three-day tour, including flight and accommodation. At weekends you can also reach the island by boat. The *Successor* leaves Balboa at 8 am, arrives in Contadora at 10 am and returns at 4.30 pm. A return ticket, available from Paradise Tours, tel 230679, costs US$30 and you'll have to pay another US$10 to spend the day in the hotel complex.

However, Contadora is only one of the archipelago's many islands, all of which are beautiful, if a little difficult to visit (although you should be able to arrange a boat from

Contadora). The largest is the Isla del Rey, which is largely covered by dense tropical forest. There are weekly flights to its main village, San Miguel. The other islands, many of which are just a few hundred metres long, are sparsely populated, dotted with small fishing villages and spectacular beaches.

THE PANAMÁ CANAL

We bought it, we paid for it, it's ours, and we should tell Torrijos and company that we are going to keep it.

Ronald Reagan

Panamanians are keen to stress that there's more to Panamá than the canal, but the fact of the matter is that it lies at the nation's heart in every way. More than two-thirds of the population live in the canal corridor and it provides the basis for the nation's transit economy, including the banks, shops and drug deals. Locals tend to have mixed feelings about the canal, aware that it's a huge asset but wary of the instability and dependence that it has brought to their corner of Central America. Control of the canal remains Panamá's most explosive political issue, and we can be sure that the 26,000 US troops who touched down here in December 1989 didn't come to save the rainforest.

The Canal Route

A trip to Panamá without visiting the canal would be almost unthinkable. Fifty years on it remains one of the wonders of the world and has a rugged, industrial beauty; ocean-going vessels waft through the jungle, huge Spanish freighters are gently nudged into the locks and rusting Russian trawlers steam off towards the open sea.

GETTING THERE AND AROUND
Sadly the railway from Panamá City to Colón, which provided the best views of the canal, suspended its passenger services following the US invasion. But a good road, with plenty of buses, runs parallel to the canal from Panamá City to Gamboa. The best places to admire the workings of the canal are the Miraflores and Gatún locks, both of which have facilities for visitors.

Buses to Balboa run every ten minutes or so from the Plaza 5 de Mayo off Avenida Central in Panamá City, heading for Paraíso or Gamboa. If you get off in Balboa you can flag down another to continue to the Miraflores Locks or the Summit gardens.

However, the ideal way to grasp the enormity of the canal is to travel through it by boat. **Reisa Tours**, tel 254728, offer boat trips from Balboa through the Miraflores and Pedro Miguel locks to the Galliard Cut and back again. Or, if you've got a day or two to spare, you can work your way through the canal as a line-handler. Small yachts transiting the canal take on line-handlers to catch the ropes which secure them as they pass through the locks. Yachts are generally taken through the canal twice a week, on Tuesday and Thursday, and they always need extras to help out. If you hang around the yacht club in either Colón or Balboa you should be able to get on a boat. The trip should only take a day, although hold-ups are common.

History

The idea of an inter-ocean canal spanning the waist of the Americas dates back to 1534, when Charles I of Spain ordered the first survey of the isthmus. It took more than three hundred years for the idea to take shape and even then the project was only completed at the second attempt. The first attempt, which began in 1881, was directed by Ferdinand de Lesseps, an inspired Frenchman who had recently completed the Suez Canal. The French plan was for a sea-level canal along the Chagras River. After eight years of digging in the jungle the sheer size of the task eventually overcame them; by early 1889 the canal company was bankrupt. The attempt had cost US$287 million and the lives of at least 20,000 labourers.

In 1903 the project was taken on by the US government, which was initially convinced that the best route would be through Nicaragua, where the San Juan River and Lake Nicaragua would help cover the distance. However, when the French offered to sell their remaining machinery at the bargain price of US$40 million the US government gradually came around to the idea of cutting through Panamá. Nevertheless they insisted on total control of the project and didn't begin to dig until they had engineered a coup in Panamá and on 3 November 1903 manipulated its independence from Colombia.

The completion of the canal took the Americans ten years and cost them some US$387 million. It was a massive and unparalleled feat of engineering, directed by the engineer George Goethals but largely inspired by President Roosevelt. A labour force of 75,000 was imported from around the world, along with everything from dredgers to donkeys. The key to their success was in the design. Instead of digging straight through, from ocean to ocean, as the French had planned, the Americans dammed the Chagras River to create Gatún Lake, forming an artificial Lake Nicaragua, with locks to the north and south lifting ships up into the lake so that they could cross the continental divide. The canal began operating on 15 August 1914 and much of the machinery, including the massive lock gates, is original, maintained with meticulous care at a cost of around US$2 million a week.

The canal is just 83 km long and 150 m wide in most places. It takes eight to ten hours for a ship to pass from ocean to ocean. Around 5% of all ocean trade passes through the canal with over 70% of it going to or from the US. About 30 ships transit the canal each day, paying an average toll of US$26,000, which brings in around a million dollars a day. Tolls are calculated on a net tonnage basis; the highest ever was US$107,000 paid by the *Queen Elizabeth II* in 1988, the lowest 36 c, paid by Richard Halliburton, who swam the canal in 1928.

The canal's future remains somewhat uncertain, overshadowed by tension between Panamá and the US. The Canal Zone, which includes a huge tract of land either side of the waterway, is currently owned and administered by the US, although according to a 1977 treaty the entire operation will be handed over to Panamá in 1999. At the moment it is operated by the Panamá Canal Commission, a US government agency which has a seven member supervisory board—three Panamanians and four Americans. Early in

1990, in accordance with the 1977 treaty, the post of chief administrator was given to a Panamanian, although only after President Bush had vetoed the first Panamanian nomination. The Canal Commission, which has its headquarters in Balboa, currently employs around 1000 US citizens and 6000 Panamanians.

At present the canal is large enough to take 95% of the world's ships but that last 5% carries a huge percentage of world trade and to remain viable the canal must be expanded. Possible developments include creating a fourth set of locks, building a second sea-level canal, and enlarging and improving the existing system. One plan is to widen the Gaillard Cut, which would take 10 years and make two-way traffic possible.

WHAT TO SEE

Ships entering the canal from the Pacific steam under the great span of the **Puente de las Américas**. Beneath the bridge on the eastern bank of the canal is **Balboa**, the home of the Canal Commission, which is an archetypal Canal Zone town: crisp, quiet and extremely well organized. The streets are litter-free, the grass groomed, the houses white and the palm trees arranged in well-drilled ranks. The entire Canal Zone has a deep obsession with discipline and signs tell you what to wear, where to walk, what to touch and how to behave: a desperate effort to impose order on Panamá's unpredictable spontaneity. According to Paul Theroux, who passed through here in 1979, life in the Zone is comfortably cushioned: 'The Zonian is living in a company house; he drives on company roads, send his children to a company school, banks at the company bank ... the system is maddening but if the Zonian is driven crazy there is a company psychiatrist'.

Balboa is made up of US bases, port facilities and canal administration buildings, a large YMCA, where anyone can eat but only company men can stay, and an abundance of churches. The town's grand avenue (on your right as you enter town from Panamá City) is the **El Prado Boulevard**, a tree-lined avenue which leads up to the Canal Commission's Administration building, a huge white block which serves as a monument to US colonial muscle. Alongside the boulevard are patches of grass which duplicate the exact dimensions of the canal's locks and at its bottom end is the **Stevens Circle**, where Kuna Indians usually sell their wares. At the other end, beneath the Canal Administration building, is a **memorial to George Goethals**, who succeeded Stevens and was the canal's chief engineer from 1907 until its completion in 1914. The monument is made up of a large marble shaft, intended to represent the continental divide, which stands in the centre of a fountain. The water runs off into three small basins representing the locks.

From the monument a grand staircase leads up to the **Administration Building**, in front of which is a chunk of rock from the Gaillard Cut, extracted when the cut was widened in the 1960s. The entrance to the building (open 7.15–4.15) is around the back and visitors are allowed in to look at the murals inside the *rotonda*, four superb, strident images, depicting the building of the canal: the digging of the Gaillard Cut, the construction of the Gatún Locks, the slipway of the Gatún Dam and the Miraflores Locks. At the centre of the *rotonda* is a bust of Roosevelt; in the shadows behind is Ferdinand de Lesseps.

The Miraflores Locks

North of Balboa the main road to Gamboa runs past Fort Clayton and the **Albrook Air Force Base** to a busy US military establishment with fleets of helicopters shuttling in and out. Opposite this base are the two **Miraflores Locks**, the first stage in a ship's passage from the Pacific to Gatún Lake. The lower of these locks is the largest in the canal and has to cope with the extreme tidal variations of the Pacific—from 380–640 cm.

Ships entering the locks are tied to several locomotives known as 'mules', which haul them with amazing accuracy. The original 'mules' were made in the US, although these days they're supplied by Mitsubishi. Once the ship is secure millions of gallons of water flood in and lift it gracefully to the height of the next section.

Alongside the locks is an observation platform (open 8–5) from where you get an excellent view of passing ships and the operation of the locks. A Canal Commission guide gives a commentary in Spanish and English, explaining the mechanics of the canal and giving a brief history of its construction.

Just 1.5 km north of the Miraflores Locks, across the Miraflores Lake, are the Pedro Miguel Locks, which lift ships to the height of Gatún Lake and mark the entrance to the notorious Gaillard Cut. It was this stretch, spanning the continental divide, which was by far the hardest challenge for the builders of the canal. Its unstable structure and steep sides combined to unleash countless landslides and the same sections had to be dug time and time again.

The Summit Gardens, Gamboa and Gatún Lake

A few kilometres beyond the Pedro Miguel Locks the road runs through dense forest as it climbs the continental divide, which is marked by the **Summit Botanical Garden**: a small zoo and huge collection of tropical plants and trees, which includes some 15,000 species. The gardens (open 8–4) were created by the Canal Commission in 1923 but under the 1977 canal treaty they were handed back to Panamá in 1979. Buses heading to Gamboa from the Plaza 5 de Mayo in Panamá City pass the Summit Gardens.

Heading north the road drops through the forest and crosses the Chagres River to reach Gamboa, yet another neat and regimented Canal Zone town. Ships emerge from the Gaillard Cut at Gamboa and enter the huge **Gatún Lake**: a great forest bowl, the size of Barbados, which was flooded for the creation of the canal. Large parts of the lake are perilously shallow and outside the shipping lanes dead trees still show above the surface. The lake also serves as a massive reservoir, maintaining the water level at 26 m above sea-level and feeding the locks. However, large amounts of silt, washed out of the deforested mountains, are now clogging the channels and despite the best efforts of the dredging division the problem has to be stopped at source and the surrounding area has now been declared a forest reserve to prevent further soil erosion.

When Gatún Lake was flooded the forest animals fled onto several hills, which eventually became islands. The largest of these, **Barro Colorado Island**, is a nature reserve and research station operated by the Smithsonian Institute and an excellent place to see wildlife. The island is home to an enormous population of tropical animals and birds, including a semi-tame tapir, and there's a nature trail. (The institute publish a guide, which is available at their offices in Ancón.) Access to the island is restricted so you need to book in advance. Trips are made on Tuesdays, for individuals, and on Saturdays for groups, leaving Gamboa at 8 am, returning at 4.30 pm. Reservations must be made through Maria Morello at the Smithsonian Institute in Ancón, tel 276022.

Gatún Locks and Fort San Lorenzo

At the northern end of the canal are the **Gatún Locks,** three massive locks which lift ships a total of 28 m, taking them directly between Gatún Lake and the Caribbean. A small **visitors' centre** offers superb views of the activity here. The viewing platform is only metres from the edge of the lock and you can see down into the depths and watch the line-handlers struggling to control ships as they ease into the locks. Gatún is a little harder to get to, reached by road from Colón. Buses from Colón run every couple of hours, heading for Chapira.

To the west of Gatún Locks is Gatún Dam, a massive concrete span which is the key to the canal's design, blocking the Chagras River and holding back the waters of Gatún Lake. A road runs from the locks to the dam, crossing the river below the dam.

Further west still, at the mouth of the Chagres River are the **ruins of the Spanish forts** of San Lorenzo, a squat, solid structure which dates from the 16th century, although there are also some 18th-century additions. The fort, which guarded Panamá's backdoor, is perched on a cliff high above the river. The sight is superb, with expansive views across the river and into surrounding jungle. The fort is about an hour's drive from Colón. Take the road to Gatún, where you can cross the canal below the locks and then head out past Fort Sherman.

COLÓN AND THE CARIBBEAN COAST

Panamá's second city has a daunting reputation for drugs. US troops, heading for a night on the town, are now warned that they are 'entering the most dangerous place in the world!' Forty years of economic decline has left Colón at the mercy of drugs, violence, poverty and unemployment, its bold colonial architecture now cracked and crumbling.

Nevertheless Colón is an amazing place: a steamy tropical port, steeped in history and alive with Caribbean hustle, wit and warmth, offering sailors the chance to indulge in every imaginable sin! Its clubs and bars are wildly cosmopolitan, their clientele ranging from Polish deckhands to Colombian prostitutes. Few travellers are sufficiently tempted by the city's attractions to take on the risks and it's even avoided by the majority of Panamanians. If you do decide to brave the streets of Colón then there is a very real possibility that you'll be robbed. To minimize this likelihood stick to the main streets and don't wear jewellery or carry luggage. Always travel by taxi at night.

History

Founded in 1850 Colón is a transit terminal, originally created as the railway's northern terminus. John Lloyd Stevens, diplomat, explorer and director of the railway christened the town Aspinwall, after one of the founders of the railway, but the Colombians insisted on calling it Colón, after Christopher Columbus—a dispute which dragged on for decades, although today Colón is uncontested. During the building of the canal the town was a hotbed of poverty, disease and prostitution, although some of the outlying suburbs became immensely wealthy.

Colón functioned as the country's main port and all essential equipment for the canal, from shovels to shoes, arrived here from Europe and the US, along with French prostitutes—known as 'lobsters'—and fortune-hunters from around the globe. In 1885 the entire town was set on fire by rebels during the Prestan uprising—which was prompted by rivalry between Colombian liberals and conservatives. Railway engineers swiftly rebuilt the city but it soon sunk back into its former squalor.

With the canal up and running, Colón became one of the great port cities of the Americas: cruise liners and merchant ships from around the world called in to indulge in the traditional pleasures of port life. Goods from every corner of the globe could be bought on Front Street and the city's clubs and bars offered some of the most outrageous cabaret in Latin America.

Today around 15,000 ships pass through Cristóbal—Colón's Canal Zone sister town—every year and the port handles over two million tons of cargo, much of it associated with the Colón Free Zone. Nevertheless a large proportion of Colón's population live in desperate poverty and the city has an air of terminal decline, its main streets dotted with empty buildings which soon give way to rough, overcrowded slums.

GETTING THERE AND AROUND

Express buses for Colón leave from Avenida Central and Calle B in Panamá City. The journey takes an hour and a half. Buses from Colón to Panamá City, Portobelo, La Guaira (for Isla Grande) and Cuipo (for Gatún Locks) all leave from the bus terminal on Avenida Bolívar. There are also hourly flights from the Paitilla airport in Panamá City to Colón with Aeroperlas, tel 694555.

If you don't have a car the best way to see Colón is to travel on the city buses—the 'Ruta Circular' runs a large loop through the city, beside the Free Zone, past the hospital, down Avenida Bolívar and back up Avenida Central. To get to the Free Zone get on any bus marked 'Zona Libre'.

WHAT TO SEE

Among the horror of contemporary Colón lies the remains of a planned colonial town, modelled on New Orleans, with sweeping colonial structures and broad balconies. There are three main streets: Avenida Bolívar, which is lined with busts of the city's famous sons; Avenida Central, which is where you'll find most of the shops, bars and cafés; and Front Street, which is home to up-market boutiques, travel agents and car-hire companies. The more impressive older buildings are the **railway station**, the **cathedral** and the grand **Hotel Washington**, which is at the north western tip of the city, surrounded by rough slums. Across the railway tracks to the west is **Cristóbal**: the contrast is astonishing as you pass clean white buildings and quiet streets, the discipline of the Canal Zone replacing the desperate vitality of Colón.

The Colón Free Zone

Occupying a huge block in the southwest of the city is the **Colón Free Zone**, the city's commercial tax haven: a bizarre, bulk-buy, international shopping centre where US$4 billion worth of goods changes hands every year.

Opened in 1948, in a bid to stave off the city's post-war depression, this is now the second-largest free zone in the world, matched only by Hong Kong. Some 500 companies, from all around the world, employ over 5000 people in warehousing, regional distribution, manufacturing and sales, accounting for 3% of Panamá's gross national product. Companies located here are free from almost all government interference; they require no licence to trade and pay no taxes and the US government has repeatedly alleged that the Zone is used to launder drug money. But while the streets of the Free Zone are as clean and prosperous as a Californian suburb, little of this wealth has filtered through the fence and the city itself still has more in common with Calcutta.

The Free Zone makes an interesting excursion from Colón—if only to experience the extreme culture shock. The Zone is sealed within a massive fence, with an entrance on Calle 13, where you'll need to show your passport. Most goods are sold in bulk but some shops also sell to the public. According to the rules goods bought here are held in bond and flown directly to the international airport in Panamá City, where you pick them up from the customs department when you leave. However with smaller items, and particularly clothing, you can usually just walk out the gate.

WHERE TO STAY AND EAT
When it comes to finding a hotel in Colón security has to be top priority, although things are really only in doubt at the cheaper end of the market. The **Hotel Washington**, tel 471870, is the city's oldest and grandest hotel and even if you're only in Colón for the day then this is an excellent place for lunch, as is the restaurant in the **Yacht Club**. Other more moderate hotels worth a try are the **Hotel Internacional**, tel 452930, or the **Ancón**, both on Bolívar, the **Andros**, tel 478921, the **Atlantic**, on Avenida Central, while for inexpensive accommodation the **Hotel Plaza** is safe.

Portobelo and Isla Grande

About 50 km northeast of Colón is Portobelo, a small town at the back of a magnificent bay, which once provided a vital link in Spain's communications with its Latin American empire, a role which still echoes around the world, with this forgotten corner of Panamá lending its name to markets, towns and ports from Scotland to New Zealand.

The Spanish founded a settlement here in 1597, after their fort at Nombre de Dios was sacked by English pirates. For two centuries Portobelo stood at the northern end of the Camino Real, 'the royal road'. Thousands of tons of gold and silver, looted from Latin America, arrived here from Panamá City on mule trains and was stored in the *Aduana* or customs house, until an armada of galleons arrived to take it home. The site was an obvious target for pirate raids and it was probably with this is mind that the Spaniards chose the bay, with its steep sides and west-facing entrance protecting it from pirate attacks and Caribbean storms. Nevertheless, in November 1737 a handful of English pirates, under the command of Admiral Vernon, managed to take control of the town. They were, however, six weeks too late: the *Aduana* was empty, its massive gold reserves already bound for Spain. Seething with frustration, the Admiral stayed in Portobelo for six weeks, dismantling the surrounding fortifications.

WHAT TO SEE

Today Portobelo is small and extremely sleepy. The deep bay is popular with passing yachtsmen, and the ruined *Aduana* remains one of the largest buildings in town. The bay is extremely beautiful, ringed by steep-sided hills and dotted with the remains of **Spanish forts** where great lead cannons rest idly on their battlements. Two impressive forts flank the town although the large, three-tiered fort on the other side of the bay is perhaps the most beautiful, with fantastic views from its hilltop site—you should have no trouble persuading someone to take you across for a couple of dollars.

Portobelo itself is dominated by the ruined *Aduana* and a large 18th-century **Cathedral**, which houses the town's famous wooden **Black Christ**. The image was rescued from a sinking Spanish galleon and several miracles have been attributed to it. During the town's **fiesta**, on 21 October, which is a crazy mix of religious passion, drink and dance, the statue is paraded through the streets.

The surrounding coastline is lush with tropical forest and scattered with beaches, coral reefs and small offshore islands. The road from Colón runs just behind the shore, passing the black sand beaches of **Playa Langosta** and **María Chiquita**. Several other beaches can be reached from Portobelo, including those on the **Isla de Drake**, a small uninhabited island just outside the bay, and **Drake's Cove**, which is said to be the final resting place of Sir Francis Drake, who was buried at sea in a lead coffin. If you want to head off in search of lead coffins or sandy beaches then Carlos Palmer, who lives in Portobelo, at the entrance to the town, hires out his services as a boatman and guide.

Isla Grande

To the northwest of Portobelo, surrounded by the turquoise waters of the Caribbean, is the beautiful **Isla Grande**, a great forested mound which rises out of the water a kilometre or so offshore. The island is about 2 km in width and perhaps double that in length, and there's really only one thing to do here—enjoy the sun and the sand! The southern side of the island is inhabited and the southwestern tip, which has the finest beach, is occupied by the **Hotel Isla Grande**, where you can hire water-sports equipment. On the heavily forested northern side is a steel lighthouse built by the French in 1893. The island is popular with Panamanian tourists and US troops, at the weekends, but virtually deserted during the week when hotel prices are significantly lower.

Isla Mamey

To the west of the Isla Grande is the more remote **Isla Mamey**, one of the best places to dive in Panamá. Dive sites include several colonial shipwrecks, a crashed plane and a maze of mangrove swamps. **Reisa Tours** in Panamá City offer one-day and overnight tours to the island, or if you'd like to visit Isla Mamey under your own steam, call **Scuba Mamey** in Panamá City, tel 618003, to make a reservation. Facilities on the island are fairly basic and camping is allowed.

GETTING THERE

Buses from Colón's bus terminal run to Portobelo every hour or so. From Panamá City, change buses at Sabanitas, a couple of km before Colón. To get to Isla Grande you'll need to take a bus to La Guaira—you can pick these up in Colón, Sabanitas or Portobelo.

The journey from Colón to Portobelo takes 1½ hrs, and it's another 45 minutes to La Guaira. The last bus leaves Colón at about 5. There's a steady shuttle of boats taking passengers from the village to Isla Grande.

WHERE TO STAY
Sadly there are no hotels in Portobelo so you'll have to head on through and stay on or near Isla Grande. In La Guaira, the village opposite Isla Grande, is **Cabañas Monte Carlo**, while on the island itself are several moderately priced hotels. The best is the **Hotel Isla Grande**, tel 643046 or 614211, a beautiful beach hotel with cabins scattered beneath the palm trees. There's a choice of bungalows or rooms and Abraham Sadd, who runs the hotel, is immensely accommodating. Accommodation is also available at **Cabanas Jackson** and **La Cholita**, which has a range of air-conditioned cabins.

The San Blás Islands

Safe in their island stronghold Panamá's Kuna Indians have fought off outsiders for more than 400 years and are among the most sophisticated and successful tribes in Central America. Their home is the San Blás Islands, a chain of some 365 islands which stretches for 300 km along Panamá's northeast coast, and are a superb mix of crystal-clear waters, coral reefs, thick tropical forest and palm-fringed beaches.

Before the arrival of the Spanish the Kuna lived in Panamá's jungles, but pressure applied by the Spanish and local Choco Indians gradually forced them north, and in the mid-18th century they began relocating onto the San Blás islands. The Spanish had visited the islands as early as 1501 but had little interest. Over the next 100 years it became a Kuna homeland, occasionally visited by traders and pirates. However, by the mid-19th century the Kuna came into increasing conflict with outsiders and on several occasions used violence to expel European traders and colonists. During the building of the Panamá canal, engineers searching for high-quality sand found huge reserves here, but the Kuna declared that the land, water and sand were gifts from God. The engineers were permitted to anchor overnight on the condition that they left at dawn and never returned.

Matters eventually came to a head in 1925, when the Kuna staged a bloody revolt against the mounting pressure from Catholic missionaries and the Panamanian government. This led to the recognition of all Kuna territory as the Comarca de San Blás, which was given partial autonomy and in which non-Kunas are not permitted to own land. Inside the Comarca, Kuna run the majority of businesses, including transport, hotels and shops. The Comarca is administered by the Kuna National Congress, which meets twice a year, and is presided over by three national chiefs, who represent the Kuna in national politics. Kuna society is matrilineal, rooted in a traditional religion focused on an Earth Mother deity. Their economy is based on farming and fishing. Kuna women wear incredibly beautiful, hand-made costumes, including *molas*—embroidered blouses—and huge amounts of gold jewellery. (They charge 25c for a photograph.)

In 1985 the Kuna became the first indigenous group in Central America to create their own forest reserve, **The Kuna Wildlife Project**, which covers 60,000 acres of mainland forest and is being preserved using traditional Kuna techniques. Inside the reserve is a learning centre, where non-Kunas are instructed in rainforest management techniques and scientists are carrying out research. The reserve is situated where the road to Cartí enters the Comarca and was intended to protect the forest from the exploitation which usually accompanies road-building.

GETTING AROUND AND TOURS

Several travel companies offer trips to the San Blás, ranging from one day to a week. These include **Reisa tours**, tel 254728, **Happy Tours**, tel 645001, **Por El Mundo**, tel 646152, **Chadwick Travel Service**, tel 522942. If you are prepared to be flexible you can organize your own trip by simply flying to El Porvenir and arranging travel and accommodation once you arrive. ANSA, tel 267891 or 266881, fly daily from the Paitilla airport in Panamá City to the island of El Porvenir at 6 am, returning at 5 pm. From El Porvenir, which is a small island and government outpost, you can take a boat to one of the other islands or arrange a one-day tour taking in several islands.

WHERE TO STAY AND EAT

The Kuna have restricted tourist development to a handful of simple but expensive hotels. The **Hotel El Porvenir** is on the island of the same name, near the landing strip; the management can arrange a tour of the islands or a boat to any of the other islands. The other hotels are on the islands to the east. **The Hotel Anay**, tel 206596, is situated on the beautiful Wichub Wala island, and the cheapest hotel on the islands is the **Hotel Nargana**, on Nargana island. Further east still is the **Hotel Las Palmeras**, tel 223096, on Ailigandí. All the hotels have restaurants, serving superb local seafood.

WESTERN PANAMÁ

Western Panamá is cut off from the capital by the canal, a gulf which is bridged by the massive span of the Puente de las Américas, completed in 1962, which offers superb views of the docks at Balboa and of ocean liners approaching the Miraflores Locks. Across the bridge the highway skirts the perimeter of several US bases and heads up into the hills.

The Cerro Campana National Park

The Cerro Campana is Panamá's most developed National Park. Situated just 50 km from the capital it covers some 4800 hectares, embracing at least five distinct ecosystems, from dry tropical forest to cloud forest. But don't get too excited; not only is it difficult to get to the park, the area has only basic facilities and just a couple of simple trails. There are no buses to the park so those without cars must walk the 8 km from the highway, along a road which branches off just beyond the village of Capira. Camping is permitted but bring your own food.

The Pacific Beaches

Beyond Cerro Campana the highway swings around to the south and drops out of the mountains towards the Pacific, with views of the coast opening out ahead. Once it reaches sea level the road runs parallel to the shore for some 60 km, within a couple of kilometres of the Pacific and providing excellent access to a continuous string of beautiful sandy beaches.

Jutting out into the ocean at the end of this stretch is **Punta Chame**, a narrow spit of sand with a handful of hotels and restaurants. The spit provided the bulk of sand used in mixing concrete for the canal, but plenty remains. Heading on west you pass the beaches at **Nueva Gorgona, Playa Coronado**, which is the most popular, **San Carlos, El Palmar, Río Mar**, which has the best surf; **Santa Clara** and finally **Fallaron**. So if you're driving it's easy to sample three or four places before choosing where to spend the night or heading back to Panamá City.

El Valle

In the mountains behind this Panamanian riviera the resort town of **El Valle** (pronounced 'ballet') is tucked into a massive forested bowl which was once the cone of a volcano. El Valle is a favourite weekend destination for Panamanians, who spend their nights in the cool of the mountains and descend to the beaches during the day. A large tourist market is held here on Sundays and the surrounding hills offer excellent walking. The forests on the east side of the bowl are famous for their square-trunked trees and golden toads, both of which can also be seen in the Cerro Campana National Park, and there are also several small waterfalls within easy walking distance. The best is **El Chorro Macho**—to get there walk through the village, past the church, cross the bridge and turn right, and then left after the second bridge. Another popular walk is to **El Indio Durmiendo**, a softly rounded peak to the west, which gives good views of the valley below.

GETTING AROUND
Buses to and from the Avenida B terminal in Panamá City operate every 30 minutes or so along the highway, from 5 am to 9 pm. There are no direct buses to the beaches. Buses to El Valle leave the terminal every couple of hours.

WHERE TO STAY AND EAT
The first good-quality hotels you'll come across are on the Pacific beaches. There are some excellent moderately priced places at Punta Chame (the **Motel Punta Chame**, tel 231747, and the **Club Bahía**, tel 691065), in San Carlos (the **Hotel Playa Río Mar**, tel 642272, the **Hotel El Palmar** and the **Cabañas Río Mar**), at Santa Clara (the **Cabañas Pericar** and **Cabañas Las Sirena**), at Fallaron (the **Hotel Fallaron**) and at Nueva Gorgona (the **Hotel Gorgona Jayes**, tel 237775). All the above are in the expensive range and have swimming pools and restaurants, while some also offer air conditioning. For inexpensive accommodation San Carlos and Coronado are your best bet. There are also several good hotels in El Valle and the surrounding area. The best is the luxury **Hotel Campestre**, tel 936146, a beautiful hacienda-style building raised up on the western side of the valley with superb views of the surrounding hills and a small collection of tropical birds. Alternatively you could settle for the moderately priced **Hotel Greco** which is on the main entrance road, or the inexpensive **Pensión Niña Delia**, which offers the cheapest accommodation.

The Azuero Peninsula

Jutting south into the Pacific the **Azuero Peninsula** is a stronghold of Panamanian rural traditions, famous for its hospitality, fiestas and Saturday-night drinking binges. The land is scattered with cattle farms and rice fields. During the rainy season the hills and grassland are lush with greenery, but under the scorching sun they soon turn a sandy brown and bus travellers are coated in soft yellow dust. The central area is covered with low-lying hills and few roads penetrate the southwestern tip of the peninsula, where the only settlements are small coastal villages.

The people here are deeply conservative, their lives bound up in rural traditions, including the manufacture of traditional pottery and old-style cowboy culture, united by an all-pervading air of colonial formality. Life revolves around the family and farming; at weekends young couples promenade in village plazas and horsemen parade through the streets, flaunting their skills, horses and traditional silver saddle-work.

Chitré and Los Santos

The twin towns of Chitré and Los Santos are the main centres of population and the gulf between the two says a lot about the region. The larger, **Chitré**, is a bustling commercial centre, its streets busy with traffic, its shops packed with goods. Here the plaza is dominated by a huge, cool church, with a stern, dark-wood ceiling, while the market behind sells locally woven straw hats and traditional pottery, most of which is made in the nearby village of Arena. The town also has a small regional museum, the **Museo de Herrera** (open 8.30–noon and 1–4, Tues–Sat; 9–noon on Sun), housed in an old-style mansion on the corner of the Parque La Bandera. The museum focuses clearly on the traditions of Herrera; the ground floor is devoted to pre-Columbian history, with interesting artefacts from local Indian tribes, while upstairs exhibits focus on colonial traditions and modern fiestas. Chitré's own **fiesta**, the Feria de Azuero, is held in April.

Just 4 km to the south **Los Santos** has preserved a peaceful, old-world atmosphere. Sleepy and sedate, the town feels almost deserted. Not to be outdone it has its own small museum, **The Museum of Panamanian Nationality** (open 9–noon and 2–4.30, Mon–Sat; 1–4 on Sun), in the central plaza.

A Back Route Through Ocú and Las Minas

West from Chitré an interesting alternative to the Pan-American Highway is to travel the back roads through the hills at the heart of the peninsula. From Chitré the road heads west through several small villages, including **Los Pozos, Pese, Las Minas** and **Ocú**, all of which are deeply traditional communities. The road rises high in the hills; the massive plains spread out below. Minibuses from Chitré run as far as Las Minas, a journey of 2–3 hrs, from where there are two or three minibuses a day to Ocú, another 40 minutes, from where there is a regular shuttle to Santiago.

Las Tablas, Pedasí and the Southern Beaches

Another 27 km south of Los Santos is **Las Tablas**, a smaller farming centre which is the official provincial capital. The town is pervaded by an air of formality, most notably at weekends, when young lovers walk around the plaza hand-in-hand, families wander through the streets and groups of men spend the entire weekend drinking. Further south is **Pedasí**, yet another small and traditional farming town, from where you can reach a number of good beaches. To the east of the town the beaches at **El Toro** and **La Arenal** are both about 25 minutes' walk along dirt tracks (passable with four-wheel-drive). By far the best beach on the peninsula is **Playa Venao**, another 15 km to the south, a beautiful sweep of sand, blocked at either end by steep, forested hills. The beach is popular with surfers and the eastern end, sheltered by a rocky outcrop, provides excellent safe swimming.

To avoid returning by the same route it is possible to head back to Las Tablas or Los Santos via Tonosí. A couple of minibuses provide the only public transport along this route and four-wheel-drive is necessary.

GETTING AROUND
Buses between Chitré and Panamá City (the Avenida B terminal) run every hour or so throughout the day. From Chitré minibuses from behind the church run to Los Santos, Las Tablas and Pedasi. From Pedasi three of four daily minibuses to Canas and Tonosi run past Playa Venao.

WHERE TO STAY
All the best hotels on the peninsula are in Chitré. On the main plaza is the moderately priced **Hotel Rex**, tel 964310, which has the benefit of air conditioning. The next best option is the **Hotel El Prado**, tel 964621, on Avenida Herrera, or the **Hotel Santa Rita**, tel 964610, on Calle Manuel Macorrea. The best of the inexpensive hotels is the **Pensión Herrera**, on Avenida Herrera, but avoid the front rooms where the noise of traffic is deafening.

In Los Santos, beside the entrance road, is the moderately priced **Hotel La Villa**, tel 964845, but there's little to recommend it and you might as well stay in Chitré.

In Las Tablas the best hotel is the **Hotel Piamonte**, tel 946372, but there are also a couple of basic inexpensive hotels: the **Pensión Mariela**, opposite the Piamonte, which is the better of the two, and the **Pensión Marta**. In Pedasi the **Pensión Moscoso**, a delightful and friendly hotel, provides inexpensive accommodation. None of the beaches immediately to the east have accommodation, although you can always camp, or rent a cabin at the **Playa Venao**, where there's also a simple restaurant.

Santiago

Billed as 'The City Of the Future' Santiago is far from promising. With a population of some 30,000 the city occupies an important commercial position, halfway between Panamá City and David, but is dominated by rough commercial activity, its main street bursting with cut-price shops, cheap restaurants, grimy bars and truckers' hotels. There's plenty of action and the town has an invigorating energy, but there are no formal tourist attractions and the architecture is modern and unremarkable. From a practical point of view the town has a couple of banks, an abundance of restaurants and a single cinema.

North to San Francisco and the Caribbean

To the north of Santiago a paved road struggles up into the mountains, rollercoasting through the foothills. It passes through **San Francisco**, a small farming village with a beautiful colonial church; decades of decay severely damaged the building's roof, which was recently replaced, although the original carved beams and altar have been carefully preserved.

Up above San Francisco the village of *Santa Fé* nestles in a beautiful bowl-shaped valley, overshadowed by superb, sharp peaks. Blessed with the clear air and a cool climate the village is popular at weekends, when people from Santiago come to escape the heat and enjoy a cockfight. It is also a good place to enjoy the mountains; horses can sometimes be hired here, or you can climb one of the surrounding peaks. The most impressive of these is the Cerro de los Gringos, which towers above the village to the west and is named after a group of North Americans who claim to have been the first to reach the summit—the peak is marked by a plaque celebrating their achievement. The mountain can be climbed in a day, but to see it at its best you should spend a night near the top, either camping out or sleeping in one of the caves. A much easier climb is the Cerro Tuto, which stands in front of the Cerro de los Gringos and is a comfortable day trip. There are trails to both peaks although you'll certainly need a guide.

GETTING AROUND

Buses run between Santiago and Panamá City every half hour or so. In Panamá they leave from the Avenida B terminal and in Santiago from the purpose-built terminal on the edge of town, which is halfway between the centre of town and the highway. From here you'll also find hourly buses to Santa Fé, San Francisco, Chitré and Los Santos, Ocú and David.

WHERE TO STAY

If you do choose to stay in Santiago the best hotel is the **Piramidical**, tel 982571, which is an expensive hotel outside the town on the highway. If that's full then try the nearby **Hotel Gran David**, tel 984510, also on the highway. In the town itself the best option is the inexpensive **Hotel Santiago**, tel 984824, to the left of the church, which is good, clean and air-conditioned. In Santa Fé there's a very basic *pensión* in one of the houses on the plaza and up above the village is a hotel with double cabins. The hotel has a cock-fighting pit and is popular and noisy when fights are scheduled, but empty at other times.

Chiriquí

Panamá's extreme western province of Chiriquí has little in common with either the aggression of Panamá City or the poverty of Colón and has developed independently, largely on the basis of its abundant natural resources. Locals often argue that the province would be better off on its own.

493

Northern Chiriquí is dominated by a marvellously beautiful section of the Cordillera Central, dotted with volcanic peaks, coffee plantations and tracts of dense forest. To the south the fertile coastal plain produces rice, beef, sugar, shrimp, beer, rum, bananas, fish and corn. The province is also home to the majority of Panamá's Guayami Indians, who live scattered in the highlands and around the small town of Tolé, to the east of David. There are a total of 45,000 Guayami in Panamá, spread across the provinces of Chiriquí, Veraguas and Bocas del Toro. Guayami women are unmistakable, wearing vivid traditional dresses, made with bold primary colours, and can often be seen on the streets of David. Meanwhile among the *ladino* population the traditions associated with Panamá's cowboy culture are strong here, including rodeos, cock fights and heavy drinking.

David

Wealthy, sedate and, by Panamanian standards, deeply civilized, **David**—pronounced Da-veed—is Panamá's third city and the only large town that's not inextricably bound up with the canal. The city is the centre of a prosperous agricultural area and serves as a focus of transport and commerce, although it has little to offer the visitor beyond an array of urban pleasures. Founded in colonial times the city is laid out on a strict grid pattern, centred on a pleasant plaza, known as the **Parque Cervantes**, where shoeshine boys and waiting taxis are shaded by massive trees. To the north of the plaza is a roughish part of town, centred on the busy market and bus terminal, while to the east you'll find up-market shops, hotels and smart residential districts. The city's church is modern, as are the majority of the other buildings and the only tourist attraction is the **Museo de Historia y de Arte**, Tues–Sat, 8–4, on 8 Avenida Este, in a beautiful old colonial mansion just south of the junction with Calle A Norte. The building itself justifies a visit and the museum, though small, includes some interesting artefacts relating both to the region and to Panamá as a whole. The ground floor is devoted to pre-Columbian history and Indian heritage, while upstairs you'll find a series of displays relating to the colonial era, the church and, inevitably, the building of the canal.

WHERE TO STAY
David's finest hotel is the **Hotel Fiesta**, an expensive, modern hotel outside the town on the Pan-American Highway. Much more convenient for enjoying the city itself is the **Hotel Nacional**, at the corner of Calle Central and Avenida 1a Este, two blocks west of the plaza. The hotel has a casino, pool and tennis court. Right in the centre of town, on the plaza, is the **Hotel Iris**, which is moderately priced, clean, air conditioned, but windowless. Also on the plaza and similarly priced is the **Hotel Occidental**, also air conditioned. A couple of blocks to the south of the plaza is the **Hotel Panamá Rey**, at the junction of Avenida 3a Este and Calle A Sur, which is the tallest building in town. Inexpensive hotels in David are rough and rare: of the **Hotel La Fortuna**, on Calle A Norte, and the **Hotel Rocio**, on Avenida 5a Este, the latter is marginally better.

EATING OUT
The **Café Jimar**, a block west of the plaza, serves filling Panamanian food and is at the heart of daily life in David, while around the corner, along Avenida 3a Este, are several

cheaper places and a couple of Chinese restaurants. For something a little more up-market there are a number of good restaurants in the streets around the **Hotel Nacional**, including **Sarti**, which serves a good range of pizzas and **Los Churrascos**, a block west of the plaza on Avenida 2 Este, which does formidable Panamanian-style steaks.

ACTIVITIES

David's delights are strictly urban: there's a **bowling alley** (open 3–11, beside the Hotel Nacional on Avenida 1a Este; two **cinemas**, the Cine David at the far southern end of Avenida 1a Este and the Cine Plaza on Calle B Norte—the films of the day are advertised in the plaza; and plenty of **pool halls**, on Avenida 3a Este. The **casino** and **swimming pool** at the Hotel Nacional are open to non-residents for a small fee.

GETTING THERE

Express buses run from Panamá City to David every hour or so from 7 to 7, with an express service at midnight. In Panamá City they leave from a separate terminal just south of the main Avenida B terminal and in David from the main bus terminal which is on Avenida Obaldia, three blocks northwest of the plaza. The journey takes about 8 hrs. Also from the terminal in David there are buses every 20 minutes to the border with Costa Rica (2½ hrs); to Puerto Armuelles (2½ hrs) every hour; to Río Sereno (3 hrs) every two hours from 7 to 5; to Boquete (1 hr) every hour from 6 am to 7 pm; to Volcán del Hato (1½ hrs) every hour; to Cerro Punta (2 hrs) every hour; and to Chiriquí Grande (3 hrs) every two hours from 6 to 5.

There are four flights daily from the Paitilla airport in Panamá City to David. The journey takes about an hour and costs US$50 one-way. To confirm the schedule contact **Aeroperlas**, in Panamá on 694555, or in David on 754362, or **Alas Chiricanas** on 646448. There are also daily flights from David to Changuinola in Bocas del Toro.

USEFUL INFORMATION

The **Panamanian Tourist Board** has an office in the southeast corner of the plaza above the 'Fino' clothes store. The entrance is on Avenida 4 Este, beneath the ITAP sign, and the office is open Mon–Fri, 8.30–4.30. You have to work hard to extract any useful information from the staff.

The **Post Office**, open Mon–Sat, 7–5.45, is on Calle C Norte—a block north of the plaza—as is the **phone company**, INTEL, open Mon–Sat, 8–noon and 1–4.

There are branches of **Citibank** and the **Banco Nacional** on the plaza. Neither are particularly enthusiastic about changing traveller's cheques, although Citibank will usually change at least US$100 worth.

If you need a visa (US$20) to enter Costa Rica there's a **Costa Rican consul**, Avenida 3 Oeste and Calle E Norte, open Mon–Fri, 9–1. There's also a **Panamanian Immigration office** in Calle C Sur, between Avenidas 1 Este and Central.

Budget Car Hire have an office in David on Avenida 7 Este, tel 755597, as do **Hertz**, tel 756829.

THE CORDILLERA CENTRAL

To the north of David are Panamá's tallest and wildest mountains, **the Cordillera Central**, a range of sharp peaks and dense forests, amongst which are several small towns and villages in the high valleys. Two routes penetrate this complex landscape, winding up through lush valleys, coffee plantations and pine forests, alongside fresh, clear streams.

Concepción, Río Sereno, Volcán and Cerro Punta

To the west of David is **Concepción**, a traditional town which lies at the heart of cowboy country and is the centre of the saddle-making industry. At weekends the town is a popular venue for cockfighting, which is now illegal in Costa Rica but remains a national passion in Panamá, particularly in the Chiriquí area. Fights are staged in specially made 'pits'. Visitors are always welcome, and the atmosphere is both exhilarating and horrific as the audience is swept up in a heady atmosphere of alchohol, blood and betting!

From Concepción an excellent paved road climbs into mountains, twisting through superb cattle country with fantastic views across the coastal plain. The town of **Volcán del Hato** (known as Volcán) is the first place that you reach, resting on the edge of a level plateau on the western side of the Barú volcano, with views of the steep, forested mountains to the north. The town is a popular weekend resort and has several hotels and a few small restaurants, although it has no real centre and is sprawled around a road junction—right for **Cerro Punta** and straight on for the mountain border with Costa Rica and the village of **Río Sereno**. Three kilometres northwest of the volcano is the entrance to the **Volcán National Park**, a large protected area of forest where quetzals can occasionally be seen. A good road leads to the park but little has been done to make the forest accessible to visitors.

Taking a left turn at the junction in the centre of Volcán you head west along the side of the Cordillera, into a landscape that is dominated by coffee production, the hillside delicately terraced, with every last inch occupied by groomed coffee bushes. The big names in Panamanian coffee, including 'Café Duran' and 'Café Sitton' have huge plantations here.

The paved road comes to an end at the mountain village of **Río Sereno**, from where you can continue into **Costa Rica**, either by bus or on foot. Buses leave from the gravel area outside the 'Almacén Xelia' at 5.30, 8.30, 11.30 am and 5.30 pm. Before you leave drop in at the **Panamanian Immigration Office**, which is in a small camouflage hut to the right of the shop. Inside Costa Rica you can get an entrance stamp at the immigration office in **Sabalito**, open Mon–Fri, 8–noon and 1–4 and Sat, 8–1.

Cerro Punta and Walking to Boquete

From Volcán a paved road heads high up onto the western slopes of the Barú volcano to the small town of **Cerro Punta**, which is perched on the side of a massive bowl-shaped valley at some 2000 metres. The air here is fresh and clear, the nights crisp.

From Cerro Punta a tough 8–10 hr hike takes you over the shoulder of Barú volcano to the town of Boquete. The first part of this walk is easy enough. Follow the main road up through the town and beyond—left at the T-junction. In due course the tarmac ends and the road climbs through the forest to a high pass (about 2 hrs' walk from Cerro Punta). If you just want to take a gentle stroll from the town then you can walk this far, marvel at the views—which stretch out for miles across a series of densely forested peaks—and then head back to town. Alternatively you can push on to Boquete, by continuing over the pass and down into the river valley on the other side. The trail isn't easy to follow, plunging down the steep-sided valley and cutting through the forest, but ask anyone you meet along the way and you may even manage to pick up a guide. The walk is wildly beautiful, heading through spectacular tropical forest and crossing clear streams, and accompanied by an amazing array of tropical birds. Three or four hours before you reach Boquete you come across a couple of signs pointing the way and the trail becomes a muddy track, passing some small farms, where coffee and vegetables are grown, after which the track emerges onto a tarmac road. From here you should be able to hitch, through the village of **Los Naranjos**, to Boquete.

Boquete

The largest town in the Chiriquí highlands, **Boquete** has a distinctly European atmosphere. Touches of Swiss and German architecture testify to the presence of a large European community, who arrived here earlier in the century to farm coffee.

With the remains of a steam engine rusting away in the plaza the town is quiet and relaxed, surrounded by forested hills, volcanic peaks and heavily farmed valleys, which produce the very best in oranges, coffee and race horses. With its clear air, gushing rivers and cool nights the town is another popular Panamanian retreat. Horses can be hired here, there's trout fishing in some of the higher streams, and the walking is superb. The extinct **Barú volcano**, which towers above the town, is the highest peak in the country at 3474 m and can be climbed in about eight hours. The summit is marked by a radio mast and a roughish track reaches to the top. To follow it walk up through the town, past the church, and take a left turn, past the INTEL office. If you'd really like to explore the area then speak to Ricardo at the **Coffee Bean Café**, to the south of town. For around US$50 a day he'll take you deep into the forest and if you've a real taste for adventure he'll lead you along the '3rd of November' trail, a four or five-day hike which heads north from Boquete, emerging on the coast in Bocas del Toro. Along the way the forest is virtually untouched, containing jaguars, ocelots, tapirs and monkeys.

GETTING AROUND
Buses between Boquete and David run every hour or so from 6 am to 6.30 pm, the trip taking just under an hour. Buses between Volcán and David and between Río Sereno and David (3 hrs) run every couple of hours from 7 am to 5 pm. Bear in mind that there's nowhere to stay in Río Sereno, so if you're heading for Costa Rica set out early.

WHERE TO STAY AND EATING OUT
In Volcán the best place to stay is the **Hotel Dos Ríos**, tel 714271, a moderately priced hotel on the road to Río Sereno, although if it's full you might try the **Motel California**,

tel 714272. For inexpensive accommodation there are a number of cabañas-style hotels including the **Cabañas Morales**. Restaurants in Volcán include a couple of pizza places on the main road and the **Panadería Molleck**, at the main junction, which does good cakes. Off the road between Volcán and Cerro Punta is a massive luxury hotel and casino, **The Bambito**, tel 714265, where the restaurant serves delicious mountain trout from the hotel's own fish farm.

In **Cerro Punta** itself you'll find the **Hotel Cerro Punta**, tel 712020, a good, moderately priced small hotel and the **Pensión Primavera**, a musty little inexpensive hotel, a kilometre down a road which branches off to the left. The **5 Star** restaurant on the main street serves excellent and simple Panamanian food.

Boquete has something of a reputation as an upper-class resort and as such it has several excellent hotels. The **Hotel Panamonte**, tel 701327, is perhaps the most famous, counting Greta Garbo and Richard Nixon among its former guests. Just as good is the **Hotel Fundadores**, tel 701298, on the entrance road from David, where you'll be lulled to sleep by a stream which gushes through the grounds. To the right as you enter town is the **Hotel Rebequet**, another excellent hotel, which is more moderately priced with a good restaurant. Opposite the Rebequet is the **Pensión Marilos**, which is very good value and inexpensive. The **Pensión Virginia**, on the plaza, is an overpriced budget hotel, but does however have a classic 1950s-style restaurant, but the decor outclasses the food. However, there are several good restaurants in Boquete including the **Restaurant Lourdes**, a couple of pizza places and, for cheap food, the restaurant **Don Robin**. A couple of kilometres to the south of town is the **Coffee Bean Café**, an excellent place for a sandwich, a cool beer and a superb cup of coffee. Among the residents at the Coffee Bean is Elsa, a massive 10-year-old lioness, which Ricardo, the owner, saved from life in the circus.

BOCAS DEL TORO

Hidden away in northeast Panamá the province of Bocas del Toro has, until recently, been in a world of its own. Until the last decade the only way to reach the area by road was through Costa Rica. As you might expect, the area is very different from the rest of Panamá: entirely dominated by the banana industry and largely populated by English-speaking blacks. For the visitor the area offers a refreshingly new angle or Panamanian culture as well as two beautiful Caribbean islands, where you can swim and snorkel to your heart's content.

Gualaca and Chiriquí Grande

The road from David to Chiriquí Grande, straddling the high, forested peaks of the Cordillera Central is among the most spectacular trips in Panamá. Heading out of David you travel east along the Pan-American Highway, before branching off towards the village of **Gualaca**, where you can stop off for a swim in the cool waters of the Río Chiriquí. To get to the river follow the sign for the 'Cangilones de Gualaca'.

Above Gualaca the road winds up into the mountains; beneath you the lowlands stretch out to the sea, while to the west rises the cone of the Barú volcano. Cut from the side of the mountains the road slips through a gash in the ridge and drops into a beautiful, forested wilderness. Here a huge mountain valley is suspended between the peaks, at the bottom of which is the **Fortuna hydroelectric dam**. For the benefit of both the wildlife and the electricity company the area has been declared a forest reserve and is one of the few places in Panamá where you can get close to the one of the country's tropical forests. At the bottom of the valley a bridge spans the lake, beyond which the road climbs out of the valley and drops towards Chiriquí Grande.

The town of **Chiriquí Grande** is perched on the edge of a wilderness, peering out across a huge lagoon and surrounded by dense forest. The town is a half-built collection of ramshackle wooden huts, cheap hotels, and crumbling docks. Beside it is the northern end of the trans-Panamá pipeline, which is used to transport huge quantities of Alaskan crude across the isthmus; ocean-going tankers frequently lie offshore. There's little to do in Chiriquí Grande, apart from revel in the atmosphere of tropical chaos, trade and transport, but you may easily find yourself spending the night here, waiting for the ferry.

GETTING AROUND

There are buses from David to Chiriquí Grande (3 hrs) every couple of hours. From Chiriquí Grande there's a daily ferry to Almirante, to the northwest, which is quite an experience in itself with its Russian crew, meatball stew and 9-hour crossing. The trip can also be done, in just an hour, by speedboat, for US$10 per person—beware of overcharging—with boats leaving for Almirante every couple of hours, depending on the number of people who want to travel, the last at around 3 pm. If you'd like to explore the area around the lagoon, or head east along the Caribbean coast then you can hitch a ride on one of the small cargo boats which leave from the docks beside the main pier.

Bocas del Toro and Bastimentos

The island of **Bocas del Toro** is the place to make for, surrounded by crystal-clear waters and basking in the relaxed atmosphere of the Caribbean. There are three hotels and you can feast on traditional Caribbean food: coconut bread, Johnny Cakes and the finest lobster. The town of Bocas del Toro occupies a narrow spit at the island's southern tip and is centred around a single main street.

A narrow strip of water separates Bocas del Toro from the neighbouring island of **Bastimentos**. There's nowhere to stay on Bastimentos but it makes an excellent day trip and is the site of Panamá's only marine wildlife reserve. Officially called the **Marino Isla Bastimentos**, the reserve covers some 13,226 hectares, including a small area of primary forest, offshore cayes and coral reefs. To get to Bastimentos you can simply wander down to the dock in Bocas del Toro and pay one of the boats to take you across, or if you'd like to be shown around then Lee Paget at the **Botel Thomas** will be able to give you a guided tour. Snorkelling gear can be hired from one of the hotels in Bocas.

GETTING AROUND

A ferry service operates from Almirante to Bocas del Toro, every day except Wednesday. The schedule is a masterpiece of creative routing and is extremely difficult to grasp.

However, the first departure from Almirante is usually at around 7 am, on Monday, Thursday and Saturday and at noon on Sunday and Tuesday, although it's well worth checking the night before. There are also daily flights to the island from Changuinola and Panamá City with **Alas Chiricanas**, tel 646448.

WHERE TO STAY

There are three hotels on Bocas del Toro, all moderately priced. The best is the **Hotel Bahía**, tel 789211, but the **Hotel Thomas**, tel 789248, is a close second and its owners are particularly friendly. The hotel also has a very fine restaurant, perched above the sea. The cheapest place to stay, down the street towards the fire station, is the **Pensión Peck**.

Almirante and Changuinola

Almirante and Changuinola owe their existence to the humble banana. This entire area was developed in the 19th century by the United Fruit Company and despite disease, earthquake and wild price fluctuations the banana industry continues to dominate the area, now largely in the hands of the Chiriquí Land Company. Almirante is the main port of exit for the packaged bananas, with a large port facility and railway marshalling. Recent migration from the surrounding countryside has swelled the town's Indian population and it is now developing some economic activity that's independent of banana business.

To the west of Almirante is **Changuinola**, a long straggle of a town that clings to the railway tracks. Typical of Central American banana towns it occupies a tiny island in the sea of bananas, with looming banana plants pressing in on all sides. Its bus terminal is a testament to the general lack of imagination that's involved in banana production with a steady stream of buses heading out to plantations named finca 1, finca 7, finca 42, etc.

Buses run every hour or so between Almirante, Changuinola and Guabito.

WHERE TO STAY AND EAT

There are a couple of hotels in Changuinola, both intended to cater for those on banana business they are overpriced but still in the moderate range. Beside the airport is the **Hotel Changuinola**, tel 788451, which offers air conditioning, and in the centre of town is the **Hotel Carol**. In Almirante all accommodation is in the inexpensive bracket. The best hotel is the **Hotel Bambi**, although the **Hotel Hong Kong** and **Hospedaje San Francisco** are a little cheaper, and the **Pensión Colón** even more so.

Guabito and the Border with Costa Rica

About 15 km to the west of Changuinola the border with Costa Rica is marked by the muddy waters of the Río Sixaola and spanned by a steel railway bridge. On the Panamanian side is the border town of **Guabito**, a roughish spot made up of a couple of rows of cut-price clothes shops. The town is kept alive by a steady flow of Costa Rican shoppers who cross the border to buy cheap Panamanian clothing. To maintain the trade balance Panamanians go into Costa Rica to take advantage of cheaper food and drink. There's nowhere to stay in Guabito (although there are some basic hotels on the Costa Rican side) and the border is open from 8–6, Panamanian time (which is 7–5 in Costa Rica).

Buses run between Changuinola and Guabito (30 minutes) every hour or so from 5–5. In Changuinola take any bus marked 'Frontera' or 'Las Tablas'.

EASTERN PANAMÁ AND THE DARIÉN GAP

Eastern Panamá is one of Latin America's great wildernesses: a swampy and impenetrable expanse of dense tropical forest, tortuous rivers and low, rugged hills, inhabited almost exclusively by indigenous Indians. Few Panamanians ever venture in this direction and the area is commonly known as El Tapón—the stopper. The Pan-American Highway, which stretches from Alaska to Tierra del Fuego, ends in Yaviza, from where all travel is on foot or by boat. The area is inhabited by Kuna and Choco Indians, who moved into the area in the late 18th century. Much of the forest is now protected by law, including the Darién Biosphere Reserve which covers a total of 579,000 hectares along the border with Colombia.

Travel in this part of Panamá is for the adventurous, the hazards are many and unpredictable: tropical downpours, potholed roads and an almost total lack of infrastructure can play havoc with the best-laid plans. Above all you'll need plenty of time and patience, but despite all this the area is undeniably fascinating, rich in indigenous culture, wildlife, fauna, flora and with a wild frontier atmosphere. The highway runs south from Panamá City as far as **Yaviza**, and there are a couple of buses a day along this route, as well as flights from Panamá City. There are basic hotels in Yaviza and food is available here. If you plan to go any further you will need a tent or hammock and a mosquito net. Colombia is at least a week's walk away, while other towns and villages can be reached either on foot, by boat or in a plane. For more information on crossing the Darién Gap consult *Backpacking in Mexico and Central America* by Hilary Bradt and Rob Rachowiecki (Bradt Publications 1985), which gives the best account of the route.

501

LANGUAGE

Excepting Belize, where the majority speak English, the most widely used language in Central America is Spanish, followed closely by the many Maya Indian languages spoken predominantly in Guatemala. There are at least ten major language groups for the Maya people and among those the variety of dialects is staggering. Even communication from one region to the next can be impossible, and foreigners cannot hope to learn about the indigenous linguistic complexities on a short visit. Suffice it to say that most Maya can speak Spanish, and only in very remote areas will you find villagers unable to use it.

Few people have a working knowledge of English or other European languages, and your visit will be immeasurably improved if you can at least communicate in basic Spanish. There are plenty of language schools in Central America, most notably in Antigua, Guatemala, and many travellers find that even one or two weeks of tuition makes all the difference. The courses are also much cheaper here than in the West, and tuition is generally one-to-one, making your advance very rapid. One week of daily four-hour sessions can cost you as little as US$45 or around US$100, depending on which language school you choose (see p. 103 for Antigua's practical information).

Formal Greetings

Buenos días	Good morning
Buenas tardes	Good afternoon
Buenas noches	Good evening
Buenos días, don (doña)...	Good morning Mr (Mrs)...
¡Señor!	Sir/Madam (applied to both)
¿Como está (usted)?	How are you?
Adiós	Goodbye

Informal Greetings

Hola!	Hello!
¿Qué tal?	How's it going?
Adiós	Hello (in passing)
Hasta pronto	See you soon
Que te vaya bien	Stay well
Dios te cuida	May God keep you

Travel

Disculpe	Excuse me/sorry
Lo siento	Sorry
¿Habla inglés?	Do you speak English?
Dónde está...	Where is?
Terminal de buses	Bus station

502

Camioneta	Bus
Estación de tren	Train station
Aeropuerto	Airport
Parada	Bus stop
Barco	Boat
Puerto	Port
Aduana	Customs
Cuánto cuesta...	How much?
¿A qué hora sale el bus?	What time does the bus depart?
¿Cuándo sale el próximo?	When does the next one leave?
¿De dónde?	From where?
¿Cuánto es el pasaje?	How much is the bus fare?
El boleto	Ticket
Ida y vuelta	Return ticket
Solo ida	Just one way
¿Hasta dónde?	Where to?
Hasta Antigua	To Antigua
Asiento	Seat
Lleno	Full
Atrás hay lugares	There are seats at the back
¡Buen viaje!	Have a good trip!
Quiero un taxi	I'm looking for (want) a taxi

Directions and Locations

Izquierda	Left
Derecha	Right
Adelante	Forward
Atrás	Backward
Arriba	Up
Abajo	Down
Dos cuadras de aquí	Two blocks from here
Lejos	Far/distant
Cerca	Near/close
Recto	Straight (ahead)
Norte	North
Sur	South
Oeste	West
Este	East
Entrada	Entrance
Salida	Exit
Esquina	Corner (exterior)
Rincón	Corner (interior)

Accommodation

Hotel/Posada	Hotel
Hospedaje/Pensión	Guest house

503

¿Hay cuartos?	Do you have rooms?
Para una persona	For one person
Para dos (tres) personas	For two (three) people
¿Cuánto son or *A cómo son?*	How much are they?
¿Hay con baño privado?	Are there rooms with private bath?
¿Hay unos con cama matrimonial?	Do you have ones with double beds?
Con dos camas	With two beds
¿Hay cuartos más barato?	Do you have cheaper rooms?
Hay agua caliente?	Do you have hot water?
Funcionar	to work/function/to be in working order
Está bien	That is good (I accept)
¿A qué hora hay desayuno?	What time is breakfast?
¿Hay comida?	Do you have meals/Is there food?
¿Qué hay para comer?	What do you have to eat?
¿Tiene (usted) un candado?	Do you have a padlock (for the room)?
¿Tiene (usted) candelas?	Do you have candles?
Tiene (usted) un ventilador?	Do you have a ventilator?
Quiero salir muy temprano	I wish to leave very early
Jabón	Soap
Toalla	Towel
Papel Higiénico	Toilet paper

Driving

Carro	Car
Moto	Motorbike
Bicicleta	Bicycle
Alquilar	to rent
Gasolinera	Petrol station
Gasolina	Petrol
Garaje	Garage
Carretera	Road
Camino	Path/road
Permiso (Carnet) de conducir	Driving licence
Conductor (Piloto)	Driver
Peligro	Danger

Shopping, Service, Sightseeing

Guía	Guide
Abierto	Open
Cerrado	Closed
¿A qué hora abre el museo?	What time does the museum open?
¿A qué hora cierra el museo?	What time does the museum close?
El dinero	Money
Pisto	Money/income (slang)
La tienda	Shop
La golosina/pulpería/sastrería	Shop (Honduras)

El mercado	Market
Barato/Caro	Cheap/Expensive
Cuánto vale eso?	How much is that?
Está demasiado caro	It's too expensive
Hay rebaja?	Is there a discount?
No se puede	It's not possible
No hay	There isn't any
El correo	Post office
El banco	Bank
La oficina de turismo	Tourist office
Agencia de viaje	Travel agent
La farmacia	Chemist
Artesanía	Crafts
La Policía	Police force
Comisaría	Police station
La playa	Beach
El mar	Sea
La iglesia	Church

Maya Clothes and Market Goods

Indígena	Indian/Indigenous person
Traje	Traditional costume
Artesanía/Típica	Crafts
Huipil	Blouse/Top
Corte	Skirt/Wrap
Faja	Belt/Sash
Cinta/Bola/Tzute	Headdress
Cubrecama	Bedspread/Cover
Alfombra	Carpet/Rug
Mantel	Tablecloth
Servilleta	Napkin
Cinturón	Belt
Sombrero	Hat
Joyas	Jewellery
Pulsera	Bracelet
Collar	Necklace
Anillo	Ring
Plata	Silver
Oro	Gold
Máscara	Mask
Carraca	Rattle
Escultura	Carving

Useful Words and Phrases

¡Cuidado!	Careful
¿Puedes ayudarme?	Can you help?

505

Por favor	Please
Gracias	Thank you
Lo siento/disculpe	Sorry
De nada	It's a pleasure
¿Cómo te llamas?	What's your name?
Mucho gusto conocerte	It's a pleasure meeting you
Con mucho gusto	With pleasure
Sí/No	Yes/No
Quizás	Maybe
¿Por qué?	Why?
No sé	I don't know
No entiendo	I don't understand
Déjame en paz	Leave me alone
Habla despacio	Speak slowly
¿Qué es esto?	What is that?
¿Para qué es esto?	What is that for?
Servicio/Baño	Toilet/Bathroom
Aquí	Here
Allá	There
Que	What
Quien	Who
Como	How
Cuando	When
Bueno	Good
Malo	Bad
Tengo hambre	I'm hungry
Tengo sed	I'm thirsty
Estoy cansado (masc.), *cansada* (fem.)	I'm tired
¿Tiene fuego?	Have you got a light?
No fumo	I don't smoke
Tomar	to drink (slang)
Estoy casado/a	I'm married
Marido	Husband
Esposa	Wife
Niño/a	Child
Novio/a	Boyfriend/Girlfriend
Prometido/a	Engaged
Embarazada	Pregnant
Divorciado/a	Divorced

Time

¿Qué hora es?	What time is it?
Tiempo	Time
Hace tiempo	A long time ago
Ahora	Now
Después/Más tarde	Later

506

Temprano	Early
Hoy	Today
Ayer	Yesterday
Mañana	Tomorrow
Mañana	Morning
Tarde	Afternoon (late)
Noche	Evening
Mediodía	Midday
Año	Year
Mes	Month
Semana	Week
Día	Day

Days

Lunes	Monday
Martes	Tuesday
Miércoles	Wednesday
Jueves	Thursday
Viernes	Friday
Sábado	Saturday
Domingo	Sunday
Feria	Bank holiday
Vacaciónes	Holidays

Numbers

Uno/a	One
Dos	Two
Tres	Three
Cuatro	Four
Cinco	Five
Seis	Six
Siete	Seven
Ocho	Eight
Nueve	Nine
Diez	Ten
Once	Eleven
Doce	Twelve
Trece	Thirteen
Catorce	Fourteen
Quince	Fifteen
Dieciséis	Sixteen
Diecisiete	Seventeen
Dieciocho	Eighteen
Diecinueve	Nineteen
Veinte	Twenty
Veintiuno	Twenty-one

Treinta	Thirty
Cuarenta	Forty
Cincuenta	Fifty
Sesenta	Sixty
Setenta	Seventy
Ochenta	Eighty
Noventa	Ninety
Cien	One hundred
Ciento uno	One hundred and one
Quinientos	Five hundred
Mil	One thousand

Restaurants and Food

Restaurante	Restaurant
Comedor	Eating place
Comida corriente	Meal of the day
Desayuno	Breakfast
Almuerzo	Lunch
Cena	Dinner
Pan	Bread
Mantequilla	Butter
Queso	Cheese
Jalea	Jam
Miel	Honey
Azúcar	Sugar
Pan tostado	Toast
Huevos (fritos/revueltos)	Eggs (fried/scrambled)
Huevos a la mexicana	with tomato, onion and hot sauce
Huevos rancheros	with hot sauce
Hervir	Boil
Mosh	Porridge
Pastel	Pastry/cake
Mesa	Table
Silla	Chair
Cuchillo	Knife
Tenedor	Fork
Cuchara	Spoon
Sopa	Soup
Condimento	Salt and pepper
Salsa picante	Hot sauce
Mostaza	Mustard
Cenicero	Ashtray
Cuenta	Bill
Anafre	Beanpaste snack (Honduras)
Pinchos	Meat kebabs
Chile relleno	Stuffed pepper

Chuchitos	Stuffed maize dumplings
Enchilada	Crisp tortillas with salad/meat topping
Quesadilla	Flour tortilla stuffed with cheese
Taco	Stuffed tortilla
Tamale	Maize pudding wrapped in palm leaf

Drinks

Bebidas	Drinks
Agua	Water or fizzy drink
Jugo	Fruit juice
Licuado (leche/agua)	Milkshake (with milk or water)
Cerveza	Beer
Vino	Wine
Café negro	Black coffee
Café con leche	White coffee
Té (con limón)	Tea (with lemon)

Meats

Carne	Meat
Lomito	Meat (usually beef)
Carne de res	Beef
Bistec	Steak
Marano (Cerdo)	Pork
Chorizo	Sausage
Tocino	Bacon
Jamón	Ham
Chuleta	Chop
Guisado	Stew
Milanesa	Breaded meat
Cordero	Lamb
Ternera	Veal
Venado	Venison
Pollo	Chicken
Gallina	Hen
Pato	Duck
Pavo	Turkey
Conejo	Rabbit
Tepezcuintle	A jungle rodent (good)
Hígado	Liver
Asado	Roasted
Al horno	Baked
A la parrilla	Grilled

Fish and Shellfish

Pescado entero	Whole fish

Pescado frito	Fried fish
Tiburón	Shark
Bacalao	Cod
Trucha	Trout
Atún	Tuna
Ceviche	Raw fish salad
Mariscos	Shellfish
Camarones	Shrimp
Langosta	Lobster
Calamares	Squid
Cangrejo	Crab

Vegetables

Verduras	Vegetables
Ajo	Garlic
Cebolla	Onion
Papas	Potatoes
Arroz	Rice
Maíz	Maize/Corn
Frijoles	Beans
Tomate	Tomato
Hongos	Mushrooms
Aguacate	Avocado
Col	Cabbage
Coliflor	Cauliflower
Lechuga	Lettuce
Pepino	Cucumber
Zanahoria	Carrot

Fruit

Coco	Coconut
Plátano	Banana
Papaya	Pawpaw
Melón	Honeymelon
Sandía	Watermelon
Durazno (Melocotón)	Peach
Piña	Pineapple
Pitaya	Guatemalan fruit (purple inside)
Fresas	Strawberries
Guayaba	Guava
Limón	Lemon
Naranja	Orange
Manzana	Apple
Toronja	Grapefruit
Uvas	Grapes

FURTHER READING

Travel and the Maya

Cockburn, J., *A Journey Overland from the Gulf of Honduras to the Great South Sea*, London, C. Rivington, 1735

Coe, M. D., *The Maya*, London, Thames & Hudson, 1986

Coe, W. R., *Tikal*, University of Pennsylvania, 1967

Dampier, W., *A New Voyage Round the World*, London, A. & C. Black, 1937

Daniels, A., *Sweet Waist of America*, London, Arrow, 1991

Exquemeling, J., *The Buccaneers of America*, London, Routledge & Sons, 1924

Gage, T., *The English American*, London, Routledge, 1928

Hagen, V. (von), *Jungle in the Clouds*, London, Hale, 1945

Huxley, A., *Beyond the Mexique Bay*, London, Chatto & Windus, 1936

Keenagh, P., *Mosquito Coast*, London, Chatto & Windus, 1937

Lester, M., *A Lady's Ride Across Spanish Honduras*, Edinburgh, Blackwood, 1884

Marnham, P., *So Far from God*, London, Penguin, 1986

Maslow, J. E., *Bird of Life, Bird of Death*, London, Penguin, 1987

Morris, M., *Nothing to Declare*, London, Paladin, 1990

Namuth, H., *Los Todos Santeros*, London, Nishen, 1989

O'Rourke, P. J., *Holidays in Hell*, London, Picador, 1989

Rushdie, S., *The Jaguar Smile: A Nicaraguan Journey*, London, Cape, 1987

Squier, E. G., *Adventures on the Mosquito Shore*, New York, Worthington Co., 1891

Stephens, J. L., *Incidents of Travel in Central America, Chiapas and Yucatán*, London, Dover, 1970

Time Life Books, *The Jungles of Central America*

Theroux, P., *The Old Patagonian Express*, London, Penguin, 1979

Thompson, J. E. S., *The Maya of Belize: Historical Chapters Since Columbus*, Belize, Cubola Productions, 1988

Thompson, J. E. S., *The Rise and Fall of Maya Civilization*, University of Oklahoma Press, 1968

Thompson, J. E. S. (ed.), *Thomas Gage's Travels in the New World*, University of Oklahoma Press

Warlords and Maize Men: A Guide to the Maya Sites of Belize, Belize, Cubola Productions, 1989

Wells, W. V., *Explorations and Adventures in Honduras*, New York, Harper & Bros., 1857

Wright, R., *Time Among the Maya*, London, Bodley Head, 1989

History and Analysis

Asturias de Barrios, L., *Comalapa: Native Dress and its Significance*, Guatemala, Ixchel, 1985

Belize: A Country Guide, Albuquerque, Resource Center, 1990

Bethell, L. (ed.), *Central America Since Independence*, CUP, 1991

511

Costa Rica: A Country Guide, Albuquerque, Resource Center, 1989

Dobson, N., *A History of Belize*, Longman, 1973

El Salvador: A Country Guide, Albuquerque, Resource Center, 1990

Floyd, T. S., *The Anglo-Spanish Struggle for Mosquitia*, University of New Mexico, 1967

Grant, C. H., *The Making of Modern Belize*, Cambridge University Press, 1976

Guatemala: A Country Guide, Albuquerque, Resource Center, 1990

Guatemala: False Hope, False Freedom, London, Latin America Bureau, 1989

Handy, J., *Gift of the Devil*, London, Between the Lines, 1984

Henderson, G., *An Account of the British Settlement of Honduras*, London, Baldwin, 1809

Honduras: A Country Guide, Albuquerque, Resource Center, 1990

Honduras, State for Sale, London, Latin America Bureau, 1985

Long, T. & Bell, E., *Antigua Guatemala*, Guatemala, 1990

Mayan de Castellanos, G., *Tzute and Hierarchy in Sololá*, Guatemala, Ixchel, 1988

Menchu, R., I . . . Rigoberta Menchu. *An Indian Woman in Guatemala*, London, Verso, 1984

Nairn, A., 'The Guns of Guatemala: the merciless mission of Ríos Montt's army' in *The New Republic 188*. 14:17–21, 1983

Nicaragua: A Country Guide, Albuquerque, Resource Center, 1989

Oakes, M., *Beyond the Windy Place: Life in the Guatemalan*

Oakes, M., *The Two Crosses of Todos Santos: Survivals of Maya Religious Rituals*, New York, Pantheon, 1951

Highlands, New York, Farrar, Straus and Young, 1951

Panama: A Country Guide, Albuquerque, Resource Center, 1990

Pearce, J., *Under the Eagle: US Intervention in Central America and the Caribbean*, London, Latin America Bureau, 1982

Schlesinger, S. & Kinzer, S., *Bitter Fruit: The Untold Story of the American Coup in Guatemala*, London, Anchor Books, 1983

Sexton, J. D. (trans. and ed.), *Son of Tecún Umán, A Maya Indian Tells His Life Story*, Tucson, University of Arizona Press, 1981

Sexton, J. D. (trans. and ed.), *Campesino, The Diary of a Guatemalan Indian*, Tucson, University of Arizona Press, 1985

Simon, J.-M., *Eternal Spring—Eternal Tyranny*, New York, Norton, 1987

Tedlock, D. (trans.), *Popol Vuh*, New York, Simon & Schuster, 1985

Werne, P., *The Maya of Guatemala*, London, Minority Rights Group, 1989

Woodward Jr, R. L., *Central America: A Nation Divided*, Oxford, OUP, 1985

512

COUNTRY INDEX

The following seven **Country Indexes** contain references to place names, and all practical information that is relevant to the country in question.

On page 526 the **General Index** contains non-specific references to subjects and activities, major players and events—such as tobacco, bird-watching, the Maya, Christopher Columbus and the Spanish Conquest.

Note: Page references in **bold** type indicate maps; those in *italics* indicate illustrations.

GENERAL INDEX

Note: Page references in **bold** type indicate maps; those in *italics* indicate illustrations.

527